Capri II Owners Workshop Manual

by J H Haynes
Member of the Guild of Motoring Writers
and Peter Ward

Models covered

UK: Capri II, 1593 cc and 1993 cc
USA: Mercury Capri II, 140 cu in (2298 cc)
Covers models introduced in March 1978, sometimes known as Series III
Does not cover ohv and V6 models

ISBN 0 85696 795 5

ABCDE
FGHI

Printed in England (283-6H3)

HAYNES PUBLISHING GROUP
SPARKFORD YEOVIL SOMERSET BA22 7JJ ENGLAND
distributed in the USA by
HAYNES PUBLICATIONS INC
861 LAWRENCE DRIVE
NEWBURY PARK
CALIFORNIA 91320
USA

Acknowledgements

Special thanks are due to the Ford Motor Company in the UK and USA for the supply of technical information and certain illustrations. Castrol Limited provided lubrication data, and the Champion Sparking Plug Company supplied the illustrations showing the various spark plug conditions. The bodywork repair photographs used in this manual were provided by Holt Lloyd Limited who supply 'Turtle Wax', 'Dupli-color Holts', and other Holts range products.

About this manual

Its aim

The aim of this manual is to help you get the best value from your vehicle. It can do so in several ways. It can help you decide what work must be done (even should you choose to get it done by a garage), provide information on routine maintenance and servicing, and give a logical course of action and diagnosis when random faults occur. However, it is hoped that you will use the manual by tackling the work yourself. On simpler jobs it may even be quicker than booking the car into a garage and going there twice, to leave and collect it. Perhaps most important, a lot of money can be saved by avoiding the costs a garage must charge to cover its labour and overheads.

The manual has drawings and descriptions to show the function of the various components so that their layout can be understood. Then the tasks are described and photographed in a step-by-step sequence so that even a novice can do the work.

Its arrangement

The manual is divided into thirteen Chapters, each covering a logical sub-division of the vehicle. The Chapters are each divided into Sections, numbered with single figures, eg 5; and the Sections into paragraphs (or sub-sections), with decimal numbers following on from the Section they are in, eg 5.1, 5.2, 5.3 etc.

It is freely illustrated, especially in those parts where there is a detailed sequence of operations to be carried out. There are two forms of illustration: figures and photographs. The figures are numbered in sequence with decimal numbers, according to their position in the Chapter – eg Fig. 6.4 is the fourth drawing/illustration in Chapter 6. Photographs carry the same number (either individually or in related groups) as the Section or sub-section to which they relate.

There is an alphabetical index at the back of the manual as well as a contents list at the front. Each Chapter is also preceded by its own individual contents list.

Throughout the manual the abbreviations FoB, FoG and RPO are used. These indicate:

FoB	Ford of Britain
FoG	Ford of Germany
RPO	Regular Production Option

References to the 'left' or 'right' of the vehicle are in the sense of a person in the driver's seat facing forwards.

Unless otherwise stated, nuts and bolts are removed by turning anti-clockwise, and tightened by turning clockwise.

Vehicle manufacturers continually make changes to specifications and recommendations, and these, when notified, are incorporated into our manuals at the earliest opportunity.

Whilst every care is taken to ensure that the information in this manual is correct, no liability can be accepted by the authors or publishers for loss, damage or injury caused by any errors in, or omissions from, the information given.

Introduction to the Capri II

The Capri II models were first introduced in the United Kingdom in February 1974 using a wide range of engines previously used on other Ford vehicles; the models covered in this manual use the 1.6 litre and 2.0 litre overhead camshaft engines developed by Ford of Germany. In 1975 a similarly styled Capri II was introduced in the United States using either an existing V6 ohv engine or the new 2.3 litre ohc engine already used in the Pinto and Mustang; the models covered in this Manual use the 2.3 litre engine.

The car is conventional in mechanical layout, drive from the engine being transmitted to the rear axle via a 4-speed manual or 3-speed automatic gearbox and a one or two-piece propeller shaft according to the particular model.

Although the U.K. version is only 1 inch longer and 2¼ inches wider than the previous Ford Capri, the appearance of a larger car is obtained by the sleeker lines which evolved with the re-styling. This is even more apparent from the inside due to the increased load-space and opening tailgate.

A wide variety of optional extras is available but the basic equipment including emission control items, is governed by the particular model and intended market.

Reference should be made to Chapter 13 (Supplement) for changes in the Capri with the introduction of the Series III in March 1978.

Contents

Ford Capri II 2.0 Ghia (UK model)

Ford Capri II 1.6 GL (UK model)

General dimensions and weights

	Capri II	Mercury Capri II
Overall length	172.2 in (4373 mm)	179.1 in (4549 mm)
Overall width	66.9 in (1699 mm)	69.1 in (1755 mm)
Overall height	50.7 in (1288 mm)	51.4 in (1306 mm)
Wheelbase	100.9 in (2563 mm)	100.4 in (2550 mm)
Front track	53.3 in (1354 mm)	56.6 in (1438 mm)
Rear track	54.5 in (1384 mm)	57.0 in (1448 mm)
Kerb weight	2204 lb (1000 kg)	2623 lb (1191 kg)
Maximum towing weight	1200 lb (545 kg)	1200 lb (545 kg)
Maximum roof rack load	75 lb (34 kg)	75 lb (34 kg)

Buying spare parts and vehicle identification numbers

Buying spare parts

Spare parts are available from many sources. Ford have many dealers throughout the UK and the USA, and other dealers, accessory stores and motor factors will also stock Ford spare parts.

Our advice regarding spare part sources is as follows:

Officially appointed vehicle main dealers – This is the best source of parts which are peculiar to your vehicle and are otherwise not generally available (eg complete cylinder heads, internal transmission components, badges, interior trim etc). It is also the only place at which you should buy parts if your vehicle is still under warranty. To be sure of obtaining the correct parts it will always be necessary to give the storeman your vehicle's engine and chassis number, and if possible, to take the 'old' part along for positive identification. Remember that many parts are available on a factory exchange scheme – any parts returned should always be clean! It obviously makes good sense to go straight to the specialists on your vehicle for this type of part, for they are best equipped to supply you.

Other dealers and auto accessory stores – These are often very good places to buy materials and components needed for the maintenance of your vehicle (eg oil filters, spark plugs, bulbs, fan belts, oils and greases, touch-up paint, filler paste etc). They also sell general accessories, usually have convenient opening hours, charge lower prices and can often be found not far from home.

Motor factors – Good factors will stock all of the more important components which wear out relatively quickly (eg clutch components, pistons, valves, exhaust systems, brake cylinders/pipes/hoses/seals/shoes and pads etc). Motor factors will often provide new or reconditioned components on a part exchange basis – this can save a considerable amount of money.

Vehicle identification numbers

Although many individual parts, and in some cases sub-assemblies, fit a number of different models, it is dangerous to assume that just because they look the same, they are the same. Differences are not always easy to detect except by serial numbers. Make sure therefore, that the appropriate identity number for the model or sub-assembly is known and quoted when a spare part is ordered.

Capri II

The ***vehicle identification plate*** is mounted on the right-hand front wing (fender) apron, and may be seen once the bonnet is open. Record the numbers from your car on the blank spaces of the accompanying illustration. You can then take the manual with you when buying parts; also the exploded drawings throughout the manual can be used to point out and identify the components required.

Mercury Capri II

The ***vehicle identification number*** is stamped on a metal tab attached to the inside of the windshield pillar (driver's side) and repeated on the vehicle patent plate located in the engine compartment. The vehicle identification number is also included on the Vehicle Certification label which is attached to the left-hand centre pillar. This label is specially formulated to self-destruct if tampered with or removed.

Vehicle loading and tyre pressures are shown on a label fixed to the edge of the passenger door.

Emission control decal. All Mercury Capri II models have an emission control decal in the engine compartment. This gives information such as spark plug type and gap setting, ignition initial advance setting, idle speeds, maintenance schedule code letter and basic details of engine tune-up procedures. A typical decal is shown in the illustration.

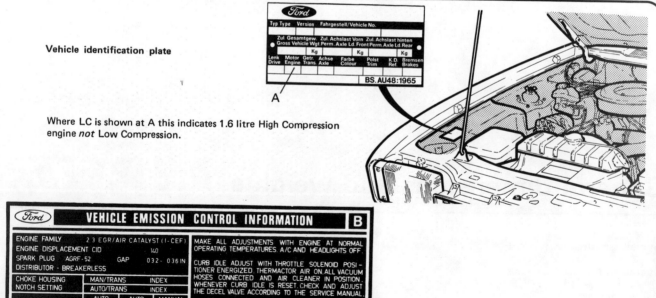

Vehicle identification plate

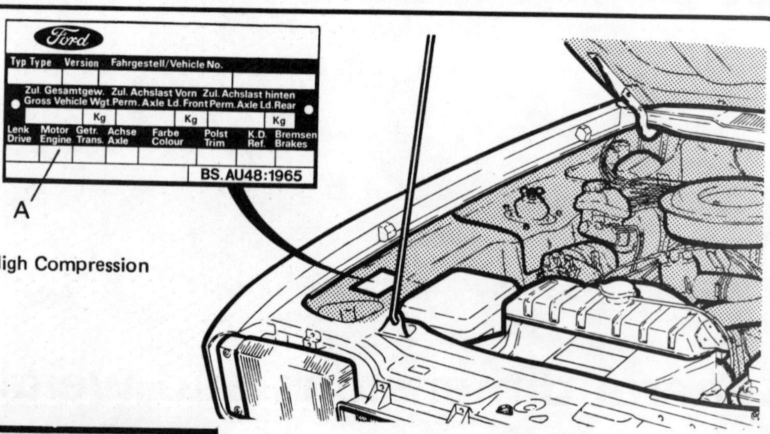

Where LC is shown at A this indicates 1.6 litre High Compression engine *not* Low Compression.

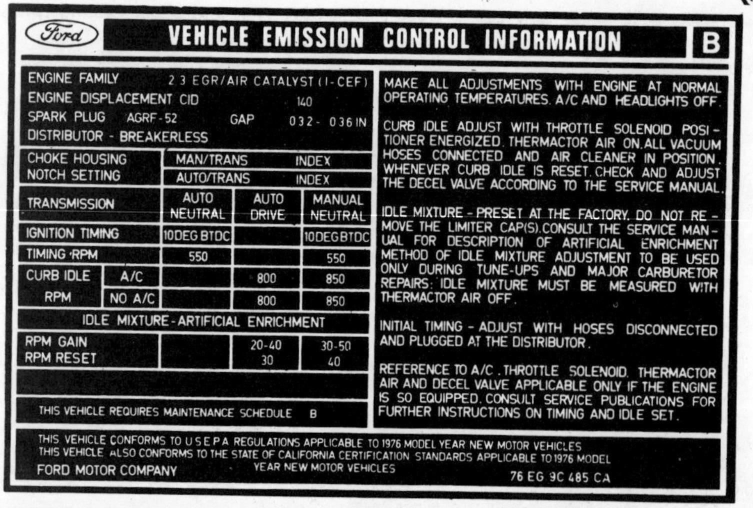

VEHICLE EMISSION CONTROL INFORMATION — B

ENGINE FAMILY 2 3 EGR/AIR CATALYST (I-CEF)
ENGINE DISPLACEMENT CID 140
SPARK PLUG AGRF-52 GAP 032- 036 IN
DISTRIBUTOR - BREAKERLESS

CHOKE HOUSING NOTCH SETTING	MAN/TRANS INDEX		
	AUTO/TRANS INDEX		
TRANSMISSION	AUTO NEUTRAL	AUTO DRIVE	MANUAL NEUTRAL
IGNITION TIMING	10DEG BTDC		10DEG BTDC
TIMING RPM	550		550
CURB IDLE RPM A/C		800	850
CURB IDLE RPM NO A/C		800	850
IDLE MIXTURE - ARTIFICIAL ENRICHMENT			
RPM GAIN		20-40	30-50
RPM RESET		30	40

THIS VEHICLE REQUIRES MAINTENANCE SCHEDULE B

MAKE ALL ADJUSTMENTS WITH ENGINE AT NORMAL OPERATING TEMPERATURES. A/C AND HEADLIGHTS OFF.

CURB IDLE ADJUST WITH THROTTLE SOLENOID POSITIONER ENERGIZED. THERMACTOR AIR ON. ALL VACUUM HOSES CONNECTED AND AIR CLEANER IN POSITION. WHENEVER CURB IDLE IS RESET, CHECK AND ADJUST THE DECEL VALVE ACCORDING TO THE SERVICE MANUAL.

IDLE MIXTURE - PRESET AT THE FACTORY. DO NOT REMOVE THE LIMITER CAP(S). CONSULT THE SERVICE MANUAL FOR DESCRIPTION OF ARTIFICIAL ENRICHMENT METHOD OF IDLE MIXTURE ADJUSTMENT TO BE USED ONLY DURING TUNE-UPS AND MAJOR CARBURETOR REPAIRS: IDLE MIXTURE MUST BE MEASURED WITH THERMACTOR AIR OFF.

INITIAL TIMING - ADJUST WITH HOSES DISCONNECTED AND PLUGGED AT THE DISTRIBUTOR.

REFERENCE TO A/C, THROTTLE SOLENOID, THERMACTOR AIR AND DECEL VALVE APPLICABLE ONLY IF THE ENGINE IS SO EQUIPPED. CONSULT SERVICE PUBLICATIONS FOR FURTHER INSTRUCTIONS ON TIMING AND IDLE SET.

THIS VEHICLE CONFORMS TO U S E P A REGULATIONS APPLICABLE TO 1976 MODEL YEAR NEW MOTOR VEHICLES
THIS VEHICLE ALSO CONFORMS TO THE STATE OF CALIFORNIA CERTIFICATION STANDARDS APPLICABLE TO 1976 MODEL YEAR NEW MOTOR VEHICLES
FORD MOTOR COMPANY 76 EG 9C 485 CA

Emission Control Decal (Mercury Capri II)

Tools and working facilities

Introduction

A selection of good tools is a fundamental requirement for anyone contemplating the maintenance and repair of a motor vehicle. For the owner who does not possess any, their purchase will prove a considerable expense, offsetting some of the savings made by doing-it-yourself. However, provided that the tools purchased are of good quality, they will last for many years and prove an extemely worthwhile investment.

To help the average owner to decide which tools are needed to carry out the various tasks detailed in this manual, we have compiled three lists of tools under the following headings: *Maintenance and minor repair, Repair and overhaul,* and *Special.* The newcomer to practical mechanics should start off with the *Maintenance and minor repair* tool kit and confine himself to the simpler jobs around the vehicle. Then, as his confidence and experience grows, he can undertake more difficult tasks, buying extra tools as, and when, they are needed. In this way, a *Maintenance and minor repair* tool kit can be built-up into a *Repair and overhaul* tool kit over a considerable period of time without any major cash outlays. The experienced do-it-yourselfer will have a tool kit good enough for most repair and overhaul procedures and will add tools from the *Special* category when he feels the expense is justified by the amount of use these tools will be put to.

It is obviously not possible to cover the subject of tools fully here. For those who wish to learn more about tools and their use there is a book entitled *How to Choose and Use Car Tools* available from the publishers of this manual.

Maintenance and minor repair tool kit

The tools given in this list should be considered as a minimum requirement if routine maintenance, servicing and minor repair operations are to be undertaken. We recommend the purchase of combination spanners (ring one end, open-ended the other); although more expensive than open-ended ones they do give the advantages of both types of spanner.

Combination spanners – 10, 11, 13, 14, 17 mm
Adjustable spanner – 9 inch
Engine sump/gearbox/rear axle drain plug key (where applicable)
Spark plug spanner (with rubber insert)
Spark plug gap adjustment tool
Set of feeler gauges
Brake adjuster spanner (where applicable)
Brake bleed nipple spanner
Screwdriver – 4 in long x ¼ in dia (flat blade)
Screwdriver – 4 in long x ¼ in dia (cross blade)
Combination pliers – 6 inch
Hacksaw, junior
Tyre pump
Tyre pressure gauge
Grease gun (where applicable)
Oil can
Fine emery cloth (1 sheet)
Wire brush (small)
Funnel (medium size)

Repair and overhaul tool kit

These tools are virtually essential for anyone undertaking any major repairs to a motor vehicle, and are additional to those given in the *Maintenance and minor repair* list. Included in this list is a comprehensive set of sockets. Although these are expensive they will be found invaluable as they are so versatile - particularly if various drives are included in the set. We recommend the ½ in square drive type, as this can be used with most proprietary torque wrenches. If you cannot afford a socket set, even bought piecemeal, then inexpensive tubular box spanners are a useful alternative.

The tools in this list will occasionally need to be supplemented by tools from the *Special* list.

Sockets (or box spanners) to cover range in previous list
Reversible ratchet drive (for use with sockets)
Extension piece, 10 inch (for use with sockets)
Universal joint (for use with sockets)
Torque wrench (for use with sockets)
'Mole' wrench – 8 inch
Ball pein hammer
Soft-faced hammer, plastic or rubber
Screwdriver – 6 in long x 5/16 in dia (flat blade)
Screwdriver – 2 in long x 5/16 in square (flat blade)
Screwdriver – 1½ in long x ¼ in dia (cross blade)
Screwdriver – 3 in long x 1/8 in dia (electricians)
Pliers – electricians side cutters
Pliers – needle nosed
Pliers – circlip (internal and external)
Cold chisel – ½ inch
Scriber – (this can be made by grinding the end of a broken hacksaw blade)
Scraper – (this can be made by flattening and sharpening one end of a piece of copper pipe)
Centre punch
Pin punch
Hacksaw
Valve grinding tool
Steel rule/straight edge
Allen keys
Selection of files
Wire brush (large)
Axle stands
Jack (strong scissor or hydraulic type)

Special tools

The tools in this list are those which are not used regularly, are expensive to buy, or which need to be used in accordance with their manufacturers' instructions. Unless relatively difficult mechanical jobs are undertaken frequently, it will not be economic to buy many of these tools. Where this is the case, you could consider clubbing together with friends (or a motorists' club) to make a joint purchase, or borrowing the tools against a deposit from a local garage or tool hire specialist.

The following list contains only those tools and instruments freely available to the public, and not those special tools produced by the vehicle manufacturer specifically for its dealer network. You will find occasional references to these manufacturers' special tools in the text of this manual. Generally, an alternative method of doing the job without the vehicle manufacturers' special tool is given. However, sometimes, there is no alternative to using them. Where this is the case and the relevant tool cannot be bought or borrowed you will have to entrust the work to a franchised garage.

Valve spring compressor
Piston ring compressor
Balljoint separator
Universal hub/bearing puller
Impact screwdriver
Micrometer and/or vernier gauge
Carburettor flow balancing device (where applicable)
Dial gauge
Stroboscopic timing light
Dwell angle meter/tachometer
Universal electrical multi-meter
Cylinder compression gauge
Lifting tackle (see photo)
Trolley jack
Light with extension lead

Buying tools

For practically all tools, a tool factor is the best source since he will have a very comprehensive range compared with the average garage or accessory shop. Having said that, accessory shops often offer excellent quality tools at discount prices, so it pays to shop around.

Remember, you don't have to buy the most expensive items on the shelf, but it is always advisable to steer clear of the very cheap tools. There are plenty of good tools around at reasonable prices, so ask the proprietor or manager of the shop for advice before making a purchase.

Care and maintenance of tools

Having purchased a reasonable tool kit, it is necessary to keep the tools in a clean serviceable condition. After use, always wipe off any dirt, grease and metal particles using a clean, dry cloth, before putting the tools away. Never leave them lying around after they have been used. A simple tool rack on the garage or workshop wall, for items such as screwdrivers and pliers is a good idea. Store all normal spanners and sockets in a metal box. Any measuring instruments, gauges, meters, etc., must be carefully stored where they cannot be damaged or become rusty.

Take a little care when tools are used. Hammer heads inevitably become marked and screwdrivers lose the keen edge on their blades from time-to-time. A little timely attention with emery cloth or a file will soon restore items like this to a good serviceable finish.

Working facilities

Not to be forgotten when discussing tools, is the workshop itself. If anything more than routine maintenance is to be carried out, some form of suitable working area becomes essential.

It is appreciated that many an owner mechanic is forced by circumstances to remove an engine or similar item, without the benefit of a garage or workshop. Having done this, any repairs should always be done under the cover of a roof.

Wherever possible, any dismantling should be done on a clean flat workbench or table at a suitable working height.

Any workbench needs a vice: one with a jaw opening of 4 in (100 mm) is suitable for most jobs. As mentioned previously, some clean dry storage space is also required for tools, as well as the lubricants, cleaning fluids, touch-up paints and so on which become necessary.

Another item which may be required, and which has a much more general usage, is an electric drill with a chuck capacity of at least 5/16 in (8 mm). This, together with a good range of twist drills, is virtually essential for fitting accessories such as wing mirrors and reversing lights.

SPANNER JAW GAP COMPARISON TABLE

Jaw gap (in)	Spanner size
0.250	¼ in AF
0.275	7 mm AF
0.312	5/16 in AF
0.315	8 mm AF
0.340	11/32 in AF; 1/8 in Whitworth
0.354	9 mm AF
0.375	3/8 in AF
0.393	10 mm AF
0.433	11 mm AF
0.437	7/16 in AF
0.445	3/16 in Whitworth; ¼ in BSF
0.472	12 mm AF
0.500	½ in AF
0.512	13 mm AF
0.525	¼ in Whitworth; 5/16 in BSF
0.551	14 mm AF
0.562	9/16 in AF
0.590	15 mm AF
0.600	5/16 in Whitworth; 3/8 in BSF
0.625	5/8 in AF
0.629	16 mm AF
0.669	17 mm AF
0.687	11/16 in AF
0.708	18 mm AF
0.710	3/8 in Whitworth; 7/16 in BSF
0.748	19 mm AF
0.750	¾ in AF
0.812	13/16 in AF
0.820	7/16 in Whitworth; ½ in BSF
0.866	22 mm AF
0.875	7/8 in AF
0.920	½ in Whitworth; 9/16 in BSF
0.937	15/16 in AF
0.944	24 mm AF
1.000	1 in AF
1.010	9/16 in Whitworth; 5/8 in BSF
1.023	26 mm AF
1.062	1 1/16 in AF; 27 mm AF
1.100	5/8 in Whitworth; 11/16 in BSF
1.125	1 1/8 in AF
1.181	30 mm AF
1.200	11/16 in Whitworth; ¾ in BSF
1.250	1¼ in AF
1.259	32 mm AF
1.300	¾ in Whitworth; 7/8 in BSF
1.312	1 5/16 in AF
1.390	13/16 in Whitworth; 15/16 in BSF
1.417	36 mm AF
1.437	1 7/16 in AF
1.480	7/8 in Whitworth; 1 in BSF
1.500	1½ in AF
1.574	40 mm AF; 15/16 in Whitworth
1.614	41 mm AF
1.625	1 5/8 in AF
1.670	1 in Whitworth; 1 1/8 in BSF
1.687	1 11/16 in AF
1.811	46 mm AF
1.812	1 13/16 in AF
1.860	1 1/8 in Whitworth; 1¼ in BSF
1.875	1 7/8 in AF
1.968	50 mm AF
2.000	2 in AF
2.050	1¼ in Whitworth; 1 3/8 in BSF
2.165	55 mm AF
2.362	60 mm AF

A Haltrac hoist and gantry in use during a typical engine removal sequence

Jacking and towing

Jacking points

To change a wheel in an emergency, use the jack supplied with the vehicle. Ensure that the roadwheel nuts are released before jacking up the car and make sure that the arm of the jack is fully engaged with the body bracket and that the base of the jack is standing on a firm surface.

The jack supplied with the vehicle is not suitable for use when raising the vehicle for maintenance or repair operations. For this work, use a trolley, hydraulic or screw type jack located under the front crossmember, bodyframe side-members or rear axle casing, as illustrated. Always supplement the jack with axle stands or blocks before crawling beneath the car.

Towing points

If your vehicle is being towed, make sure that the tow rope is attached to the front crossmember. If the vehicle is equipped with automatic transmission, the distance towed must not exceed 15 miles (24 km), nor the speed 30 mph (48 km/h), otherwise serious damage to the transmission may result. If these limits are likely to be exceeded, disconnect and remove the propeller shaft.

If you are towing another vehicle, attach the tow rope to the lower shock absorber mounting bracket at the axle tube.

On some later vehicles, towing eyes are fitted at the front and rear of the vehicles.

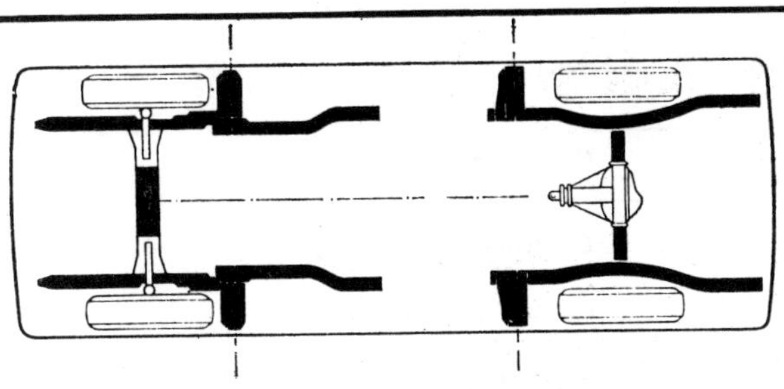

Jacking points

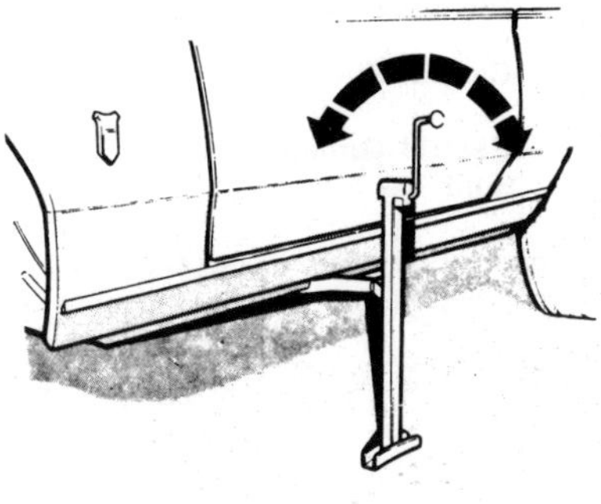

Using the vehicle jack

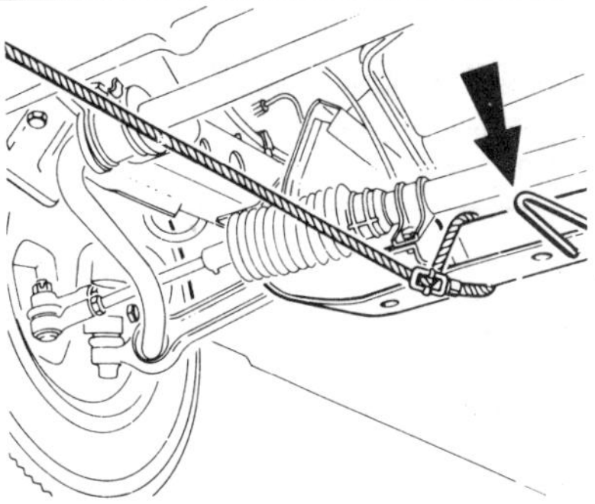

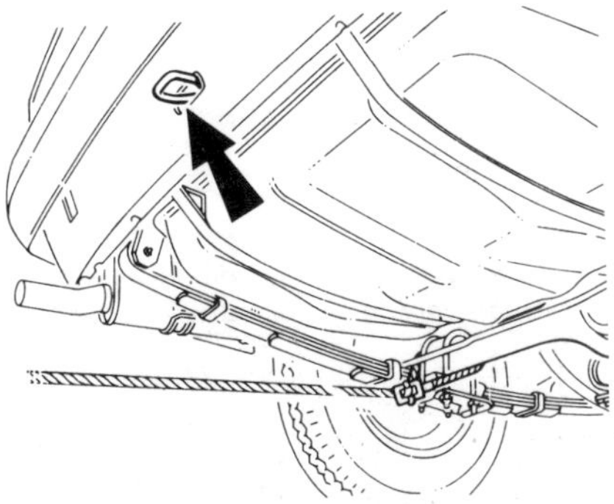

Attachment points for towing

(Above) *Front* *(Below)* *Rear*

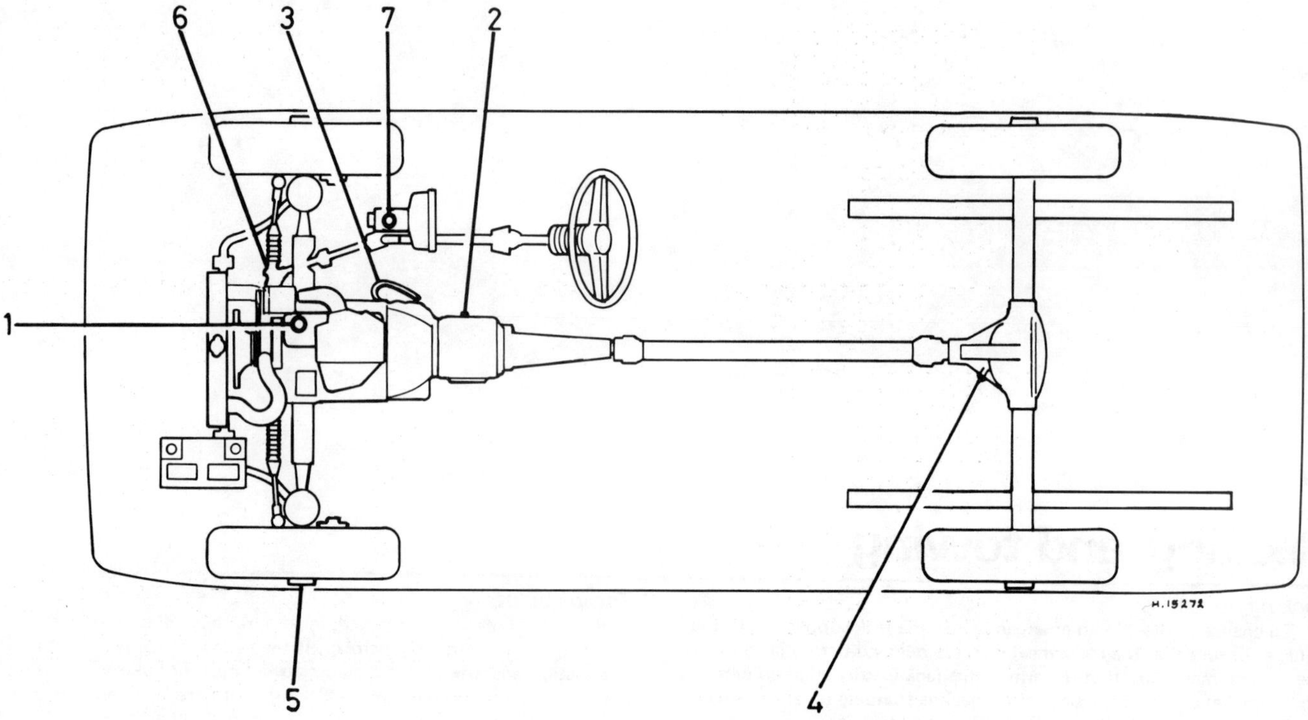

Recommended lubricants and fluids

Component or system	Lubricant type or specification	Castrol product
Engine (1)	Multigrade engine oil	Castrol GTX
Manual gearbox (2)	SAE 80EP gear oil	Castrol Hypoy Light
Automatic transmission (3)	Type F automatic transmission fluid	Castrol TQF
Rear axle (4)	SAE 90EP gear oil	Castrol Hypoy B
Front wheel bearings (5)	Multi-purpose lithium based grease	Castrol LM grease
Steering gear (6)	SAE 90EP gear oil	Castrol Hypoy B
Brake master cylinder	SAE J1703 hydraulic fluid	Castrol Girling Universal Brake & Clutch fluid

Note: *The above are general recommendations only. Lubrication requirements vary from territory-to-territory and depend on vehicle usage. If in doubt, consult the operator's handbook supplied with the vehicle, or your nearest dealer.*

Routine maintenance

Maintenance is essential for ensuring safety, and desirable for the purpose of getting the best in terms of performance and economy from your car. Over the years the need for periodic lubrication - oiling, greasing and so on - has been drastically reduced, if not totally eliminated. This has unfortunately tended to lead some owners to think that because no such action is required, components either no longer exist, or will last forever. This is a serious delusion. It follows therefore that the largest initial element of maintenance is visual examination and a general sense of awareness. This may lead to repairs or renewals, but should help to avoid roadside breakdowns.

In compiling this routine maintenance schedule, the author was confronted with a slight dilemma. For example, why should the maintenance interval for checking the brake fluid reservoir be recommended as 6000 miles (10000 km) for a Capri II when it is 30000 miles for a Mercury Capri II? The author therefore has made slight alterations to the manufacturer's schedule for some maintenance tasks since, for example, it is felt that it is better to check and rectify a noticeable drop in fluid level rather than wait for a warning light to tell the driver that something is wrong. Also, an item such as the brake fluid check already mentioned, takes so little time compared with its importance, that a much more frequent check is recommended.

For vehicles used in the USA two different maintenance schedules are given, according to the maintenance schedule code letter to be found on the engine compartment emission control decal or glovebox door.

It must be appreciated that not all maintenance tasks are applicable to all vehicles; therefore the owner must select those applicable to his particular car.

Revised servicing interval - Capri II (March 1978 on): In order to contain the ever increasing servicing charges and to prevent escalation of work entering their dealerships which results automatically from increased sales of new vehicles, the manufacturers now recommend a major (12 000 mile) and an interim (minor) service every 6000 miles. This extension of the service period is not recommended to the home mechanic however and the intervals specified in this manual should be observed as an aid to preventive maintenance and early fault diagnosis. This is bound to save money by avoiding the cost of renewing expensive components or assemblies damaged through failure to diagnose a malfunction early enough.

All models

Every 250 miles (400 km), weekly or before a long journey

Steering
- Check tyre pressures (when cold)
- Examine tyres for wear and damage
- Check steering for smooth and accurate operation

Brakes
- Check reservoir fluid level. If this has fallen noticeably, check for fluid leakage (photo).
- Check for satisfactory brake operation

Lights, wipers, horns, instruments
- Check operation of all lights
- Check operation of windscreen wipers and washers
- Check that the horn operates
- Check that all instruments and gauges are operating

Engine compartment
- Check engine oil level; top-up if necessary (photo)
- Check radiator coolant level
- Check battery electrolyte level

Capri II and Mercury Capri II: Schedules A, B and C

At first 3000 miles (5000 km), and for vehicles which operate under continuous stop/start conditions every subsequent 3000 miles (5000 km)

- Renew engine oil
- Renew engine oil filter at first 3000 miles (5000 km) (photo)
- Check automatic transmission fluid level

The engine oil filter location

Topping-up engine oil

Brake fluid reservoir - typical

Mercury Capri II: Schedules A and B

Every 5000 miles (8000 km) or 5 months, whichever occurs first

Renew the engine oil
Check the ignition timing
Adjust engine idle speeds and mixture
Check operation of fuel deceleration valve

Capri II and Mercury Capri II: Schedule C

Every 6000 miles (10000 km) or 6 months, whichever occurs first

Renew engine oil and oil filter
Clean distributor points and reset gap (Capri II only)
Lubricate distributor (Capri II only)
Clean spark plugs and reset gaps
Clean all HT leads and top of ignition coil
Check ignition timing (Capri II only)
Check valve clearances (Capri II only)
With rocker cover removed, remove distributor rotor and crank engine on starter motor. Check that oil is discharged from the lubrication tube nozzles onto the cam followers (Capri II only)
Check tightness of inlet and exhaust manifold bolts
Check condition of exhaust system
Check condition and tension of all drivebelts
Renew fuel filter (Mercury Capri II)
Check condition of pipes and hoses in emission control system
Lubricate accelerator linkage
Adjust engine idle speeds and mixture
Examine cooling system hoses and check for leaks
Clean/tighten battery terminals
Check gearbox oil level
Check rear axle oil level
Check clutch adjustment
Check front brake pads for wear (photo)
Check rear brake linings for wear (photo)
Examine brake hoses for leaks and chafing
Check handbrake adjustment
Check steering linkage for wear and damage and condition of ball joint covers
Check front suspension linkage for wear and damage
Check front wheel toe-in
Check operation of all doors, catches and hinges. Lubricate as necessary
Check condition of seatbelts and operation of buckles and inertia reels

Mercury Capri II: Schedules A and B

Every 10000 miles (16000 km) or 10 months, whichever occurs first

Carry out the maintenance tasks listed at intervals of 6000 miles (10000 km) for schedule C vehicles, except where this is a duplication of the items checked every 5000 miles.

Capri II and Mercury Capri II: Schedule C

Every 12000 miles (20000 km) or 12 months, whichever occurs first

Renew the contact breaker points (Capri II only)
Renew spark plugs
Check condition of distributor cap and rotor
Clean the positive crankcase ventilation (PCV) system
Arrange for your Ford dealer to check the emission control system operation (Mercury Capri II)
Check automatic transmission fluid level
Arrange for your Ford dealer to adjust the automatic transmission bands

Mercury Capri II: Schedules A and B

Every 15000 miles (24000 km) or 15 months, whichever occurs first

Carry out the maintenance tasks listed at intervals of 12000 miles for schedule C vehicles.

All models

Every 18000 miles (30000 km) or 18 months, whichever occurs first

Check tightness of rear spring mountings
Renew air cleaner element
Drain and refill automatic transmission (dusty or arduous conditions only)

All models

Every 24000 miles (40000 km) or 2 years, whichever occurs first

Adjust front wheel bearings
Renew all rubber seals and hoses in braking system. Renew brake fluid
Drain engine coolant. Renew antifreeze or inhibitor coolant mixture
Lubricate front suspension (Mercury only)

Check the disc brake pads for wear

Check the rear brake linings for wear

Chapter 1 Part A: 1600 and 2000 engines (Capri II)

For modifications, and information applicable to later models, see Supplement at end of manual

Contents

Specifications - Capri II

Engine (general)

Engine identification:	
1.6 litre	LCE
1.6 litre GT	LEC
2.0 litre	NEE
Camshaft location	Within cylinder head
Valve gear operation	Rockers, via camshaft and toothed belt
Firing order	1 3 4 2
Bore:	
1.6 litre, 1.6 litre GT	3.451 in (87.65 mm)
2.0 litre	3.575 in (90.8 mm)
Stroke:	
1.6 litre, 1.6 litre GT	2.6 in (66 mm)
2.0 litre	3.03 in (76.95 mm)
Cubic capacity:	
1.6 litre, 1.6 litre GT	1593 cc
2.0 litre	1993 cc
Compression ratio	9.2 : 1
Compression pressure at cranking speed	142 to 170 lb f/in^2 (10 to 12 kgf/cm^2)
Engine idle speed	See Specifications, Chapter 3 and Chapter 13

Max. continuous engine speed:	
1.6 litre	6000 rpm
1.6 litre GT	6300 rpm
2.0 litre	5850 rpm
Engine horsepower (DIN):	
1.6 litre	72 BHP at 5500 rpm
1.6 litre GT	88 BHP at 6300 rpm
2.0 litre	98 BHP at 5500 rpm
Torque (DIN):	
1.6 litre	87 lbf ft (12 kg fm) at 2700 rpm
1.6 litre GT	92 lbf ft (12.7 kg fm) at 4000 rpm
2.0 litre	111 lbf ft (15.4 kg fm) at 3500 rpm

Cylinder block

	1.6 litre, 1.6 litre GT	2.0 litre
Cast identification marks	16	20
Number of main bearings	5	5
Cylinder bore diameter in. (mm) grades:		
Standard grade:		
1	3.4508 - 3.4512 (87.650 - 87.660)	3.5748 - 3.5752 (90.800 - 90.810)
2	3.4512 - 3.4516 (87.660 - 87.670)	3.5752 - 3.5756 (90.810 - 90.820)
3	3.4516 - 3.4520 (87.670 - 87.680)	3.5756 - 3.5760 (90.820 - 90.830)
4	3.4520 - 3.4524 (87.680 - 87.690)	3.5760 - 3.5764 (90.830 - 90.840)
Oversize A in (mm)	3.4709 - 3.4713 (88.160 - 88.170)	3.5949 - 3.5953 (91.310 - 91.320)
Oversize B in (mm)	3.4713 - 3.4717 (88.170 - 88.180)	3.5953 - 3.5957 (91.320 - 91.330)
Oversize C in (mm)	3.4717 - 3.4720 (88.180 - 88.190)	3.5957 - 3.5961 (91.330 - 91.340)
Standard service replacement in (mm)	3.4520 - 3.4524 (87.680 - 87.690)	3.5760 - 3.5764 (90.830 - 90.840)
Oversize 0.5 in (mm)	3.4717 - 3.4720 (88.180 - 88.190)	3.5957 - 3.5961 (91.330 - 91.340)
Oversize 1.0 in (mm)	3.4913 - 3.4917 (88.680 - 88.690)	3.6154 - 3.6157 (91.830 - 91.840)

	All engines
Centre main bearing width - in (mm)	1.070 - 1.072 (27.17 - 27.22)
Main bearing liners (inner diameter, standard) - in (mm)	2.2441 - 2.2454 (57.000 - 57.033)
Undersize:	
0.25 in (mm)	2.2343 - 2.5901 (56.750 - 56.788)
0.50 in (mm)	2.2244 - 2.2259 (56.50 - 56.538)
0.75 in (mm)	2.2146 - 2.2161 (56.25 - 56.288)
1.00 in (mm)	2.2047 - 2.2062 (56.00 - 56.038)
Main bearing basic bore diameter:	
Standard in (mm)	2.3866 - 2.3874 (60.62 - 60.64)
Oversize in (mm)	2.4024 - 2.4032 (61.02 - 61.04)

Crankshaft

Main bearing journal diameters:	
Standard in (mm)	2.2429 - 2.2437 (56.97 - 56.99)
Undersize:	
0.25 in (mm)	2.2331 - 2.2339 (56.72 - 56.74)
0.50 in (mm)	2.2332 - 2.2240 (56.47 - 56.49)
0.75 in (mm)	2.2134 - 2.2142 (56.22 - 56.24)
1.00 in (mm)	2.2035 - 2.2043 (55.97 - 55.99)
Thrust washer thickness:	
Standard in (mm)	0.091 - 0.0925 (2.3 - 2.35)
Oversize in (mm)	0.098 - 0.100 (2.5 - 2.55)
Main bearing clearance:	
Aluminium - in (mm)	0.0004 - 0.0025 (0.010 - 0.064)
Compound - in (mm)	0.0004 - 0.0027 (0.010 - 0.068)
Crankpin journal diameter:	
Standard - in (mm)	2.0465 - 2.0472 (51.98 - 52.00)
Undersize:	
0.25 in (mm)	2.0366 - 2.0374 (51.73 - 51.75)
0.50 in (mm)	2.0268 - 2.0276 (51.48 - 51.50)
0.75 in (mm)	2.0169 - 2.0177 (51.23 - 51.25)
1.00 in (mm)	2.0071 - 2.0079 (50.98 - 51.00)
Endfloat - in (mm)	0.0032 - 0.0110 (0.08 - 0.28)

Camshaft

Drive	Toothed belt	
Thrust plate thickness - in (mm)	0.157 - 0.158 (3.98 - 4.01)	
Width of camshaft groove - in (mm)	$0.1600^{+0.0028}_{-0.0000}$	$(4.064^{+0.070}_{-0.000})$
	1.6 litre, 1.6 litre GT	**2.0 litre**
Cam lift - in (mm)	0.2348 (5.9639)	0.2493 (6.3323)
Cam heel to toe dimension - in (mm)	1.4118 - 1.4280 (35.86 - 36.27)	1.4264 - 1.4425 (36.23 - 36.64)
Camshaft identification colour	White	Yellow

	All engines
Journal diameter:	
Front - in (mm)	1.6531 - 1.6539 (41.99 - 42.01)
Centre - in (mm)	1.7563 - 1.7571 (44.61 - 44.63)
Rear - in (mm)	1.7713 - 1.7720 (44.99 - 45.01)
Bearing - inside diameter:	
Front - in (mm)	16.549 - 16.557 (42.035 - 42.055)
Centre - in (mm)	1.7415 - 1.7578 (44.655 - 44.675)
Rear - in (mm)	1.7730 - 1.7381 (45.035 - 45.055)
Camshaft endfloat - in (mm)	0.0035 - 0.0067 (0.09 - 0.17 mm)

Auxiliary shaft

Endfloat - in (mm)	0.00157 - 0.0047 (0.04 - 0.12)

Pistons

	1.6 litre, 1.6 litre GT	**2.0 litre**
Piston diameter:		
Standard - Grade 1 - in (mm)	3.4494 - 3.4498 (87.615 - 87.625)	3.5734 - 3.5738 (90.765 - 90.775)
Grade 2 - in (mm)	3.4498 - 3.4502 (87.625 - 87.635)	3.5738 - 3.5742 (90.775 - 90.785)
Grade 3 - in (mm)	3.4502 - 3.4506 (87.635 - 87.645)	3.5742 - 3.5746 (90.785 - 90.795)
Grade 4 - in (mm)	3.4506 - 3.4510 (87.645 - 87.655)	3.5746 - 3.5750 (90.795 - 90.805)
Standard service replacement - in (mm)	3.4500 - 3.4510 (87.630 - 87.655)	3.5740 - 3.5750 (90.780 - 90.805)
Oversize service replacement:		
0.5 - in (mm)	3.4697 - 3.4707 (88.130 - 88.155)	3.5937 - 3.5947 (91.280 - 91.305)
1.0 - in (mm)	3.4894 - 3.4904 (88.630 - 88.655)	3.6134 - 3.6144 (91.780 - 91.805)

	All engines
Piston clearance in cylinder bore - in (mm)	0.001 - 0.0024 (0.025 - 0.060)
Ring gap (in-situ):	
Top - in (mm)	0.015 - 0.023 (0.38 - 0.58)
Centre - in (mm)	0.015 - 0.023 (0.38 - 0.58)
Bottom - in (mm)	0.0157 - 0.055 (0.4 - 1.4)
Ring gap position:	
Top	150° from one side of the helical expander gap
Centre	150° from the side opposite the helical expander gap, top mark towards piston crown
Bottom	Helical expander: opposite the marked piston front side Intermediate rings: 1 in (25 mm) each side of helical expander gap

Gudgeon pins

Length - in (mm)	2.83 - 2.87 (72 - 72.8)
Diameter RED - in (mm)	0.94465 - 0.94476 (23.994 - 23.997)
BLUE - in (mm)	0.94476 - 0.94488 (23.997 - 24.000)
YELLOW - in (mm)	0.94488 - 0.94500 (24.000 - 24.003)
Clearance in piston - in (mm)	0.0003 - 0.00055 (0.008 - 0.014)
Interference in small end bush - in (mm)	0.0007 - 0.00153 (0.018 - 0.039)

Connecting rod

Big-end bore - in (mm)	2.1653 - 2.1661 (55.00 - 55.02)
Small end bush diameter - in (mm)	0.9434 - 0.9439 (23.964 - 23.976)
Inside diameter:	
Standard - in (mm)	2.0475 - 2.0490 (52.006 - 52.044)
Undersize 0.25 - in (mm)	2.0376 - 2.0391 (51.756 - 51.794)
0.50 - in (mm)	2.0278 - 2.0293 (51.506 - 51.544)
0.75 - in (mm)	2.0180 - 2.0194 (51.256 - 51.294)
1.00 - in (mm)	2.0081 - 2.0096 (51.006 - 51.044)
Crankpin to bearing liner clearance:	
Aluminium - in (mm)	0.0002 - 0.0027 (0.006 - 0.069)
Compound - in (mm)	0.0002 - 0.0025 (0.006 - 0.064)

Cylinder head

	1.6 litre, 1.6 litre GT	**2.0 litre**
Cast identification number	6	0

	All engines
Valve seat angle	44° 30' - 45°
Valve guide inside diameter, inlet and exhaust (standard) - in (mm)	0.3174 - 0.3184 (8.063 - 8.088)
Oversize 0.2 - in (mm)	0.3253 - 0.3263 (8.263 - 8.288)
0.4 - in (mm)	0.3332 - 0.3342 (8.463 - 8.488)

Parent bore for camshaft bearing liners:	
Front - in (mm)	1.6549 - 1.6557 (42.035 - 42.055)
Centre - in (mm)	1.7580 - 1.7589 (44.655 - 44.675)
Rear - in (mm)	1.7730 - 1.7738 (45.035 - 45.055)

Valves

Valve clearance (cold):	
Inlet	0.008 (0.20)
Exhaust	0.010 (0.25)

	1.6 litre, 1.6 litre GT	2.0 litre
Inlet opens	22° BTDC	24° BTDC
Inlet closes	54° ABDC	64° ABDC
Exhaust opens	64° BBDC	70° BBDC
Exhaust closes	12° ATDC	18° ATDC

Inlet valve

Length - in (mm)	4.449 ± 0.016 (113 ± 0.4)	4.3760 (111.15)
Valve head diameter - in (mm)	1.516 ± 0.008 (38.5 ± 0.2)	1.654 ± 0.008 (42 ± 0.2)

	All engines
Valve stem diameter:	
Standard - in (mm)	0.3159 - 0.3167 (8.025 - 8.043)
Oversize 0.2 - in (mm)	0.3238 - 0.3245 (8.225 - 8.243)
0.4 - in (mm)	0.3317 - 0.3324 (8.425 - 8.443)
Valve stem to guide clearance - in (mm)	0.0008 - 0.0025 (0.020 - 0.063)

	1.6 litre, 1.6 litre GT	2.0 litre GT
Valve lift - in (mm)	0.3730 (9.474)	0.3993 (10.142)
Spring load, valve open - lb f (kg f)	169.4 ± 6.6 (77 ± 3)	176 ± 6 (80 ± 3)

	All engines
Spring load, valve closed - lb f (kg f)	68 ± 4 (31 ± 2)
Spring length, compressed - in (mm)	0.945 (24)
Spring free-length - in (mm)	1.73 (44)

Exhaust valve

	1.6 litre, 1.6 litre GT	2.0 litre
Length - in (mm)	4.449 ± 0.19 (113 ± 0.5)	4.37 ± 0.19 (111 ± 0.5)

	1.6 litre	1.6 litre GT	2.0 litre
Valve head diameter - in	1.18 ± 0.08	1.34 ± 0.08	1.42 ± 0.08
mm	30 ± 0.2	34 ± 0.2	36 ± 0.2

	All engines
Valve stem diameter:	
Standard - in (mm)	0.3149 - 0.3156 (7.999 - 8.017)
Oversize 0.2 - in (mm)	0.3228 - 0.3235 (8.199 - 8.217)
0.4 - in (mm)	0.3307 - 0.3314 (8.399 - 8.417)
Valve stem to guide clearance - in (mm)	0.0018 - 0.0035 (0.046 - 0.089)
Valve spring free-length - in (mm)	1.7321 (44)

	1.6 litre, 1.6 litre GT	2.0 litre
Valve lift	0.3741 (9.5034)	0.3985 (10.1211)
Spring force:		
Valve open - lb f (kg f)	160 ± 6.6 (72.5 ± 3)	166 ± 6.6 (75.3 ± 3)
Valve closed - lb f (kg f)	66 ± 4.4 (30 ± 2)	66 ± 4.4 (30 ± 2)
Spring length, compressed - in (mm)	1.0366 (26.33)	1.0197 (25.9)

Engine lubrication data

Initial sump capacity, including filter:	
Imp. pint (litre)	6.6 (3.75)
Oil change without renewal of filter	
Imp. pint (litre)	5.3 (3.0)
Minimum oil pressure at:	
700 rpm lb f/in² (kgf/cm²)	16 (1.1)
1500 rpm lb f/in² (kgf/cm²)	36 (2.5)
Relief valve opens at - lb f/in² (kgf/cm²)	57 - 67 (4.0 - 4.7)
Oil pump outer rotor and housing clearance - in (mm)	0.006 - 0.012 (0.15 - 0.30)
Inner and outer rotor clearance - in (mm)	0.002 - 0.008 (0.05 - 0.20)
Inner and outer rotor endfloat - in (mm)	0.0011 - 0.0041 (0.028 - 0.104)
Oil pressure warning light illuminates at lb f/in² (kg f/cm²)	4 to 9 (0.3 to 0.6)
Engine oil type	Multigrade

Note: In the above Specifications it will be seen that a figure is given after the word Undersize or Oversize. This figure refers to the service replacement part and is measured in millimetres.

Torque wrench settings	lbf ft	kgf m
Main bearing caps	64.5 - 74.5	9.0 - 10.4
Flywheel	46.5 - 50.9	6.5 - 7.1
Connecting rod bolts	30 - 35	4.1 - 4.8
Crankshaft pulley	41 - 44	5.7 - 6.1
Camshaft gear	33 - 37	4.6 - 5.1
Oil pump	12 - 15	1.6 - 2.1
Oil pump cover	6.4 - 9.3	0.9 - 1.3
Oil sump (stage 1)	0.7 - 1.4	0.1 - 0.2
Oil sump (stage 2)	4.3 - 5.7	0.6 - 0.8
After 20 minutes running re-tighten (stage 3)	4.3 - 5.7	0.6 - 0.8
Oil drain plug	15 - 20	2.1 - 2.8
Oil pressure switch	9 - 11	1.2 - 1.5
Valve adjustment ball pins	33 - 37	4.6 - 5.1
Cylinder head (stage 1)	15 - 30	2.0 - 4.0
Cylinder head (stage 2)	36 - 51	4.9 - 6.9
After 20 minutes wait re-tighten (stage 3)	54 - 61	7.3 - 8.3
After 15 minutes running at 1000 rpm, re-tighten (stage 4)	70 - 85	9.5 - 11.5
Rocker cover:		
1st to 6th bolt	(1) 3.6 - 5	0.5 - 0.7
7th to 8th bolt	(2) 1.4 - 1.8	0.2 - 0.25
9th and 10th bolt	(3) 3.6 - 5	0.5 - 0.7
7th and 8th bolt	(4) 3.6 - 5	0.5 - 0.7
Front cover	10 - 13	1.4 - 1.8
Inlet manifold	13 - 15	1.8 - 2.1
Exhaust manifold	15 - 18	2.1 - 2.5
Spark plugs	See Chapter 4 Specifications	

1 General description

Engines fitted to models covered by this Section of the manual are of the four cylinder overhead camshaft design and available in two capacities, 1.6 litre and 2.0 litre. An exploded view identifying the main components is shown in Fig. 1.1.

The cylinder head is of the crossflow design with the inlet manifold one side and the exhaust manifold on the other. As flat top pistons are used, the combustion chambers are contained in the cylinder head.

The combined crankcase and cylinder block is made of cast iron and houses the pistons and crankshaft. Attached to the underside of the crankcase is a pressed steel sump which acts as a reservoir for the engine oil. Full information on the lubricating system will be found in Section 24.

The cast iron cylinder head is mounted on top of the cylinder block and acts as a support for the overhead camshaft. The slightly angled valves operate directly in the cylinder head and are controlled by the camshaft via cam followers. The camshaft is operated by a toothed reinforced composite rubber belt from the crankshaft. To eliminate backlash and prevent slackness of the belt a spring loaded tensioner in the form of a jockey wheel is in contact with the back of the belt. It serves two further functions, to keep the belt away from the water pump and also to increase the contact area of the camshaft and crankshaft sprocket.

The drive belt also drives the balance shaft sprocket and it is from this shaft that the oil pump, distributor and fuel pump operate.

The inlet manifold is mounted on the left-hand side of the cylinder head and to this the carburettor is fitted. A water jacket is incorporated in the inlet manifold so that the petrol air charge may be correctly prepared before entering the combustion chambers.

The exhaust manifold is mounted on the right-hand side of the cylinder head and connects to a single downpipe and silencer system.

Aluminium alloy pistons are connected to the crankshaft by 'H' section forged steel connecting rods and gudgeon pins. The gudgeon pin is a press fit in the small end of the connecting rod but a floating fit in the piston boss. Two compression rings and one scraper ring, all located above the gudgeon pin, are fitted.

The forged crankshaft runs in five main bearings and endfloat is accommodated by fitting thrust washers either side of the centre main bearing.

Before commencing any overhaul work on the engine refer to Section 8, where information is given about special tools that are required to remove the cylinder head, drivebelt tensioner and oil pump.

2 Major operations possible with engine in car

The following major operations can be carried out as the engine with it in place:

1 *Removal and refitting of cylinder head*
2 *Removal and refitting of camshaft drivebelt*
3 *Removal and refitting of engine front mountings*

The camshaft can be removed after removal of the cylinder head.

3 Major operations requiring engine removal

The following major operations can be carried out with the engine out of the body frame on the bench or floor:

1 *Removal and refitting of the main bearings*
2 *Removal and refitting of the crankshaft*
3 *Removal and refitting of the flywheel*
4 *Removal and refitting of the crankshaft rear oil seal*
5 *Removal and refitting of the sump*
6 *Removal and refitting of the pistons, connecting rods and big-end bearings*
7 *Removal and refitting of auxiliary (balance) shaft*

4 Methods of engine removal

The engine may be lifted out either on its own or in unit with the gearbox. On models fitted with automatic transmission it is recommended that the engine be lifted out on its own, unless a substantial crane or overhead hoist is available, because of the weight factor. If the engine and gearbox are removed as a unit they have to be lifted out at a very steep angle, so make sure that there is sufficient lifting height available.

5 Engine - removal (with gearbox)

1 The do-it-yourself owner should be able to remove the power unit fairly easily in about 3 hours. It is essential to have a good hoist and two axle stands if an inspection pit is not available.
2 The sequence of operations listed in this Section is not critical as the position of the person undertaking the work, or the tool in his hand, will determine to a certain extent the order in which the work is

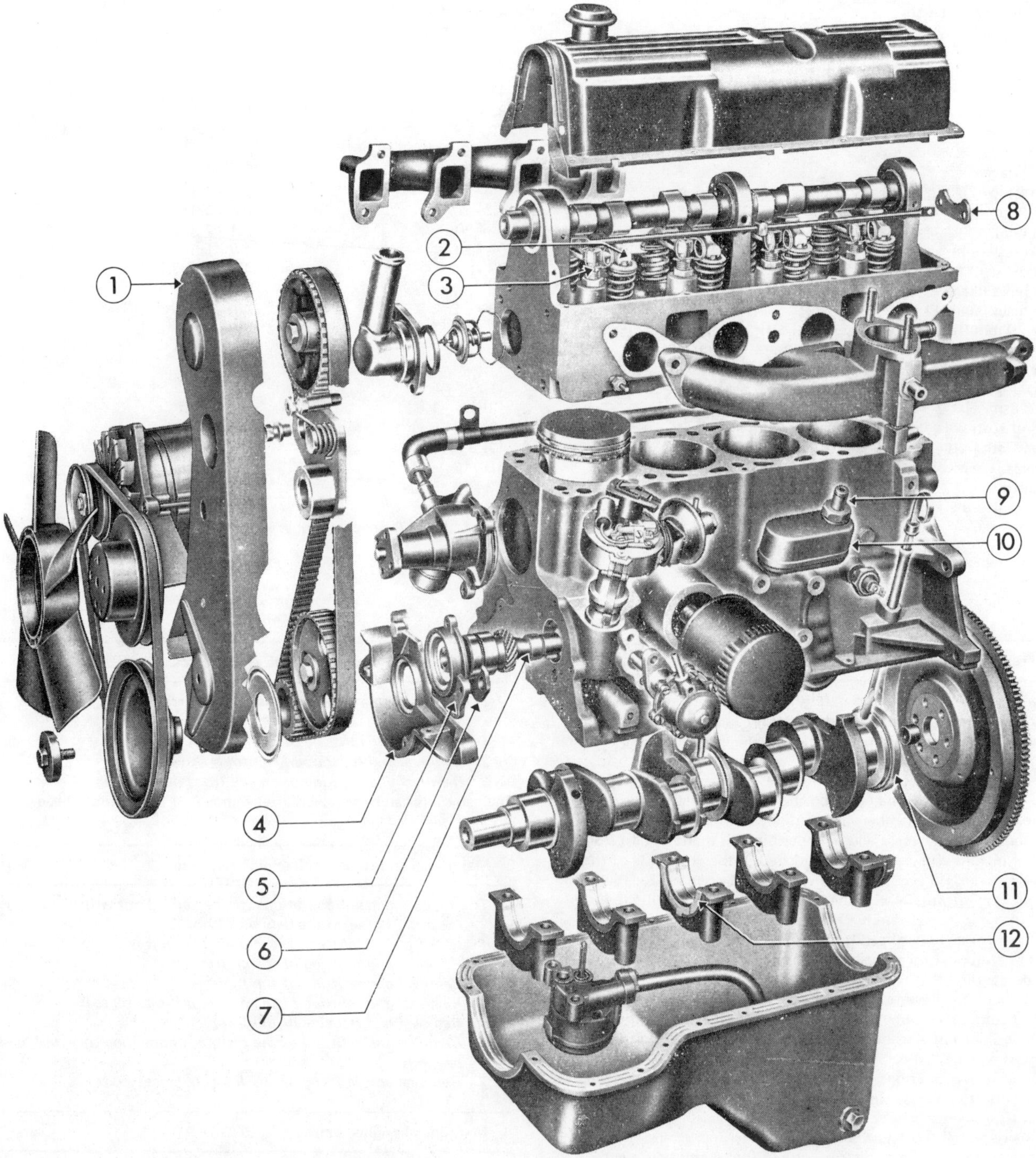

Fig. 1.1. Major components of the engine (Sec. 1)

1 Guard, toothed belt drive
2 Cam follower
3 Cam follower spring
4 Timing cover, crankshaft
5 Timing cover, auxiliary shaft
6 Thrust plate, auxiliary shaft
7 Auxiliary shaft
8 Thrust plate, camshaft
9 Ventilation valve
10 Oil seaparator
11 Oil seal, crankshaft
12 Central main bearing

tackled.
3 Open the bonnet and using a soft pencil mark the outline positon of both the hinges at the bonnet to act as a datum for refitting.
4 With the help of a second person to take the weight of the bonnet undo and remove the hinge to bonnet securing bolts with plain and spring washers. There are two bolts to each hinge.
5 Lift away the bonnet and put in a safe place where it will not be scratched. Remove the battery as described in Chapter 10.
6 Place a container having a capacity of at least 8 Imp. pints (4.55 litres) under the engine sump and remove the oil drain plug. Allow the oil to drain out and then refit the plug using a new sealing washer.
7 Refer to Chapter 3, and remove the air cleaner assembly from the top of the carburettor.
8 Mark the HT leads so that they may be refitted in their original positions and detach from the spark plugs.
9 Release the HT lead rubber moulding from the clip on the top of the cover.
10 Spring back the clips securing the distributor cap to the distributor body. Lift off the distributor cap.
11 Detach the HT lead from the centre of the ignition coil. Remove the distributor cap from the engine compartment.
12 Refer to Chapter 2 and drain the cooling system.
13 Slacken the clip that secures the heater hose to the water pump. Pull off the hose.
14 Slacken the clip that secures the heater hose to the heater unit; pull off the hose.
15 Slacken the clips that secure the hoses to the automatic choke and pull off the two hoses (automatic choke).
16 Slacken the clip securing the water hose to the adaptor elbow on the side of the inlet manifold and pull off the hose.
17 Slacken the clips that secure the fuel pipes to the carburettor float chamber and pull off the hoses. Plug the ends to stop dirt ingress or fuel loss due to syphoning.
18 Detach the throttle control inner cable from the operating rod then, unscrew the throttle control outer cable securing nut. Detach the cable from the mounting bracket (photo).
19 Slacken the choke outer cable securing clip screw and detach the inner cable from the choke linkage (manual choke) (photo).
20 Detach the vacuum pipe from the vacuum unit on the side of the distributor.
21 Undo and remove the four nuts and washers that secure the carburettor to the inlet manifold. Carefully lift the carburettor up and away from the studs on the manifold.
22 The combined insulation spacer and gasket may now be lifted from the studs. Note that it is marked 'TOP FRONT' and it must be refitted the correct way round.
23 Slacken the clips securing the hoses to the manifold; pull off the hoses.
24 Detach the brake servo hose from the manifold and move it to one side.
25 Undo and remove the self lock nuts and bolts securing the inlet manifold to the side of the cylinder head.
26 Note that one of the manifold securing bolts also retains the air cleaner support bracket on some models.
27 Lift away the inlet manifold.
28 Carefully lift away the inlet manifold gasket.
29 Undo and remove the two nuts that secure the exhaust downpipe clamp plate to the exhaust manifold.
30 Slide the clamp plate down the exhaust pipe.
31 Refer to Chapter 2 and remove the radiator.
32 Detach the thermal transmitter electric cable from the inlet manifold side of the cylinder head.
33 Pull the crankcase ventilation valve and hose from the oil separator located on the left-hand side of the cylinder block.
34 Detach the oil pressure warning light cable from the switch located below the oil separator, or unscrew the oil pressure gauge pipe fitting (as applicable).
35 *Pre-engaged starter:* Detach the Lucar terminal connector from the starter motor solenoid. Also detach the terminal connector from the rear of the alternator. If tight a screwdriver will be of assistance. Make a note of the electrical cable connections on the rear of the starter motor solenoid and detach the cables.
36 *Inertia starter:* Detach the single cable from the front end of the starter motor.
37 Undo and remove the distributor clamp bolt and clamp. Lift away the distributor.
38 Undo and remove the bolt that secures the earth cable terminal to the crossmember just in front of the fuel pump.
39 Undo and remove the two bolts and spring washers that secure the fuel pump to the cylinder block.
40 Remove the fuel pump. Withdraw the pump operating rod from the cylinder block and put in a safe place.
41 Slacken the alternator securing bolts and push the alternator towards the engine. Lift away the fan belt.
42 Undo and remove the four bolts that secure the fan pulley to the water pump pulley hub. Lift away the fan and pulley.
43 Working under the car slacken the exhaust downpipe to silencer clamp.
44 Detach the exhaust pipe rubber mounting from the body mounted bracket and pull the exhaust system to one side to give better access. Tie in position with string or wire.
45 *Type C gearbox:* From inside the car remove the gear lever as described in Chapter 6.
46 *Type H gearbox:* From beneath the car detach the gearshift rods as described in Chapter 6.
47 Mark the mating position of the propeller shaft flanges then remove the shaft. For further information refer to Chapter 7.
48 Wrap some polythene around the end of the gearbox and secure with string or wire to stop oil running out.
49 Pull off the plug attached to the reverse light switch located on the

5.18 Detach the throttle cable connection

5.19 Detach the choke cable connection

side of the remote control housing.
50 Using a pair of circlip pliers remove the circlip retaining the speedometer drive cable end to the gearbox extension housing.
51 Pull the speedometer drive cable away from the side of the extension housing.
52 Using a pair of pliers detach the clutch operating cable from the actuating arm that protrudes from the side of the clutch housing. On some models it will be necessary to pull back the rubber gaiter first.
53 Pull the clutch cable assembly through the locating hole in the flange on the clutch housing.
54 Suitably support the weight of the gearbox by either using a jack or an axle stand. Using a sling passed under the engine mountings support the weight of the engine.
55 Undo and remove the one bolt that secures the rubber mounting to the gearbox extension housing.
56 Undo and remove the four bolts, spring and plain washers that secure the gearbox support crossmember to the body. Lift away the crossmember.
57 Undo and remove the two engine mountings lower securing nut and large plain washer.
58 Check that no electric cables or controls have been left connected and are tucked well out of the way.
59 The complete unit may now be removed from the car. Commence by removing the support from the rear of the gearbox and carefully lower the end to the ground. It will be beneficial if a piece of wood planking is placed between the end of the gearbox and the floor so that it can act as a skid.
60 Carefully raise the engine and pull slightly forward. It will now be necessary to tilt the engine at a very steep angle so that the sump clears the front grille panels. Continue to raise the engine until the sump is just above the front panel (photo). When all is clear lower the unit to the floor.
61 Thoroughly wash the exterior with paraffin (kerosene) or a water soluble solvent. Wash off with a strong water jet and dry thoroughly.
62 The gearbox may now be separated from the engine. Undo and remove the two bolts that secure the starter motor to the bellhousing flange. Lift away the starter motor.
63 Remove the rear engine cover plate and bracket assembly from the clutch housing.
64 Undo and remove the remaining bolts that secure the clutch bellhousing to the rear of the engine. The gearbox may now be parted from the engine. **Do not** allow the weight of the gearbox to hang on the input shaft (first motion shaft) whilst it is still engaged in the clutch driven plate hub.

6 Engine - removal (without gearbox)

1 Follow the instructions given in Section 5, paragraphs 1 to 44, inclusive.
2 Suitably support the weight of the gearbox by either using a jack or an axle stand. Using a rope sling passed under the engine mountings support the weight of the engine.

5.60 The approximate angle for lifting out the engine

3 Undo and remove the two engine mounting lower securing nuts and large plain washer.
4 *Pre-engaged starter:* Undo and remove the two bolts that secure the starter motor to the gearbox flange. Lift away the starter motor.
5 Remove the rear engine cover plate and bracket assembly from the clutch housing. Detach the bracket assembly from the cylinder block and swing it back out of the way.
6 Undo and remove the remaining bolts that secure the clutch bellhousing to the rear of the engine.
7 Follow the instructions given in Section 5, paragraphs 58, 60 and 61.

7 Engine - removal (without automatic transmission)

Because of the weight considerations it is advisable to detach and remove the automatic transmission first, as described in Chapter 6, and then remove the engine, as described in Section 6 of this Chapter.

8 Engine - dismantling (general)

1 It is best to mount the engine on a dismantling stand, but if this is not available, stand the engine on a strong bench at a comfortable working height. Failing this, it will have to be stripped down on the floor.
2 During the dismantling process, the greatest care should be taken to keep the exposed parts free from dirt. As an aid to achieving this thoroughly clean down the outside of the engine, first removing all traces of oil and congealed dirt.
3 A good grease solvent will make the job much easier, for, after the solvent has been applied and allowed to stand for a time, a vigorous jet of water will wash off the solvent and grease with it. If the dirt is thick and deeply embedded, work the solvent into it with a strong stiff brush.
4 Finally, wipe down the exterior of the engine with a rag and only then, when it is quite clean, should the dismantling process begin. As the engine is stripped, clean each part in a bath of paraffin or petrol.
5 Never immerse parts with oilways in paraffin (eg; crankshaft and camshaft). To clean these parts, wipe down carefully with a petrol dampened rag. Oilways can be cleaned out with wire. If an air-line is available, all parts can be blown dry and the oilways blown through as an added precaution.
6 Re-use of old gaskets is false economy. To avoid the possibility of trouble after the engine has been reassembled **always** use new gaskets throughout.
7 Do not throw away the old gaskets, for sometimes it happens that an immediate replacement cannot be found and the old gasket is then very useful as a template. Hang up the gaskets as they are removed.
8 To strip the engine, it is best to work from the top down. When the stage is reached where the crankshaft must be removed, the engine can be turned on its side and all other work carried out with it in this position.
9 Wherever possible, refit nuts, bolts and washers finger tight from wherever they were removed. This helps to avoid loss and muddle. If they cannot be refitted then arrange them in a fashion that it is clear from whence they came.
10 Before dismantling begins it is important that three special tools are obtained otherwise certain work cannot be carried out. The special tools are shown in the photo, and will enable the cylinder head bolts, the oil pump bolts and the valve springs to be removed.

9 Engine - removing ancillary components

Before basic engine dismantling begins, it is necessary to strip it of ancillary components.

a) Fuel components
Carburettor and manifold assembly
Exhaust manifold
Fuel pump
Fuel line

b) Ignition system components
Spark plugs
Distributor

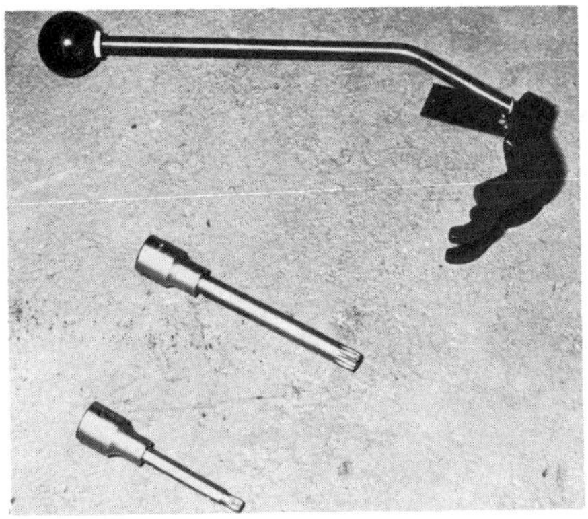

8.10 Three special tools necessary for dismantling

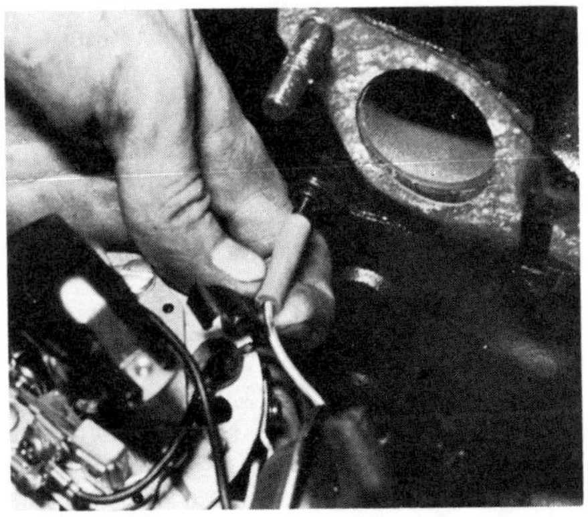

10.19 Thermal transmitter cable detachment

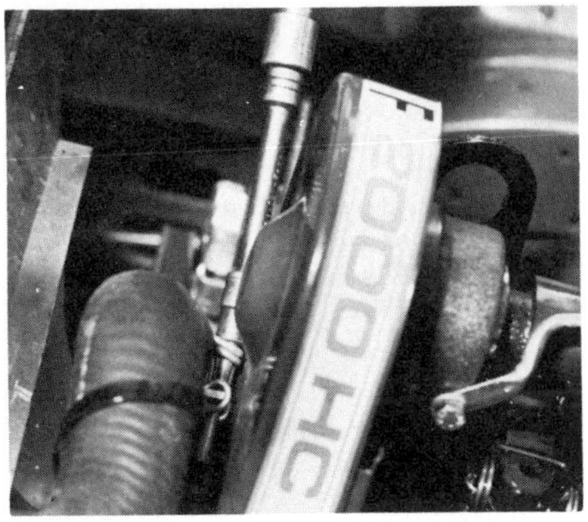

10.20 Slackening radiator top hose clip

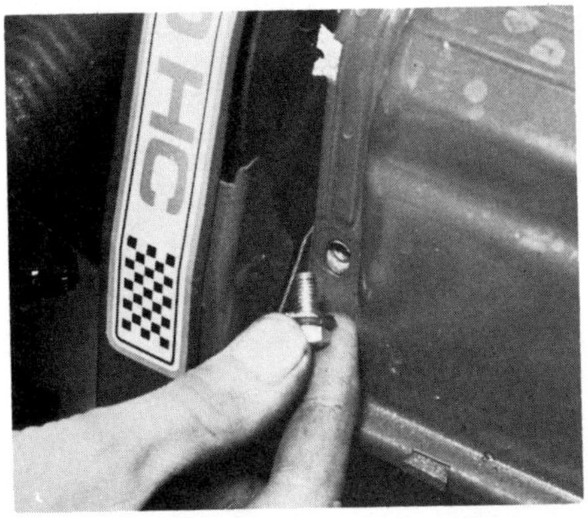

10.21A Top cover flange securing bolts

10.21B Top cover flange securing bolts

10.22 Top cover removal

10.23 Heat deflector plate removal

10.24 Belt guard securing bolts removal

10.25 Belt guard removal

10.26 Releasing belt tensioner mounting plate securing bolt

10.27 Removing belt from camshaft sprocket

10.28 Slackening cylinder head securing bolts

c) *Electrical system components*
Alternator
Starter motor
d) *Cooling system components*
Fan and hub
Water pump
Thermostat housing and thermostat
Water temperature indicator sender unit
e) *Engine*
Oil filter
Oil pressure sender unit
Oil level dipstick
Oil filler cap and top cover
Engine mountings
Crankcase ventilation valve and oil separator
f) *Clutch*
Clutch pressure plate assembly
Clutch friction plate assembly
g) *Where emission control systems are installed (see Chapter 3), remove any additional items bolted to the cylinder block.*

Some of these items have to be removed for individual servicing or renewal periodically and details can be found in the appropriate Chapter.

10 Cylinder head - removal (engine in car)

1 Open the bonnet and using a soft pencil mark the outline of both the hinges at the bonnet to act as a datum for refitting.
2 With the help of a second person to take the weight of the bonnet undo and remove the hinge to bonnet securing bolts with plain and spring washers. There are two bolts to each hinge.
3 Lift away the bonnet and put in a safe place where it will not be scratched.
4 Refer to Chapter 10, and remove the battery.
5 Refer to Chapter 3, and remove the air cleaner assembly from the top of the carburettor.
6 Mark the HT leads so that they may be refitted in their original positions and detach from the spark plugs.
7 Release the HT lead rubber moulding from the clip on the top of the cover.
8 Spring back the clips securing the distributor cap to the distributor body. Lift off the distributor cap.
9 Detach the HT lead from the centre of the ignition coil. Remove the distributor cap from the engine compartment.
10 Refer to Chapter 2, and drain the cooling system.
11 Refer to Chapter 3, and remove the carburettor.
12 The combined insulation spacer and gasket may now be lifted from the studs. Note that it is marked 'TOP FRONT' and it must be refitted the correct way round.
13 Slacken the clip securing the hose to the inlet manifold branch pipe adaptor and pull off the hose.
14 Slacken the clip securing the hose to the adaptor at the centre of the manifold and pull off the hose.
15 Undo and remove the self lock nuts and bolts securing the inlet manifold to the side of the cylinder head. Note that one of the manifold securing bolts also retains the air cleaner support bracket on some models.
16 Lift away the inlet manifold and recover the manifold gasket.
17 Undo and remove the two nuts that secure the exhaust downpipe and clamp plate to the exhaust manifold.
18 Slide the clamp plate down the exhaust pipe.
19 Detach the thermal transmitter cable from the inlet manifold side of the cylinder head (photo).
20 Slacken the radiator top hose clips and completely remove the hose (photo).
21 Undo and remove the bolts, spring and plain washers that secure the top cover to the cylinder head (photos).
22 Lift away the top cover (photo).
23 Undo and remove the two self locking nuts that secure the heat deflector plate to the top of the exhaust manifold. Lift away the deflector plate (photo).
24 Undo and remove the bolts, spring and plain washers that secure the toothed drivebelt guard (photo).
25 Lift away the guard (photo).
26 Release the tension from the drivebelt by slackening the spring loaded roller mounting plate securing bolt (photo).
27 Lift the toothed drivebelt from the camshaft sprocket (photo).
28 Using the special tool 21 - 002 together with a socket wrench (photo), slacken the cylinder head securing bolts in a diagonal and progressive manner until all are free from tension. Remove the ten bolts noting that because of the special shape of the bolt head no washers are used. Unfortunately there is no other tool suitable to slot into the bolt head so do not attempt to improvise which will only cause damage to the bolt (Fig. 1.2).
29 The cylinder head may now be removed by lifting upwards (photo). If the head is stuck, try to rock it to break the seal. Under no circumstances try to prise it apart from the cylinder block with a screwdriver or cold chisel, as damage may be done to the faces of the cylinder head and block. If the head will not readily free, temporarily refit the battery and turn the engine over using the starter motor, as the compression in the cylinders will often break the cylinder head joint. If this fails to work, strike the head sharply with a plastic headed or wooden hammer, or with a metal hammer with an interposed piece of wood to cushion the blow. Under no circumstances hit the head directly with a metal hammer as this may cause the casting to fracture. Several sharp taps with the hammer, at the same time pulling upwards, should free the head. Lift the head off and place to one side (photo).

Fig. 1.2. Correct order for slackening or tightening cylinder head bolts (secs. 10 and 58)

10.29A Cylinder head removal

10.20B Engine with cylinder head removed

12.1 Auxiliary shaft sprocket securing bolt removal

12.2 Balance shaft timing cover securing bolts removal

12.3 Balance shaft timing cover removal

12.4 Removal of thrust plate securing screws

12.5 Lifting away thrust plate

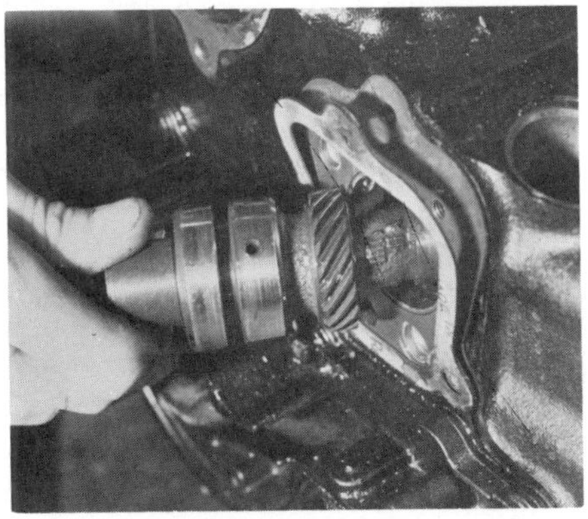
12.6 Withdrawal of auxiliary shaft

13.1 Flywheel securing bolts removal

13.2 Lifting away flywheel

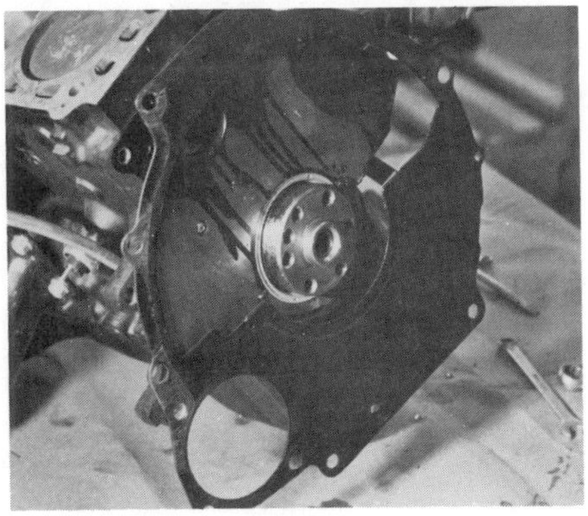
13.3 Backplate removal

14.1 Removal of sump securing bolts

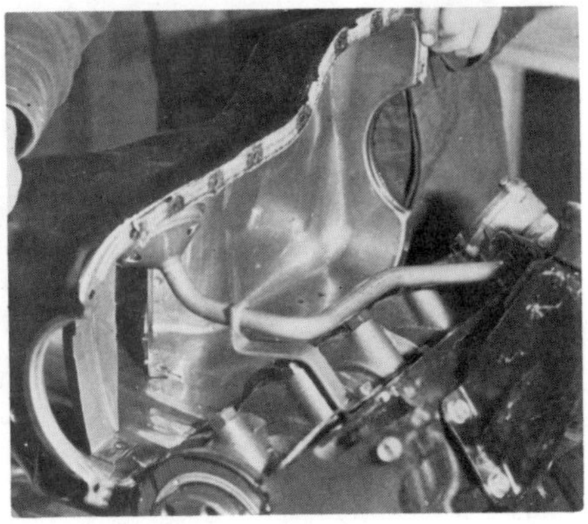
14.2 Lifting away sump

11 Cylinder head - removal (engine on bench)

The procedure for removing the cylinder head with the engine on the bench is similar to that for removal when the engine is in the car, with the exception of disconnecting the controls and services. Refer to Section 10, and follow the sequence given in paragraphs 21 to 29 inclusive.

12 Auxiliary shaft removal

1 Using a metal bar lock the shaft sprocket and with an open ended spanner undo and remove the bolt and washer that secures the sprocket to the shaft (photo).
2 Undo and remove the three bolts and spring washers that secure the shaft timing cover to the cylinder block (photo).
3 Lift away the timing cover (photo).
4 Undo and remove the two crosshead screws that secure the thrust plate to the cylinder block (photo).
5 Lift away the thrust plate (photo).
6 The shaft may now be drawn forwards and then lifted away (photo).

13 Flywheel and backplate - removal

1 With the clutch removed, as described in Chapter 5, lock the flywheel using a screwdriver in mesh with the starter ring gear and undo the six bolts that secure the flywheel to the crankshaft in a diagonal and progressive manner (photo). Lift away the bolts.
2 Mark the relative position of the flywheel and crankshaft and then lift away the flywheel (photo).
3 Undo the remaining engine backplate securing bolts and ease the backplate from the two dowels. Lift away the backplate (photo).

14 Sump, oil pump and strainer - removal

1 Undo and remove the bolts that secure the sump to the underside of the crankcase (photo).
2 Lift away the sump and its gasket (photo).
3 Undo and remove the screw and spring washer that secures the oil pump pick up pipe support bracket to the crankcase.
4 Using special tool (21 - 020) undo the two special bolts that secure the oil pump to the underside of the crankcase. Unfortunately there is no other tool suitable to slot into the screw head so do not attempt to improvise which will only cause damage to the screw (photo).
5 Lift away the oil pump and strainer assembly (photo).
6 Carefully lift away the oil pump drive making a special note of which way round it is fitted (photo).

15 Crankshaft pulley, sprocket and timing cover - removal

1 Lock the crankshaft using a block of soft wood placed between a crankshaft web and the crankcase then using a socket and suitable extension, undo the bolt that secures the crankshaft pulley. Recover the large diameter plain washer.
2 Using a large screwdriver ease the pulley from the crankshaft. Recover the large diameter thrust washer.
3 Again using the screwdriver ease the sprocket from the crankshaft (photo).
4 Undo and remove the bolts and spring washers that secure the timing cover to the front of the crankcase.
5 Lift away the timing cover and the gasket (photo).

16 Pistons, connecting rods and big-end bearings - removal

1 Note that the pistons have an arrow marked on the crown showing the forward facing side (photo). Inspect the big-end bearing caps and

14.4 Oil pump securing bolts removal

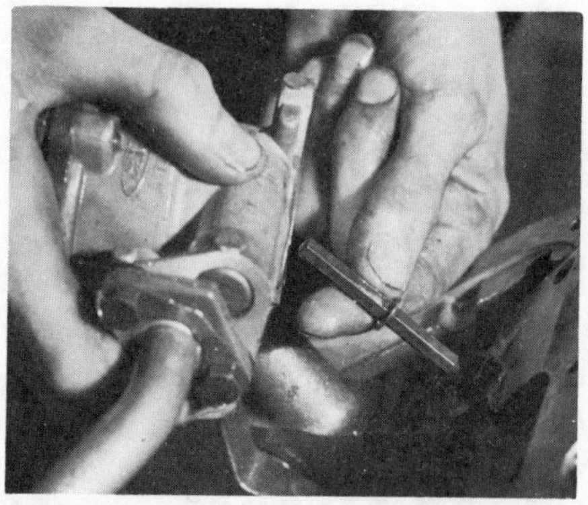

14.5 Lifting away oil pump and pick-up pipe

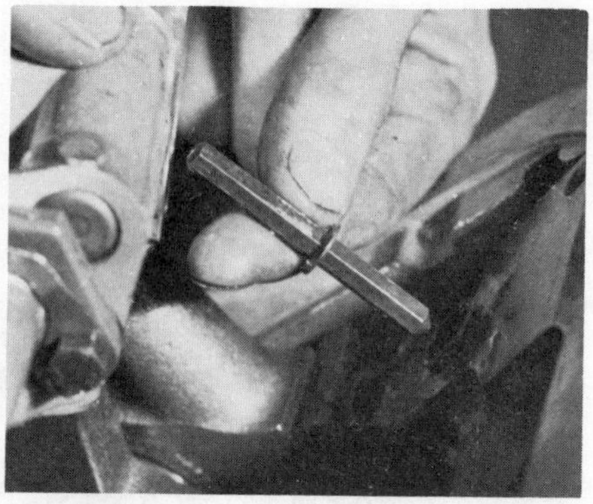

14.6 Oil pump drive shaft removal

15.3 Removal of sprocket from crankshaft

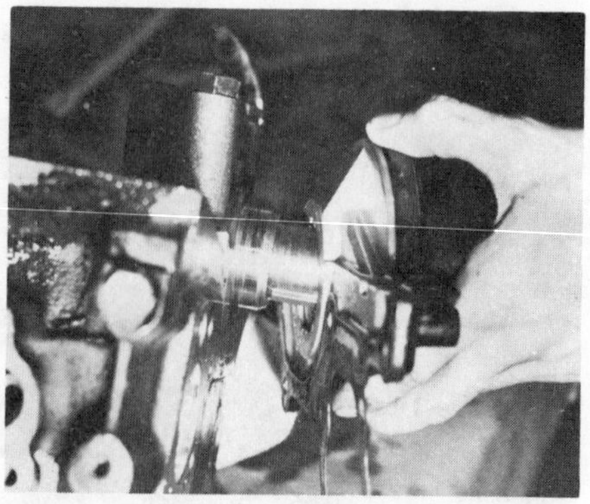

15.5 Timing cover and gasket removal

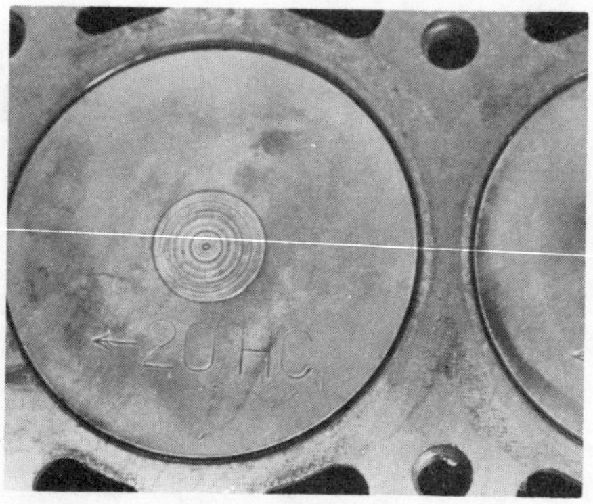

16.1 Piston crown identification marks

connecting rods to make sure identification marks are visible. This is to ensure that the correct end caps are fitted to the correct connecting rods and the connecting rods placed in their respective bores (Fig. 1.3).
2 Undo the big-end nuts and place to one side in the order in which they were removed.
3 Remove the big-end caps, taking care to keep them in the right order and the correct way round. Also ensure that the shell bearings are kept with their correct connecting rods unless the rods are to be renewed (photo).
4 If the big-end caps are difficult to remove, they may be gently tapped with a soft faced hammer.
5 To remove the shell bearings, press the bearing opposite the groove in both the connecting rod and its cap, and the bearing will slide out easily.
6 Withdraw the pistons and connecting rods upwards and ensure they are kept in the correct order for replacement in the same bore as they were originally fitted.

Fig. 1.3. Big-end bearing cap and connecting rod identification marks (Sec. 16)

17 Crankshaft and main bearings - removal

With the engine removed from the car and separated from the gearbox, and the drivebelt, crankshaft pulley and sprocket, flywheel and backplate, oil pump, big-end bearings and pistons all removed:
1 Make sure that identification marks are visible on the main bearing end caps, so that they may be refitted in their original positions and also the correct way round (photo).
2 Undo by one turn at a time the bolts which hold the five bearing caps.
3 Lift away each main bearing cap and the bottom half of each bearing shell, taking care to keep the bearing shell in the right caps (photo).
4 When removing the rear main bearing end cap note that this also retains the crankshaft rear oil seal (photo).
5 When removing the centre main bearing, note the bottom semi-circular halves of the thrust washers, one half lying on either side of the main bearing. Lay them with the centre main bearing along the correct side.
6 As the centre and rear bearing end caps are accurately located by dowels it may be necessary to gently tap the end caps to release them.
7 Slightly rotate the crankshaft to free the upper halves of the bearing shells and thrust washers which can be extracted and placed over the correct bearing cap.
8 Carefully lift away the crankshaft rear oil seal (photo).
9 Remove the crankshaft by lifting it away from the crankcase (photo).

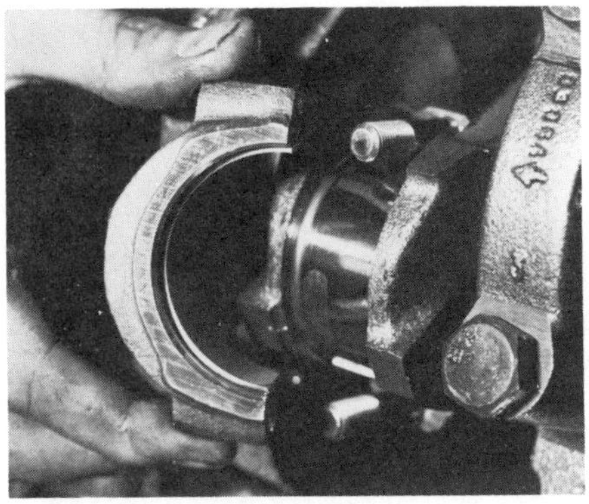

16.3 Lifting away big-end cap

17.1 Main bearing cap identification marks

17.3 Lifting away No2 main bearing cap

17.4 Rear main bearing cap removal

17.8 Lifting away crankshaft rear oil seal

17.9 Cylinder block and crankcase with crankshaft removal

18 Camshaft drivebelt - removal (engine in the car)

It is possible to remove the camshaft drivebelt with the engine in-situ but experience is such that this type of belt is very reliable and unlikely to break or stretch considerably. However, during a major engine overhaul it is recommended that a new belt is fitted. To renew the belt, engine in the car:

1 Refer to Chapter 2, and drain the cooling system. Slacken the top hose securing clips and remove the top hose.

2 Slacken the alternator mounting bolts and push the unit towards the engine. Lift away the fan belt.

3 Undo and remove the bolts that secure the drivebelt guard to the front of the engine. Lift away the guard.

4 Slacken the belt tensioner mounting plate securing bolt and release the tension on the belt.

5 Place the car in gear (manual gearbox only), and apply the brakes firmly. Undo and remove the bolt and plain washer that secure the crankshaft pulley to the nose of the crankshaft. On vehicles fitted with automatic transmission, the starter must be removed and the ring gear jammed to prevent the crankshaft from rotating.

6 Using a suitable extractor (or even a large screwdriver) carefully ease off the pulley (photo).

7 Recover the large diameter belt guide washer.

8 The drivebelt may now be lifted away (photo).

19 Valves - removal

1 To enable the valves to be removed a special valve spring compressor is required. This has a part number of '21 - 005'. However, it was found that it was just possible to use a universal valve spring compressor provided extreme caution was taken.

2 Make a special note of how the cam follower springs are fitted and using a screwdriver remove these from the cam followers (photo).

3 Back off fully the cam follower adjustment and remove the cam followers. Keep these in their respective order so that they can be refitted in their original positions.

4 Using the valve spring compressor, compress the valve springs and lift out the collets (photo).

5 Remove the spring cap and spring and, using a screwdriver prise the oil retainer caps out of their seats. Remove each valve and keep in their respective order unless they are so badly worn that they are to be renewed. If they are going to be used again, place them in a sheet of card having eight numbered holes corresponding with the relative positions of the valves when fitted. Also keep the valve springs cups etc., in the correct order.

6 If necessary unscrew the ball head bolts.

20 Camshaft - removal

It is not necessary to remove the engine from the car in order to remove the camshaft. However, it will be necessary to remove the cylinder head first (Section 10) as the camshaft has to be withdrawn from the rear.

1 Undo and remove the bolts, and spring washers and bracket that secure the camshaft lubrication pipe. Lift away the pipe (photo).

2 Carefully inspect the fine oil drillings in the pipe to make sure that none are blocked (photo).

3 Using a metal bar, lock the camshaft drive sprocket then undo and remove the sprocket securing bolt and washer (photo).

4 Using a soft faced hammer or screwdriver ease the sprocket from the camshaft (photo).

5 Undo and remove the two bolts and spring washers that secure the camshaft thrust plate to the rear bearing support (photo).

6 Lift away the thrust plate noting which way round it is fitted (photo).

7 Remove the cam follower springs and then the cam followers as detailed in Section 19, paragraphs 2 and 3.

8 The camshaft may now be removed by using a soft faced hammer and tapping rearwards. Take care not to cut the fingers when the

18.6 Lifting away crankshaft pulley

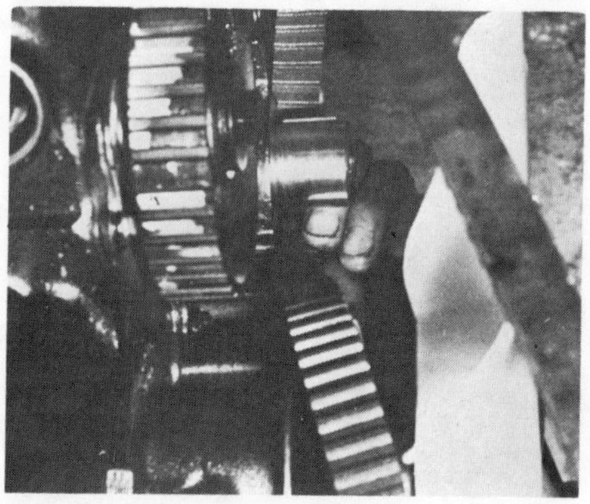

18.8 Drive belt removal

19.2 Cam follower spring removal

19.4 Compressing valve spring

20.1 Camshaft lubrication pipe removal

20.2 Camshaft lubrication pipe oil holes

20.3 Using a metal bar to lock camshaft sprocket

20.4 Removal of camshaft sprocket

20.5 Camshaft thrust plate securing bolts removal

20.6 Camshaft thrust plate removal

20.8 Tapping camshaft through bearings

20.9 Camshaft removal

20.10 Oil seal removal

21.3 Thermostat housing removal

21.4A Belt tensioner mounting plate securing bolt removal

21.4B Easing off the spring tension with a screwdriver

21.5 Using special tool to remove mounting plate and spring securing bolt from belt tensioner

camshaft is being handled as the sides of the lobes can be sharp (photo).
9 Lift the camshaft through the bearing inserts as the lobes can damage the soft metal bearing surfaces (photo).
10 If the oil seal has hardened or become damaged, it may be removed by prising it out with a screwdriver (photo).

21 Thermostat housing and belt tensioner - removal

1 Removal of these parts will usually only be necessary if the cylinder head is to be completely dismantled.
2 Undo and remove the two bolts and spring washers that secure the thermostat housing to the front face of the cylinder head. to).
3 Lift away the thermostat housing and recover its gasket (photo).
4 Undo and remove the bolt and spring washer that secures the belt tensioner to the cylinder head. It will be necessary to override the tension using a screwdriver as a lever (photos).
5 Using tool number '21 - 012', (the tool for removal of the oil pump securing bolts), unscrew the tensioner mounting plate and spring shaped bolt and lift away the tensioner assembly (photo).

22 Gudgeon pin - removal

A press type gudgeon pin is used and it is important that no damage is caused during removal and refitting. Because of this, should it be necessary to fit new pistons, take the parts along to the local Ford garage who will have the special equipment to do this job.

23 Piston rings - removal

1 To remove the piston rings, slide them carefully over the top of the piston, taking care not to scratch the aluminium alloy, never slide them off the bottom of the piston skirt. It is very easy to break the cast iron piston rings if they are pulled off roughly, so this operation should be done with extreme care. It is helpful to make use of an old 0.020 inch (0.5 mm) feeler gauge.
2 Lift one end of the piston ring to be removed out of its groove and insert under it the end of the feeler gauge.
3 Turn the feeler gauge slowly round the piston and, as the ring comes out of its groove, apply slight upward pressure so that it rests on the hand above. It can then be eased off the piston with the feeler gauge stopping it from slipping into an empty groove if it is any but the top piston that is being removed.

24 Lubrication and crankcase ventilation systems - description

1 The pressed steel oil sump is attached to the underside of the crankcase and acts as a reservoir for the engine oil. The oil pump draws oil through a strainer located under the oil surface, passes it along a short passage and into the full-flow oil filter. The freshly filtered oil flows from the centre of the filter element and enters the main gallery. Five small drillings connect the main gallery to the five main bearings. The big-end bearings are supplied with oil by the front and rear main bearings via skew oil bores. When the crankshaft is rotating, oil is thrown from the hole in each big-end bearings and splashes the thrust side of the piston.
2 The auxiliary shaft is lubricated directly from the main oil gallery. The distributor shaft is supplied with oil passing along a drilling inside the auxiliary shaft.
3 A further three drillings connect the main oil gallery to the overhead camshaft. The centre camshaft bearing has a semi-circular groove from which oil is passed along a pipe running parallel with the camshaft. The pipe is drilled opposite to each cam and cam follower so providing lubrication to the cams and cam followers. Oil then passes back to the sump via large drillings in the cylinder head and cylinder block.
4 A semi enclosed engine ventilation system is used to control crankcase vapour. It is controlled by the amount of air drawn in by the engine when running and the throughput of the regulator valve (Fig. 1.5).
5 The system is known as the PCV (Positive Crankcase Ventilation)

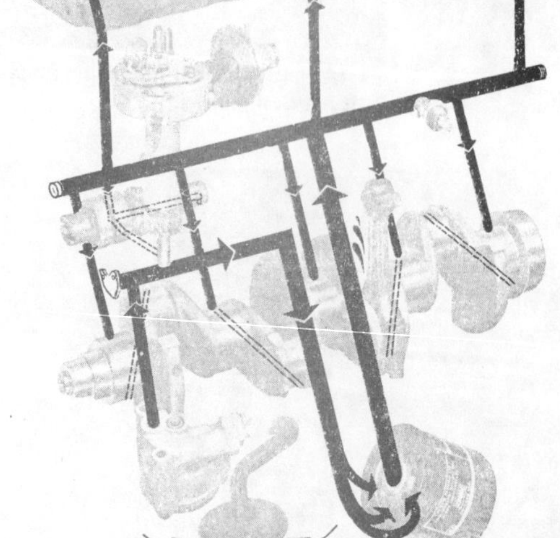

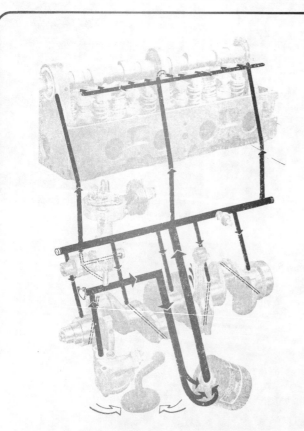

Fig. 1.4. Circulation of lubricant through the engine (Sec. 24)

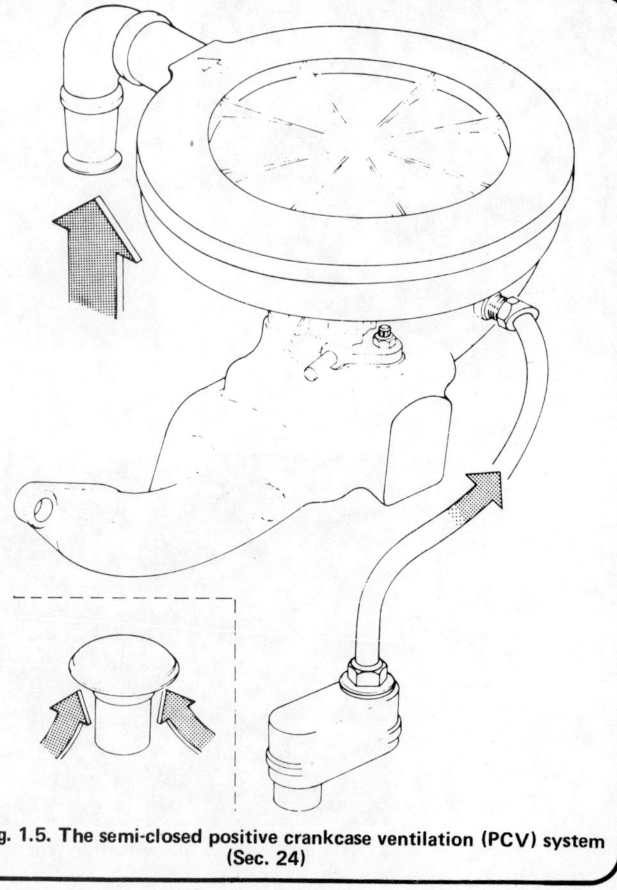

Fig. 1.5. The semi-closed positive crankcase ventilation (PCV) system (Sec. 24)

system. The advantage of this system is that should the 'blow-by' exceed the capacity of the PCV valve, excess fumes are fed into the engine through the air cleaner. This is effected by the rise in crankcase pressure which creates a reverse flow in the air intake pipe.

6 Periodically pull the valve and hose from the rubber grommet of the oil separator and inspect the valve for free-movement. If it is sticky in action or is clogged with sludge, dismantle it and clean the component parts.

7 Occasionally check the security and condition of the system connecting hoses.

25 Oil pump - dismantling, inspection and reassembly

1 If oil pump wear is suspected it is possible to obtain a repair kit. Check for wear first as described later in this section and if confirmed obtain an overhaul kit or a new pump. The two rotors are a matched pair and form a single replacement unit. Where the rotor assembly is to be re-used the outer rotor, prior to dismantling, must be marked on its front face in order to ensure correct reassembly.

2 Undo and remove the two bolts and spring washers that secure the intake cowl to the oil pump body. Lift away the cowl and its gasket (Fig. 1.6).

3 Note the relative position of the oil pump cover and body and then undo and remove the three bolts and spring washers. Lift away the cover.

4 Carefully remove the rotors from the housing.

5 Using a centre-punch tap a hole in the centre of the pressure relief valve sealing plug, (make a note to obtain a new one).

6 Screw in a self-tapping screw and using an open-ended spanner withdraw the sealing plug as shown in Fig. 1.7.

7 Thoroughly clean all parts in petrol or paraffin and wipe dry using a lint-free cloth. The necessary clearances may now be checked using a machined straight-edge (a good steel rule) and a set of feeler gauges. The critical clearances are between the lobes of the centre rotor and convex faces of the outer rotor, between the rotor and the pump body and between both rotors and the end cover plate.

8 The rotor lobe clearances may be checked using feeler gauges and should be within the limits 0.002 - 0.008 in (0.05 - 0.20 mm).

9 The clearance between the outer rotor and pump body should be within the limits 0.006 - 0.012 in (0.15 - 0.30 mm) (Fig. 1.8).

10 The endfloat clearance may be measured by placing a steel straight-edge across the end of the pump and measuring the gap between the rotors and the straight-edge. The gap in either rotor should be within the limits 0.0011 - 0.0041 in (0.028 - 0.104 mm), as shown in Fig. 1.9.

11 If the only excessive clearances are endfloat it is possible to reduce them by removing the rotors and lapping the face of the body on a flat bed until the necessary clearances are obtained. It must be emphasised, however, that the face of the body must remain perfectly flat and square to the axis of the rotor spindle otherwise the clearances will not be equal and the end cover will not be a pressure tight fit to the body. It is worth trying, of course, if the pump is in need of renewal anyway but unless done properly it could seriously jeopardise the rest of the overhaul. Any variations in the other two clearances should be overcome with a new unit.

12 With all parts scrupulously clean first refit the relief valve and spring and lightly lubricate with engine oil

13 Using a suitable diameter drift drive in a new sealing plug, flat side outwards until it is flush with the intake cowl bearing face.

14 Well lubricate both rotors with engine oil and insert into the body. Fit the oil pump cover and secure with the three bolts in a diagonal and progressive manner to the specified torque.

15 Fit the intermediate shaft into the rotor drive shaft and make sure that the rotors turn freely.

16 Fit the cowl to the pump body, using a new gasket and secure with the two bolts.

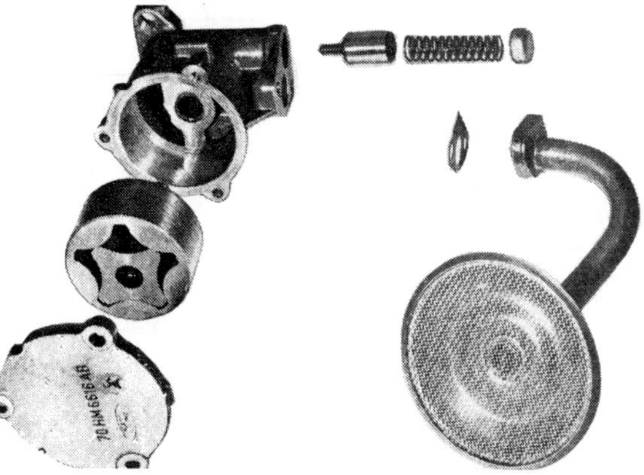

Fig. 1.6. Components of the oil pump (Sec. 25)

Fig. 1.7. Removal of sealing plug (Sec. 25)

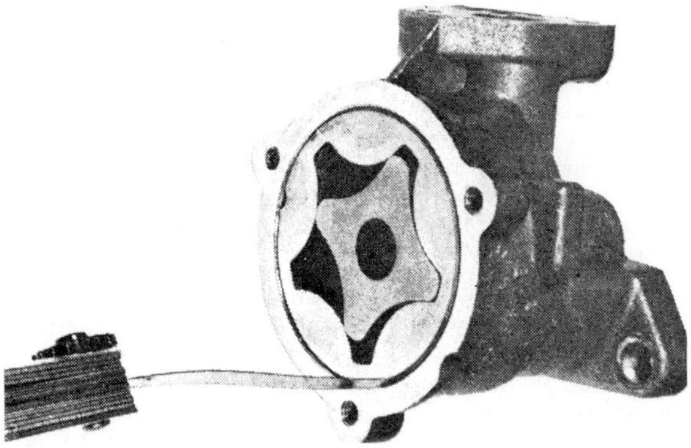

Fig. 1.8. Checking outer rotor and pump body clearance (Sec. 25)

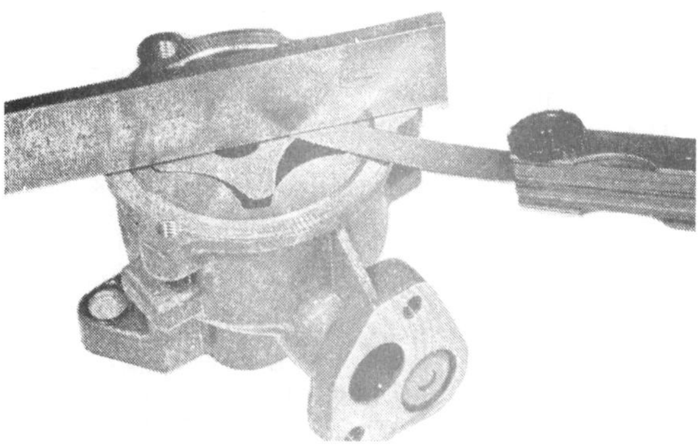

Fig. 1.9. Checking endfloat clearance (Sec. 25)

26 Oil filter - removal and refitting

The oil filter is a complete throw away cartridge screwed into the left-hand side of the cylinder block. Simply unscrew the old unit, clean the seating on the block and lubricate with engine oil. Screw the new one into position taking care not to cross the thread. Continue until the sealing ring just touches the block face then tighten one half turn by hand only. Always run the engine and check for signs of leaks after installation.

27 Engine components - examination for wear

When the engine has been stripped down and all parts properly cleaned decisions have to be made as to what needs renewal and the following Sections tell the examiner what to look for. In any border line case it is always best to decide in favour of a new part. Even if a part may still be serviceable its life will have been reduced by wear and the degree of trouble needed to replace it in the future must be taken into consideration. However, these things are relative and it depends on whether a quick 'survival' job is being done or whether the car as a whole is being regarded as having many thousands of miles of useful and economical life remaining.

28 Crankshaft - examination and renovation

1 Look at the main bearing journals and the crankpins, and if there are any scratches or score marks then the shaft will need regrinding. Such conditions will nearly always be accompanied by similar deterioration in the matching bearing shells.

2 Each bearing journal should also be round and can be checked with a micrometer or caliper gauge around the periphery at several points. If there is more than 0.001 in of ovality regrinding is necessary. Also see Figs. 1.10 and 1.11.

3 A main Ford Agent or motor engineering specialist will be able to decide to what extent regrinding is necessary and also supply the special undersize shell bearing to match whatever may need grinding off.

4 Before taking the crankshaft for regrinding check also the cylinder bores and pistons as it may be advantageous to have the whole engine done at the same time.

5 During any major engine repair, prise out the clutch pilot bearing from the rear end of the crankshaft; this may require the use of a hook-ended tool to get behind the bearing. Fit the replacement bearing with the seal outwards (where applicable) so that it is just below the surface of the crankshaft flange.

29 Crankshaft, main and big-end bearings - examination and renovation

1 With the careful servicing and regular oil and filter changes, bearings will last for a very long time but they can still fail for unforeseen reasons. With big-end bearings the indication is a regular rhythmic load knocking from the crankcase. The frequency depends on engine speed and is particularly noticeable when the engine is under load. This symptom is accompanied by a fall in oil pressure although this is not normally noticeable unless an oil pressure gauge is fitted. Main bearing failure is usually indicated by serious vibration, particularly at higher engine revolutions, accompanied by a more significant drop in oil pressure and a 'rumbling' noise.

2 Bearing shells in good condition have bearing surfaces with a smooth, even matt silver/grey colour all over. Worn bearings will show patches of a different colour when the bearing metal has worn away and exposed the underlay. Damaged bearings will be pitted or scored. It is always well worthwhile fitting new shells as their cost is relatively low. If the crankshaft is in good condition it is merely a question of obtaining another set of standard size. A reground crankshaft will need new bearing shells as a matter of course.

30 Cylinder bores - examination and renovation

1 A new cylinder is perfectly round and the walls parallel throughout its length. The action of the piston tends to wear the walls at right angles to the gudgeon pin due to side thrust. This wear takes place principally on that section of the cylinder swept by the piston rings.

2 It is possible to get an indication of bore wear by removing the cylinder heads with the engine still in the car. With the piston down in the bore first signs of wear can be seen and felt just below the top of the bore where the top piston ring reaches and there will be a noticeable lip. If there is no lip it is fairly reasonable to expect that bore wear is not severe and any lack of compression or excessive oil consumption is due to worn or broken piston rings or pistons (see Section 31).

3 If it is possible to obtain a bore measuring micrometer measure the bore in the thrust plane below the lip and again at the bottom of the cylinder in the same plane. If the difference is more than 0.003 inch (0.08 mm) then a rebore is necessary. Similarly, a difference of 0.003 inch (0.08 mm) or more across the bore diameter is a sign of ovality calling for rebore.

4 Any bore which is significantly scratched or scored will need reboring. This symptom usually indicates that the piston or rings are damaged also. In the event of only one cylinder being in need of reboring, it will still be necessary for all four to be bored and fitted with new oversize pistons and rings. Your Ford agent or local motor engineering specialist will be able to rebore and obtain the necessary matched pistons. If the crankshaft is undergoing regrinding also, it is a good idea to let the same firm renovate and reassemble the crankshaft and pistons to the block. A reputable firm normally gives a guarantee for such work. In cases where engines have been rebored already to their maximum, new cylinder liners are available which may be fitted. In such cases the same reboring processes have to be followed and the services of a specialist engineering firm are required.

31 Pistons and piston rings - inspection and testing

1 Worn pistons and rings can usually be diagnosed when the symptoms of excessive oil consumption and lower compression occur and are sometimes, though not always, associated with worn cylinder bores. Compression testers that fit into the spark plug hole are available and these can indicate where low compression is occuring. Wear usually accelerates the more it is left so when the symptoms occur early action can possibly save the expense of a rebore.

2 Another symptom of piston wear is piston slap - a knocking noise from the crankcase not to be confused with the big-end bearing failure. It can be heard clearly at low engine speed when there is no load (idling for example) and is much less audible when the engine speed increases. Piston wear usually occurs in the skirt or lower end of the piston and is indicated by vertical streaks in the worn area which is always on the thrust side. It can also be seen where the skirt thickness is different.

3 Piston ring wear can be checked by first removing the rings from the pistons as described in Section 23. Then place the rings in the cylinder bores from the top, pushing them down about 1½ inches (38 mm) with the head of a piston (from which the rings have been removed), so that they rest square in the cylinder. Then measure the gap at the ends of the ring with a feeler gauge. If it exceeds that given in the Specifications, they need renewal.

4 The grooves in which the rings locate in the piston can also become enlarged in use. The clearance between ring and piston, in the groove, should not exceed that given in the Specifications.

5 However, it is rare that a piston is only worn in the ring grooves and the need to replace them for this fault alone is hardly ever encountered. Wherever pistons are renewed the weight of the four piston/connecting rod assemblies should be kept within the limit variations of 8 gms. to maintain engine balance.

32 Connecting rods and gudgeon pins - examination and renovation

1 Gudgeon pins are a shrink fit into the connecting rods. Neither of these would normally need replacement unless the pistons were being changed, in which case the new pistons would automatically be supplied with new gudgeon pins.

2 Connecting rods are not subject to wear but in extreme circumstances such as engine seizure they could be distorted. Such

A A standard size parent bore in the cylinder block is unmarked. Bores which are 0.016 in (0.4 mm) oversize have a white stripe on the main bearing caps

B Main bearing journals of standard size are unmarked. Journals which are 0.010 in (0.25 mm) undersize have a green stripe on the web adjacent to the particular journal

Fig. 1.10. Crankshaft identification codes (Sec. 28)

A If the big end journals are undersize the front side of the counter-weight is marked with a green paint spot

B If the main bearing and big end bearing journals have been ground undersize, the crankshaft is marked by a green paint stripe and a green paint spot on the front web

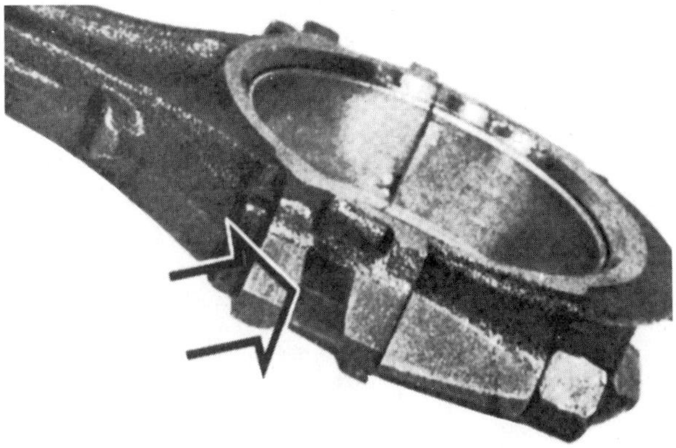

C The red paint spots for connecting rod identification are adjacent on the same side

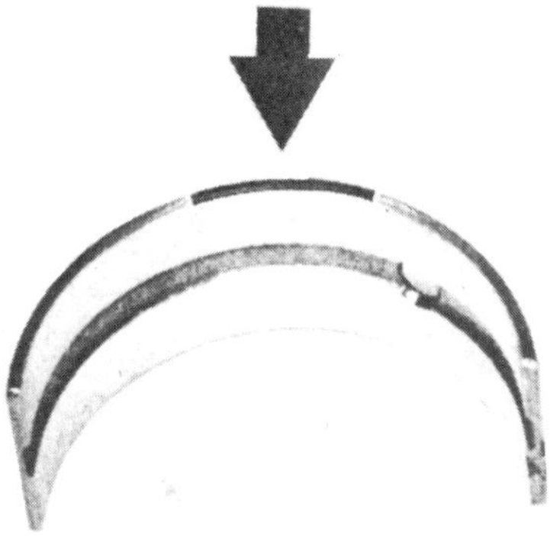

D A green paint spot for bearing shell identification is on the outer edge of the shell. If oversize shells are fitted they are marked on their backs - see specification

Fig. 1.11. Crankshaft and big-end identification codes (Sec. 28)

conditions may be visually apparent but where doubt exists they should be changed. The bearing caps should also be examined for indications of filing down which may have been attempted in the mistaken idea that bearing slackness could be remedied in this way. If there are such signs then the connecting rods should be renewed.

33 Camshaft and camshaft bearings - examination and renovation

1 The camshaft bearing bushes should be examined for signs of scoring and pitting. If they need renewal they will have to be dealt with professionally as, although it may be relatively easy to remove the old bushes, the correct fitting of new ones requires special tools. If they are not fitted evenly and square from the very start they can be distorted thus causing localised wear in a very short time. See your Ford dealer or local engineering specialist for this work.
2 The camshaft itself may show signs of wear on the bearing journals or cam lobes. The main decision to take is what degree of wear justifies replacement, which is costly. Any signs of scoring or damage to the bearing journals cannot be removed by grinding. Renewal of the whole camshaft is the only solution. **Note:** Where excessive cam lobe wear is evident, refer to the note in the following Section.
3 The cam lobes themselves may show signs of ridging or pitting on the high points. If ridging is light then it may be possible to smooth it out with fine emery. The cam lobes however, are surface hardened and once this is penetrated, wear will be very rapid thereafter.
4 Ensure that the camshaft oilways are unobstructed.

34 Cam followers - examination

1 The faces of the cam followers which bear on the camshaft should show no signs of pitting, scoring or other forms of wear. They should not be a loose sloppy fit on the ballheaded bolt.
2 Inspect the face which bears onto the valve stem and if pitted the cam follower must be renewed.
3 If excessive cam follower wear is evident (and possibly excessive cam lobe wear), this may be due to a malfunction of the valve drive lubrication tube. If this has occurred, renew the tube and the cam follower. If more than one cam follower is excessively worn, renew the camshaft, all the cam followers and the lubrication tube, this also applies where excessive cam lobe wear is found.
4 During any operation which requires removal of the valve rocker cover ensure that oil is being discharged from the lubrication tube nozzles by cranking the engine on the starter motor. During routine maintenance operations, this can be done after checking the valve clearances.

35 Auxiliary shaft and bearings - examination and renovation

1 The procedure for the auxiliary shaft and bearings is similar to that described in Section 33 for the camshaft.
2 Examine the skew gear for wear and damaged teeth. If either is evident, a replacement shaft must be obtained.

36 Valves and valve seats - examination and renovation

1 With the valves removed from the cylinder heads examine the heads for signs of cracking, burning away and pitting of the edge where it seats in the port. The seats of the valves in the cylinder head should also be examined for the same signs. Usually it is the valve that deteriorates first but if a bad valve is not rectified the seat will suffer and this is more difficult to repair.
2 Provided there are no obvious signs of serious pitting the valve should be ground with its seat. This may be done by placing a smear of carborundum paste on the edge of the valve and, using a suction type valve holder, grinding the valve in situ. This is done with a semi-rotary action, rotating the handle of the valve holder between the hands and lifting it occasionally to re-distribute the traces of paste. Use a coarse paste to start with. As soon as a matt grey unbroken line appears on both the valve and seat the valve is 'ground in'. All traces of carbon should also be cleaned from the head and neck of the valve stem. A wire brush mounted in a power drill is a quick and effective way of doing this.

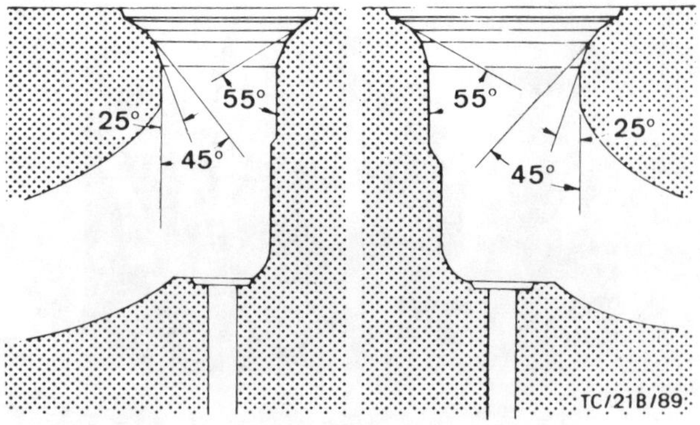

Fig. 1.12. Valve seat angles (Sec. 36)

3 If the valve requires renewal it should be ground into the seat in the same way as the old valve.
4 Another form of valve wear can occur on the stem where it runs in the guide in the cylinder head. This can be detected by trying to rock the valve from side to side. If there is any movement at all it is an indication that the valve stem or guide is worn. Check the stem first with a micrometer at points along and around its length and if they are not within the specified size new valves will probably solve the problem. If the guides are worn, however, they will need reboring for oversize valves or for fitting guide inserts. The valve seats will also need recutting to ensure they are concentric with the stems. This work should be entrusted to your Ford dealer or local auto-engineering works.
5 When valve seats are badly burnt or pitted, requiring renewal, inserts may be fitted - or replaced if already fitted once before - and once again this is a specialist task to be carried out by a suitable engineering firm.
6 When all valve grinding is completed it is essential that every trace of grinding paste is removed from the valves and ports in the cylinder head. This should be done by thorough washing in petrol or paraffin and blowing out with a jet of air. If particles of carborundum should work their way into the engine they would cause havoc with bearings or cylinder walls.

37 Timing gears and belt - examination

1 Any wear which takes place in the timing mechanism will be on the teeth of the drive belt or due to stretch of the fabric. Whenever the engine is to be stripped for major overhaul a new belt should be fitted.
2 It is very unusual for the timing gears (sprockets) to wear at the teeth. If the securing bolt/nuts have been loose it is possible for the keyway or hub bore to wear. Check these two points and if damage or wear is evident a new gear must be obtained.

38 Flywheel - examination and renovation

1 If the ring gear is badly worn or has missing teeth it should be renewed. The old ring can be removed from the flywheel by cutting a notch between two teeth with a hacksaw and then splitting it with a cold chisel.
2 To fit a new ring gear requires heating the ring to 400°F (204°C). This can be done by polishing four equally spaced sections of the gear laying it on a suitable heat resistance surface (such as fire bricks) and heating it evenly with a blow lamp or torch until the polished areas turn a light yellow tinge. Do not overheat or the hard wearing properties will be lost. The gear has a chamfered inner edge which should go against the shoulder when put on the flywheel. When hot enough place the gear in position quickly, tapping it home, if necessary and let it cool naturally without quenching it any way.

39 Cylinder head and piston crowns - decarbonisation

1 When the cylinder head is removed, either in the course of an overhaul or for inspection of bores or valve condition when the engine is in the car, it is normal to remove all carbon deposits from the piston crowns and heads.

2 This is best done with a cup shaped wire brush and an electric drill and is fairly straightforward when the engine is dismantled and the pistons removed. Sometimes hard spots of carbon are not easily removed except by a scraper. When cleaning the pistons with a scraper, take care not to damage the surface of the piston in any way.

3 When the engine is in the car, certain precautions must be taken when decarbonising the piston crowns in order to prevent dislodged pieces of carbon falling into the interior of the engine which could cause damage to cylinder bores, piston and rings - or if allowed into the water passages - damage to the water pump. Turn the engine so that the piston being worked on is at the top of its stroke and then mask off the adjacent cylinder bores and all surrounding water jacket orifices with paper and adhesive tape. Press grease into the gap all round the piston to keep carbon particles out and then scrape all carbon away by hand carefully. Do not use a power drill and wire brush when the engine is in the car as it will virtually be impossible to keep all the carbon dust clear of the engine. When completed carefully clear out the grease around the rim of the piston with a matchstick or something similar - bringing any carbon particles with it. Repeat the process on the other piston crown. It is not recommended that a ring of carbon is left round the edge of the piston on the theory that it will aid oil consumption. This was valid in the earlier days of long stroke low revving engines but modern engines, fuels and lubricants cause less carbon deposits anyway and any left behind tends merely to cause hot spots.

40 Valve guides - inspection

Examine the valve guides internally for wear. If the valves are a very loose fit in the guides and there is the slightest suspicion of lateral rocking using a new valve, then the guides will have to be reamed and oversize valves fitted. This is a job best left to the local Ford dealer.

41 Sump - inspection

Wash out the sump in petrol and wipe dry. Inspect the exterior for signs of damage or excessive rust. If evident, a new sump must be obtained. To ensure an oil tight joint scrape away all traces of the old gasket from the cylinder block mating face.

42 Engine reassembly - general

All components of the engine must be cleaned of oil, sludge and old gasket and the working area should also be cleared and clean. In addition to the normal range of good quality socket spanners and general tools which are essential the following must be available before reassembling begins:

1 *Complete set of new gaskets.*
2 *Supply of clean lint-free cloths.*
3 *Clean oil can full of clean engine oil.*
4 *Torque wrench.*
5 *All new spare parts as necessary.*

43 Crankshaft - refitting

Ensure that the crankcase is thoroughly clean and that all oilways are clear. A thin twist drill or a piece of wire is useful for cleaning them out. If possible blow them out with compressed air.

Treat the crankshaft in the same fashion, and then inject engine oil into the crankshaft oilways.

Commence work of rebuilding the engine by refitting the crankshaft and main bearings:

1 Wipe the bearing shell locations in the crankcase with a lint-free cloth.
2 Wipe the crankshaft journals with a soft lint-free cloth.
3 If the old main bearing shells are to be renewed (not to do so is a false economy unless they are virtually new) fit the five upper halves of the main bearing shells to their location in the crankcase (photo).
4 Identify each main bearing cap and place in order. The number is cast onto the cap and with intermediate caps an arrow is also marked so that the cap is fitted the correct way round. (photo)
5 Wipe the end cap bearing shell location with a soft non-fluffy rag.
6 Fit the bearing half shell onto each main bearing cap (photo).
7 Fit the bearing half shell into each location in the crankcase.
8 Apply a little grease to either side of the centre main bearing so as to retain the thrust washers (photo).
9 Fit the upper halves of the thrust washers into their grooves either side of the main bearing. The slots must face outwards (photo).
10 Lubricate the crankshaft journals and the upper and lower main bearing shells with engine oil (photo).
11 Carefully lower the crankshaft into the crankcase (photo).
12 Lubricate the crankshaft main bearing journals again and then fit No. 1 bearing cap (photo). Fit the two securing bolts but do not tighten yet.
13 Apply a little non-setting gasket sealant to the crankshaft rear main bearing end cap location (photo).
14 Next fit No. 5 end cap (photo). Fit the two securing bolts but as before do not tighten yet.
15 Apply a little grease to either side of the centre main bearing end cap so as to retain the thrust washers. Fit the thrust washers with the tag located in the groove and the slots facing outwards (photo).
16 Fit the centre main bearing end cap and the two securing bolts. Then refit the intermediate main bearing end caps. Make sure that the arrows always point towards the front of the engine (photo).

43.3 Inserting bearing shells into crankcase

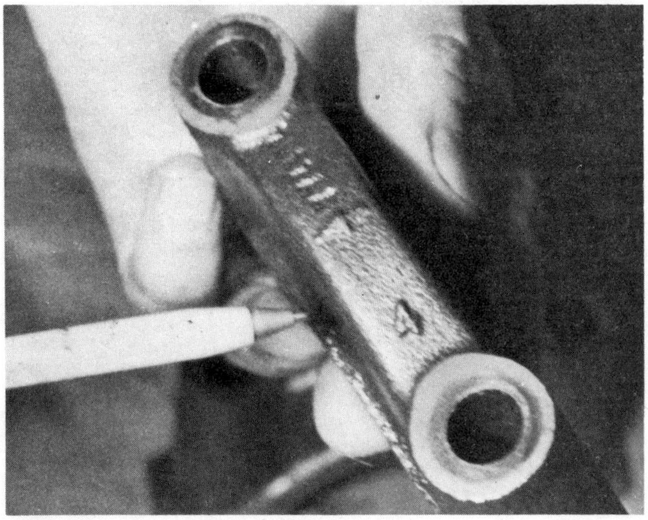

43.4 Main bearing cap identification marks

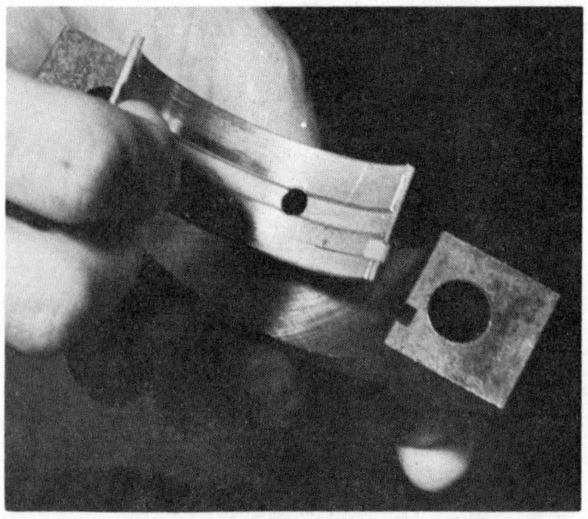
43.6 Fitting bearing shell to main bearing cap

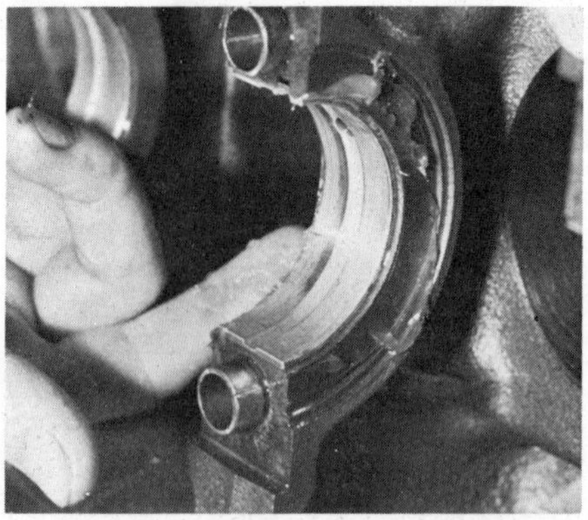
43.8 Applying grease to either side of centre main bearing

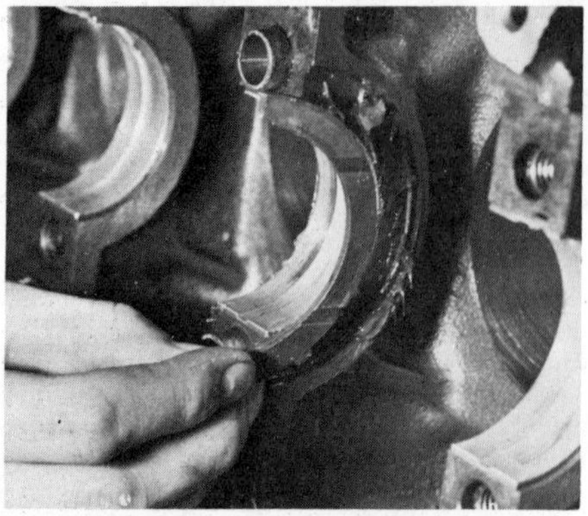
43.9 Fitting thrust washers to centre main bearing

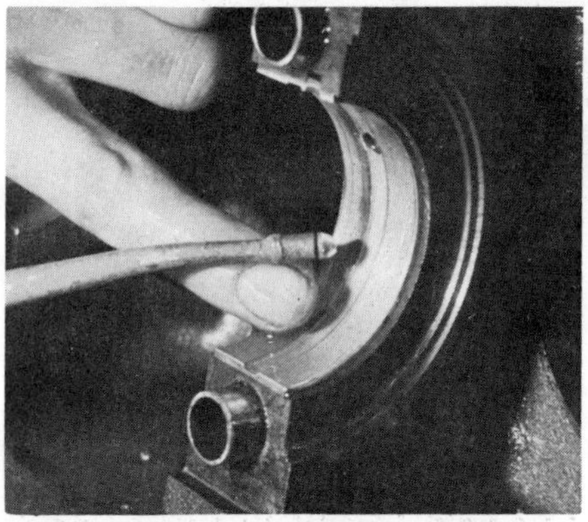
43.10 Lubricating bearing shells

43.11 Fitting crankshaft to crankcase

43.12 Refitting No 1 main bearing cap. Note identification mark

43.13 Applying gasket sealant to rear main bearing cap location

43.14 Refitting rear main bearing cap

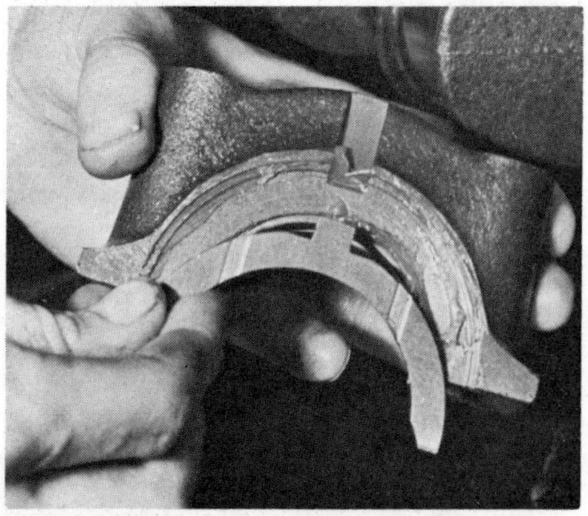
43.15 Fitting thrust washers to centre main bearing cap

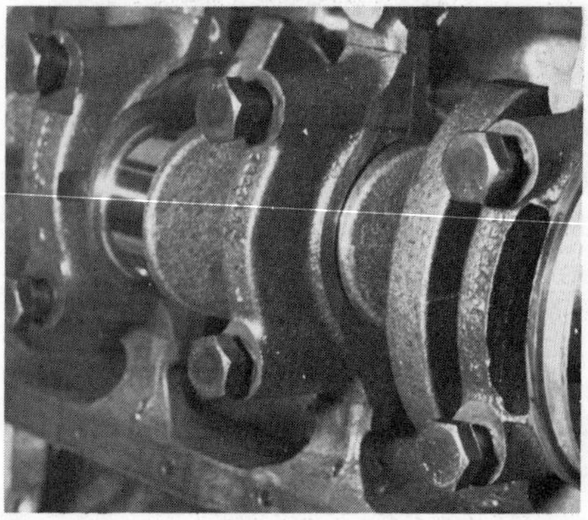
43.16 All main bearing caps in position

43.17 Tightening main bearing cap securing bolts

43.18 Using feeler gauge to check endfloat

17 Lightly tighten all main cap securing bolts and then fully tighten in a progressive manner to a final torque wrench setting as specified (photo).
18 Using a screwdriver ease the crankshaft fully forwards and with feeler gauges check the clearance between the crankshaft journal side and the thrust washers. The clearance must not exceed that given in the Specifications. Oversize thrust washers are available (photo).
19 Test the crankshaft for freedom of rotation. Should it be stiff to turn or possess high spots, a most careful inspection must be made with a micrometer, preferably by a qualified mechanic, to get to the root of the trouble. It is very seldom that any trouble of this nature will be experienced when fitting the crankshaft.

44 Pistons and connecting rods - reassembly

As a press type gudgeon pin is used (see Section 22) this operation must be carried out by the local Ford dealer.

45 Piston rings - refitting

1 Check that the piston ring grooves and oilways are thoroughly clean and unblocked. Piston rings must always be fitted over the head of the piston and never from the bottom.
2 The easiest method to use when fitting rings is to wrap a 0.020 in (0.5 mm) feeler gauge round the top of the piston and place the rings one at a time, starting with the bottom oil control ring, over the feeler gauge.
3 The feeler gauge, complete with ring can then be slid down the piston over the other piston ring grooves until the correct groove is reached. The piston ring is then slid gently off the feeler gauge into the groove.
4 An alternative method is to fit the rings by holding them slightly open with the thumbs and both of the index fingers. This method requires a steady hand and great care as it is easy to open the ring too much and break it.

46 Pistons - refitting

The piston, complete with connecting rods, can be fitted to the cylinder bores in the following sequence:
1 With a wad of clean rag wipe the cylinder bores clean.
2 The pistons, complete with connecting rods, are fitted to their bores from the top of the block.
3 Locate the piston ring gaps in the following manner:
Top: 150° from one side of the helical expander gap.
Centre: 150° from the side opposite the helical expander gap.
Bottom: Helical expander: opposite the marked piston front side.
Intermediate rings: 1 inch (25 mm) each side of the helical expander gap (photo).
4 Well lubricate the piston and rings with engine oil (photo).
5 Fit a universal piston ring compressor and prepare to inset the first piston into the bore. Make sure it is the correct piston-connecting rod assembly for that particular bore, that the connecting rod is the correct way round and that the front of the piston is towards the front of the bore, ie; towards the front of the engine (photo).
6 Again lubricate the piston skirt and insert into the bore up to the bottom of the piston ring compressor (photos).
7 Gently but firmly tap the piston through the piston ring compressor and into the cylinder bore with a wooden, or plastic faced, hammer (photo).

47 Connecting rods to crankshaft - refitting

1 Wipe clean the connecting rod half of the big-end bearing cap and the underside of the shell bearing, and fit the shell bearing in position with its locating tongue engaged with the corresponding cut out in the rod.
2 If the old bearings are nearly new and are being refitted then ensure they are refitted in their correct locations on the correct rods.
3 Generously lubricate the crankpin journals with engine oil and turn the crankshaft so that the crankpin is in the most advantageous position for the connecting rods to be drawn onto it.
4 Wipe clean the connecting rod bearing cap and back of the shell bearing, and fit the shell bearing in position ensuring that the locating tongue at the back of the bearing engages with the locating groove in the connecting rod cap.
5 Generously lubricate the shell bearing and offer up the connecting rod bearing cap to the connecting rod.
6 Refit the connecting rod nuts and pinch them tight (photo).
7 Tighten the bolts with a torque wrench to the specified torque (photo).
8 When all the connecting rods have been fitted, rotate the crankshaft to check that everything is free, and that there are no high spots causing binding. The bottom half of the engine is now nearly built up.

Fig. 1.13. Piston identification mark relative to piston lubrication jet hole (Sec. 46)

46.3 Positioning ring gaps

46.4 Lubricating pistons prior to refitting

46.6a Inserting connecting rod into cylinder bore

46.6b Piston ring compressor correctly positioned

46.7 Pushing piston down bore

47.6 Refitting big-end cap securing nuts

47.7 Tightening big-end cap securing nuts

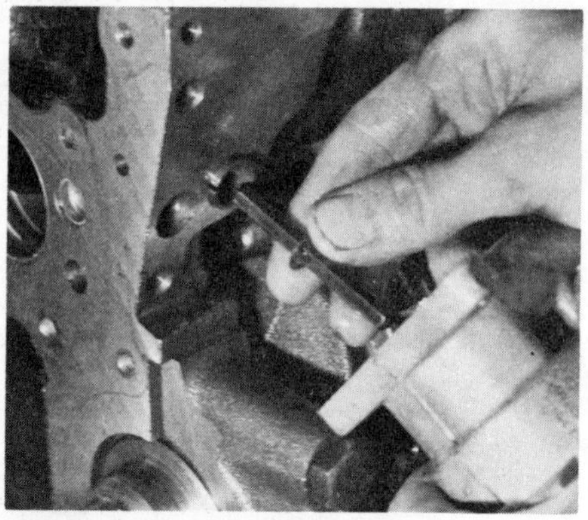

48.2 Inserting oil pump drive shaft

48.3 Tightening oil pump securing bolts

49.1 Refitting rectangular shaped seals to rear of crankshaft

49.2 Fitting seal into rear main bearing cap

49.3 Refitting crankshaft rear oil seal

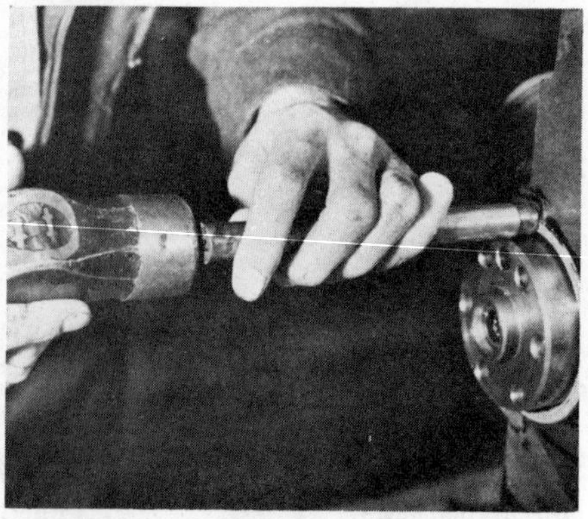

49.4 Tapping oil seal into position

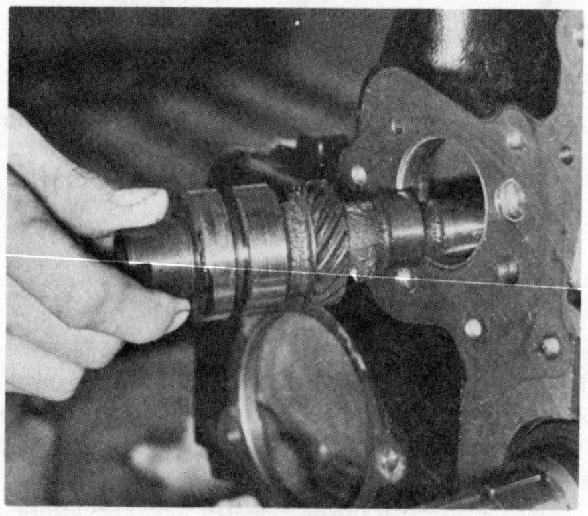

50.1 Refitting auxiliary shaft

48 Oil pump and strainer - refitting

1 Wipe the mating faces of the oil pump and underside of the cylinder block.
2 Insert the hexagonal driveshaft into the end of the oil pump (photo).
3 Offer up the oil pump and refit the two special bolts. Using special tool '21 - 020' and a torque wrench tighten the two bolts to the specified torque (photo).
4 Refit the one bolt and spring washer that secures the oil pump pick-up pipe support bracket to the crankcase.

49 Crankshaft rear oil seal - installation

1 Apply some non-setting gasket sealant to the slot on either side of the rear main bearing end cap and insert a rectangular shaped seal (photo).
2 Apply some non-setting gasket sealant to the slot in the rear main bearing end cap and carefully insert the shaped seal (photo).
3 Lightly smear some grease on the crankshaft rear oil seal and carefully ease over it the end of the crankshaft. The spring must be inwards (photo).
4 Using a soft metal drift carefully tap the seal into position (photo).

50 Auxiliary shaft and timing cover - refitting

1 Carefully insert the auxiliary shaft into the front face of the cylinder block (photo).
2 Position the thrust plate into its groove in the shaft - countersunk faces of the holes facing outwards - and refit the two crosshead screws (photo).
3 Tighten the two crosshead screws using a crosshead screwdriver and an open ended spanner (photo).
4 Smear some grease on the cylinder block face of a new gasket and carefully fit into position (photo).
5 Apply some non-setting gasket sealant to the slot in the underside of the crankshaft timing cover. Insert the shaped seal.
6 Offer up the timing cover and secure with the bolts and spring washers (photos).
7 Smear some grease onto the seal located in the auxiliary shaft timing cover and carefully ease the cover over the end of the auxiliary shaft.
8 Secure the auxiliary shaft timing cover with the four bolts and spring washers (photo).

51 Sump - refitting

1 Wipe the mating faces of the underside of the crankcase and the sump.
2 Smear some non-setting gasket sealant on the underside of the crankcase.
3 Fit the sump gasket and end seals making sure that the bolt holes line up (Fig. 1.14).
4 Offer the sump up to the gaskets taking care not to dislodge, and secure in position with the bolts (photo).
5 Tighten the sump bolts in a progressive manner, to a final torque wrench setting as specified, in the order shown in Fig. 1.15.

52 Crankshaft sprocket and pulley and auxiliary shaft sprocket - refitting

1 Check that the keyways in the end of the crankshaft are clean and the keys are free of burrs. Fit the keys into the keyways (photo).
2 Slide the sprocket into position on the crankshaft. This sprocket is the small diameter one (photo).
3 Ease the drivebelt into mesh with the crankshaft sprocket (photo).
4 Slide the large diameter plain washer onto the crankshaft (photo).
5 Check that the keyway in the end of the balance shaft is clean and the key is free of burrs. Fit the key to the keyway.
6 Slide the sprocket onto the end of the auxiliary shaft (photo).
7 Slide the pulley onto the end of the crankshaft (photo).
8 Refit the bolt and thick plain washer to the end of the crankshaft (photo).
9 Lock the crankshaft pulley with a metal bar and using a socket wrench fully tighten the bolt (photo).

53 Water pump - refitting

1 Make sure that all traces of the old gasket are removed and then smear some grease on the gasket face of the cylinder block.
2 Fit a new gasket to the cylinder block.
3 Offer up the water pump and secure in position with the four bolts and spring washers (photo).

54 Backplate, flywheel and clutch - refitting

1 Remove all traces of the shaped seal from the backplate and apply a little adhesive to the backplate. Fit a new seal to the backplate (photo).
2 Wipe the mating faces of the backplate and cylinder block and carefully fit the backplate to the two dowels (photo).
3 Wipe the mating faces of the flywheel and crankshaft and offer up the flywheel to the crankshaft aligning the previously made marks unless new parts have been fitted.
4 Fit the six crankshaft securing bolts and lightly tighten.
5 Lock the flywheel using a screwdriver engaged in the starter ring gear and tighten the securing bolts in a diagonal and progressive manner to a final torque wrench setting as specified (photo).
6 Refit the clutch disc and pressure plate assembly to the flywheel making sure the disc is the right way round (photo).
7 Secure the pressure plate assembly with the six retaining bolts and spring washers.
8 Centralise the clutch disc using an old input shaft or piece of wooden dowel, and fully tighten the retaining bolts (photo).

50.2 Locating auxiliary shaft thrust plate

50.3 Tightening thrust plate securing screws

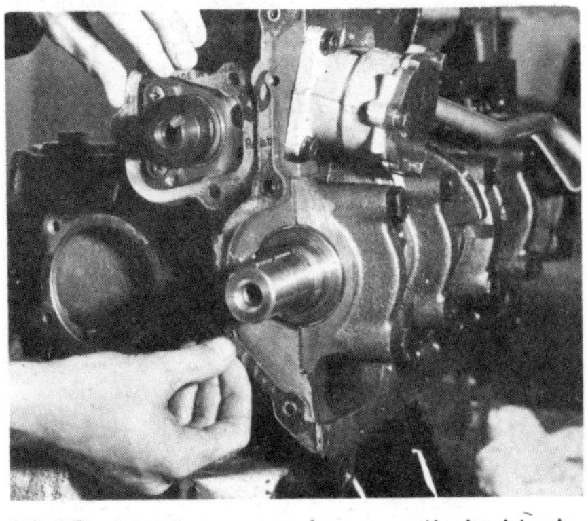
50.4 Positioning new gasket on cylinder block front-face

50.6a Refitting crankshaft timing cover.

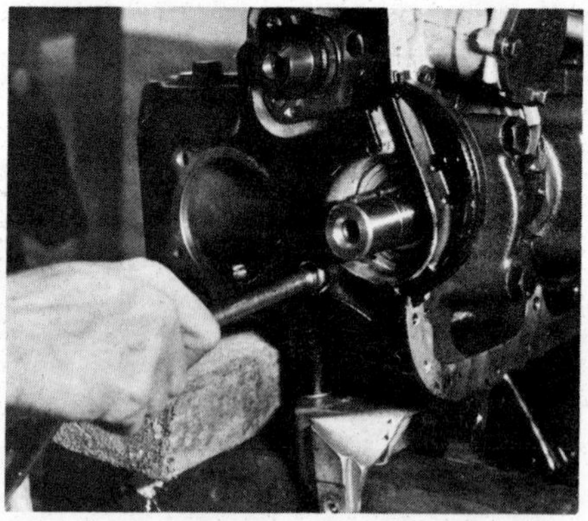

50.6b Tightening crankshaft timing cover and securing bolts

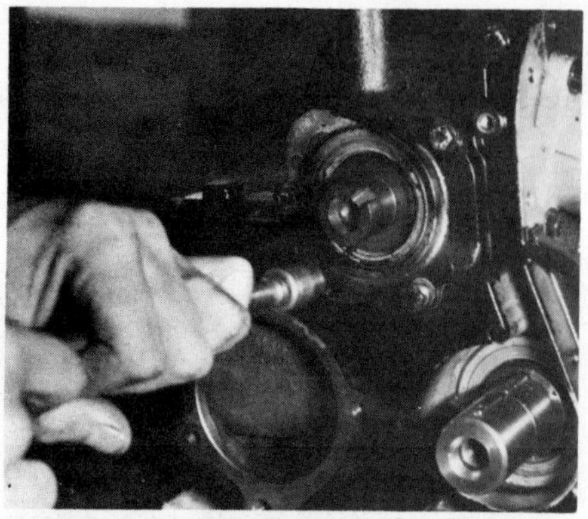

50.8 Tightening auxiliary shaft timing cover securing bolts

51.4 New gaskets fitted to greased underside of crankcase, ready for sump

52.1 Refitting Woodruff Key to crankshaft

52.2 Sliding on crankshaft sprocket

Fig. 1.14. Correct fitment of sump gasket end seals (Sec. 51)

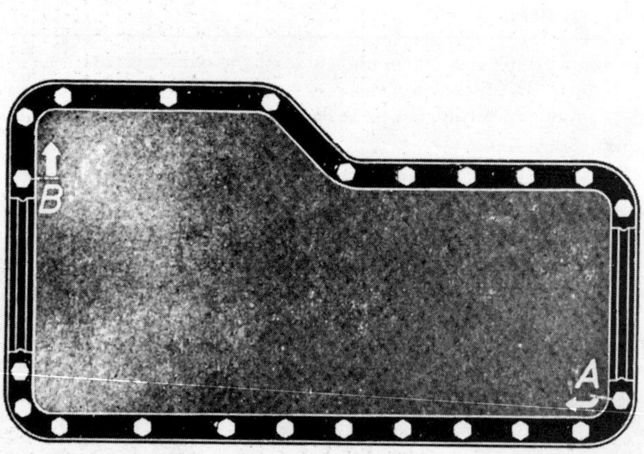

Fig. 1.15. Correct order for tightening sump bolts (Sec. 51)

52.3 Fitting drive belt to crankshaft sprocket

52.4 Refitting large diameter plain washer

52.6 Fitting sprocket to auxiliary shaft

52.7 Refitting crankshaft pulley

52.8 Crankshaft pulley securing bolt and large washer

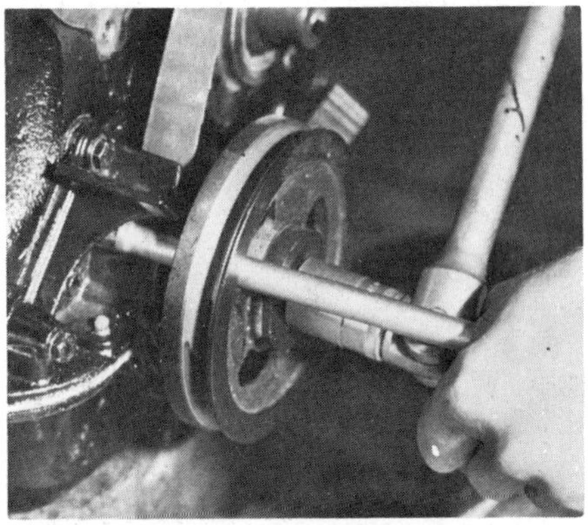
52.9 Tightening crankshaft pulley securing bolt

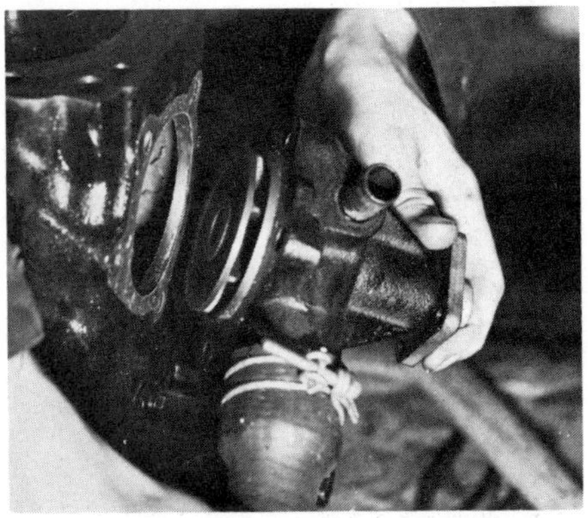
53.3 Water pump is offered up to mating face fitted with new gasket

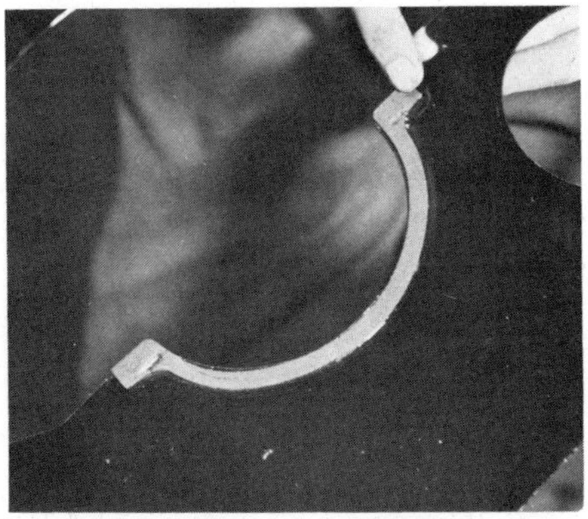
54.1 Fitting new gasket to backplate

54.2 Backplate located on dowels in rear of cylinder block

54.5 Fully tightening flywheel securing bolts

54.6 Refitting clutch

54.8 Fully tightening clutch securing bolts once disc has been centralised

55 Valves - refitting

1 With the valves suitably ground in (see Section 36) and kept in their correct order, start with no. 1 cylinder and insert the valve into its guide (photo).
2 Lubricate the valve stem with engine oil and slide on a new oil seal. The spring must be uppermost as shown in the photo.
3 Fit the valve spring and cap (photo).
4 Using a universal valve spring compressor, compress the valve spring until the split collets can be slid into position (photo). Note these collets have serrations which engage in slots in the valve stem. Release the valve spring compressor.
5 Repeat this procedure until all eight valves and valve springs are fitted.

56 Camshaft - refitting

1 If the oil seal was removed (Section 20) a new one should be fitted taking care that it is fitted the correct way round. Gently tap it into position so that it does not tilt (photo).
2 Apply some grease to the lip of the oil seal. Wipe the three bearing surfaces with a clean lint-free cloth then lubricate them with SAE 90EP gear oil.
3 Lift the camshaft through the bearing taking care not to damage the bearing surfaces with the sharp edges of the cam lobes. Also take care not to cut the fingers (photo).
4 When the journals are ready to be inserted into the bearings lubricate the bearings with engine oil (photo).
5 Push the camshaft through the bearings until the locating groove in the rear of the camshaft is just rearwards of the bearing carrier.
6 Slide the thrust plate into engagement with the camshaft taking care to fit it the correct way round as previously noted (photo).
7 Secure the thrust plate with the two bolts and spring washers (photo).
8 Check that the keyway in the end of the camshaft is clean and the key is free of burrs. Fit the key into the keyway (photo).
9 Locate the tag on the camshaft sprocket backplate and this must locate in the second groove in the camshaft sprocket (photo).
10 Fit the camshaft sprocket backplate, tag facing outwards (photo).
11 Fit the camshaft sprocket to the end of the camshaft and with a soft faced hammer make sure it is fully home (photo).
12 Refit the sprocket securing bolt and thick plain washer (photo).

57 Cam followers - refitting

1 Undo the ball headed bolt locknut and screw down the bolt fully. This will facilitate refitting the cam followers (photo).
2 Rotate the camshaft until the cam lobe is away from the top of the cylinder head. Pass the cam follower under the back of the cam until the cup is over the ball headed bolt (photo).
3 Engage the cup with the ball headed bolt (photo).
4 Refit the cam follower spring by engaging the ends of the spring with the anchor on the ball headed bolt (photo).
5 Using the fingers pull the spring up and then over the top of the cam follower (photos).
6 Repeat the above sequence for the remaining seven cam followers.
7 Check that the jet holes in the camshaft lubrication pipe are free and offer up to the camshaft bearing pedestals (photo).
8 Refit the pipe securing bolts and spring washers.

58 Cylinder head - refitting

1 Wipe the mating faces of the cylinder head and cylinder block.
2 Carefully place a new gasket on the cylinder block and check to ensure that it is the correct way up and the right way round (photo).
3 Gently lower the cylinder head being as accurate as possible first time so that the gasket is not dislodged (photo).
4 Refit the cylinder head bolts taking care not to damage the gasket

55.1 Inserting valve into valve guide

55.2 Sliding seal down valve stem

55.3 Replacing valve spring cap

55.4 Refitting valve collets

56.1 Camshaft oil seal correctly fitted

56.3 Threading camshaft through bearings

56.4 Lubricating camshaft bearings

56.6 Locating camshaft thrust plate

56.7 Tightening camshaft thrust plate retaining bolts

56.8 Fitting Woodruff key to camshaft

56.9 Camshaft sprocket backplate tag

56.10 Camshaft sprocket backplate refitted

56.11 Refitting camshaft sprocket

56.12 Camshaft sprocket securing bolt and plain washer

57.1 Slackening ball-headed bolt locknut

57.2 Passing cam follower under camshaft

57.3 Cup located over ball-headed bolt

57.4 Cam follower spring engaged with the anchor

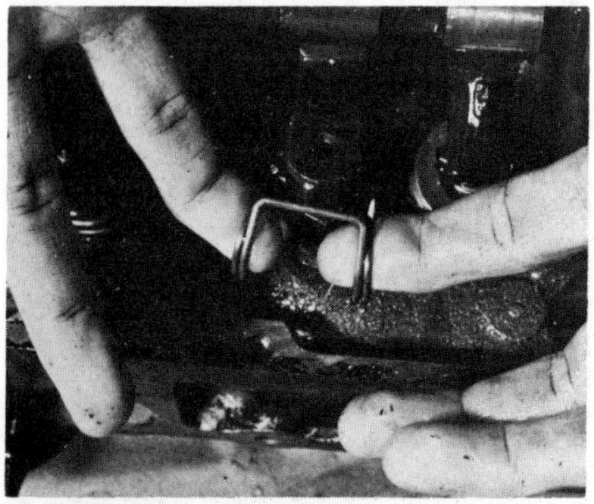

57.5a Cam follower spring bearing lifted over cam follower.

57.5b Cam follower spring correctly fitted.

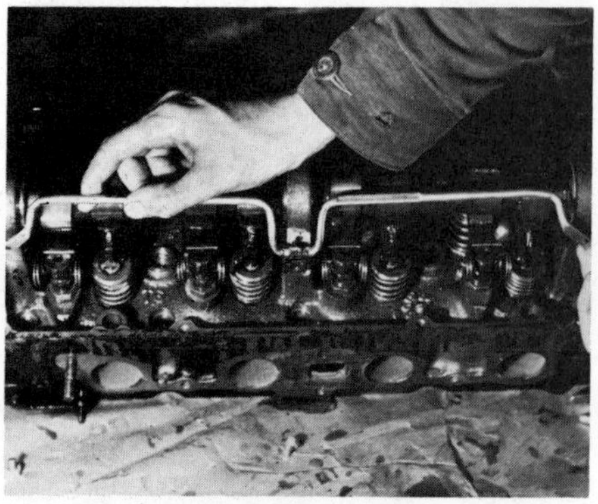

57.7 Replacing lubrication pipe.

58.2 Positioning cylinder head gasket on top of cylinder block.

58.3 Lowering cylinder head onto gasket.

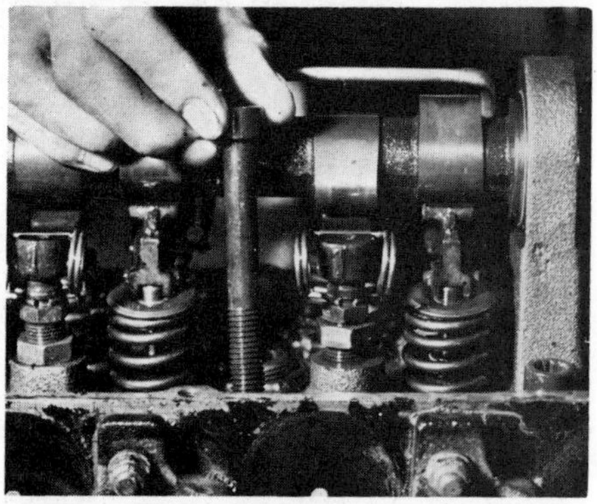

58.4 Refitting cylinder head bolts.

58.5 Special tool engaged in cylinder head bolt.

58.6 Tightening cylinder head bolts.

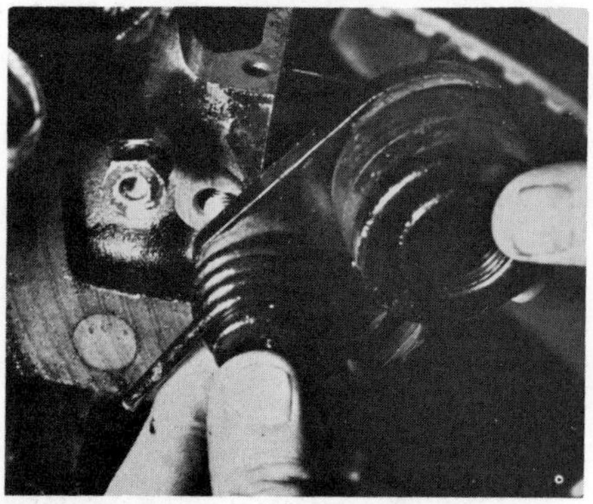

59.1 Refitting drive belt tensioner.

if it has moved (photo).

5 Using the special tool '21 - 002' lightly tighten all the bolts (photo).

6 Tighten the cylinder head bolts progressively to a torque wrench setting as specified, in the order shown in Fig. 1.2 (photo). After running the engine for 15 minutes at about 1000 rpm, slacken each bolt by $\frac{1}{2}$ turn, one at a time, in the correct sequence then retighten to the specified torque.

59 Drive belt tensioner and thermostat housing - refitting

1 Thread the shaped bolt through the spring and tensioner plate and screw the bolt into the cylinder head (photo).

2 Tighten the bolt securely using special tool '21 - 020'.

3 Using a screwdriver to overcome the tension of the springs positon the plate so that its securing bolt can be screwed into the cylinder head (photo).

4 Clean the mating faces of the cylinder head and thermostat housing and fit a new gasket.

5 Offer up the thermostat housing and secure in position with the two bolts and spring washers.

6 Tighten the bolts to the specified torque.

60 Camshaft drivebelt - refitting and camshaft timing

1 Rotate the crankshaft until No. 1 piston is at its TDC position. This is indicated by the crankshaft sprocket keyway being uppermost or, if the pulley is in position, by the TDC mark being in alignment with the pointer. If the distributor is in position, check that the rotor is pointing to No. 1 spark plug contact in the distributor cap (Fig. 1.16).

2 Rotate the camshaft until the pointer is in alignment with the dot mark on the front bearing pedestal (photo). To achieve this always rotate the camshaft in the direction shown in Fig. 1.16.

3 Engage the drivebelt with the crankshaft sprocket and auxiliary shaft sprocket. Pass the back of the belt over the tensioner jockey wheel and then slide it into mesh with the camshaft sprocket.

4 Slacken the tensioner plate securing bolt and allow the tensioner to settle by rotating the crankshaft twice. Retighten the tensioner plate securing bolt.

59.3 Using screwdriver to relieve tension of spring.

60.2 Lining up camshaft timing marks.

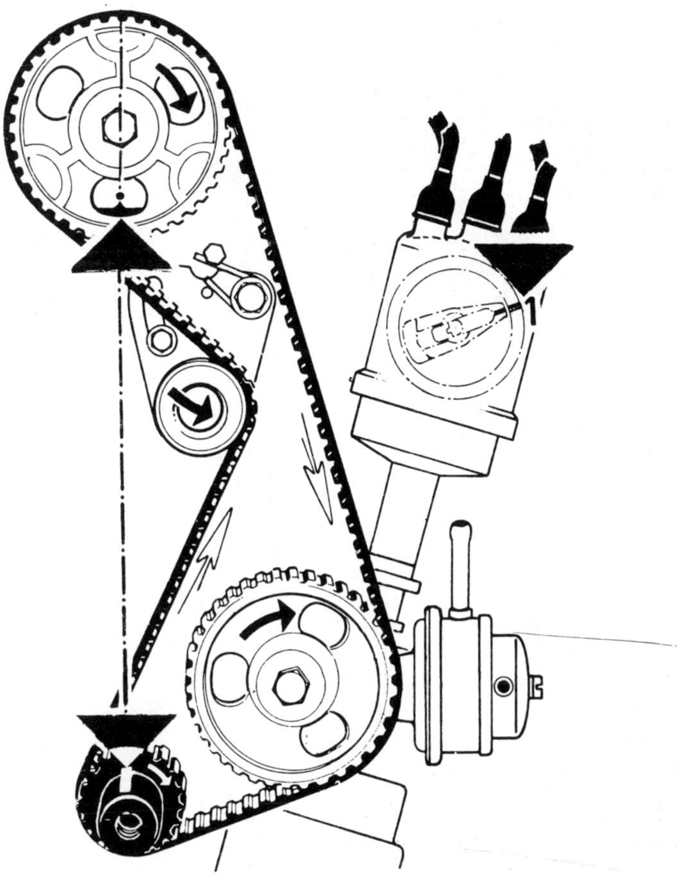

Fig. 1.16. Camshaft, ignition and crankshaft timing (Sec. 60)

60.5 Drive belt fitted.

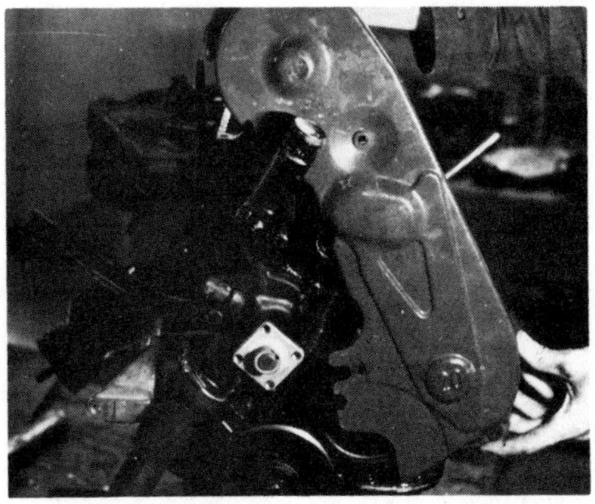

60.6a Refitting drive belt guard.

60.6b Locating guard between washer and pedestal.

5 Line up the timing marks and check that these are correct indicating the belt has been correctly refitted (photo).
6 Refit the drivebelt guard, easing the guard into engagement with the bolt and large plain washer located under the water pump (photos).

61 Valve clearances - checking and adjustment

1 With the engine top cover removed, turn the crankshaft until the two cams of one cylinder point upwards to form a 'V'. This will ensure that the cam follower will be at the back of the cam (Fig. 1.17).
2 Using feeler gauges as shown in this photo check the clearance which should be as follows:

Inlet 0.008 in (0.20 mm)
Exhaust 0.010 in (0.25 mm)

3 If adjustment is necessary using open-ended spanners slacken the ball headed bolt securing locknut (photo).
4 Screw the ball headed bolt up or down as necessary until the required clearance is obtained (photo). Retighten the locknut.

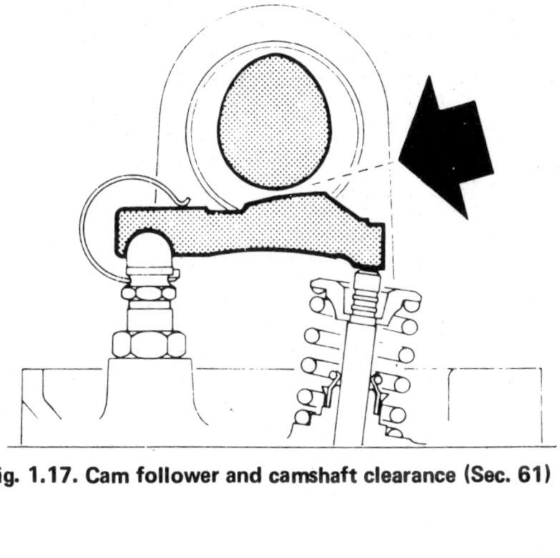

Fig. 1.17. Cam follower and camshaft clearance (Sec. 61)

61.2 Checking cam follower clearance

61.3 Slackening ball-headed bolt locknut

61.4 Adjusting ball headed bolt

5 An alternative method of adjustment is to work to the following table:

Valves open	Valves to adjust
1 ex and 4 in	*6 in and 7 ex*
6 in and 7 ex	*1 ex and 4 in*
2 in and 5 ex	*3 ex and 8 in*
3 ex and 8 in	*2 in and 5 ex*

62 Engine/gearbox - reconnecting

If the engine was removed in unit with the gearbox it may be re-attached in the following manner:

1 With the engine on the floor and a wood block under the front of the sump, lift up the gearbox and insert the gearbox input shaft in the centre of the clutch and push so that the input shaft splines pass through the internal splines of the clutch disc.
2 If difficulty is experienced in engaging the splines try turning the gearbox slightly but on no account allow the weight of the gearbox to rest on the input shaft as it is easily bent.
3 With the gearbox correctly positioned on the engine backplate support its weight using a wooden block (photo).
4 Secure the gearbox to the engine and backplate with the bolts and spring washers.
5 Refit the starter motor to its aperture in the backplate and secure with the two bolts and spring washers (photos).
6 Refit the support bar located between the engine and clutch bell housing (photo).

63 Engine/gearbox - refitting

1 Pass a rope sling around the engine mountings and raise the complete power unit from the floor.
2 Check that all cables and controls in the engine compartment are tucked out of the way and that the exhaust downpipe is tied to the steering column.
3 Place an old blanket over the front of the car to avoid scratching of the grille or front panel. Lift up the power unit sufficiently so that the sump passes over the front panel.
4 An assistant should now lift up the gearbox extension housing whilst the engine is pushed rearwards. Ease the gearbox through the engine compartment and then gradually lower the engine.
5 If a trolley jack is available have it ready under the car to accept the weight of the rear of the gearbox. Alternatively use a piece of wood.
6 Continue to lower the engine and ease the gearbox rearwards until the engine is central within the engine compartment.
7 Locate the engine front mounting studs within the bracket in the front crossmember using a metal bar.
8 Jack-up the rear of the gearbox and secure the engine mountings with the nuts and plain washers.
9 Attach the gearbox crossmember to the gearbox extension housing and secure with the shaped metal plate and bolt.
10 Secure the gearbox crossmember to the body attached brackets using the four special dowel bolts and spring washers.
11 Remove the engine suspension rope and the trolley jack (if used) from the gearbox.
12 Working under the car first reconnect the reverse light switch terminal connector.
13 Reconnect the speedometer inner cable to the drive gear and push the outer cable fully up to the extension housing machined recess.
14 Secure the speedometer cable to the gearbox using the circlip. Make sure that it is correctly seated.
15 Check that the clutch release cable nylon bush is correctly located in the gearbox clutch housing flange and fixed through the clutch release cable.
16 Thread the clutch cable through the rubber gaiter (if fitted) and reconnect the clutch inner cable to the release arm.
17 Adjust the cable as described in Chapter 5.
18 Refit the rubber gaiter (if fitted).
19 Wipe clean the gearbox mainshaft splines and lubricate with a little EP 80 oil.
20 Refit the propeller shaft as described in Chapter 7. Ensure that the alignment marks coincide.
21 Release the exhaust downpipe and offer up to the exhaust manifold. Push up the clamp plate and secure with the two nuts. These nuts should be tightened a turn at a time to ensure that the downpipe seats correctly.
22 Reconnect the exhaust pipe intermediate support rubber to the body mounted bracket.
23 Remove the gearbox drain plug and check the oil level. Top-up as necessary with gearbox oil.
24 Refit the drain plug and tighten.
25 Now turning to the engine compartment reconnect the cable(s) to the starter motor.
26 The distributor may now be refitted. Look up the initial static advance for the particular model in the Specifications given in Chapter 4.
27 Turn the engine until No. 1 piston is coming up to TDC on the compression stroke. This can be checked by removing No. 1 spark plug and feeling the pressure being developed in the cylinder. Alternatively remove the oil filler cap and note when the cam is in the upright position.
28 Refer to Chapter 4 and refit the distributor to the engine.
29 Wipe the oil filter mating face of the cylinder block and smear a little grease on the oil filter seal. Screw the new unit into position taking care not to cross the thread. Continue until the sealing ring just touches the block face then tighten a half turn.
30 Insert the fuel pump operating rod in the side of the cylinder block just below the distributor body.
31 Refit the fuel pump and insulation washer and secure with the two bolts and spring washers.
32 Refit the earth cables to the side of the cylinder block just below the fuel pump and secure them with the bolt and washer.
33 Refit the main fuel line connection to the fuel pump.
34 Refit the water pump pulley and fan blades to the water pump hub and secure with the four bolts, plain and spring washers. Tighten these bolts to the specified torque.
35 Remove all traces of old gasket from the inlet manifold side of the cylinder head and inlet manifold. Fit a new gasket.
36 Refit the inlet manifold to the side of the cylinder head.
37 Secure the inlet manifold with the nuts, bolts and washers.
38 Fit the insulator washer to the inlet manifold taking care to ensure that it is the correct way round.

62.3 Gearbox located ready for attachment to engine

62.5a Refitting starter motor

62.5b Securing starter motor to engine

62.6 The support bar

39 Refit the carburettor to the inlet manifold.
40 Reconnect the brake servo hose.
41 *Automatic choke:* Reconnect the hose located between the automatic choke and inlet manifold. Tighten the two clips.
42 Reconnect the crankcase breather pipe to the union adjacent to the water hose connection on the inlet manifold. Tighten the hose clip.
43 *Manual choke:* Reconnect the choke operating cable to the choke linkage.
44 Reconnect the throttle control rod to the carburettor and the throttle control cable to the throttle operating rod.
45 Refit the fuel pipes to the carburettor. Tighten the hose clips.
46 Reconnect the throttle return spring.
47 The alternator may now be refitted. Offer it up to its mounting bracket on the right-hand side of the cylinder block and insert the two lower mounting bolts with spring washers and spacer on the bolt and plain washer on the front.
48 Refit the adjustment link to the side of the cylinder block and then attach the alternator to the adjustment link. Adjust the tension until there is 0.5 in (12.7 mm) of lateral movement at the mid point position of the belt run between the alternator pulley and the water pump. Tighten all securing bolts.
49 Refit the terminal connector to the rear of the alternator.
50 Secure the terminal connector with the spring clip.
51 Carefully refit the radiator. Refer to Chapter 2 if necessary.
52 Locate the cowl in the rear of the radiator (if fitted) and secure with the four bolts and washers.
53 Reconnect the radiator top and bottom hoses and tighten the hose clips.
54 Refit the heater hose to the union on the side of the water pump and secure with the clips.
55 Place new gaskets on the engine top cover and position on the top of the cylinder head.
56 Secure the top cover with the ten bolts and spring washers: see Fig. 1.18.

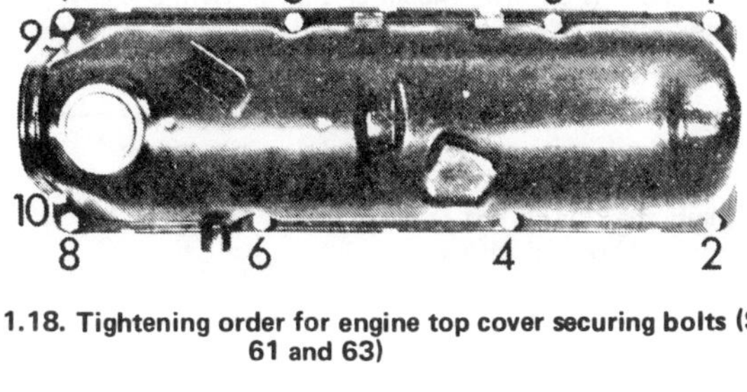

Fig. 1.18. Tightening order for engine top cover securing bolts (Secs. 61 and 63)

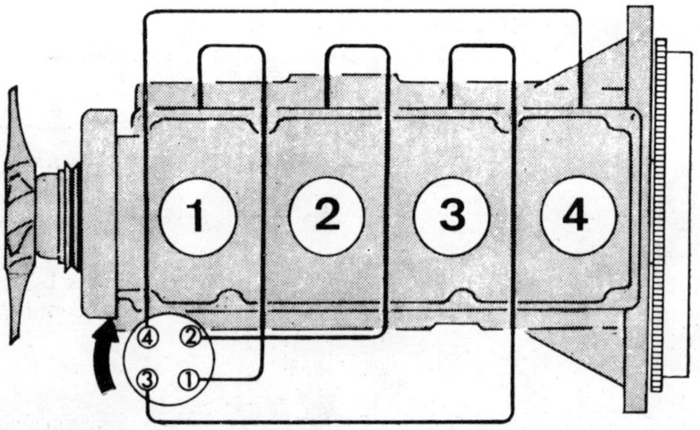

Fig. 1.19. Correct fitment of HT leads (Sec. 63)

57 Make sure the sump drain plug is tight and then refill the engine with engine oil.
58 *Automatic choke:* Reconnect the lower heater hose to the thermostatic choke union on the side of the carburettor. Secure with the hose clip.
59 Place the battery on its tray and secure with the clamp, bolt and washers.
60 Reconnect the battery positive and then negative terminals. Also reconnect the distributor HT leads to the spark plugs and to the centre of the ignition coil.
61 Refit the oil pressure gauge pipe or warning light lead.
62 Refit the water temperature sender lead.
63 Fit the oil separator to the left-hand side of the engine and insert the PCV valve in the top.
64 Refit the air cleaner to the carburettor, as described in Chapter 3.
65 Reconnect the LT cable to the side of the distributor.
66 Refill the cooling system as described in Chapter 2.
67 Reconnect the gearshift lever or linkage according to the gearbox type, referring to Chapter 6, as necessary.
68 With the help of an assistant refit the bonnet and secure the hinges with the bolts, spring and plain washers in their original positions.
69 Generally check that all wires, hoses, controls and attachments have been reconnected and the engine should be ready to start.
70 On vehicles having emission control systems, refit the components and hoses.

64 Engine - refitting (without gearbox)

1 The sequence of operations is basically identical to that for refitting the engine with the gearbox attached. The exception being work carried out on detaching the gearbox. Then differences will have become evident during the removal stage. Follow the instructions found in Section 63, leaving out the paragraphs referring to the gearbox.
2 If a reconditioned engine is being fitted, make sure that the following items are worth refitting. If not, obtain new assemblies.

Clutch and release bearing
Flywheel and ring gear
Starter motor drive
Distributor drive

3 In addition, clean the carburettor and fuel pump, then flush the radiator.
4 Always fit a new oil filter and air cleaner element and apply a little grease to the clutch release lever pivots and input shaft splines.

65 Engine - initial start-up after overhaul or major repair

1 Make sure that the battery is fully charged and that all lubricants, coolant and fuel are replenished.

66.1 Remove the nuts from the rubber engine mounting insulators.

2 If the fuel system has been dismantled it will require several revolutions of the engine on the starter motor to pump the petrol up to the carburettor.
3 As soon as the engine fires and runs, keep it going at a fast idle only (no faster) and bring it up to normal working temperature. When the thermostat opens the coolant level will fall and must therefore be topped-up again as necessary.
4 As the engine warms up there will be odd smells and some smoke from parts getting hot and burning off oil deposits. The signs to look for are leaks of water or oil which will be obvious, if serious. Check also the exhaust pipe and manifold connections as these do not always find their exact gastight position until the warmth and vibration have acted on them and it is almost certain that they will need tightening further. This should be done, of course, with the engine stopped.
5 When normal running temperature has been reached, adjust the engine idle speed, as described in Chapter 3.
6 Stop the engine and wait a few minutes to see if any lubricant or coolant is dripping out when the engine is stationary.
7 After the engine has run for 15 minutes remove the engine top cover and recheck the tightness of the cylinder head bolts. Also check the tightness of the sump bolts. In both cases use a torque wrench.
8 Road test the car to check that the timing is correct and that the engine is giving the necessary smoothness and power. Do not race the engine; if new bearings and/or pistons have been fitted it should be treated as a new engine and run in at a reduced speed for the first 1000 miles (2000 km).

66 Engine/gearbox mountings - renewal

Front mountings

1 Remove the nuts from the rubber insulator(s) (photo).
2 Raise the engine just high enough to permit the insulator(s) to be removed by carefully jacking-up beneath the mounting support bracket(s).
3 Refitting is a direct reversal of the removal procedure.

Rear mounting

4 Support the gearbox using a jack then detach the right-hand and left-hand bracket from the sidemembers.
5 Unscrew the centre bolt and remove the bracket.
6 Detach the rubber block and mounting plate from the bracket.
7 Refitting is the reverse of the removal procedure but do not fully tighten the bolts until the jack has been removed.

67 Fault diagnosis - Engine (all types)

Symptom	Reason/s	Remedy
Engine fails to turn over when starter button operated	Discharged or defective battery	Charge or renew battery, push-start car (manual gearbox only)
	Dirty or loose battery leads	Clean and tighten both terminals and earth ends of earth lead.
	Defective starter solenoid or switch	Run a heavy duty cable direct from the battery to the starter motor or bypass the solenoid.
	Engine earth strap disconnected	Check and retighten strap.
	Defective starter motor	Remove and repair.
Engine turns over but will not start	Ignition damp or wet	Wipe dry the distributor cap and ignition leads.
	Ignition leads to spark plugs loose	Check and tighten at both spark plug and distributor cap ends.
	Shorted or disconnected low tension leads	Check the wiring on the CB and SW terminals of the coil and to the distributor.
	Dirty, incorrectly set or pitted contact breaker points	Clean, file smooth and adjust.
	Faulty condenser	Check contact breaker points for arcing, remove and fit new condenser.
	Defective ignition switch	Bypass switch with wire.
	Ignition LT leads connected wrong way round	Remove and replace leads to coil in correct order.
	Faulty coil	Remove and fit new coil.
	Contact breaker point spring earthed or broken	Check spring is not touching metal part of distributor. Check insulator washers are correctly placed. Renew points if the spring is broken.
	No petrol in petrol tank	Refill tank.
	Vapour lock in fuel line (in hot conditions or at high altitude)	Blow into petrol tank, allow engine to cool, or apply a cold wet rag to the fuel line in engine compartment.
	Blocked float chamber needle valve	Remove, clean and replace.
	Fuel pump filter blocked	Remove, clean and replace.
	Choked or blocked carburettor jets	Dismantle and clean.
	Faulty fuel pump	Remove, overhaul and replace.
	Too much choke allowing too rich a mixture to wet plugs (manual choke)	Remove and dry spark plugs or with wide open throttle, push-start the car.
	Float damaged or leaking, or needle not seating	Remove, examine, clean and replace float and needle valve as necessary.
	Float lever incorrectly adjusted	Remove and adjust correctly.
Engine stalls and will not start	Ignition failure - sudden	Check over low and high tension circuits for breaks in wiring.
	Ignition failure - misfiring	Check contact breaker points, clean and adjust. Renew condenser if faulty.
	Ignition failure - in severe rain or after traversing water splash	Dry out ignition leads and distributor cap.
	No petrol in petrol tank	Refill tank.
	Petrol tank breather choked	Remove petrol cap and clean out breather hole or pipe.
	Sudden obstruction in carburettor	Check jets, filter, and needle valve in float chamber for blockage.
	Water in fuel system	Drain tank and blow out fuel lines.
Engine misfires or idles unevenly	Ignition leads loose	Check and tighten as necessary at spark plug and distributor cap ends.
	Battery leads loose on terminals	Check and tighten terminal leads.
	Battery earth strap loose on body attachment point	Check and tighten earth lead to body attachment point.
	Engine earth lead loose	Tighten lead.
	Low tension leads to terminals on coil loose	Check and tighten leads if found loose.
	Low tension lead from distributor loose	Check and tighten if found loose.
	Dirty, or incorrectly gapped spark plugs	Remove, clean and regap.
	Dirty, incorrectly set or pitted contact breaker points	Clean, file smooth and adjust.
	Tracking across distributor cap	Remove and fit new cap.
	Ignition too retarded	Check and adjust ignition timing
	Faulty coil	Remove and fit new coil.
	Mixture too weak	Check jets, float chamber needle valve and filters for obstruction. Clean as necessary. Carburettor incorrectly adjusted.

Symptom	Reason/s	Remedy
	Air leak in carburettor	Remove and overhaul carburettor.
	Air leak at inlet manifold to cylinder head, or inlet manifold to carburettor	Test by pouring oil along joints. Bubbles indicate leak. Renew manifold gasket as appropriate.
	Incorrect valve clearances	Adjust cam follower clearances (Capri II)
	Collapsed lash adjuster	Renew/overhaul lash adjuster (Mercury Capri II).
	Burnt out exhaust valves	Remove cylinder head and renew defective valves.
	Sticking or leaking valves	Remove cylinder head, clean, check and renew valves as necessary.
	Weak or broken valve springs	Check and renew as necessary.
	Worn valve guides or stems	Renew valves.
	Worn pistons and piston rings	Dismantle engine, renew pistons and rings.
Lack of power and poor compression	Burnt out exhaust valves	Remove cylinder head, renew defective valves.
	Sticking or leaking valves	Remove cylinder head, clean, check and renew valves as necessary.
	Worn valve guides and stems	Remove cylinder head and renew valves.
	Weak or broken valve springs	Remove cylinder head, renew defective springs.
	Blown cylinder head gasket (accompanied by increase in noise)	Remove cylinder head and fit new gasket.
	Worn pistons and piston rings	Dismantle engine, renew pistons and rings.
	Worn or scored cylinder bores	Dismantle engine, rebore, renew pistons and rings.
	Ignition timing wrongly set. Too advanced or retarded	Check and reset ignition timing.
	Contact breaker points incorrectly gapped	Check and reset contact breaker points.
	Incorrect valve clearances	Adjust cam follower clearances.
	Incorrect set spark plugs	Remove, clean and regap.
	Carburettor too rich or too weak	Tune carburettor for optimum performance.
	Dirty contact breaker points	Remove, clean and replace.
	Fuel filters blocked causing top end fuel starvation	Dismantle, inspect, clean, and replace all fuel filters
	Distributor automatic advance weights or vacuum advance and retard mechanisms not functioning correctly	Overhaul distributor.
	Faulty fuel pump giving top end fuel starvation	Remove, overhaul, or fit exchange reconditioned fuel pump.
Excessive oil consumption	Badly worn, perished or missing valve stem oil seals	Remove, fit new oil seals to valve stems.
	Excessively worn valve stems and valve guides	Remove cylinder head and fit new valves.
	Worn piston rings	Fit oil control rings to existing pistons or purchase new pistons.
	Worn pistons and cylinder bores	Fit new pistons and rings, rebore cylinders.
	Excessive piston ring gap allowing blow-by	Fit new piston rings and set gap correctly.
	Piston oil return holes choked	Decarbonise engine and pistons.
Oil being lost due to leaks	Leaking oil filter gasket	Inspect and fit new gasket as necessary.
	Leaking rocker cover gasket	Inspect and fit new gasket as necessary.
	Leaking timing case gasket	Inspect and fit new gasket as necessary.
	Leaking sump gasket	Inspect and fit new gasket as necessary.
	Loose sump plug	Tighten, fit new gasket as necessary.
Unusual noises from engine	Worn valve gear (noisy tapping from top cover)	Inspect and renew cam follower and ball headed bolts (CapriII).
	Worn big-end bearing (regular heavy knocking)	Fit new bearings.
	Worn main bearings (rumbling and vibration)	Fit new bearings.
	Worn crankshaft (knocking, rumbling and vibration	Regrind crankshaft, fit new main and big-end bearings.

Chapter 1 Part B: 2300 engine (Mercury Capri II)

Contents

Specifications

Engine (general)

Engine type	Four in-line, single overhead camshaft
Firing order	1, 3, 4, 2
Bore	3.78 in (96 mm)
Stroke	3.126 in (79.4 mm)
Cubic capacity	2300 cc (140 cu in)
Compression pressure	Lowest reading within 75% of highest reading
Oil pressure, hot	40 to 60 lb f/in^2 (2.8 to 4.2 kg f/cm^2)
Engine idle speed	See engine compartment emission control decal

Cylinder head

Valve guide bore diameter	0.3433 to 0.3443 in (8.720 to 8.745 mm)
Valve seat width:	
Intake	0.060 to 0.090 in (1.524 to 2.286 mm)
Exhaust	0.070 to 0.090 in (1.778 to 2.286 mm)
Valve seat angle	45°
Valve seat runout, max.	0.0016 in (0.041 mm)
Valve arrangement, front to rear	EI, EI, EI, EI
Gasket surface flatness	0.003 in (0.076 mm) in any 6 in (152.4 mm): 0.006 in (0.152 mm) overall
Head gasket surface finish	60 to 150 rms

Valve springs

Spring load	71 to 79 lb at 1.56 in (32.23 to 35.87 kg at 39.6 mm) 180 to 198 lb at 1.16 in (81.72 to 89.82 kg at 29.46 mm)
Spring free-length (approx.)	1.824 in (46.33 mm)
Valve spring assembled height, pad to retainer	1 17/32 in (38.89 mm)
Valve spring out of square (max.)	0.078 in (1.98 mm)

Valves

Stem to guide clearance:	
Intake	0.0010 to 0.0027 in (0.0254 to 0.069 mm)
Exhaust	0.0015 to 0.0032 in (0.0381 to 0.081 mm)
Wear limit	0.0055 in (0.1397 mm)
Valve head diameter:	
Intake	1.728 to 1.744 in (43.89 to 44.298 mm)
Exhaust	1.492 to 1.508 in (37.897 to 38.30 mm)
Valve face angle	44°
Valve face runout, max.	0.002 in (0.051 mm)
Stem diameter, standard:	
Intake	0.3416 to 0.3423 in (8.676 to 8.694 mm)
Exhaust	0.3411 to 0.3418 in (8.664 to 8.682 mm)
Oversize 0.008 in:	
Intake	0.3446 to 0.3453 in (8.751 to 8.771 mm)
Exhaust	0.3441 to 0.3448 in (8.740 to 8.756 mm)
Oversize 0.016 in:	
Intake	0.3566 to 0.3573 in (9.058 to 9.075 mm)
Exhaust	0.3561 to 0.3568 in (9.045 to 9.063 mm)
Oversize 0.032 in:	
Intake	0.3716 to 0.3723 in (9.439 to 9.456 mm)
Exhaust	0.3711 to 0.3718 in (9.426 to 9.444 mm)

Cylinder block

Bore diameter, standard	3.7795 to 3.7831 in (96 to 96.09 mm)
Maximum out of round	0.001 in (0.0254 mm)
Wear limit	0.005 in (0.127 mm)
Bore	18.88 rms
Taper wear limit	0.01 in (0.254 mm)
Bore diameter 0.003 in oversize	3.7825 to 3.7861 in (96.08 to 96.17 mm)
Main bearing bore diameter	2.5902 to 2.5910 in (65.79 to 65.81 mm)
Head gasket surface flatness	0.003 in (0.076 mm) in any 6 in (152.4 mm) 0.006 in (0.152 mm) overall
Head gasket surface finish	60 to 150 rms

Camshaft

Lobe lift	0.2437 in (6.19 mm)
Max. permissible lobe lift loss	0.005 in (0.127 mm)
Endplay	0.001 to 0.007 in (0.0254 to 0.178 mm)
Wear limit	0.009 in (0.229 mm)
Camshaft journal to bearing clearance	0.001 to 0.003 in (0.0254 to 0.076 mm)
Wear limit	0.006 in (0.152 mm)
Camshaft journal diameter	1.7713 to 1.772 in (44.99 to 45.01 mm)
Camshaft bearings inside diameter	1.773 to 1.7742 (45.03 to 45.06 mm)

Camshaft drive mechanism

Face run-out, max. assembled:	
Camshaft gear	0.007 in (0.178 mm)
Crankshaft gear	0.005 in (0.127 mm)

Hydraulic lash adjuster

Standard diameter	0.8422 to 0.8427 in (21.39 to 21.40 mm)
Clearance to bore	0.0007 to 0.0027 in (0.018 to 0.069 mm)
Leak-down rate for 1/8 in (3.175 mm) of travel	2 to 8 seconds
Collapsed adjuster gap at cam (allowable)	0.035 to 0.055 in (0.89 to 1.34 mm)
Collapsed adjuster gap at cam (desired)	0.040 to 0.050 in (1.0 to 1.27 mm)

Auxiliary shaft

Endplay	0.001 to 0.007 in (0.025 to 0.178 mm)
Bearing clearance	0.001 to 0.0028 in (0.025 to 0.071 mm)

Crankshaft and flywheel

Main bearing journal diameter	2.3892 to 2.399 in (60.686 to 60.935 mm)
Main bearing journal run-out, max.	0.002 in (0.051 mm)
Wear limit	0.005 in (0.127 mm)
Main bearing journal thrust face run-out, max.	0.001 in (0.0254 mm)
Connecting rod journal diameter	2.0464 to 2.0472 in (51.979 to 51.999 mm)
Crankshaft free-endplay	0.004 to 0.008 in (0.102 to 0.203 mm)
Wear limit	0.012 in (0.305 mm)
Flywheel clutch face run-out	0.008 in (0.203 mm)

Crankshaft bearings

Connecting rod bearing-to-crankshaft clearance	0.0008 to 0.0026 in (0.02 to 0.066 mm)
Wall thickness, standard	0.0619 to 0.0624 in (1.572 to 1.585 mm)
Wall thickness, 0.002 in undersize	0.0629 to 0.0634 in (1.598 to 1.61 mm)
Main bearing-to-crankshaft clearance	0.0008 to 0.0015 in (0.02 to 0.038 mm)
Wall thickness, standard	0.0951 to 0.0956 in (2.416 to 2.428 mm)
Wall thickness, 0.002 in undersize	0.0961 to 0.0966 in (2.441 to 2.454 mm)

Connecting rod

Piston pin bore	0.9104 to 0.9112 in (23.12 to 23.14 mm)
Connecting rod bearing bore diameter	2.172 to 2.1728 in (55.169 to 55.189 mm)
Connecting rod side clearance (assembled to crankshaft)	0.0035 to 0.0105 in (0.089 to 0.267 mm)
Wear limit	0.014 in (0.356 mm)

Piston

Diameter:	
Standard	3.7780 to 3.7786 in (95.96 to 95.976 mm)
Coded blue	3.7792 to 3.7798 in (95.99 to 96.007)
0.003 in oversize	3.7804 to 3.7810 in (96.02 to 96.037 mm)
Piston to bore clearance	0.0014 to 0.0022 in (0.035 to 0.056 mm)
Piston pin bore diameter	0.9123 to 0.9126 in (23.17 to 23.18 mm)
Ring groove width:	
Compression rings	0.08 to 0.081 in (2.03 to 2.056 mm)
Oil control ring	0.188 to 0.189 in (4.78 to 4.80 mm)

Piston pin

Length	3.01 to 3.04 in (76.45 to 77.22 mm)
Diameter, standard:	0.912 to 0.9123 in (23.16 to 23.17 mm)
0.001 in oversize	0.913 to 0.9133 in (23.19 to 23.198 mm)
0.002 in oversize	0.914 to 0.9143 in (23.21 to 23.22 mm)
Pin to piston clearance	0.0002 to 0.0004 in (0.005 to 0.01 mm)
Pin to connecting rod bushing clearance	Interference fit

Piston rings

Compression ring width	0.077 to 0.08 in (1.956 to 2.03 mm)
Compression ring side clearance	0.002 to 0.004 in (0.05 to 0.10 mm)
Wear limit	0.006 in (0.152 mm)
Oil control ring	Snug fit
Compression ring gap width	0.01 to 0.02 in (0.254 to 0.51 mm)
Oil control ring gap width	0.015 to 0.055 in (0.38 to 1.397 mm)

Oil pump

Relief valve spring tension	7.54 to 8.33 lb (3.4 to 3.78 kg) at 1.54 in (39.12 mm)
Driveshaft to housing clearance	0.0015 to 0.0029 in (0.038 to 0.074 mm)
Relief valve clearance	0.0015 to 0.0029 in (0.038 to 0.074 mm)
Rotor assembly end-clearance	0.001 to 0.004 in (0.025 to 0.102 mm)
Outer race-to-housing radial clearance	0.001 to 0.007 in (0.025 to 0.178 mm)
Oil pan capacity (approx.)	8¼ Imp. pints (4.7 litre/10 US pints)
Oil type:	**Multi-viscosity**
Below + 32°F (0°C)	5W-30/10W-30
−10°F to + 90°F (−23°C to + 32°C)	10W-30
−10°F to above 90°F (−23°C to above + 32°C)	10W-40
Above 90°F (32°C)	20W-40

Torque wrench settings

	lbf ft	**kgf m**
Auxiliary shaft gear bolt	28/40	3.9/5.5
Auxiliary shaft thrust plate bolt	6/9	0.83/1.2
Belt tensioner bolt:		
Pivot	28/40	3.9/5.5
Adjuster	14/21	1.9/2.9
Camshaft gear bolt	50/71	6.9/9.8
Camshaft thrust plate bolt	6/9	0.83/1.2
Carburettor to carburettor spacer stud	7.5/15	1.0/2.1
Carburettor to spacer nut	10/14	1.4/1.9
Carburettor spacer to manifold bolt	14/21	1.9/2.9
Connecting rod nut	30/36	4.1/5.0
Crankshaft damper/pulley bolt	80/114	11/15.7
Cylinder head bolt	80/90	11/12.5
Distributor clamp bolt	20/28	2.8/3.9
Distributor vacuum tube to inlet manifold - adapter	5/8	0.7/1.1
Exhaust manifold to cylinder head nut or bolt	16/23	2.2/3.2
Flywheel to crankshaft bolt	54/64	7.5/8.8
Fuel pump to cylinder block bolt	14/21	1.9/2.9
Intake manifold to cylinder head nut or bolt	14/21	1.9/2.9
Main bearing cap bolt	80/90	11/12.5
Oil pressure sending unit to cylinder block	8/18	1.1/2.5

Torque wrench settings	lbf ft	kgf m
Oil pump pick-up tube to oil pump	14/21	1.9/2.9
Oil pump pick-up tube to cylinder block	14/21	1.9/2.9
Oil pan drain plug	15/25	2.1/3.5
Oil pan to cylinder block bolts:		
M6 bolts	7/9	1.0/1.2
M8 bolts	11/13	1.5/1.8
Oil filter insert to block	20/25	2.8/3.5
Rocker arm cover bolt	4/7	0.6/1.0
Spark plug to cylinder head	10/15	1.4/2.1
Temperature sending unit to cylinder head	8/18	1.1/2.5
Water jacket drain plug	23/28	3.2/3.9
Water pump to cylinder block bolt	14/21	1.9/2.9
Exhaust manifold to EGR pipe - connector	25/35	3.5/4.8
EGR valve to spacer bolt	14/21	1.9/2.9
EGR tube to exhaust manifold - connector	8/12	1.1/1.6
EGR tube nut	8/12	1.1/1.6
Auxiliary shaft cover bolt	6/9	0.8/1.2
Cylinder front cover bolt	6/9	0.8/1.2
Water outlet connection bolt	14/21	1.9/2.9
Inner timing belt cover stud	14/21	1.9/2.9
Outer timing belt cover bolt	6/9	0.8/1.2
Rocker arm cover shield bolt	28/40	3.9/5.5
Thermactor check valve to manifold	25/35	3.5/4.8

68 General description

The engine used on models covered by this manual is a 4-cylinder, 2300 cc, overhead camshaft type of lightweight iron construction.

The crankshaft runs in five main bearings, and the camshaft runs in four. The main, connecting rod (big-end), camshaft and auxiliary shaft bearings are all replaceable.

The camshaft is driven from the crankshaft by a toothed belt, which also operates the auxiliary shaft. The auxiliary shaft drives the oil pump and distributor, and operates the fuel pump through an eccentric. Tension on the cam drivebelt is maintained by a preloaded idler pulley which runs on the outside of the belt.

A separate V-belt is used to drive the water pump, fan and alternator. V-belts are also used to drive the engine driven accessories.

Hydraulic valve lash adjusters are used, these operating on the fulcrum point of the cam followers (rocker arms). The cylinder head is drilled to provide oil feed and return pipes for their operation.

A positive, closed-type crankcase ventilation system is used to recycle crankcase blow-by vapors back to the intake manifold.

69 Major operations possible with engine in car

Refer to the information given in Section 2 of this Chapter for the 1.6 and 2.0 litre engines.

70 Major operations requiring engine removal

Refer to the information given in Section 3 of this Chapter for the 1.6 and 2.0 litre engines.

71 Methods of engine removal

The engine may be lifted out either on its own or in unit with the transmission. On models fitted with automatic transmission, it is recommended that the engine be lifted out on its own, unless a substantial crane or overhead hoist is available, because of the weight factor. If the engine and transmission are removed as a unit they have to be lifted out at a very steep angle, so make sure that there is sufficient lifting height available.

72 Engine - removal (without transmission)

1 The do-it-yourself owner should be able to remove the engine in about 4 hours provided that a good selection of tools and a hoist is available. Also, for access beneath the car a jack and/or axle stands will be required. Although not essential, it may be found useful to have help from an assistant, particularly during the lifting operations.

Caution: Where air-conditioning is installed, ensure that the refrigerant lines are disconnected by a qualified refrigerant specialist.

2 Open the engine compartment hood and disconnect the battery ground lead.

3 Remove the air cleaner assembly referring to Chapter 3, as necessary. It is recommended that a sketch is made showing the various pipe connections to avoid confusion when refitting.

4 Using a soft-lead pencil or chalk, mark the outline of the hood hinges. Remove the hood, referring to Chapter 12, if necessary.

5 If possible, raise the car on a hoist or place it over an inspection pit. If neither of these is available, jack-up the car on the body side members for access beneath. (Refer to the Introductory Sections for the jacking points).

6 Where applicable, remove the engine shield.

7 Remove the radiator bottom hose and drain the engine coolant mixture into a suitable container. This can be re-used if less than two years old; however, if it is discolored in any way it should be discarded.

8 Remove the starter motor. Further details will be found in Chapter 10, if required.

9 *On automatic transmission models:* remove the torque converter bolt access plug. Remove the three flywheel-to-converter bolts. Remove the converter housing cover and disconnect the converter from the flywheel.

10 *On manual transmission models:* remove the flywheel cover.

11 Remove the flywheel or converter housing cover, as applicable.

12 Detach the exhaust pipe from the exhaust manifold. Remove the packing washer.

13 Where applicable, remove the automatic transmission oil cooler lines from the radiator.

14 Remove the nuts from the engine mountings.

15 Removethe oil pan drain plug and drain the oil into a container of adequate capacity.

16 Detach the fuel lines from the fuel pump, plugging the lines to prevent fuel spillage.

17 Where applicable, remove the power steering pump drivebelt and draw off the pulley. The drivebelt arrangement is shown in Chapter 2; refer to Chapter 11 for further information on the pump.

18 Remove the lower bolt securing the power steering pump to the bracket.

19 Lower the car to the ground.

20 Remove the engine-to-radiator top hose, fan shroud and radiator. For further information on these items refer to Chapter 2.

21 Disconnect the heater and vacuum hoses from the engine. It is recommended that a sketch is made showing the various connections to avoid confusion when refitting.

22 Disconnect the power brake hose.

23 Remove the oil pressure union from the connection on the rear left-hand side of the cylinder head.

24 Detach the carburetor cable (s).

25 Disconnect the wire to the throttle solenoid and choke heater.

26 Detach the wire from the water temperature sender on the rear left-hand side of the cylinder block.
27 Disconnect the lines from the vacuum amplifier.
28 From the distributor, disconnect the coil wire and vacuum line.
29 Pull off the multi-plug from the alternator, followed by the ground wire.
30 Remove the bolt from the alternator adjusting arm.
31 Remove the remaining power steering pump-to-bracket bolts, and remove the pump.
32 Support the weight of the transmission on a suitable jack, with a wood block interposed between the jack head and the transmission.
33 Attach the hoist hooks to the engine lifting brackets and lift the engine a little.
34 Draw the engine forward to disengage the transmission, ensuring that the transmission is still satisfactorily supported.
35 Lift the engine out, ensuring that no damage occurs to the hoses etc., in the engine compartment or to the engine mounting equipment. Transfer the engine to a suitable working area and detach the accessories. These will vary according to the engine, but would typically be:

Alternator
Thermactor pump
Air-conditioning compressor
Clutch

36 Clean the outside of the engine using a water soluble solvent then transfer it to where it is to be dismantled. On the assumption that engine overhaul is to be carried out, remove the fuel pump, oil filter (unscrew), spark plugs, distributor (index mark the distributor body and block to assist with installation), fan, water pump, thermostat, oil pressure and water temperature senders, emission control ancillaries, etc. Refer to the appropriate Sections in this and other Chapters for further information.

73 Engine - removal (with manual transmission)

1 The procedure for removing the engine and transmission together is basically similar to that described in the previous Section. However, the following differences should be noted:

a) *Disconnect the gearshift linkage from the transmission, referring to Chapter 6, as necessary.*
b) *Detach the propeller shaft following the procedure given in Chapter 7.*
c) *Disconnect the clutch operating cable from the release arm.*
d) *Do not remove the clutch housing bolts. These items are removed after the assembly has been removed from the car. Further information on this will be found in Chapter 6.*
e) *Remove the speedometer drive cable, and the transmission electrical connections. If there is any possibility of them being mixed up, suitably label them or make a sketch showing their installed positions.*
f) *Support the weight of the transmission in a similar manner to that described in the previous Section, paragraph 32, while the rear mounting is being detached.*
g) *It is a good idea to do the preliminary cleaning of the engine with the transmission still attached.*

74 Engine - dismantling (general)

1 It is best to mount the engine on a dismantling stand, but if this is not available, stand the engine on a strong bench at a comfortable working height. Failing this, it can be stripped down on the floor.
2 During the dismantling process, the greatest care should be taken to keep the exposed parts free from dirt. As an aid to achieving this thoroughly clean down the outside of the engine, first removing all traces of oil and congealed dirt.
3 A good grease solvent will make the job much easier, for, after the solvent has been applied and allowed to stand for a time, a vigorous jet of water will wash off the solvent and grease with it. If the dirt is thick and deeply embedded, work the solvent into it with a strong stiff brush.
4 Finally wipe down the exterior of the engine with a rag and only then, when it is quite clean, should the dismantling process begin. As the engine is stripped, clean each part in a bath of kerosene or gasoline.
5 Never immerse parts with oilways in kerosene (eg; crankshaft and camshaft). To clean these parts, wipe down carefully with a gasoline dampened rag. Oilways can be cleaned out with wire. If an air line is available, all parts can be blown dry and the oilways blown through as an added precaution.
6 Re-use of old gaskets is false economy. To avoid the possibility of trouble after the engine has been reassembled **always** use new gaskets throughout.
7 Do not throw away the old gaskets, for sometimes it happens that an immediate replacement cannot be found and the old gasket is then very useful as a template. Hang up the gaskets as they are removed.
8 To strip the engine, it is best to work from the top down. When the stage is reached where the crankshaft must be removed, the engine can be turned on its side and all other work carried out with it in this position.
9 Wherever possible, refit nuts, bolts and washers finger-tight from wherever they were removed. This helps to avoid loss and muddle. If they cannot be refitted then arrange them in a fashion that it is clear from whence they came.
10 Before dismantling begins it is important that a special tool is obtained for compressing the lash adjusters. This has the Ford number T74P-6565-B.

75 Cylinder head removal - engine out of the car

1 Remove the carburettor from the intake manifold using a suitable cranked wrench. For further information see Chapter 3.
2 Take off the gasket. Remove the EGR spacer, followed by the second gasket.
3 Remove any emission control system hoses and fittings from the intake manifold, carefully noting their installed positions to assist in reassembly later.
4 Loosen the intake manifold securing bolts by about ½ turn each, in the reverse order to that shown in Fig. 1.22. Then remove the bolts completely and lift away the manifold. Note the lifting eye on the No. 7 bolt.
5 Remove the timing belt outer cover (4 bolts). Note the spacers used with two of the bolts adjacent to the auxiliary shaft sprocket.
6 If major engine dismantling is going to be carried out, remove the nut and washer retaining the crankshaft pulley. If this is found difficult because the engine tends to turn over, either wedge a screwdriver in the flywheel teeth or lock the pulley using a suitable bar in the slots.

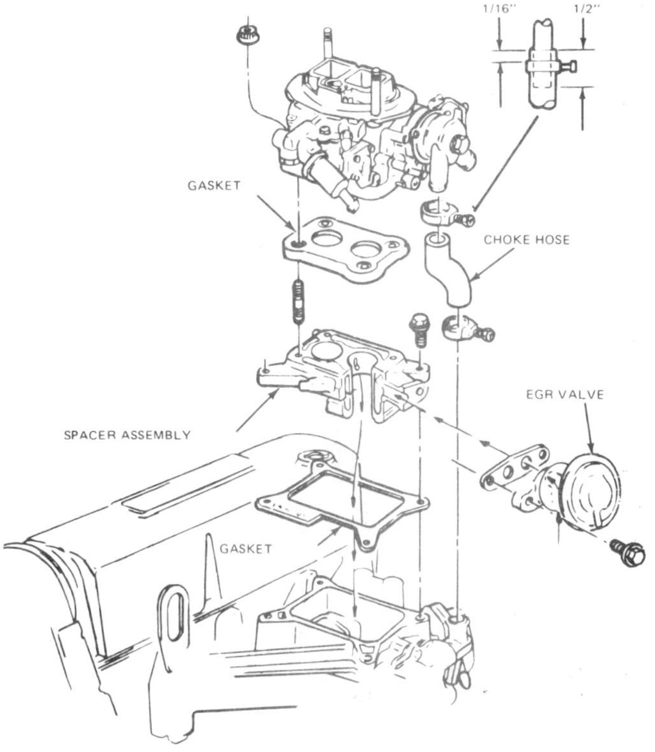

Fig. 1.20. The carburettor, EGR spacer and associated parts (Secs. 75 and 130)

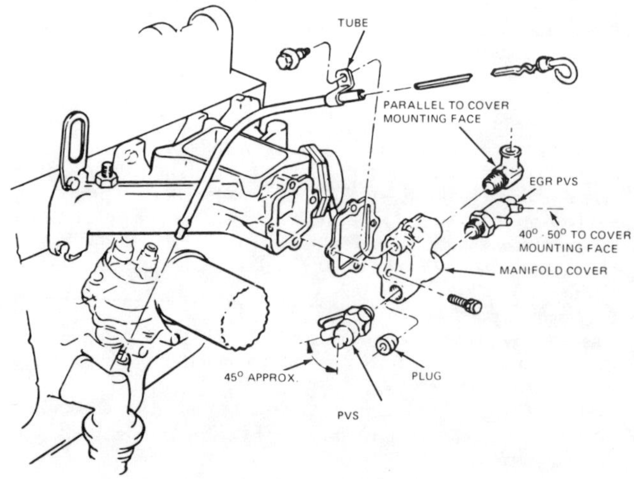

Fig. 1.21. Intake manifold ancillaries (Secs. 75 and 130)

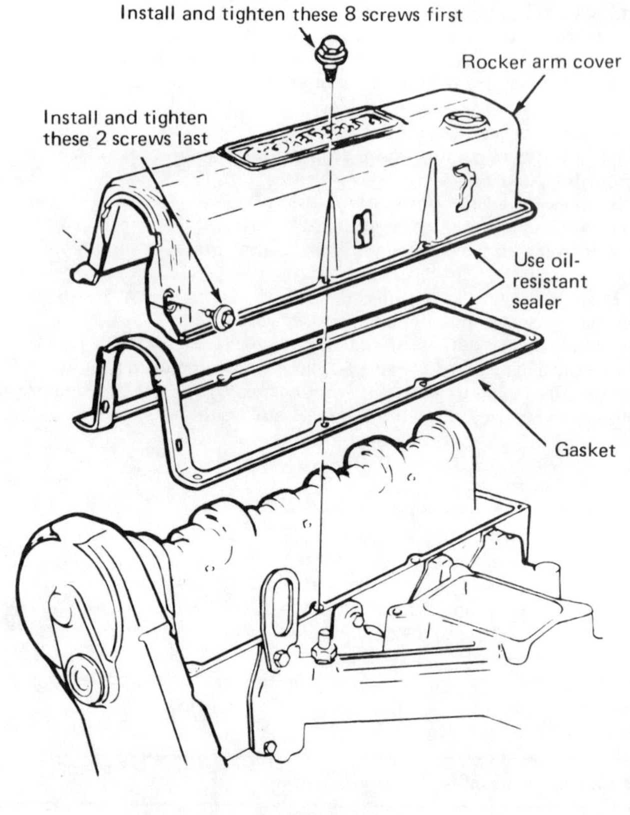

Fig. 1.24. Rocker arm cover (Sec. 75)

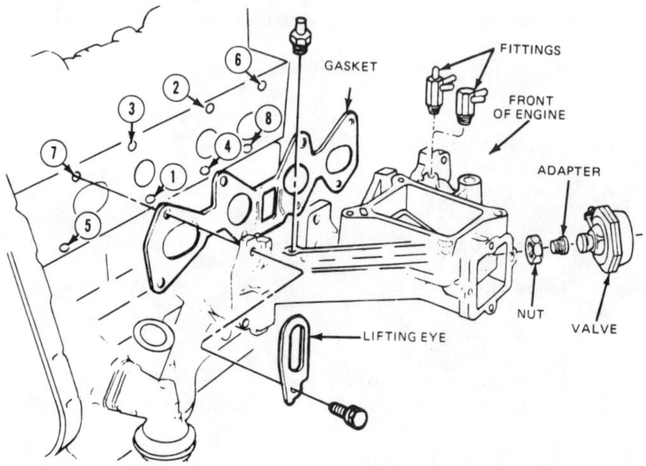

Fig. 1.22. Intake manifold and gaskets (Secs. 75 and 130)

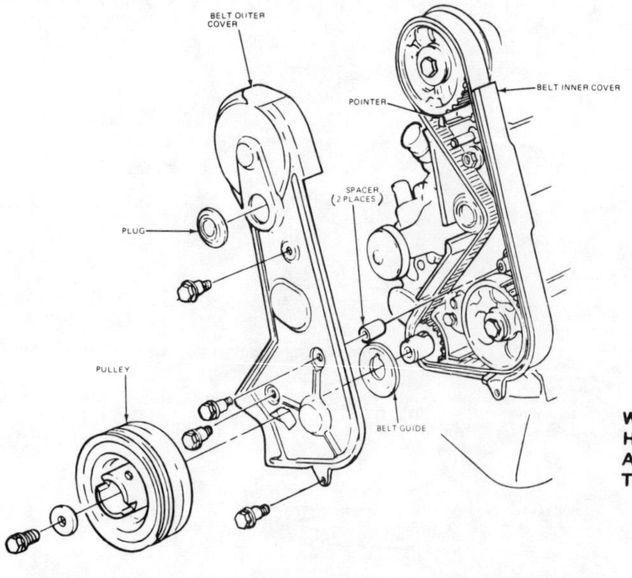

Fig. 1.23. Crankshaft pulley/damper and belt outer cover (Sec. 75)

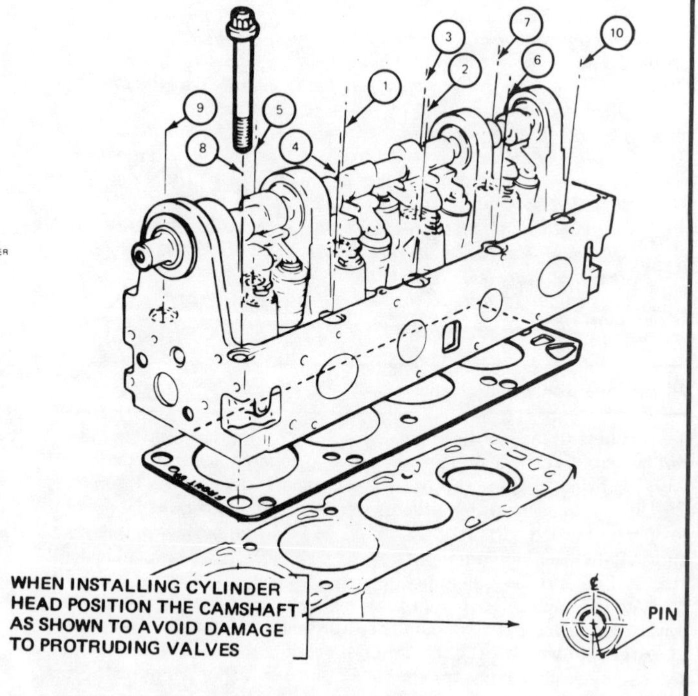

Fig. 1.25. Cylinder head (Secs. 75 and 123)

7 Draw off the pulley using a suitable puller (or carefully pry it off using a large screwdriver), then remove the belt guide.
8 Loosen the timing belt tensioner adjustment bolt to relieve the belt tension.
9 Remove the timing belt by drawing it off the sprockets.
10 Remove the timing belt tensioner from the front end of the cylinder head (2 bolts).
11 Remove the single stud and washer from the upper attachment point of the inner timing belt cover.
12 Loosen the eight screws from around the rocker arm cover flange and the two screws at the front end. Remove the screws, lift off the cover and remove the gasket.
13 Loosen each cylinder head bolt slightly in the reverse order to that shown in Fig. 1.25. Then remove all the bolts with the exception of Nos. 7 and 8 which should be unscrewed so that only about two threads are engaged.
14 Using the exhaust manifold for leverage, lift it up to break the cylinder head/gasket seal.
15 Loosen the exhaust manifold retaining bolts in the reverse order to that shown in Fig. 1.26. Remove the bolts whilst supporting the manifold then remove the manifold from the engine. Note the lifting eye on the rear bolt.
16 Remove the two remaining cylinder head bolts and lift off the head. Transfer it to a suitable workbench for further dismantling. Remove the old gasket from the block.

76 Cylinder head removal - engine in the car

1 Removal of the cylinder head with the engine in the car is very similar to the procedure given in the previous Section. However, the following points should be noted:

a) First remove the engine compartment hood for improved access.
b) Disconnect the battery ground lead.
c) Drain the engine coolant and remove the hoses connected to the cylinder head. Refer to Chapter 2, if necessary.
d) Remove the air cleaner, carburettor and emission control system items attached to the carburettor and manifolds. Refer to Chapter 3 if necessary. It is recommended that a sketch is made showing the various pipe connections to avoid confusion when refitting.
e) The camshaft drivebelt need not be completely removed unless it is to be renewed. This means that the crankshaft pulley and belt guide need not be removed.

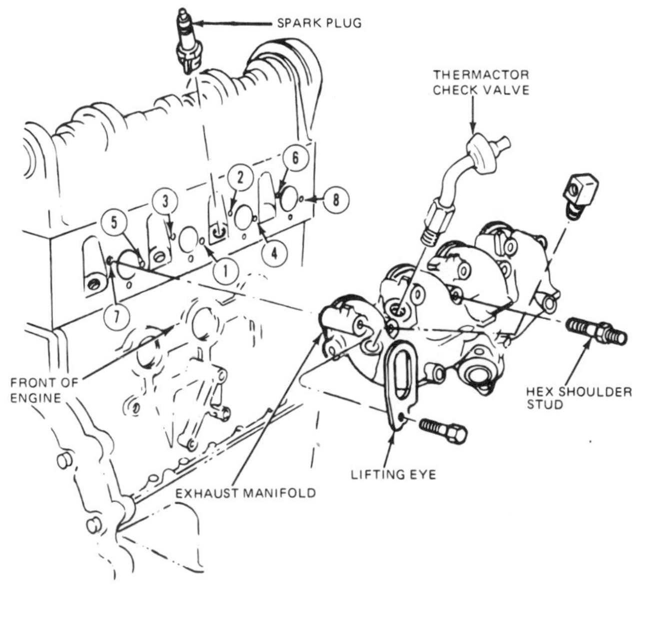

Fig. 1.26. Exhaust manifold and ancillaries (Secs. 75 and 130)

f) Remove the appropriate drivebelts from the engine driven accessories as necessary to permit the drivebelt outer cover to be removed.
g) If air-conditioning refrigerant lines need to be disconnected, this must be carried out by a qualified refrigeration specialist.
h) Detach the spark plug leads and the oil pressure gauge connection.

77 Auxiliary shaft - removal

1 Using a metal bar to lock the auxiliary shaft sprocket, remove the sprocket retaining bolt and washer.
2 Pull off the sprocket using a universal puller, and remove the sprocket locking pin.
3 Remove the auxiliary shaft front cover (3 screws).
4 Remove the auxiliary shaft retaining plate (2 screws).
5 Withdraw the auxiliary shaft. If this is tight, refit the bolt and washer, then use a pry bar and a spacer block to pry out the shaft.

78 Flywheel and backplate - removal

Refer to the procedure given in Section 13 of this Chapter for the 1.6 and 2.0 litre engine. Fig. 1.29 shows the relevant parts; note that the rear oil seal is of a different type and is integral with the crankshaft rear bearing shell.

79 Oil pan, oil pump and strainer - removal

Refer to the procedure given in Section 14 of this Chapter for the 1.6 and 2.0 litre engines, ignoring the tool reference number.

80 Crankshaft sprocket, drivebelt inner cover and cylinder front cover - removal

1 Having already removed the crankshaft pulley (Section 75), very carefully pry off the crankshaft sprocket using a large screwdriver.
2 Remove the remaining bolt and take off the engine front cover.
3 Remove the two bolts and take off the cylinder front cover.
4 Remove the gasket.
5 If the crankshaft key is not a tight fit in the keyway, remove it at this stage to prevent it from being lost.

81 Pistons, connecting rods and connecting rod bearings - removal

The procedure is generally as described in Section 16 of this Chapter for the 1.6 and 2.0 litre engines. Observe the piston crown and bearing cap markings which should be as shown in the illustration (Fig. 1.32).

82 Crankshaft and main bearings - removal

The procedure is generally as described in Section 17 of this Chapter for the 1.6 and 2.0 litre engines. If the bearing caps are not marked already, ensure that they are marked as they are removed so that they can be refitted later in their correct positions.

83 Camshaft drivebelt - removal (engine in the car)

The procedure is generally as described in Section 18 of this Chapter for the 1.6 and 2.0 litre engines. However, it will be necessary to remove the drivebelts from all the engine belt driven items.

84 Valves and lash adjusters - removal

1 Remove the spring clip from the hydraulic valve lash adjuster end of the cam followers (where applicable).
2 Using special tool T74P-6565-B inserted beneath the camshaft, fully compress the lash adjuster of the valve (s) to be removed, ensuring

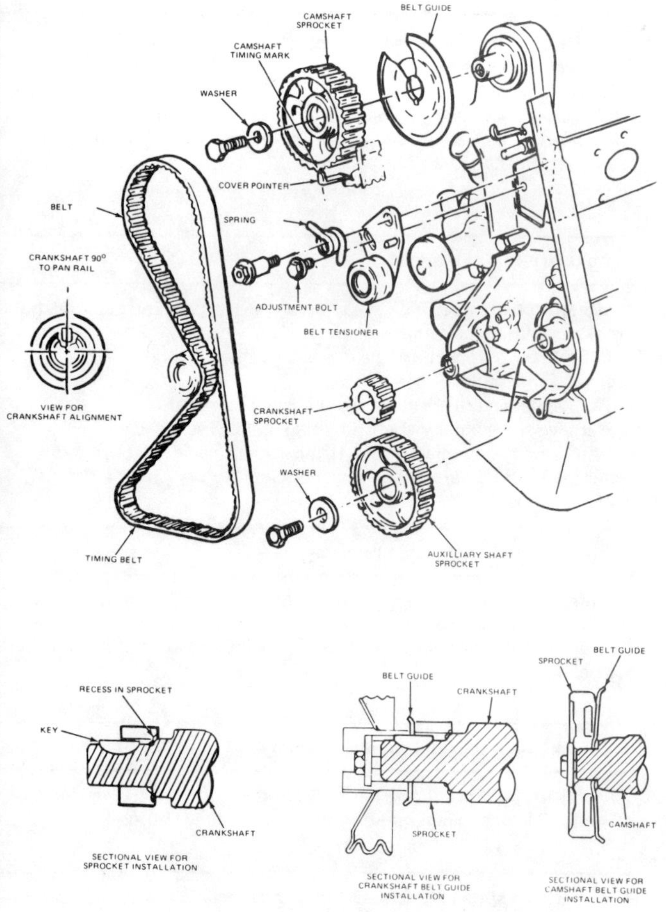

Fig. 1.27. Camshaft belt, sprockets and tensioner (Sec. 76)

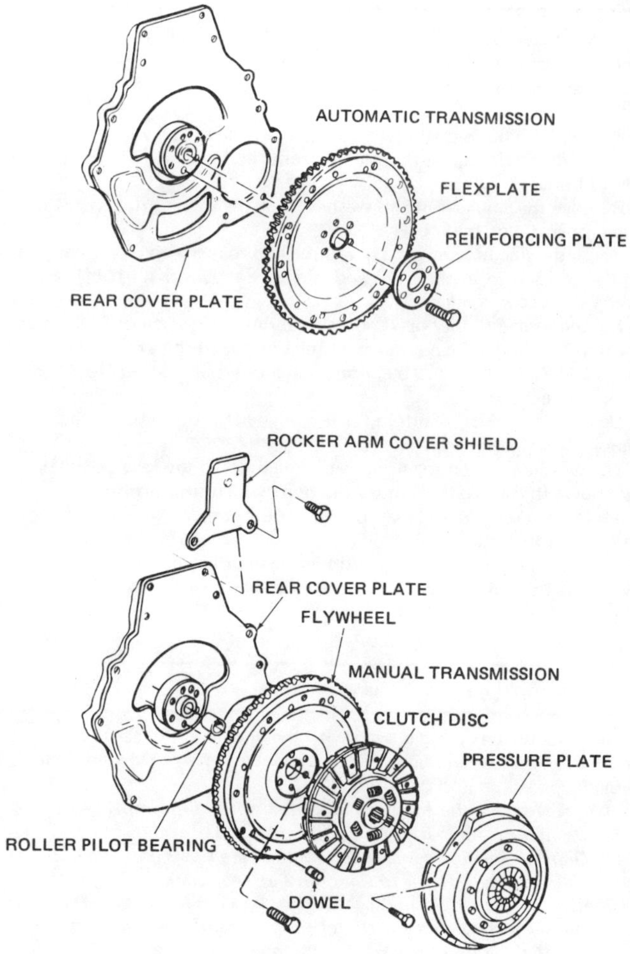

Fig. 1.29. Flywheel and associated parts (Sec. 78)

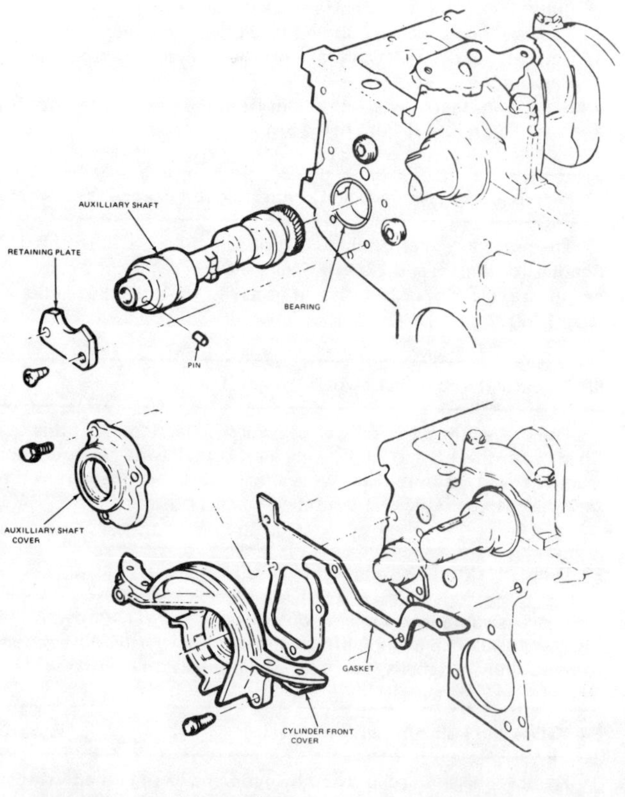

Fig. 1.28. Auxiliary shaft and front covers (Sec. 77)

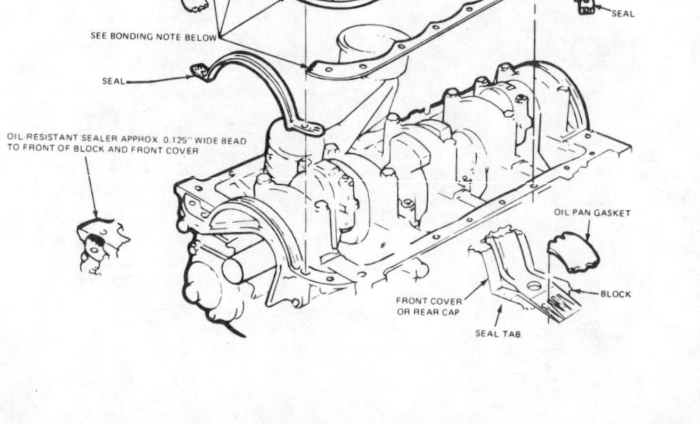

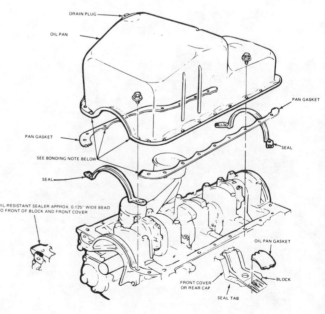

Fig. 1.30. Oil pan (Sec. 79)

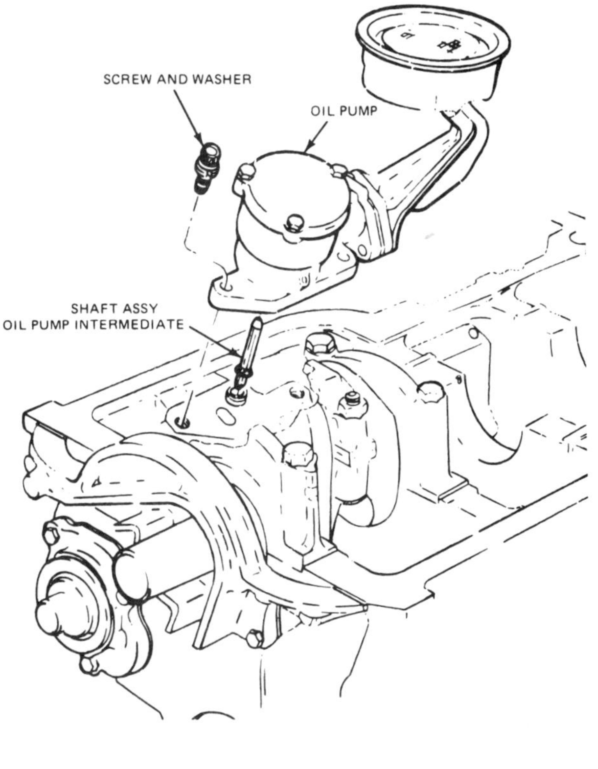

Fig. 1.31. Oil pump (Sec. 79)

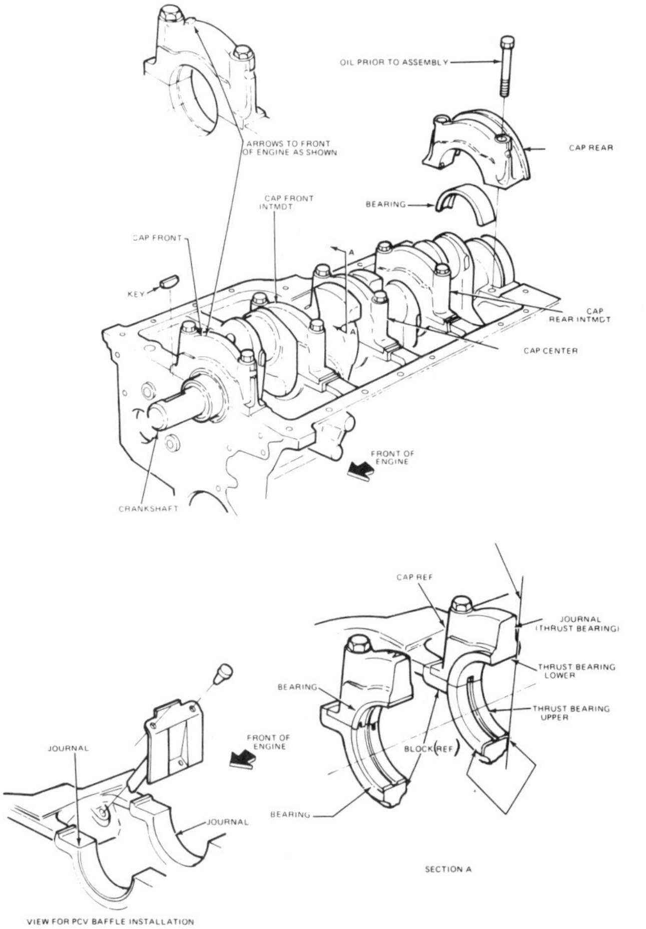

Fig. 1.33. Crankshaft and main bearings (Sec. 82)

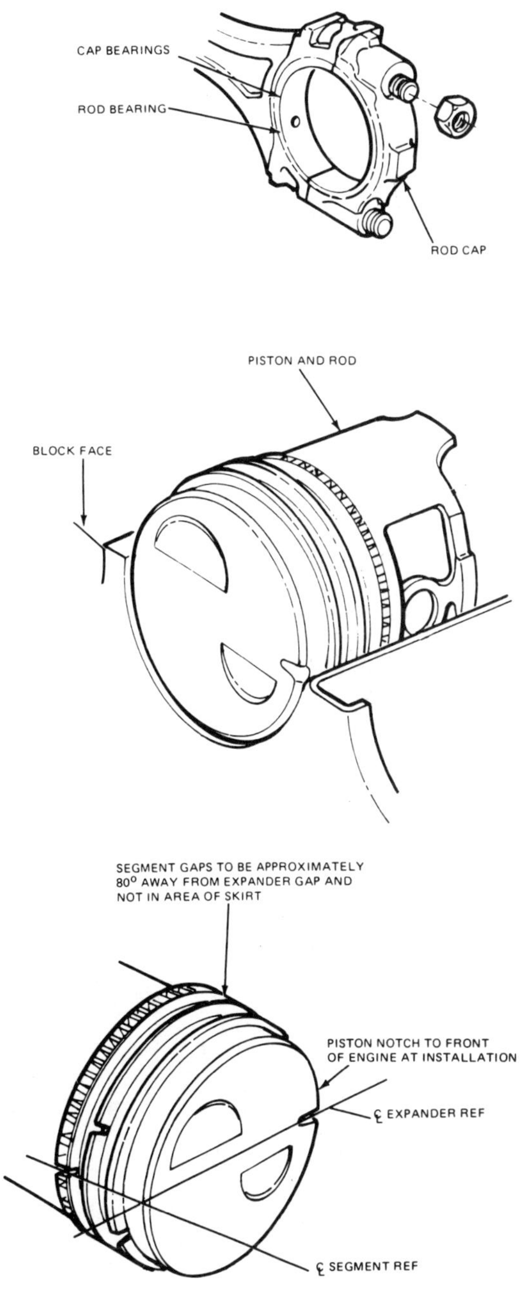

Fig. 1.32. Pistons, piston rings and piston markings (Secs. 81 and 112)

that the cam peak is facing away from the follower. This will permit the cam followers to be removed. Keep the cam followers in order so that they can be refitted in their original positions. **Note:** on some valves it may be found necessary to compress the valve spring slightly as well, in order to remove the cam followers.

3 Using a valve spring compressor, compress the valve springs and lift out the keys.

4 Remove the spring retainer and valve spring, then pry off the valve seal from the valve stem.

5 Push out the valve and keep it with its cam follower. Repeat this for the other valves.

6 Lift out the hydraulic lash adjusters, keeping each one with its respective cam follower and valve.

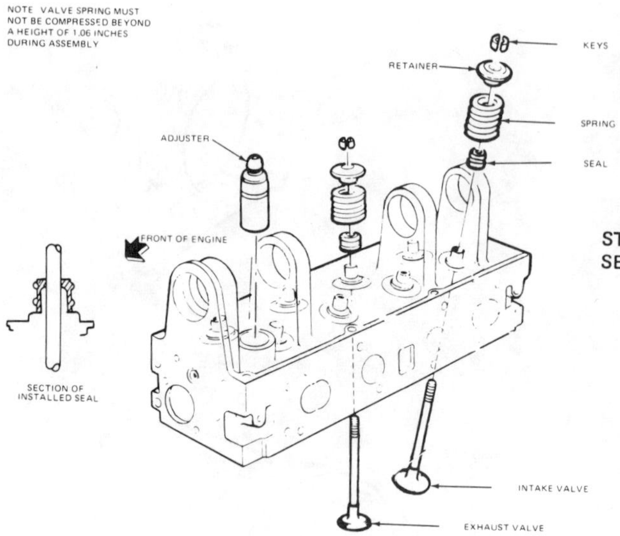

Fig. 1.34. Valves and associated parts (Sec. 84)

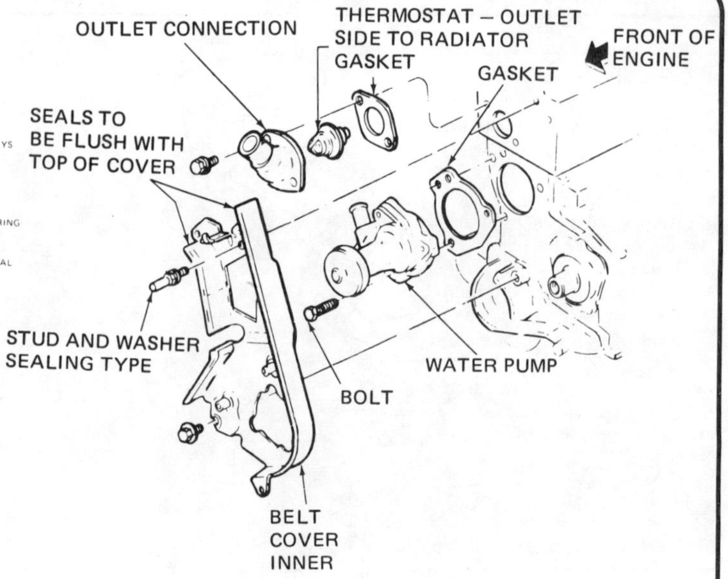

Fig. 1.36. Thermostat and water pump (Sec. 86)

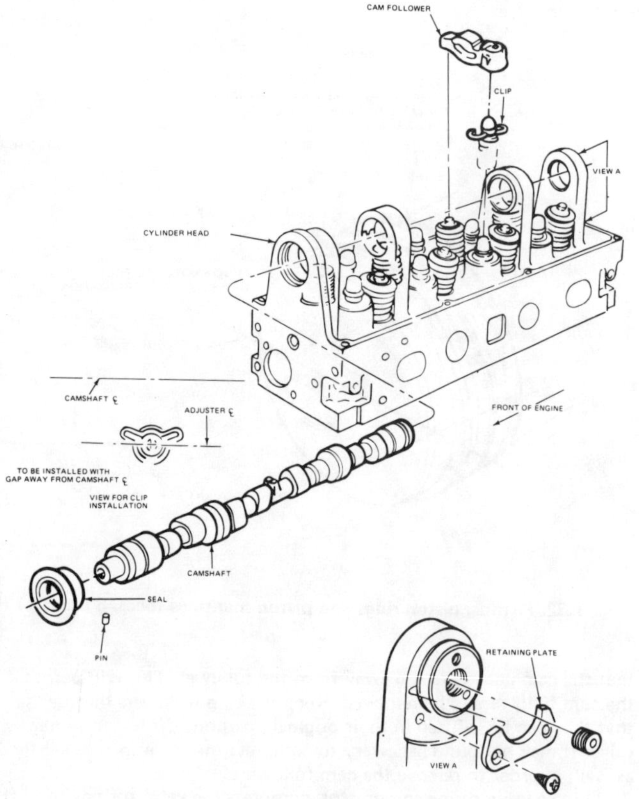

Fig. 1.35. Camshaft and associated parts (Sec. 85)

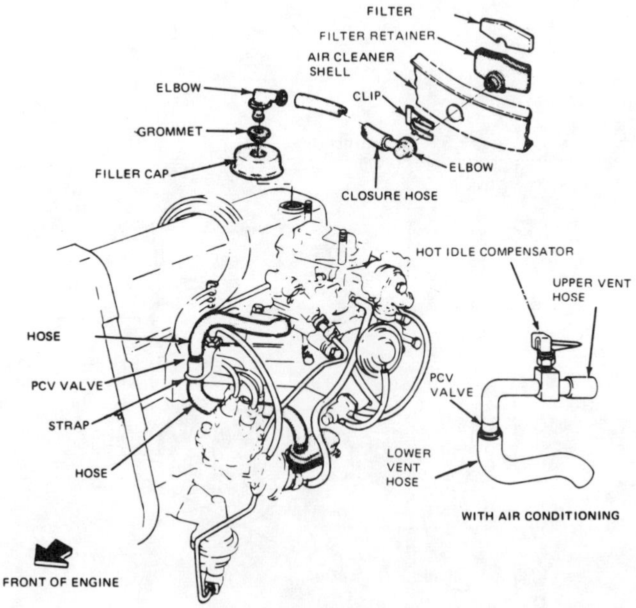

Fig. 1.37. Positive crankcase ventilation (PCV) system components (Sec. 89)

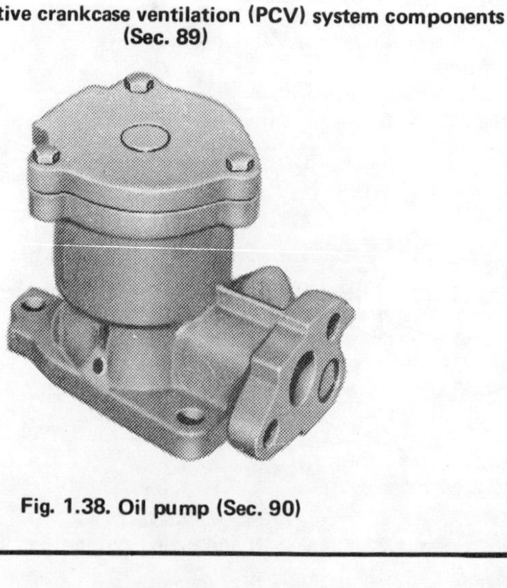

Fig. 1.38. Oil pump (Sec. 90)

85 Camshaft - removal

It is not necessary to remove the engine from the car to remove the camshaft. However, it will be necessary to remove the cylinder head as described earlier in this Chapter and the cam followers as described in Section 84.

1 Using a metal bar, lock the camshaft drive sprocket. Remove the securing bolt and washer.

2 Draw off the sprocket using a suitable puller (or carefully pry it off using a large screwdriver), then remove the belt guide.

3 Remove the sprocket locating pin from the end of the camshaft.

4 From the rear bearing pedestal, remove the camshaft retaining plate (2 screws).

5 Using a hammer and a brass or aluminium drift, drive out the camshaft towards the front of the engine, taking the front seal with it. Take great care that the camshaft bearings and journals are not damaged as it is pushed out.

86 Thermostat and water pump - removal

If the cylinder head and block are being completely dismantled, the thermostat and housing, and water pump should be removed. Further information on these procedures will be found in Chapter 2.

87 Piston pin - removal

Refer to the procedure given in Section 22 of this Chapter for the 1.6 and 2.0 litre engines.

88 Piston ring - removal

Refer to the procedure given in Section 23 of this Chapter for the 1.6 and 2.0 litre engines.

89 Lubrication and crankcase ventilation systems - description

These systems are basically as described in Section 24 for the 1.6 and 2.0 litre engines, with the exception that the cam followers are lubricated through drillings in the base circle of the cams.

90 Oil pump - inspection

1 The oil pump cannot be dismantled or repaired in any way. If there is any obvious damage, or in the case of major engine overhaul, a replacement item must be fitted.

2 Detach the oil intake pipe and screen (2 screws and spring washers), and clean the parts thoroughly in gasoline.

3 Refit the intake pipe and screen, using a new gasket.

91 Oil filter - removal and refitting

Refer to the procedure given in Section 26 of this Chapter for the 1.6 and 2.0 litre engines.

92 Engine components - examination for wear

Refer to the procedure given in Section 27 of this Chapter for the 1.6 and 2.0 litre engines.

93 Crankshaft - examination and renovation

Refer to the procedure given in Section 28 of this Chapter for the 1.6 and 2.0 litre engines.

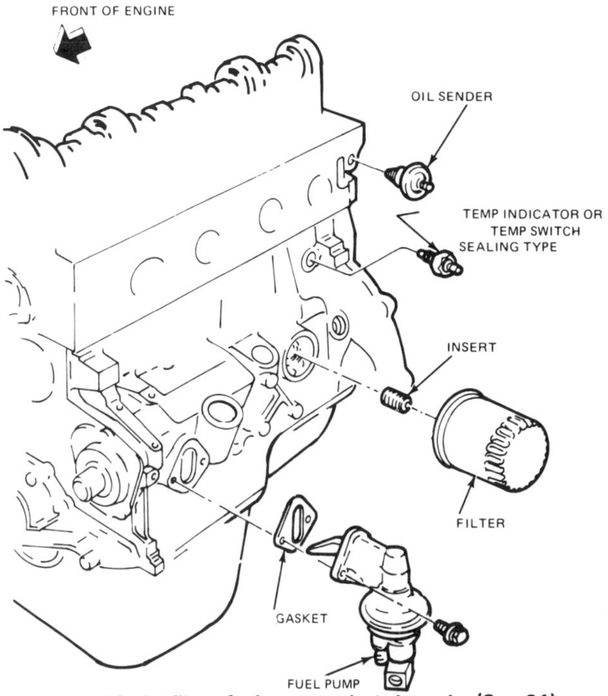

Fig. 1.39. Oil filter, fuel pump and sender units (Sec. 91)

94 Crankshaft, main and connecting rod bearings - examination and renovation

Refer to the procedure given in Section 29 of this Chapter for the 1.6 and 2.0 litre engines.

95 Cylinder bores - examination and renovation

Refer to the procedure given in Section 30 of this Chapter for the 1.6 and 2.0 litre engines.

96 Pistons and piston rings - inspection and testing

Refer to the procedure given in Section 31 of this Chapter for the 1.6 and 2.0 litre engines.

97 Connecting rods and piston pins - examination and renovation

Refer to the procedure given in Section 32 of this Chapter for the 1.6 and 2.0 litre engines.

98 Camshaft and camshaft bearings - examination and renovation

1 The procedure is generally as described in Section 33 of this Chapter for the 1.6 and 2.0 litre engines. However, due to the different method of lubrication of the cam followers, ignore the references to the oil nozzles in paragraph 2.

2 Position the camshaft into its location in the cylinder head and fit the thrust plate at the rear. Using a dial gauge, check the total shaft endfloat by tapping the camshaft carefully back-and-forth along its length. If the endplay is outside the specified limit, renew the thrust plate.

99 Cam followers - examination

Refer to the procedure given in Section 34 of this Chapter for the 1.6 and 2.0 litre engines.

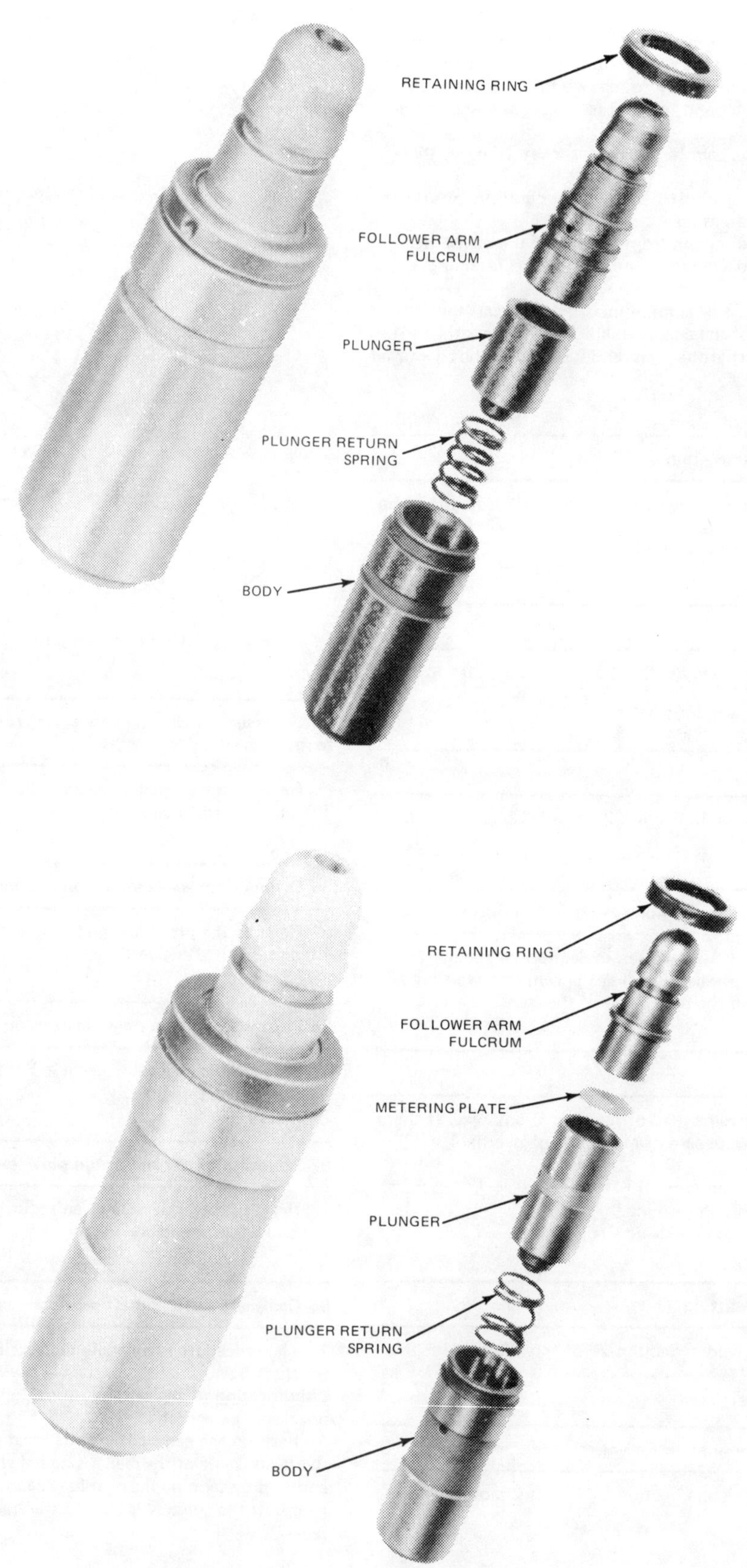

Fig. 1.40. Alternative types of lash adjusters (Sec. 102)

100 Auxiliary shaft and bearings - examination

Refer to the procedure given in Section 35 of this Chapter for the 1.6 and 2.0 litre engines.

101 Valves and valve seats - examination and renovation

Refer to the procedure given in Section 36 of this Chapter for the 1.6 and 2.0 litre engines.

102 Hydraulic lash adjusters - examination and renovation

1 Examine the outside of each lash adjuster for wear and scoring. If lightly scored, very fine emery cloth can be used to polish out the marks. However, if wear is evident, it is recommended that the complete adjuster is renewed.
2 Carefully pry off the retaining ring, take out the follower arm fulcrum and dismantle the complete adjuster. The component parts of the two different types in common use are shown in Fig. 1.40.
3 Examine all the parts of each adjuster for damage, wear, corrosion and gum deposits; obtain replacement parts for any which are unserviceable. Do not mix up the parts from the different adjusters.
4 Reassemble the adjusters, lightly lubricating the parts with engine oil. Do not attempt to fill them with oil.
5 Testing of the lifters is not practicable without the use of special equipment. However, this is available at Ford dealers or most auto engineering workshops and can be very useful where there is any doubt about serviceability.

103 Timing gears and belt - examination

Refer to the procedure given in Section 37 of this Chapter for the 1.6 and 2.0 litre engines.

104 Flywheel - examination and renovation

Refer to the procedure given in Section 38 of this Chapter for the 1.6 and 2.0 litre engines.

105 Cylinder head and piston crowns - decarbonisation

Refer to the procedure given in Section 39 of this Chapter for the 1.6 and 2.0 litre engines.

106 Valve guides - inspection

Refer to the procedure given in Section 40 of this Chapter for the 1.6 and 2.0 litre engines.

107 Oil pan - inspection

Refer to the procedure given in Section 41 of this Chapter for the 1.6 and 2.0 litre engines.

108 Engine reassembly - general

Refer to the procedure given in Section 42 of this Chapter for 1.6 and 2.0 litre engines.

109 Crankshaft - refitting

The procedure is generally as described in Section 43 of this Chapter for the 1.6 and 2.0 litre engines. However, the 2300 cc engine uses a two-piece seal which is located in the rear main bearing cap and in a groove in the crankcase, instead of a one-piece seal. It is important that the seal halves are lubricated with engine oil before installation,

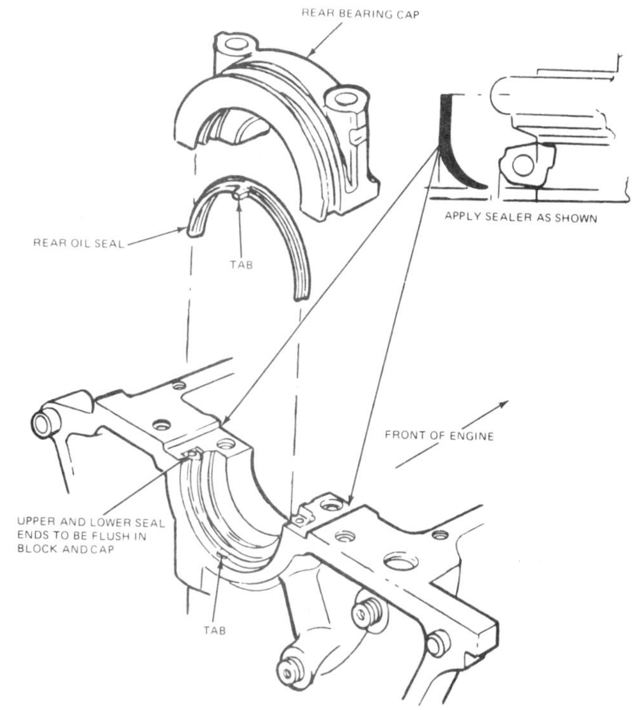

Fig. 1.41. Rear bearing cap showing the oil seal (Sec. 109)

and that the ends are flush with the block face and bearing cap after installation. Also apply a non-setting gasket sealant to the two points as indicated in Fig. 1.41.

110 Pistons and connecting rods - reassembly

Refer to the procedure given in Section 44 of this Chapter for the 1.6 and 2.0 litre engines, and to Section 81. Note that the notch in the piston must eventually face towards the front of the engine.

111 Piston rings - refitting

Refer to the procedure given in Section 45 of this Chapter for the 1.6 litre and 2.0 litre engines.

112 Pistons - refitting

1 The procedure is generally as described in Section 46 of this Chapter for the 1.6 and 2.0 litre engines. However, it is important that the piston ring gaps are positioned as follows:

a) The piston ring gaps should be positioned as shown in Fig. 1.32.
b) The oil control ring segment gaps are to be approximately 80° away from the expander gap and not in the area of the skirt.
c) The piston should be installed in the block so that the expander gap is towards the front and the segment gap is towards the rear.

113 Connecting rods to crankshaft - refitting

Refer to the procedure given in Section 47 of this Chapter for the 1.6 and 2.0 litre engines.

114 Oil pump and strainer - refitting

Refer to the procedure given in Section 48 of this Chapter for the 1.6 and 2.0 litre engines.

115 Auxiliary shaft - refitting

1 Lubricate the auxiliary shaft bearing surfaces with engine oil then insert the shaft into the block. Tap it gently with a soft-faced hammer to ensure that it is fully home.
2 Fit the retaining plate and secure it with the two screws.

116 Auxiliary shaft front cover and cylinder front covers - refitting

Note: If only one of the covers has been removed, the existing gasket may be cut away and a new gasket suitably cut.
1 Lubricate a new auxiliary shaft seal with engine oil and fit it into the auxiliary shaft cover so that the seal lips are towards the cylinder block face.
2 Position a new gasket on the cylinder block endface, position the auxiliary shaft cover over the spigot of the shaft.
3 Fit the cover retaining bolts but do not tighten them until the cylinder front cover has been fitted or the gasket may distort.
4 Fit the cylinder front cover in a similar manner to that described for the auxiliary shaft front cover.
5 Position the front cover over the crankshaft spigot and loosely fit the retaining bolts.
6 Using the crankshaft sprocket as a centralizing tool, tighten the front cover bolts to the specified torque.
7 Tighten the auxiliary shaft cover bolts to the specified torque.

117 Oil pan - refitting

Refer to the procedure given in Section 48 of this Chapter for the 1.6 and 2.0 litre engines.

118 Water pump - refitting

Refit the water pump to the cylinder block (if removed), referring to Chapter 2 as necessary.

119 Backplate, flywheel and clutch - refitting

The procedure is generally as described in Section 54 of this Chapter for the 1.6 and 2.0 litre engines. However, note that no seal is used between the rear cover plate (backplate) and the cylinder block.

120 Valves - refitting

Refer to the procedure given in Section 55 of this Chapter for the 1.6 and 2.0 litre engines.

121 Camshaft - refitting

1 Lubricate the camshaft journals and bearings with SAE 90 EP gear oil then carefully install the shaft in the cylinder head.
2 Fit the retainer plate and screws at the rear end.
3 Lubricate a new camshaft seal with engine oil and carefully tap it into position at the front of the cylinder head.
4 Fit the belt guide and pin to the front end of the camshaft, and carefully tap on the sprocket.
5 Fit a new sprocket bolt and tighten it to the specified torque.

122 Hydraulic lash adjusters and cam followers - refitting

1 Smear the hydraulic lash adjusters with SAE 90 EP gear oil then install each one into its respective position.
2 Smear the rubbing surfaces of the camshaft lobes and cam followers with a molybdenum disulphide grease.
3 Using special tool T74P-6565-B to compress each lash adjuster, position each cam follower on its respective valve end and adjuster, ensuring that the camshaft is rotated as necessary. Fit the retaining spring clips (where applicable). **Note:** On some valves it may be found

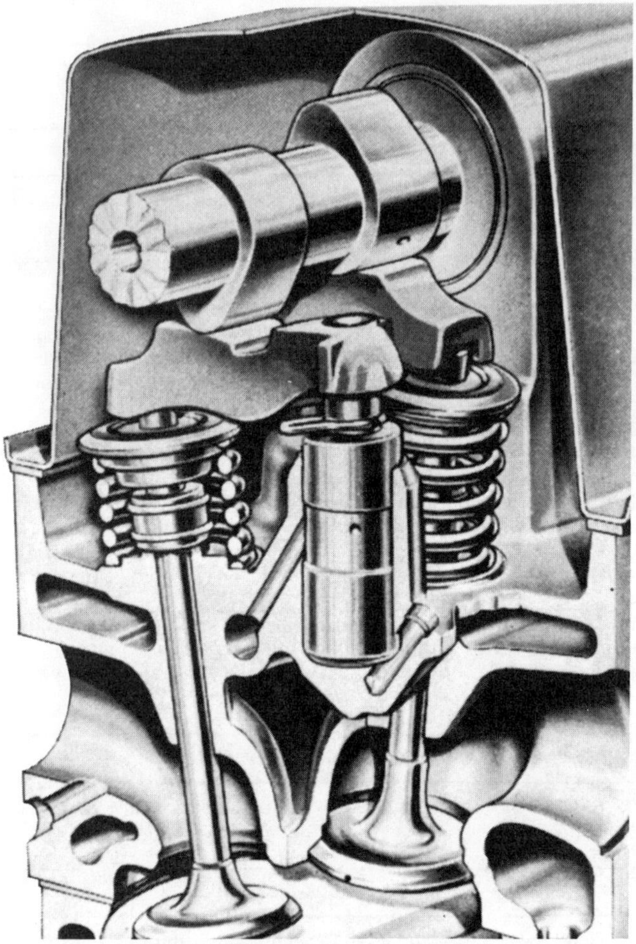

Fig. 1.42. Cutaway view of the valve train (Sec. 122)

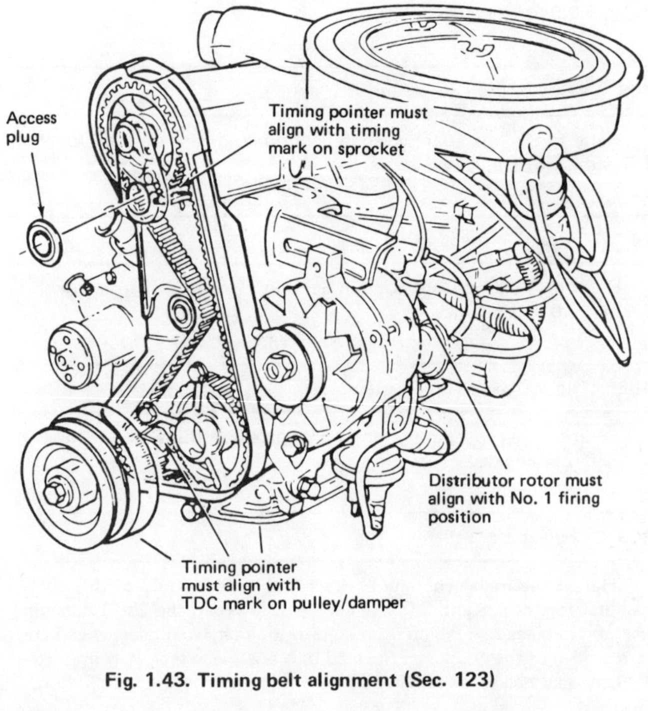

Fig. 1.43. Timing belt alignment (Sec. 123)

necessary to compress the valve spring slightly when fitting the cam followers.

123 Cylinder head - refitting

1 Wipe the mating surfaces of the cyllnder head and cylinder block.
2 Carefully place a new gasket on the cylinder block, ensuring that it is the correct way up (each gasket is marked 'FRONT UP'.)
3 Rotate the camshaft so that the sprocket retaining pin is in the position shown in Fig. 1.43, then position the head on the block. If the crankshaft needs to be rotated for any reason, ensure that the pistons are approximately halfway down the bores or they may contact the valves.
4 Fit and tighten the cylinder head bolts progressively to the specified torque, in the order shown in Fig. 1.25.

124 Thermostat housing and thermostat - refitting

Refit the thermostat housing and thermostat to the cylinder head (if removed), referring to Chapter 2, if necessary.

125 Inner belt cover, auxiliary shaft sprocket and crankshaft sprocket - refitting

1 Refit the engine front cover to the cylinder block (two bolts).
2 Ensure that the crankshaft sprocket key is in position then carefully tap on the sprocket.
3 Ensure that the auxiliary shaft sprocket locking pin is in position then carefully tap on the sprocket.
4 Fit the auxiliary shaft washer and nut, and tighten to the specified torque.

126 Timing belt tensioner and timing belt - refitting

1 Rotate the camshaft until the index mark on the sprocket aligns with the timing pointer on the belt inner cover.
2 Rotate the crankshaft until No. 1 piston is at top-dead-centre (TDC). This position can be checked either by rotating the crankshaft whilst carefully inserting a screwdriver through a spark plug hole, or by positioning the belt outer cover and sprocket on the engine to align the pulley 'O' mark with the timing pointer.
3 Without disturbing the crankshaft and camshaft positions, refit the belt tensioner but do not tighten the bolt yet.
4 Install the timing belt over the crankshaft sprocket, then counter-clockwise over the auxiliary shaft and camshaft sprockets, then behind the tensioner jockey wheel. If difficulty is experienced, use a lever to pull the tensioner jockey wheel away from the belt.
5 Rotate the crankshaft two full turns in a clockwise direction to remove all slack from the belt.
6 Ensure that the timing marks are correctly aligned then tighten the adjuster/bolts to the specified torque.

127 Belt outer cover and crankshaft pulley - refitting

1 Position the belt guide on the end of the crankshaft.
2 Install the belt outer cover, noting that spacers are used on two of the bolts.
3 Fit the crankshaft pulley, washer and retaining bolt. Tighten the bolt to the specified torque.

128 Valve lash - adjustment

1 With the engine top cover removed, rotate the crankshaft so that the base circle of the camshaft lobe of the first valve to be checked, is facing the cam follower.
2 Using special tool T74P-6565-B, compress the valve lash adjuster fully and hold it in this position.
3 Using a suitable feeler gauge, check that the gap is as given in the Specifications for the hydraulic lash adjuster.
4 If outside the allowable limit, either the cam follower is worn, the valve spring assembled height is incorrect, the camshaft is worn, or the lash adjuster is unserviceable.

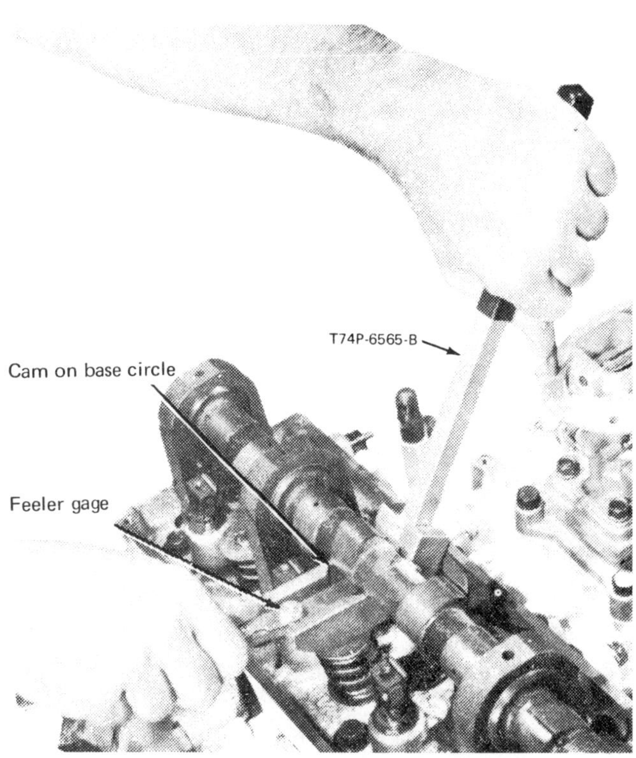

Fig. 1.44. Checking lash adjustment (Sec. 128)

129 Rocker arm cover - refitting

1 Clean the mating surfaces of the rocker arm cover and cylinder head, then lightly smear on a little non-setting gasket sealant.
2 Position a new gasket in the rocker arm cover, ensuring that the locating tabs are correctly positioned in the slots.
3 Fit the rocker cover. Fit and tighten the eight screws around the base to the specified torque.
4 Fit and tighten the two screws at the front end of the cover to the specified torque.

130 Engine - preparation for refitting

1 Having completed the engine rebuilding, it is now necessary to refit the items which were taken off prior to the commencement of major dismantling. These will differ according to the extent of the work done and the original equipment fitted, but will typically be:
a) Oil pressure sender: Coat threads with a non-setting gasket sealant and screw into cylinder head.
b) Water temperature sender: Coat threads with a non-setting gasket sealant and screw into cylinder block.
c) Fan: Refer to Chapter 2, if necessary.
d) Exhaust manifold: Ensure that the mating surfaces are clean then apply a light even film of graphite grease. Install the manifold and tighten the bolts in two steps to the specified torque in the order shown in Fig. 1.26. Do not forget the lifting eye at No. 7 bolt.
e) Spark plugs: Fit new spark plugs of the type stated on the engine emission control decal.
f) Intake manifold: Ensure that the mating surfaces of the manifold and cylinder head are clean then install the manifold using a new gasket. Tighten the bolts in two steps to the specified torque in the order shown in Fig. 1.22. Do not forget the lifting eye at No. 7 bolt.
g) Manifold ancillaries: Refit the manifold ancillaries. These will vary according to the particular vehicle, but will typically be as shown in Figs. 1.21 and 1.22.
h) Carburettor: Install the carburettor, EGR valve and spacer assembly

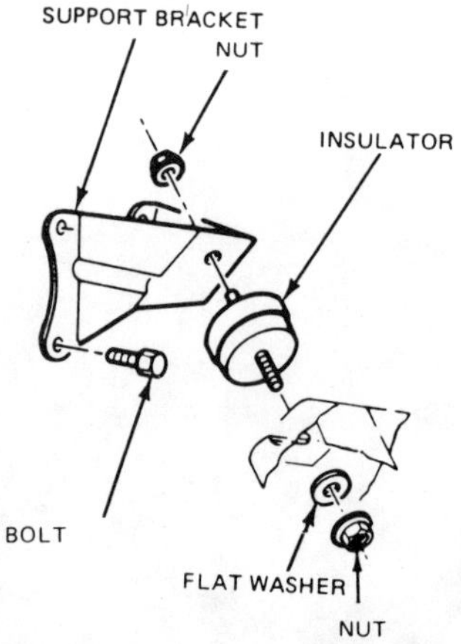

Fig. 1.45. Engine front mounting (Sec. 134)

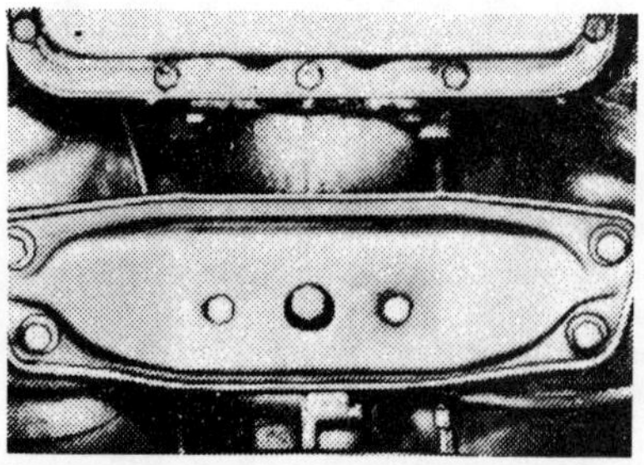

Fig. 1.46. Rear mounting - automatic transmission (Sec. 134)

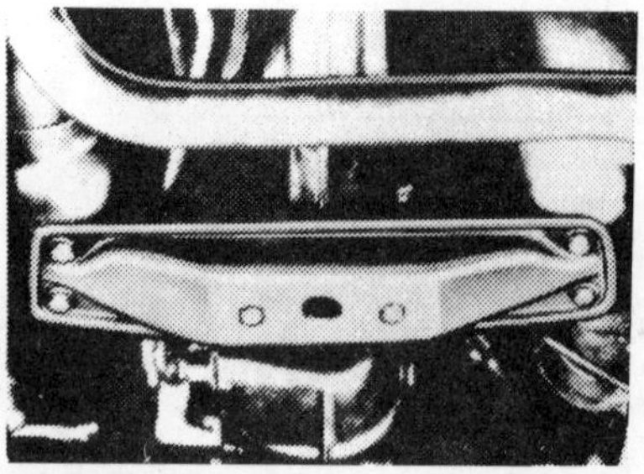

Fig. 1.47. Rear mounting - manual transmission (Sec. 134)

using new gaskets. The layout of the components is shown in Fig. 1.20. Do not forget the choke hose; do not fit the air cleaner at this stage.

j) Fan: Refer to Chapter 2 if necessary.

k) Distributor: Align the index marks and refer to Chapter 4 to ensure that the ignition timing is correct.

l) Oil filter: If not already fitted, refer to Section 91.

m) Fuel pump: Refer to Chapter 3 if necessary.

n) Alternator: Refit loosely; do not fit the drivebelt.

p) Thermactor pump, compressor, PCV system, oil level dipstick, miscellaneous emission control items and associated interconnecting hoses etc.

131 Engine - refitting (without transmission)

1 Raise the engine on the hoist and position it over the car engine compartment so that the rear end is sloping downward.
2 Lower the engine so that the exhaust manifold lines up approximately with the exhaust muffler inlet pipe.
3 *Automatic transmission:* Start the converter pilot into the crankshaft.
4 *Manual transmission:* Start the transmission main drive gear (input shaft) into the clutch hub. If necessary rotate the engine slightly *clockwise* to align the splines.
5 Ensure that the engine is settled on its mounts then detach the hoist chains.
6 From beneath the car install the flywheel housing or converter upper attaching bolts.
7 *Automatic transmission:* Attach the converter to the flywheel and tighten the nuts to the specified torque. Refer to Chapter 7 for further information if necessary. Install the converter bolt access plug.
8 Fit the front engine mount nuts.
9 Connect the exhaust pipe to the manifold, using a new gasket (if applicable).
10 Refit the starter motor and electrical cables.
11 Remove the plugs from the fuel lines and reconnect them to the fuel pump. If not already done, reconnect the fuel line to the carburetor.
12 Position the power steering pump on its brackets and install the upper bolts.
13 Fit the engine shield.
14 From inside the engine compartment fit the power steering pump pulley.
15 Reconnect the engine ground lead.
16 Fit the alternator adjusting arm bolt and the electrical connector(s).
17 Connect the wire to the electrically assisted choke.
18 Connect the coil wire and vacuum hose to the distributor.
19 Connect the vacuum amplifier.
20 Connect the wire to the water temperature sender in the cylinder block.
21 Connect the idle solenoid wires.
22 Position the accelerator cable on the ball stud and install the ball stud on the clip. Snap the bracket clip into position on the bracket. Where applicable, install the kick-down cable.
23 Refit the line to the oil pressure sender.
24 Refit the brake vacuum unit hose.
25 Reconnect the engine heater and vacuum hoses.
26 Refit the drivebelts to the engine driven accessories. Refer to Chapter 2 for the correct tension.
27 Refit the radiator. Refer to Chapter 2 if necessary.
28 Refit the oil cooler lines (where applicable).
29 Refit the radiator hoses.
30 Where applicable, refit the fan shroud.
31 Refill the cooling system with the correct amount of water/antifreeze (or inhibitor) mixture. Refer to Chapter 2 as necessary.
32 Fill the crankcase with the specified amount and type of oil.
33 Refit the air cleaner and the vacuum hoses. Refer to Chapter 3 if necessary.
34 Connect the battery leads.
35 Have a last look round the engine compartment to ensure that no hoses and electrical connections have been left off.

132 Engine - refitting (with manual transmission)

1 The procedure for refitting the engine and manual transmission is basically as described in the previous Section. However, the following differences should be noted:

a) Support the weight of the transmission with a trolley jack prior to fitting the rear mounting.

b) Do not forget to reconnect the speedometer cable and transmission electrical connections. Refer to Chapter 6 for further information, if necessary.

c) Check the clutch adjustment after the cable has been reconnected. Refer to Chapter 5 for further information.

d) When reconnecting the propeller shaft, ensure that the index marks are correctly aligned. Refer to Chapter 7 for further information if necessary.

e) Reconnect and adjust the gearshift linkage, as described in Chapter 6.

133 Engine - initial start-up after overhaul or major repair

The procedure is generally as described in Section 65 of this Chapter for the 1.6 and 2.0 litre engines.

134 Engine/transmission mountings - renewal

Refer to the procedure given in Section 66 of this Chapter for the 1.6 and 2.0 litre engines.

135 Fault diagnosis - engine

Refer to the procedure given in Section 67 of this Chapter for the 1.6 and 2.0 litre engines.

Chapter 2 Cooling system

Contents

Specifications

System type	Pressurised, assisted by pump and fan	
Thermostat		
Type	Wax	
Location	Front of cylinder head	
Starts to open	85 to 89°C (185 to 192°F)	
Fully open	99 to 102°C (210 to 216°F)	
Operating tolerance for used thermostat	± 3°C (± 5°F)	
Radiator		
Type	Corrugated fin	
Pressure cap setting	13 lb f/in^2 (0.91 kg f/cm^2)	
Water pump		
Type	Centrifugal	
Fan belt		
Free-play	0.5 in (13 mm) at midpoint of longest span of belt	
Cooling system capacity, including heater		
Capri II - 1.6 litre	10.15 Imp. pints (5.8 litre/12.2 US pints)	
Capri II - 2.0 litre	10.8 Imp. pints (6.13 litre/13 US pints)	
Mercury Capri II	12.7 Imp. pints (7.2 litre/15.2 US pints)	
Torque wrench settings	**lbf ft**	**kgf m**
Fan blades:		
Capri II	5 to 7	0.7 to 1.0
Mercury Capri II	7 to 9	1.0 to 1.2
Water pump	5 to 7	0.7 to 1.0
Thermostat housing	12 to 15	1.66 to 2.1
Alternator mounting and adjustment bolts	15 to 18	2.1 to 2.5

1 General description

1 The engine cooling water is circulated by a thermo-syphon water pump assisted system, and the whole system is pressurised. This is both to prevent the loss of water down the overflow pipe with the radiator cap in position and to prevent premature boiling in adverse conditions. The radiator cap is pressurised to 13 lbf/in^2 (0.91 kgf/cm^2). This has the effect of considerably increasing the boiling point of the coolant. If the water temperature goes above the increased boiling point the extra pressure in the system forces the internal part of the cap off its seat, thus exposing the overflow pipe down which the steam from the boiling water escapes thereby relieving the pressure. It is, therefore, important to check that the radiator cap is in good condition and that the spring behind the sealing washer has not weakened. The cooling system comprises the radiator, top and bottom water hoses, heater hoses, the impeller water pump (mounted on the front of the engine, it carries the fan blades, and is driven by the fan belt), the thermostat and the two drain taps. The inlet manifold is water heated. The fan used on Mercury Capri II cars is a viscous-coupled type.

2 The system functions in the following fashion. Cold water in the bottom of the radiator circulates up the lower radiator hose to the water pump where it is pushed round the water passages in the cylinder block, helping to keep the cylinder bores and pistons cool.

3 The water then travels up into the cylinder head and circulates round the combustion spaces and valve seats absorbing more heat, and then, when the engine is at its correct operating temperature, travels out of the cylinder head, past the open thermostat into the upper radiator hose and so into the radiator header tank.

4 The water travels down the radiator where it is rapidly cooled

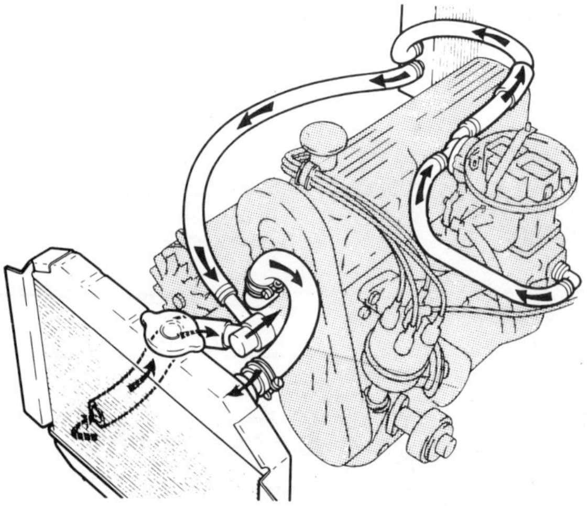

Fig. 2.1. Capri II cooling system

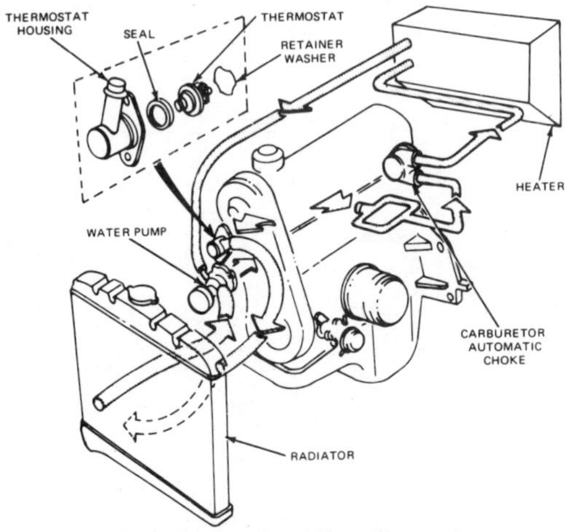

Fig. 2.2. Mercury Capri II cooling system

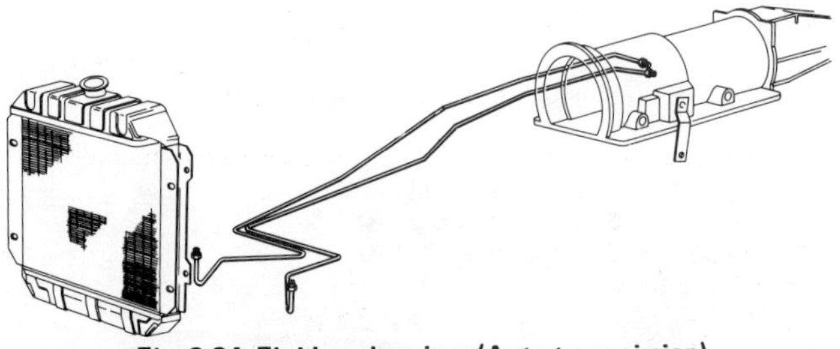

Fig. 2.2A Fluid cooler pipes (Auto transmission)

by the in-rush of cold air through the radiator core, which is created by both the fan and the motion of the car. The water, now much cooler, reaches the bottom of the radiator when the cycle is repeated.

5 When the engine is cold the thermostat (which is a valve that opens and closes according to the temperature of the water) maintains the circulation of the same water in the engine.

6 Only when the correct minimum operating temperature has been reached, as shown in the Specifications, does the thermostat begin to open, allowing water to return to the radiator.

7 On cars fitted with automatic transmission, a transmission fluid cooler is incorporated within the base of the radiator.

2 Cooling system - draining

1 If the engine is cold, remove the filler cap from the radiator by turning the cap anti-clockwise. If the engine is hot, then turn the filler cap very slightly until pressure in the system has had time to be released. Use a rag over the cap to protect your hand from escaping steam. If with the engine very hot the cap is released suddenly, the drop in pressure can result in the water boiling. With the pressure released the cap can be removed.

2 If antifreeze is used in the cooling system, drain it into a bowl having a capacity of at least that of the cooling system for re-use.

3 Open the drain plug located on the rear of the radiator lower tank next to the bottom hose or remove the bottom radiator hose. Also remove the engine drain plug which is located at the rear left-hand side of the cylinder block (photo). If the heater has a water control valve, open this also to drain the heat exchanger.

4 When the water has finished running, probe the drain plug orifices with a short piece of wire to dislodge any particles of rust or sediment which may be causing a blockage.

5 It is important to note that the heater on most models cannot be drained completely during the cold weather so an antifreeze solution must be used. Always use an antifreeze with an ethylene-glycol base.

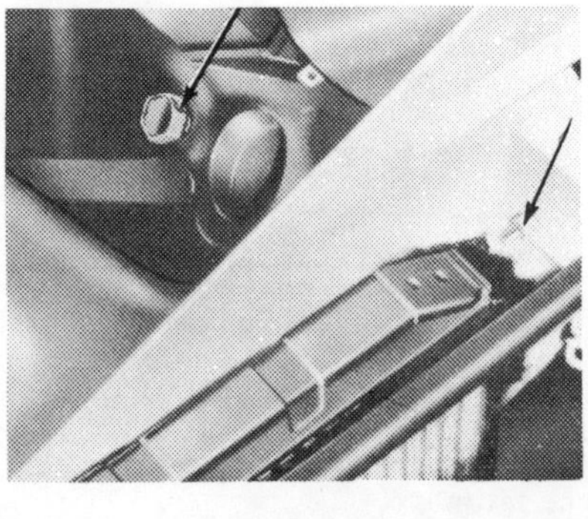

Fig. 2.3 Radiator and cylinder block drain plugs - Mercury Capri II (Sec. 2)

2.3 Cylinder block drain plug removal.

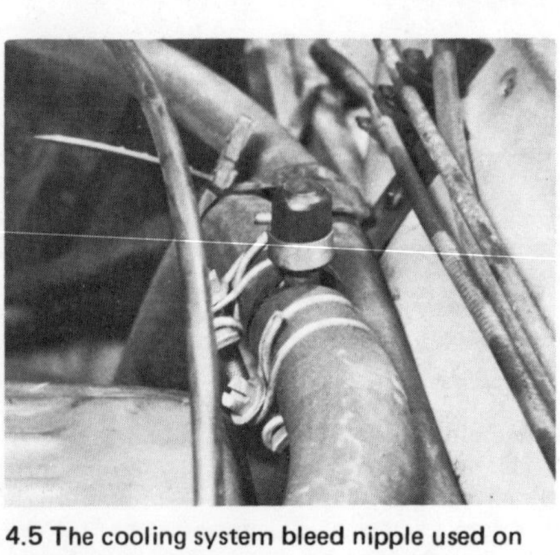

4.5 The cooling system bleed nipple used on some cars.

5.5 Radiator removal.

3 Cooling system - flushing

1 In time the cooling system will gradually lose its efficiency as the radiator becomes choked with rust, scale deposits from the water, and other sediment. To clean the system out, remove the radiator filler cap and drain plug and leave a hose running in the filler cap neck for ten to fifteen minutes.
2 In very bad cases the radiator should be reverse flushed. This can be done with the radiator in position. The cylinder block plug is removed and a hose with a suitable tapered adaptor placed in the drain plug hole. Water under pressure is then forced through the radiator and out of the header tank filler cap neck.
3 It is recommended that some polythene sheeting is placed over the engine to stop water finding its way into the electrical system.
4 The hose should now be removed and placed in the radiator cap filler neck, and the radiator washed out in the usual manner.

4 Cooling system - filling

1 Refit the cylinder block and radiator drain plugs.
2 Fill the system slowly to ensure that no air lock develops. If the heater has a water control valve check that it is open (control at hot), otherwise an air lock may form in the heater. The best type of water to use in the cooling system is rain water; use this whenever possible.
3 Do not fill the system higher than within ½ inch (13 mm) of the filler neck. Overfilling will merely result in wastage, which is especially to be avoided when antifreeze is in use.
4 It is usually found that air locks develop in the heater radiator so the system should be vented during refilling by detaching the heater supply hose from the elbow connection on the water outlet housing.
5 Pour coolant into the radiator filler neck whilst the end of the heater supply hose is held at the elbow connection height. When a constant stream of water flows from the supply hose quickly refit the hose. If venting is not carried out it is possible for the engine to overheat. Should the engine overheat for no apparent reason then the system should be vented before seeking other causes. On some models a bleed nipple is incorparated in the coolant hose which runs at the rear of the engine (photo).
6 Only use antifreeze mixture with a glycerine or ethylene glycol base, or a cooling system inhibitor.
7 Refit the filler cap and turn it firmly clockwise to lock it in position.

5 Radiator - removal, inspection and cleaning

1 Drain the cooling system as described in Section 2 of this Chapter
2 Slacken the two clips which hold the top and bottom radiator hoses on the radiator and carefully pull off the two hoses.
3 As applicable, remove radiator upper splash shield and disconnect the pipes from the automatic transmission oil cooler.
4 Undo and remove the four bolts that secure the radiator shroud to the radiator side panels and move the shroud over the fan blades. This is only applicable when a shroud is fitted.
5 Undo and remove the four bolts that secure the radiator to the front panel. The radiator may now be lifted upwards and away from the engine compartment. The fragile matrix must not be touched by the fan blades as it easily punctures (photo).
6 Lift the radiator shroud from over the fan blades and remove from the engine compartment.
7 With the radiator away from the car any leaks can be soldered or repaired with a suitable proprietary substance. Clean out the inside of the radiator by flushing as described earlier in this Chapter. When the radiator is out of the car it is advantageous to turn it upside down and reverse flush. Clean the exterior of the radiator by carefully using a compressed air jet or a strong jet of water to clear away any road dirt, flies etc.
8 Inspect the radiator hoses for cracks, internal or external perishing and damage by overtightening of the securing clips. Also inspect the overflow pipe. Renew the hoses if suspect. Examine the radiator hose clips and renew them if they are rusted or distorted.
9 The drain plug and washer should be renewed if leaking or with worn threads, but first ensure the leak is not caused by a faulty fibre washer.

6 Radiator - refitting

1 Refitting the radiator and shroud (if fitted) is the reverse sequence to removal (see Section 5).
2 If new hoses are to be fitted they can be a little difficult to fit on to the radiator so lubricate them with a little soap. Ensure that a clearance of 0.8 in (20 mm) is maintained between the bottom hose and the stabilizer bar to prevent chafing. Also ensure that the upper end of the hose is pushed well up onto the water pump.
3 Refill the cooling system, as described in Section 4.
4 On automatic transmission models, reconnect the pipes to the fluid cooler. When the car is operational, check the transmission fluid level and top-up if necessary (see Chapter 6).

7 Thermostat - removal, testing and refitting

1 Partially drain the cooling system as described in Section 2.
2 Slacken the top radiator hose to the thermostat housing and remove the hose.
3 Undo and remove the two bolts and spring washers that secure the thermostat housing to the cylinder head.
4 Carefully lift the thermostat housing away from the cylinder head. Recover the joint washer adhering to either the housing or cylinder head.
5 Using a screwdriver ease the clip securing the thermostat to the housing (Fig. 2.4). Note which way round the thermostat is fitted in the housing and also that the bridge is 90° to the outlet (photo).

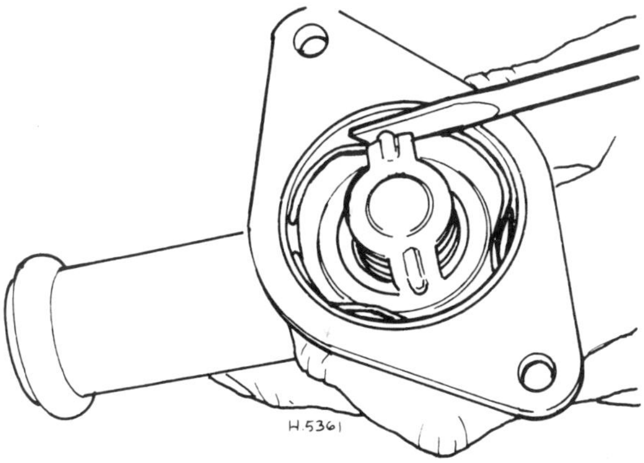

Fig. 2.4. Using a screwdriver to release the thermostat retaining clip (Sec. 7)

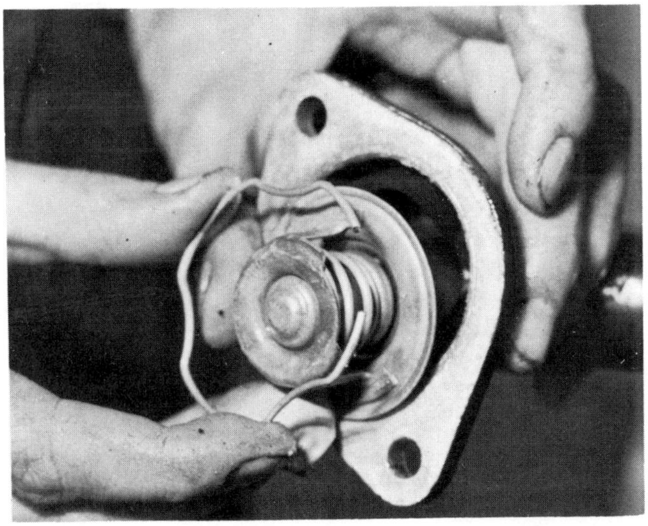

7.5 Removal of thermostat retaining clips

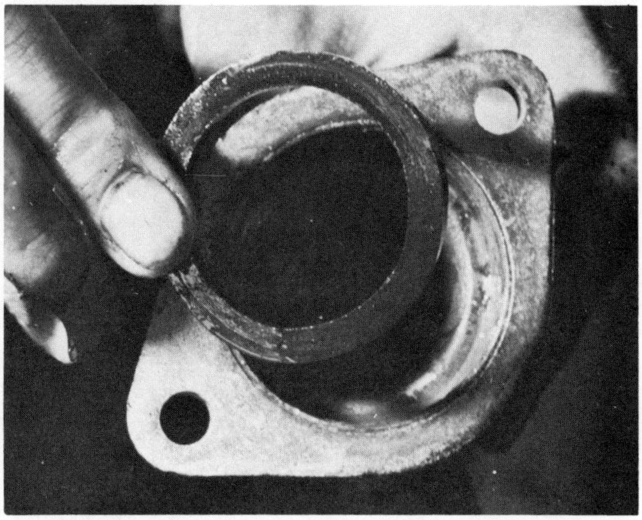

7.6 Removal of sealing ring

6 The thermostat may now be withdrawn from the housing. Recover the seal from the inside the housing (photo).
7 Test the thermostat for correct functioning by suspending it on a string in a saucepan of cold water together with a thermometer. Heat the water and note the temperature at which the thermostat begins to open. This should be as given in the Specifications. Continue heating the water until the thermostat is fully open. Then let it cool down naturally.
8 If the thermostat does not fully open in boiling water, or does not close down as the water cools, then it must be discarded and a new one fitted. Should the thermostat be stuck open when cold this will usually be apparent when removing it from the housing.
9 Refitting the thermostat is the reverse sequence to removal. Always ensure that the thermostat housing and cylinder head mating faces are clean and flat. If the thermostat housing is badly corroded fit a new housing. Always use a new gasket. Tighten the two securing bolts to the specified torque.

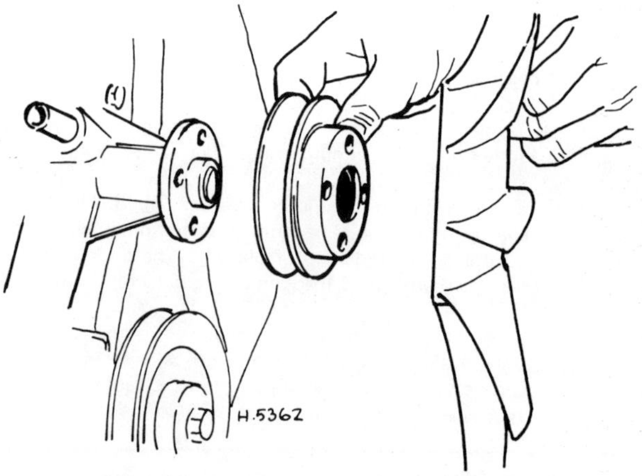

Fig. 2.5. Fan and pulley removal (Sec. 8)

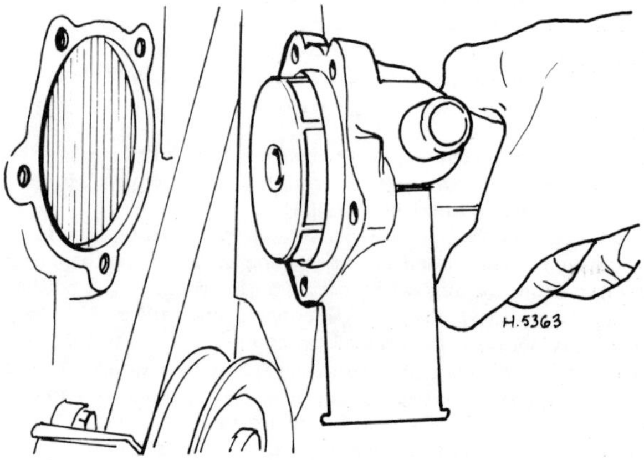

Fig. 2.6. Water pump removal (Sec. 8)

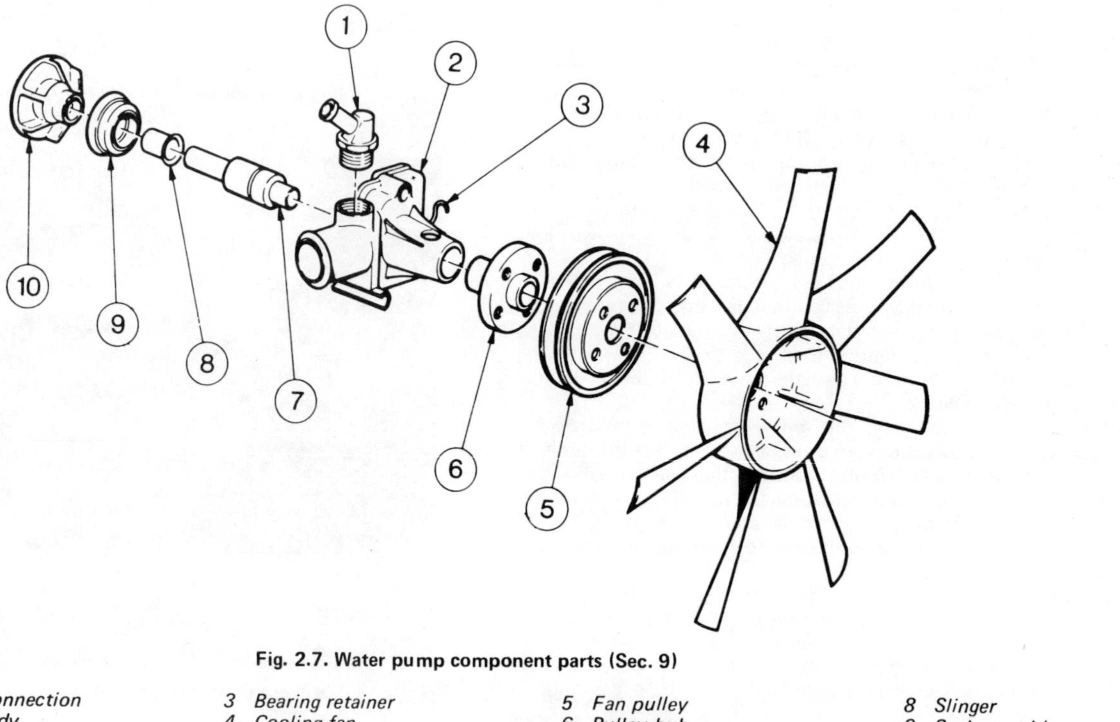

Fig. 2.7. Water pump component parts (Sec. 9)

1 Heater connection
2 Pump body
3 Bearing retainer
4 Cooling fan
5 Fan pulley
6 Pulley hub
7 Shaft and bearing assembly
8 Slinger
9 Seal assembly
10 Impeller

8 Water pump (Capri II) - removal and refitting

1 Drain the cooling system, as described in Section 2.
2 Refer to Section 5 and remove the radiator (and shroud if fitted).
3 Slacken the alternator mounting bolts and push the alternator towards the cylinder block. Lift away the fan belt.
4 Undo and remove the four bolts and washers that secure the fan assembly to the water pump spindle hub. Lift away the fan and pulley (Fig. 2.5).
5 Slacken the clip that secures the heater hose to the water pump. Pull the hose from its union on the water pump.
6 Undo and remove the four bolts and spring washers that secure the water pump to the cylinder block. Lift away the water pump and recover the gasket (Fig. 2.6).
7 Refitting the water pump is the reverse sequence to removal. The following additional points should however be noted:

a) Make sure the mating faces of the cylinder block and water pump are clean. Always use a new gasket.
b) Tighten the water pump and fan bolts to the specified torque.

9 Water pump (Capri II) - dismantling and overhaul

1 Before undertaking the dismantling of the water pump to effect a repair, check that all parts are available. It may be quicker and more economical to replace the complete unit.
2 Refer to Fig. 2.7 and using a universal three legged puller and suitable thrust block draw the hub from the shaft.
3 Carefully pull out the bearing retaining clip from the slot in the water pump housing. On some water pumps this clip is not fitted.
4 Using a soft faced hammer drive the shaft and bearing assembly out towards the rear of the pump body.
5 The impeller vane is removed from the spindle by using a universal three legged puller and suitable thrust block.
6 Remove the seal and the slinger by splitting the latter with the aid of a sharp cold chisel.
7 Carefully inspect the condition of the shaft and bearing assembly and if it shows signs of wear or corrosion, new parts should be obtained. If it was found that the coolant was leaking from the pump a new seal should be obtained. If it was evident that the pulley hub or impeller were a loose fit they must be renewed. The repair kit available comprises a new shaft and bearing assembly, a slinger seal, bush, clip and gasket.
8 To reassemble the water pump first fit the shaft and bearing assembly to the housing, larger end of the shaft to the front of the housing, and press the assembly into the housing until the front of the bearing is flush with the pump housing.
9 Refit the bearing retaining clip.
10 Next press the pump pulley onto the front end of the shaft until the end of the shaft is flush with the end of the hub.
11 Press the new slinger flanged end first onto the shaft until the non-flanged end is approximately 0.5 in (13mm) from the shaft end. To act as a rough guide the flanged end on the slinger will be just in line with the impeller side of the window in the water pump body.
12 Place the new seal over the shaft and into the counterbore in the water pump housing and then press the impeller onto the shaft until a clearance of 0.03 inch (0.76 mm) is obtained between the impeller and the housing face (Fig. 2.8). Whilst this is being carried out the slinger will be pushed into its final position by the impeller.

10 Water pump (Mercury Capri II) - general

1 The procedure for removal of the water pump is basically as described for Capri II models. However, because engine driven components vary according to the particular model, these will need to be removed as necessary. Removal of the Mercury Capri II fan is dealt with in Section 11.
2 In the event of water pump failure, a replacement item must be fitted.

11 Viscous cooling fan (Mercury Capri II) - removal and refitting

1 Remove the radiator, as described in Section 5.
2 Remove the centre bolt attaching the fan assembly to the extension shaft and remove the fan.
3 Remove the four nuts and bolts securing the viscous-clutch to the fan, and separate the parts.
4 Refitting is the reverse of the removal procedure.

12 Fan belt (Capri II) - removal and refitting

If the fan belt is worn or has stretched unduly, it should be renewed. The most usual reason for repacement is that the belt has broken in service. It is recommended that a spare belt be always carried in the car.
1 Loosen the alternator mounting bolts and move the alternator towards the engine.
2 Slip the old belt over the crankshaft, alternator and water pump pulley wheels and lift it off over the fan blades.
3 Put a new belt onto the three pulleys and adjust it as described in Section 11. **Note:** After fitting a new belt it will require adjustment after 250 miles (400 km).

13 Fan belt (Capri II) - adjustment

1 It is important to keep the fan belt correctly adjusted and it is considered that this should be a regular maintenance task every 6000 miles (10000 km). If the belt is loose it will slip, wear rapidly and cause the alternator and water pump to malfunction. If the belt is too tight the alternator and water pump bearings will wear rapidly causing premature failure of these components.
2 The fan belt tension is correct when there is 0.5 in (13 mm) of lateral movement at the mid point position of the belt run between the alternator pulley and the water pump.
3 To adjust the fan belt, slacken the alternator securing bolts and move the alternator in or out until the correct tension is obtained. It is easier

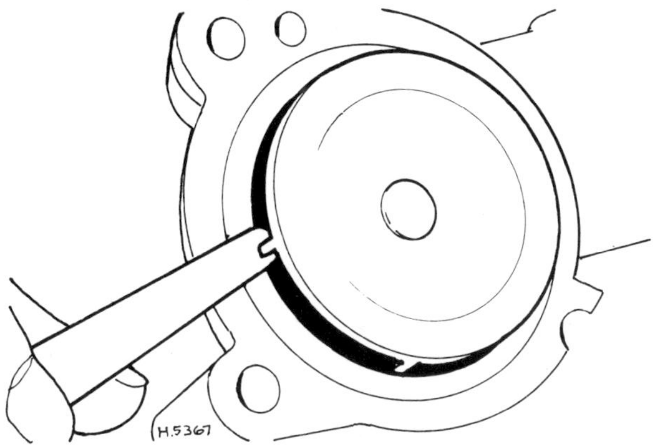

Fig. 2.8. Checking impeller clearance with feeler gauge (Sec. 9)

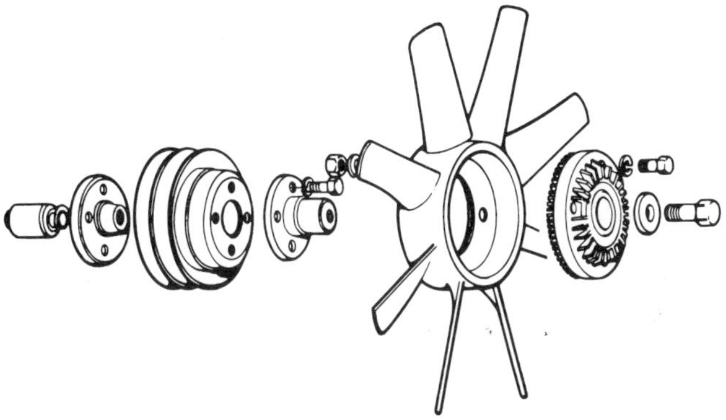

Fig. 2.9. The Mercury Capri II viscous fan assembly - typical (Sec. 11)

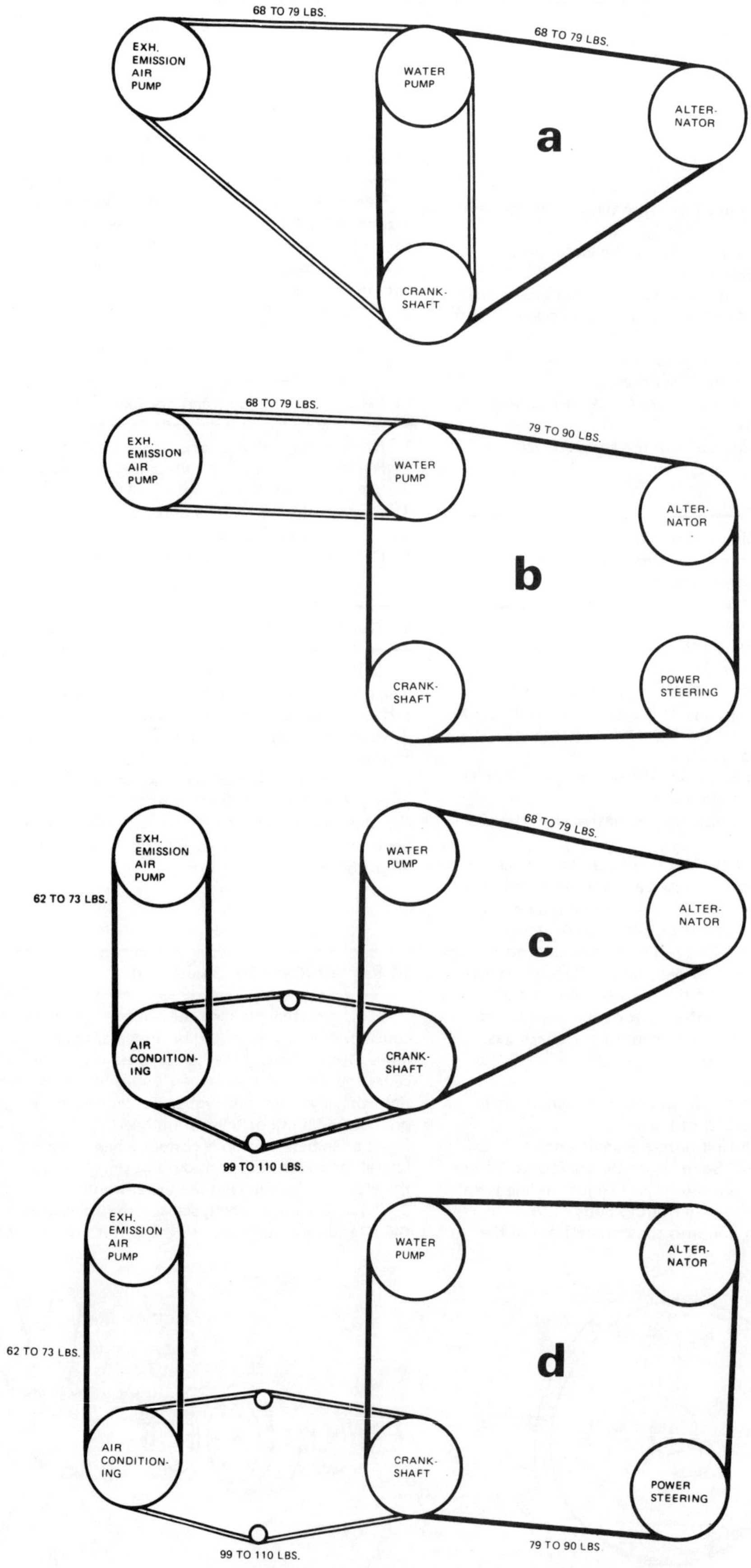

Fig. 2.10. Mercury Capri II drivebelts and belt tensions (Sec. 14)

a Manual steering without air conditioning
b Power steering without air conditioning
c Manual steering with air conditioning
d Power steering with air conditioning

if the alternator bolts are only slackened a little so it requires some effort to move the alternator. In this way the tension of the belt can be arrived at more quickly than by making frequent adjustments.
4 When the correct adjustment has been obtained fully tighten the alternator mounting bolts.

14 Drivebelts (Mercury Capri II) - general

1 Drivebelts for the various pieces of engine driven equipment are shown in Fig. 2.10 The removal and refitting procedure is basically as described in Section 12.
2 Drivebelt adjustment should be carried out using a belt tension gauge, the actual values being as shown alongside the belts in the illustrations. In the event of a belt tension gauge not being available, an adjustment can be obtained by checking for a deflection of ½ inch (13 mm) midway between pulleys under moderate hand pressure.

15 Temperature gauge - fault diagnosis

1 If the temperature gauge fails to work, either the gauge, the sender unit, the wiring or the connections are at fault.
2 It is not possible to repair the gauge or the sender unit and they must be replaced by new units if at fault.
3 First check that the wiring connections are sound. Check the wiring for breaks using an ohmmeter. The sender unit and gauge should be tested by substitution.

16 Temperature gauge and sender unit - removal and refitting

1 Information on the removal of the gauge will be found in Chapter 10.
2 To remove the sender unit, disconnect the wire leading into the unit at its connector and unscrew the unit with a spanner. The unit is locked in the cylinder head just below the manifold on the left-hand side on Capri II models, and on the cylinder block just below the oil pressure switch on Mercury Capri II models. Refitting is the reverse sequence to removal.

17 Antifreeze and corrosion inhibitors

1 In circumstances where it is likely that the temperature will drop below freezing it is essential that some of the water is drained and an adequate amount of ethylene glycol antifreeze is added to the cooling system. If antifreeze is not used, it is essential to use a corrosion inhibitor in the cooling system in the proportion recommended by the inhibitor manufacturer.
2 Any antifreeze which conforms with specifications BS3151 or BS3152 can be used. Never use an antifreeze with an alcohol base as evaporation is too high.
3 Castrol antifreeze with an anti-corrosion additive can be left in the cooling system for up to two years, but after six months it is advisable to have the specific gravity of the coolant checked at your local garage, and thereafter once every three months.
4 The table below gives the proportion of antifreeze and degree of protection:

Antifreeze	Commences to freeze		Frozen solid	
%	°C	°F	°C	°F
25	-13	9	-26	-15
33 1/3	-19	-2	-36	-33
50	-36	-33	-48	-53

Note: Never use antifreeze in the windscreen washer reservoir as it will cause damage to the paintwork.

18 Fault diagnosis - Cooling system

Symptom	Reason/s	Remedy
Overheating	Insufficient water in cooling system	Top up radiator.
	Fan belt slipping (accompanied by a shrieking noise on rapid engine acceleration)	Tighten fan belt to recommended tension or replace if worn.
	Radiator core blocked or radiator grille restricted	Reverse flush radiator, remove obstructions.
	Bottom water hose collapsed, impeding flow	Remove and fit new hose.
	Thermostat not opening properly	Remove and fit new thermostat.
	Ignition advance and retard incorrectly set (accompanied by loss of power, and perhaps, misfiring)	Check and reset ignition timing.
	Carburettor incorrectly adjusted (mixture too weak)	Tune carburettor.
	Exhaust system partially blocked	Check exhaust pipe for constrictive dents and blockages.
	Oil level in sump too low	Top up sump to full mark on dipstick.
	Blown cylinder head gasket (water/steam being forced down the radiator overflow pipe under pressure)	Remove cylinder head, fit new gasket.
	Engine not yet run-in	Run-in slowly and carefully.
	Brakes binding	Check and adjust brakes if necessary.
Underheating	Thermostat jammed open	Remove and renew thermostat.
	Incorrect thermostat fitted allowing premature opening of valve	Remove and replace with new thermostat which opens at a higher temperature.
	Thermostat missing	Check and fit correct thermostat.
Loss of cooling water	Loose clips on water hoses	Check and tighten clips if necessary.
	Top, bottom, or by-pass water hoses perished and leaking	Check and replace any faulty hoses.
	Radiator core leaking	Remove radiator and repair.
	Thermostat gasket leaking	Inspect and renew gasket.
	Radiator pressure cap spring worn or seal ineffective	Renew radiator pressure cap.
	Blown cylinder head gasket (pressure in system forcing water/steam down overflow pipe)	Remove cylinder head and fit new gasket.
	Cylinder wall or head cracked	Dismantle engine, despatch to engineering works for repair.

Chapter 3 Carburation; fuel, exhaust and emission control systems

For modifications, and information applicable to later models, see Supplement at end of manual

Contents

Specifications

Fuel pump

Type	Mechanical, driven from auxiliary shaft
Delivery pressure	4.0 to 5.0 lb f/in^2 (0.27 to 0.35 kg f/cm^2)

Fuel tank

Capacity	12.8 Imp. gallons (58 litres/15.3 US gallons)

Fuel filter	Nylon mesh, located in fuel pump
Air cleaner	Replaceable paper element

Carburettor (Capri II)

Type:	
1.6 litre	Motorcraft single venturi, manual or automatic choke according to transmission type
1.6 litre GT, 2.0 litre	Weber dual venturi, automatic choke

Carburettor specifications (Capri II) *(1974/75 models)	1.6 litre	1.6 litre GT	2.0 litre
Throttle bore diameter:			
Primary	1.42 in (36.0 mm)	1.26 in (32.0 mm)	1.26 in (32.0 mm)
Secondary	–	1.42 in (36.0 mm)	1.42 in (36.0 mm)
Venturi diameter:			
Primary	1.10 in (28.0 mm)	1.02 in (26.0 mm)	1.02 in (26.0 mm)

Secondary	–	1.06 in (27.0 mm)	1.06 in (27.0 mm)
Main jets:			
Primary	137	135 or 140	140
Secondary	–	150 or 140	135
Air correction jet:			
Primary	140	170	160
Secondary	–	140	140
Idling jet:			
Primary	80	50	50
Secondary	–	45	50
Idle air bleed:			
1st	110	170	170
2nd	100	70	70
Accelerator pump jet	55	50	50
Enrichment pipe jet	–	F50	F50
Power jet	90	100	100
Float needle valve	2.0 mm	2.0 mm	2.0 mm
Float level (raised)	1.1 in (28.0 mm)	1.38 in (35.0 mm)	1.38 in (35.0 mm)
Float level (hanging)	1.38 in (35.0 mm)	2.0 in (51.0 mm)	2.0 in (51.0 mm)
Choke plate pull down	0.12 to 0.14 in (3.05 to 3.55 mm)	0.12 to 0.24 in (3.0 to 6.0 mm)	0.12 to 0.24 in (3.0 to 6.0 mm)
De-choke dimension	0.19 to 0.23 in (4.8 to 5.8 mm)	0.138 to 0.158 in (3.5 to 4.0 mm)	0.138 to 0.158 in (3.5 to 4.0 mm)
Accelerator pump stroke	0.115 to 0.125 in (2.87 to 3.13 mm)	–	–
Idling speed:			
Manual gearbox	725 to 775 rpm	725 to 775 rpm	725 to 775 rpm
Automatic transmission (in 'N')	725 to 775 rpm	725 to 775 rpm	725 to 775 rpm
Fast idle speed (rpm)			
Manual choke	900 to 1100	–	–
Auto choke	3000	3000	3000

** Note: These carburettor specifications were compiled from the latest information available at the time of publication. In cases of doubt, it is recommended that further information is sought from the nearest Ford dealer with regard to jet sizes, etc. For specifications applicable to later models, see Chapter 13.*

Carburettor (Mercury Capri II)

Type	Motorcraft model 5200 dual venturi, automatic choke

No detailed carburettor specifications available at the time of publication. Where necessary, consult your Ford dealer for information regarding jet sizes, etc.

Fast idle speed	1800 rpm
TSP-off idle speed	500 rpm
Curb idle speed	See engine compartment decal
Electric choke heater resistance	1.3 to 3.5 ohms
Automatic choke setting	1NL
Choke plate pulldown	0.178 to 0.218 in (4.5 to 5.5 mm)
Dry float setting	0.46 in (11.7 mm)
Accelerator pump setting	No. 2
Fast idle cam setting	0.1 in (2.5 mm)

Torque wrench settings (Capri II)

	lbf ft	kgf m
1.6 litre		
Air cleaner to carburettor or rocker cover	4 to 7	0.6 to 0.9
Air cleaner lid to body	4 to 5	0.5 to 0.7
Carburettor to manifold	12 to 15	1.7 to 2.1
Fuel pump to engine	12 to 15	1.7 to 2.1
1.6 litre GT and 2.0 litre		
Air cleaner to carburettor or rocker cover	6 to 9	0.8 to 1.2
Carburettor to manifold	5 to 7	0.7 to 1.0
Fuel pump to engine	12 to 15	1.7 to 2.1
All versions		
Exhaust manifold to downpipe bolts	15 to 20	2.1 to 2.8
U-bolts and clamps	28 to 33	3.9 to 4.6
Muffler box clamps	9 to 12	1.2 to 1.6

The fuel tank retaining straps are tightened until 1.4 to 1.6 in (35 to 40 mm) of thread is protruding through the nut.

Torque wrench settings (Mercury Capri II)

	lbf ft	kgf m
Air cleaner wing nuts	1.5	0.2
Exhaust manifold flange bolts	15 to 20	2.1 to 2.8
U-bolts and clamps	28 to 33	3.9 to 4.5
Strap-type clamps	9 to 12	1.2 to 1.6
Fuel filter to carburettor	6 to 9	0.9 to 1.15

1 General description

1 The fuel system on all models comprises a rear mounted fuel tank, a fuel pump which is mechanically operated from an eccentric on the engine auxiliary shaft, a carburettor and the interconnecting pipes, hoses and controls.

2 The Capri II models use a Motorcraft single venturi carburettor for the 1.6 litre models which has a manual or automatic choke according to the transmission type. The 1.6 litre GT and 2.0 litre models use a Weber dual venturi with an automatic choke. Mercury Capri II models use a Motorcraft dual venturi carburettor with an automatic choke.

3 It is important that all models use the appropriate grade of fuel. All Capri II models should use 97 octane (UK 4-star rating fuel). Mercury Capri II either require unleaded gasoline or regular grade fuel, depending whether or not a catalytic converter is incorporated in the exhaust system. The fuel filler pipe is of a smaller diameter where unleaded fuel must be used, so that only fuel from the special low-lead dispensing pumps can be used; also a label is fitted on the instrument panel and fuel filler door to this effect.

4 Separate parts of this Chapter are allocated to the Capri II, Mercury Capri II and emission control systems for convenience of presentation.

Fig. 3.1. Air cleaner mounting plate (locking tabs arrowed) (Sec. 2)

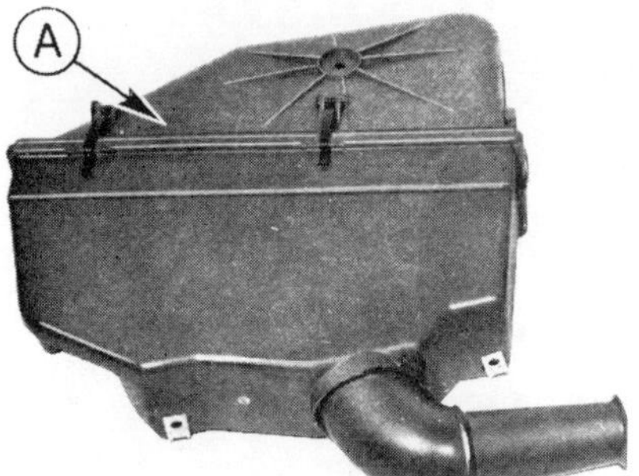

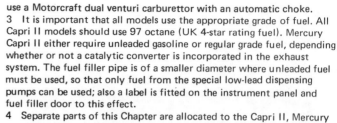

Fig. 3.2. Air cleaner, 1.6 and 2.0 litre GT (Sec. 2)

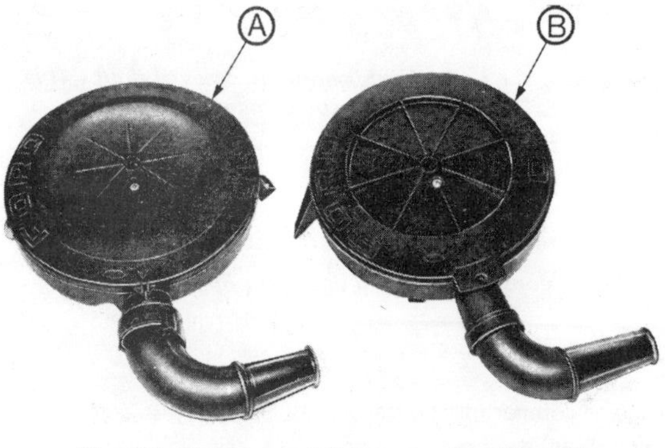

Fig. 3.3. Air cleaner, 1.6 litre standard (Sec. 2)
A Ford of Britain *B Ford of Germany*

Fig. 3.4. Alternative types of fuel pump connections (Sec. 5)

3.2 The air cleaner element in position, 1.6 litre

4.1 Fuel pump location

Part A: Capri II

2 Air cleaner - removal and refitting

1 Disconnect the battery earth lead.
2 *1.6 litre:* Remove the three bolts securing the air cleaner stays to the rocker cover, manifold and accelerator bracket.
3 *1.6 litre GT, 2.0 litre:* Remove the two bolts securing the stay bars to the air cleaner; remove the single nut located above the carburettor and loosen the carburettor-to-air cleaner clamp.
4 *All models:* Remove the air cleaner and take out the element, as described in the following Section.
5 Refitting is the reverse of the removal procedure. On 1.6 litre models the stays must only be nipped tight; overtightening will open out the hole. Adjust the air cleaner to the summer or winter position, as necessary.

3 Air cleaner element - removal and refitting

1 Disconnect the battery earth lead.
2 *1.6 litre:* Remove the self-tapping screws, unclip the air cleaner lid and remove the element (photo).
3 *1.6 litre GT, 2.0 litre:* Remove the air cleaner assembly, as described in the previous Section, then snap-off the six retaining clips to open the assembly; remove the element.
4 Refitting is the reverse of the removal procedure, but ensure that any dust inside the air cleaner body is carefully wiped out. Do not allow dust to enter the carburettor.

4 Fuel pump - description

1 The mechanical fuel pump is mounted on the left-hand side of the engine and is driven by an auxiliary shaft. This type of pump cannot be dismantled for repair other than cleaning the filter and sediment cap. Should a fault appear in the pump it may be tested and if confirmed it must be discarded and a new one obtained. One of two designs may be fitted, this depends on the availability at the production time of the car (photo).

5 Fuel pump - removal and refitting

1 Remove the inlet and outlet hoses at the pump and plug the ends to stop petrol loss or dirt finding its way into the fuel system. If crimped type hose clips are fitted as original equipment, cut them off and use screw type clamps for replacement.
2 Undo and remove two bolts and spring washers that secure the pump to the cylinder block.
3 Lift away the fuel pump and gasket and recover the pushrod.
4 Refitting the fuel pump is the reverse sequence to removal but there are several additional points that should be noted:

a) Do not forget to refit the pushrod.
b) Tighten the pump securing bolts to the specified torque.
c) Before reconnecting the pipe from the fuel tank to the pump inlet, move the end to a position lower than the fuel tank so that fuel can syphon out. Quickly connect the pipe to the pump inlet.
d) Disconnect the pipe at the carburettor and turn the engine over until petrol issues from the open end. Quickly connect the pipe to the carburettor union. This last operation will help to prime the pump.

6 Fuel pump - testing

Assuming that the fuel lines and unions are in good condition and that there are no leaks anywhere, check the performance of the fuel pump in the following manner. Disconnect the fuel pipe at the carburettor inlet union, and the high tension lead to the coil and, with a suitable container or large rag in position to catch the ejected fuel, turn the engine over. A good spurt of petrol should emerge from the end of the pipe every second revolution.

7 Fuel pump - cleaning

1 Detach the fuel pipe from the pump inlet tube.
2 Undo and remove the centre screw and 'O' ring and lift off the sediment cap, filter and seal (photo).
3 Thoroughly clean the sediment cap, filter and pumping chamber using a paintbrush and clean petrol to remove any sediment (photo).
4 To reassemble is the reverse sequence to dismantling. Do not overtighten the centre screw as it could distort the sediment cap.

8 Carburettors - general description

1 *Single venturi carburettor:* This carburettor incorporates idling, main, power valve and accelerator pump systems. The float chamber is externally vented. The carburettor comprises two castings, the upper and lower bodies. The upper body incorporates the float chamber cover and pivot brackets, fuel inlet components, choke plate and the main and power valve system, idling system and accelerator pump discharge nozzle. The lower body incorporates the float chamber, the throttle barrel and venturi, throttle valve components, adjustment screws, accelerator pump and distributor vacuum connection.
2 *Dual venturi carburettors:* These carburettors operate on similar principles to the single venturi type and incorporate a fully automatic strangler type choke to ensure easy starting whilst the engine is cold.

7.2 Lifting away fuel pump sediment cap, filter and seal.

7.3 Removal of filter from fuel pump sediment cap.

The float chamber is internally vented.

The carburettor body comprises two castings which form the upper and lower bodies. The upper incorporates the float chamber cover, float pivot brackets, fuel inlet union, gauze filter, spring-loaded needle valve, twin air intakes, choke plates and the section of the power valve controlled by vacuum.

Incorporated in the lower body is the float chamber, accelerator pump, two throttle barrels and integral main venturies, throttle plates, spindles, levers, jets and the petrol power valve.

The throttle plate opening is in a preset sequence so that the primary starts to open first and is then followed by the secondary in such a manner that both plates reach full throttle position at the same time. The primary barrel, throttle plate and venturi are smaller than the secondary, whereas the auxiliary venturi size is identical in both the primary and secondary barrels.

All the carburation systems are located in the lower body and the main progression systems operate in both barrels, whilst the idling and the power valve systems operate in the primary barrel only and the full load enrichment system in the secondary barrel.

The accelerator pump discharges fuel into the primary barrel.

A connection for the vacuum required to control the distributor advance/retard vacuum unit is located on the lower body.

9 Motorcraft single venturi and Weber dual venturi carburettors - slow running adjustment

1 Run the engine until normal operating temperature is reached.
2 Adjust the throttle speed screw until the specified idling speed is obtained.
3 Now unscrew (anticlockwise) the mixture control screw until the engine begins to run unevenly ('hunts').
4 Screw the mixture control screw in, until the engine runs evenly and then re-adjust the throttle speed screw, if necessary, to obtain the correct slow running speed.
5 This method of adjustment is basic and it is recommended that a final tuning is made using a device such as a Colortune, a vacuum gauge or an exhaust gas analyser in accordance with the manufacturer's instructions.

10 Carburettor - removal and refitting

1 Disconnect the battery earth lead.
2 Remove the air cleaner, as described in Section 2.
3 On Weber carburettors, peen back the lock tabs then remove the four nuts and take off the air cleaner mounting plate.
4 *Automatic choke:* Remove, then refit, the radiator cap to depressurize the cooling system. Disconnect the water hoses from the choke housing, then plug the hose ends to prevent loss of coolant.
5 *Manual choke:* Disconnect the choke inner and outer cables from the carburettor linkage and bracket.
6 Disconnect the throttle cable from the carburettor. Where applicable, disconnect the kick-down linkage.
7 Disconnect the fuel, vacuum, emission control and vent pipes from the carburettor. Where crimped hoses are used, the clips must be prised open.
8 Remove the retaining nuts and lift off the carburettor. Remove the gasket (and spacer, if fitted).
9 Installation is the reverse of the removal procedure, but the following points must be noted:

a) Ensure that all mating surfaces are clean and that new gaskets are used.
b) Where a spacer is used, position a gasket on each side of it.
c) Screw-type hose clips should be used as replacements for crimped-type clips.
d) Top-up the cooling system before running the engine (automatic choke models).
e) On manual choke models adjust the choke cable by pulling out the dash knob approximately ¼ in (6 mm), then connect the cable to the carburettor, eliminating all the cable slackness.
f) Adjust the carburettor, as described in Section 9.

11 Carburettors - dismantling and reassembly (general)

1 With time, the component parts of the carburettor will wear and petrol consumption increase. The diameter of drillings and jets may alter, and air and fuel leaks may develop round spindles and other moving parts. Because of the high degree of precision involved it is best to purchase an exchange carburettor. This is one of the few instances where it is better to take the latter course rather than to rebuild the component oneself.
2 It may be necessary to partially dismantle the carburettor to clear a blocked jet. The accelerator pump itself may need attention and gaskets may need renewal, providing care is taken there is no reason why the carburettor may not be completely reconditioned at home, but ensure a full repair kit can be obtained before you strip the carburettor down. **Never** poke out jets with wire or similar to clean them, but blow them out with compressed air or air from a car tyre pump.

12 Motorcraft single venturi carburettor - cleaning, inspection and adjustment

1 Initially remove the carburettor from the car as described in Section 10, then clean the exterior with a water soluble solvent.
2 *Manual choke:* Remove the six screws and lift off the carburettor body. Disconnect the choke link and move it clear of the carburettor body.
3 *Automatic choke:* Remove the six screws and lift off the carburettor body. Disconnect the choke mechanism by removing the single screw

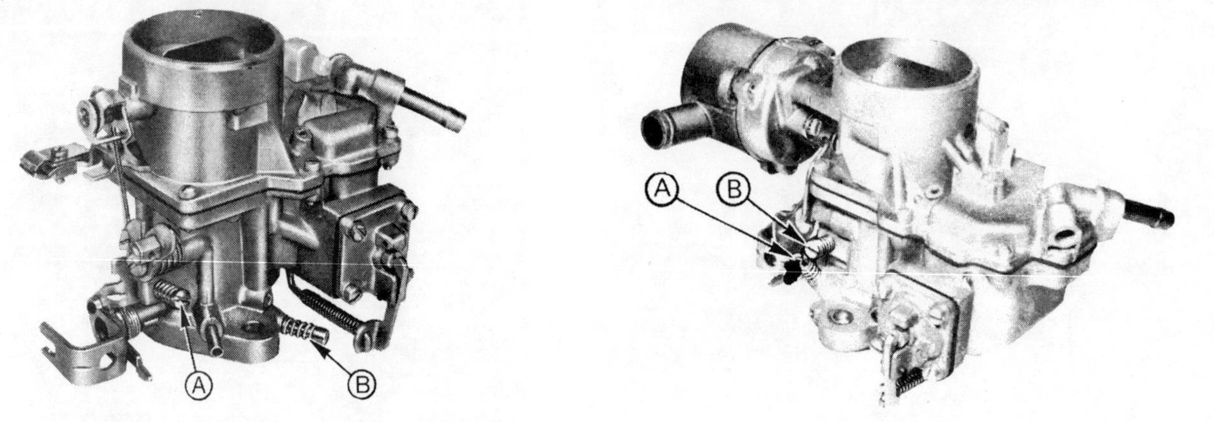

Fig. 3.5. Motorcraft single venturi carburettor (Sec. 9)

Left - Manual choke
Right - Automatic choke

A Mixture adjustment screw
B Idle adjustment screw

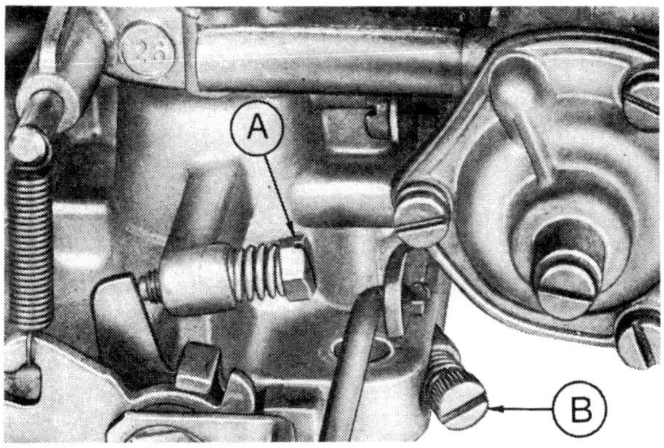

Fig. 3.6. Weber dual venturi carburettor adjustment screws (Sec. 9)

A Idle adjustment screw *B Mixture adjustment screw*

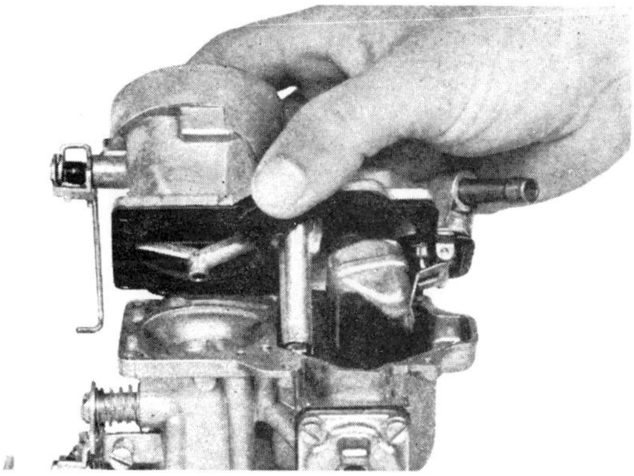

Fig. 3.7. Removal of the carburettor upper body - Motorcraft single venturi carburettor (Sec. 12)

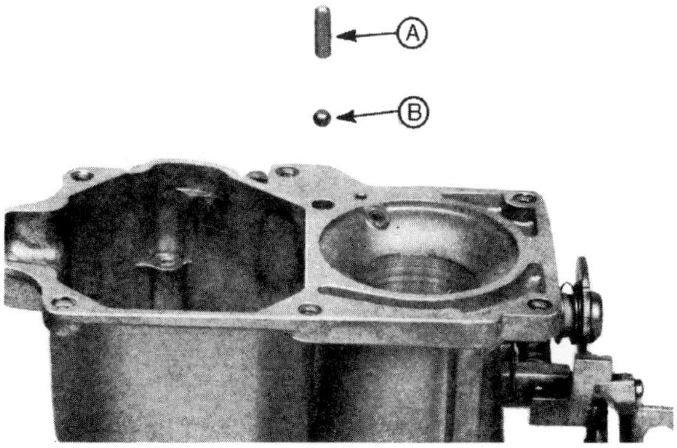

Fig. 3.8. Accelerator ball valve (B) and weight (A) (Sec. 12)

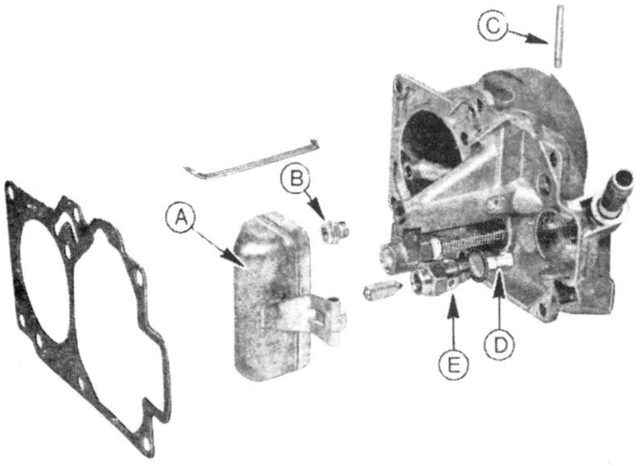

Fig. 3.9. Upper body of carburettor dismantled (Sec. 12)

A Float
B Main jet
C Float retaining pin
D Fuel filter
E Valve housing

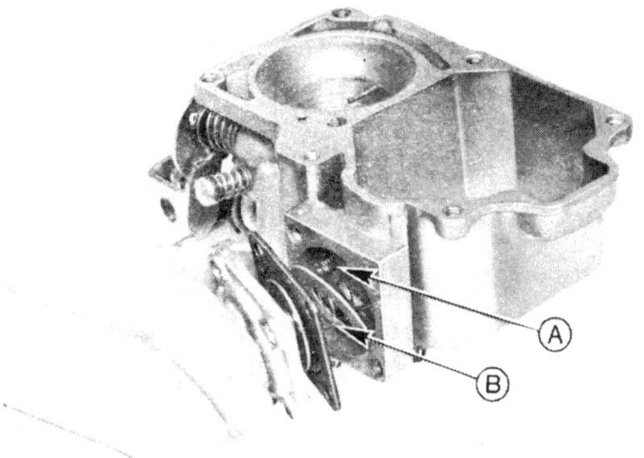

Fig. 3.10. Dismantling the accelerator pump (Sec. 12)

A Check valve spring *B Diaphragm assembly return spring*

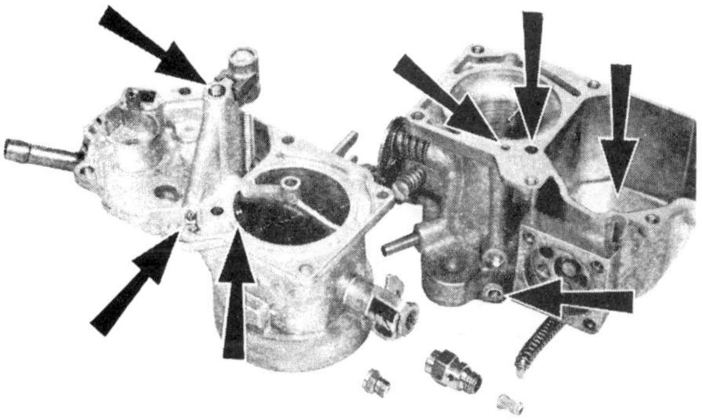

Fig. 3.11. The main items to be cleaned (Sec. 12)

securing the fast idle cam to the main body of the carburettor.
4 Invert the carburettor and allow the accelerator weight and ball valve to fall out.
5 Tap out the float retaining pin and lift out the float and needle valve.
6 Unscrew the valve housing and detach the filter.
7 Unscrew the main jet.
8 Remove the screws from the accelerator pump assembly, take off the cover then remove the component parts. Do not lose the two return springs.
9 Carefully screw in the mixture screw until it *just* contacts its seat, noting the number of turns so that it can eventually be refitted in the same position. Unscrew the mixture screw.
10 Unscrew the jets.
11 Clean the jets and passageways shown in Fig. 3.11 using clean, dry compressed air.
12 Check the float for signs of damage or leaking. Inspect the pump diaphragm and gasket for splits or deterioration. Examine the mixture screw, throttle spindle and needle valve seat for signs of wear. Replace parts as necessary.
13 When reassembling first fit the mixture screw and spring in the same position as originally fitted.

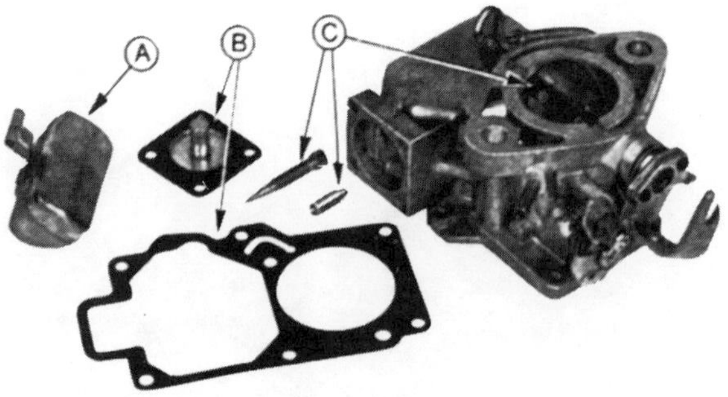

Fig. 3.12. Carburettor main body parts (Sec. 12)

A Float - check for leaks
B Diaphragm and gasket - check for splits or damage
C Check for wear and damage

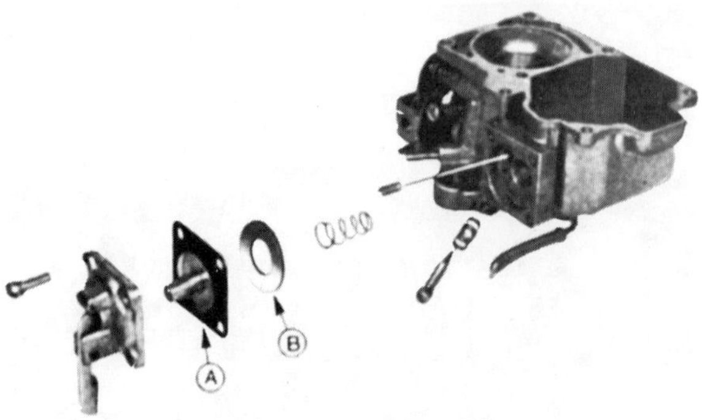

Fig. 3.13. Accelerator pump parts (Sec. 12)

A Pump diaphragm *B Sealing washer*

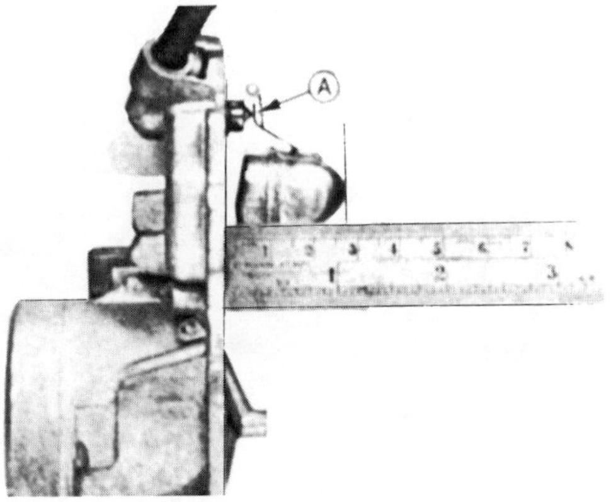

Fig. 3.14. Float level adjustment (Sec. 12)

A Float adjusting tag

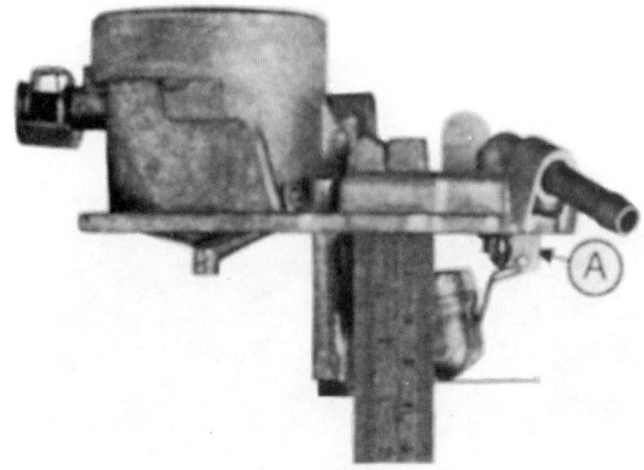

Fig. 3.15. Float travel adjustment (Sec. 12)

A Float adjustment tag

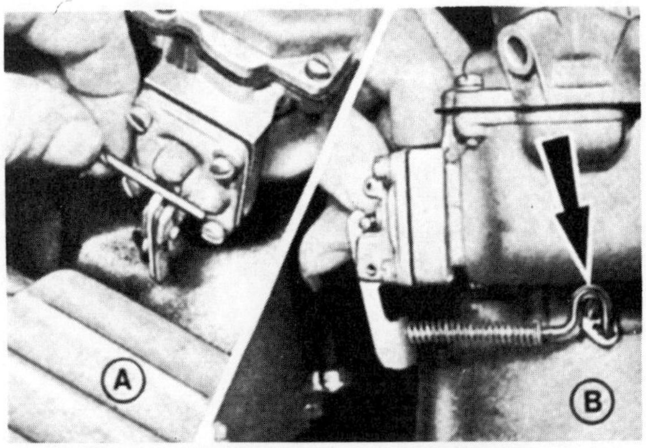

Fig. 3.16. Accelerator pump adjustment (Sec. 12)

A Checking the pump stroke *B Adjustment position*

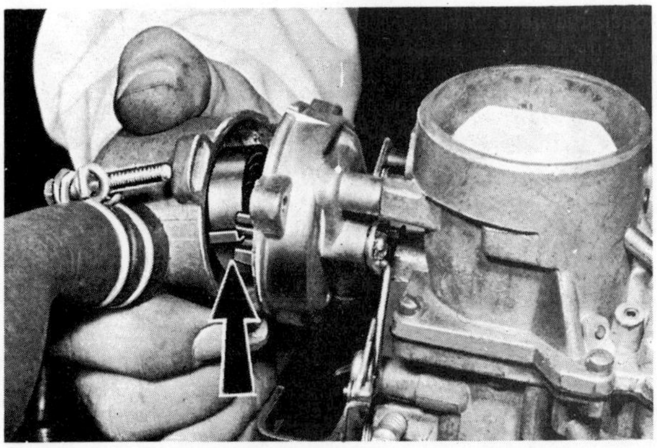

Fig. 3.17. Removing the choke cover - Motorcraft single venturi carburettor (Sec. 13)

14 Reassemble the accelerator pump. The sealing washer is fitted with the steel side outwards and the main return spring has the smaller diameter inwards.
15 Refit the needle valve assembly and float. Ensure that the filter and sealing washer are fitted to the valve housing before fitting to the carburettor upper body.
16 *Float level adjustment:* Hold the upper body vertically so that the needle valve is closed by the float, then measure the dimension from the face of the upper body to the base of the float. Repeat this check with the upper body horizontal so that the float hangs under its own weight. Bend the tag 'A' (Figs. 3.14 and 3.15), to obtain the dimensions given in the Specifications.
17 Refit the main jet.
18 Refit the accelerator ball valve and weight.
19 Using a new gasket, fit the upper body to the main body, and reconnect the choke operating linkage. On manual choke carburettors hold the choke mechanism fully closed so that the cam does not go over-centre when the upper body is fitted.
20 *Accelerator pump stroke:* Screw the idle adjusting screw clear of the linkage, so that the throttle is fully closed. Push the accelerator pump diaphragm fully in and measure the clearance between the pump lever and the diaphragm. Bend the control link at the U-section to

obtain the dimension given in the Specifications.
21 Refit the automatic choke (Section 13).

13 Motorcraft single venturi carburettor automatic choke - removal, overhaul and refitting

1 Disconnect the battery earth lead.
2 Remove the air cleaner, as described in Section 2.
3 Remove the three choke cover retaining screws, detach the cover and move it clear of the carburettor. Remove the gasket.
4 Remove the two screws securing the choke body and the single screw securing the linkage to the operating spindle. Detach the choke assembly.
5 Remove the single screw, detach the choke operating spindle, and pull out the linkage and piston.
6 Clean all the components, inspect them for damage and wipe them dry with a lint-free cloth. Do not use any lubricants during reassembly.
7 Reassemble the vacuum piston, operating spindle and operating linkage; do not forget the plastic sleeve on the spindle and ensure that link rod of the piston assembly is in the outer hole of the lever.
8 Position the sealing rubber between the main choke body and the carburettor. Reconnect the choke linkage to the spindle and fit the choke body.
9 Adjust the V-mark setting, de-choke setting and vacuum pulldown as described in Section 14.
10 Using a new gasket on the choke cover, connect the bi-metal spring into the top slot in the operating link, position the cover and loosely fit the three retaining screws.
11 Rotate the cover until the marks are aligned then tighten the three screws (Fig. 3.21).
12 Reconnect the battery, run the engine and adjust the fast idle speed as described in Section 14.
13 Refit the air cleaner (Section 2).

14 Motorcraft single venturi carburettor automatic choke - adjustment

Note: The procedure is described for a carburettor which is fitted in the car but, with the exception of fast idle speed adjustment, can be carried out on the bench if required where the carburettor has been removed.
1 Disconnect the battery earth lead.
2 Remove the air cleaner, as described in Section 2.

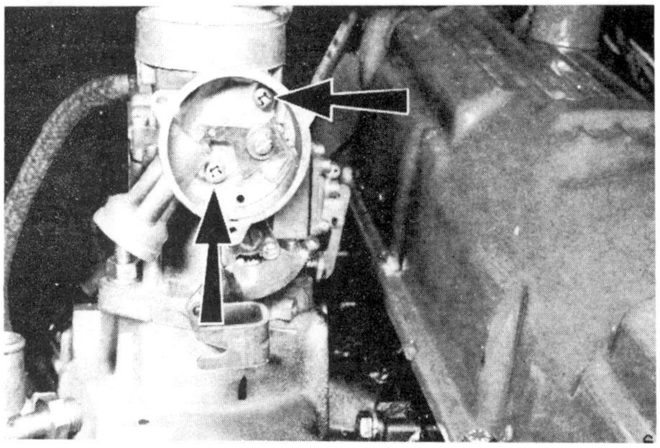

Fig. 3.18. The choke housing retaining screws (Sec. 13)

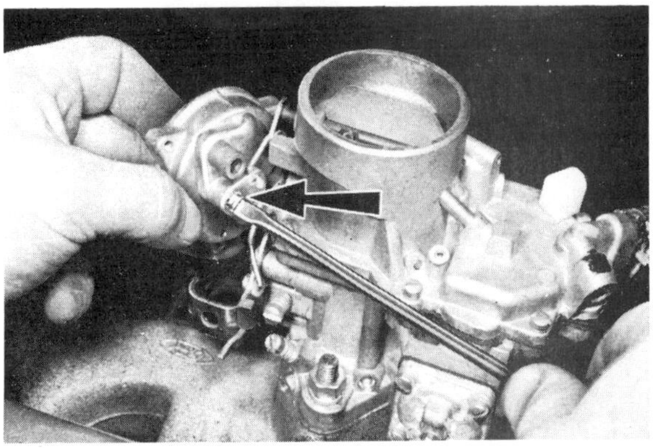

Fig. 3.19. Detaching the choke linkage (Sec. 13)

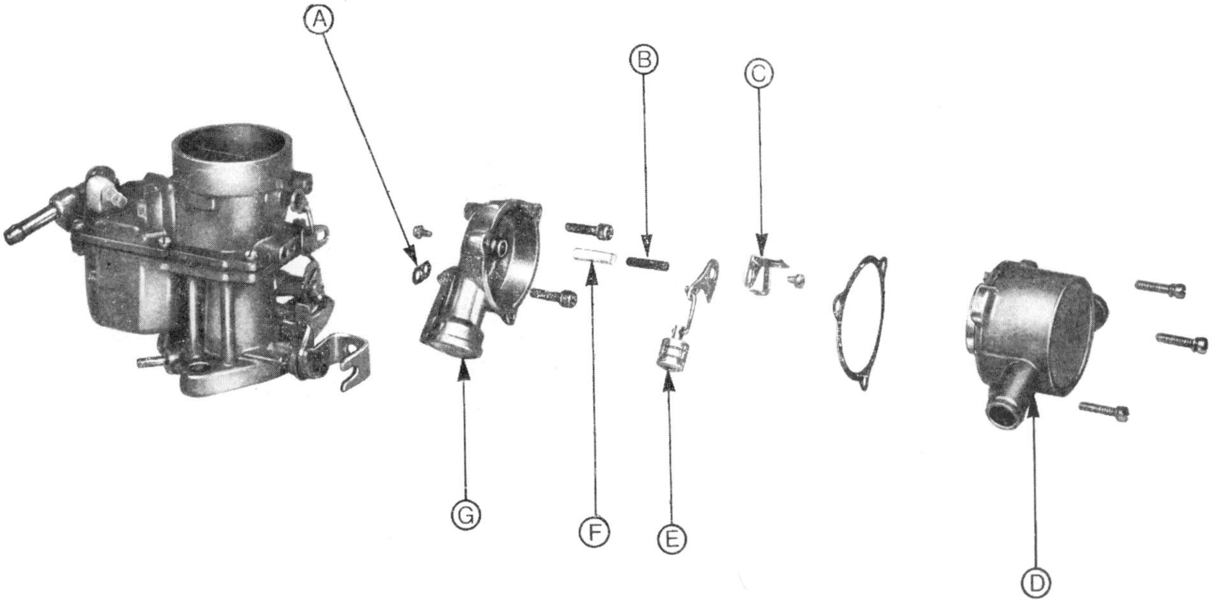

Fig. 3.20. The automatic choke assembly (Sec. 13)

A Gasket
B Choke spindle
C Operating link
D Housing and bi-metal assembly
E Vacuum piston assembly
F Spindle sleeve
G Main choke housing

Fig. 3.21. Choke cover alignment marks (arrowed) (Sec. 13)

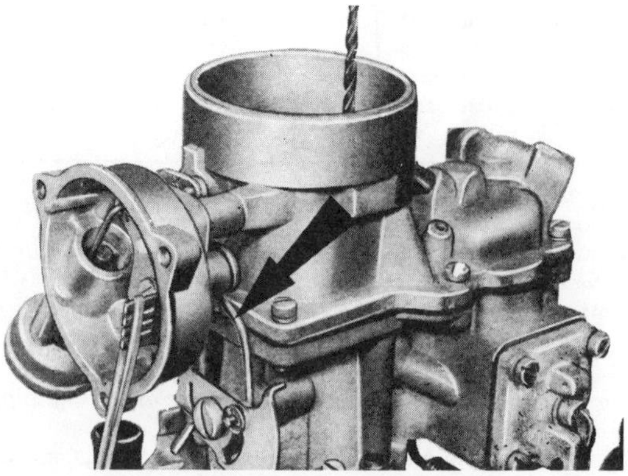

Fig. 3.22. Bending the control rod where arrowed to obtain the correct V-mark setting (Sec. 14)

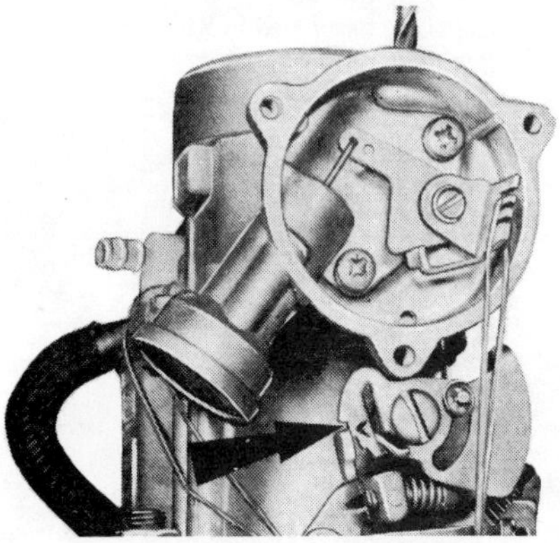

Fig. 3.23. Choke V-mark setting (Sec. 14)

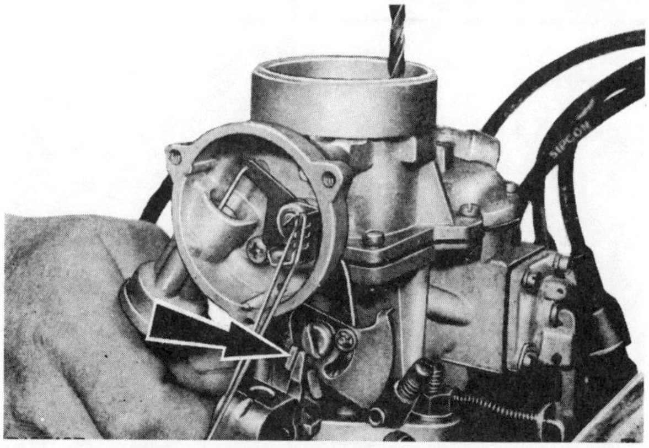

Fig. 3.24. De-choke adjustment - adjusting tag arrowed (Sec. 14)

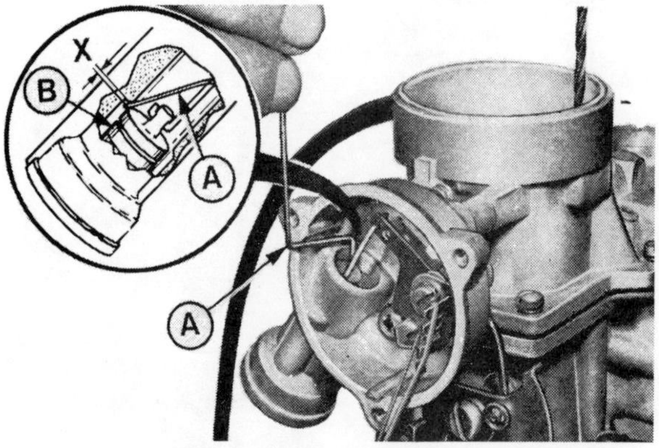

Fig. 3.25. Vacuum pull down adjustment (Sec. 14)

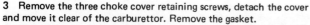

A Stiff wire
B Vacuum piston
Dimension X = 0.04 in (1 mm)

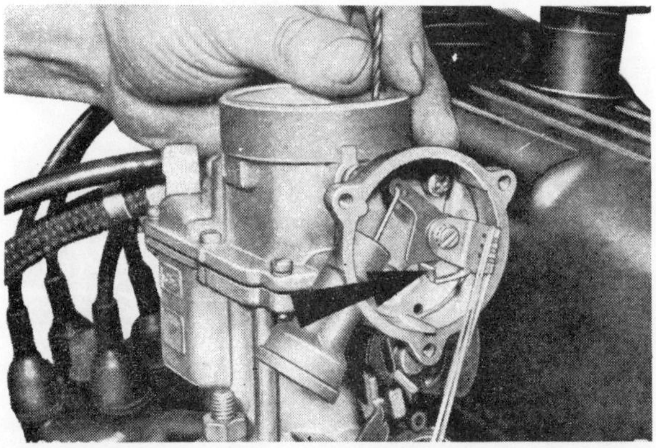

Fig. 3.26. Vacuum pull down adjustment tag (arrowed) (Sec. 14)

3 Remove the three choke cover retaining screws, detach the cover and move it clear of the carburettor. Remove the gasket.

4 *V-mark setting:* Fit an elastic band to the choke lever plate so that the plate is held closed. Open, then release, the throttle to ensure that the choke plate closes fully. Position an unmarked No. 18 (0.169 in/ 4.25 mm) twist drill shank between the edge of the choke plate and the air horn wall on the accelerator pump side of the carburettor. Partially open the throttle to allow the fast idle cam to drop into its operating position. With the choke control rod located at the end of the slot in the fast idle cam, bend the rod at the point arrowed in Fig. 3.22 so that the V-mark on the cam alings with the end of the throttle lever (Fig. 3.23). Remove the twist drill.

5 *De-choke setting:* Hold the choke lever plate closed with the elastic band as described in the previous paragraph. Fully open the throttle and check that the de-choke operates just before full throttle is reached. The adjustment is checked by measuring between the edge of the choke plate and the air horn wall on the accelerator pump side of the carburettor using an unmarked drill shank; the de-choke lever is bent to obtain a dimension of 0.19 to 0.23 in (4.8 to 5.8 mm). **Note:** No. 11 drill is 0.191 in; No. 1 drill is 0.228 in; 7/32 in drill is 0.219 in. Take care that the drill does not fall into the inlet manifold as the choke plate opens. Remove the drill.

6 *Vacuum pull-down:* Hold the choke lever plate closed with the elastic band as previously described. Partially open the throttle and choke mechanism. Obtain a thin piece of stiff wire of approximately 0.04 in (1 mm) diameter which can be suitably bent (a paper clip will probably be satisfactory) and insert it in the slot located inside the front edge of the piston bore (Fig. 3.25). Release the throttle and choke mechanism so that the piston traps the wire. Now measure the gap between the choke plate and the air horn wall on the accelerator pump side of the carburettor using an unmarked drill shank. Adjust the pull-down adjustment tag (arrowed in Fig. 3.26), to obtain a gap of 0.09 ± 0.01 in (2.25 ± 0.25 mm). **Note:** No. 39 drill is 0.0995 in; No. 46 drill is 0.081 in.
7 Remove the elastic band, position the gasket on the choke cover and connect the bi-metal spring into the top slot in the operating link. Position the cover and loosely fit the retaining screws.
8 Rotate the cover until the marks are aligned then tighten the three retaining screws.
9 Reconnect the battery, run the engine and adjust the fast idle speed, as described in the following paragraph.
10 *Fast idle speed adjustment:* **Note** - Ideally a tachometer will be required in order to set the fast idle rpm to the specified value. Run the engine up to normal operating temperature then switch off and connect the tachometer (where available). Open the throttle and locate the fast idle cam in the fast idle position (with the V-mark in line with the throttle lever). Release the throttle to hold the cam in this position and check that the choke plate is fully open (if it is not fully open, the assembly is faulty or the engine is not at operating temperature). Without touching the accelerator pedal, start the engine and bend the tag on the throttle lever as necessary to obtain the correct fast idle rpm.
11 Finally refit the air cleaner (Section 2).

15 Weber dual venturi carburettor - cleaning, inspection and adjustment

1 Initially remove the carburettor from the car as described in Section 10, then clean the exterior with a water soluble solvent.
2 Carefully prise out the U-circlip with a screwdriver and disconnect the choke plate operating link.
3 Remove the six screws and detach the carburettor upper body.
4 Unscrew the brass nut located at the fuel intake and detach the fuel filter.
5 Tap out the float retaining pin, and detach the float and needle valve.
6 Remove the three screws and detach the power valve diaphragm assembly.
7 Unscrew the needle valve housing.
8 Unscrew the jets and jet plugs from the carburettor body, noting the positions in which they are fitted.
9 From beneath the carburettor, remove the two primary diffuser tubes.
10 Remove four screws and detach the accelerator pump diaphragm, taking care that the spring is not lost (Fig. 3.31).
11 Carefully screw in the mixture screw until it just contacts its seat, noting the number of turns so that it can eventually be refitted in the same position. Unscrew the mixture screw.
12 Clean the jets and passageways using clean, dry compressed air. Check the float assembly for signs of damage or leaking. Inspect the power valve and pump diaphragms and gaskets for splits or deterioration. Examine the mixture screw, needle valve seat and throttle spindle for signs of wear. Replace parts as necessary (Fig. 3.35).
13 When reassembling, refit the accelerator pump diaphragm assembly.
14 Fit the mixture screw and spring in the same position as originally fitted.
15 Slide the two diffuser tubes into position then refit the jets and jet plugs.
16 Loosely fit the three screws to retain the power valve diaphragm assembly, then compress the return spring so that the diaphragm is not twisted or distorted. Lock the retaining screws and release the return spring.
17 Hold the diaphragm down, block the air bleed with a finger then release the diaphragm. If the diaphragm stays down it has correctly sealed to the housing.
18 Refit the needle valve housing, needle valve and float assembly to the upper body.

Fig. 3.27. The choke link U-circlip (arrowed) (Sec. 15)

Fig. 3.28. Location of the carburettor fuel filter - Weber dual venturi carburettor (Sec. 15)

Fig. 3.29. Jets and jet plugs (arrowed) (Sec. 15)

X Main correction jet location

19 *Float level adjustment:* Hold the upper body vertically so that the needle valve is closed by the float, then measure the dimension from the face of the upper body to the base of the float. Repeat this check with the upper body horizontal so that the float hangs under its own weight. Bend the tags arrowed in Figs. 3.36 and 3.37 to obtain the dimensions given in the Specifications.
20 Refit the fuel inlet filter and brass nut.
21 Position a new gasket and refit the carburettor upper body to the main body. Ensure that the choke link locates correctly through the upper body.
22 Reconnect the choke link and refit the U-circlip.

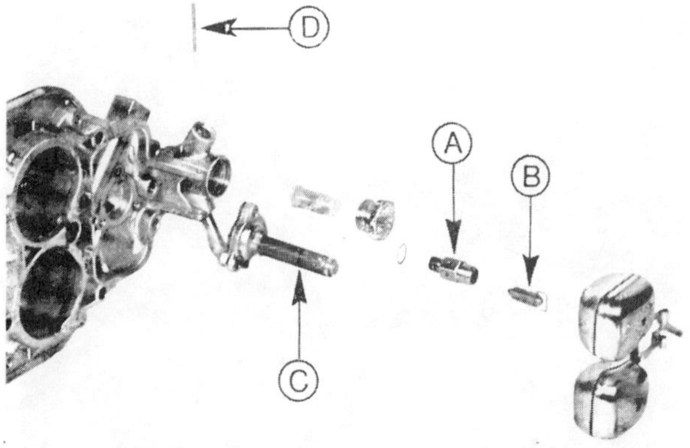

Fig. 3.30. Carburettor upper body parts (Sec. 15)

A Valve housing
B Needle valve
C Power valve
D Float retaining pin

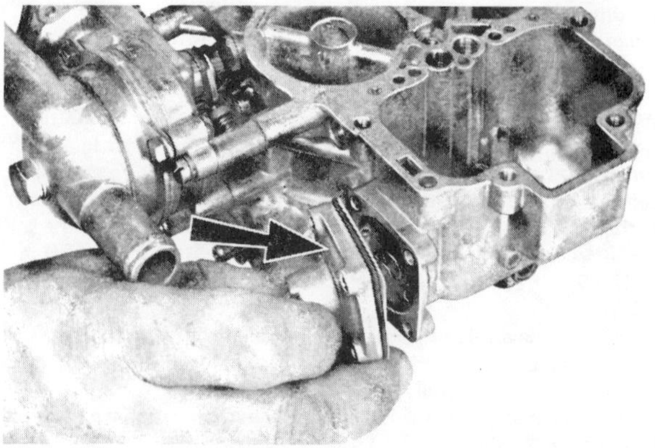

Fig. 3.31. Removing the accelerator pump diaphragm (Sec. 15)

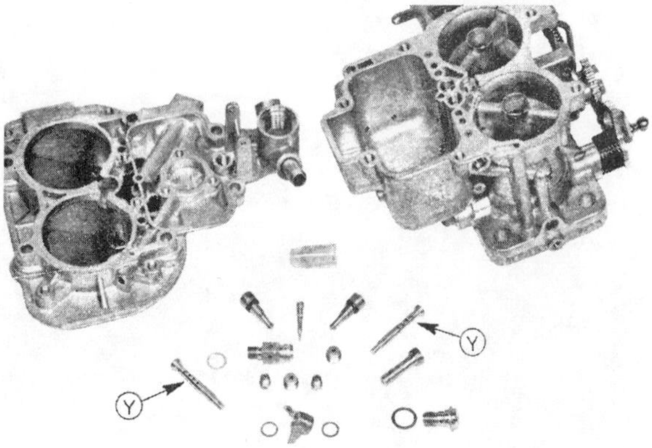

Fig. 3.32. Carburettor jets and body halves (Sec. 15)

Y Diffuser tubes

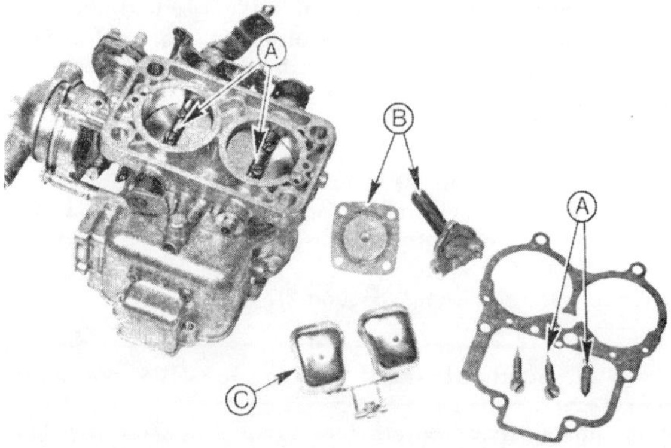

Fig. 3.33. Carburettor main body parts (Sec. 15)

A Needle seats - check for damage or wear
B Diaphragms - check for splits or damage
C Floats - check for leaks

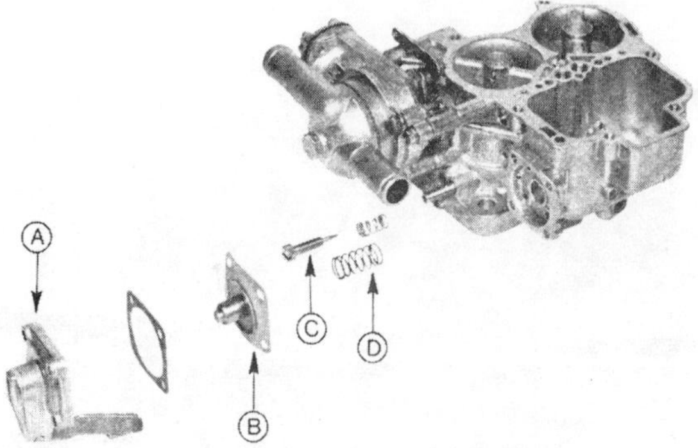

Fig. 3.34. Accelerator pump parts (Sec. 15)

A Pump housing
B Pu.np diaphragm
C Mixture screw
D Pump return spring

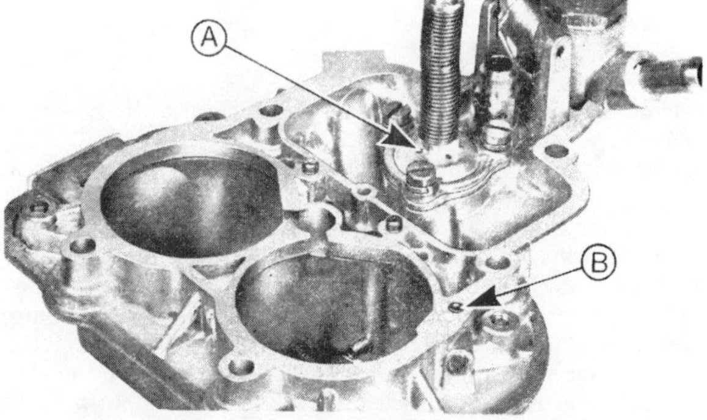

Fig. 3.35. Power valve diaphragm (Sec. 15)

A Power valve
B Diaphragm bleed hole

16 Weber dual venturi carburettor automatic choke - removal, overhaul and refitting

1 Disconnect the battery earth lead.
2 Remove the air cleaner, as described in Section 2.
3 Remove the three screws, detach the cover and move it clear of the carburettor. For access to the lower screw it will be necessary to make up a suitably cranked screwdriver.
4 Detach the internal heat shield.
5 Remove the single U-circlip and disconnect the choke plate operating link.
6 Remove the three screws, disconnect the choke link at the operating lever and detach the choke assembly. For access to the lower screw the cranked screwdriver will again be required.
7 Remove the three screws and detach the vacuum diaphragm assembly.
8 Dismantle the remaining parts of the choke mechanism.
9 Clean all the components, inspect them for wear and damage and wipe them dry with a lint-free cloth. Do not use any lubricants during reassembly.
10 Reassemble the choke mechanism.

Fig. 3.36. Float level adjustment (adjusting tag arrowed) (Sec. 15)

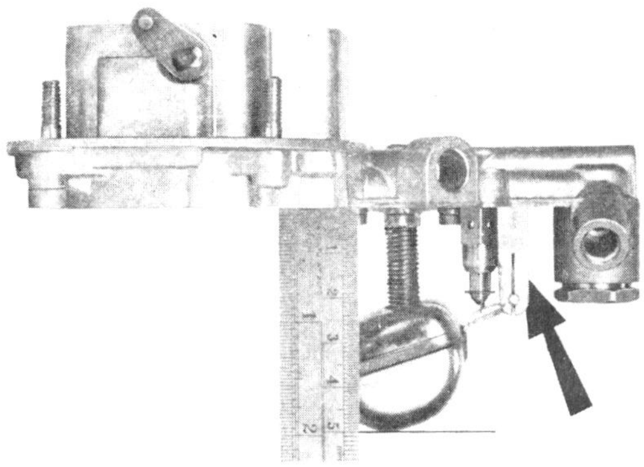

Fig. 3.37. Float travel adjustment (adjusting tag arrowed) (Sec. 15)

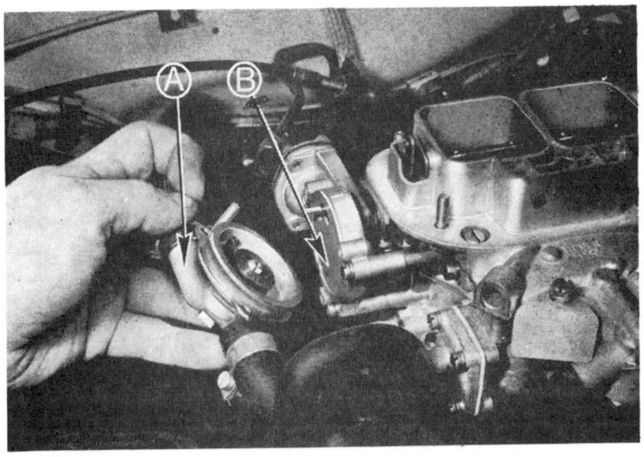

Fig. 3.38. Removing the choke cover (Sec. 16)

A Outer cover *B Internal heat shield*

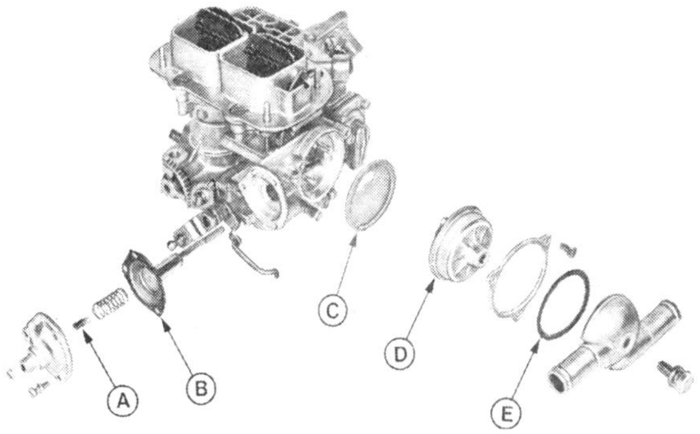

Fig. 3.39. Vacuum diaphragm and outer cover (Sec. 16)

A Diaphragm adjusting screw
B Diaphragm
C Internal heat shield
D Bimetal spring and housing assembly
E Outer sealing gasket

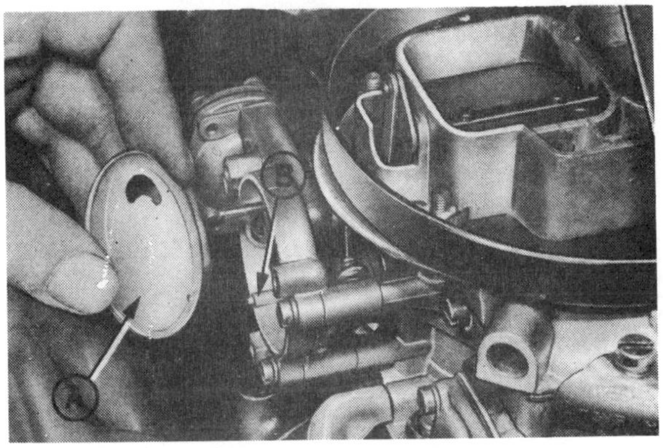

Fig. 3.40. Fitting the internal heat shield (Sec 16)

A Heat shield *B Locating peg*

Fig. 3.41. Alignment marks on choke housing (Sec. 16)

11 Refit the vacuum diaphragm and housing, ensuring that the diaphragm is flat before the housing is fitted.
12 Ensure that the O-ring is correctly located in the choke housing then reconnect the lower choke link. Position the assembly and secure it with the three screws; ensure that the upper choke link locates correctly through the carburettor body.
13 Reconnect the upper choke link to the choke spindle.
14 Check the vacuum pull-down and choke phasing, as described in Section 17.
15 Refit the internal heat shield ensuring that the hole in thecover locates correctly onto the peg cast in the housing.
16 Connect the bi-metal spring to the choke lever, position the choke cover and loosely fit the three retaining screws.
17 Rotate the cover until the marks are aligned, then tighten the three screws.
18 Reconnect the battery, run the engine and adjust the fast idle speed, as described in Section 17.
19 Refit the air cleaner (Section 2).

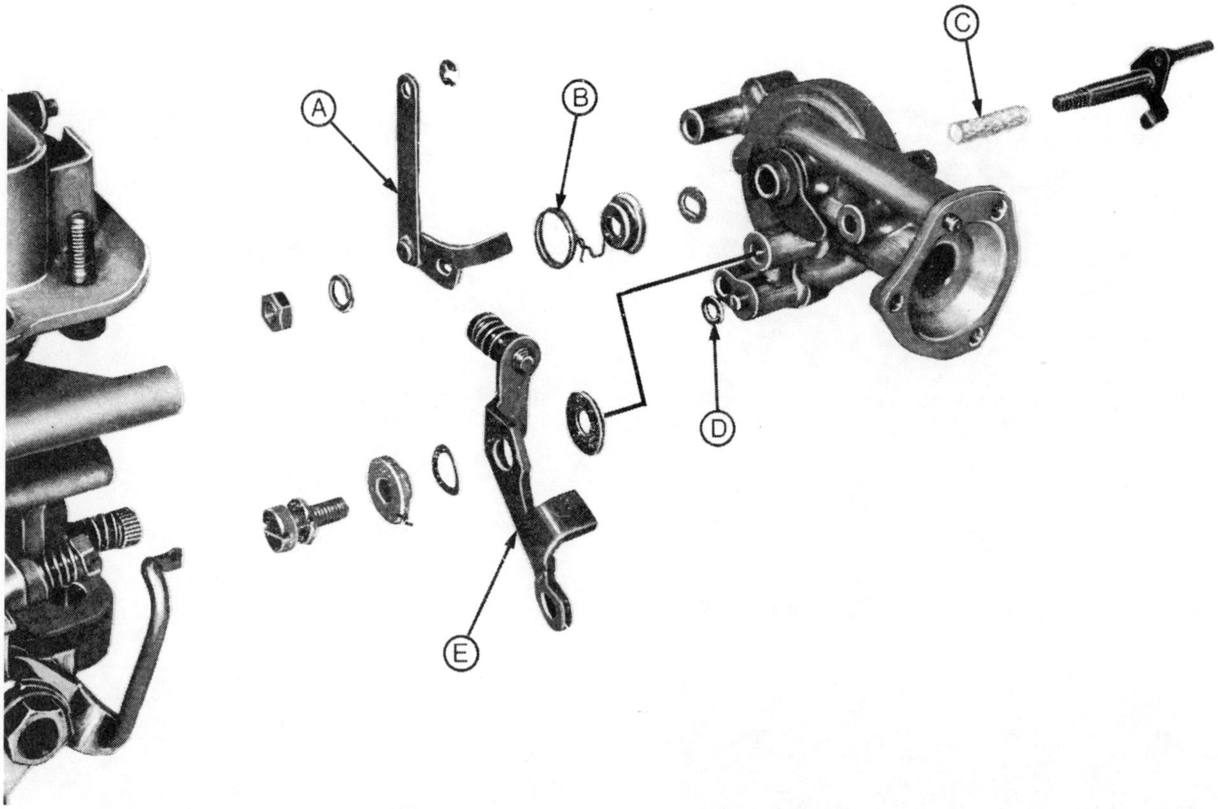

Fig. 3.42. Automatic choke assembly (Sec. 16)

A Upper choke operating link
B Fast idle cam return spring
C Spindle sleeve
D Seal ring
E Choke link

Fig. 3.43 Checking vacuum pull down (Sec. 17)

Fig. 3.44 Adjusting vacuum pull down (Sec. 17)

17 Weber dual venturi carburettor automatic choke - adjustment

Note: The procedure is described for a carburettor which is fitted in the car but with the exception of fast idle speed adjustment, can be carried out on the bench if required where the carburettor has been removed.

1 Disconnect the battery earth lead.
2 Remove the air cleaner, as described in Section 2.
3 Remove the three screws, detach the choke cover and move it clear of the carburettor. For access to the lower screw it will be necessary to make up a suitable cranked screwdriver.
4 Detach the internal heat shield.
5 *Vacuum pull-down:* Fit an elastic band to the choke plate lever and position it so that the choke plates are held closed. Open, then release, the throttle to ensure that the choke plates close fully. Unscrew the plug from the diaphragm unit then manually push open the diaphragm up to its stop from inside the choke housing. Do not push on the rod as it is spring loaded but push on the diaphragm plug body. The choke plate pull-down should now be measured, using an unmarked twist drill shank between the edge of the choke plate and the air horn wall, and compared with the specified figure. Adjust, if necessary, by screwing the adjusting screw in or out, using a very short bladed screwdriver. Refit the end plug and detach the elastic band on completion.
6 *Choke phasing:* Hold the throttle partly open and position the fast idle cam so that the fast idle adjusting screw locates on the upper

section of the cam. Release the throttle to hold the cam in this position then push the choke plates down until the step on the cam jams against the adjusting screw. Measure the clearance between the edge of the choke plate and the air horn wall using an unmarked 2 mm/0.08 in twist drill shank (a No. 46 drill is 0.081 in). Adjust if necessary, by bending the tag arrowed in Fig. 3.46.

7 Refit the internal heat shield ensuring that the hole in the cover locates correctly onto the peg cast in the housing.

8 Connect the bi-metal spring to the choke lever, position the choke cover and loosely fit the three retaining screws.

9 Rotate the cover until the marks are aligned then tighten the three screws.

10 Reconnect the battery, run the engine and adjust the fast idle speed as described in the following paragraph.

11 *Fast idle speed adjustment.* **Note:** Ideally a tachometer will be required in order to set the fast idle rpm to the specified value. Run the engine up to normal operating temperature, then switch off and connect the tachometer (where available). Open the throttle partially, hold the choke plates fully closed then release the throttle so that the choke mechanism is held in the high cam/fast idle position. Release the choke plates, checking that they remain fully open (if they are not open, the assembly is faulty or the engine is not at operating temperature). Without touching the accelerator pedal, start the engine and adjust the fast idle screw as necessary to obtain the correct fast idle rpm.

12 Finally refit the air cleaner (Section 2).

18 Fuel tank - removal and refitting

1 Disconnect the battery earth lead.

2 Using a length of flexible tubing, syphon as much fuel out of the tank as possible.

3 Jack-up the rear of the car and suitably support it for access beneath.

4 Disconnect the fuel feed pipe at the tank and detach it from the clips along the tank front edge.

5 Disconnect the electrical leads from the sender unit.

6 Unclip the vent pipe from the chassis and disconnect the breather pipe at the T-connection.

7 Loosen the tank securing straps then support the tank weight while the straps are unclipped.

8 Remove the tank (and guard, where applicable), leaving the fuel filler pipe in position.

9 If it is necessary to remove the sender unit, this can be unscrewed from the tank using the appropriate Ford tool. Alternatively a suitable C-spanner or drift can probably be used, but great care should be taken that the flange is not damaged and that there is no danger from sparks if a hammer has to be resorted to.

10 Taking care not to damage the sealing washer, prise out the tank-to-filler pipe seal.

11 When refitting, ensure that the rubber pads are stuck in position as shown in Fig. 3.48.

12 Refit the filler pipe seal.

13 Refit the sender unit using a new seal as the original one will almost certainly be damaged.

14 The remainder of the refitting procedure is the reverse of removal. A smear of grease on the tank filler pipe exterior will aid its fitment. Refer to the Torque Wrench Settings for the tank retaining strap nuts.

19 Fuel tank - cleaning and repair

1 With time it is likely that sediment will collect in the bottom of the fuel tank. Condensation, resulting in rust and other impurities will

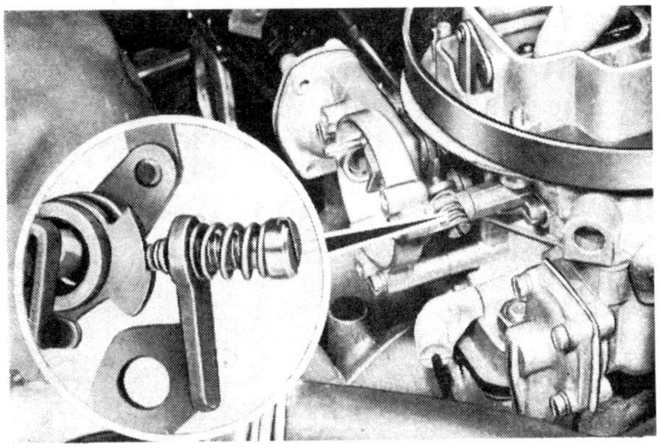

Fig. 3.45. Checking the choke phasing (Sec. 17)

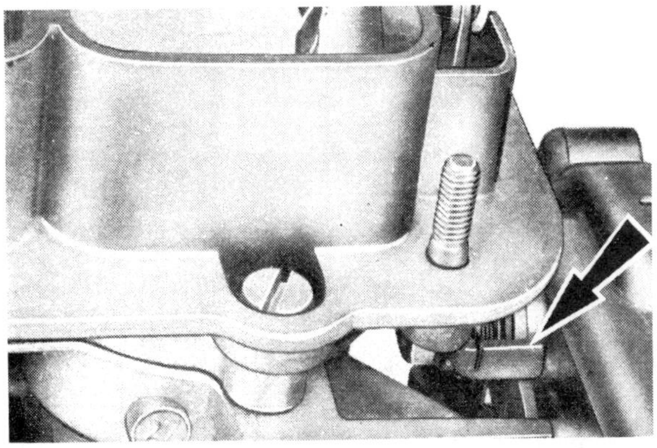

Fig. 3.46. Choke phasing adjustment tag (arrowed) (Sec. 17)

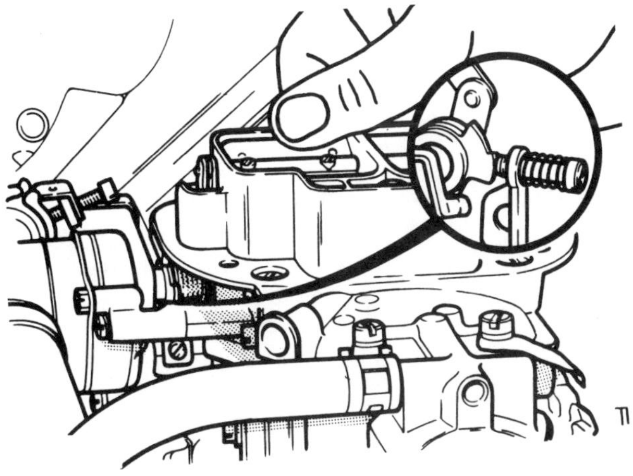

Fig. 3.47 Fast idle adjustment with choke mechanism held in high cam/fast idle position (Sec 17)

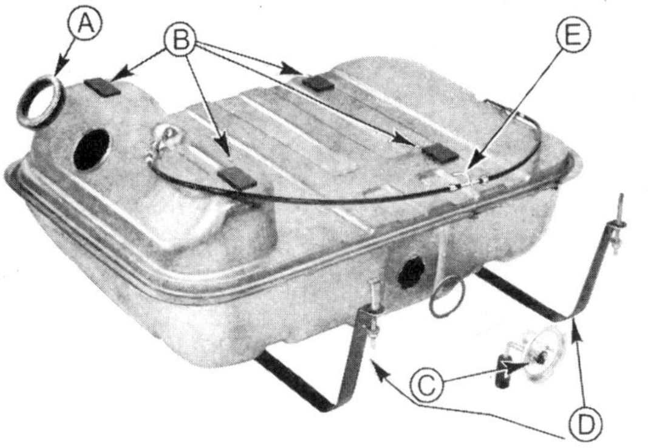

Fig. 3.48. Capri II fuel tank (Sec. 18)

A Seal
B Rubber pads
C Sender unit
D Securing straps
E T-connection

usually be found in the fuel tank of any car more than three or four years old.
2 When the tank is removed it should be vigorously flushed out with hot water and detergent and, if facilities are available, steam cleaned.
3 Never weld, solder or bring a naked light close to an empty fuel tank, unless it has been cleaned as described in the previous paragraph for at least two hours.

20 Accelerator and kick-down cable - removal, refitting and adjustment

1 Disconnect the battery earth lead.
2 Disconnect the accelerator inner cable at the throttle link, turn back the locknut then detach the outer cable from the bracket.
3 Detach the outer cable from the bulkhead (1 screw).
4 From inside the car, remove the dash lower insulator panel. It is retained by five screws (r.h.d.) or three screws (l.h.d.), along the rear edge and can then be unclipped from the front edge.
5 Remove the retaining clip from the pedal shaft by depressing at point 'A' and lifting at point 'B' (Fig. 3.49), then pull the inner cable through the shaft and lift it out of the slot.
6 Refitting is the reverse of the removal procedure, the clip on the shaft being pressed in to secure the cable end.
7 To adjust the cable, remove the air cleaner (Section 2) and detach the throttle return spring.
8 Fully slacken the outer cable adjusting nut and locknut.
9 Jam the throttle pedal in the wide open position using a block of wood or similar item.
10 Wind back the accelerator cable adjusting nut to a point where the carburettor linkage is just in the fully open position, then securely tighten the locknut.
11 On automatic transmission models, adjust the kick-down cable as described in Chapter 6, Section 20.
12 Reconnect the throttle return spring then check the pedal action.
13 Refit the air cleaner (Section 2) and reconnect the battery earth lead.

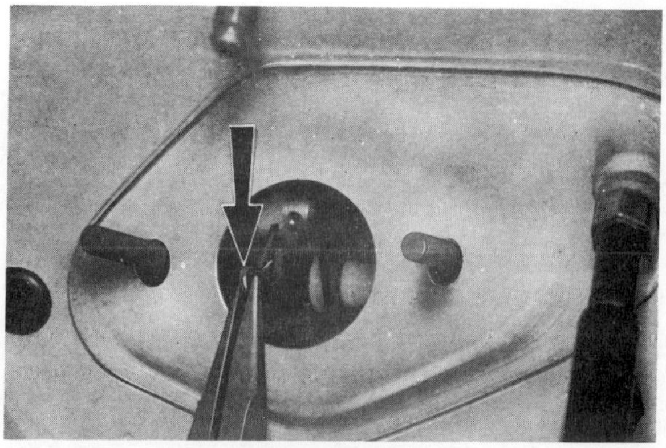

Fig. 3.49. Removal of the shaft end securing clip (Sec. 20)

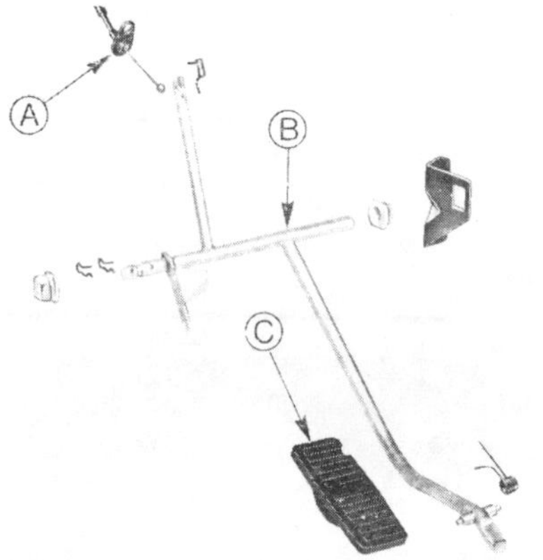

Fig. 3.50. Accelerator shaft assembly (rhd) (Sec. 21)

A Throttle cable B Accelerator shaft C Pedal

21 Accelerator pedal and pedal shaft - removal and refitting

Note: If the pedal only is to be removed refer to paragraph 12.
1 Disconnect the battery earth lead.
2 From inside the car remove the dash lower insulator panel. It is retained by five screws (r.h.d.) or three screws (l.h.d.) along the rear edge and can then be unclipped from the front edge.
3 Remove the accelerator cable from the pedal shaft as described in the previous Section.

R.h.d. variants

4 Disconnect the brake operating rod at the brake pedal, then remove the master cylinder and servo unit. Refer to Chapter 9 for further information.
5 Working through the rear bulkhead in the engine compartment, pull out the shaft end securing clip.
6 Rotate the right-hand shaft mounting bush through 45° in either direction and pull it out.
7 Detach the accelerator shaft assembly.

L.h.d. variants

8 Loosen the clamp and detach the shaft extension rod.
9 Carefully drive out the right-hand mounting bush retaining clip from the shaft then slide out the shaft until it fouls the heater box.
10 Detach the right-hand mounting bush from the pedal box by rotating it through 45° in either direction, then pulling it out. The accelerator shaft assembly can now be removed.

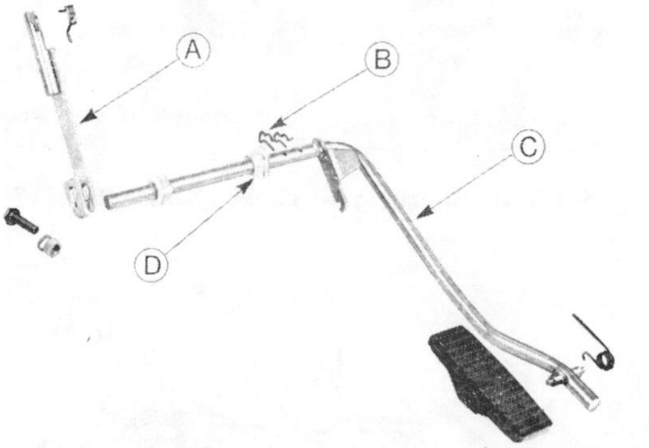

Fig. 3.51. Accelerator shaft assembly (lhd) (Sec. 21)

A Shaft extension rod
B Spring clip
C Accelerator shaft
D End mounting bush

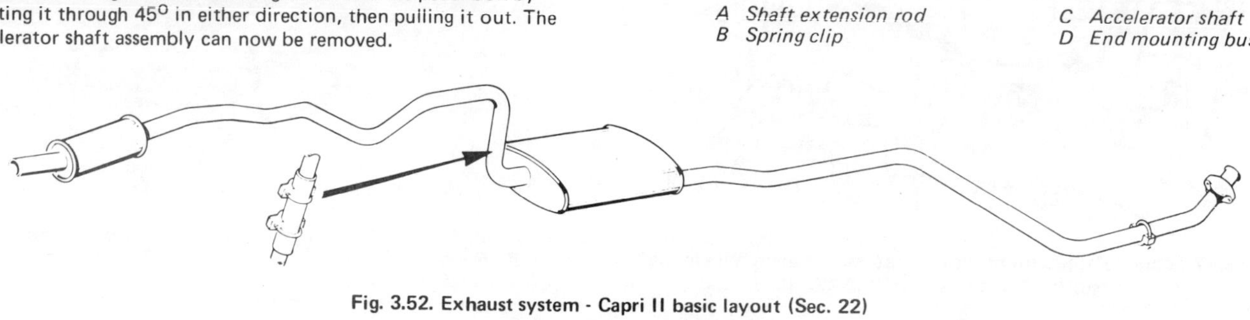

Fig. 3.52. Exhaust system - Capri II basic layout (Sec. 22)

All models

11 Detach the remaining bush and clip from the shaft.
12 To remove the pedal, prise the flange away from the spigot on the shaft, then remove the pedal and spring.
13 When refitting the pedal, locate the spring on the spigot shaft then clip the flanges onto the spigots and check that the pedal pivots correctly.
14 Refitting the pedal shaft is the reverse of the removal procedure, following which it will be necessary to adjust the cable, as described in Section 20. On r.h.d. variants check that the pedal has 0.24 to 0.55 in (6 to 14 mm) lift from the idle position; if necessary adjust the pedal lift-up stop to achieve this.

22 Exhaust system - general description

1 The exhaust system is a single piece type comprising a front pipe, front resonator and rear muffler.
2 The resonator and muffler are flexibly attached to the floor pan by two circular rubber mountings and one circular mounting respectively.
3 At regular intervals the system should be checked for corrosion, joint leakage, the condition and security of the flexible mountings and the tightness of the joints.

23 Exhaust system - replacement

Note: This Section describes the procedures for replacement of the complete one-piece exhaust system. If only the front resonator is to be replaced it is not necessary to remove the rear muffler. If only the rear muffler is to be replaced it is not necessary to remove the front resonator. However, if either of these parts is to be replaced individually, it is important to make the sawcut described in paragraph 5 in the position stated. Where a replacement muffler or resonator is being used on what was originally a one-piece exhaust system, a service sleeve and U-clamps will be required to connect the two parts of the system.

1 Disconnect the battery earth lead.
2 If possible, raise the car on a ramp or place it over an inspection pit. Alternatively jack up the car and support it to obtain the maximum amount of working room underneath.
3 Lift up the resonator and slide out the two mounting rubbers.
4 Disconnect the front pipe at the manifold, detach the sealing ring and lower the front section of the exhaust.
5 Cut through the exhaust with a hacksaw on the short vertical section to the rear of the resonator. If the complete exhaust is being replaced the position of the sawcut is not important. If the resonator only is being replaced the sawcut should be made 9.5 in (241 mm) from the rear face of the resonator for 1.6 litre models or 8.5 in (216 mm) for 1.6 litre GT and 2.0 litre models. If the muffler only is being replaced the sawcut should be made 9 in (229 mm) from the rear face of the resonator for the 1.6 litre models or 8 in (203 mm) for the 1.6 litre GT and 2.0 litre models. Ensure that the sawcut is at 90° to the pipe. Where a 2-piece exhaust system is fitted, separate the two parts by removing the U-clamps at the service sleeve behind the resonator.
6 Remove the single nut securing the rear muffler bracket clamp, swing the bracket clear of the exhaust and detach the rear section.
7 Detach the rear mounting rubber and bracket clamp.
8 Remove the front U-clamp and drift off the front pipe. Detach the resonator mounting and the tail trim pipe (where fitted).
9 When fitting the new system parts, measure back from the resonator outlet pipe end and/or the muffler inlet pipe end, 1.8 in (45 mm) and scribe a line.
10 Assemble the front pipe to the resonator pipe and loosely fit the U-clamp.
11 Position the resonator mounting bracket to the body and refit the mounting rubbers.
12 Position the muffler mounting bracket to the body and refit the mounting rubber.
13 Position the resonator and front pipe assembly. Loosely secure the bracket and manifold connection.
14 Slide the service sleeve onto the resonator pipe up to the scribed line (paragraph 9).

Fig. 3.53. Position of the sawcut when renewing the resonator (Sec. 23)

Dimension A = 8.5 in (216 mm) or 9.5 in (241 mm) - see text

Fig. 3.54. Position of the sawcut when renewing the muffler (Sec. 23)

Dimension B = 8.0 in (203 mm) or 9.0 in (229 mm) - see text

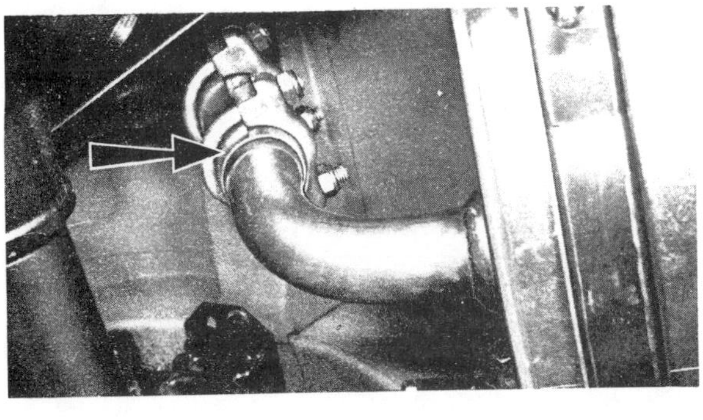

Fig. 3.55. Service sleeve and U-clamps in position (Sec. 23)

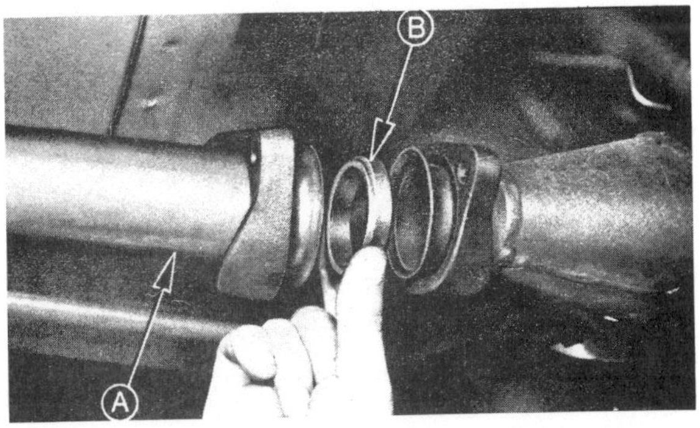

Fig. 3.56. Fitting the manifold connection - typical (Sec. 23)

A Exhaust front pipe *B Sealing ring*

15 Position the muffler pipe into the sleeve up to the scribed mark, and loosely secure it to the rear mounting bracket. Ensure that the angled end of the clamp is at the top.
16 Align the exhaust system ensuring that there is a minimum clearance of 1 in (25 mm) between any part of the system and the body or body components. Tighten the manifold connection to the specified torque. Tighten the resonator mounting bracket until there is a thread protrusion of 0.5 in (13 mm).
17 Fit the service sleeve U-clamps and tighten them. Where applicable fit the tailpipe trim.
18 Reconnect the battery, run the engine and check for exhaust leaks.
19 Lower the car to the ground.

Part B: Mercury Capri II

24 Thermostatic air cleaner and duct system - general description

1 The air cleaner on Mercury Capri II models is mounted on studs projecting from the top of the carburettor air horn and is similar in style to the Capri II air cleaner described in Part A of this Chapter.
2 An additional feature is the control system for intake air to ensure that fuel atomisation within the carburetor takes place using air at the correct temperature. This is effected by a duct system which draws in fresh air, or pre-heated air from a heat shroud around the engine exhaust manifold. The component parts of a typical system are shown in Fig. 3.57.
3 Operation of the system can be summarized as follows:

When the engine is cold, heated air is directed from the exhaust manifold into the air cleaner, but as the engine warms up cold air is progressively mixed with this warm air to maintain a carburettor air temperature of 105 to 130°F (40.5 to 76.8°C). At high ambient temperatures the hot air intake is closed off completely.

The mixing of air is regulated by a vacuum operated motor on the air cleaner inlet duct, which is controlled by a bi-metal temperature sensor and cold weather modulator valve. Operation of the system is best understood by referring to Fig. 3.59 which shows the routing of the intake air under different temperature conditions.

An additional feature on cars with catalytic converters or Cold Temperature Actuated Vacuum (CTAV) systems is an ambient temperature sensor mounted within the air cleaner. This switch is operated by ambient temperature changes and under certain conditions will override the cold weather modulator system. For further information see Section 44.

25 Thermostatic air cleaner - testing

Vacuum motor and valve assembly

1 Check that the valve is open when the engine is switched off. Start the engine, and check that the valve closes when idling (except where the engine is hot). If this fails to happen, check for disconnected or leaking vacuum lines, and for correct operation of the bi-metal sensor (see below).
2 If the valve closes, open and close the throttle rapidly. The valve should open at temperatures above 55°F (12.7°C) during the throttle operation. If this does not happen, check the valve for binding.

Bi-metal switch

3 The bi-metal switch can be checked by subjecting it to heated air, either from the engine or from an external source (eg; a hair dryer). **Do not immerse it in water or damage may occur.**

Cold weather modulator valve

4 Without the use of a supply of refrigerant R-12 and a vacuum source, testing is impractical. If the modulator valve is suspected of being faulty it should be tested by your Ford dealer.

26 Air cleaner and element - removal and refitting

Note: It is not recommended that the air cleaner element is removed unless the air cleaner has been removed from the carburettor. This is to prevent dirt entering the carburettor.
1 Disconnect the vacuum hoses from the vacuum motor and intake manifold (or T-connection).
2 Detach the air intake ducts.
3 Remove the wing nuts attaching the air cleaner body to the carburetor air horn studs.
4 Where applicable, detach the catalyst switch connectors and any remaining vacuum hoses, noting where they were fitted, and remove the air cleaner.
5 Remove the air cleaner top cover, and take out the element.
6 Refitting is the reverse of the removal procedures, using new gaskets as applicable.

27 Fuel pump

1 The fuel pump used on Mercury Capri II engines is similar in design to that used on Capri II engines, except that no internal filter is fitted and it is operated from the engine auxiliary shaft through an actuating lever on the pump rather than a pushrod.
2 With the above differences in mind, refer to Part A for fuel pump description, testing, removal and refitting. No other service procedures are applicable.

28 Fuel filter - renewal

1 Initially remove the carburettor air cleaner.
2 Loosen the fuel line clips at the filter, pull off the fuel lines and discard the clips.
3 Fit the replacement filter using new clips, start the engine and check for fuel leaks. **Note:** If the replacement filter shows the direction of fuel flow, take care that it is fitted the correct way round.
4 Refit the air cleaner.

29 Carburation - warning

1 Before making any adjustment or alteration to the carburettor or emission control systems (see Part C of this Chapter), the owner is advised to make himself aware of any Federal, State or Provincial laws which may be contravened by making any such adjustment or alteration.
2 Setting dimensions and specifications are given in this Chapter where relevant to adjustment procedures. Where these differ from those given on the engine tune-up decal, the decal information should be assumed to be correct.
3 Where the use of special test equipment is called-up (eg; exhaust gas CO analyzer, engine tachometer, etc.), and this equipment is not available, any setting or calibration should be regarded as a temporary measure only and should be rechecked by a suitably equipped Ford dealer or carburation/emission control specialist at the earliest opportunity.
4 Before attempting any carburettor adjustments, first ascertain that the following items are serviceable or correctly set:

a) All vacuum hoses and connections.
b) Ignition system.
c) Spark plugs.
d) Ignition initial advance.

5 If satisfactory adjustment cannot be obtained check the following points:

a) Carburettor fuel level.
b) Crankcase ventilation system.
c) Valve clearance.
d) Engine compression.
e) Idle mixture.

30 Motorcraft model 5200 carburettor - general description

The component parts of this carburettor are shown in Fig. 3.68. It will be seen that it is of the dual barrel, vertical downdraught design, incorporating an automatic strangler-type water heated, electrically assisted choke. The float chamber is internally vented.

The carburettor body comprises two castings which form the upper and lower bodies. The upper incorporates the float chamber cover, float pivot brackets, fuel inlet union, gauze filter, spring loaded needle valve, twin air intakes, choke plates and the section of the power valve

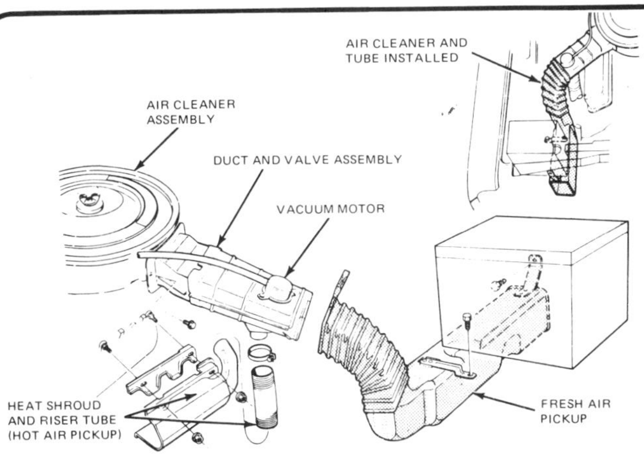

Fig. 3.57. Air cleaner and duct system - typical (Sec. 24)

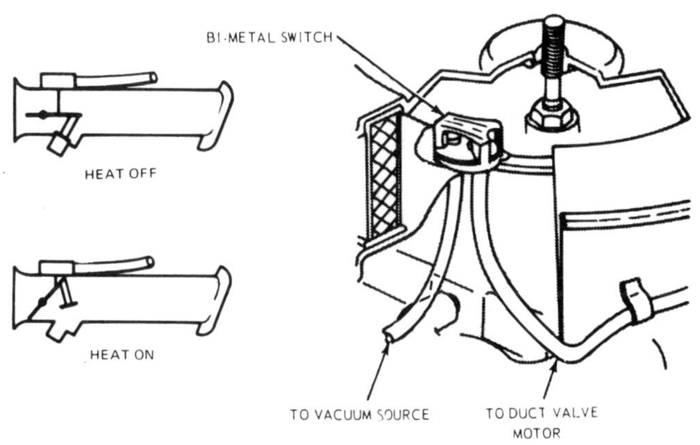

Fig. 3.58. Operation of the duct and valve assembly (Sec. 24)

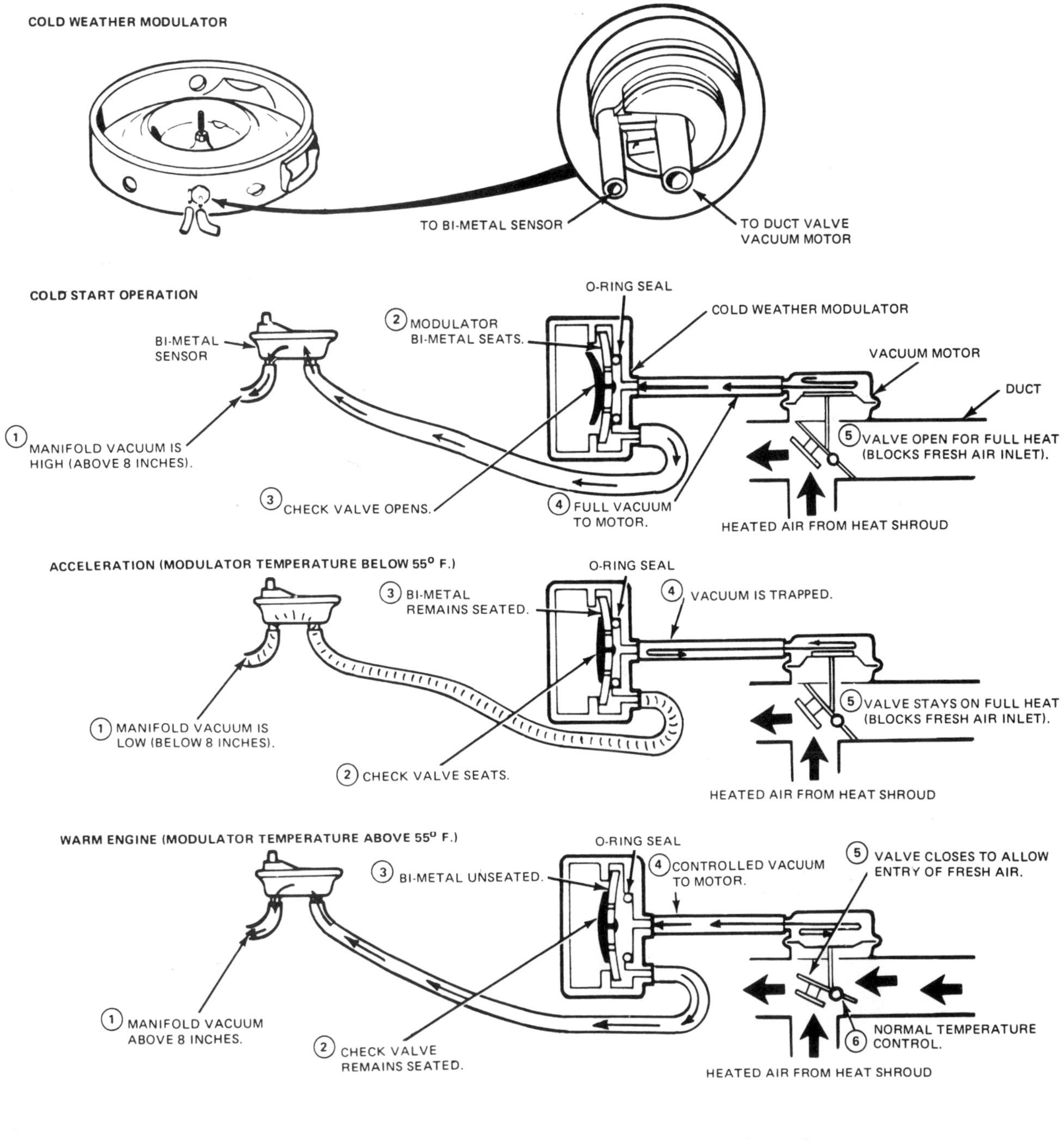

Fig. 3.59. Thermostatic air cleaner - cold weather modulator system (Sec. 24)

controlled by vacuum.

Incorporated in the lower body is the float chamber, accelerator pump, two throttle barrels and integral main venturis, throttle plates, spindles, levers, jets and the enrichment valve.

The throttle plate opening is in a preset sequence so that the primary starts to open first and is then followed by the secondary in such a manner that both plates reach full throttle position at the same time.

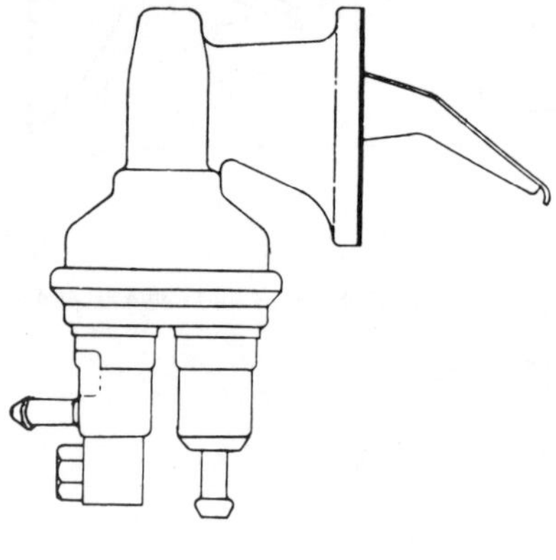

Fig. 3.60. Fuel pump (Sec. 27)

The primary barrel, throttle plate and venturi size is identical in both the primary and secondary barrels.

All the carburation systems are located in the lower body and the main progression systems operate in both barrels, whilst the idling and the power valve systems operate in the primary barrel only and the full load enrichment system in the secondary barrel.

The accelerator pump discharges fuel into the primary barrel.

A connection for the vacuum required to control the distributor advance/retard vacuum unit is located on the lower body.

A solenoid throttle positioner (TSP) assembly is incorporated on certain versions to prevent dieseling (running-on) after the ignition has been switched off, by allowing the throttle plates to close beyond the point required for idling.

31 Motorcraft model 5200 carburettor - curb idle, TSP-off and fast idle speed adjustments

Note: Read Section 30 before commencing.

1 Remove the air cleaner and plug all vacuum lines at the vacuum source end.

2 Apply the parking brake and block the roadwheels.

3 Check, and adjust if necessary, the choke and throttle linkage for freedom of movement.

4 Connect an engine speed tachometer (where available) in accordance with the maker's instructions.

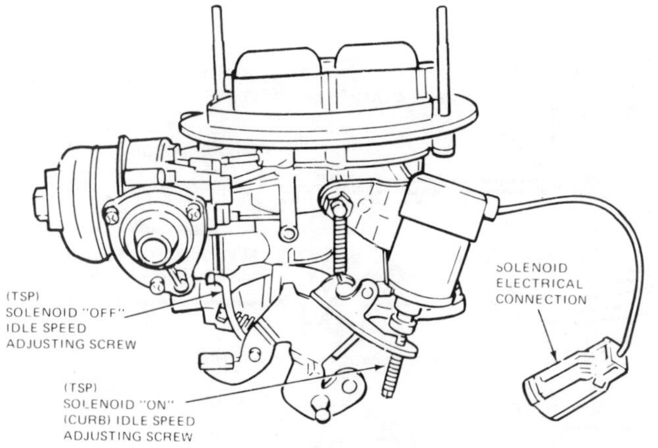

Fig. 3.61. Motorcraft model 5200 (with solenoid throttle positioner) idle speed adjustment points (Sec. 31)

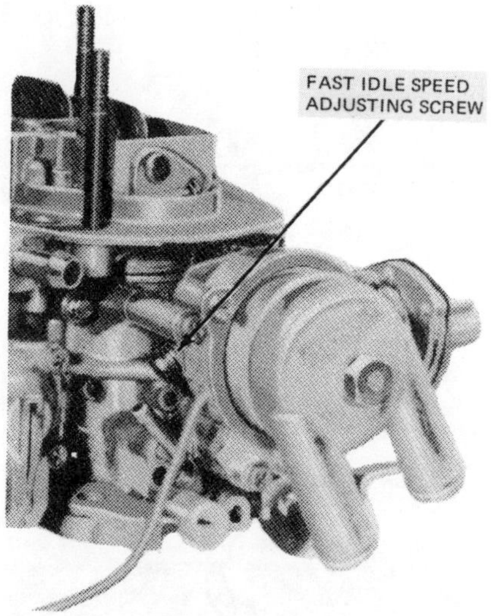

Fig. 3.62. Fast idle adjustment screw - Motorcraft 5200 (Sec. 31)

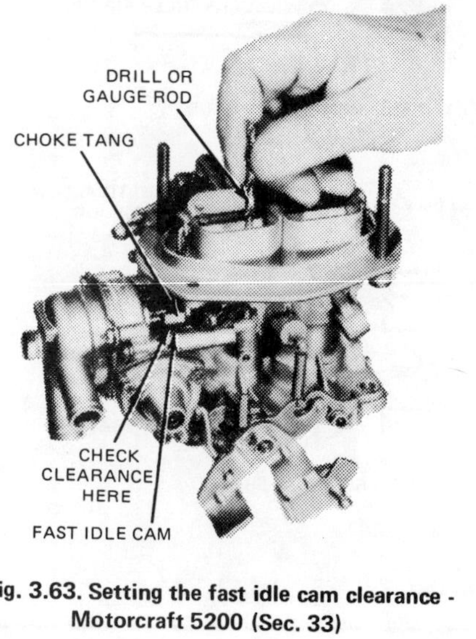

Fig. 3.63. Setting the fast idle cam clearance - Motorcraft 5200 (Sec. 33)

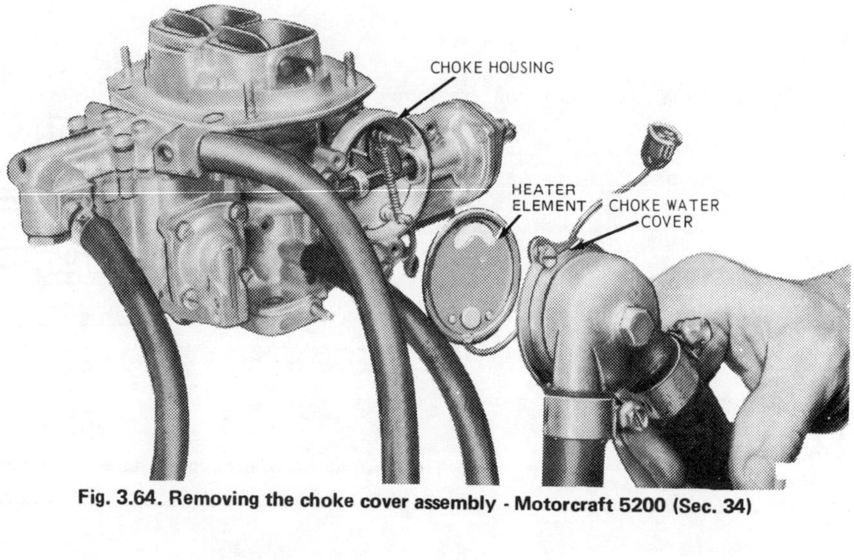

Fig. 3.64. Removing the choke cover assembly - Motorcraft 5200 (Sec. 34)

5 Start the engine and run it up to normal operating temperature.
6 Disconnect the EGR vacuum line at the valve, and plug the line.
7 Where applicable, set the Air-Conditioning to Off.
8 Where applicable, remove the spark delay valve and route the primary advance vacuum signal directly to the distributor vacuum diaphragm unit (advance side).
9 Set the automatic transmission to Park or manual transmission to Neutral, then run the engine at normal operating temperature. Check that the choke plates are closed then set the throttle so that the fast idle adjustment screw contacts the kick-down step of the choke cam; adjust the fast idle adjusting screw to obtain the specified rpm.
10 Set the throttle to the high step of the choke cam and allow the engine to run for 5 seconds (approximately).
11 Rotate the choke cam until the fast idle adjustment screw contacts the choke cam kick-down step. Allow the engine speed to stabilize then recheck the fast idle rpm, as described in paragraphs 9 and 10; readjust if necessary then repeat the procedure given in the first sentence of this paragraph to ensure repeatability.
12 Allow the engine to return to the normal idle, then for automatic transmission models select Drive.
13 Where no TSP assembly is fitted, adjust the curb idle screw in or out to obtain the specified curb idle speed then proceed to paragraph 16.
14 Where a TSP assembly is fitted, adjust the curb idle screw which contacts the solenoid plunger to obtain the specified curb idle speed (the solenoid is energized and the plunger extended when the ignition is On).
15 Now collapse the solenoid plunger by forcing the throttle linkage against the plunger, grasping the throttle lever and solenoid housing between the thumb and index finger to alleviate movement of the solenoid assembly position.
16 Adjust the TSP-off adjusting screw to obtain the specified TSP-off idle speed.
17 Open the throttle slightly to allow the solenoid plunger to extend.
18 Provided that all adjustments are now satisfactory, stop the engine then install the air cleaner and its associated vacuum lines. If the adjustments are not satisfactory, refer to paragraph 5 in Section 29.
19 Restart the engine and if necessary run it up to normal operating temperature. With the engine running at 2000 rpm (approximately) select Park (automatic transmission/or Neutral (manual transmission). Allow 5 seconds (approximately) for the speed to stabilize then let the engine return to idle; set automatic transmission models to Drive. Recheck the curb idle speed, and if necessary readjust as described in paragraph 13 onwards.
20 Refit all vacuum lines and disconnect the tachometer (if used).

32 Motorcraft model 5200 carburettor - idle mixture adjustment

Note: Idle mixture adjustment can only be satisfactorily carried out by the artificial enrichment method using special test equipment. The procedure given in this Section allows approximate settings to be obtained should this be necessary (e.g. after carburettor overhaul). Read Section 29 before commencing.
1 Obtain the best possible idle speed using the method given in Section 31. If the idle speed is unsteady, it should be increased sufficiently for the engine to continue running.
2 Rotate the idle mixture screws within the range of the limiting caps to obtain the most satisfactory idle speed. Where the idle mixture is too rich, indicated by a 'sooty' exhaust smoke and the engine 'hunting' (slowing down and running 'lumpily'), rotate the screws clockwise. Where the idle mixture is too lean, indicated by the engine speed tending to increase and then decrease, and possibly a 'hollow' exhaust note, rotate the screws counter-clockwise.
3 Reset the idle speed as soon as the mixture is satisfactorily set, following the procedure given in Section 31.
4 If the idle mixture cannot be set satisfactorily within the range of the limiting caps, pull off the caps and adjust the mixture screws but refit the caps afterwards. In caseit is not possible to obtain a satisfactory setting, rotate each screw in turn, counting the exact number of turns to just seat it, then back off the same number of turns. This will give a datum point from which adjustment can commence. Both screws can be expected to be the same number of turns from the seat when correctly set, after which the limiting cap must be refitted.
5 On completion of *any* idle mixture adjustment, ensure that the setting is checked by a Ford dealer or carburettor/emission control specialist at the earliest opportunity.

33 Motorcraft model 5200 carburettor - fast idle cam clearance

1 Remove the air cleaner if the carburettor is installed on the engine.
2 Insert the unmarked shank of a twist drill 0.1 in (2.5 mm) diameter between the lower edge of the choke plate and the air horn wall. **Note:** No. 38 drill is 0.1015 in; No. 39 drill is 0.0995 in.
3 With the fast idle screw held on the bottom step of the fast idle cam, against the top step, the choke lever tang and the fast idle cam arm should *just* be in contact. Bend the choke lever tang up or down as necessary.

34 Motorcraft model 5200 carburettor - choke plate vacuum pull down

1 Remove the air cleaner if the carburettor is installed on the engine.
2 Remove the three screws and the ring retaining the choke thermostatic spring cover. Do not remove the screw retaining the water cover.
3 Pull the cover assembly away and remove the electric assist assembly.
4 Set the fast idle cam on the top step then use a screwdriver to push the diaphragm stem back against its stop.
5 Insert the unmarked shank of a twist drill 0.20 in (5 mm) between the lower edge of the choke plate and the air horn wall. **Note:** No. 7 drill is 0.201 in; No. 8 drill is 0.199 in.
6 Adjust the choke plate-to-air horn wall clearance by turning the vacuum diaphragm adjusting screw, as necessary, with a hexagonal wrench.

35 Motorcraft model 5200 carburettor - dry float setting

1 The dry float setting can only be checked at the appropriate stage of carburettor disassembly.
2 With the bowl cover inverted, and the float tang resting lightly on the spring loaded fuel inlet needle, measure the clearance between the edge of the float and the bowl cover using the unmarked shank of a twist drill of 0.44/0.48 in (11.2/12.2 mm) diameter. **Note:** 7/16 in (0.4375 in) drill plus feeler gauges can be used.
3 To adjust the clearance, bend the float tang as necessary so that both floats are equally adjusted. Do not scratch or otherwise damage the float tang.

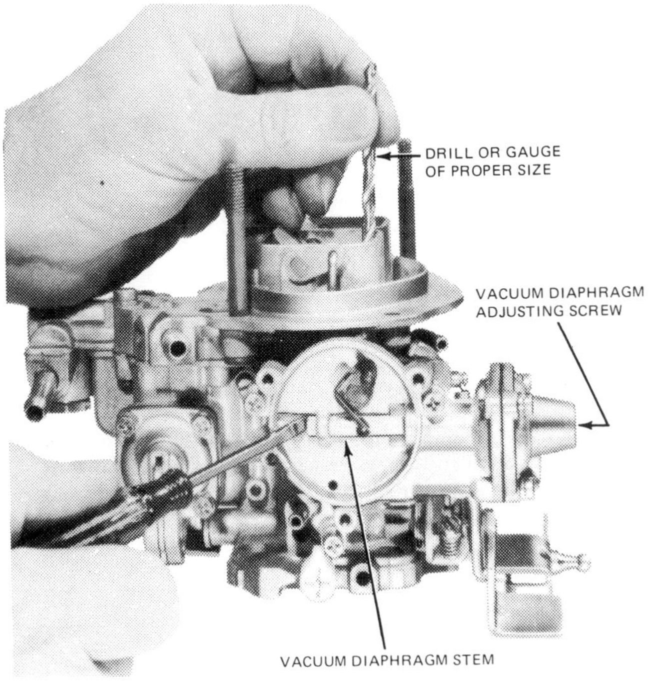

Fig. 3.65. Checking the choke plate pull down - Motorcraft 5200 (Sec. 34)

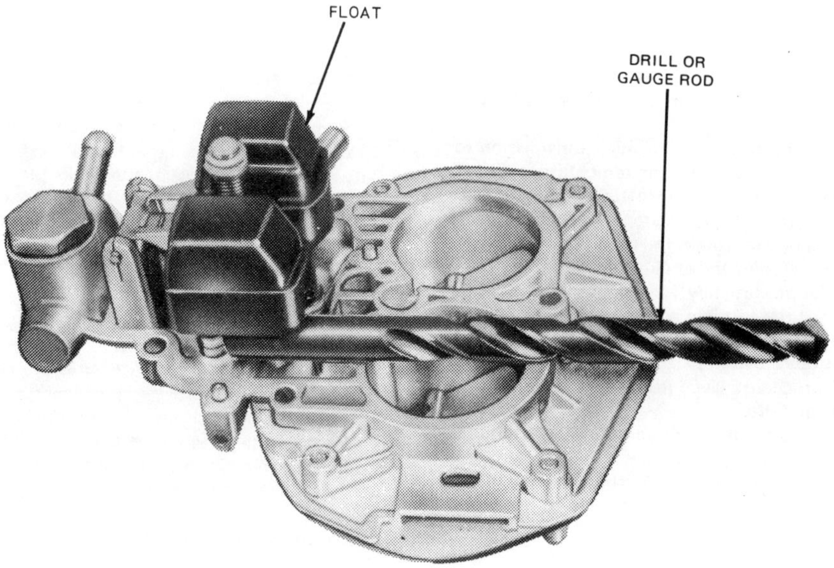

Fig. 3.66. Dry float setting - Motorcraft 5200 (Sec. 35)

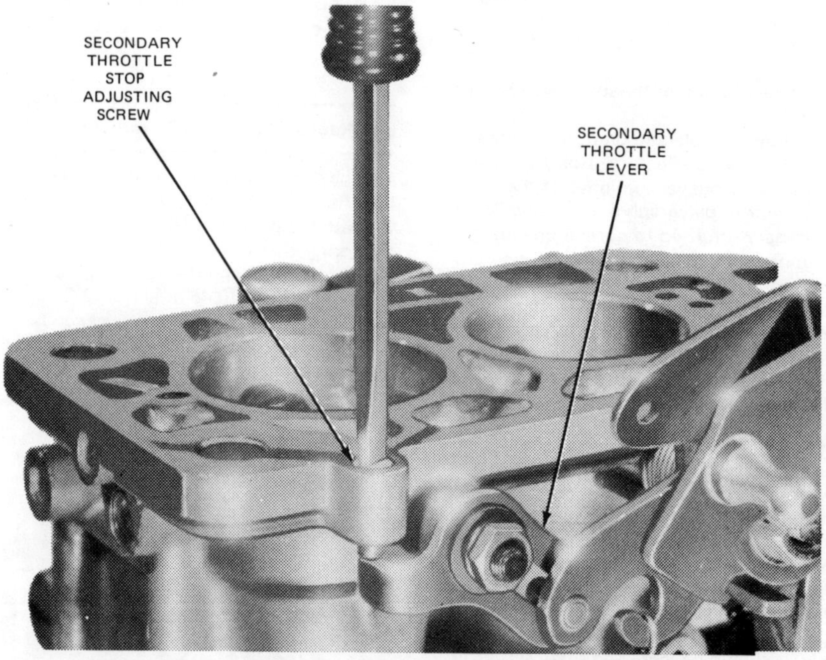

Fig. 3.67. Secondary throttle stop screw adjustment - Motorcraft 5200

36 Motorcraft model 5200 carburettor - secondary throttle stop screw

1 The secondary throttle stop screw can only be set at the appropriate stage of carburettor disassembly.
2 Back off the screw until the secondary throttle plate seats in its bore.
3 Turn the screw until it touches the tab on the secondary throttle lever, then turn it an additional ¼ turn.

37 Motorcraft model 5200 carburettor - removal and refitting

1 Remove the air cleaner as described in Section 26.
2 Disconnect the fuel feed line from the carburettor.
3 Disconnect the electrical leads and vacuum lines from the carburettor.
4 Disconnect the throttle cable/kick-down cable from the carburettor. For further information see Section 41.
5 Partially drain the cooling system and disconnect the water hoses from the choke housing (refer to Chapter 2, if necessary).
6 Using suitably cranked ring/socket wrenches, remove the carburettor mounting nuts. Lift off the carburettor and gasket.
7 Refitting the carburettor is basically the reverse of the removal procedure, but ensure that a new flange gasket is used.

38 Motorcraft model 5200 carburettor - dismantling and reassembly

1 Before dismantling wash the exterior of the carburettor and wipe dry using a non-fluffy rag. Select a clean area of the workbench and lay several layers of newspaper on the top. Obtain several small containers for putting some of the small parts in, which could be easily lost. Whenever a part is to be removed look at it first so that it may be refitted in its original position. As each part is removed place it in order along one edge of the newspaper so that by using this method reassembly

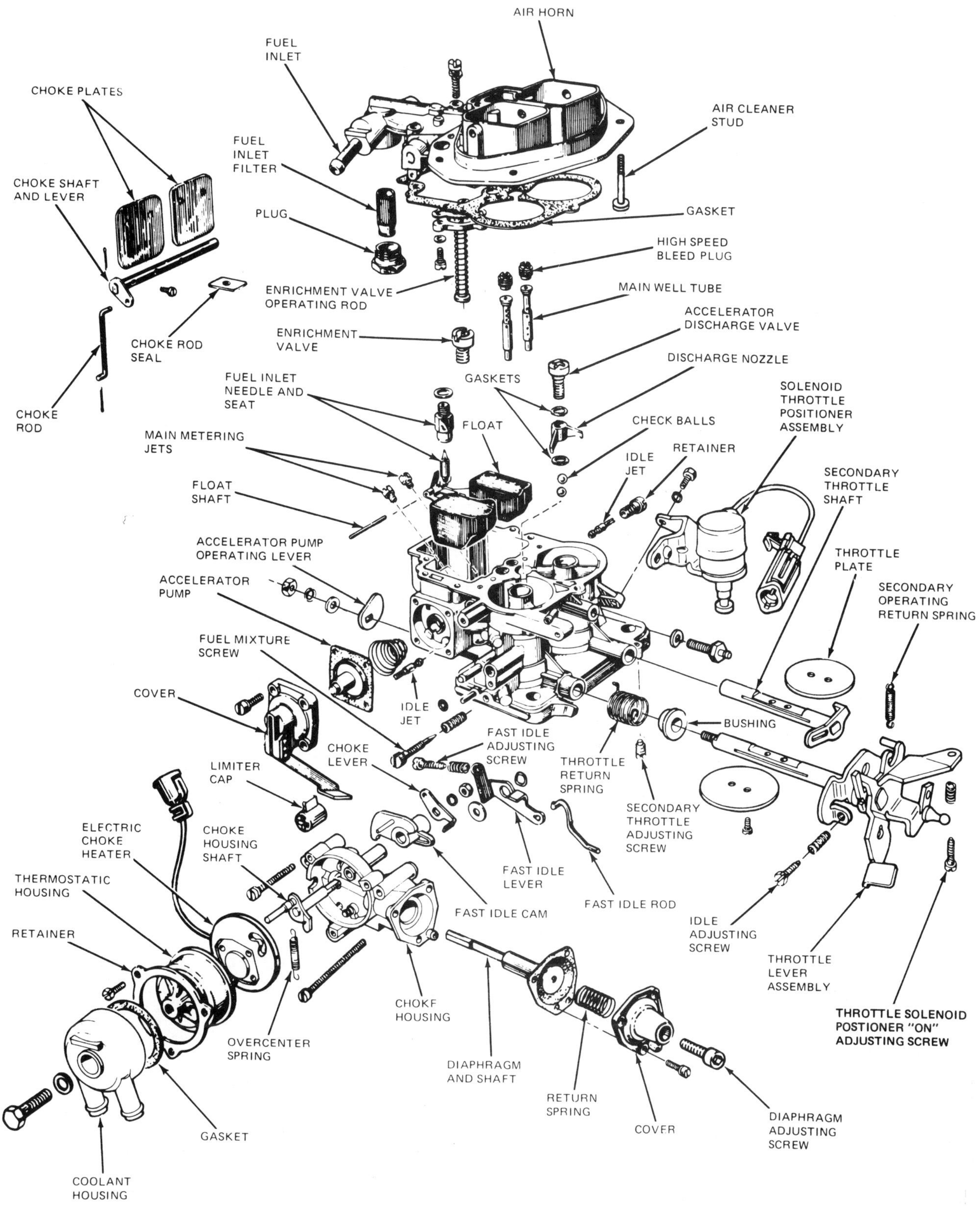
AIR HORN
FUEL INLET
CHOKE PLATES
AIR CLEANER STUD
FUEL INLET FILTER
CHOKE SHAFT AND LEVER
PLUG
GASKET
HIGH SPEED BLEED PLUG
ENRICHMENT VALVE OPERATING ROD
MAIN WELL TUBE
CHOKE ROD SEAL
ENRICHMENT VALVE
ACCELERATOR DISCHARGE VALVE
DISCHARGE NOZZLE
FUEL INLET NEEDLE AND SEAT
GASKETS
SOLENOID THROTTLE POSITIONER ASSEMBLY
CHOKE ROD
FLOAT
CHECK BALLS
MAIN METERING JETS
IDLE JET
RETAINER
SECONDARY THROTTLE SHAFT
FLOAT SHAFT
ACCELERATOR PUMP OPERATING LEVER
THROTTLE PLATE
ACCELERATOR PUMP
SECONDARY OPERATING RETURN SPRING
FUEL MIXTURE SCREW
COVER
IDLE JET
BUSHING
FAST IDLE ADJUSTING SCREW
CHOKE LEVER
LIMITER CAP
THROTTLE RETURN SPRING
SECONDARY THROTTLE ADJUSTING SCREW
ELECTRIC CHOKE HEATER
CHOKE HOUSING SHAFT
FAST IDLE LEVER
THERMOSTATIC HOUSING
FAST IDLE ROD
FAST IDLE CAM
IDLE ADJUSTING SCREW
RETAINER
THROTTLE LEVER ASSEMBLY
CHOKE HOUSING
THROTTLE SOLENOID POSTIONER "ON" ADJUSTING SCREW
OVERCENTER SPRING
DIAPHRAGM AND SHAFT
RETURN SPRING
COVER
DIAPHRAGM ADJUSTING SCREW
GASKET
COOLANT HOUSING

Fig. 3.68. Exploded view of the model 5200 carburettor (Secs. 30 and 38)

is made easier.

Carburettor bowl cover

2 Unscrew and remove the fuel filter retainer from the upper body. Recover the filter.

3 Disconnect the choke plate operating rod at its upper end.

4 Undo and remove the screws and spring washers that retain the upper body to the lower body. Lift away the upper body and the gasket.

5 Carefully extract the float pivot pin and lift out the float assembly followed by the needle valve.

6 Unscrew the needle valve seat and remove the gasket.

7 Remove the three enrichment valve vacuum diaphragm screws. Remove the washers and diaphragm.

Automatic choke

8 Remove the single screw and washer from the choke housing. Remove the cover and gasket.

9 Remove the thermostatic spring housing retaining ring screws. Remove the retaining ring, housing and electric choke heater.

10 Remove the choke housing assembly screws; note the long screw on the long leg of the assembly. Move the housing away from the main body, disengaging the fast idle rod. Remove the O-ring from the vacuum port.

11 Remove the choke shaft nut, lockwasher, lever and fast idle cam.

12 Remove the fast idle lever retaining screw, the fast idle lever and the spacer. Take off the screw and spring from the lever.

13 Remove the choke diaphragm cover screws. Remove the cover, spring and diaphragm/shaft.

Accelerator pump

14 Remove the four pump cover screws and the pump cover. Remove the pump diaphragm and spring.

15 Remove the pump discharge screw assembly, the discharge nozzle and the two gaskets. Remove the two discharge check balls.

Main body

16 Remove the primary high speed bleed plug and the main well tube.

17 Remove the secondary high speed bleed plug and the main well tube. Note the size of the primary and secondary plugs and tubes to ensure correct assembly.

18 Remove the primary and secondary main jets, noting their sizes to ensure correct assembly.

19 Remove the enrichment valve and gasket.

20 From the side of the carburettor body, remove the idle jet retainers and idle jets.

21 Turn the idle limiter cap counter-clockwise to the rich stop. Remove the cap then count the exact number of turns to *just* seat the idle mixture needle. Remove the needle and spring.

22 Detach the secondary operating lever return spring.

23 Remove the primary throttle lever nut and locking tab. Remove the lever and flat washer followed by the secondary lever assembly and lever bushing.

24 Remove the idle adjustment lever spring and shaft washer. Note how the primary throttle return spring is hooked over the idle adjustment lever and the carburettor body.

25 Remove the idle speed screw and spring from the idle adjustment lever.

26 Remove the secondary throttle lever nut, lockwasher, flat washer and the lever itself.

27 Remove the secondary idle adjustment screw.

28 Remove the solenoid throttle positioner (TSP) from the carburettor body if considered necessary.

29 Dismantling is now complete and all parts should be thoroughly washed and cleaned in gasoline. Remove any sediment in the float chamber and drillings but take care not to scratch the fine drillings whilst doing so. Remove all traces of old gaskets using a sharp knife. When all parts are clean reassembly can begin.

30 Reassembly of the carburettor is essentially the reverse of the removal procedure, but careful attention should be paid to the following points:

Motorcraft 5200

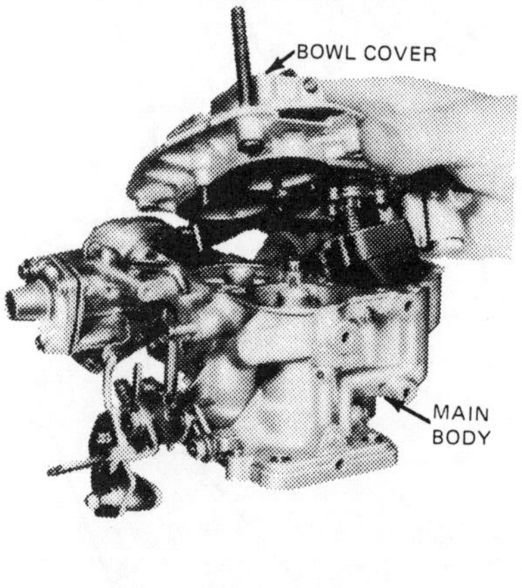

Fig. 3.69. Removing the bowl cover (air horn) (Sec. 38)

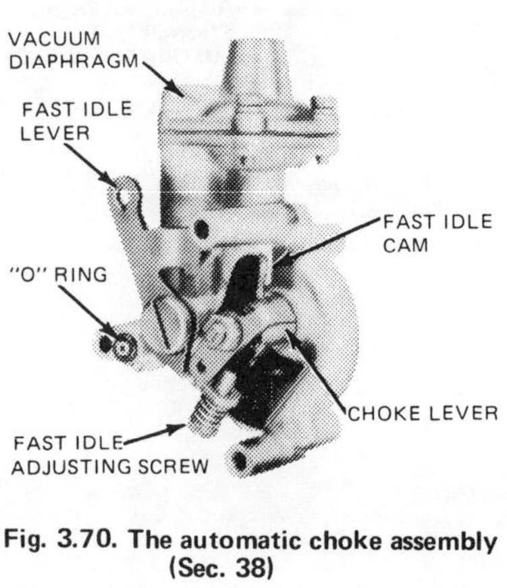

Fig. 3.70. The automatic choke assembly (Sec. 38)

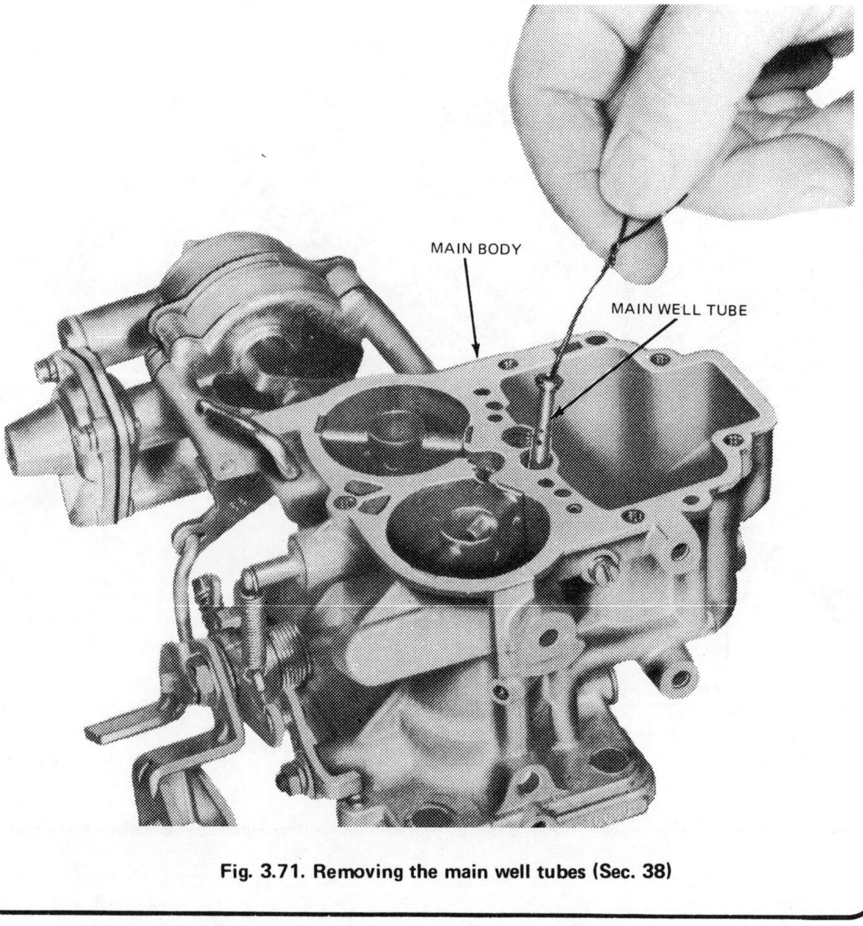

Fig. 3.71. Removing the main well tubes (Sec. 38)

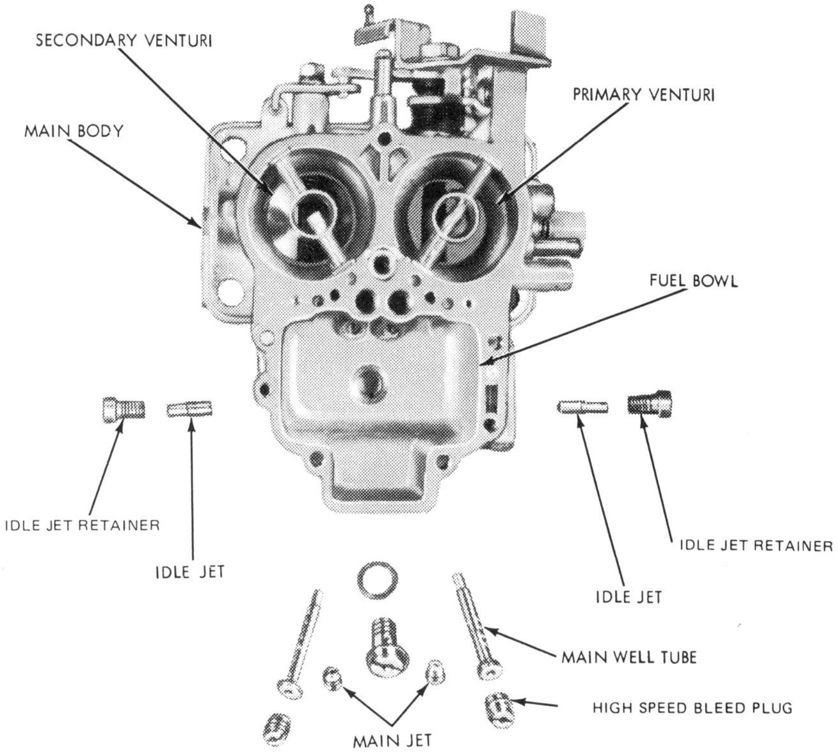

Fig. 3.72. Removing the main metering jets and idle jets - Motorcraft 5200 (Sec. 38)

a) Main body: Ensure that the idle mixture screws are refitted in exactly the same position as determined at paragraph 21 then install a new limiter cap with the stop tab against the rich side of the stop on the carburettor body. Now ensure that the main jets, primary and secondary main well tubes, and high speed bleeds are correctly fitted in their respective positions.

b) Accelerator pump: When refitting the return spring and pump diaphragm assembly, start the four cover screws then hold the pump lever partly open to align the gasket; then tighten the screws.

c) Automatic choke: When installing the diaphragm adjusting screw, initially adjust it so that the threads are flush with the inside of the cover. Fit the fast idle rod with the end which has one tab in the fast idle adjustment lever, and the end which has two tabs in the primary throttle lever. Adjust the choke plate pull down as described in Section 34. Before installing the electric choke heater ensure that the choke plate is either fully open or fully closed.

d) Bowl cover: When refitting the enrichment valve vacuum diaphragm, depress the spring and fit the screws and washers finger-tight. Hold the stem so that the diaphragm is horizontal then tighten the screws evenly. Adjust the dry float setting as described in Section 35.

39 Fuel tank - removal and refitting

1 Refer to the procedure given in Part A but note that on some models a fuel return line may additionally be fitted.

40 Fuel tank - cleaning and repair

1 Refer to the procedure given in Part A.

41 Accelerator and kick-down cable - removal, refitting and adjustment

1 Refer to the procedure given in Part A.

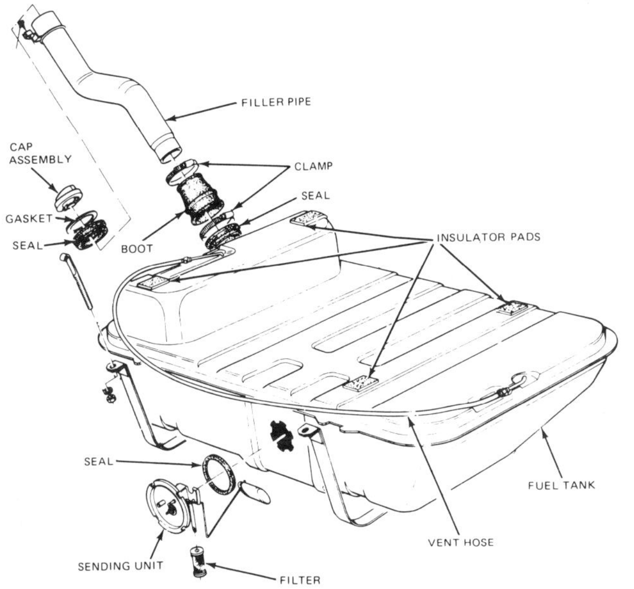

Fig. 3.73. Fuel tank - Mercury Capri II (Sec. 39)

42 Accelerator pedal and pedal shaft - removal and refitting

1 Refer to the procedure given in Part A.

43 Exhaust system - general

1 For details of the basic exhaust system which is similar to that used on 2.0 litre Capri II cars, refer to Part A.

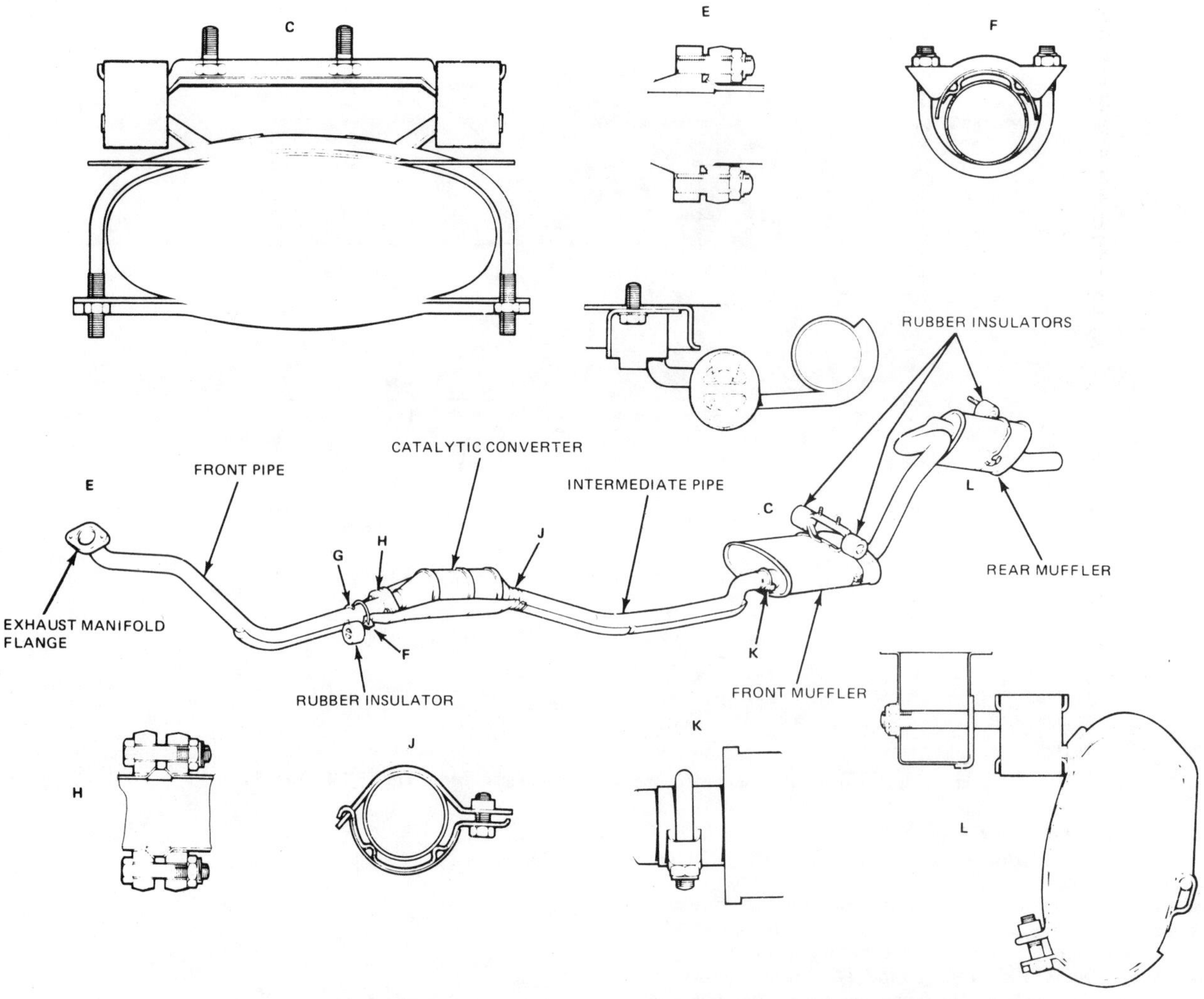

Fig. 3.74. Layout of the exhaust system where a catalytic converter is incorporated (Sec. 43)

Catalytic converter

2 Cars manufactured for California incorporate a catalytic converter in the exhaust system upstream of the front muffler (see Fig. 3.74).
3 Removal is straightforward. Remove the converter shield clamps, remove the shield, loosen the clamp at the front muffler then detach the converter at the flange joint.
4 Refitting is the reverse of the removal procedure but do not tighten the clamps until all joints have been loosely refitted. Check for leaks before refitting the converter shield.

Part C: Emission control

44 Emission control system - general description

Note: The information given in this Section is not generally applicable to Capri II models, although for some markets certain items may be relevant. It must also be appreciated that applicability for Mercury Capri II models will be dependent upon the operating territory.
1 In order to reduce the emission pollutants to a minimum, a comprehensive emission control system is incorporated on many vehicles. This system can be broken down into the following sub-systems:

Improved combustion (IMCO) system

2 The main features of this system are covered by the design of the engine and carburettor, and therefore require no special information. However, an electrically assisted choke heater is used as an aid to fast choke release for better emission characteristics during engine warm-up.
3 The heater is a constant temperature, positive temperature co-efficient (PTC) unit, energised from the alternator field (IND) terminal, and is energised when the engine is running.
4 Incorporated with the unit is a fast idle cam latch, which holds the cam on the high position until the choke heats up and the bi-metal latch backs off to allow the latch pin and fast idle cam to rotate to the normal run position.
5 An overcenter spring assists in closing the choke plate for initial starting of a cold engine in high ambient temperatures. This spring has no effect after initial choke pull-down occurs.

Positive crankcase ventilation (PCV) system

6 The PCV system operates by drawing in air and mixing it with the vapors which have escaped past the piston rings (blow-by vapors). This mixture is then drawn into the combustion chamber through an oil separator and PCV valve. An illustration of the system will be found in Chapter 1, Part B.

Evaporative emission control

7 This system is designed to limit the emission of fuel vapors to the atmosphere. It comprises the fuel tank, pressure and vacuum sensitive fuel filler cap, a restrictor bleed orifice, a charcoal canister and the associated connecting lines.
8 When the fuel tank is filled, vapors are discharged to atmosphere through the filler tube, and a space between the inner filler tube and the outer neck. When fuel covers the filler control tube, vapors can no longer escape and a vapor lock is created by the orifice; therefore there can be no flow to the vapor charcoal canister.

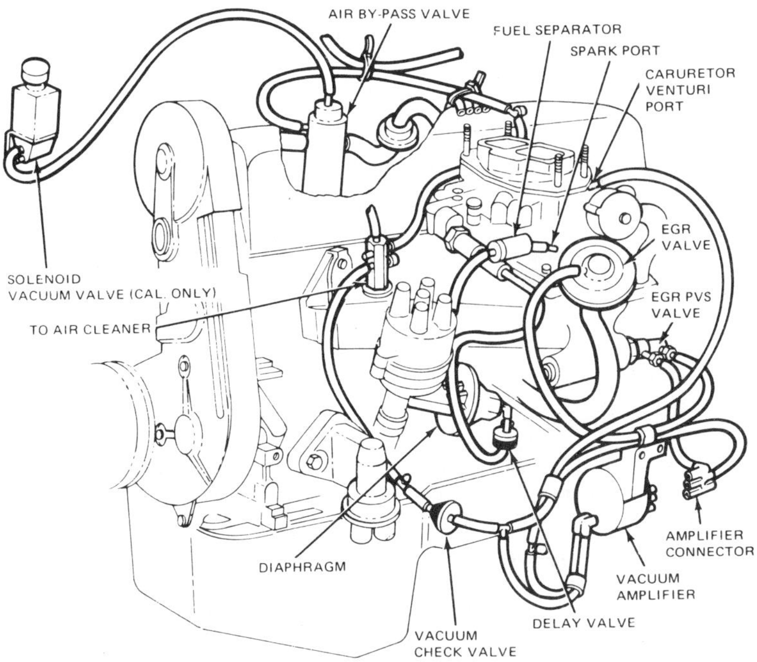

Fig. 3.75. Layout of the emission control system (Sec. 44)

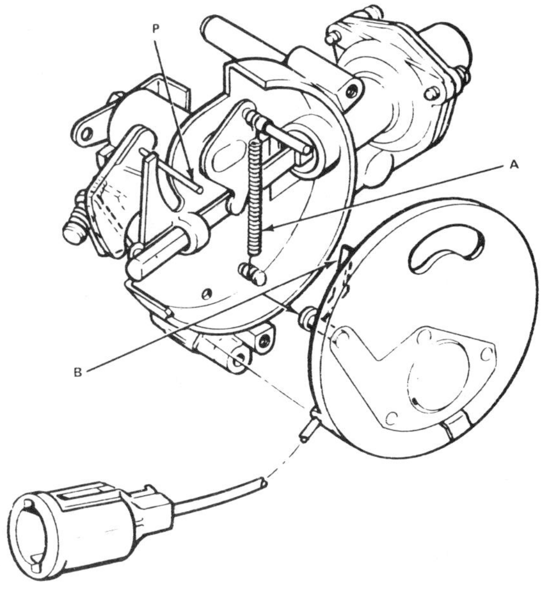

Fig. 3.76. Electrically assisted choke (Sec. 44)

A Overcenter spring *P Latch pin*
B Fast idle cam latch

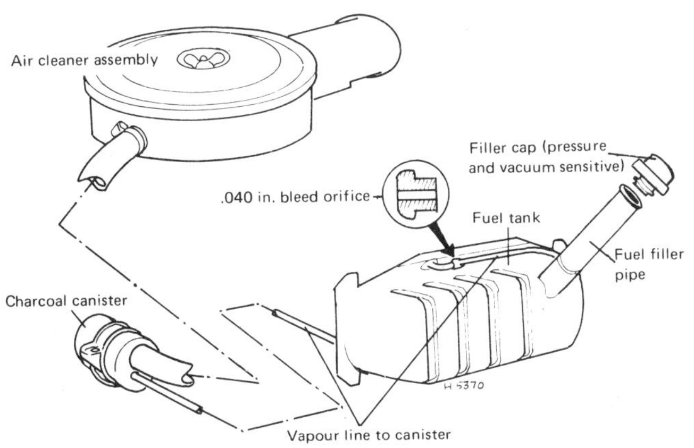

Fig. 3.77. Evaporative emission control system - typical (Sec. 44)

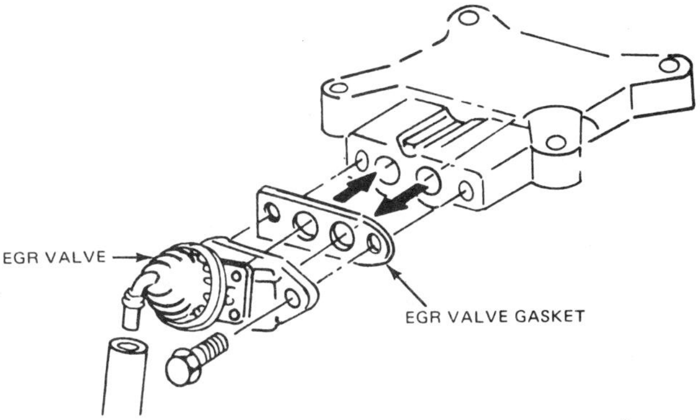

Fig. 3.78. Components of a typical EGRsystem (Sec. 44)

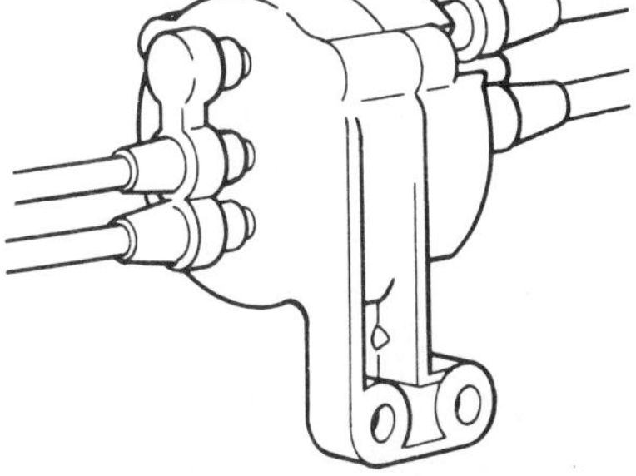

Fig. 3.79. The venturi vacuum amplifier (Sec. 44)

9 When thermal expansion occurs in the fuel tank, vapor is forced through the orifice to the canister, where it is stored when the engine is not running and is drawn into the carburettor intake system as soon as the engine is started.

Exhaust gas recirculation (EGR) system

10 This system is designed to reintroduce small amounts of exhaust gas into the combustion cycle to reduce the generation of oxides of nitrogen (NOx). The amount of gas reintroduced is governed by engine vacuum and temperature.

11 The EGR valve is mounted on a spacer block between the carburettor and manifold. A venturi vacuum amplifier (VVA) is used to change the relatively weak vacuum signal in the carburettor throat to a strong signal for operation of the EGR valve.

12 A relief valve is also used to modify the output EGR signal whenever venturi vacuum is equal to, or greater than, manifold vacuum. This allows the EGR valve to close at or near, wide open throttle, when maximum engine power is required.

13 The EGR/CSC (cold start cycle) regulates the distributor spark advance and EGR valve operation according to the engine coolant temperature, by sequentially switching the vacuum signals. When the coolant temperature is below 82°F (27.8°C), the EGR ported vacuum switch (PVS) admits carburettor EGR port vacuum (which occurs at approximately 2500 rpm) directly to the distributor advance diaphragm through the one-way check valve. At the same time the PVS

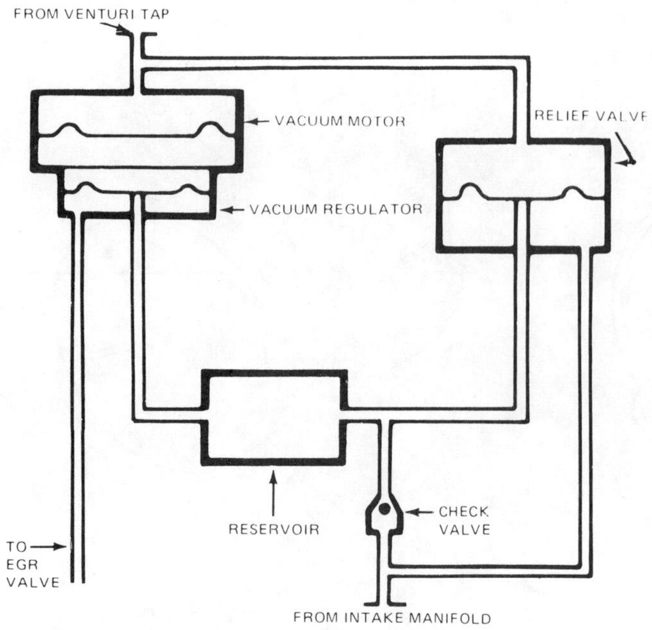

Fig. 3.80. Schematic diagram of a venturi vacuum amplifier (Sec. 44)

shuts off the carburettor vacuum to the EGR valve.

14 When the engine coolant is 95°F (35°C) or above, the EGR-PVS directs carburettor vacuum to the EGR valve.

15 At temperatures between 82 and 95°F (27.8 and 35°C), the EGR-PVS may be closed, open or in the mid-position.

16 A spark delay valve (SDV) is incorporated in the system to delay the carburettor spark vacuum to the distributor diaphragm unit for a predetermined time. During acceleration, little or no vacuum is admitted to the distributor diaphragm unit until acceleration is completed because of the time delay of the SDV and the re-routing of the EGR port vacuum at temperatures above 95°F (32°C). The check valve blocks the vacuum signal from the SDV to the EGR-PVS, so that carburettor spark vacuum will not be dissipated at temperature above 95°F.

17 The 235°F (113°C) PVS is not strictly part of the EGR system, but is connected to the distributor vacuum advance unit to prevent overheating while idling with a hot engine. At idle speeds, no vacuum is generated at either of the carburettor ports and the engine timing is fully retarded. However, when the coolant temperature reaches 235°F (113°C) the PVS is actuated to admit intake manifold vacuum to the distributor advance diaphragm. The engine timing is thus advanced, idling speed is correspondingly increased and the engine temperature is lowered due to increased fan speed and coolant flow.

Catalytic converter

18 On some models a catalytic converter is incorporated upstream of the exhaust front muffler (see Part B, Section 43). The converter comprises a ceramic honeycomb-like core housed in a stainless steel pipe. The core is coated with a platinum and palladium catalyst which converts unburned carbon monoxide and hydrocarbons into carbon

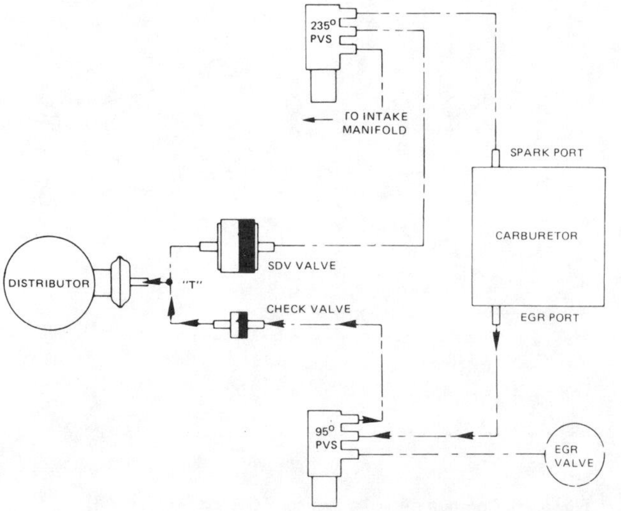

Fig. 3.81. EGR/CSC system operation below 82°F (Sec. 44)

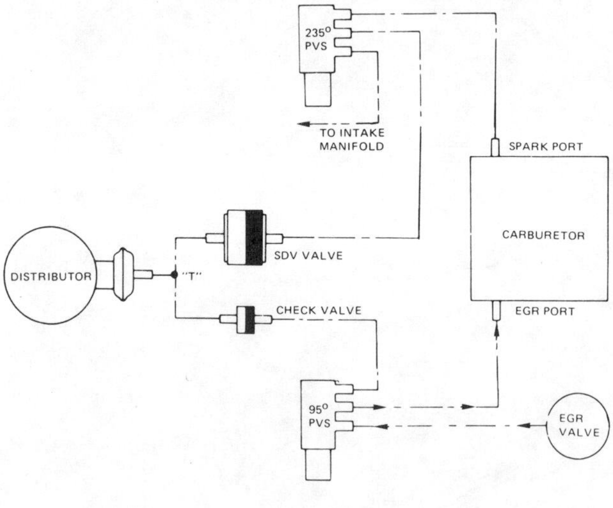

Fig. 3.82. EGR/CSC system operation above 95°F (Sec. 44)

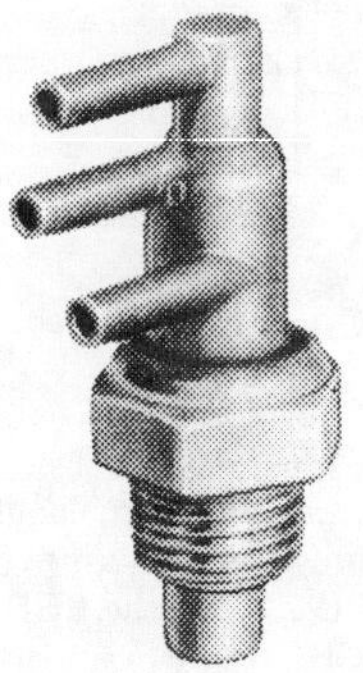

Fig. 3.83. Typical ported vacuum switch (PVS) (Sec. 44)

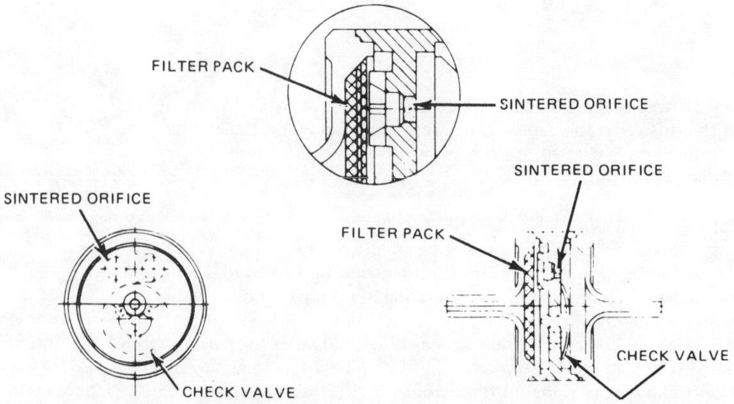

Fig. 3.84. Typical spark delay valve (SDV) (Sec. 44)

dioxide and water by a chemical reaction.
19 No special maintenance of the converter is required, but it can be damaged by the use of leaded fuels, engine misfiring, excessive richness of the carburettor mixture, incorrect operation of the Thermactor system or running out of gasoline.

Inlet air temperature regulation

20 Inlet air temperature regulation is accomplished by the use of a thermostatic air cleaner and duct system (see Part B, Section 24).
21 An additional feature, incorporated on some models, is the cold temperature actuated vacuum (CTAV) system. This is designed to select either carburettor spark port vacuum or carburettor EGR port vacuum, as a function of ambient air temperature. The selected vacuum source is used to control the distributor diaphragm unit.
22 The system comprises an ambient temperature switch, a three-way solenoid valve, an external vacuum bleed and a latching relay.
23 The temperature switch activates the solenoid, which is open at temperatures below 49°F (9.5°C) and is closed above 65°F (18.3°C). Within this temperature range the solenoid valve may be open or closed.
24 Below 49°F (9.5°C) the system is inoperative and the distributor diaphragm receives carburettor spark port vacuum while the EGR valve recieves EGR port vacuum.
25 When the temperature switch closes (above 65°F/18.3°C) the three way solenoid valve is energized from the ignition switch and the carburettor EGR port vacuum is delivered to the distributor advance diaphragm as well as to the EGR valve. The latching relay is also energized by the temperature switch closing, and will remain energized until the ignition switch is turned off, regardless of the temperature switch being open or closed.

Thermactor exhaust control system

26 This system is designed to reduce the hydrocarbon and carbon monoxide content of the exhaust gases by continuing the oxidation of unburnt gases after they leave the combustion chamber. This is achieved by using an engine driven air pump to inject fresh air into the hot exhaust stream after it leaves the combustion chamber. This air mixes with the hot exhaust gases and promotes further oxidation, thus reducing their concentration and converting some of them into carbon dioxide and water.
27 The air pump draws in air through an impeller type, centrifugal fan and exhausts it from the exhaust manifold through a vacuum controlled

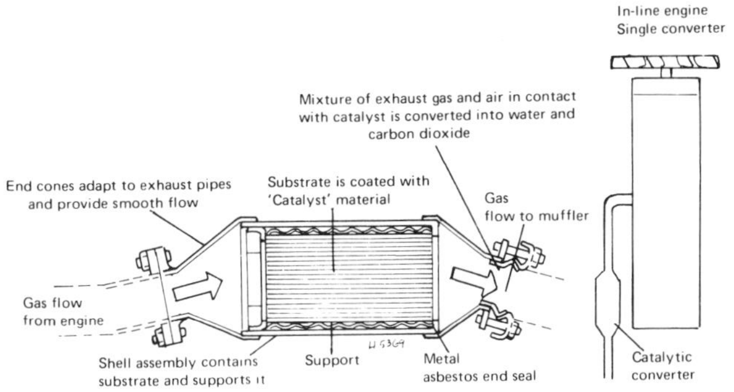

Fig. 3.85. Typical catalytic converter (Sec. 44)

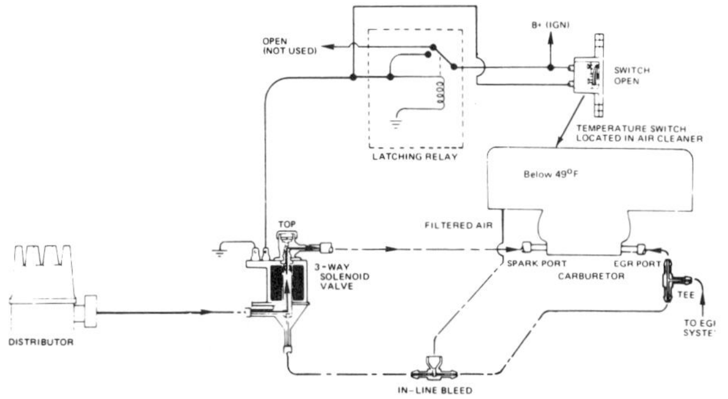

Fig. 3.86. Typical CTAV system operation below 49°F (Sec. 44)

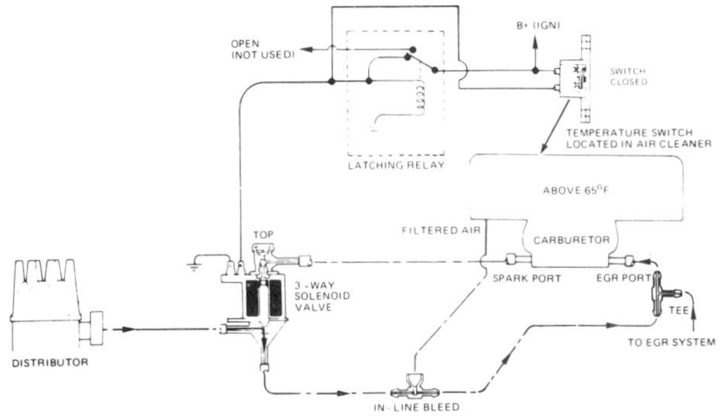

Fig. 3.87. Typical CTAV system operation above 65°F (Sec. 44)

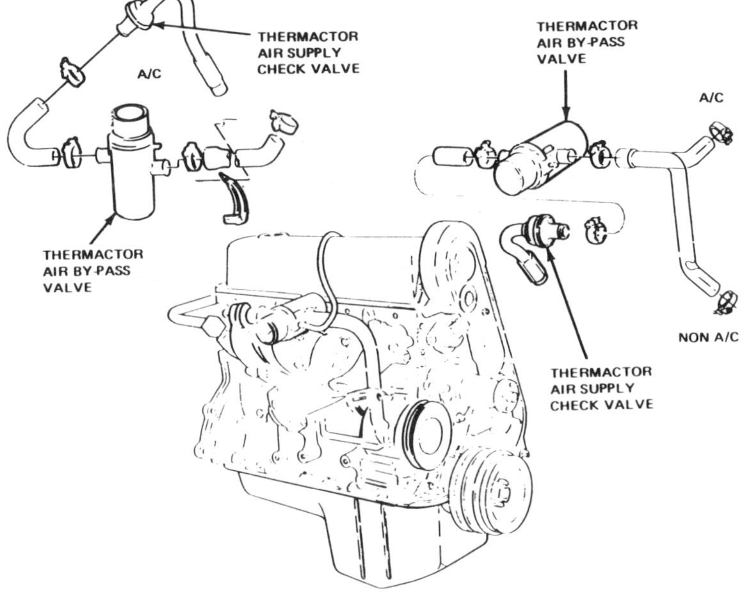

Fig. 3.88. Basic thermactor system (Sec. 44)

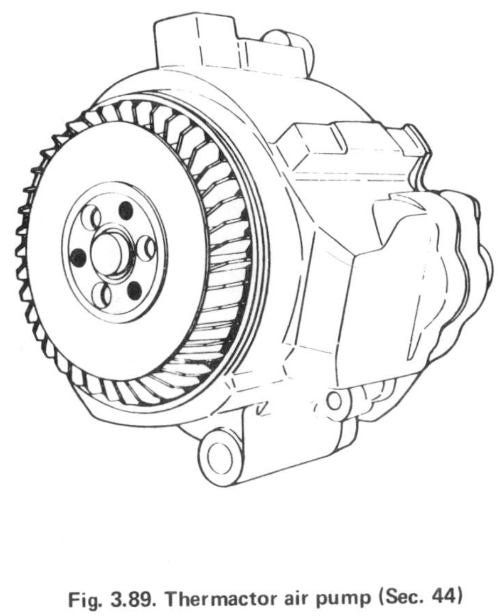

Fig. 3.89. Thermactor air pump (Sec. 44)

air bypass valve and check valve. Under normal conditions thermactor air passes straight through the bypass valve, but during deceleration, when there is a high level of intake manifold vacuum, the diaphragm check valve operates to shut off the thermactor air to the air supply check valve and exhaust it to atmosphere. The air supply check valve is a non-return valve which will allow thermactor air to pass to the exhaust manifold but will not allow exhaust gases to flow in the reverse direction.

28 A slightly modified system may be used on some later vehicles which have catalytic converters in the exhaust system; this may incorporate a vacuum delay valve (VDV). A typical system is shown in the illustrations.

45 Emission control system - maintenance and testing

Note: Read Part B, Section 29, paragraph 1 before commencing any maintenance or testing.

1 In view of the special test equipment and procedures there is little that can be done in the way of maintenance and testing for the emission control system. In the event of a suspected malfunction of the system, check the security and condition of all pneumatic and electrical connections then, where applicable, refer to the following paragraphs for further information.

Electrically assisted choke heater

2 The only test that can be carried out on this assembly, without special test equipment, is a continuity check of the heater coil. If an ohmmeter is available, check for the specified resistance. If no ohmmeter is available, disconnect the stator lead from the choke cap terminal and connect one terminal of a 12V low wattage bulb (eg; instrument panel bulb). Ground (earth) the other terminal of the bulb and check that it illuminates when the engine is running. If it fails to illuminate, check the alternator output and the choke lead for continuity. If the bulb illuminates, disconnect the bulb ground terminal and reconnect it to the choke lead. If the bulb does not illuminate when the engine is warm, a faulty choke unit is indicated.

PCV system

3 Remove all the hoses and components of the system and clean them in kerosene or gasoline. Ensure that all hoses are free from any obstruction and are in a serviceable condition. Where applicable, similarly clean the crankcase breather cap and shake it dry. Replace parts as necessary then refit them to the car.

Charcoal canister

4 The charcoal canister is located on the right-hand dash panel in the engine compartment. To remove it, disconnect the two hoses, then remove the three nuts securing the canister bracket to the dash panel. Remove the canister and bracket. Refitting is the reverse of the removal procedure.

EGR system

5 The EGR valve can be removed for cleaning, but where it is damaged, corroded or extremely dirty it is preferable to fit a replacement. If the valve is to be cleaned, check that the orifice in the body is clear but take care not to enlarge it. If the valve can be dismantled, internal deposits can be removed with a small power driven rotary wire brush. Deposits around the valve stem and disc can be removed by using a steel blade or shim approximately 0.028 in (7 mm) thick in a sawing motion around the stem shoulder at both sides of the disc. Clean the cavity and passages in the main body; ensure that the poppet wobbles and moves axially before reassembly.

CTAV system

6 Without special equipment it is only possible to carry out electrical tests of the system circuitry. Connect one terminal of a 12V low wattage bulb (eg; instrument panel bulb) to the car ground (earth). Connect the other terminal to point 'B' (Fig. 3.96) and remove the connector at point 'D'. Turn on the ignition, if the light illuminates, replace the latching relay. If there is no light, reconnect at point 'D'; there should now be a light. If there is none, check the temperature switch and the wiring back to the ignition switch. Provided that there is a light, disconnect at point 'D' again. There should now be a light; if there is none, replace the latching relay. If it is possible to cool the temperature switch below 49°F (9.5°C), check that the contacts are open at or below this temperature.

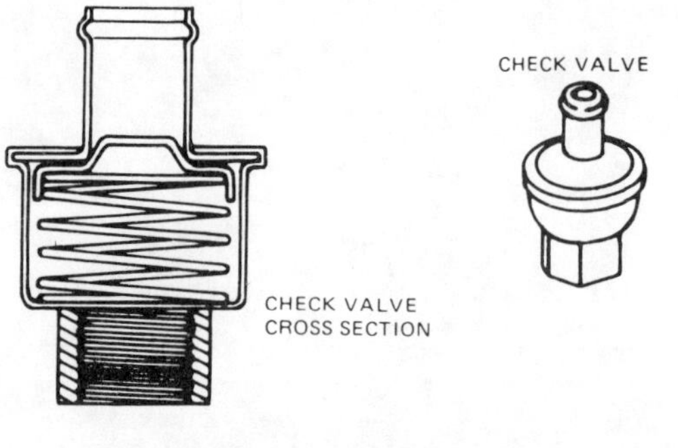

Fig. 3.90. Air supply check valve (Sec. 44) - Thermactor system

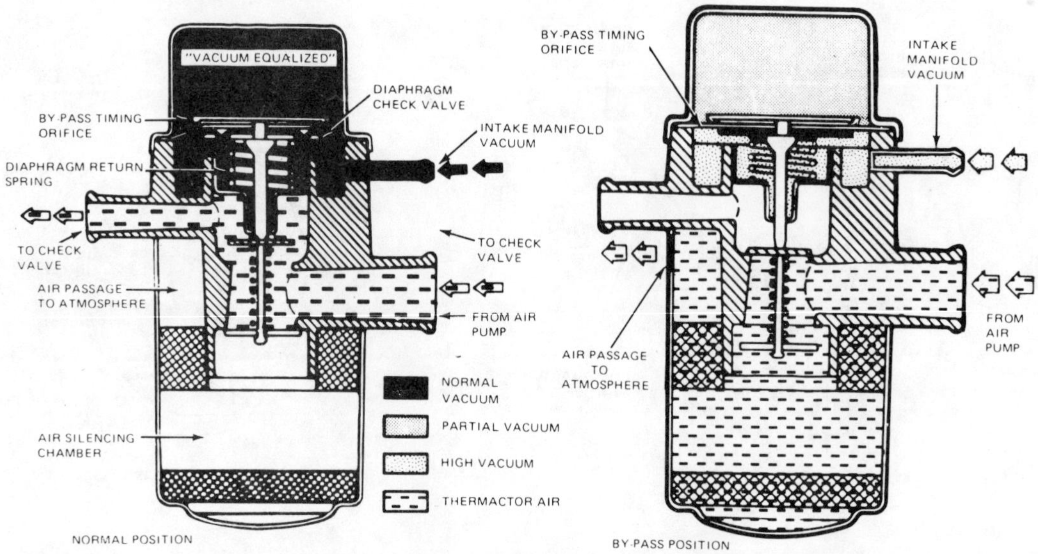

Fig. 3.91. Thermactor system by-pass valve (Sec. 44)

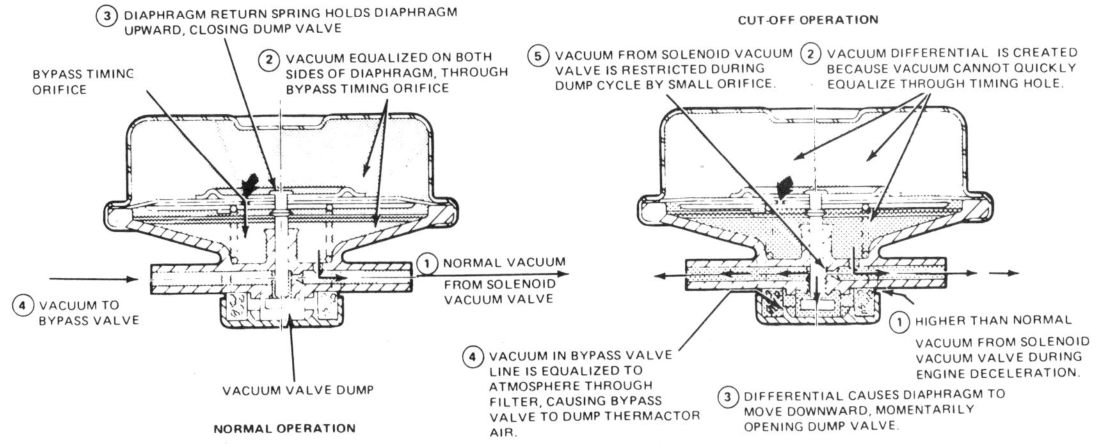

Fig. 3.92. Later type thermactor system by-pass valve (Sec. 44)

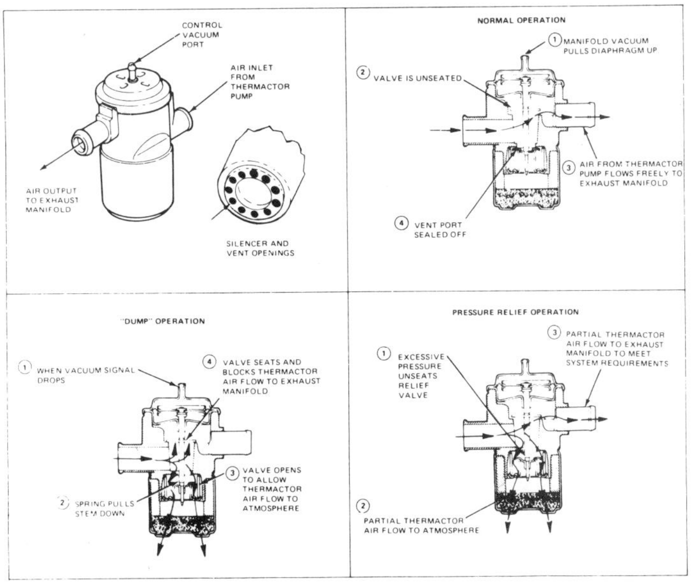

Fig. 3.93. Vacuum differential valve used on some systems (Sec. 44)

Thermactor system

7 Apart from checking the condition of the drivebelt and pipe connections, and checking the pump drivebelt tension, there is little that can be done without the use of special test equipment. Drivebelt tension should be checked using a special tension gauge, the tension reading being as given in Chapter 2. However, this is approximately equal to ½ in (13 mm) of belt movement between the longest pulley run under moderate hand pressure.

Deceleration valve

8 A deceleration valve is fitted to engines operating in certain territories. This device contributes to the reduction of noxious gases during periods of deceleration on overrun conditions.

9 Faulty adjustment of the valve or 'sticky operation' can give rise to excessively high engine idle speeds. Where this occurs, carry out the following checks.

10 The deceleration valve should be checked and adjusted, if necessary, any time the engine idle speed or fuel mixture has been adjusted. This will assure that factory specifications are met for this system.

11 Incorrect initial ignition timing and/or an over rich mixture can cause a properly functioning valve to stick open. Obviously, any adjustment that affects manifold vacuum also affects the deceleration valve opening and closing points. The higher the vacuum, the sooner the valve opens and the later it closes. When checking the deceleration valve, idle vacuum should not exceed 18.5 inches Hg for engines with dual-diaphragm distributors, or 19.5 inches Hg with a single diaphragm distributor.

12 Attach a tachometer to the engine.

13 Operate the engine for twenty minutes at 1200 rpm to stabilize engine temperature. Disconnect the rubber hose between the deceleration valve and the carburettor at the deceleration valve end and cap the nipple on the valve.

14 Verify that ignition timing, idle speed and carburettor mixtures are set to specifications.

15 Increase engine speed to 3000 rpm and hold for approximately 5 seconds; then, release the throttle. If engine does not return to normal idle speed, check for throttle linkage free movement and correct, if necessary, before continuing.

16 Remove cap from deceleration valve nipple, "Tee" a vacuum gauge into the hose between the deceleration valve and carburettor.

17 Increase engine speed to 3000 rpm and hold for approximately 5 seconds. Release the throttle and measure the time required for the vacuum reading to drop to zero. This should take from 2 to 5 seconds. If the valve is not within specifications, adjust as required to meet specifications (2 to 5 seconds).

18 Turning the adjusting screw inward reduces the time the valve is open; outward increases the open time. If the valve cannot be adjusted within the limits of the adjusting screw, renew the valve.

19 If the valve closes sooner than specified, the engine deceleration mixture will be too lean. If the valve stays open longer than 5 seconds, excessive engine speed will be experienced during deceleration when the accelerator pedal is released.

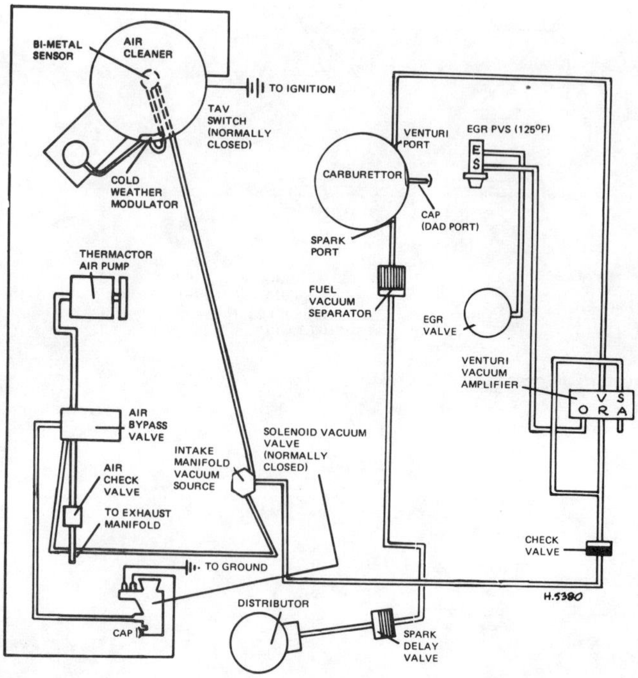

Vacuum diagram - A

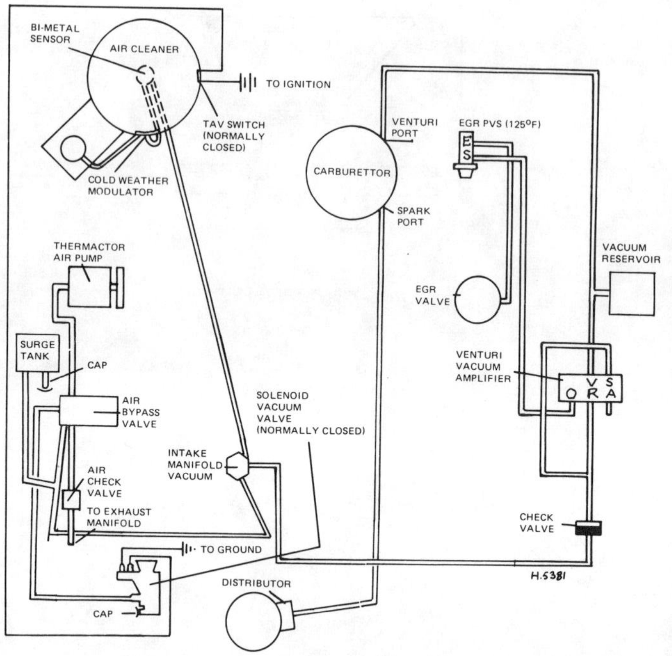

Vacuum diagram - B

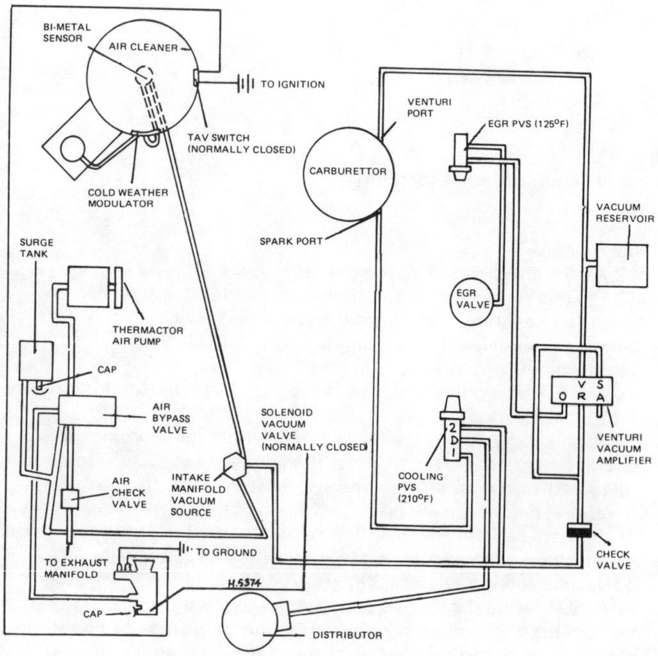

Vacuum diagram - C

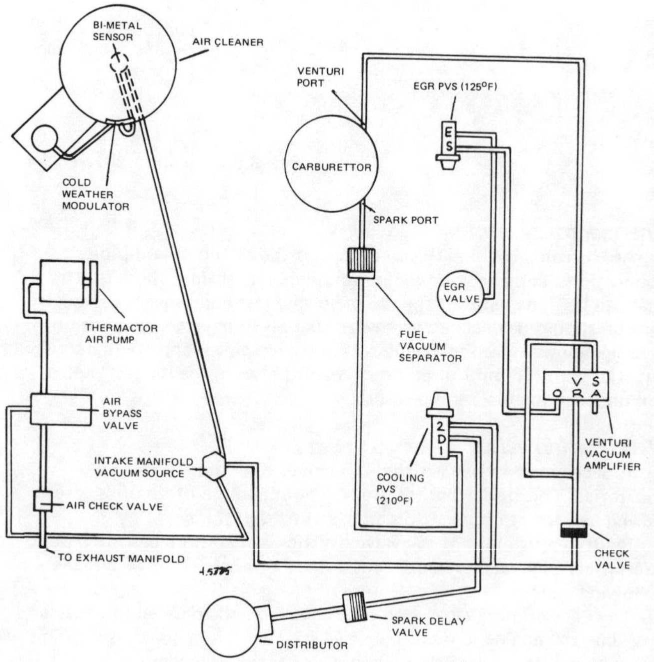

Vacuum diagram - D

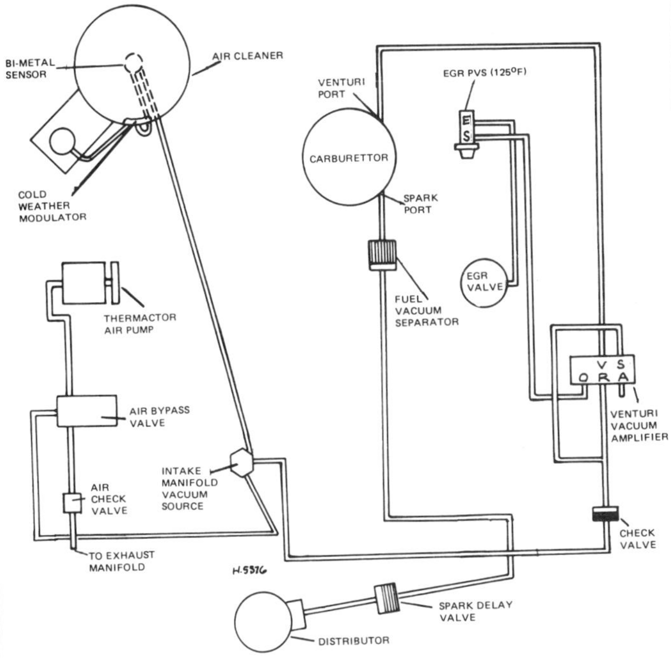

Vacuum diagram - E

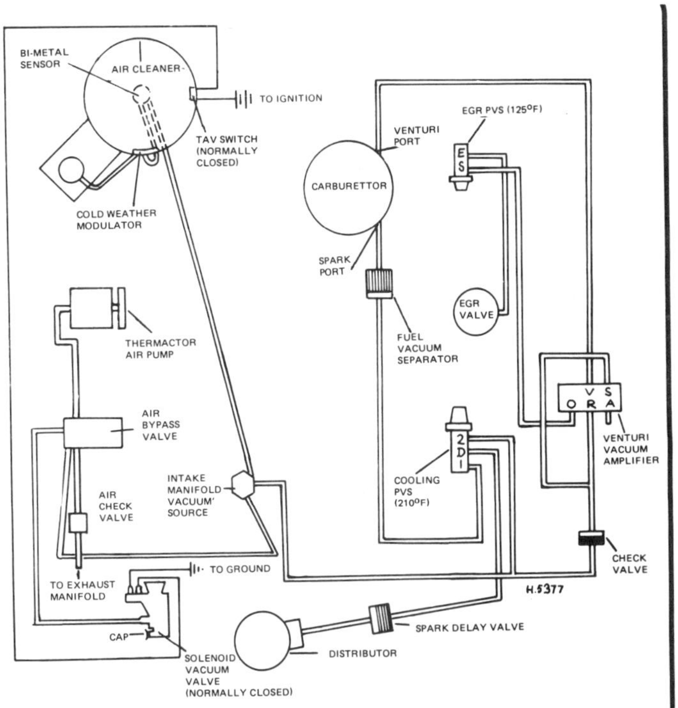

Vacuum diagram - F

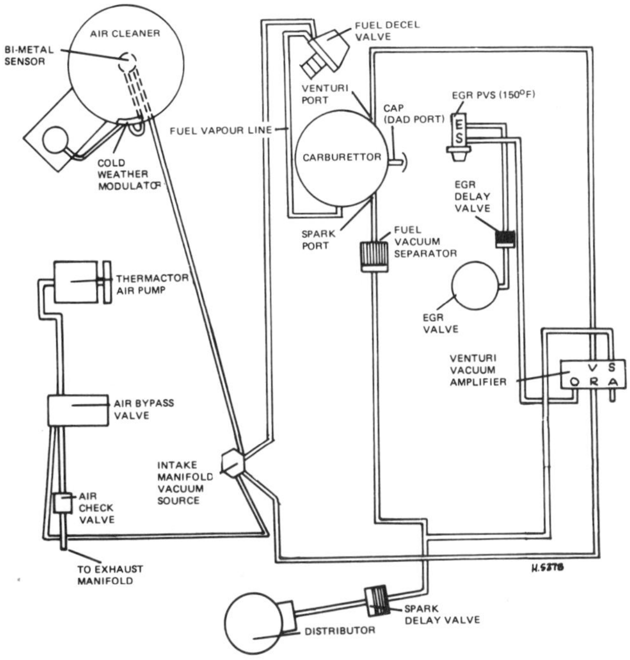

Vacuum diagram - G

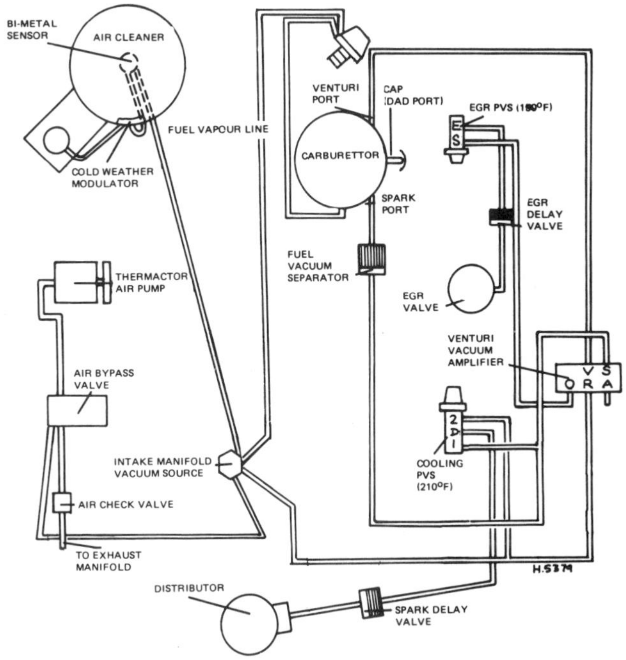

Vacuum diagram - H

Fig. 3.94. Typical vacuum diagrams (Sec. 44)

These diagrams are reproduced as a guide only, and do not necessarily cover all models or systems

A California, automatic transmission, no air conditioning
B California, manual transmission, no air conditioning
C California, manual transmission, air conditioning
D Federal, automatic transmission, air conditioning
E Federal, automatic transmission, no air conditioning
F California, automatic transmission, air conditioning
G Federal, manual transmission, no air conditioning
H Federal, manual transmission, air conditioning

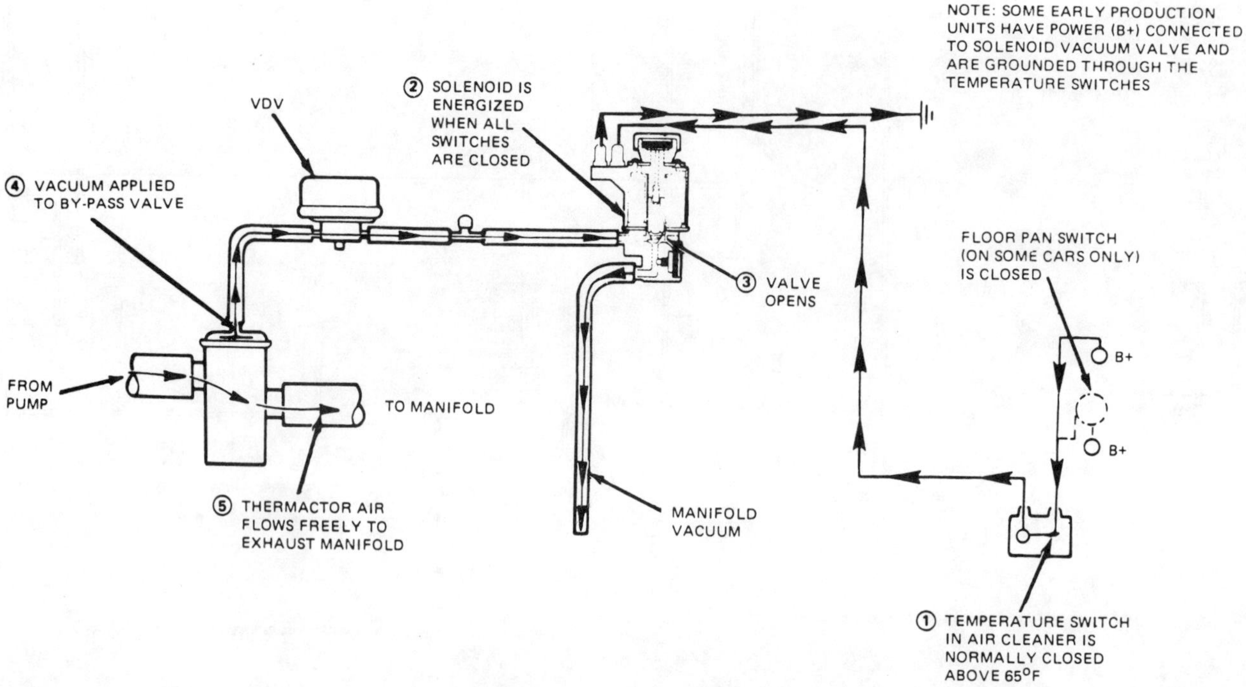

Fig. 3.95. Schematic diagram of typical thermactor system (Sec. 44)

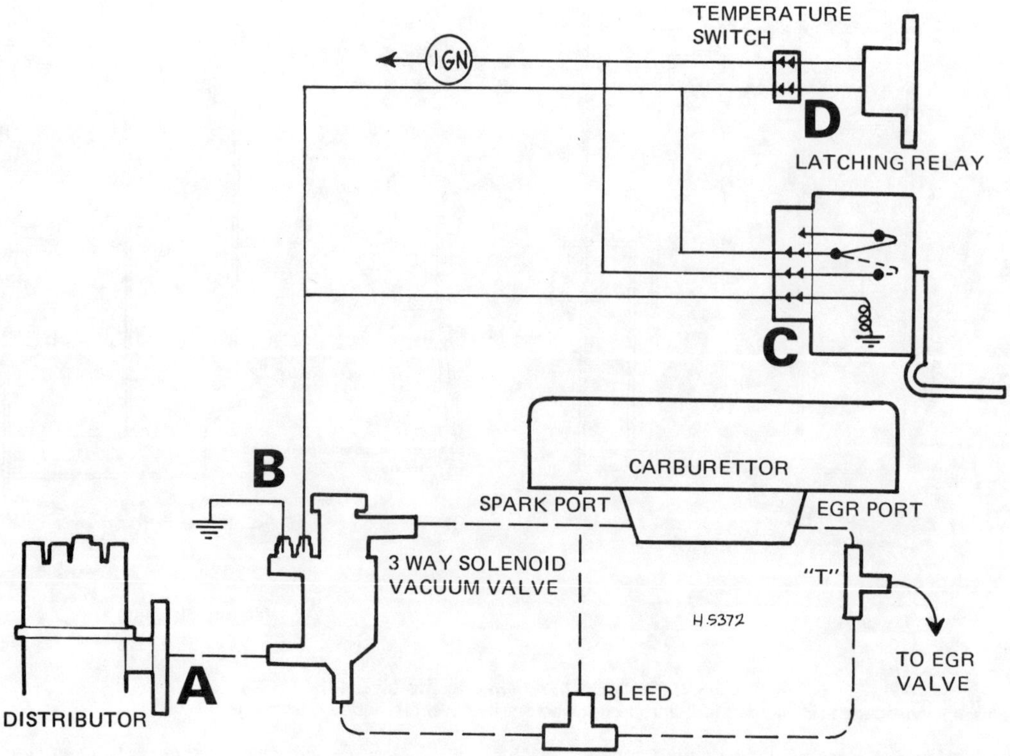

Fig. 3.96. Test connection points for the CTAV system (Sec. 45)

Part D: Fault diagnosis

46 Fault diagnosis - Fuel system

Symptom	Reason/s
Excessive fuel consumption *	Air cleaner choked or inlet duct system inoperative. General leaks from fuel system. Float chamber fuel level too high. Rich mixture. Incorrect valve clearances. Dragging brakes. Tyres under-inflated. Faulty choke operation.

** May also be due to faulty condenser or advance/retard system in distributor OR an emission control system fault.*

Symptom	Reason/s
Insufficient fuel delivery or weak mixture	Clogged fuel line or carburettor filter. Fuel inlet needle valve stuck. Faulty fuel pump. Leaking pipe connections. Leaking inlet manifold gasket. Leaking carburettor mounting flange gasket. Weak carburettor mixture setting.

47 Fault diagnosis - Emission control system

The following list is for guidance only, since a combination of faults may produce symptoms which are difficult to diagnose. It is therefore essential that a Ford dealer or emission control specialist is consulted in the event of problems occurring.

Symptom	Reason/s
Electrically assisted choke heater Long engine warm-up time	Faulty choke heater.
PCV system Fumes escaping from engine	Clogged PCV valve. Split or collapsed hoses.
Evaporative control system Fuel odour or rough engine running	Choked carbon canister. Stuck filler cap valve. Split or collapsed hoses.
Thermactor system Fume emission from exhaust	Air pump drivebelt incorrectly tensioned. Damaged air supply pipes. Split or collapsed sensing hoses. Defective air pump. Faulty pressure relief valve.
EGR system Rough idling	Faulty or dirty EGR valve. Split or collapsed hoses. Leaking valve gasket.
Catalytic converter Fume emission from exhaust	Damaged or clogged catalyst.

ABBREVIATIONS – EMISSION CONTROL

IMCO	Improved combustion system
PCV	Positive crankcase ventilation
PTC	Positive temperature co-efficient
EGR	Exhaust gas recirculation
VVA	Venturi vacuum amplifier
CSC	Cold start cycle
SVV	Solenoid vacuum valve
SDV	Spark delay valve
PSV	Ported vacuum switch
CTAV	Cold temperature actuated vacuum
VDV	Vacuum delay valve
TAV	Temperature actuated vacuum
DAD	Distributor advance diaphragm

Chapter 4 Ignition system

For modifications, and information applicable to later models, see Supplement at end of manual

Contents

Specifications

Capri II

Spark plugs

Type:	
1.6 litre	Motorcraft BF22, taper seat
2.0 litre	Motorcraft BF 32, taper seat
Thread size	18 mm
Electrode gap	0.025 in (0.64 mm)

Coil

Type	8 volt
Manufacture:	
FOB	Motorcraft
FOG	Bosch
Ballast resistor wire	1.5 ohms

Distributor

Manufacture	Motorcraft (black cap) or Bosch (red cap)
Automatic advance	Centrifugal and vacuum
Rotation	Clockwise
Condenser capacity	0.21 to 0.25 mfd
Contact breaker points gap:	
Motorcraft	0.025 in (0.64 mm)
Bosch	0.016 to 0.020 in (0.4 to 0.5 mm)
Dwell angle	48 to 52°
Distributor drive endfloat:	
Motorcraft	0.024 to 0.041 in (0.61 to 1.04 mm)
Bosch	0.021 to 0.051 in (0.53 to 1.31 mm)
Static advance (initial):	
1.6 litre	6 to 8° BTDC
2.0 litre	4° BTDC
Firing order	1, 3, 4, 2

Torque wrench settings (Capri II)	**lbf ft**	**kgf m**
Spark plugs	15 to 21	2.0 to 2.8

Mercury Capri II

System type	Bosch breakerless type with distributor and amplifier module

Distributor

Direction of rotation	Clockwise
Rotor air gap maximum voltage drop	7.5 kv
Distributor shaft endplay (distributor removed)	0.022 to 0.033 in (0.6 to 0.84 mm)
Ignition timing	Refer to vehicle engine decal
Firing order	1, 3, 4, 2

Coil

Primary resistance	1.3 to 1.6 ohms
Secondary resistance	7000 to 9000 ohms

Primary circuit resistor

Resistance at 68°F (20°C) ... ... 1.3 to 1.6 ohms

Spark plug type and gap ... ... Refer to vehicle engine decal

Torque wrench settings (Mercury Capri II)	**lbf ft**	**kgf m**
Spark plugs	10 to 15	1.4 to 2.1

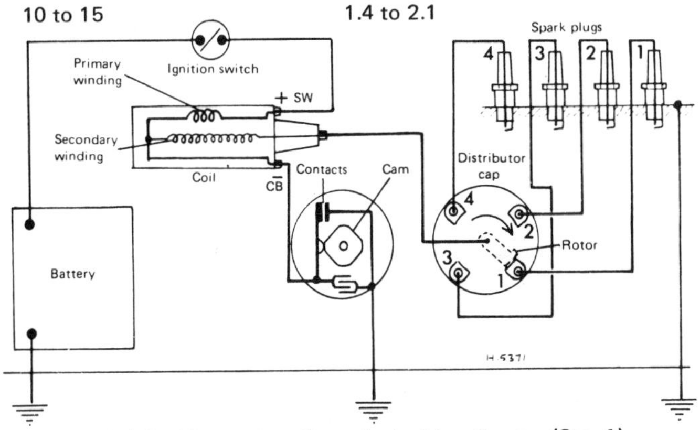

Fig. 4.1. Ignition system theoretical wiring diagram (Sec. 1)

1 General description

1 In order that the engine can run correctly it is necessary for an electrical spark to ignite the fuel/air mixture in the combustion chamber at exactly the right moment in relation to engine speed and load. The ignition system is based on feeding low tension voltage from the battery to the coil where it is converted to high tension voltage. The high tension voltage is powerful enough to jump the spark plug gap in the cylinders many times a second under high compression pressures, providing that the system is in good condition and that all adjustments are correct.

The ignition system is divided into two circuits, low tension and high tension.

The low tension circuit (sometimes known as the primary) consists of the battery lead to the ignition switch, ballast resistor lead from the ignition switch to the low tension or primary coil winding (terminal 15 or +), and the lead from the low tension coil winding (terminal 1 or –) to the contact breaker points and condenser in the distributor.

The high tension circuit consists of the high tension or secondary coil winding, the heavy ignition lead from the centre of the coil to the centre of the distributor cap, the rotor arm, the spark plug leads and spark plugs.

The system functions in the following manner. Lower tension.voltage is changed in the coil into high tension voltage by the opening of the contract breaker points in the low tension circuit. High tension voltage is then fed via the carbon brush in the centre of the distributor cap to the rotor arm of the distributor, and each time it comes in line with one of the four metal segments in the cap, which are connected to the spark plug leads, the opening of the contact breaker points causes the high tension voltage to build up, jump the gap from the rotor arm to the appropriate metal segment and so via the spark plug lead to the spark plug, where it finally jumps the spark plug gap before going to earth.

The ignition is advanced and retarded automatically, to ensure the spark occurs at just the right instant for the particular load at the prevailing engine speed.

The ignition advance is controlled both mechanically and by a vacuum operated system. The mechanical governor comprises two weights, which move out from the distributor shaft as the engine speed rises due to centrifugal force. As they move outwards they rotate the cam relative to the distributor shaft, and so advance the spark. The weights are held in position by two light springs and it is the tension of the springs which is largely responsible for correct spark advancement.

The vacuum control consists of a diaphragm, one side of which is connected via a small bore tube to the carburettor, and the other side to the contact breaker plate. Depression in the inlet manifold and carburettor, which varies with the engine speed and throttle opening, causes the diaphragm to move, so moving the contact breaker plate, and advancing the spark. A spring within the vacuum unit returns the breaker plate to the normal position when the amount of manifold depression is reduced.

The wiring harness includes a high resistance wire in the ignition coil feed circuit and it is very important that only a 'ballast resistor' type ignition coil is used. The starter solenoid has an extra terminal so that a wire from the solenoid to the coil supplies voltage direct to the coil when the starter motor is operated. The ballast resistor wire is therefore bypassed and battery voltage is fed to the ignition system so giving easier starting.

On some models where an F.M. radio is fitted a 'screening can' is fitted around the distributor to suppress interference. This is easily removable for access to the distributor.

2 Contact breaker points - adjustment

1 To adjust the contact breaker points to the correct gap, first release the two clips securing the distributor cap to the distributor body, and lift away the cap. Clean the cap inside and out with a dry cloth. It is unlikely that the four segments will be badly burned or scored, but if they are the cap will have to be renewed.

2 Inspect the carbon brush contact located in the top of the cap to ensure that it is not broken and stands proud of the plastic surface.

3 Lift away the rotor arm and check the contact spring on the top of the rotor arm. It must be clean and have adequate tension to ensure good contact.

4 Gently prise the contact breaker points open to examine the condition of their faces. If they are rough, pitted or dirty it will be necessary to remove them for resurfacing, or for replacement points to be fitted.

5 Presuming the points are satisfactory, or that they have been cleaned or replaced, measure the gap between the points with feeler gauges by turning the crankshaft until the heel of the breaker arm is on the highest point of the cam. The gap should be as given in the Specifications.

6 If the gap varies from the amount slacken the contact plate securing screw/s, Bosch distributor 1 screw, Ford distributor 2 screws (photo).

7 Adjust the contact gap by inserting a screwdriver in the notched hole in the contact breaker plate. Turn clockwise to increase, and anti-clockwise to decrease the gap. When the gap is correct, tighten the securing screw/s and check the gap again (photo).

8 Replace the rotor arm and distributor cap. Retain in position with the two clips.

Dwell angle

9 On modern engines, setting the contact breaker gap with feeler blades must be considered as an initial adjustment. For optimum performance, check and adjust the dwell angle.

10 The dwell angle is the number of degrees through which the distributor cam turns whilst the contact breaker points are closed. It can only be checked using a dwell meter.

11 Connect the dwell meter in accordance with the maker's instructions and with the engine running at the specified idling speed, check the dwell angle on the meter.

12 If the dwell angle is larger than that specified, switch off the engine and increase the points gap, if it is too small, decrease the gap. Re-check the dwell angle.

3 Contact breaker points - removal and refitting

1 If the contact breaker points are burned, pitted or badly worn, they must be removed and either replaced or their faces must be filed smooth. The contact breaker points fitted to the Ford distributor are mounted on the breaker plate and the assembly must be renewed as a complete unit as opposed to the Bosch distributor where the contact breaker points may be renewed as a set.

2 Lift off the rotor arm by pulling it straight up from the top end of the cam spindle.

2.6 Slackening contact plate screw (Ford)

2.7 Resetting contact breaker points

Bosch

a) Detach the low tension lead terminal from the internal terminal post and then undo and remove the screw that retains the contact breaker assembly to the base plate. Lift away the two contact breaker points.

b) To refit the points first locate the fixed point and lightly tighten the retaining screws. Smear a trace of grease onto the cam to lubricate the moving point heel and then fit the moving point pivot and reset the gap as described in Section 2.

Ford

a) Slacken the self-tapping screw that secures the condenser and low tension lead to the contact breaker point assembly. Slide out the forked ends of the lead terminals.

b) Undo and remove the two screws that secure the contact breaker points base plate to the distributor base plate. Lift away the points assembly.

c) To refit the points is the reverse sequence to removal. Smear a trace of grease onto the cam to lubricate the moving point heel, and then reset the gap, as described in Section 2.

3 Should the contact breaker points be badly worn, a new set must be fitted. As an emergency measure clean the faces with fine emery paper folded over a thin steel rule. It is necessary to rub the pitted point right down to the stage where all the pitting has disappeared. When the surfaces are flat a feeler gauge can be used to reset the gap.

4 Finally replace the rotor arm and distributor cap. Retain in position with the two clips.

4 Condenser - removal, testing and refitting

1 The purpose of the condenser (sometimes known as a capacitor) is to ensure that when the contact breaker points open there is no sparking across them which would waste voltage and cause wear.

2 The condenser is fitted in parallel with the contact breaker points. If it develops a short circuit, it will cause ignition failure as the contact breaker points will be prevented from correctly interrupting the low tension circuit.

3 If the engine becomes very difficult to start or begins to miss after several miles of running and the breaker points show signs of excessive burning, then the condition of the condenser must be suspect. One further test can be made by separating the points by hand with the ignition switched on. If this is accompanied by a bright flash, it is indicative that the condenser has failed.

4 Without special test equipment the only safe way to diagnose condenser trouble is to replace a suspected unit with a new one and note if there is any improvement.

5 To remove the condenser from the distributor take off the distributor cap and rotor arm.

6 *Bosch:* Release the condenser cable from the side of the distributor body and then undo and remove the screw that secures the condenser to the side of the distributor body. Lift away the condenser.

7 *Ford:* Slacken the self-tapping screw holding the condenser lead and low tension lead to the contact breaker points. Slide out the forked terminal on the end of the condenser low tension lead. Undo and remove the condenser retaining screw and remove the condenser from the breaker plate.

8 To refit the condenser, simply reverse the order of removal.

5 Distributor - lubrication

1 It is important that the distributor cam is lubricated with petroleum jelly or grease at 6000 miles (10000 km) or 6 monthly intervals. Also the automatic timing control weights and cam spindle are lubricated with engine oil.

2 Great care should be taken not to use too much lubricant as any excess that finds its way onto the contact breaker points could cause burning and misfiring.

3 To gain access to the cam spindle, lift away the distributor cap and rotor arm. Apply no more than two drops of engine oil onto the felt pad. This will run down the spindle when the engine is hot and lubricate the bearings.

4 To lubricate the automatic timing control allow a few drops of oil to pass through the holes in the contact breaker base plate through which the four sided cam emerges. Apply not more than one drop of oil to the pivot post of the moving contact breaker point. Wipe away excess oil and refit the rotor arm and distributor cap.

6 Distributor - removal

1 To remove the distributor from the engine, mark the four spark plug leads so that they may be refitted to the correct plugs and pull off the four spark plugs lead connectors.

2 Disconnect the high tension lead from the centre of the distributor cap by gripping the end cap and pulling. Also disconnect the low tension lead.

3 Pull off the rubber union holding the vacuum pipe to the distributor vacuum advance housing. Refer to the note in paragraph 5.

4 Remove the distributor body clamp bolt which holds the distributor clamp plate to the engine and lift out the distributor (Fig. 4.2).

5 **Note:** If it is not wished to disturb the timing, turn the crankshaft until the timing marks are in line and the rotor arm is pointing to number one spark plug segment in the distributor cap. Mark the position of the rotor in relation to the distributor body. This will facilitate refitting the distributor providing the crankshaft is not moved whilst the distributor is away from the engine.

7 Distributor -(Bosch) - dismantling

1 With the distributor on the bench, release the two spring clips retaining the cap and lift away the cap (Fig. 4.5).
2 Pull the rotor arm off the distributor cam spindle.
3 Remove the contact breaker points, as described in Section 3.
4 Unscrew and remove the condenser securing screw and lift away the condenser and connector.
5 Next carefully remove the 'U' shaped clip from the pull rod of the vacuum unit.
6 Undo and remove the two screws that secure the vacuum unit to the side of the distributor body. Lift away the vacuum unit.
7 Undo and remove the screws that secure the distributor cap spring clip retainer to the side of the distributor body. Lift away the two clips and retainers. This will also release the breaker plate assembly.
8 Lift away the contact breaker plate assembly from the inside of the distributor body.
9 Separate the breaker plate by removing the spring clip that holds the lower and upper plates together.
10 It is important that the primary and secondary springs of the automatic advance system are refitted in their original position during reassembly so the springs, weights and upper plate must be marked accordingly.
11 Refer to Fig. 4.3 and unhook the springs from the posts on the centrifugal weights.
12 Using a screwdriver as shown in Fig. 4.4 release the cam from the cam spindle and recover the felt pad, lock ring, and thrust washers from the cam. Release the two springs from the cam plate and lift away the centrifugal weights and washers.
13 Should it be necessary to remove the drive gear, using a suitable diameter parallel pin punch tap out the gear lock pin.
14 The gear may now be drawn off the shaft with a universal puller. If there are no means of holding the legs these must be bound together with wire to stop them springing apart during removal.
15 Finally withdraw the shaft from the distributor body.

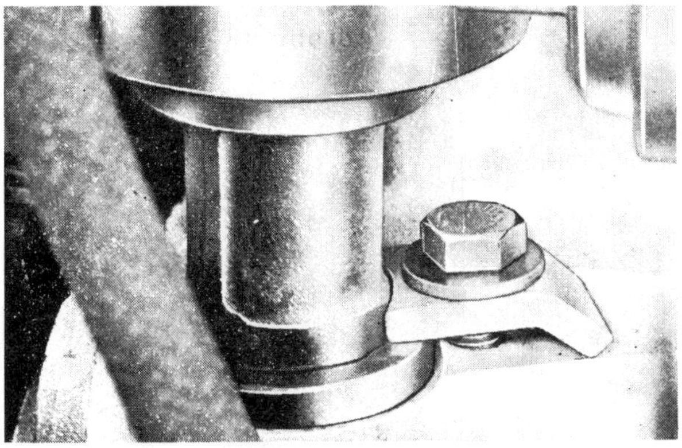

Fig. 4.2. Distributor clamp plate and bolt (Sec. 6)

Fig. 4.3. Correct installation of centrifugal weights and springs (Bosch) (Sec. 7)

Fig. 4.4. Removal of cam from cam spindle (Bosch) (Sec. 7)

8 Distributor (Ford) - dismantling

1 Refer to Section 7, and follow the instructions given in paragraphs 1 and 2. The component parts are shown in Fig. 4.6.
2 Next prise off the small circlip from the vacuum unit pivot post.
3 Take out the two screws that hold the breaker plate to the distributor body and lift away.
4 Undo and remove the condenser retaining screw and lift away the condenser.
5 Take off the circlip, flat washer and wave washer from the pivot post. Separate the two plates by bringing the holding down screw through the keyhole slot in the lower plate. Be careful not to lose the spring now left on the pivot post.
6 Pull the low tension wire and grommet from the lower plate.
7 Undo the two screws holding the vacuum unit to the body. Take off the unit.
8 To dismantle the vacuum unit, unscrew the bolt on the end of the unit and withdraw the vacuum spring, stop and shims.
9 The mechanical advance is next removed but first make a careful note of the assembly particularly which spring fits which post and the position of the advance springs. Then remove the advance springs (photo).
10 Prise off the circlips from the governor weight pivot pins and take out the weights.
11 Dismantle the spindle by taking out the felt pad in the top of the spindle. Expand the exposed circlip and take it out.
12 Now mark which slot in the mechanical advance plate is occupied by

8.9 Centifugal advance mechanism and springs (Ford)

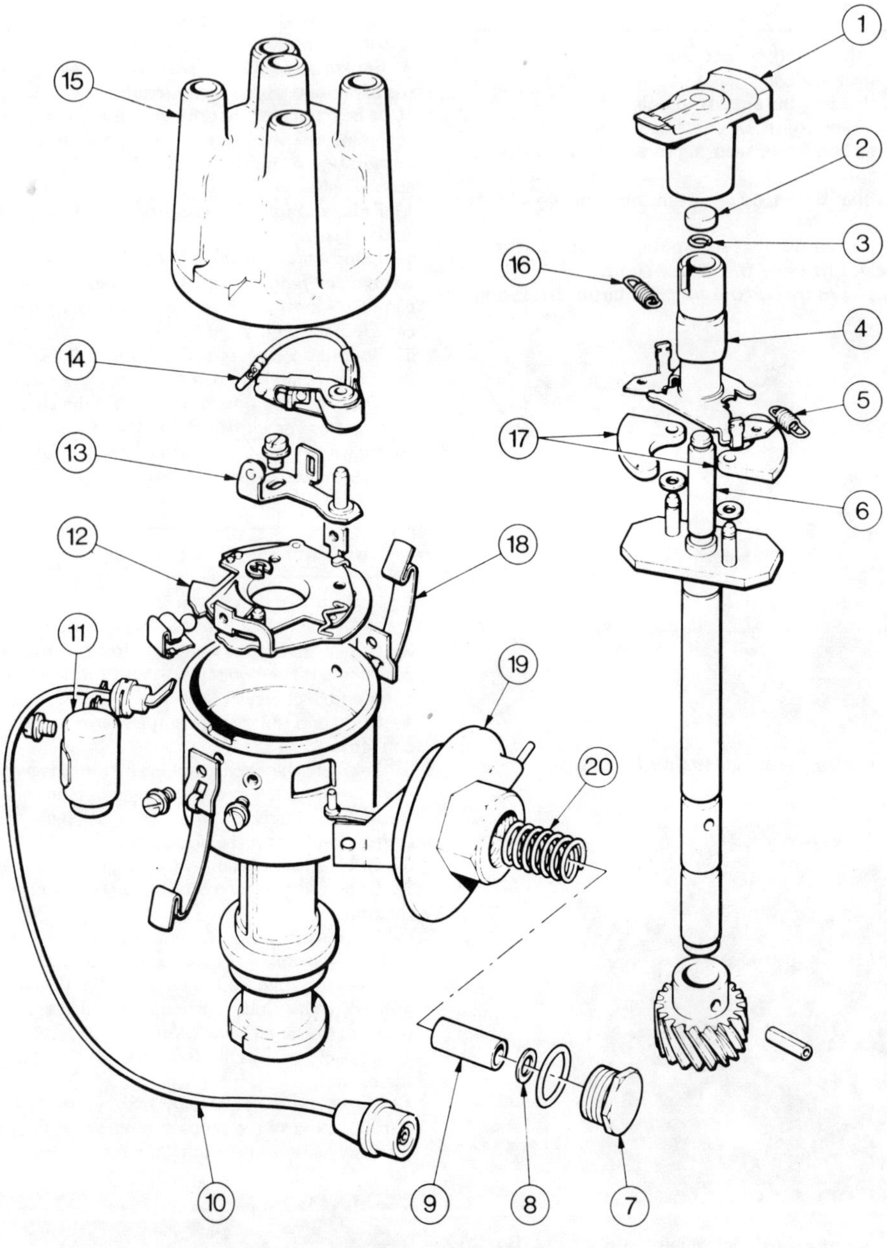

Fig. 4.5. Component parts of Bosch distributor (Sec. 7)
Note: Some distributors may vary slightly in detail from that shown

1 Rotor
2 Felt lubrication pad
3 Circlip
4 Cam
5 Advance spring
6 Shaft
7 Plug
8 Plate
9 Spacer
10 LT lead
11 Condenser
12 Base plate
13 Points assembly
14 Points assembly
15 Cap
16 Spring
17 Advance weights
18 Clip
19 Vacuum unit
20 Spring

the advance stop which stands up from the action plate, and lift the cam from the spindle.
13 It is only necessary to remove the spindle and lower plate if it is excessively worn. If this is the case, with a suitable diameter parallel pin punch tap out the gear lock pin.
14 The gear may now be drawn off the shaft with a universal puller. If there are no means of holding the legs these must be bound together with wire to stop them springing apart during removal.
15 Finally withdraw the shaft from the distributor body.

9 Distributor - inspection and repair

1 Check the contact breaker points for wear, as described in Section 3. Check the distributor cap for signs of tracking indicated by a thin black line between the segments. Replace the cap if any signs of tracking are found.
2 If the metal portion of the rotor arm is badly burned or loose, renew the arm. If only slightly burned clean the end with a fine file. Check that

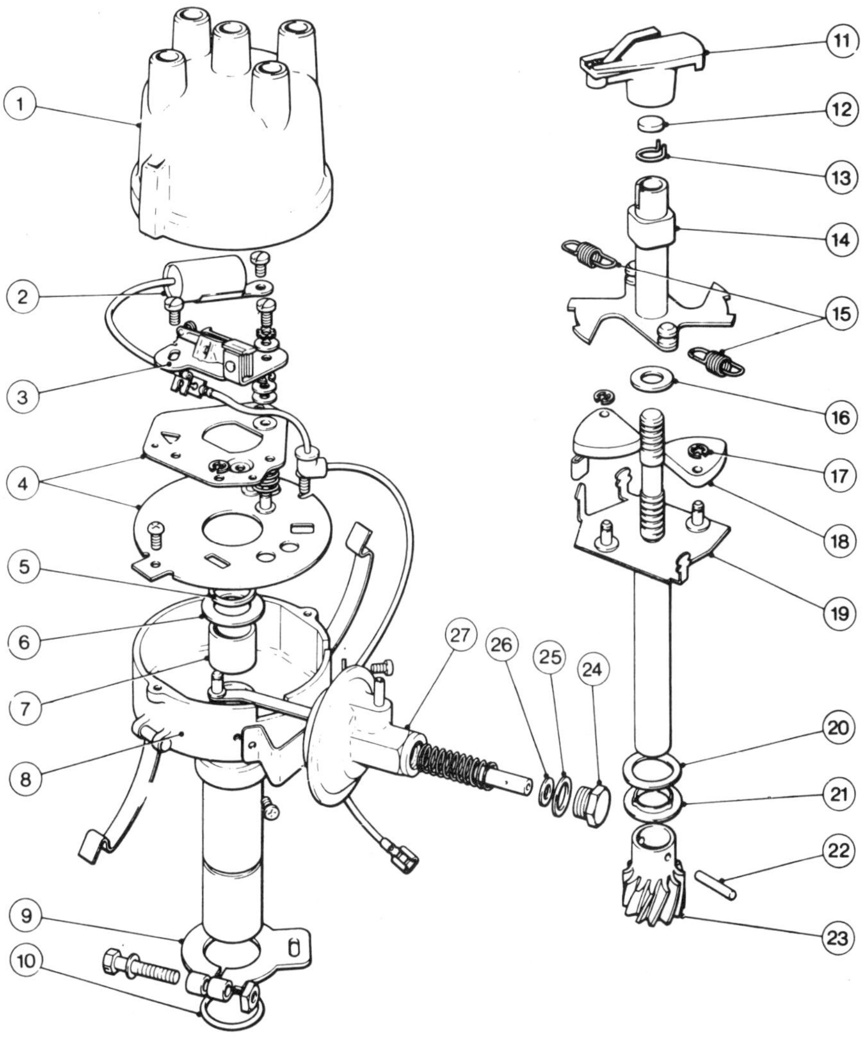

Fig. 4.6. Component parts of Ford distributor (Sec. 8)

1	*Cap*	*7*	*Bush*	*14*	*Cam*	*21*	*Washer*
2	*Condenser*	*8*	*Body*	*15*	*Advance springs*	*22*	*Pin*
3	*Points assembly*	*9*	*Clamp plate*	*16*	*Washers*	*23*	*Gear*
4	*Base plate*	*10*	*Seal*	*17*	*Circlip*	*24*	*Nut*
5	*Thrust washers*	*11*	*Rotor*	*18*	*Advance weight*	*25*	*Washer*
6	*Thrust washers*	*12*	*Felt wick*	*19*	*Shaft*	*26*	*Plate*
		13	*Circlip*	*20*	*Spacer*	*27*	*Vacuum unit*

the contact spring has adequate pressure and the bearing surface is clean and in good condition.

3 Check that the carbon brush in the distributor cap is unbroken and stands proud of its holder.

4 Examine the centrifugal weights and pivots for wear and the advance springs for slackness. They can best be checked by comparing with new parts. If they are slack they must be renewed.

5 Check the points assembly for fit on the breaker plate, and the cam follower for wear.

6 Examine the fit of the spindle in the distributor body. If there is excessive side movement it will be necessary to either fit a new bush or obtain a new body.

10 Distributor (Bosch) - reassembly

1 To reassemble first refit the two centrifugal weight washers onto the cam spindle. Smear a little grease onto the centrifugal weight contact faces and pivots and replace the weights in their original positions.

2 Lubricate the upper end of the spindle with engine oil and slide on the cam. Hook the two springs onto the weight retainers so that they are refitted in their original positions.

3 Position the thrust washer and lock ring in the cam. Carefully manipulate the lock ring into position using a thin electrician's screwdriver.

4 Refit the felt pad and thoroughly soak with engine oil.

5 Lubricate the distributor spindle with engine oil and insert it into the housing. The gear may now be tapped into position taking care to line up the lock pin holes in the gear and spindle. Support the spindle whilst performing this operation.

6 Fit a new lock pin to the gear and spindle and make sure that it is symmetrically positioned.

7 Locate the lower breaker plate in the distributor body. Place the distributor cap retaining spring clip and retainers on the outside of the distributor body and secure the retainers and lower breaker plate with the two screws.

8 Position the contact breaker point assembly in the breaker plate in such a manner that the entire lower surface of the assembly contacts the plate. Refit the contact breaker point assembly securing screw but do not fully tighten yet.

9 Hook the diaphragm assembly pull rod into contact with the pivot pin.

10 Secure the diaphragm to the distributor body with the two screws. Also refit the condenser to the terminal side of the diaphragm bracket securing screw. The condenser must firmly contact its lower stop on the housing.
11 Apply a little grease or petroleum jelly to the cam and also to the heel of the breaker lever.
12 Reset the contact breaker points, as described in Section 2, and then replace the rotor arm and distributor cap.

11 Distributor (Ford) - reassembly

1 Reassembly is a straightforward reversal of the dismantling process but there are several points which must be noted.
2 Lubricate with engine oil the balance weights and other parts of the mechanical advance mechanism, the distributor shaft and the portion of the shaft on which the cam bears, during assembly. Do not oil excessively but ensure these parts are adequately lubricated.
3 When fitting the spindle, first replace the thrust washers below the lower breaker plate before inserting into the distributor body. Next fit the wave washer at the lower end and replace the drive gear. Secure it with a new pin.
4 Assemble the upper and lower spindle with the advance stop in the correct slot (the one which was marked) in the mechanical advance plate.
5 After assembling the advance weights and springs, check that they move freely without binding.
6 Before assembling the breaker plates make sure that the nylon bearing studs are correctly located in their holes in the upper breaker plate, and the small earth spring is fitted on the pivot post (photo).
7 As the upper breaker plate is being refitted pass the holding down stud through the keyhole slot in the lower plate (photo).
8 Hold the upper plate in position and refit the wave washer, flat washer and circlip (photo).
9 When all is assembled reset the contact breaker points, as described in Section 2.

12 Distributor - refitting

1 If a new shaft or gear has not been fitted (i.e. the original parts are still being used), it will not be necessary to retime the ignition.
2 Insert the distributor into its location with the vacuum advance assembly to the rear.
3 Notice that the rotor arm rotates as the gears mesh. The rotor arm must settle in exactly the same direction that it was in before the distributor was removed. To do this lift out the assembly far enough to rotate the shaft one tooth at a time lowering it home to check the direction of the rotor arm. When it points in the desired direction with the assembly fully home fit the distributor clamp plate, bolt and plain washer.
4 With the distributor assembly fitted reconnect the low tension lead. Reconnect the HT lead to the centre of the distributor cap and refit the rubber union of the vacuum pipe which runs from the inlet manifold to the side of the vacuum advance unit.
5 If the engine has been disturbed, refer to Section 14.
6 If the position of the rotor arm was not marked before the distributor was removed, or if a new distributor is being installed then set the crankshaft as previously explained. Hold the distributor over its recess with the vacuum unit at 45° away from the engine centre line and pointing to the rear. Turn the rotor arm (contact end) so that it points towards No. 2 spark plug.
7 Insert the distributor and as the gears mesh, the rotor arm will turn slightly. Clamp the distributor so that the contact points are just about to open.
8 Check the timing as previously described.

13 Spark plugs and HT leads

1 The correct functioning of the spark plugs is vital for the correct running and efficiency of the engine.
2 At intervals of 6000 miles (10000 km) the plugs should be removed examined, cleaned, and if worn excessively renewed. The condition of the spark plugs will also tell much about the overall condition of the engine (Fig. 4.8).
3 The plugs fitted as standard are as listed in Specifications at the beginning of this Chapter. If the tip and insulator nose are covered with hard black looking deposits, then this is indicative that the mixture is too rich. Should the plug be black and oily, then it is likely that the engine is fairly worn, as well as the mixture being too rich.
4 If the insulator nose of the spark plug is clean and white, with no deposits, this is indicative of a weak mixture, or too hot a plug (a hot plug transfers heat away from the electrode slowly - a cold plug transfers it away quickly).
5 If the insulator nose is covered with light tan to greyish brown deposits, then the mixture is correct and it is likely that the engine is in good condition.
6 If there are any traces of long brown tapering stains on the outside of the white portion of the plug, then the plug will have to be renewed, as this shows that there is a faulty joint between the plug body and the insulator, and compression is being allowed to leak away.
7 Plugs should be cleaned by a sand blasting machine which will free them from carbon more thoroughly than cleaning by hand. The machine will also test the condition of the plugs under compression. Any plug that fails to spark at the recommended pressure should be renewed.
8 The spark plug gap is of considerable importance, as, if it is too large or too small, the size of the spark and its efficiency will be seriously impaired. The spark plug should be set to the figure given in Specifications at the beginning of this Chapter.
9 To set it, measure the gap with a feeler gauge, and then bend open, or closed, the outer plug electrode until the correct gap is achieved. The centre electrode should never be bent as this may crack the insulation and cause plug failure if nothing worse.
10 When refitting the plugs refit the leads from the distributor in the correct firing order which is 1,3,4,2 (No.1. cylinder being the one nearest the radiator).
11 The plug leads require no routine attention other than being kept clean and wiped over regularly.
12 At intervals of 6000 miles (10000 km) or 6 months, however, remove the leads from the plugs and distributor (one at a time) and make sure

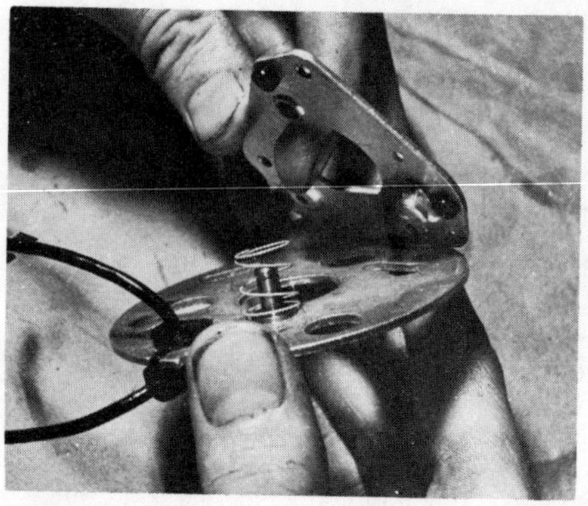
11.6 Reassembly of breaker plates (Ford).

11.7 Breaker plates correctly assembled (Ford).

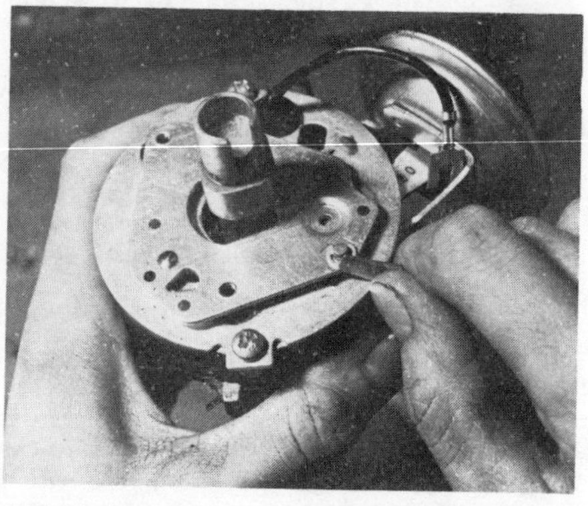
11.8 Fitting spring clip to breaker plate post (Ford)

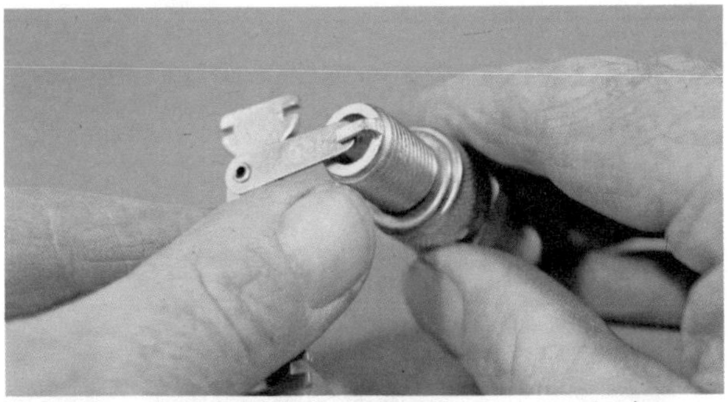

Measuring plug gap. A feeler gauge of the correct size (see ignition system specifications) should have a slight 'drag' when slid between the electrodes. Adjust gap if necessary

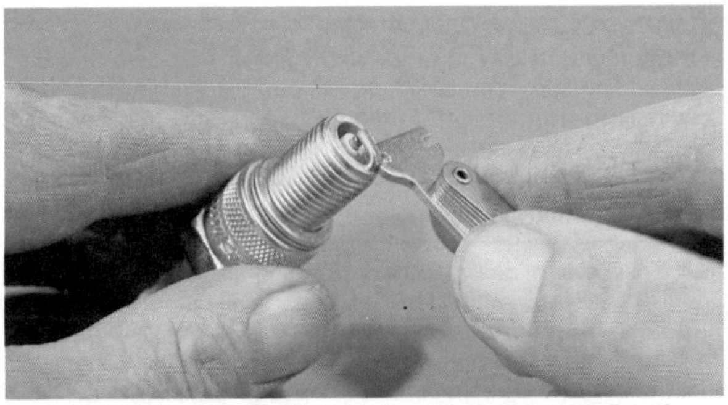

Adjusting plug gap. The plug gap is adjusted by bending the earth electrode inwards, or outwards, as necessary until the correct clearance is obtained. Note the use of the correct tool

Normal. Grey-brown deposits, lightly coated core nose. Gap increasing by around 0.001 in (0.025 mm) per 1000 miles (1600 km). Plugs ideally suited to engine, and engine in good condition

Carbon fouling. Dry, black, sooty deposits. Will cause weak spark and eventually misfire. Fault: over-rich fuel mixture. Check: carburettor mixture settings, float level and jet sizes; choke operation and cleanliness of air filter. Plugs can be re-used after cleaning

Oil fouling. Wet, oily deposits. Will cause weak spark and eventually misfire. Fault: worn bores/piston rings or valve guides; sometimes occurs (temporarily) during running-in period. Plugs can be re-used after thorough cleaning

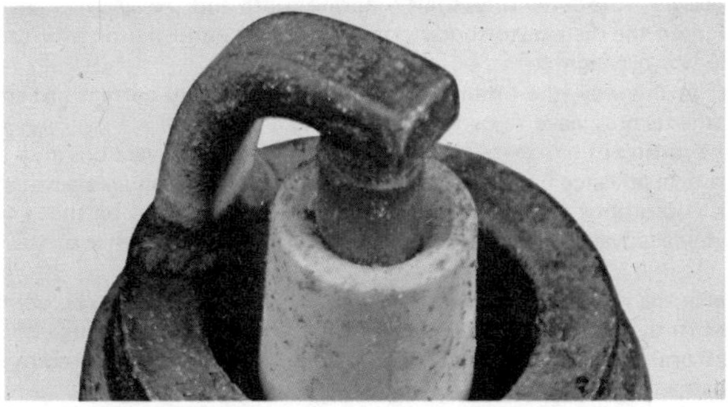

Overheating. Electrodes have glazed appearance, core nose very white – few deposits. Fault: plug overheating. Check: plug value, ignition timing, fuel octane rating (too low) and fuel mixture (too weak). Discard plugs and cure fault immediately

Electrode damage. Electrodes burned away; core nose has burned, glazed appearance. Fault: pre-ignition. Check: as for 'Overheating' but may be more severe. Discard plugs and remedy fault before piston or valve damage occurs

Split core nose (may appear initially as a crack). Damage is self-evident, but cracks will only show after cleaning. Fault: pre-ignition or wrong gap-setting technique. Check: ignition timing, cooling system, fuel octane rating (too low) and fuel mixture (too weak). Discard plugs, rectify fault immediately

no water has found its way onto the connections. Take care that the plug lead end fitting only is pulled; do not pull the leads or they may become detached from the end fitting.

14 Static ignition timing - (initial advance)

1 When a new gear or shaft has been fitted, or the engine has been rotated, or if a new assembly is being fitted, it will be necessary to retime the ignition. Carry it out this way:
2 Look up the initial advance (static) for the particular model in the Specifications at the beginning of this Chapter.
3 Turn the engine until No.1. piston is coming up to TDC on the compression stroke. This can be checked by removing No.1 spark plug and feeling the pressure being developed in the cylinder or by removing the oil filler cap and noting when the cam is in the upright position. If this check is not made it is all too easy to set the timing 180° out. The engine can most easily be turned by engaging top gear and edging the car along (except automatic).
4 Continue turning the engine until the appropriate static timing mark on the crankshaft pulley is in line with the pointer (Fig 4.9).
5 Now, with the vacuum advance unit pointing to the rear of the engine and the rotor arm in the same position as was noted before removal, insert the distributor into its location. Notice that the rotor arm rotates as the gears mesh. Lift out the distributor far enough to rotate the shaft one tooth at a time, lowering it home to check the direction of the rotor arm. When it points in the desired direction with the assembly fully home fit the distributor clamp plate, bolt and plain washer. Do not fully tighten yet.
6 Gently turn the distributor body until the contact breaker points are just opening when the rotor is pointing to the contact in the distributor cap which is connected to No.1 spark plug. A convenient way is to put a mark on the outside of the distributor body in line with the segment in the cover, so that it shows when the cover is removed.
7 If this position cannot be reached, check that the drive gear has meshed on the correct tooth by lifting out the distributor once more. If necessary, rotate the driveshaft gear one tooth and try again.
8 Tighten the distributor body clamp enough to hold the distributor, but do not overtighten.
9 Set in this way, the timing should be approximately correct but small adjustments may have to be made following a road test.
10 The setting of a distributor including the amount of vacuum and mechanical advance can only be accurately carried out on an electrical tester. Alterations to the vacuum advance shims or tension on the mechanical advance unit springs will change the characteristics of the unit.
11 Since the ignition timing setting enables the firing point to be correctly related to the grade of fuel used, the fullest advantage of a change of grade from that recommended for the engine will only be attained by readjustment of the ignition setting.

15 Ignition system - fault diagnosis

By far the majority of breakdown and running troubles are caused by faults in the ignition system either in the low tension or high tension circuits.

There are two main symptoms indicating faults. Either the engine will not start or fire, or the engine is difficult to start and misfires. If it is a regular misfire, (i.e. the engine is running on only two or three cylinders), the fault is almost sure to be in the secondary or high tension circuit. If the misfiring is intermittent the fault could be in either the high or low tension circuits. If the car stops suddenly, or will not start at all, it is likely that the fault is in the low tension circuit. Loss of power and overheating, apart from faulty carburation settings, are normally due to faults in the distributor or to incorrect ignition timing.

Engine fails to start

1 If the engine fails to start and the car was running normally when it was last used, first check there is fuel in the petrol tank. If the engine turns over normally on the starter motor and the battery is evidently well charged, then the fault may be in either the high or low tension circuits. First check the HT circuit. **Note:** If the battery is known to be fully charged, the ignition light comes on, and the starter motor fails to turn the engine **check the tightness of the leads on the battery terminals** and also the secureness of the earth lead to its **connection to the body.**

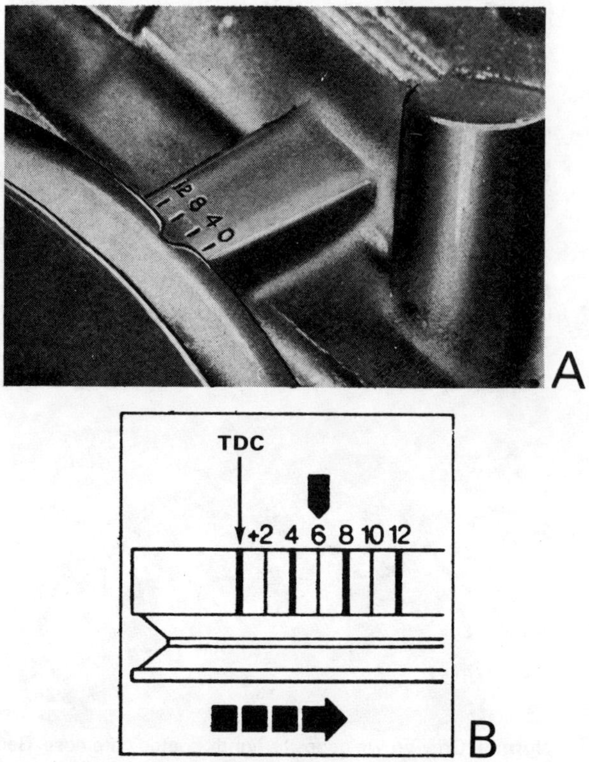

Fig. 4.9. Ignition timing marks - Capri II (Sec. 14)
A Early *B Later*

It is quite common for the leads to have worked loose, even if they look and feel secure. If one of the battery terminal posts gets very hot when trying to work the starter motor this is a sure indication of a faulty connection to that terminal.
2 One of the commonest reasons for bad starting is wet or damp spark plug leads and distributor. Remove the distributor cap. If condensation is visible internally dry the cap with a rag and also wipe over the leads. Refit the cap.
3 If the engine still fails to start, check that voltage is reaching the plugs by disconnecting each plug lead in turn at the spark plug end, and holding the end of the cable about 3/16 inch (5 mm) away from the cylinder block. Spin the engine on the starter motor.
4 Sparking between the end of the cable and the block should be fairly strong with a strong regular blue spark. (Hold the lead with rubber to avoid electric shocks). If voltage is reaching the plugs, then remove them and clean and regap them. The engine should now start.
5 If there is no spark at the plug leads, take off the HT lead from the centre of the distributor cap and hold it to the block as before. Spin the engine on the starter once more. A rapid succession of blue sparks between the end of the lead and the block indicate that the coil is in order and that the distributor cap is cracked, the rotor arm is faulty, or the carbon brush in the top of the distributor cap is not making good contact with the spring on the rotor arm. Possibly, the points are in bad condition. Clean and reset them as described in this Chapter, Section 2 or 3.
6 If there are no sparks from the end of the lead from the coil, check the connections at the coil end of the lead. If it is in order start checking the low tension circuit.
7 Use a 12v voltmeter or a 12v bulb and two lengths of wire. With the ignition switched on and the points open, test between the low tension wire to the coil (it is marked 15 or +) and earth. No reading indicates a break in the supply from the ignition switch. Check the connections at the switch to see if any are loose. Refit them and the engine should run. A reading shows a faulty coil or condenser, or broken lead between the coil and the distributor.
8 Take the condenser wire off the points assembly and with the points open test between the moving point and earth. If there now is a reading then the fault is in the condenser. Fit a new one and the fault is cleared.
9 With no reading from the moving point to earth, take a reading between earth and the — or 1 terminal of the coil. A reading here shows a broken wire which will need to be replaced between the coil and

distributor. No reading confirms that the coil has failed and must be replaced, after which the engine will run once more. Remember to refit the condenser wire to the points assembly. For these tests it is sufficient to separate the points with a piece of dry paper while testing with the points open.

Engine misfires

1 If the engine misfires regularly run it at a fast idling speed. Pull off each of the plug caps in turn and listen to the note of the engine. Hold the plug cap in a dry cloth or with a rubber glove as additional protection against a shock from the HT supply.

2 No difference in engine running will be noticed when the lead from the defective circuit is removed. Removing the lead from one of the good cylinders will accentuate the misfire.

3 Remove it about 3/16 inch (5 mm) away from the block. Re-start the engine. If the sparking is fairly strong and regular, the fault must lie in the spark plug.

4 The plug may be loose, the insulation may be cracked, or the points may have burnt away giving too wide a gap for the spark to jump. Worse still, one of the points may have broken off. Either renew the plug, or clean it, reset the gap, and then test it.

5 If there is no spark at the end of the plug lead, or if it is weak and intermittent, check the ignition lead from the distributor to the plug. If the insulation is cracked or perished, renew the lead. Check the connections at the distributor cap.

6 If there is still no spark, examine the distributor cap carefully for tracking. This can be recognised by a very thin black line running between two or more electrodes, or between an electrode and some other part of the distributor. These lines are paths which now conduct electricity across the cap thus letting it run to earth. The only answer is a new distributor cap.

7 Apart from the ignition timing being incorrect, other causes of misfiring have already been dealt with under the Section dealing with the failure of the engine to start. To recap, these are that

- *a) The coil may be faulty giving an intermittent misfire;*
- *b) There may be a damaged wire or loose connection in the low tension circuit;*
- *c) The condenser may be faulty; or*
- *d) There may be a mechanical fault in the distributor (broken driving spindle or contact breaker spring).*

8 If the ignition timing is too far retarded, it should be noted that the engine will tend to overheat, and there will be a quite noticeable drop in power. If the engine is overheating and the power is down, and the ignition timing is correct, then the carburettor should be checked, as it is likely that this is where the fault lies.

Part B: Mercury Capri II

16 General description

The component parts and layout of the Bosch breakerless ignition system are shown in Fig. 4.10.

When the ignition switch is ON, the ignition primary circuit is energized. When the distributor armature 'teeth' or 'spokes' approach the magnetic coil assembly, a voltage is induced which signals the amplifier to turn off the coil primary current. A timing circuit in the amplifier module turns on the coil current after the coil field has collapsed.

When on, current flows from the battery through the ignition switch, through the coil primary winding, through the amplifier module and then to ground. When the current is off, the magnetic field in the ignition coil collapses, inducing a high voltage in the coil secondary winding. This is conducted to the distributor cap where the rotor directs it to the appropriate spark plug. This process is repeated for each power stroke of the car engine.

The distributor is fitted with devices to control the actual point of ignition according to the engine speed and load. As the engine speed increases two centrifugal weights move outwards and alter the position of the armature in relation to the distributor shaft to advance the spark slightly. As engine load increases (for example when climbing hills or accelerating), a reduction in intake manifold depression causes the base plate assembly to move slightly in the opposite direction (clockwise) under the action of the spring in the vacuum unit, thus retarding the spark slightly and tending to counteract the centrifugal advance. Under light loading conditions (for example at moderate steady speeds) the comparatively high intake manifold depression on the vacuum advance diaphragm causes the baseplate assembly to move in a counter-clockwise direction to give a larger amount of spark advance.

For most practical do-it-yourself purposes ignition timing is carried out as for conventional ignition systems. However, a monolithic timing system is incorporated, and this has a timing receptacle mounted in the left rear of the cylinder block for use with an electronic probe. This latter system can only be used with special electronic equipment, and checks using it are beyond the scope of this manual.

Fault finding on the breakerless ignition system, which cannot be rectified by substitution of parts or cleaning/tightening connections, etc, should be entrusted to a suitably equipped Ford garage since special test procedures and equipment are required.

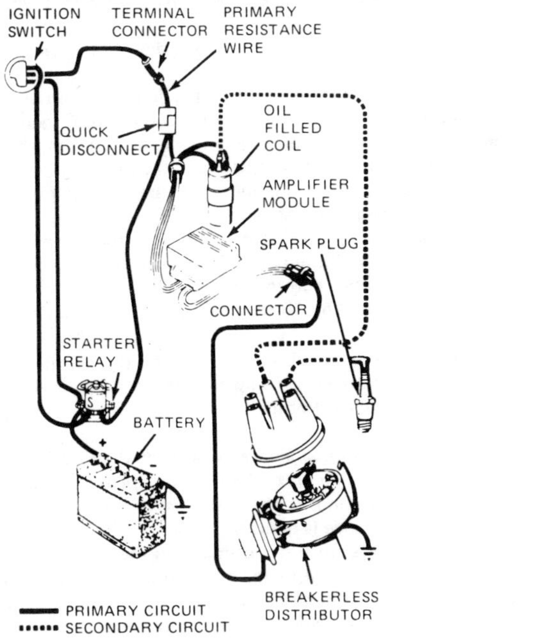

Fig. 4.10. Typical circuit for Bosch breakerless ignition system (Sec. 16)

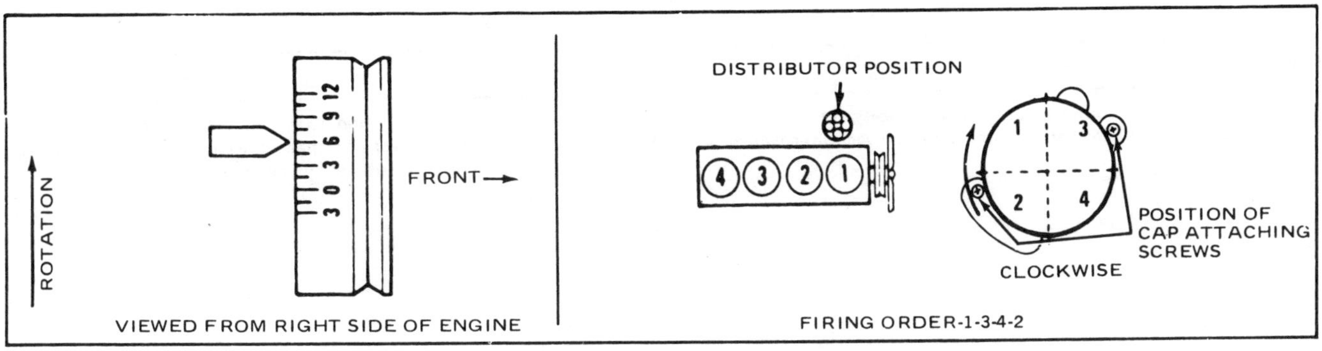

Fig. 4.11. Ignition timing marks and firing order (Sec. 17) - Mercury Capri II

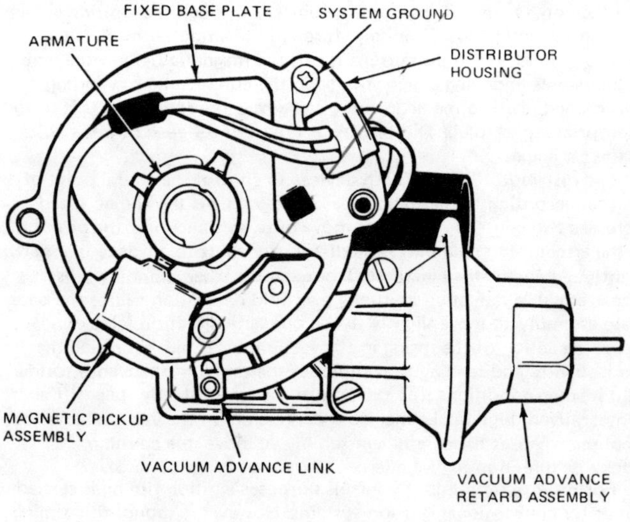

Fig. 4.12. Breakerless ignition distributor (Sec. 18)

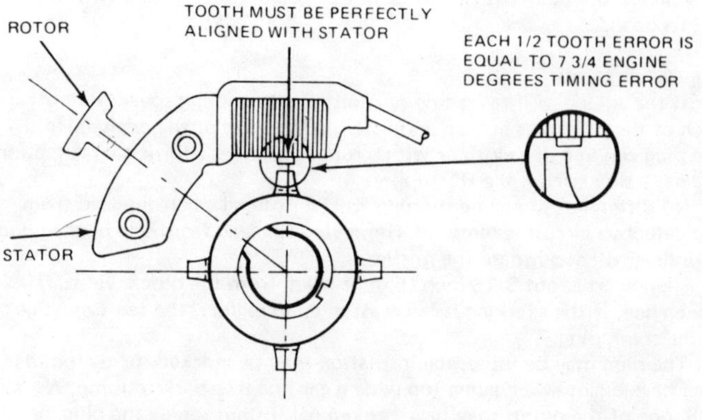

Fig. 4.13. The armature position for installation of the distributor (static timing) - Mercury Capri II (Sec. 18)

17 Ignition timing (initial advance)

1 Refer to the vehicle engine decal to obtain the ignition timing initial advance. Locate the appropriate timing mark on the engine vibration damper on the crankshaft pulley and highlight it with a white chalk or paint mark.
2 Disconnect the vacuum line from the distributor, and temporarily plug the line.
3 Connect a proprietary ignition timing light in accordance with the manufacturer's instructions to No. 1 spark plug wire, then run the engine until warm. Allow the engine to idle at 600 rpm, shine the timing light onto the vibration damper and note the position of the white line with respect to the timing pointer. If the line and pointer do not coincide, stop the engine, slacken the distributor clamp bolt, run the engine again and position the distributor until the timing marks do coincide. **Note:** If the timing marks cannot be made to coincide, or if the engine will not start and the ignition timing is suspected as being incorrect, refer to Section 18 to ensure that the distributor is correctly positioned.
4 Having set the timing, stop the engine and tighten the distributor clamp bolt, then run the engine up to 2500 rpm (approx) and check that the timing advances (indicating that the centrifugal advance is operating).
5 Stop the engine, unplug and reconnect the distributor vacuum line then again run the engine up to 2500 rpm (approx) and check that a greater amount of advance is obtained than at paragraph 4 (indicating that the vacuum advance is operating).
6 If a satisfactory result is not obtained in the tests at paragraphs 4 and 5, further investigation of the distributor should be carried out by a suitably equipped Ford dealer or ignition diagnosis specialist. Overhaul kits are not available for this type of distributor and, to the event of failure, a replacement item must be fitted.
7 On completion of any testing, ensure that all test connections are removed.

18 Distributor - removal and refitting

1 Remove the air cleaner (refer to Chapter 3, if necessary).
2 Disconnect the distributor harness connector and vacuum advance line.
3 Remove the distributor cap and move it to one side.
4 Scribe a mark on the distributor body and engine block to indicate the installed position, then remove the distributor hold-down bolt and clamp. Lift out the distributor. **Note:** To simplify the refitting procedure, do not rotate the engine after removing the distributor unless absolutely necessary.
5 Provided that the engine has not been rotated, refitting the distributor is a straightforward reversal of the removal procedure, but it is recommended that the ignition timing is checked as described in the previous Section.
6 If the engine was rotated whilst the distributor was removed it will first be necessary to bring No. 1 piston towards top-dead-centre (TDC) on its compression stroke. To do this, remove the access plug near the top of the timing belt cover, then rotate the crankshaft at the pulley in the normal direction of rotation until the timing pointer on the belt cover coincides with the 0° (TDC) marking on the crankshaft pulley vibration damper and the timing mark on the camshaft drive sprocket coincides with the timing pointer on the inner belt cover (viewed through the access plug aperture). If the vibration damper marking aligns with its pointer but the camshaft sprocket does not, rotate the engine crankshaft through 360°. (If the marks still do not coincide the valve timing should be checked, as described in Chapter 1).
7 Position the distributor in the block with one of the armature 'spokes' aligned as shown in Fig. 4.13, and the rotor in the No. 1 firing position (i.e. as if aligned with the No.1 spark plug lead terminal in the distributor cap).
8 If the distributor will not fully engage, it may be necessary to crank the engine with the starter after the distributor drive gear is partially engaged, in order to engage the oil pump intermediate shaft. Loosely install the retaining clamp and bolt, then rotate the distributor to advance the timing to a point where the armature spoke is aligned properly. Tighten the clamp bolt then refit the distributor cap, electrical leads and vacuum connection. Check the timing, as described in the previous Section.

19 Spark plugs and HT leads

1 The information given in Section 13 is generally applicable for Mercury Capri II, with the exception that service intervals are as given in the 'Routine Maintenance' Section at the beginning of the manual.

Chapter 5 Clutch

Contents

Specifications

Clutch type	Single dry plate, diaphragm spring	
Actuation	Cable	
Manufacture		
All FOG models	LUK or Fichtel and Sachs	
All FOB models	Laycock	
Size		
1.6 litre	7.5 in (190 mm)	
1.6 litre GT, 2.0 litre and Mercury Capri II	8.5 in (216 mm)	
Clutch lining thickness		
7.5 in. diameter	0.13 in (3.25 mm)	
8.5 in. diameter	0.151 in (3.85 mm)	
Clutch pedal free-travel	0.87 ± 0.16 in (2.2 ± 4.0 mm)	
Torque wrench settings	**lbf ft**	**kgf m**
Clutch pressure plate to flywheel	12 to 15	1.64 to 2.1

Clutch bellhousing torque wrench settings are given in Chapter 6.

1 General description

All models covered by this manual are fitted with a single diaphragm spring clutch. The unit comprises a steel cover which is dowelled and bolted to the rear face of the flywheel and contains the pressure plate, diaphragm spring and fulcrum rings (Fig. 5.1).

The clutch driven plate (disc) is free to slide along the splined gearbox input shaft and is held in position between the flywheel and the pressure plate by the pressure of the pressure plate spring, Friction lining material is riveted to the driven plate and it has a spring cushioned hub to absorb transmission shocks and to help ensure a smooth take off.

The circular diaphragm spring is mounted on shoulder pins and held in place in the cover by two fulcrum rings. The spring is also held to the pressure plate by three spring steel clips which are riveted in position.

The clutch is actuated by a cable controlled by the clutch pedal. The clutch release mechanism consists of a release fork and bearing which are in permanent contact with the release fingers on the pressure plate assembly. There should therefore never be any free-play at the release fork. Wear of the friction material in the clutch is adjusted out by means of a cable adjuster at the lower end of the cable where it passes through the bellhousing.

Depressing the clutch pedal actuates the clutch release arm by means of the cable. The release arm pushes the release bearing forward to bear against the release fingers so moving the centre of the diaphragm two annular rings which act as fulcrum points. As the centre of the spring is pushed in, the outside of the spring is pushed out, so moving the pressure plate backward and disengaging the pressure plate from the driven plate.

When the clutch pedal is released, the diaphragm spring forces the pressure plate into contact with the friction linings on the driven plate and at the same time pushes it a fraction of an inch forward on its splines. The driven plate is now firmly sandwiched between the pressure plate and the flywheel, so the drive is taken up.

2 Clutch - adjustment

1 At the specified service interval, adjust the clutch operating cable to compensate for wear in the driven plate linings (Fig. 5.2).
2 Release the outer cable locknut at the clutch bellhousing.
3 Have an assistant pull the clutch pedal up against its stop and then pull the outer cable forward to remove any slack.
4 Now turn the adjusting nut until there is a free-movement at the clutch pedal pad as given in the Specifications.
5 On completion, tighten the locknut and check the clutch operation during a brief test run.

3 Clutch - removal

1 Remove the gearbox, as described in Chapter 6.
2 Scribe a mating line from the clutch cover to the flywheel to ensure identical positioning on replacement and then remove the clutch

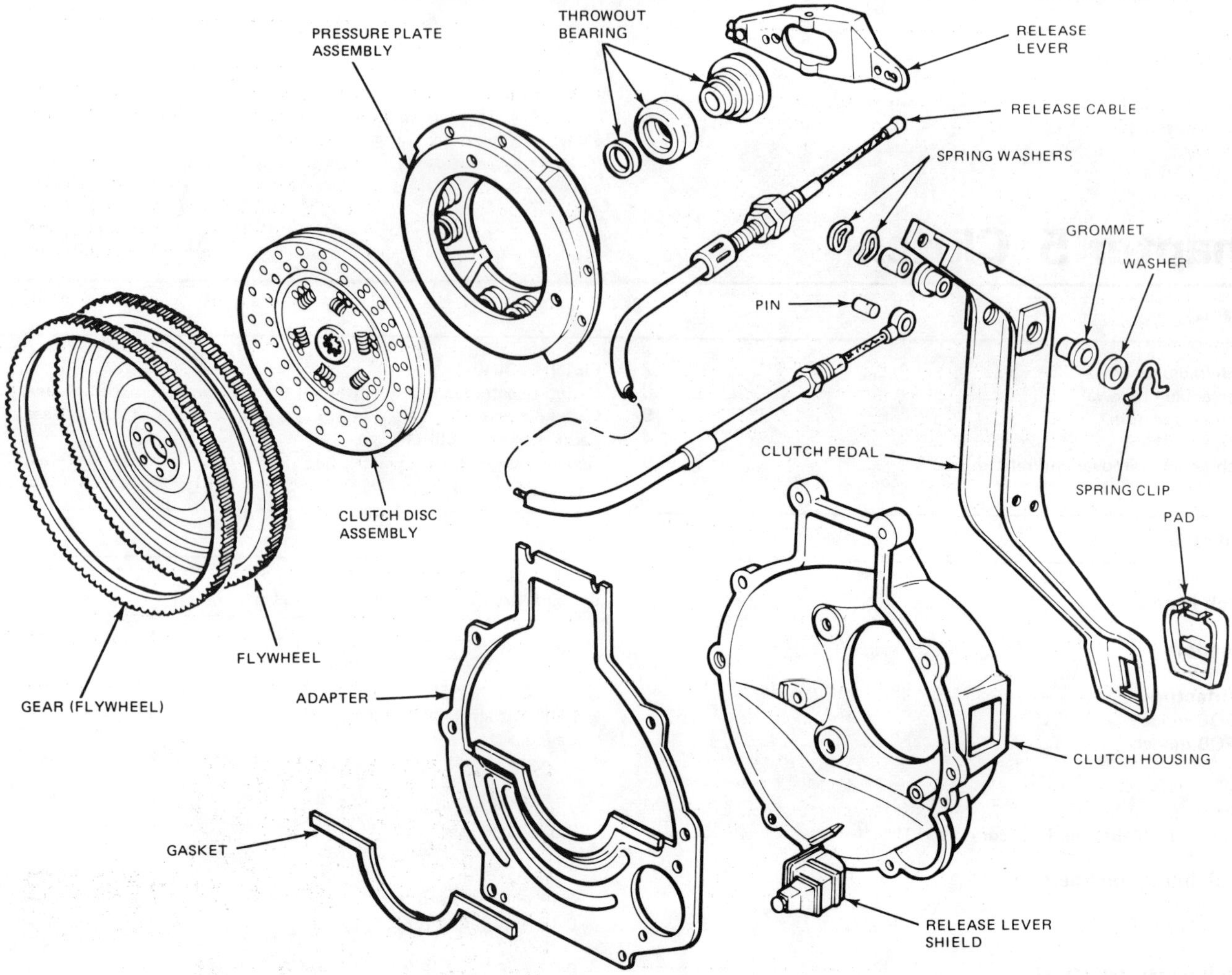

Fig. 5.1. Clutch layout - typical (Sec. 1)

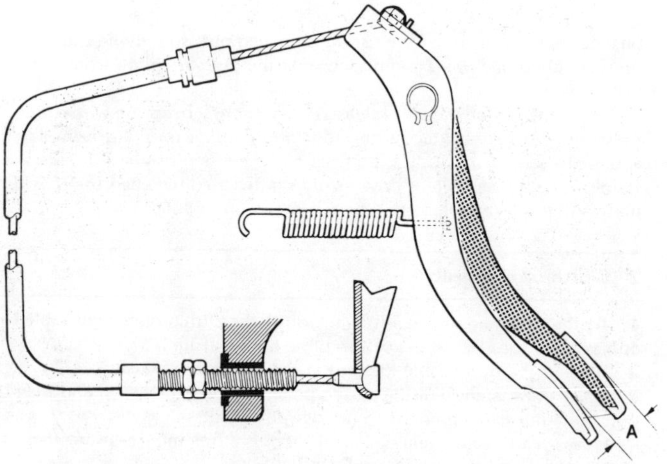

Fig. 5.2. Clutch pedal free travel adjustment (Sec. 2)

A = 0.87 ± 0.16 in (22 ± 4.0 mm)

Fig. 5.3. The clutch removed from the flywheel (Sec. 3)

assembly by unscrewing the six bolts holding the cover to the rear face of the flywheel. Unscrew the bolts diagonally, half a turn at a time, to prevent distortion to the cover flange.

3 With all the bolts and spring washers removed lift the clutch assembly off the locating dowels. The driven plate (clutch disc) may fall out at this stage as it is not attached to either the clutch cover assembly or the flywheel.

4 Clutch - overhaul

1 It is not practical to dismantle the pressure plate assembly. If a new clutch driven plate is being fitted it is false economy not to renew the release bearing at the same time. This will preclude having to replace it at a later date when wear on the clutch lining is very small.
2 If the pressure plate assembly requires renewal (see Section 5) an exchange unit must be purchased. This will have been accurately set up and balanced to very fine limits.

5 Clutch - inspection

1 Examine the clutch driven plate friction lining for wear and loose rivets and the plate for rim distortion, cracks, broken hub springs, and worn splines. The surface of the friction linings may be highly glazed, but as long as the clutch material pattern can be clearly seen this is satisfactory. Compare the amount of lining wear with a new clutch driven plate at the stores in your local garage, and if the linings are more than three quarters worn renew the driven plate.
2 It is always best to renew the clutch driven plate as an assembly to preclude further trouble, but, if it is wished to merely renew the linings, the rivets should be drilled out and not knocked out with a punch. The manufacturers do not advise that only the linings are renewed and personal experience dictates that it is far more satisfactory to renew the driven plate complete than to try and economise by fitting only new friction linings.
3 Check the machined faces of the flywheel and the pressure plate. If either is grooved it should be machined until smooth or renewed. renewed.
4 If the pressure plate is cracked or split it is essential that an exchange unit is fitted, also if the pressure of the diaphragm spring is suspect.
5 Check the release bearing for smoothness of operation. There should be no harshness and no slackness in it. It should spin reasonably freely bearing in mind it has been pre-packed with grease.
6 Check also that the clutch pilot bearing in the centre of the flywheel is serviceable. Further information on this will be found in Chapter 1, Section 28.

6 Clutch - refitting

1 It is important that no oil or grease gets on the clutch driven plate friction linings, or the pressure plate and flywheel faces. It is advisable to replace the clutch with clean hands and to wipe down the pressure plate and flywheel faces with a clean dry rag before reassembly begins.
2 Place the clutch driven plate against the flywheel, ensuring that it is the correct way round. The flywheel side of the clutch driven plate is smooth and the hub boss is longer on this side. If the driven plate is fitted the wrong way round, it will be quite impossible to operate the clutch.
3 Refit the clutch cover assembly loosely on the dowels. Refit the six bolts and spring washers, and tighten them finger tight so that the clutch driven plate is gripped but can still be moved.
4 The clutch driven plate must now be centralised so that when the engine and gearbox are mated, the gearbox input shaft splines will pass through the splines in the centre of the driven plate hub.
5 Centralisation can be carried out quite easily by inserting a round bar or long screwdriver through the hole in the centre of the clutch, so that the end of the bar rests in the small hole in the end of the crankshaft containing the input shaft pilot bush. Ideally an old input shaft should be used.
6 Using the input shaft pilot bush as a falcrum, moving the bar sideways or up and down will move the clutch driven plate in whichever direction is necessary to achieve centralisation.
7 Centralisation is easily judged by removing the bar and moving the driven plate hub in relation to the hole in the centre of the clutch cover diaphragm spring. When the hub appears exactly in the centre of the hole all is correct. Alternatively the input shaft will fit the bush and centre of the clutch hub exactly obviating the need for visual alignment.
8 Tighten the clutch bolts firmly in a diagonal sequence to ensure that the cover plate is pulled down evenly and without distortion of the flange. Finally tighten the bolts down to the specified torque.

7 Clutch release bearing - renewal

1 With the gearbox and engine separated to provide access to the clutch, attention can be given to the release bearing located in the bellhousing, over the input shaft. (photo).
2 The release bearing is a relatively inexpensive but important component and unless it is nearly new it is a mistake not to renew it during an overhaul of the clutch. Since 1977 a self-centring bearing has been fitted, interchangeable with the earlier type. If yours is a new type examine it for signs of grooving and renew if greater than 0.010 in (0.25 mm).
3 To remove the release bearing first pull off the release arm rubber gaiter.
4 The release arm and bearing assembly can then be withdrawn from the clutch housing.
5 To free the bearing from the release arm simply unhook it, and then with the aid of two blocks of wood and a vice press off the release bearing from its hub.
6 Replacement is a straightforward reversal of these instructions. On final assembly lubricate the hub bore and release lever contact face of the bearing with moly-disulphide grease.

8 Clutch cable - renewal

1 Jack-up the front of the car and support securely under the front crossmember.
2 Release the locknut on the outer cable at the bellhousing and back the adjusting nut right off.

Fig. 5.4. Centralising the clutch (Sec. 6)

7.1 The clutch release arm and bearing

3 Pull back the rubber gaiter on the end of the release arm and unhook the cable end.
4 Where applicable remove the cowl trim from the instrument panel (6 self-tapping screws).
5 Disconnect the clutch cable from the pedal by pushing the pin out of the cable eye. The clutch cable can now be withdrawn.
6 Refitting the new cable is a reverse of the removal procedure, following which it will be necessary to adjust the pedal free-travel as described in Section 2. Apply a little general purpose grease to the cable end-fitting and clutch pedal pivot.

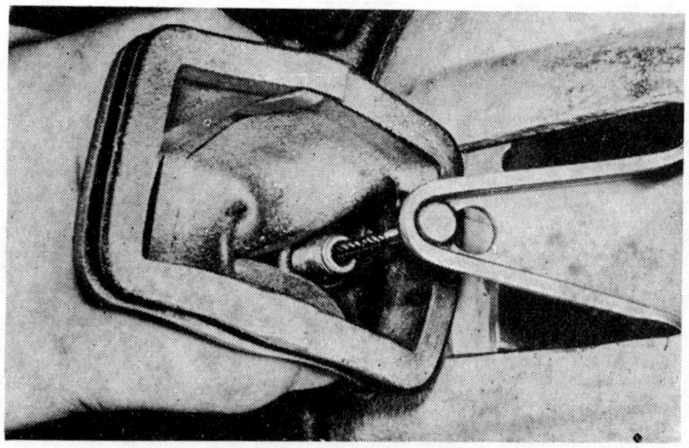

Fig. 5.5. Removing the release arm rubber gaiter - typical (Sec. 8)

9 Clutch pedal - removal and refitting

1 Where applicable remove the cowl trim from the instrument panel (6 self-tapping screws).
2 Carefully prise off the left-hand spring clip and washer from the pedal pivot shaft.
3 Unhook the clutch pedal return spring.
4 Push the pedal shaft to the side to permit the pedal to be removed.
5 Disconnect the clutch cable from the pedal by pushing the pin out of the eye.
6 Remove the clutch pedal pivot bush.
7 Refitting is the reverse of the removal procedure, but a new spring clip should be used on the pedal shaft for safety's sake, and a little general purpose grease applied to the pedal pivot. Also, if there is wear in the pivot bush, a replacement should be fitted. On completion, adjust the pedal free-travel, as described in Section 2.

10 Fault diagnosis - clutch

There are four main faults to which the clutch and release mechanism are prone. They may occur by themselves, or in conjunction with any of the other faults. They are clutch squeal, slip, spin and judder.

Clutch squeal - diagnosis and remedy.

1 If on taking up the drive or when changing gear, the clutch squeals, this is indicative of a badly worn clutch release bearing.
2 As well as regular wear due to normal use, wear of the clutch release bearing is much accentuated if the clutch is ridden or held down for long periods in gear, with the engine running. To minimise wear of this component the car should always be taken out of gear at traffic lights and for similar hold ups.
3 The clutch release bearing is not an expensive item, but is difficult to get at.

Clutch slip - diagnosis and remedy.

1 Clutch slip is a self-evident condition which occurs when the clutch driven plate is badly worn, oil or grease have got onto the flywheel or pressure plate faces, or the pressure plate itself is faulty.
2 The reason for clutch slip is that due to one of the faults above, there is either insufficient pressure from the pressure plate, or insufficient friction from the driven plate to ensure solid drive.
3 If small amounts of oil get onto the clutch, they will be burnt off under the heat of the clutch engagement, and in the process, gradually darken the linings. Excessive oil on the clutch will burn off leaving a carbon deposit which can cause quite bad slip, or fierceness, spin and judder.
4 If clutch slip is suspected, and confirmation of this condition is required, there are several tests which can be made.
5 With the engine in second or third gear and pulling lightly sudden depression of the accelerator pedal may cause the engine to increase its speed without any increase in road speed. Easing off on the accelerator will then give a definite drop in engine speed without the car slowing.
6 In extreme cases of clutch slip the engine will race under normal acceleration conditions.
7 If slip is due to oil or grease on the linings a temporary cure can sometimes be effected by squirting carbon tetrachloride into the clutch. The permanent cure is, of course, to renew the clutch driven plate and trace and rectify the oil leak.

Clutch spin - diagnosis and remedy

1 Clutch spin is a condition which occurs when there is an obstruction in the clutch, either in the gearbox input shaft or in the operating lever itself, or oil may have partially burnt off the clutch lining and have left a resinous deposit which is causing the clutch disc to stick to the pressure plate or flywheel.
2 The reason for clutch spin is that due to any, or a combination of, the faults just listed, the clutch pressure plate is not completely freeing from the driven plate even with the clutch pedal fully depressed.
3 If clutch spin is suspected, the condition can be confirmed by extreme difficulty in engaging first gear from rest, difficulty in changing gear, and very sudden take up of the clutch drive at the fully depressed end of the clutch pedal travel as the clutch is released.
4 Check the clutch cable adjustment (Section 2).
5 If these points are checked and found to be in order then the fault lies internally in the clutch, and it will be necessary to remove the clutch for examination.

Clutch judder - diagnosis and cure

1 Clutch judder is a self-evident condition which occurs when the gearbox or engine mountings are loose or too flexible, when there is oil on the face of the clutch friction plate, or when the clutch pressure plate has been incorrectly adjusted.
2 The reason for clutch judder is that due to one of the faults just listed, the clutch pressure plate is not freeing smoothly from the driven plate and is snatching.
3 Clutch judder normally occurs when the clutch pedal is released in first or reverse gears, and the whole car shudders as it moves backward or forward.

Chapter 6
Manual gearbox and automatic transmission

For modifications, and information applicable to later models, see Supplement at end of manual

Contents

Specifications

Manual gearbox

Number of gears	4 forward, 1 reverse	
Type of gears	Helical, constant mesh	
Synchromesh	All forward gears	
Gearbox type designation	Type C or H	
Gearbox application:		
Type C	1.6, 1.6GT engine (FOB)	
Type H	1.6, 1.6GT engine (FOG) 2.0 engine (FOB) and Mercury Capri II	
Gear ratios:	**Type C**	**Type H**
First	3.58 : 1	3.65 : 1
Second	2.01 : 1	1.97 : 1
Third	1.397 : 1	1.37 : 1
Fourth	1.00 : 1	1.00 : 1
Reverse	3.324 : 1	3.66 : 1
Lubricant type	SAE 80 EP gear oil	
Lubricant capacity:		
Type C	1.75 Imp pints (1.0 litre/2.1 US pints)	
Type H	2.6 Imp pints (1.45 litre/3.1 US pints)	
Mercury Capri II	2.3 Imp pints (1.3 litre/2.8 US pints)	
Countershaft cluster gear endfloat	0.006 to 0.018 in (0.15 to 0.45 mm)	
Thrust washer thickness	0.061 to 0.063 in (1.55 to 1.60 mm)	
Diameter of countershaft	0.68 in (17.3 mm)	

Automatic transmission

Manufacture	Ford
Type	Bordeaux (C3)
Selector lever positions	P, R, N, D, 2, 1
Gear ratios:	
First	2.47 : 1
Second	1.47 : 1
Third	1 : 1
Reverse	2.11 : 1
Transmission fluid specification	SQM-2C-9007-AA/ESW-M2C33-G *
Fluid capacity (approx):	
9¼ in (235 mm) torque converter (Capri II)	11.4 Imp pints (6.5 litre/13.7 US pints)
10¼ in (260 mm) torque converter (Mercury Capri II)	13.2 Imp pints (7.5 litre/15.8 US pints)

** Castrol TQF meets this specification*

Torque wrench settings (manual gearbox)

	lbf ft	kgf m
Type C		
Clutch bellhousing to transmission	31 to 35	4.3 to 4.8
Clutch bellhousing to engine:		
2 top bolts	29 to 35	4.0 to 4.8
Other bolts	22 to 27	3.0 to 3.7
Drive gear bearing retainer bolts	15 to 18	2.1 to 2.5
Extension housing retaining bolts	33 to 36	4.6 to 5.0
Transmission cover bolts	15 to 18	2.1 to 2.5
Type H		
Clutch bellhousing to transmission	43 to 51	5.9 to 7.0
Clutch bellhousing to engine	25 to 35	3.5 to 4.8
Drive gear bearing retainer bolts	15 to 18	2.1 to 2.5
Extension housing retaining bolts	33 to 36	4.6 to 5.0
Gearbox side cover bolts	15 to 18	2.1 to 2.5

Torque wrench settings (automatic transmission)

	lbf ft	kgf m
Torque converter housing to transmission	27 to 39	3.7 to 5.4
Disc to converter	27 to 30	3.7 to 4.1
Oil sump bolts	12 to 17	1.6 to 2.3
Downshift cable bracket	12 to 17	1.6 to 2.3
Downshift lever nut:		
Outer	7 to 11	1.0 to 1.5
Inner	30 to 40	4.1 to 5.5
Inhibitor switch	12 to 15	1.6 to 2.1
Brake band adjusting screw locknut	35 to 45	4.8 to 6.2
Fluid line to connector	7 to 10	1.0 to 1.4
Connector to transmission housing	10 to 15	1.4 to 2.1
Torque converter housing to engine	22 to 27	3.0 to 3.7
Torque converter drain plug	20 to 29	2.8 to 4.0
Oil cooler line to connector	12 to 15	1.6 to 2.1

1 Manual gearbox - general description

The manual gearboxes used on the models covered by this manual are equipped with four forward and one reverse gear.

All forward gears are engaged through baulk ring synchromesh units to obtain smooth, silent gearchanges. All forward gears on the mainshaft and input shaft are in constant mesh with their corresponding gears on the countershaft gear cluster and are helically cut to achieve quiet running.

The countershaft reverse gear has straight-cut spur teeth and drives the toothed 1st/2nd gear synchronizer hub on the mainshaft through an interposed sliding idler gear.

Gears are engaged either by a single selector rail and forks, or by levers in the gearbox side cover and forks. Control of the gears is from a floor mounted shift lever which connects either with the single selector rail, or the three selector levers and link rods.

Where close tolerances and limits are required during assembly of the gearbox, selective shims are used to eliminate excessive endfloat or backlash. This eliminates the need for using matched assemblies.

2 Gearbox (type C) - removal and refitting

1 If the gearbox alone is to be removed from the car, it can be taken out from below leaving the engine in position. It will mean that a considerable amount of working room is required beneath the car, and ideally ramps or an inspection pit should be used. However, provided that suitable jacks and supports are available, the task can be accomplished without the need for sophisticated equipment. A cranked spanner may be required to enable the gearshift lever to be removed.
2 Disconnect the battery earth lead.
3 If a parcel tray or centre console are fitted, remove these items (refer to Chapter 12, if necessary).
4 Remove the gearlever gaiter(s), bend back the lock tab on the retainer and unscrew the retainer using a suitably cranked spanner. Lift out the gearlever (photos).
5 Disconnect the starter motor leads; remove the starter motor (two bolts - refer to Chapter 10 if necessary).
6 Remove the propeller shaft, as described in Chapter 7. A polythene bag must be tied around the end of the gearbox to prevent loss of oil.
7 Pull back the rubber gaiter from the clutch release lever and slacken the clutch cable adjuster so that the cable can be unhooked from the release lever.
8 Remove the leads from the reverse light switch, noting which way they are fitted (photo).
9 Remove the circlip retaining the speedometer drive on the gearbox extension housing.
10 Temporarily take the gearbox weight with a trolley jack. Detach the gearbox mounting from the body (4 bolts). If wished, the mounting may also be removed from the gearbox (photo).
11 Remove the single adaptor plate bolt and the six bolts at the gearbox flange.
12 Lift the gearbox away from the engine a little then turn it through 90°. Insert a wooden block between the sump and the front engine mounting to prevent the engine from dropping, then withdraw the gearbox rearwards and downwards.
13 When refitting, ensure that the two clutch housing guide bushes are fitted to the engine and that the clutch pilot bearing in the flywheel is fitted and is serviceable. Tie the clutch release lever to the clutch housing with a piece of wire or string to prevent the release lever from slipping out.
14 Apply a little general purpose grease to the gearbox input shaft splines, then install the gearbox using the reverse procedure to that used when removing it.
15 Before removing the car from the jacks, ramps or inspection pit, top-up the oil level and adjust the clutch (refer to Chapter 5, for the latter).

3 Gearbox (type H) - removal and refitting

1 If the gearbox alone is to be removed from the car, it can be taken out from below leaving the engine in position. It will mean that a considerable amount of working room is required beneath the car, and ideally ramps or an inspection pit should be used. However, provided that suitable jacks and supports are available, the task can be accomplished without the need for sophisticated equipment. If the gearbox oil is to be drained, a rectangular section drain/filler plug wrench will be required.
2 Disconnect the battery earth lead.
3 Remove the starter motor (refer to Chapter 10, if necessary).
4 Remove the propeller shaft as described in Chapter 7. A polythene bag must be tied around the end of the gearbox to prevent loss of oil; alternatively the gearbox oil should be drained.
5 Pull back the rubber gaiter from the clutch release lever and slacken the clutch cable adjuster so that the cable can be unhooked from the release lever.

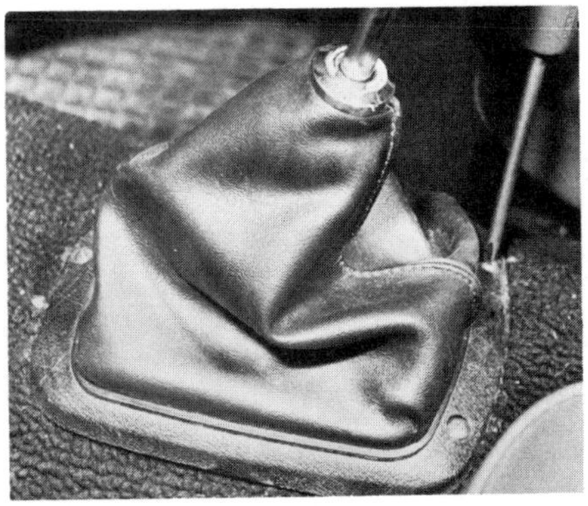

2.4a The gaiter used where there is no console

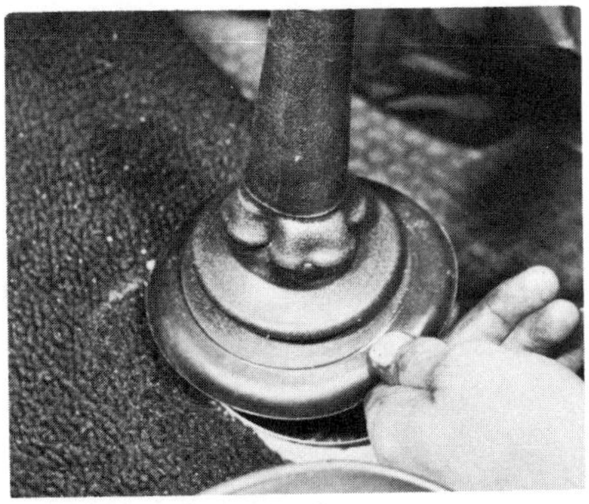

2.4b The rubber gaiter

Fig. 6.1. Type C gearshift lever removal (Sec. 2)

2.4c Removing the gear lever

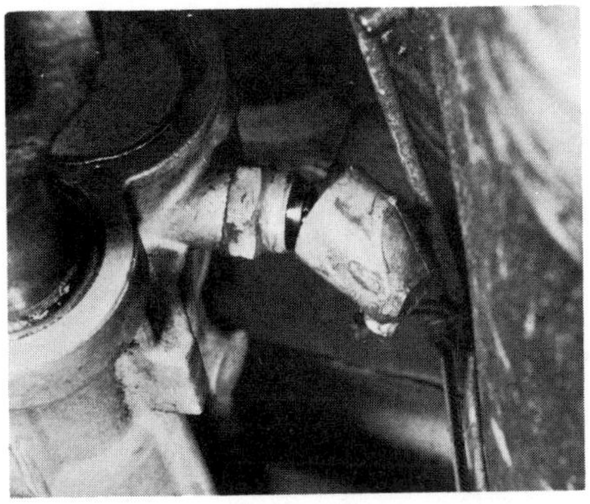

2.8 The reverse light lead cover/connector

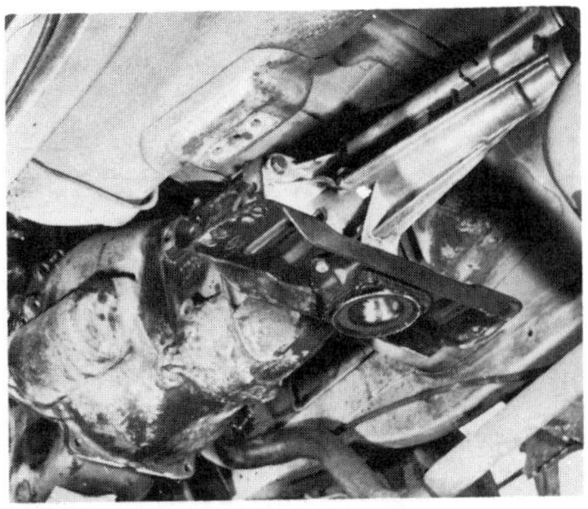

2.10 Detach the gearbox mounting

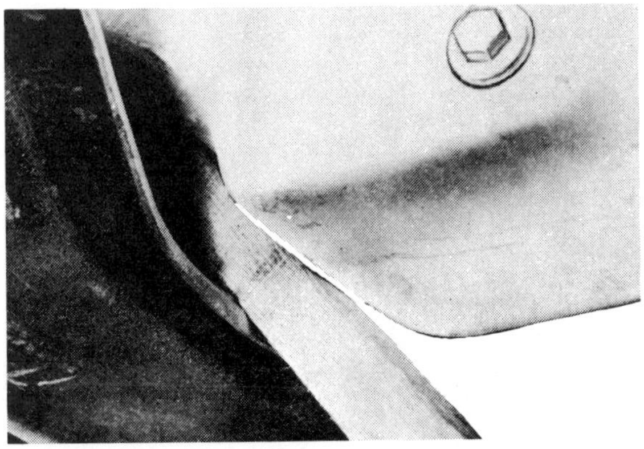

Fig. 6.2. The wooden block between the sump and the front engine mounting (Secs. 2 and 3)

Fig. 6.3. Clutch housing guide bushes (arrowed) (Secs. 2 and 3)

6 Detach the three selector shafts from the transmission.

7 Follow the procedure given in the previous Section from paragraph 8 to 14 inclusive. When refitting the selector rods to the levers on the side cover, lock the gearshift lever in the neutral position using a pin of 0.2 in (5 mm) diameter through the lock holes (Fig. 6.36). The rods should then be adjusted so that they can be inserted into the levers without strain.

8 Before removing the car from the jacks, ramps or inspection pit, top-up the oil level and adjust the clutch (refer to Chapter 5 for the latter).

4 Gearbox (type C) - dismantling

1 Remove the clutch release bearing from the gearbox input shaft (photo).

2 Then lift out the clutch release lever (photo).

3 Undo and remove the four bolts holding the bellhousing to the gearbox (photo).

4 Detach the bellhousing from the gearbox (photo).

5 Place the gearbox on a suitable workbench with blocks available to use as supports while dismantling.

6 Referring to Fig. 6.4 undo the four bolts holding the gearbox top cover (1) in place (photo A) and remove the cover (photo B).

7 Remove the spring (7) and detent ball (8). The ball can either be removed using a magnet or a screwdriver with a blob of grease on the end.

8 Tip the gearbox over on to one side and drain the oil into a suitably sized container.

9 Prise out the cup shaped speedometer drive cover (31) on the side of the gearbox extension (photo).

10 From under this seal pull out the speedometer gear (30) (photo).

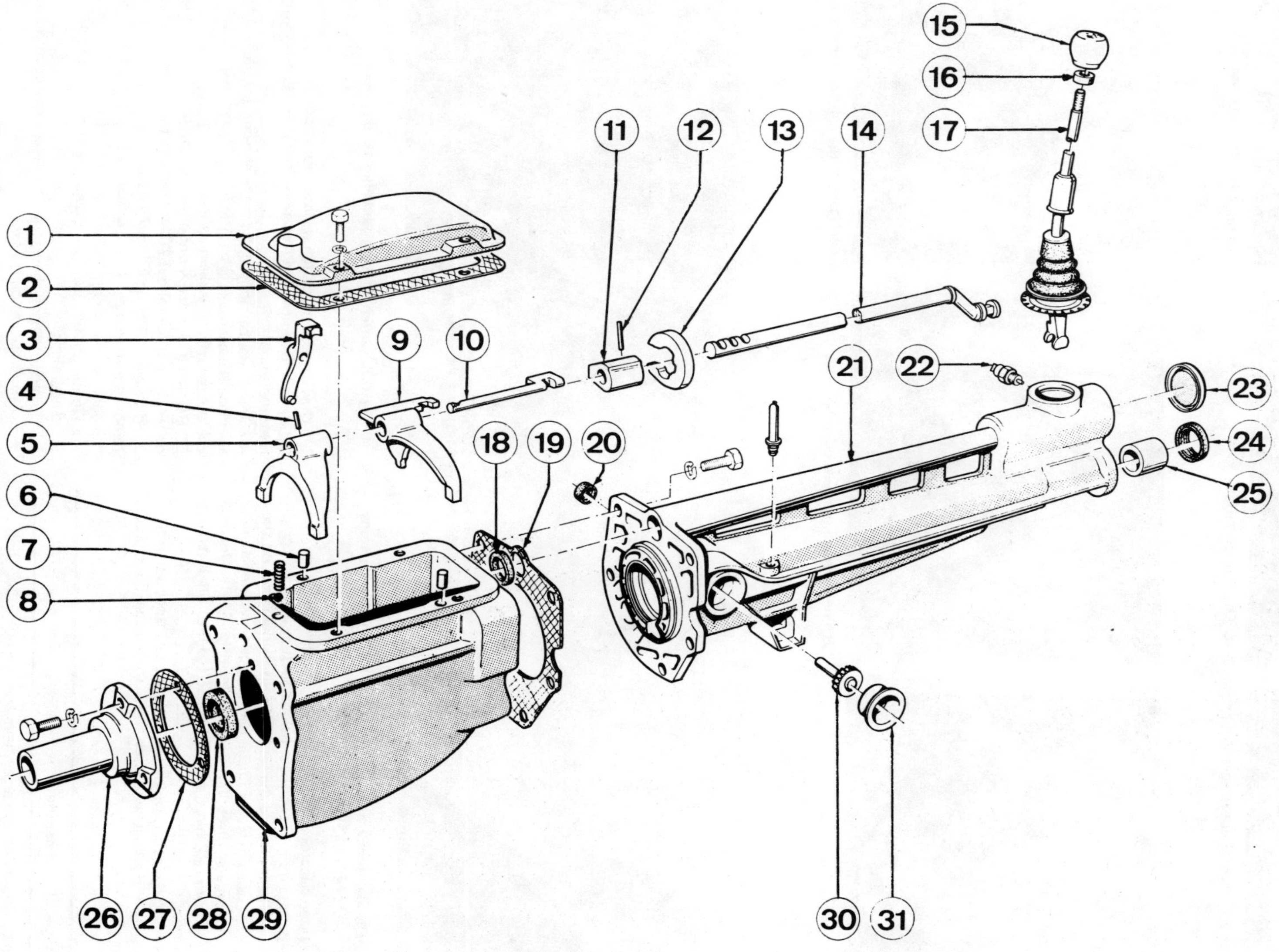

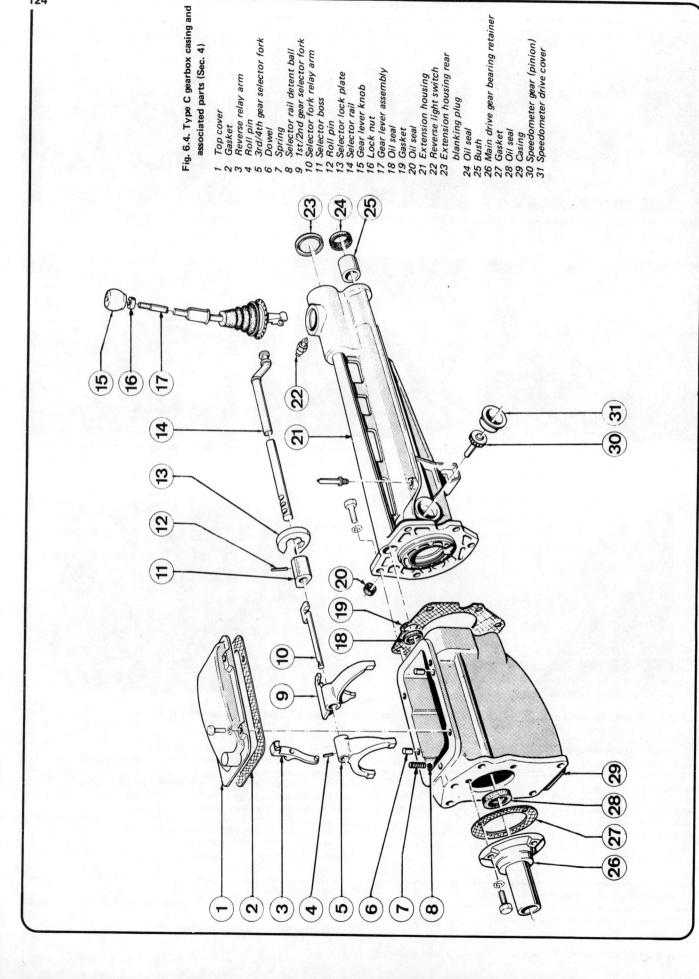

Fig. 6.4. Type C gearbox casing and associated parts (Sec. 4)

1 *Top cover*
2 *Gasket*
3 *Reverse relay arm*
4 *Roll pin*
5 *3rd/4th gear selector fork*
6 *Dowel*
7 *Spring*
8 *Selector rail detent ball*
9 *1st/2nd gear selector fork*
10 *Selector fork relay arm*
11 *Selector boss*
12 *Roll pin*
13 *Selector lock plate*
14 *Selector rail*
15 *Gear lever knob*
16 *Lock nut*
17 *Gear lever assembly*
18 *Oil seal*
19 *Gasket*
20 *Oil seal*
21 *Extension housing*
22 *Reverse light switch*
23 *Extension housing rear blanking plug*
24 *Oil seal*
25 *Bush*
26 *Main drive gear bearing retainer*
27 *Gasket*
28 *Oil seal*
29 *Casing*
30 *Speedometer gear (pinion)*
31 *Speedometer drive cover*

4.1 Remove the clutch release bearing

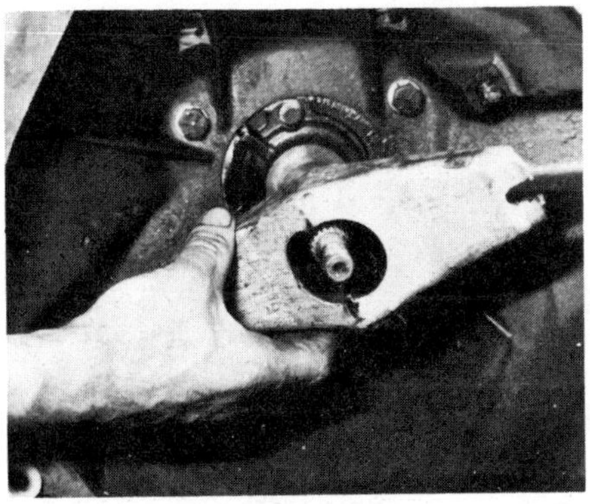
4.2 Lift out the release lever

4 3 Remove the bellhousing retaining bolts

4.4 Detach the bellhousing

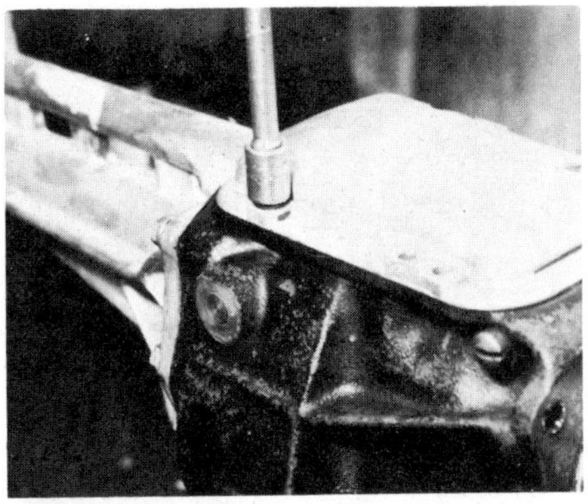
4.6a Undo the bolts...

4.6b ... and remove the top cover

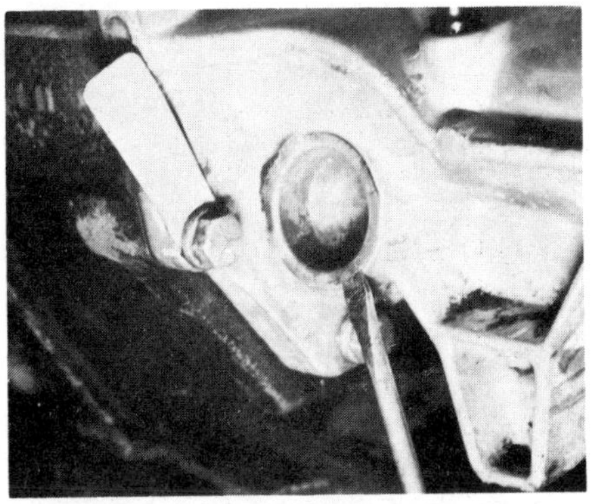
4.9 Prise out the cap shaped retainer plug

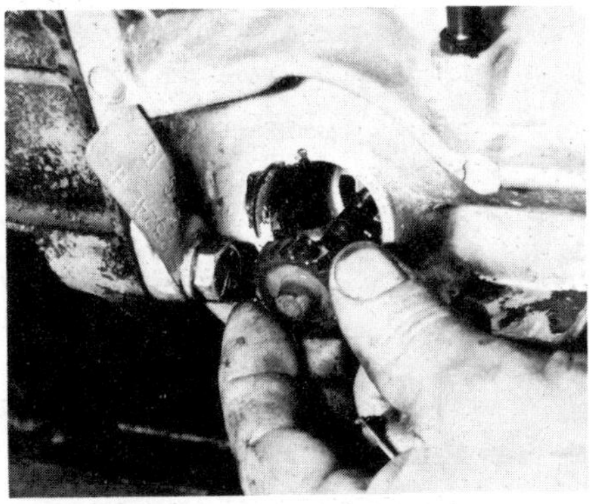
4.10 Remove the speedometer gear

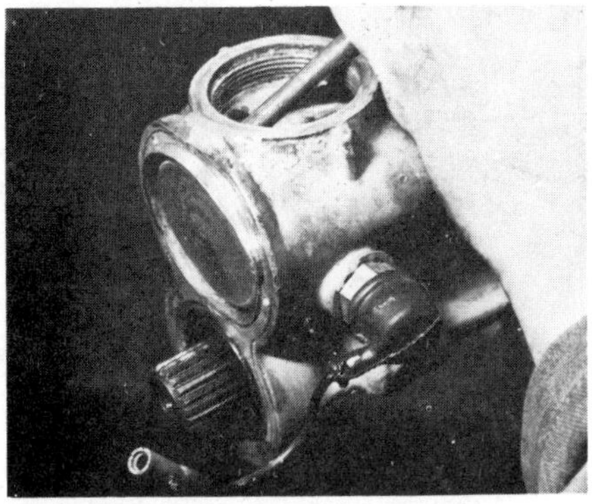
4.11 Drive out the rear extension blanking plug

To start it, it may be necessary to tap it from the other end.

11 From where the gear lever enters the extension housing, drive out the rear extension blanking plug (23) (photo).

12 Using a small punch drive out the pin holding the selector boss to the central rod (photo).

13 Now withdraw the selector rod (photo a) at the same time holding the selector boss and cam (photo b) to prevent them falling into the gearbox.

14 To remove the selector forks, it is now necessary to knock the two synchro hubs towards the front of the gearbox. This can be done with a small punch or a screwdriver; now lift out the selector forks.

15 Turn now to the gearbox extension (21) and remove the bolts and washers which hold it to the gearbox casing.

16 Knock it slightly rearwards with a soft headed hammer then rotate the whole extension until the cut-out on the extension face coincides with the rear end of the layshaft in the lower half of the gearbox casing.

17 Get hold of a metal rod to act as a dummy layshaft 6 13/16 in (173 mm) long with a diameter of 0.68 in (17.3 mm).

18 Tap the layshaft rearwards with a drift until it is just clear of the front of the gearbox casing then insert the dummy shaft and drive the layshaft out and allow the laygear cluster to drop out of mesh with the mainshaft gears into the bottom of the box.

19 Withdraw the mainshaft and extension assembly from the gearbox casing, pushing the 3rd/top synchronizer hub forward slightly to obtain the necessary clearance. A small roller bearing should come away on the nose of the mainshaft, but if it is not there it will be found in its recess in the input shaft and should be removed.

20 Moving to the front of the gearbox, remove the bolts retaining the drive gear bearing retainer (26) and take it off the shaft.

21 Remove the large circlip now exposed and then tap on the bearing outer race to remove it, and the input shaft, from inside the gearbox.

22 The laygear can now be withdrawn from the rear of the gearbox together with its thrust washers (one at either end).

23 Remove the mainshaft assembly from the gearbox extension, by taking out the large circlip adjacent to the mainshaft bearing (12), Fig. 6.5, then tapping the rear of the shaft with a soft headed hammer. Do not discard this circlip at this stage as it is required for setting-up

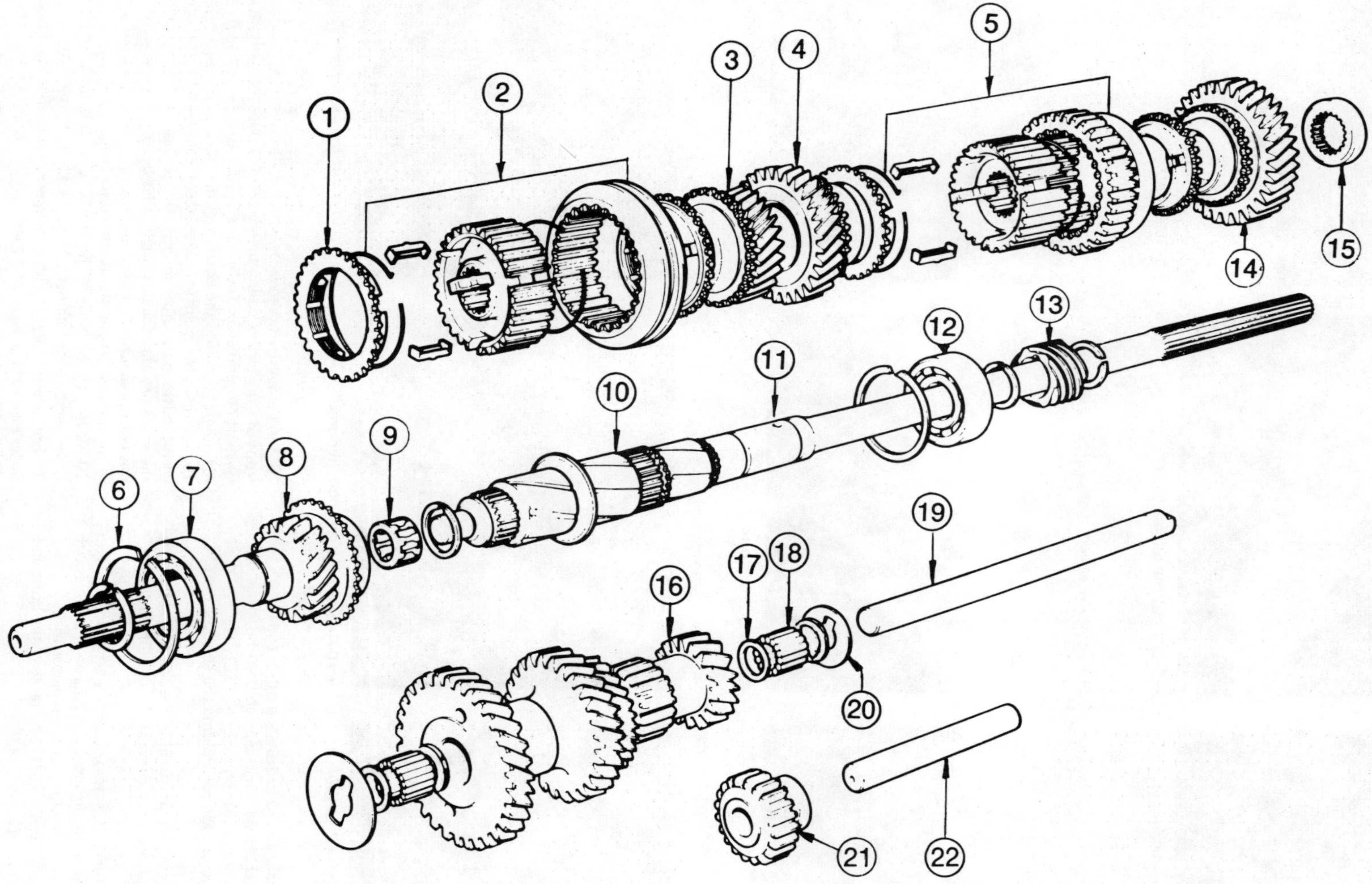

Fig. 6.5. Type C gearbox shafts and gears (Sec. 4)

1 *Synchroniser blocker ring*
2 *Synchroniser hub (3rd/4th gear)*
3 *3rd gear*
4 *2nd gear*
5 *Synchroniser hub (1st/2nd gear)*
6 *Circlip*
7 *Input shaft bearing*
8 *Input shaft (main drive gear)*
9 *Needle roller bearing*
10 *Mainshaft*
11 *Detent ball*
12 *Mainshaft bearing*
13 *Speedometer worm gear*
14 *1st gear*
15 *Oil scoop ring*
16 *Countershaft gear train*
17 *Spacer shim (layshaft)*
18 *Needle rollers (20 off)*
19 *Countershaft (layshaft)*
20 *Thrust washer*
21 *Reverse idler gear*
22 *Reverse idler shaft*

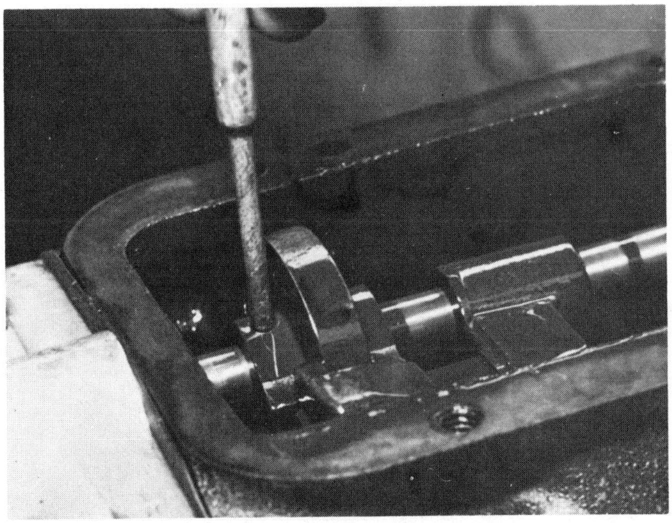

4.12 Drive out the selector boss pin

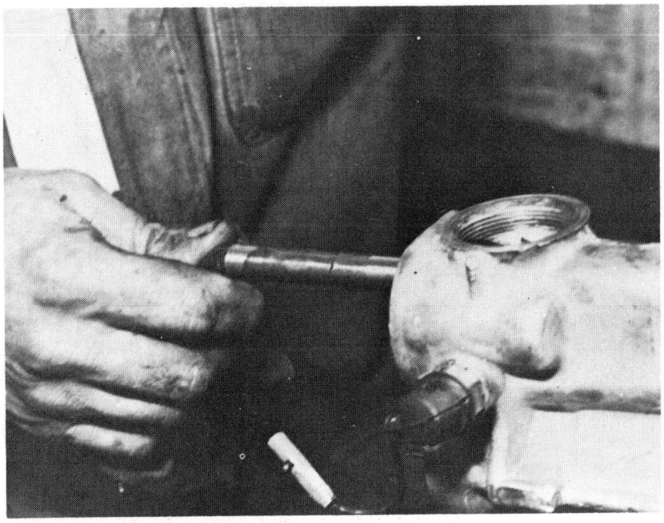

4.13a Withdraw the selector rod...

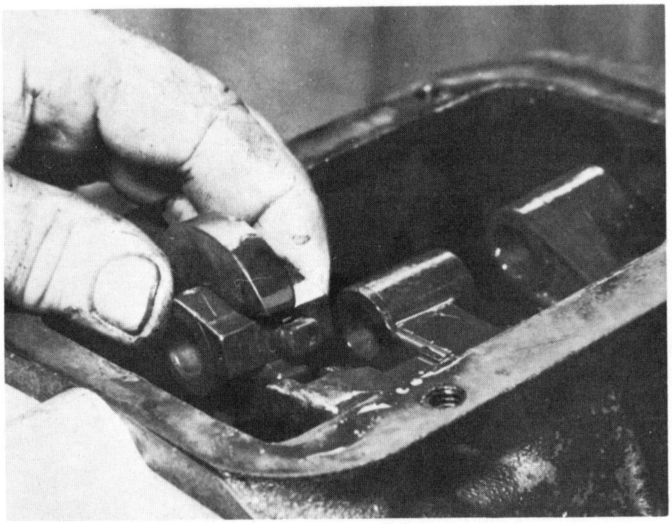

4.13b ... whilst holding the selector boss and cam

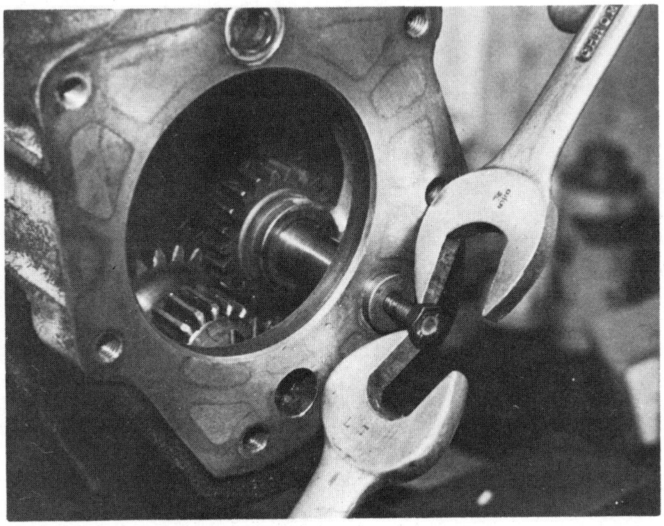

4.24 Remove the reverse idler shaft

during reassembly.

24 The reverse idler gear can be removed by screwing a suitable bolt into the end of the shaft (22) and then levering the shaft out with the aid of two large open ended spanners (photo).

25 The gearbox is now stripped right out and must be thoroughly cleaned. If there is any quantity of metal chips and fragments in the bottom of the gearbox casing it is obvious that several items will be found to be badly worn. The component parts of the gearbox and laygear should be examined for wear. The input shaft and mainshaft assemblies should be broken down further as described in the following Sections.

5 Gearbox (type C) - examination and renovation

1 Carefully clean and then examine all the component parts for general wear, distortion, slackness of fit, and damage to machined faces and threads.

2 Examine the gearwheels for excessive wear and chipping of the teeth. Renew them as necessary.

3 Examine the layshaft for signs of wear, where the laygear needle roller bearings bear. If a small ridge can be felt at either end of the shaft it will be necessary to renew it.

4 The four synchroniser rings are bound to be badly worn and it is false economy not to renew them. New rings will improve the smoothness, and speed of the gearchange considerably.

5 The needle roller bearing and cage (9) (Fig. 6.5) located between the nose of the mainshaft and the annulus in the rear of the input shaft is also liable to wear, and should be renewed as a matter of course.

6 Examine the condition of the two ball bearing assemblies, one on the input shaft (7) and one on the mainshaft (12). Check them for noisy operation, looseness between the inner and outer races, and for general wear. Normally they should be renewed on a gearbox that is being rebuilt.

7 If either of the synchroniser units (37, 38) are worn it will be necessary to buy a complete assembly as the parts are not sold individually.

8 Examine the ends of the selector forks where they rub against the channels in the periphery of the synchroniser units. If possible compare the selector forks with new units to help determine the wear that has occurred. Renew them if worn.

9 If the bush bearing in the extension housing is badly worn it is best to take the extension to your local Ford garage to have the bearing pulled out and a new one fitted.

10 The oil seals in the extension housing and main drive gear bearing retainer should be renewed as a matter of course. Drive out the old seal with the aid of a drift or broad screwdriver. It will be found that the seal comes out quite easily.

11 With a piece of wood to spread the load evenly, carefully tap a new seal into place ensuring that it enters the bore squarely.

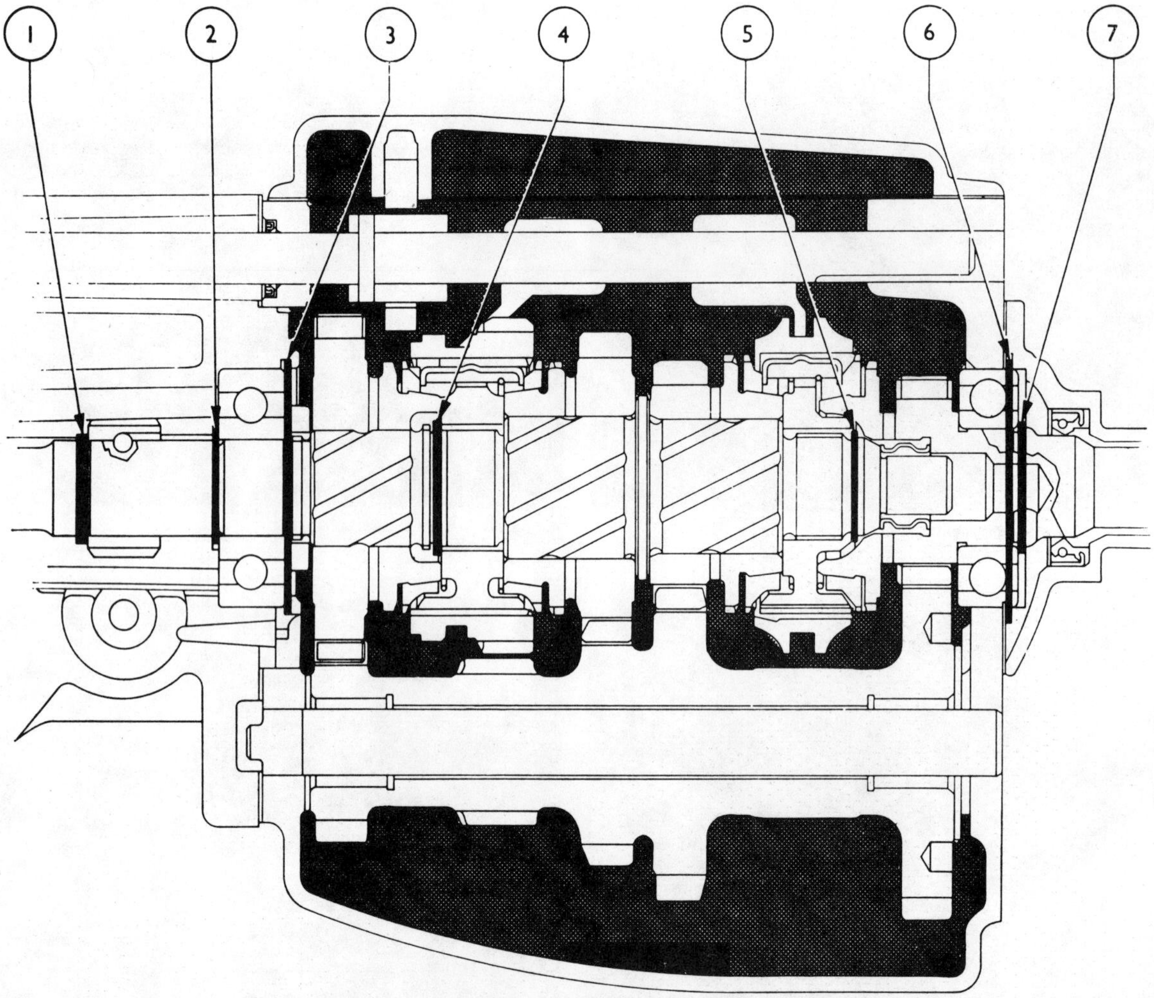

Fig. 6.6. Type C gearbox circlips: Nos. 2 and 3 are a selective fit

12 The only point on the mainshaft that is likely to be worn is the nose where it enters the input shaft. However, examine it thoroughly for any signs of scoring, picking up or flats, and if damage is apparent, renew it.

6 Input shaft (type C) - dismantling and reassembly

1 The only reason for dismantling the input shaft is to fit a new ball bearing assembly, or, if the input shaft is being renewed and the old bearing is in excellent condition, then the fitting of a new shaft to an old bearing.
2 With a pair of expanding circlip pliers remove the small circlip which secures the bearing to the input shaft.
3 With a soft-headed hammer gently tap the bearing forward and then remove it from the shaft.
4 When fitting the new bearing ensure that the groove cut in the outer periphery faces away from the gear. If the bearing is fitted the wrong way round it will not be possible to fit the large circlip which retains the bearing in the housing.
5 Using the jaws of a vice as a support behind the bearing tap the bearing squarely into place by hitting the rear of the input shaft with a plastic or hide faced hammer.
6 Finally refit the circlip which holds the bearing to the input shaft.

7 Mainshaft (type C) - dismantling and reassembly

1 The mainshaft has to be dismantled before some of the synchroniser rings can be inspected. For dismantling it is best to mount the plain portion of the shaft between two pieces of wood in a vice.
2 From the forward end of the mainshaft pull off the caged roller bearing (9) and the synchro ring (Fig. 6.5).
3 With a pair of circlip pliers remove the circlip which holds the third/fourth gear synchroniser hub in place.
4 Ease the hub (2) and third gear (3) forward by gentle leverage with a pair of long nosed pliers.
5 The hub (2) and synchro ring are then removed from the mainshaft.
6 Then slide off third gear. Nothing else can be removed from this end of the mainshaft because of the raised lip on the shaft.
7 Move to the other end of the mainshaft and remove the small circlip. Then slide off the speedometer drive, taking care not to lose the ball which locates in a groove in the gear and a small recess in the mainshaft.
8 Remove the circlip and then gently lever off the mainshaft large bearing with the aid of two tyre levers as shown in the photo.
9 The bearing, followed by the oil scoop (15) can then be pulled off. Follow these items by pulling off first gear (14) and the synchroniser ring.
10 With a pair of circlip pliers remove the circlip which retains the first and second gear synchroniser assembly in place.
11 The first and second gear synchroniser followed by second gear (4) are then simply slid off the mainshaft. The mainshaft is now completely dismantled.
12 If a new synchroniser assembly is being fitted it is necessary to take it to pieces first to clean off all the preservative. These instructions are also pertinent in instances where the outer sleeve has come off the hub accidentally before dismantling.
13 To dismantle an assembly for cleaning slide the synchroniser sleeve off the splined hub and clean all the preservative from the blocker bars, spring rings, the hub itself and the sleeve.

14 Oil the components lightly and then fit the sleeve to the hub. Note the three slots in the hub and fit a blocker bar in each.
15 Fit the two springs, one on the front and one on the rear face of the inside of the synchroniser sleeve under the blocker bars with the tagged end of each spring locating in the 'U' section of the same bar. One spring must be put on anti-clockwise, and one clockwise when viewed from the side (see Fig. 6.8). When either side of the assembly is viewed face on, the direction of rotation of the springs should then appear the same.
16 Prior to reassembling the mainshaft read paragraphs 22 and 24, to ensure that the correct thickness of selective circlips can be obtained. Reassembly commences by refitting second gear (4), gear teeth facing the raised lip, and its synchroniser ring on the rear portion of the mainshaft (photo).

7.8 Remove the large bearing

17 Next slide on the first and second gear synchroniser assembly (5) (photo a) and ensure that the cut-outs in the synchroniser ring fit over the blocker bars in the synchroniser hub (photo b); that the marks on the mainshaft and hub are in line (where made), and that the reverse gear teeth cut on the synchroniser sleeve periphery are adjacent to second gear.
18 Refit the circlip which holds the synchroniser hub in place (photo).
19 Then fit another synchroniser ring again, ensuring that the cut-outs in the ring fit over the blocker bars in the synchroniser hub.
20 Next slide on first gear (14) so that the synchronising cone portion lies inside the synchronising ring just fitted (photo).
21 Fit the oil scoop (15), large diameter facing the first gear (photo).
22 If a new mainshaft bearing (12) or a new gearbox extension is being used it will now be necessary to select a new large circlip to eliminate endfloat of the mainshaft. To do this, first fit the original circlip in its groove in the gearbox extension and draw it outwards (ie; away from the rear of the extension). Now accurately measure the dimension from the base of the bearing housing to the outer edge of the circlip and record the figure. Also accurately measure the thickness of the bearing outer track (Fig. 6.9) and subtract this figure from the depth already recorded. This will give the required shim thickness to give zero endfloat.
23 Loosely fit the selected circlip, lubricate the bearing contact surfaces then press it onto the shaft. To press the bearing home, close the jaws of the vice until they are not quite touching the mainshaft, and with the bearing resting squarely against the side of the vice jaws draw the bearing on by tapping the end of the shaft with a hide or plastic hammer (photo).
24 Refit the small circlip retaining the main bearing in place. This is also a selective circlip and must be such that all endfloat between the bearing inner track and the circlip edge is eliminated (photo).
25 Refit the small ball (11) that retains the speedometer drive in its recess in the mainshaft (photo).

Fig. 6.7. Component parts of the synchro hub (Sec. 7)

Fig. 6.8. Relative positions of synchro spring clips (Sec. 7)

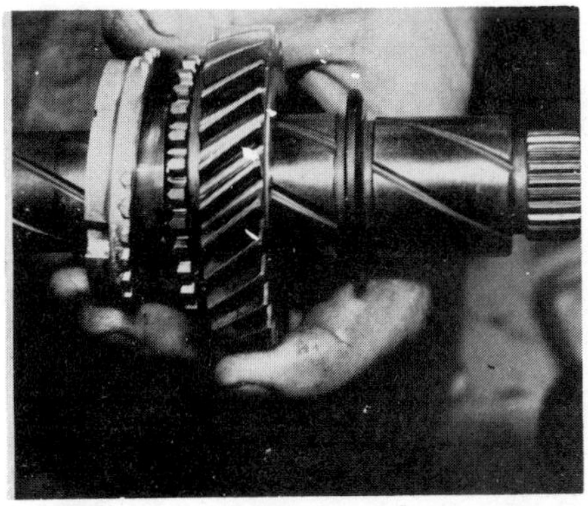

7.16 Refit the second gear and synchroniser ring

7.17a Slide on the first and second gear synchroniser assembly ...

7.17b ... and make sure that the ring fits over the blocker bars

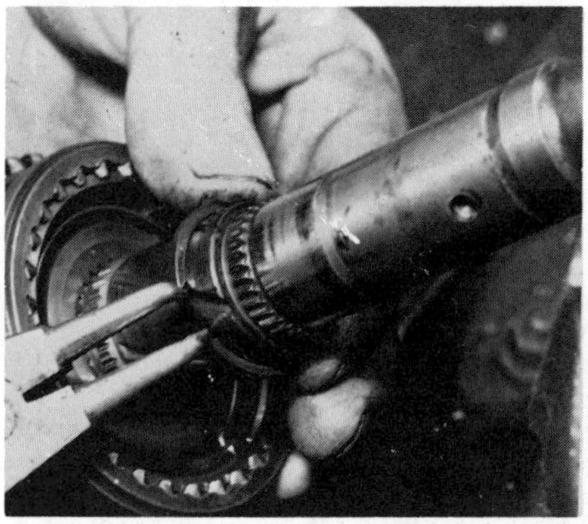

7.18 Refit the circlip

7.20 Slide on the first gear

7.21 Fit the oil scoop

Fig. 6.9. Measuring the mainshaft bearing track (Sec. 7)

7.23 Press the bearing home

7.24 Refit the main bearing selective circlip

7.25 Refit the speedometer drive retaining ball.

7.26 Slide on the speedometer drive gear

7.27 Fit the circlip.

7.28 Slide on the third gear and synchronizer ring

7.29 Fit the third and fourth gear synchronizer assembly

26 Slide on the speedometer drive noting that it can only be fitted one way round as the groove in which the ball fits does not run the whole length of the drive (photo).
27 Now fit the circlip to retain the speedometer drive (photo). Assembly of this end of the mainshaft is now complete.
28 Moving to the short end of the mainshaft slide on third gear (3) so that the machined gear teeth lie adjacent to second gear, then slide on the synchroniser ring (photo).
29 Fit the third and fourth gear synchroniser assembly (2) (photo) again ensuring that the cut-outs on the ring line up with the blocker bars.
30 With a suitable piece of metal tube over the mainshaft, tap the synchroniser fully home onto the mainshaft (photo).
31 Then fit the securing circlip in place (photo). Apart from the needle roller bearing race which fits on the nose of the mainshaft, this completes mainshaft reassembly.

8 Gearbox (type C) - reassembly

1 If removed, refit the reverse idler gear and selector lever in the gearbox, by tapping in the shaft (22) (Fig. 6.5). Once it is through the casing fit the gear wheel (21) so that its gear teeth are facing in towards the main gearbox area.
2 Fit the reverse selector lever in the groove in the idler gear then drive the shaft home with a soft headed hammer until it is flush with the gearbox casing.
3 Slide a spacer shim (17) into either end of the laygear, (16) so that they abut the internal machined shoulders.
4 Smear thick grease on the laygear roller bearing surface and fit the needle rollers (18) one at a time (photo), until all are in place. The grease will hold the rollers in position. Build up the needle roller bearings in the other end of the laygear in a similar fashion. Note that there should be 20 at each end.
5 Fit the external washer to each end of the laygear, taking care not to dislodge the roller bearings (photo).
6 Carefully slide in the dummy layshaft used previously for driving out the layshaft (photo).
7 Grease the two thrust washers (20) and position the larger of the two in the front of the gearbox so that the tongues fit into the machined recesses.
8 Fit the smaller of the thrust washers to the rear of the gearbox in the same way (photo).
9 Fit the laygear complete with dummy layshaft in the bottom of the gearbox casing taking care not to dislodge the thrust washers (photo).
10 Now from inside the gearbox, slide in the input shaft assembly (8) (photo a) and drive the bearing into place with a suitable drift (photo b).
11 Secure the bearing in position by refitting the circlip (6) (photo).
12 Fit a new gasket to the bearing retainer and smear on some non-setting jointing compound (photo).
13 Refit the retainer on the input shaft (photo A) ensuring that the oil drain hole is towards the bottom of the gearbox, and tighten down the bolts (photo B).
14 Submerge the gearbox end of the extension housing in hot water for a few minutes, then mount it in a vice and slide in the mainshaft assembly. Take care that the splines do not damage the oil seal, tape the splines if necessary (photo).
15 Secure the mainshaft to the gearbox extension by locating the circlip already placed loosely behind the main bearing into its groove in the extension (photo a). Photo b shows the circlip correctly located.
16 Fit a new gasket to the extension housing and then refit the small roller bearing on the nose of the mainshaft. Lubricate the roller bearing with gearbox oil (photo).
17 Slide the combined mainshaft and extension housing assembly into the rear of the gearbox and mate up the nose of the mainshaft with the rear of the input shaft (photo).
18 Completely invert the gearbox so that the laygear falls into mesh with the mainshaft gears.
19 Turn the extension housing round until the cut-out on it coincides with the hole for the layshaft (photo). It may be necessary to trim the gasket.
20 Push the layshaft into its hole from the rear, thereby driving out the

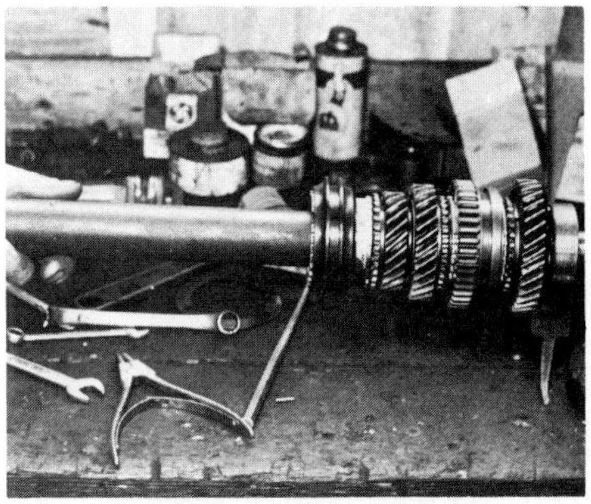
7.30 Tap the synchronizer fully home.

7.31 Fit the securing circlip.

8.4 Fit the laygear needle rollers.

8.5 Fit the external washers.

8.6 Slide in the dummy layshaft.

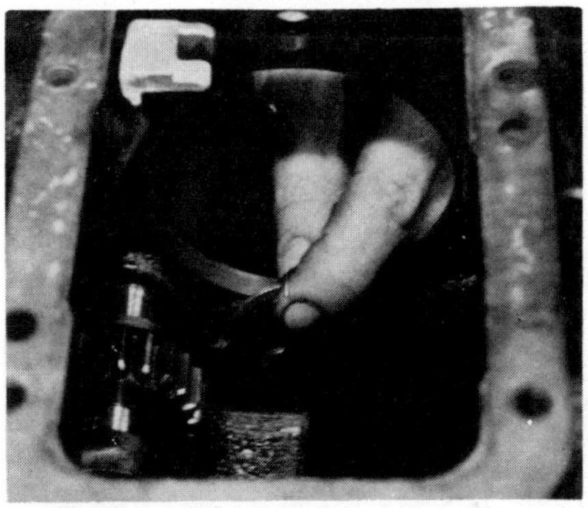
8.8 Fit the smaller thrust washer at the rear.

8.9 Fit the laygear carefully

8.10a Slide in the input shaft assembly ...

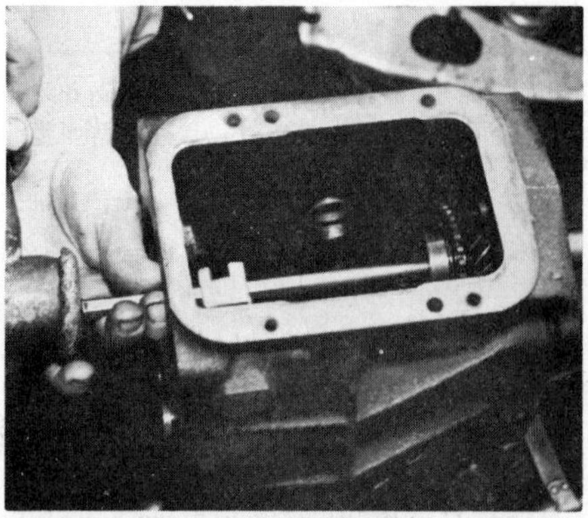

8.10b ... and drive the bearing into place

8.11 Fit the circlip to retain the bearing

8.12 Apply sealing compound to the bearing retainer

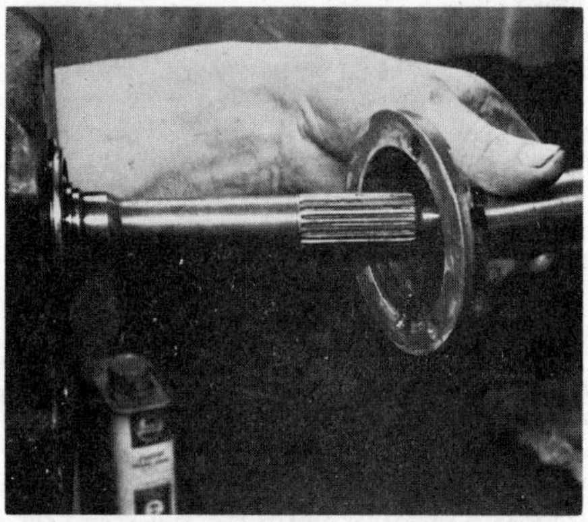

8.13a Refit the input shaft retainer ...

8.13b ... and tighten the bolts

8.14 Slide in the mainshaft assembly

8.15a Locate the circlip in the groove in the extension

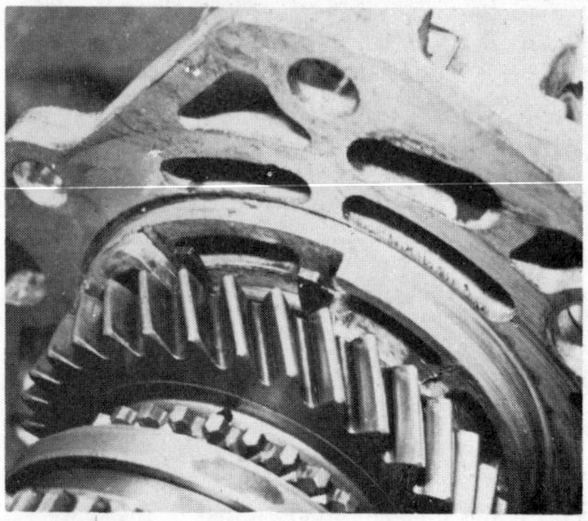

8.15b The circlip correctly located

8.16 Refit the mainshaft roller bearing

8.17 Slide the mainshaft and extension housing into the gearbox

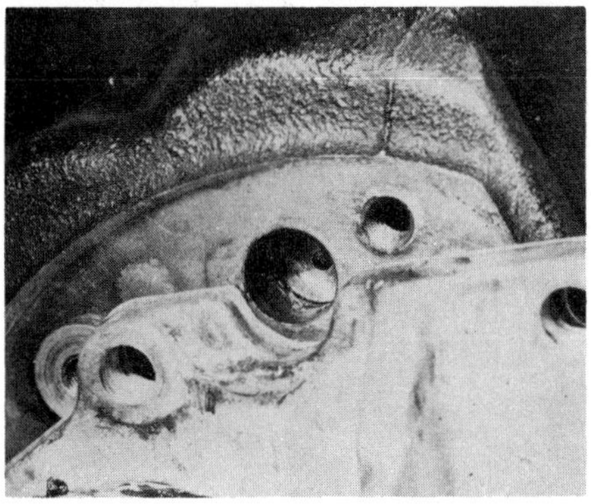
8.19 Turn the extension housing to align the cut out with the hole for the layshaft

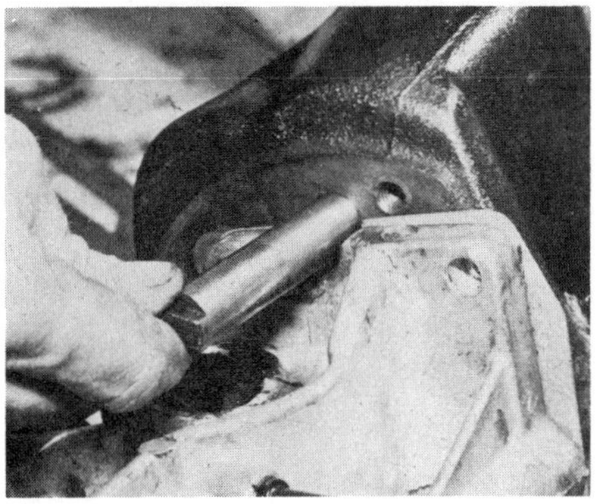
8.20 Push in the layshaft

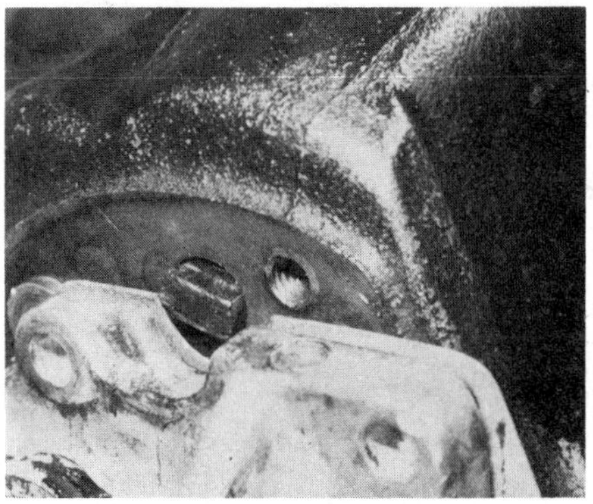
8.21 Ensure that the cut out in the end of the layshaft is in the horizontal position

8.22 Secure the extension housing to the gearbox

8.23a Push the synchroniser hub fully forward

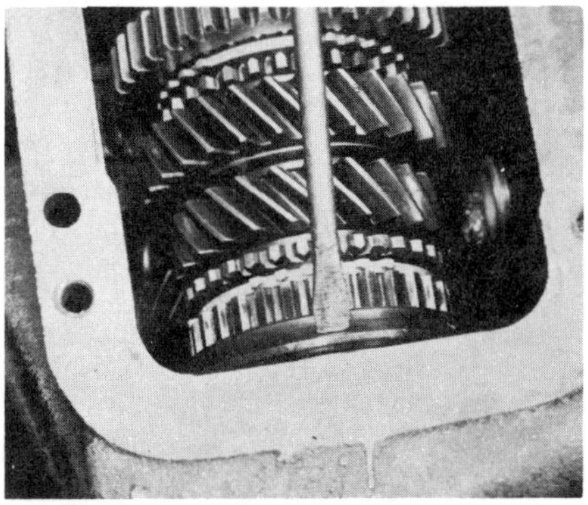
8.23b Push the synchroniser hub fully forward

8.24a Lower the selector forks into position

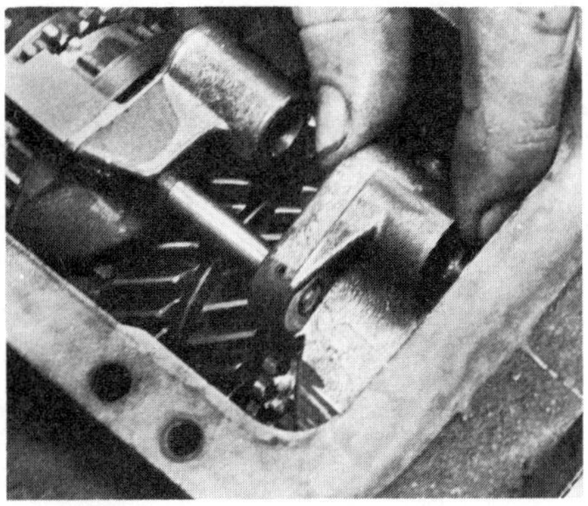
8.24b Lower the selector forks into position

dummy shaft at the same time (photo).

21 Tap the layshaft into position until its front end is flush with the gearbox casing and ensure that the cut-out on the rear end is in the horizontal position so it will fit into its recess in the extension housing flange (photo).

22 Turn the gearbox the right way up again; correctly line up the extension housing and secure it to the gearbox. Apply a non-setting jointing compound to the bolt threads before fitting them (photo).

23 The selector forks cannot be replaced until the two synchroniser hubs are pushed by means of a screwdriver or drift to their most forward positions (photos a and b).

24 Now lower the selector forks into position (photo a); it will be found that they will now drop in quite easily (photo b). Now return the synchroniser hubs to their original positions.

25 Slide the gearchange selector rail into place from the rear of the extension and as it comes into the gearbox housing slide onto it the selector boss and lock plate, having just made sure that the plate locates in the cut-outs in the selector fork extension arms.

26 Push the selector rod through the boss and the selector forks until the pin holes on the boss and rail align. Tap the pin into place thereby securing the boss to the selector rod. During this operation ensure that the cut-out on the gearbox end of the selector rail faces to the right.

27 Apply a small amount of non-setting jointing compound to the blanking plug and gently tap it into position in the rear of the extension housing behind the selector rail. Peen it with a centre punch in three or four places to retain it.

28 Insert the detent ball and spring (8 and 7 in Fig. 6.4).

29 Place a new gasket on the gearbox top cover plate, then refit the top cover and tighten down its four retaining bolts.

30 Refit the speedometer drive gear in the extension, smear the edges of its retaining plug with non-setting jointing compound and tap the plug into place.

31 Refit the bellhousing onto the gearbox, apply a non-setting jointing compound to the bolt threads then fit them.

32 Refit the clutch release fork and bearing.

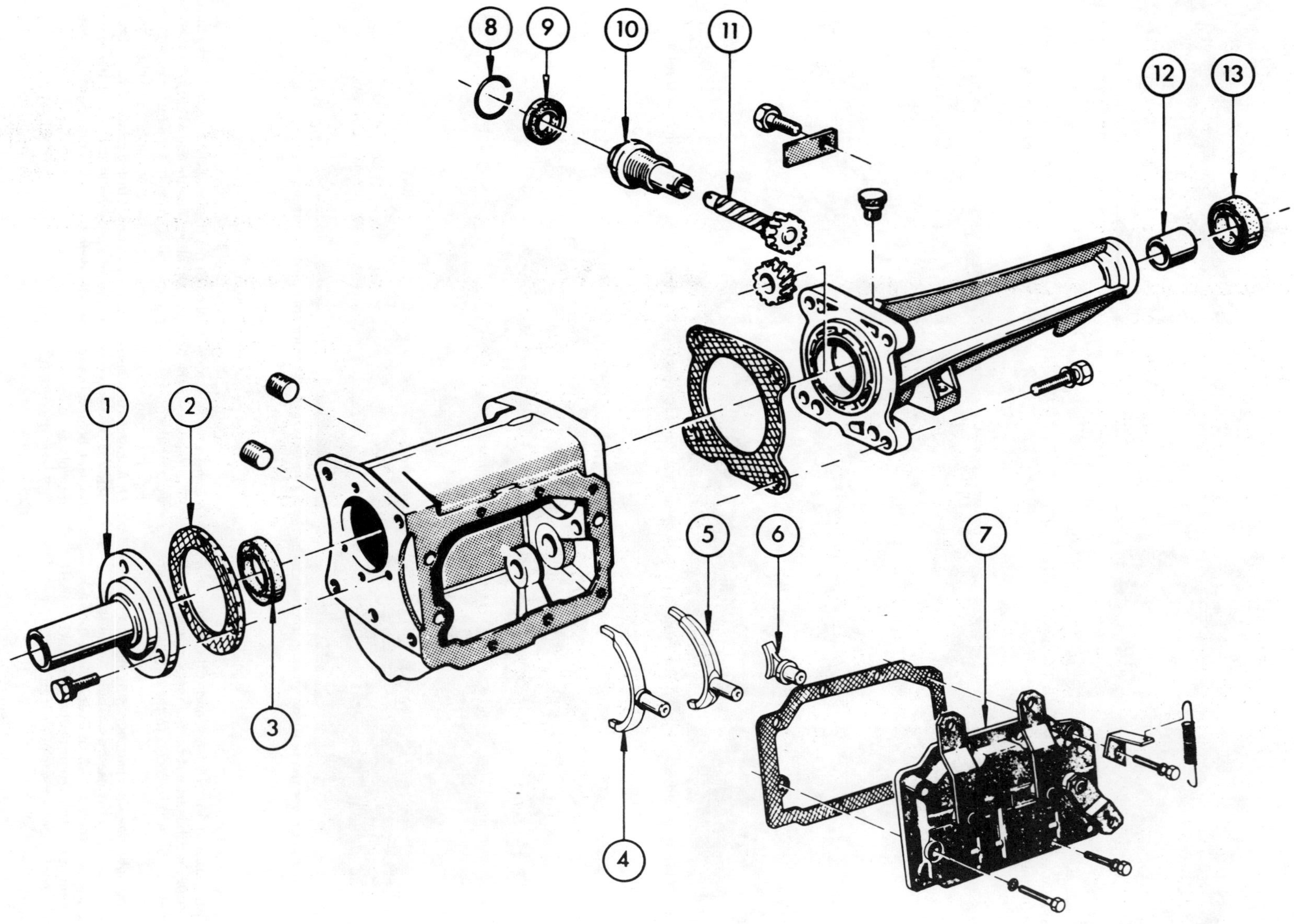

Fig. 6.10. Type H gearbox casing and associated parts (Sec. 9)

1 Main drive gear bearing retainer
2 Gasket
3 Oil seal
4 3rd/4th gear selector fork
5 1st/2nd gear selector fork
6 Reverse gear selector fork
7 Selector housing cover
8 Circlip
9 Oil seal
10 Speedometer pinion bearing
11 Speedometer gear (pinion)
12 Extension housing bush
13 Extension housing oil seal

9 Gearbox (type H) - dismantling

1 Initially follow the procedure given in paragraph 1 to 5 of Section 4. If the gearbox has not been drained of its oil, this is a convenient time to do so.

2 Referring to Fig. 6.10, remove the selector housing cover (7) together with the two supports for the reverse gear return spring, and the reversing light switch. The cover is retained by bolts.

3 Take out the selector forks from the gearbox.

4 Remove the circlip (8), oil seal (9) speedometer pinion bearing (10) and speedometer pinion (11) from the extension housing.

5 Follow the procedure given in paragraphs 15 to 18 of Section 4 but note that the dummy layshaft length recommended for the type H gearbox is 6.97 in (177 mm).

6 Remove the main drive gear bearing retainer (3 bolts and washers). Push the layshaft gear cluster to one side then withdraw the input shaft from the forward side of the gearbox.

7 Withdraw the extension housing from the rear of the gearbox, taking the assembled mainshaft with it. Do not lose the needle roller bearing from the nose of the mainshaft; if this is not there, it will be inside the counterbore of the input shaft already removed.

8 Lift out the layshaft gear cluster complete with the dummy shaft and thrust washers.

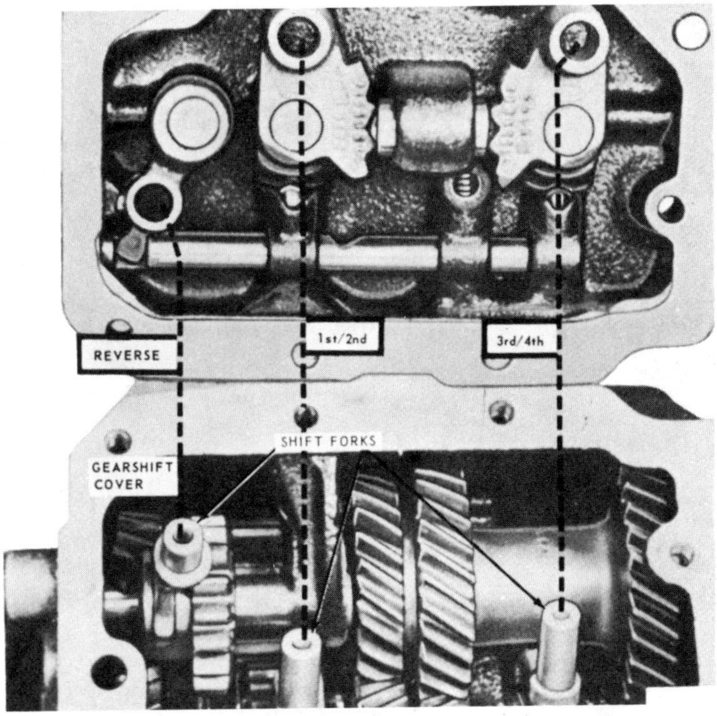

Fig. 6.11. The gearshift forks and housing cover (Sec. 9)

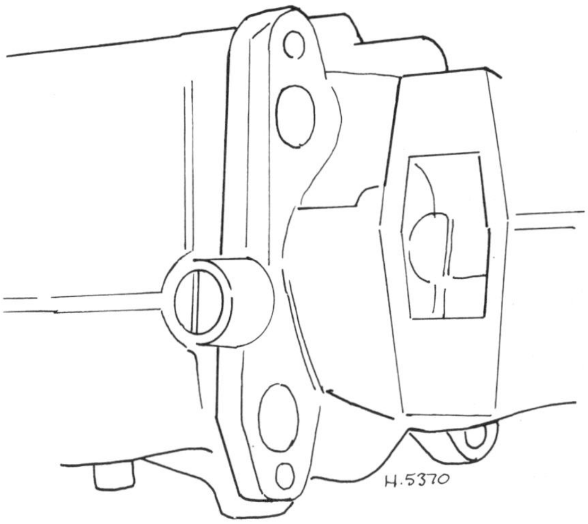

Fig. 6.12. The extension housing rotated for removing the countershaft (Sec. 9)

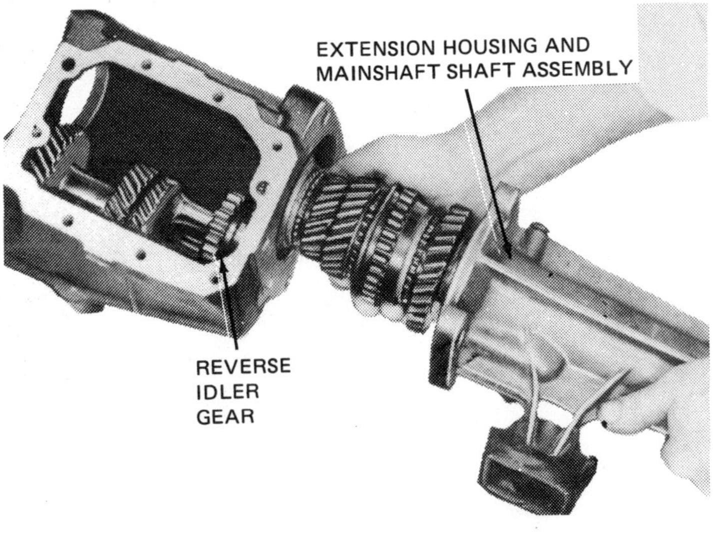

Fig. 6.13. Removing the extension housing (Sec. 9)

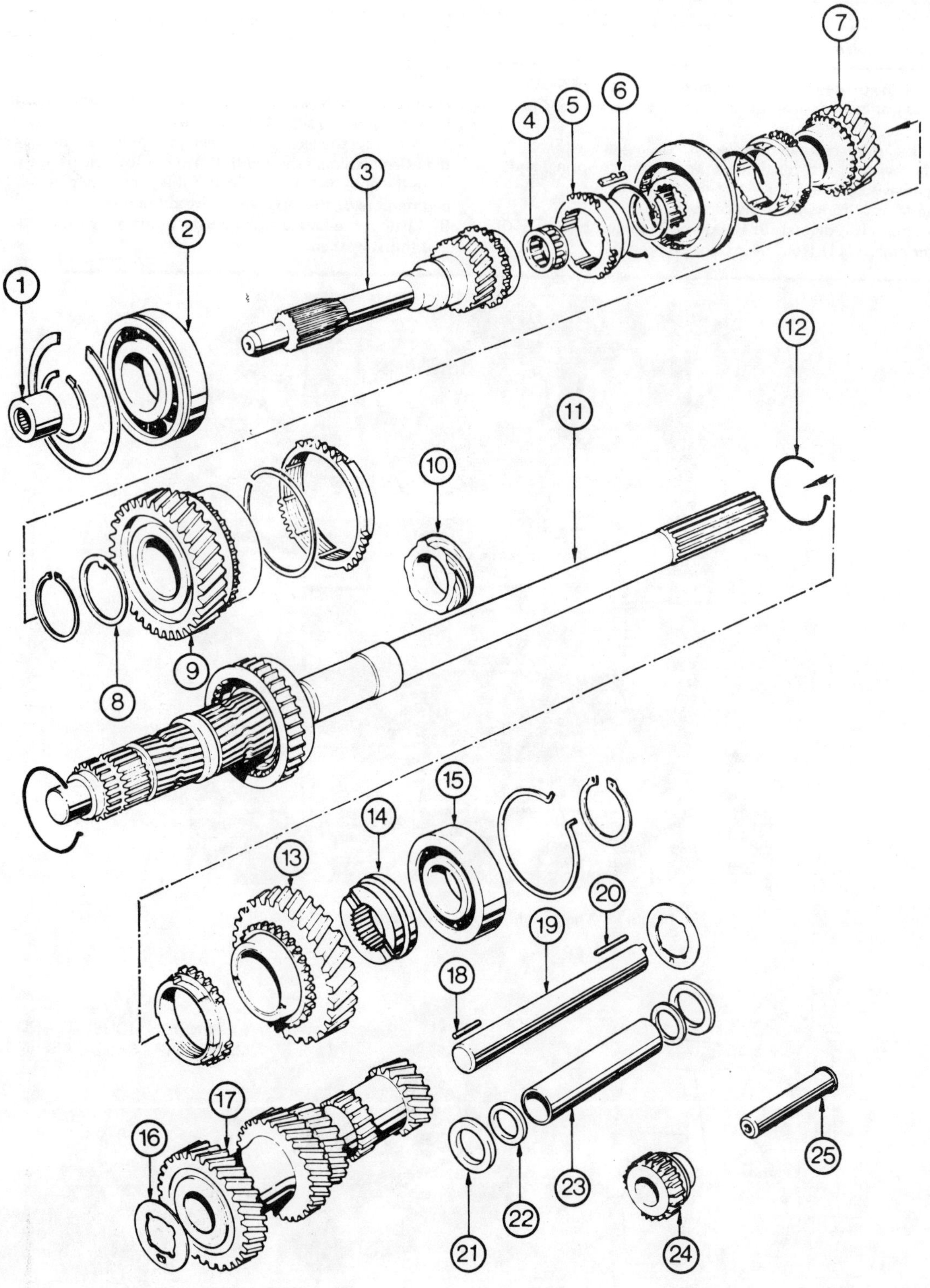

Fig. 6.14. Type H gearbox shafts and gears (Sec. 9)

1 *Input shaft bearing*
2 *Grooved ball bearing*
3 *Input shaft (main drive gear)*
4 *Needle roller bearing*
5 *Synchroniser blocker ring*
6 *Blocker bar*
7 *3rd gear*
8 *Thrust washer*
9 *2nd gear*
10 *Speedometer worm gear*
11 *Mainshaft complete with 1st/2nd gear synchroniser hub*
12 *1st/2nd gear synchroniser spring*
13 *1st gear*
14 *Oil scoop ring*
15 *Grooved ball bearing*
16 *Thrust washer*
17 *Countershaft (layshaft) cluster gear*
18 *Front needle rollers (19 off)*
19 *Countershaft (layshaft)*
20 *Rear needle rollers (19 off)*
21 *Thrust washer*
22 *Shim*
23 *Spacer tube*
24 *Reverse idler gear*
25 *Reverse idler shaft*

9 Using a suitable drift, drive out the reverse idler shaft rearwards and take out the idler gear.

10 Remove the mainshaft assembly from the gearbox extension by taking out the large circlip adjacent to the mainshaft bearing. Do not discard this circlip at this stage as it is required for setting up during reassembly.

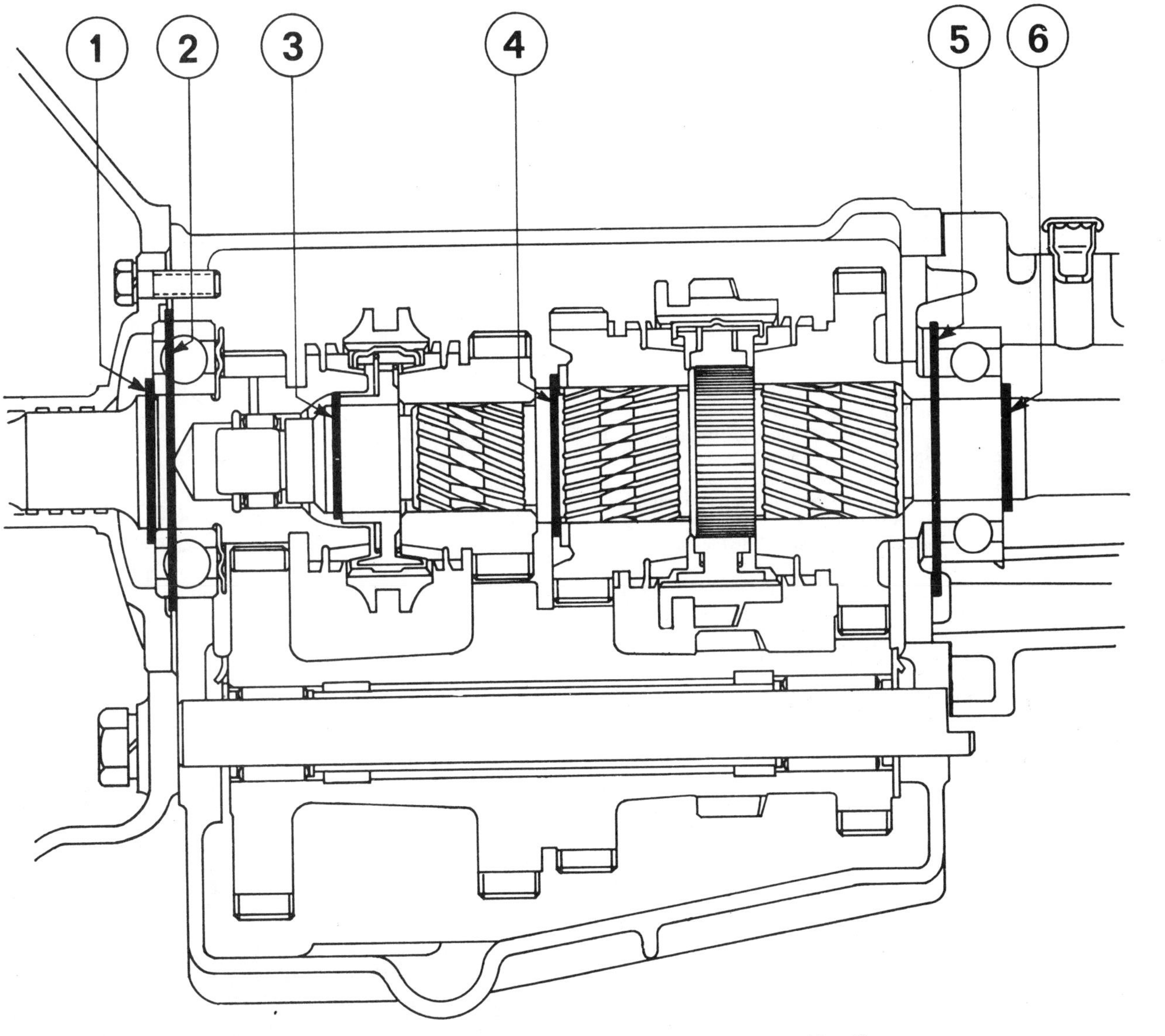

Fig. 6.15. Type H gearbox circlips: Nos. 1, 5 and 6 are a selective fit (Sec. 9)

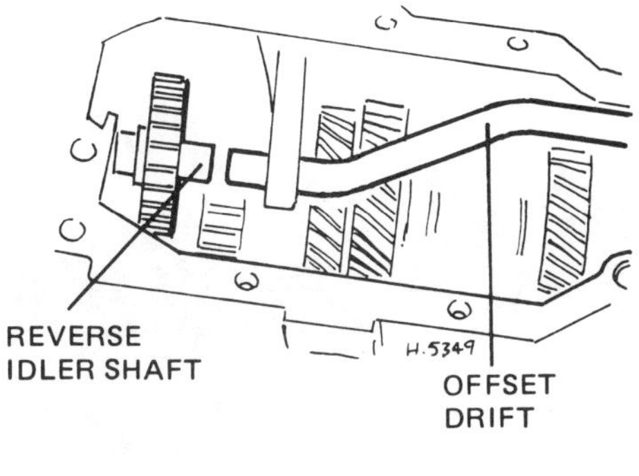

Fig. 6.16. Driving out the reverse idler shaft (Sec. 9)

Fig. 6.17. Remove the mainshaft bearing circlip (ends arrowed) from the groove in the extension housing (Sec. 9)

11 The gearbox is now stripped of its major assemblies and must be thoroughly cleaned. If there are any metal chips or fragments in the bottom of the casing it is obvious that some of the parts are worn or damaged. The component parts of the gearbox and the laygear should be examined for wear. The input shaft and mainshaft should be broken down further as described in the following Sections.

10 Gearbox (type H) - examination and renovation

1 Carefully clean and then examine all the component parts for general wear, distortion, slackness of fit, and damage to machined faces and threads.
2 Examine the gearwheels for excessive wear and chipping of the teeth. Renew them as necessary.
3 Examine the layshaft for signs of wear, where the laygear needle roller bearings bear. If a small ridge can be felt at either end of the shaft it will be necessary to renew it.
4 The four synchroniser rings are bound to be badly worn and it is false economy not to renew them. New rings will improve the smoothness and speed of the gearchange considerably.
5 The needle roller bearing and cage located between the nose of the mainshaft and the annulus in the rear of the input shaft is also liable to wear, and should be renewed as a matter of course.
6 Examine the condition of the two ball bearing assemblies, one on the input shaft and one on the mainshaft. Check them for noisy operation, looseness between the inner and outer races, and for general wear. Normally they should be renewed on a gearbox that is being rebuilt.
7 If either of the synchroniser units is worn it will be necessary to buy a complete assembly as the parts are not sold individually.
8 Examine the ends of the selector forks where they rub against the channels in the periphery of the synchroniser units. If possible compare the selector forks with new units to help determine the wear that has occurred. Renew them if worn.
9 Check for wear in the moving parts of the selector housing cover, fitting replacement parts as necessary.
10 If the bush in the extension is badly worn it is best to take the extension to your local Ford garage to have the bearing pulled out and a new one fitted.
11 The oil seals in the extension housing and main drive gear bearing retainer should be renewed as a matter of course. Drive out the old seal with the aid of a drift or broad screwdriver. It will be found that the seal comes out quite easily.
12 With a piece of wood to spread the load evenly, carefully tap a new seal into place ensuring that it enters the bore squarely.
13 The only point on the mainshaft that is likely to be worn is the nose where it enters the input shaft. However, examine it thoroughly for any signs of scoring, picking up, or flats and if damage is apparent renew it.

11 Input shaft (type H) - dismantling and reassembly

1 The only reason for dismantling the input shaft is to fit a new ball bearing assembly or, if the input shaft is being renewed and the old bearing is in excellent condition, then the fitting of a new shaft to an old bearing.
2 With a pair of expanding circlip pliers remove the circlip from the input shaft.
3 With a soft headed hammer gently tap the bearing forward and then remove it from the shaft.
4 When fitting a new bearing ensure that the groove cut in the outer periphery faces away from the gear. If the bearing is fitted the wrong way round it will not be possible to fit the large circlip which retains the bearing in the housing.
5 Using the jaws of a vice as a support behind the bearing, tap the bearing squarely into place by hitting the rear of the input shaft with a plastic or hide faced hammer.
6 Finally, refit the circlip which holds the bearing to the input shaft. Note that this is a selective fit circlip and must be such that there is no relative endfloat between the bearing inner track and the circlip groove.

12 Mainshaft (type H) - dismantling and reassembly)

1 The mainshaft has to be dismantled before some of the synchroniser rings can be inspected. For dismantling it is best to mount the plain portion of the shaft between two pieces of wood in a vice.
2 From the forward end of the mainshaft pull off the caged roller bearing (4) and the synchro ring (5) (Fig. 6.14).
3 With a pair of circlip pliers remove the circlip which holds the third/fourth gear synchroniser hub in place.
4 Ease the hub and third gear (7) forward by gentle leverage with a pair of long nosed pliers.
5 The hub and synchro ring are then removed from the mainshaft, followed by the third gear.
6 Remove the circlip and thrust washer (8) then take off the second gear.
7 The first/second synchroniser hub form a unit with the mainshaft and cannot be removed, but the synchroniser assembly can be dismantled by withdrawing the sleeve, and removing the blocker bars and springs.
8 Carefully draw or tap off the speedometer drive gear from the rear of the mainshaft.
9 If necessary, remove the circlip and press off the mainshaft rear bearing. This can be done by supporting the first gear and pressing or using a soft-faced hammer on the rear end of the mainshaft. In this way the bearing oil scoop and first gear can be removed.

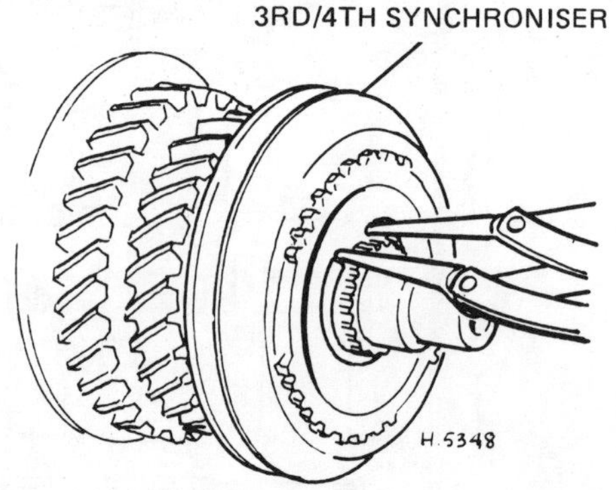

Fig. 6.18. Removing the 3rd/4th synchro hub circlip (Sec. 12)

Fig. 6.19. Removing the 2nd gear circlip (Sec. 12)

Fig. 6.20. The 1st/2nd synchro hub and mainshaft (Sec. 12)

10 If necessary, dismantle the third/top synchroniser assembly. This is similar to the first/second synchroniser apart from the hub having been removed from the mainshaft (see Fig. 6.7).
11 Clean all the parts of both synchroniser assemblies carefully then lubricate them with gearbox oil before reassembling. Insert the blocker bars then, commencing at one blocker bar insert the springs, keeping

Fig. 6.21. Selecting the small circlip which retains the mainshaft rear bearing (Sec. 12)

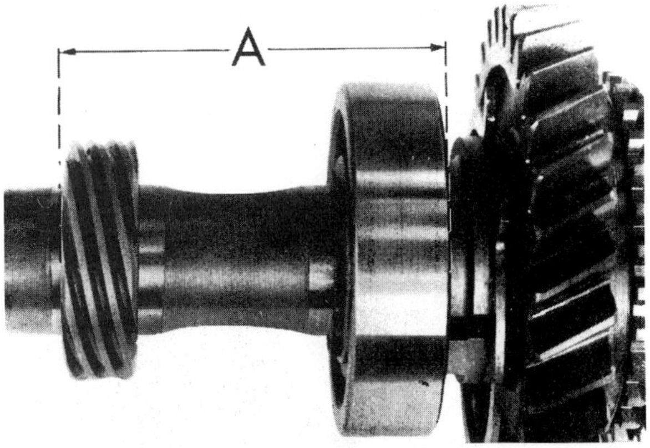

Fig. 6.22. The dimension for pressing on the speedometer drive gear (Sec. 12)

Fig. 6.24. Fitting the 3rd/4th synchro ring (Sec. 12)

to the relationship shown in Fig. 6.8. On the first/second assembly, the mark on the sleeve should coincide with the mark on the hub, and the groove should face forward.
12 The main reassembly procedure can now be commenced but first note that selective circlips will be needed at some stages during reassembly. It is therefore necessary to read through the procedure before reassembly commences so that the necessary circlips can be obtained.
13 To commence reassembly, slide the first gear and blocker ring into the mainshaft, followed by the oil scoop ring with the smaller diameter towards the first gear.
14 If a new mainshaft bearing (15) or a new gearbox extension is being used it will now be necessary to select a new large circlip to eliminate endfloat of the mainshaft. To do this, first fit the original circlip in its groove in the gearbox extension and draw it outwards (ie; away from the rear extension). Now accurately measure the dimension from the base of the bearing housing to the outer edge of the circlip and record the figure. Also accurately measure the thickness of the bearing outer track and subtract this figure from the depth already recorded. This will give the required shim thickness to give zero endfloat.
15 Loosely fit the selected circlip. Lubricate the bearing contact surfaces then press it onto the shaft. To press the bearing home, close the jaws of the vice until they are not quite touching the mainshaft and with the bearing resting squarely against the side of the vice jaws draw the bearing on by tapping the end of the shaft with a hide or plastic faced hammer.
16 Refit the small circlip retaining the main bearing in place. This is also a selective circlip and must be such that all endfloat between the bearing inner track and the circlip edge is eliminated.
17 Press on the speedometer drive gear to obtain a dimension 'A' of 3.24 in (62.25 mm) as shown in Fig. 6.22.
18 From the forward end of the mainshaft, fit the second gear together with the blocker ring, thrust washer and retaining circlip.
19 Slide the third gear and synchroniser blocker ring onto the mainshaft.
20 Slide the third/top synchroniser assembly onto the mainshaft with the long hub facing forwards, then fit the retaining circlip. Apart from the needle roller bearing which fits on the nose of the mainshaft, this completes mainshaft reassembly.

13 Gearbox (type H) - reassembly

1 Reassembly of the gearbox can be conveniently commenced by refitting the reverse idler gear; it is fitted with the groove facing towards the rear. Smear a little general purpose grease on the idler

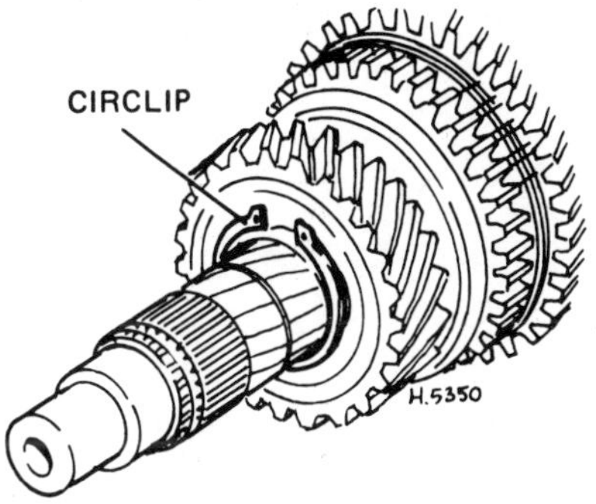

Fig. 6.23. Fitting the 2nd gear circlip (Sec. 12)

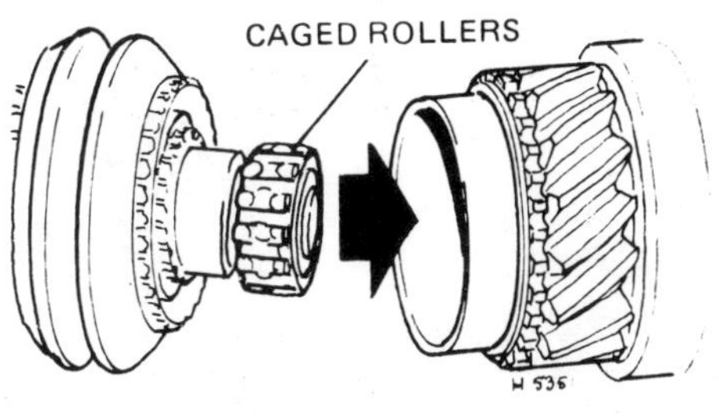

Fig. 6.25. Fitting the caged needle roller bearing to the nose of the mainshaft (Sec. 12)

shaft, then hold the gear in place and insert the shaft. Use a soft faced hammer to drive in the shaft until it is recessed by 0.008 to 0.032 in (0.2 to 0.8 mm).

2 Insert the spacer tube (23) (Fig. 6.14) into the layshaft with a shim positioned at each end. Smear thick grease on the laygear roller bearing surface and fit the needle rollers (18 and 20) one at a time until they are all in place. The grease will hold the rollers in position. Build up the needle rollers at the other end of the laygear in a similar fashion. Note that there should be 19 at each end.

3 Fit a thrust washer (21) at each end, taking care not to dislodge any of the rollers, then carefully slide in the dummy layshaft.

4 Position the two thrust washers (16) into the casing and retain them in position using thick grease. Make sure that they fit into the recesses in the end walls of the casing then place the layshaft and gear cluster into the casing taking care that the thrust washers are not dislodged.

5 Install the assembled mainshaft into the extension housing and retain it with the circlip. This will be made easier if the gearbox end of the extension housing is submerged in hot water for a few minutes to enable the bearing to be pushed into place. Take care that the splines on the end of the mainshaft do not damage the oil seal in the rear end of the housing. Tape the splines if necessary.

6 Fit the extension housing and mainshaft assembly to the gearbox casing using grease on the housing flange to hold the gasket in position. Do not fit the bolts at this stage, but turn the extension so that the layshaft entry hole is exposed.

7 Apply a little gearbox oil to the caged needle roller bearing (4) on the nose of the mainshaft. (Alternatively, the bearing may be inserted into the counterbore on the input shaft).

8 Check that the top gear synchronizer blocker ring is in position on the mainshaft, then slide the input shaft and bearing into the casing. Retain the bearing with the circlip.

9 Lightly grease the lip of the drive gear (input shaft) bearing retainer, then fit the retainer using a new gasket. Ensure that the gasket and oil return drilling are correctly mated to the drilling in the end of the gearbox casing. Apply a non-setting jointing compound to the bolt threads before they are installed.

10 Install the layshaft, by using it to drive out the dummy shaft previously fitted. Push the gear cluster in the direction of the mainshaft until the gears mesh then finally rotate the layshaft so that the flat is positioned horizontally as shown in Fig. 6.28.

11 Align the extension housing, apply a non-setting jointing compound to the bolt threads then install and torque tighten them.

12 Install the speedometer pinion, pinion bearing and oil seal and retain them with the circlip.

13 Fit the first/second and third/top selector forks into the selector housing cover so that the numbers are facing forward. The reverse selector fork is fitted with the number facing rearward.

14 Install the selector housing cover using a new gasket, ensuring that the forks align with the grooves in the synchronizer assemblies. Apply a non-setting jointing compound to the bolt threads before they are installed. Do not forget the two brackets, the reverse gear return spring and the reverse light switch (Fig. 6.30).

15 Install the clutch housing, using a non-setting jointing compound on the bolts.

16 Refit the clutch release fork and bearing.

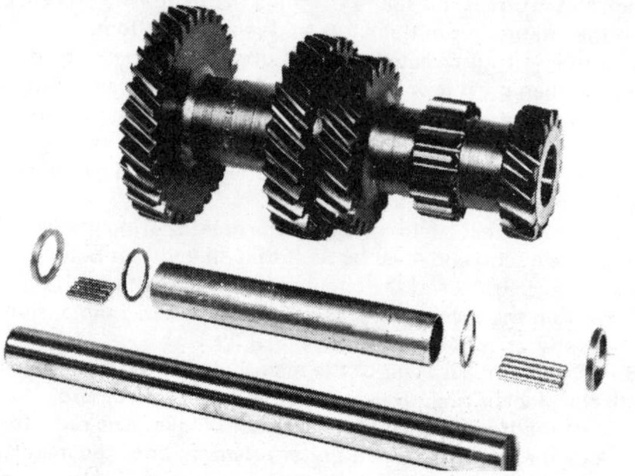

Fig. 6.26. The layshaft, gear cluster and associated parts (Sec. 13)

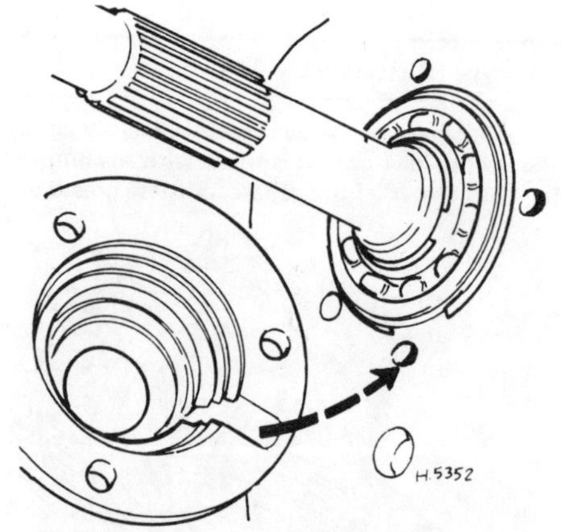

Fig. 6.27. Input shaft bearing retainer (Sec. 13)
Note location of oil drain slot

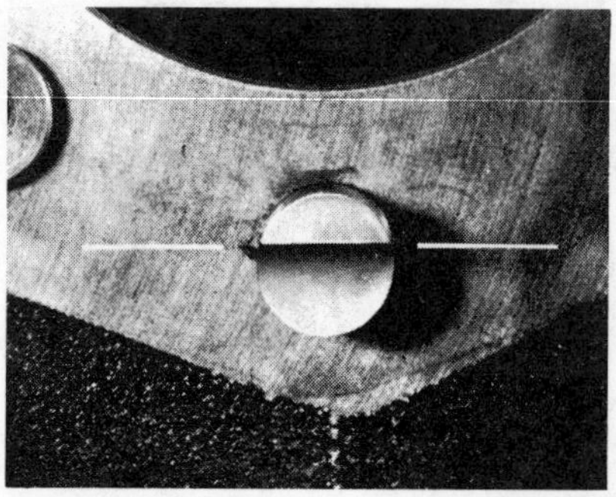

Fig. 6.28. The flat at the rear end of the layshaft (Sec. 13)

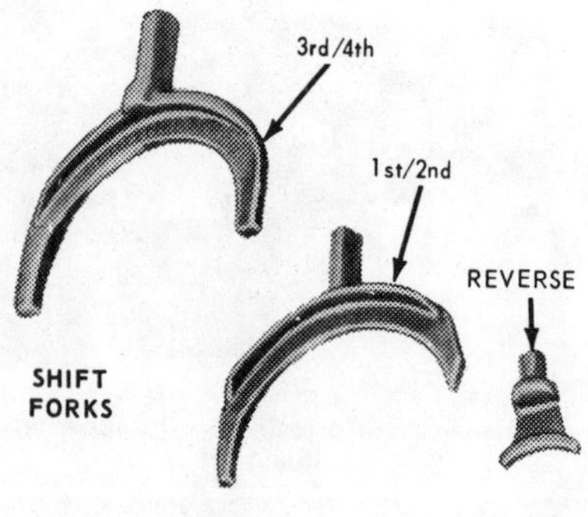

Fig. 6.29. Shift fork identification (Sec. 13)
The short leg of the 1st/2nd fork must be fitted towards the bottom of the gearbox

Fig. 6.30. The selector housing cover installed (Sec. 13)

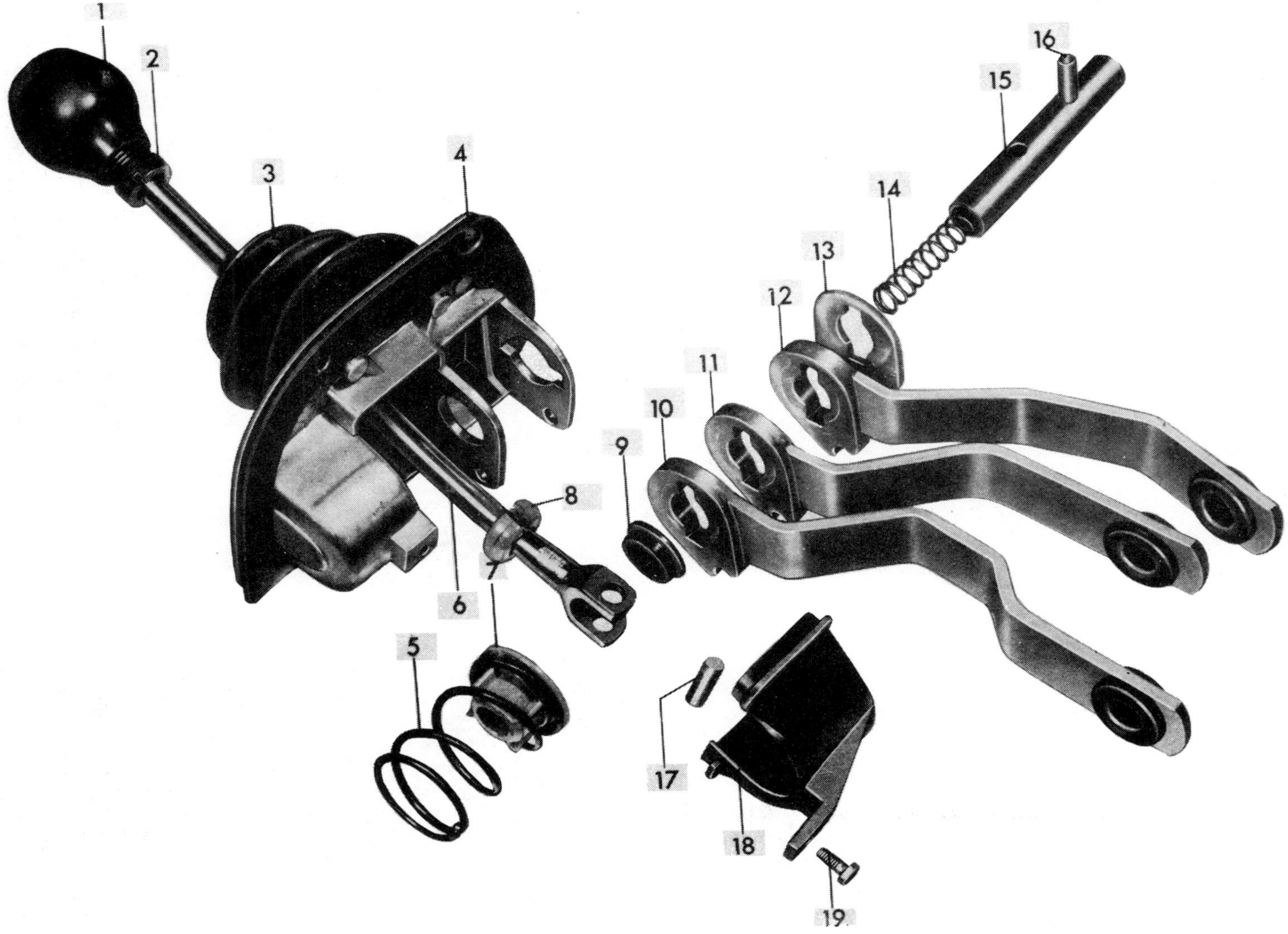

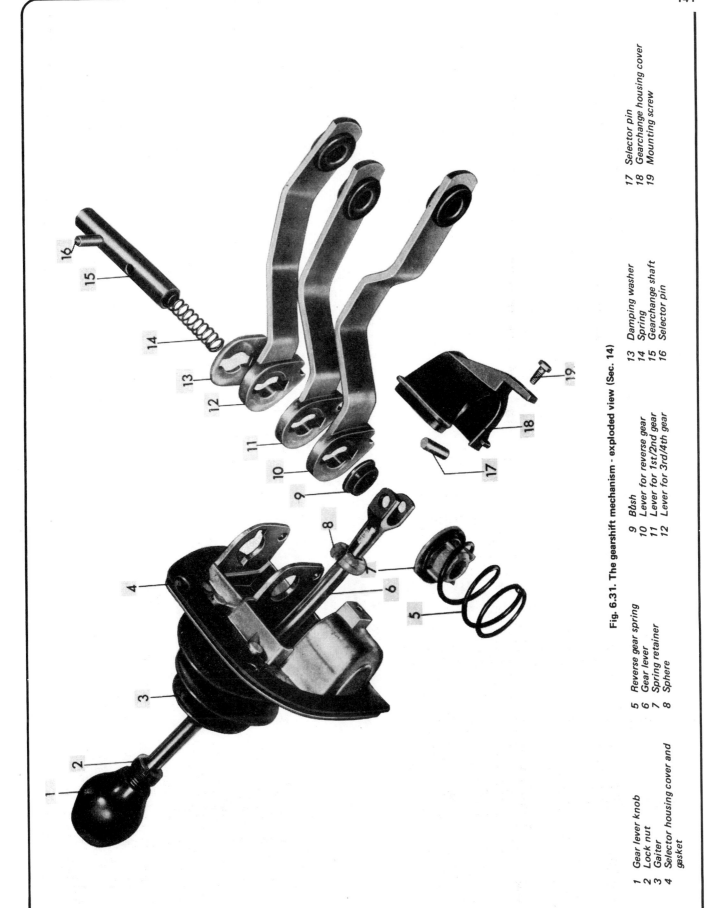

Fig. 6.31. The gearshift mechanism - exploded view (Sec. 14)

1 Gear lever knob
2 Lock nut
3 Gaiter
4 Selector housing cover and gasket
5 Reverse gear spring
6 Gear lever
7 Spring retainer
8 Sphere
9 Bush
10 Lever for reverse gear
11 Lever for 1st/2nd gear
12 Lever for 3rd/4th gear
13 Damping washer
14 Spring
15 Gearchange shaft
16 Selector pin
17 Selector pin
18 Gearchange housing cover
19 Mounting screw

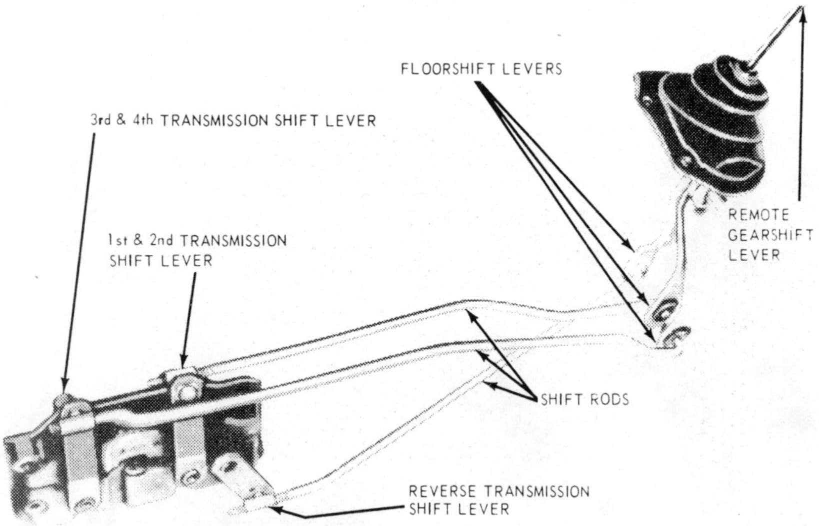

Fig. 6.32. Type H gearshift mechanism (Sec. 14)

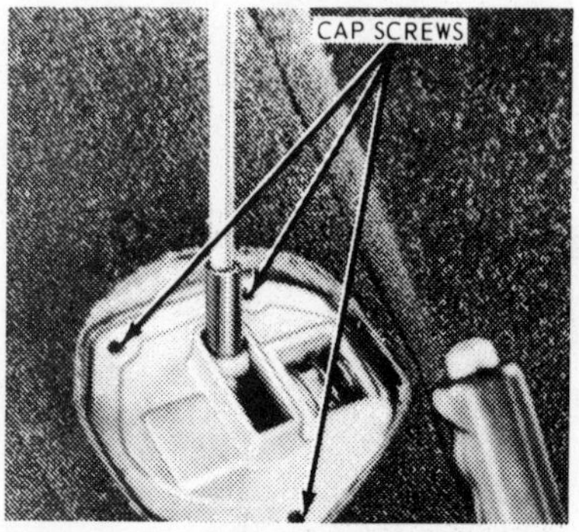

Fig. 6.33. Removing the gearshift housing cover (body)

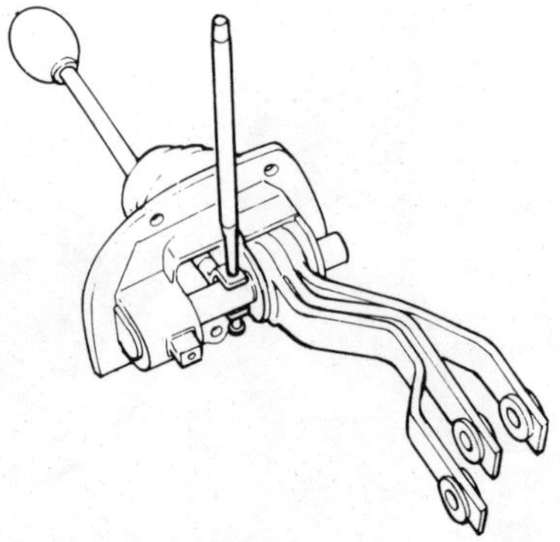

Fig. 6.34. Removing the shaft pin (Sec. 14)

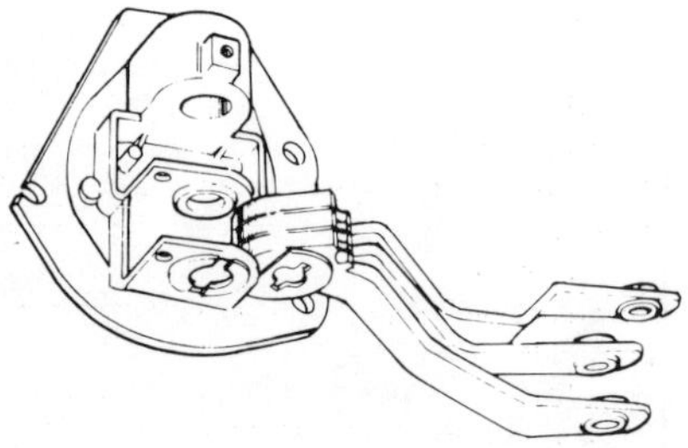

Fig. 6.35. Refitting the shift levers (Sec. 14)

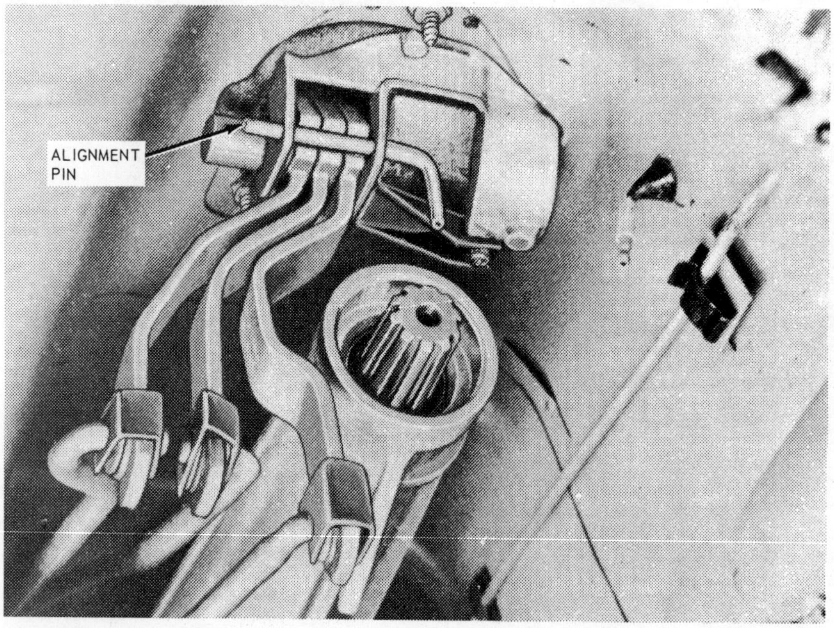

Fig. 6.36. Using an alignment pin when refitting the selector rods (Sec. 14)

14 Gearshift mechanism (type H) - removal, dismantling, reassembly and refitting

1 Raise the vehicle for access to the selector rods at the side of the gearbox.
2 Remove the reverse selector rod spring then unhook the rods from their levers on the gearbox side cover.
3 Slacken the locknut on the gear lever knob then unscrew the knob and locknut.
4 If a clock is fitted, carefully prise it out of its mounting and disconnect the electrical leads. (If a centre console is fitted, this will need to be removed beforehand - see Chapter 12).
5 Remove the three bolts from the gearshift housing cover (body) and lift out the mechanism and gasket.
6 To dismantle the mechanism, remove the gearchange housing dust

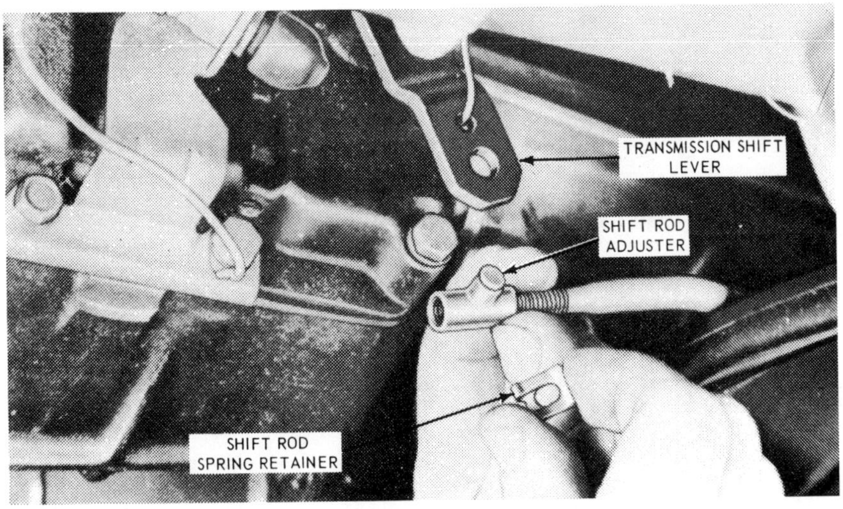

Fig. 6.37. Shift rod adjustment (Sec. 14)

cover (1 screw).

7 Using a suitable punch, drive out the gearchange shaft pin (17 in (Fig. 6.31) and withdraw the gearlever assembly from the selector channel. Remove the sphere (8).

8 Position the selector lever to the rear and withdraw the gearchange shaft (15). If necessary, press out the pin (16).

9 Withdraw the selector levers and damping washer (13).

10 Take out the small spring, and if necessary press out the bush (9).

11 Take out the large spring and spring retainer (7).

12 Reassembly is the reverse of the removal procedure, but ensure that the flat part of the damping washer is facing upwards.

13 Refitting the gearchange mechanism is the reverse of the removal procedure. However, it will be necessary to realign the selector rods with their levers on the side cover. This is done by locking the gearshift lever in the neutral position using a pin of 0.2 in (5 mm) diameter through the lock holes (Fig. 6.36). The rods should then be adjusted so that they can be inserted into the levers on the side cover without strain.

15 Reverse light switch - type C and H gearboxes

1 On type C gearboxes, the reverse light switch is screwed into the rear end of the gearbox extension. To remove the switch, disconnect the leads and unscrew it from the extension. When refitting, apply a little non-setting gasket sealant on the screw threads and refit the leads (photo).

2 On type H gearboxes, the reverse light switch is mounted on a bracket on the gearshift selector housing cover. If necessary, the switch can be adjusted once the retaining screw has been loosened.

15.1 Type C gearbox reversing light switch

16 Fault diagnosis - Manual gearboxes

Symptom	Reason/s	Remedy
Weak or ineffective synchromesh	Synchronising cones worn, split or damaged	Dismantle and overhaul gearbox. Fit new gear wheels and synchronising cones.
	Baulk ring synchromesh dogs worn, or damaged	Dismantle and overhaul gearbox. Fit new baulk ring synchromesh.
Jumps out of gear	Broken gearchange fork rod spring	Dismantle and replace spring.
	Gearbox coupling dogs badly worn	Dismantle gearbox. Fit new coupling dogs.
	Selector fork rod groove badly worn	Fit new selector fork rod.
Excessive noise	Incorrect grade of oil in gearbox or oil level too low	Drain, refill or top up gearbox with correct grade of oil.
	Bush or needle roller bearings worn or damaged	Dismantle and overhaul gearbox. Renew bearings.
	Gear teeth excessively worn or damaged	Dismantle, overhaul gearbox. Renew gear wheels.
	Countershaft thrust washers worn allowing excessive end play	Dismantle and overhaul gearbox. Renew thrust washers.
Excessive difficulty in engaging gear	Clutch cable adjustment incorrect	Adjust clutch cable correctly.

17 Automatic transmission - general description

1 The automatic transmission takes the place of the conventional clutch and gearbox, and comprises the following two main assemblies:

a) A three element hydrokinetic torque converter coupling, capable of torque multiplication at an infinitely variable ratio.

b) A torque/speed responsive and hydraulically operated epicyclic gearbox comprising a planetary gearset providing three forward ratios and one reverse ratio.

2 Due to the complexity of the automatic transmission unit, if performance is not up to standard, or overhaul is necessary, it is imperative that this be left to the local main agents who will have the special equipment for fault diagnosis and rectification. The content of the following Sections is therefore confined to supplying general information and any service information and instruction that can be used by the owner.

3 The transmission for the Capri II models is manufactured by Ford and is known as the Bordeaux or C3 type. It is similar in many ways to the Borg-Warner model 35 previously used by Ford for their smaller engined cars but the new unit has a large aluminium content which helps to reduce its overall weight and it is of compact dimensions. A transmission oil cooler is fitted as standard and ensures cooler operation of the transmission under trailer towing conditions. A vacuum connection to the inlet manifold provides smoother and more consistent downshifts under load than is the case with units not incorporating this facility.

18 Automatic transmission - fluid level checking

1 Before attempting to check the fluid level, the fluid must be at its normal operating temperature (approximately 65°C/150°F). This is best accomplished by driving the car for about 5 miles (8 km) under normal running conditions.

2 Park the car on level ground, apply the handbrake and depress the brake pedal.

3 Allow the engine to idle then move the selector through all the positions three times.

4 Select 'P' and wait for 1 to 2 minutes with the engine still idling.

5 Now withdraw the dipstick (engine still idling), wipe it clean with a lint-free cloth, replace it and withdraw it again. Note the oil level and, if necessary, top-up to maintain it between the 'MAX' and 'MIN' dipstick markings. Only fluid meeting the stated specification should be used; this is applied through the dipstick tube.

19 Automatic transmission - removal and refitting

1 If possible, raise the car on a hoist or place it over an inspection pit. Alternatively it will be necessary to jack-up the car to obtain the maximum possible amount of working room underneath.

2 Place a large drainage pan beneath the transmission sump (oil pan) then, working from the rear loosen the attaching bolts and allow the fluid to drain. Remove all the bolts except the two front ones to drain as much fluid as possible, then temporarily refit two bolts at the rear to hold it in place.

3 Remove the torque converter drain plug access cover and adapter plate bolts from the lower end of the converter housing.

4 Remove the three driveplate-to-converter attaching bolts, cranking the engine as necessary to gain access by means of a spanner on the crankshaft pulley attaching bolt. **Caution: Do not rotate the engine backwards.**

5 Rotate the engine until the converter drain plug is accessible then remove the plug, catching the fluid in the drainage pan. Fit and tighten the drain plug afterwards.

6 Remove the propeller shaft, referring to Chapter 7, as necessary. Place a polythene bag over the end of the transmission to prevent dirt from entering.

7 Detach the speedometer cable from the extension housing.

8 Disconnect the shift rod at the transmission manual lever, and the downshift rod at the transmission downshift lever.

9 Remove the starter motor retaining bolts and position the motor out of the way.

10 Disconnect the starter inhibitor (neutral start) switch leads.

11 Disconnect the vacuum lines from the vacuum unit.

12 Position a trolley jack beneath the transmission and raise it to *just* take the transmission weight.

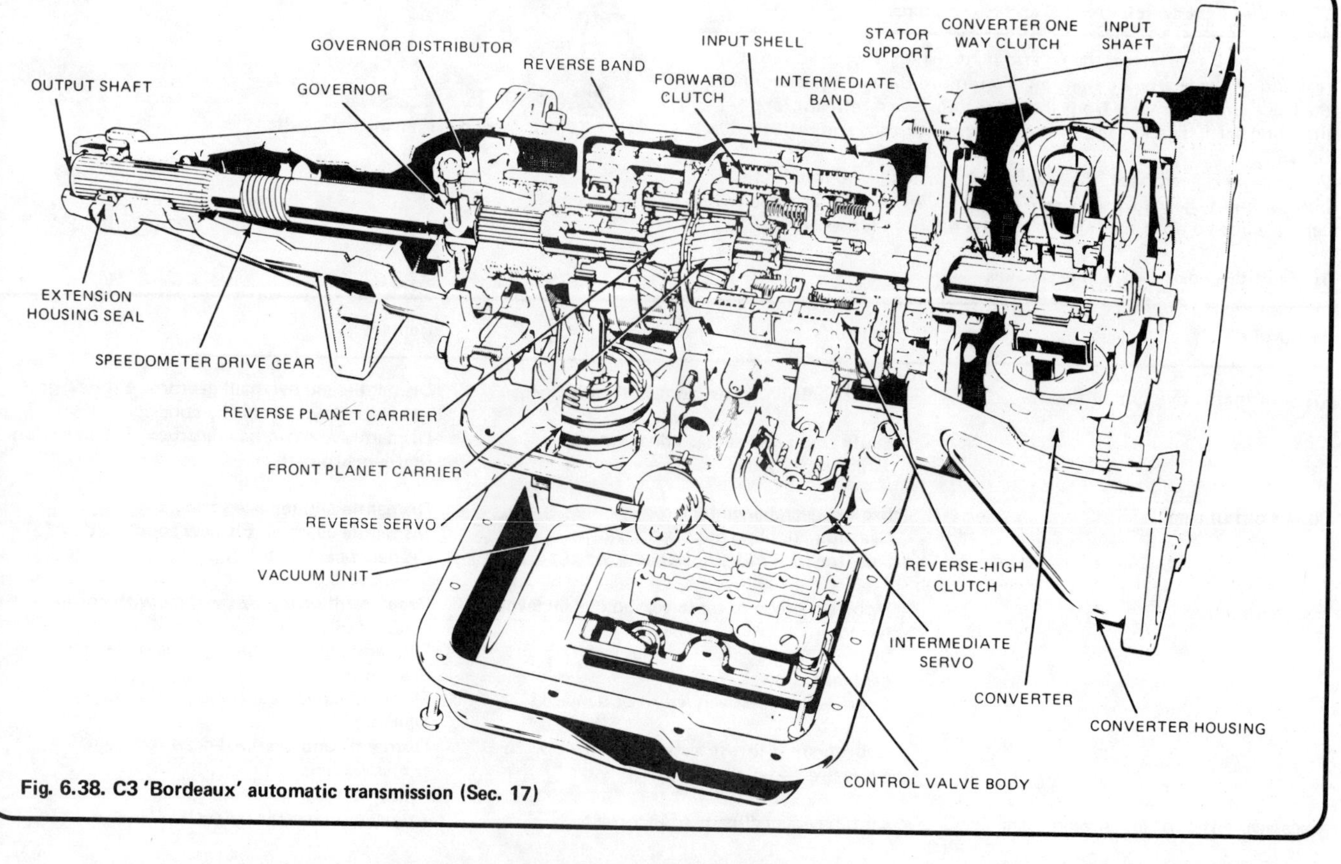

Fig. 6.38. C3 'Bordeaux' automatic transmission (Sec. 17)

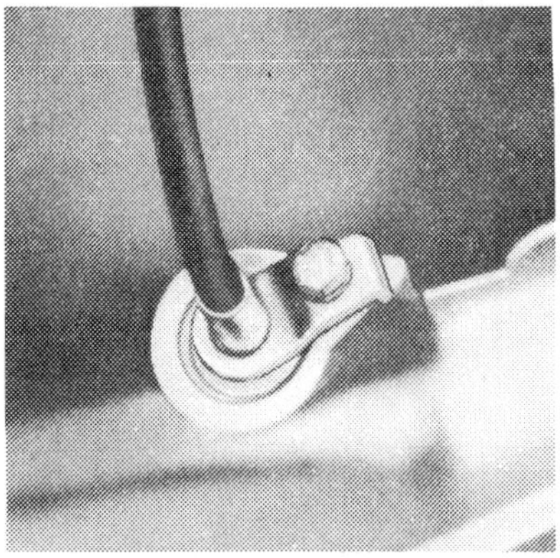

Fig. 6.39. The speedometer cable and bracket (Sec. 19)

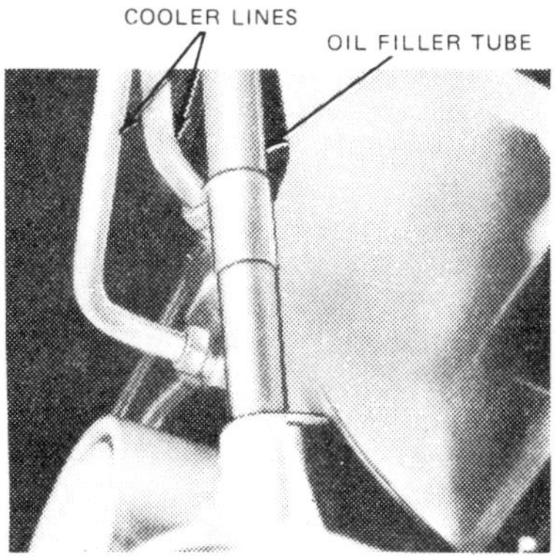

Fig. 6.40. The oil cooler lines and filler tube (Sec. 19)

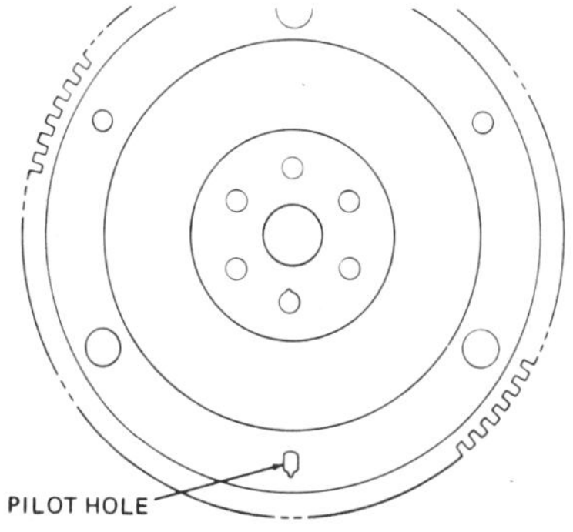

Fig. 6.41. The driveplate pilot hole (Sec. 19)

13 Remove the engine rear support-to-crossmember nut, and the crossmember-to-frame side support attaching bolts and nuts. Remove the crossmember.
14 Remove the inlet steady pipe rest from the inlet pipe and rear engine support. Disconnect the exhaust pipe at the manifold and support it to one side.
15 Lower the trolley jack slightly then place another jack to the front end of the engine. Raise the engine to gain access to the upper converter housing-to-engine attaching bolts.
16 Disconnect the oil cooler lines at the transmission and plug them to prevent dirt from entering.
17 Remove the lower converter housing-to-engine bolts, and the transmission filler tube.
18 Ensure that the transmission is securely mounted on the trolley jack then remove the two upper converter housing-to-engine bolts.
19 Carefully move the transmission rearwards and downwards, and away from the car.
20 Refitting the transmission is essentially the reverse of the removal procedure, but the following points should be noted:

- *a) Rotate the converter to align the bolt drive lugs and drain plug with their holes in the driveplate.*
- *b) Do not allow the transmission to take a 'nose-down' attitude as the converter will move forward and disengage from the pump gear.*
- *c) When installing the three driveplate-to-converter bolts position the driveplate so that the pilot hole is in the six o'clock position (see Fig. 6.41). First install one bolt through the pilot hole and torque tighten it, followed by the two remaining bolts. Do not attempt to install it in any other way.*
- *d) Adjust the downshift cable and selector linkage as necessary (see Sections 20 and 21).*
- *e) When the car has been lowered to the ground, add sufficient fluid to bring the level up to the 'MAX' mark on the dipstick with the engine not running. Having done this, check and top-up the fluid level, as described in the previous Section.*

20 Kick-down cable - adjustment

1 Slacken the inner nut on the adjuster right off and then turn the carburettor throttle rod to the fully open position. Disconnect the return spring(s).
2 Depress the accelerator pedal fully.
3 Adjust the two cable nuts so that the clearance between the throttle valve shaft and the carburettor linkage kick-down lever is between 0.020 and 0.080 in (0.8 and 2.0 mm).
4 Tighten the locknut and reconnect the return spring(s).

21 Selector linkage - adjustment

1 First check that the selector lever is correctly adjusted. To do this, use feeler gauges to check the end-clearance between the lever pawl and the quadrant notch. This should be between 0.005 and 0.010 in

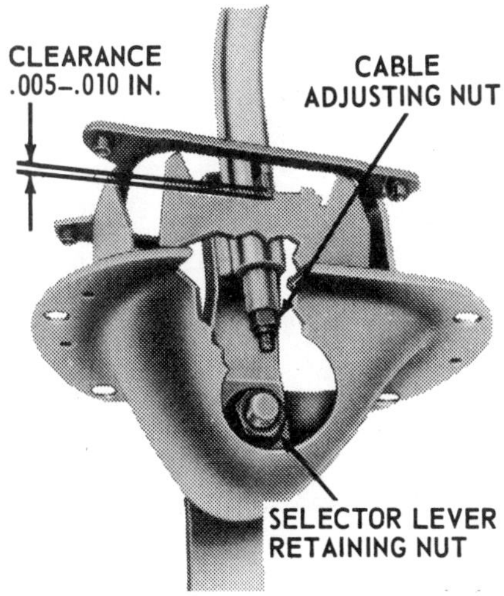

Fig. 6.42. Selector linkage adjustment (Sec. 21)

(0.13 and 0.25 mm). If necessary, adjust the cable locknut which is accessible after removal of the selector lever housing plug.
2 Disconnect the shift rod from the shift lever at the base of the hand control lever (adjustable end of rod).
3 Place the hand control lever in 'D'.
4 Place the selector lever on the side of the transmission housing in 'D'. This can be determined by counting two 'clicks' back from the fully forward position.
5 Now attempt to reconnect the shift rod to the selector hand control lever by pushing in the clevis pin. The pin should slide in without any side stress at all. If this is not the case, release the locknut on the shift rod and adjust its effective length by screwing the adjusting link in, or out.

22 Starter inhibitor (neutral start) - reverse light switch - removal and refitting

1 This switch is non-adjustable and any malfunction must be due to a wiring fault, a faulty switch or wear in the internal actuating cam.
2 When removing and installing the switch, always use a new 'O' ring seal and tighten to the specified torque.

23 Automatic transmission extension housing oil seal - renewal

1 Remove the propeller shaft, as described in Chapter 7.

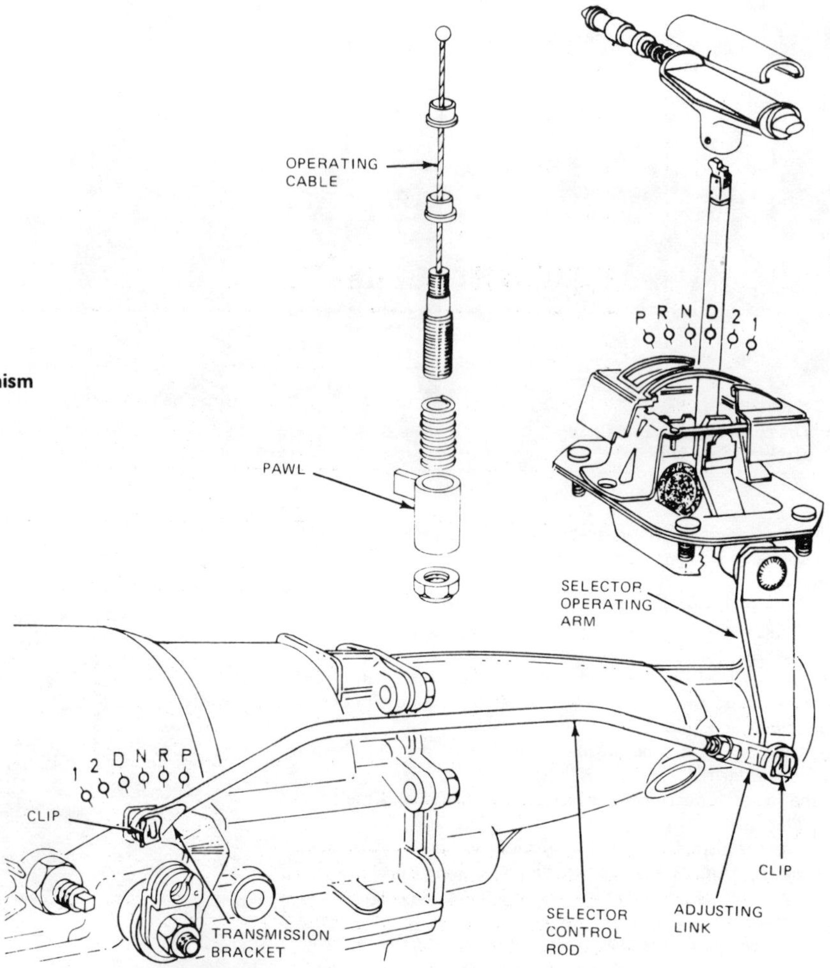

Fig. 6.43. The selector lever mechanism (Sec. 21)

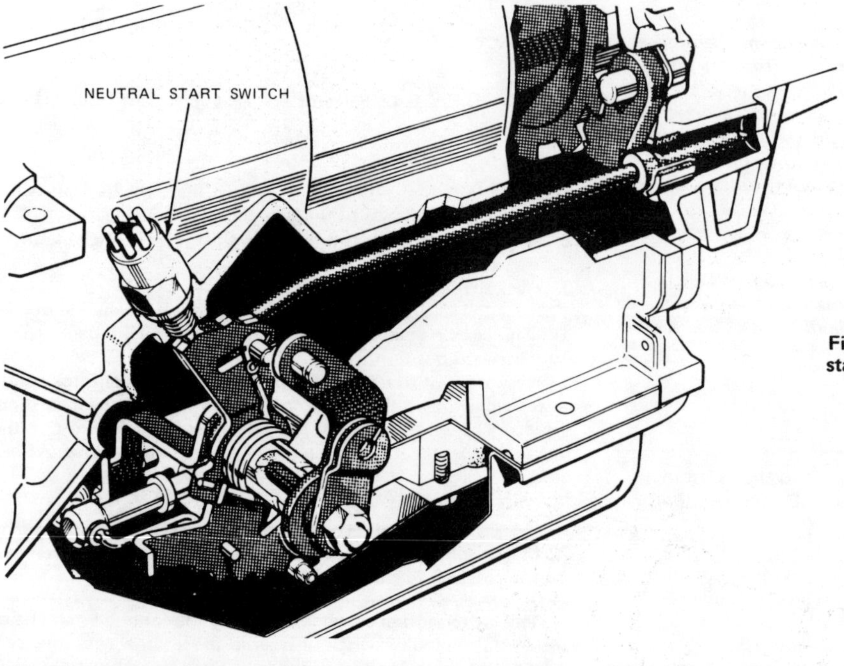

Fig. 6.44. The starter inhibitor (neutral start)/reverse light switch (Sec. 22)

2 Carefully prise out the oil seal, taking care not to damage the sealing surface in the end of the extension.

3 Ensure that the sealing surface in the extension is clean and unmarked, then press in the replacement seal, lips facing inwards, using a suitable diameter tube.

4 Refit the propeller shaft then check the fluid level, as described in Section 18.

24 Fault diagnosis - automatic transmission

Faults in these units are nearly always the result of low fluid level or incorrect adjustment of the selector linkage or downshift cable. Internal faults should be diagnosed by your main Ford dealer who has the necessary equipment to carry out the work.

Chapter 7 Propeller shaft

Contents

Specifications

Type (Capri II) ... Two piece, tubular, with rubber mounted centre bearing. Universal joints are Hardy-Spicer type, with an alternative constant velocity (CV) centre joint on some models

Type (Mercury Capri II) ... Single piece, tubular, with Hardy-Spicer type universal joints

Torque wrench settings

	lbf ft	kgf m
Centre bearing to floor assembly	13 to 17	1.8 to 2.3
Propeller shaft to drive pinion flange	44 to 48	6.1 to 6.6

1 General description

On Capri II models, drive is transmitted from the gearbox to the rear axle by means of a finely balanced tubular propeller shaft split into two halves and supported at the centre by a rubber mounted bearing. On some models, a constant velocity type centre joint is used.

Fitted to the front centre and rear of the propeller shaft assembly are universal joints which allow vertical movement of the rear axle and slight movement of the complete power unit on its rubber mountings. Each universal joint comprises a four legged centre spider, four needle roller bearings and two yokes.

Fore and aft movement of the rear axle is absorbed by a sliding spline located at the gearbox end. The yoke flange of the rear universal joint is fitted to the rear axle and is secured to the pinion flange by four bolts and lock washers.

On Mercury Capri II models a one-piece propeller shaft is used.

The propeller shaft universal joints cannot be renewed on a do-it-yourself basis since the joint spiders are staked into the yokes in a position determined during electronic balancing. When joint wear is detected (see Section 4), either a replacement propeller shaft should be obtained or the complete propeller shaft should be passed to a suitably equipped engineering workshop for repair.

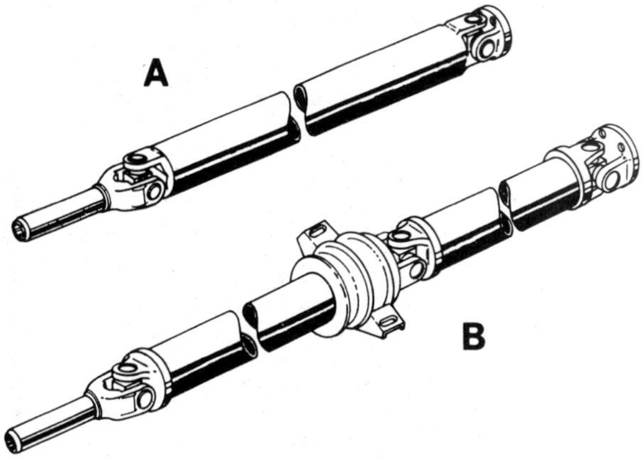

Fig. 7.1. Single-piece (A) and two-piece universal joint (B) propeller shaft (Sec. 1)

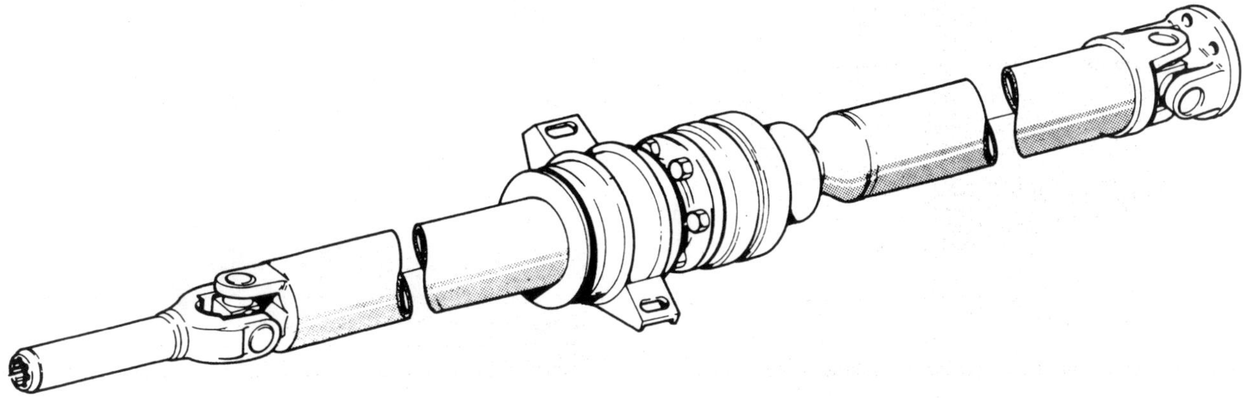

Fig. 7.2. Two-piece constant velocity joint propeller shaft (Sec. 1)

2.5 Removing the propeller shaft from the axle flange

2.6 Propeller shaft centre bearing

2.7 Disengaging the propeller shaft from the gearbox

2 Propeller shaft - removal and refitting

1 Jack-up the rear of the car, or position the rear of the car over a pit or on a ramp.
2 If the rear of the car is jacked-up, suppl ement the jack with support blocks so that danger is minimised, should the jack collapse.
3 If the rear wheels are off the ground, place the car in gear or put the handbrake on to ensure that the propeller shaft does not turn when an attempt is made to loosen the four bolts securing the propeller shaft to the rear axle companion flange.
4 The propeller shaft is carefully balanced to fine limits and it is important that it is replaced in exactly the same position it was in, prior to its removal. Scratch a mark on the propeller shaft and rear axle flanges to ensure accurate mating when the time comes for reassembly.
5 Unscrew and remove the four lock bolts and securing washers which hold the flange on the propeller shaft to the flange on the rear axle (photo).
6 Where applicable undo and remove the two bolts holding the centre bearing housing to the underframe. Note the position and number of any shims which are fitted (photo).
7 Push the shaft forward slightly to separate the two flanges at the rear, then lower the end of the shaft and pull it rearwards to disengage it from the gearbox mainshaft splines (photo).
8 Place a large can or tray under the rear of the gearbox extension to catch any oil which is likely to leak through the spline lubricating holes when the propeller shaft is removed.
9 Refitting the propeller shaft is a reversal of the above procedure Ensure that the mating marks scratched on the propeller shaft and rear axle flanges line up, and that any shims at the centre bearing are refitted.
10 Note the method of securing the flanges, either nuts and bolts or setscrews, according to type of rear axle.

3 Propeller shaft centre bearing - renewal

1 Prior to removing the centre bearing from the section of the two piece propeller shaft, carefully scratch marks on the rear yoke and on the shaft just forward of the bearing housing to ensure correct alignment on reassembly.
2 Knock back the tab washer on the centre bolt located in the jaws of the rear yoke. Slacken off the nut and remove the 'U' washer from under it.
3 With the 'U' washer removed the rear yoke can now be drawn off the splines of the front section. The centre bolt and its washer remain attached to the splined front section.
4 Slide the bearing housing with its rubber insulator from the shaft Bend back the six metal tabs on the housing and remove the rubber insulator.
5 The bearing and its protective caps should now be withdrawn from the splined section of the propeller shaft by careful levering with two large screwdrivers or tyre levers. If a suitable puller tool is available this should always be used in preference to any other method as it is less likely to cause damage to the bearing.
6 To refit the bearing, first fill the space between the bearing and caps with a general purpose grease. Select a piece of piping or tubing that is just a fraction smaller in diameter than the bearing, place the splined part of the drive shaft upright in a vice, position the bearing on the shaft and using a soft hammer on the end of the piece of tubing, drive the bearing firmly and squarely onto the shaft.
7 Refit the rubber insulator in the bearing housing ensuring that the boss on the insulator is at the top of the housing and will be adjacent to the under frame when the propeller shafts are replaced.
8 When the insulator is correctly positioned, bend back the six metal tabs and slide the housing and insulator assembly over the bearing, so that the recess (Fig. 7.5) faces towards the front of the car.
9 Slide the splined end of the shaft into the rear yoke ensuring that the previously scribed mating marks are correctly aligned.
10 Replace the 'U' washer under the centre bolt with its smooth surface facing the front section of the propeller shaft. Tighten down the centre bolt to the specified torque and bend up its tab washer to secure it.

4 Universal joints - inspection

1 Wear in the needle roller bearings is characterised by vibration in the transmission, 'clonks' on taking up the drive, and in extreme cases of lack of lubrication, metallic squeaking, and ultimately grating and shrieking sounds as the bearings break up.
2 It is easy to check if the needle roller bearings are worn with the propeller shaft in position, by trying to turn the shaft with one hand the other holding the rear axle flange when the rear universal is being checked, and the front half coupling when the front universal is being checked. Any movement between the propeller shaft and the front and the rear half couplings is indicative of considerable wear. If worn a replacement propeller shaft must be obtained, or the existing shaft overhauled by a suitably equipped engineering workshop.

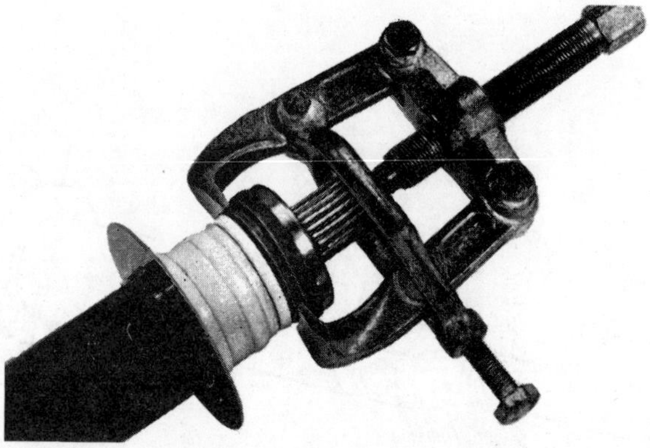

Fig. 7.3. Withdrawing the centre bearing and caps (Sec. 3)

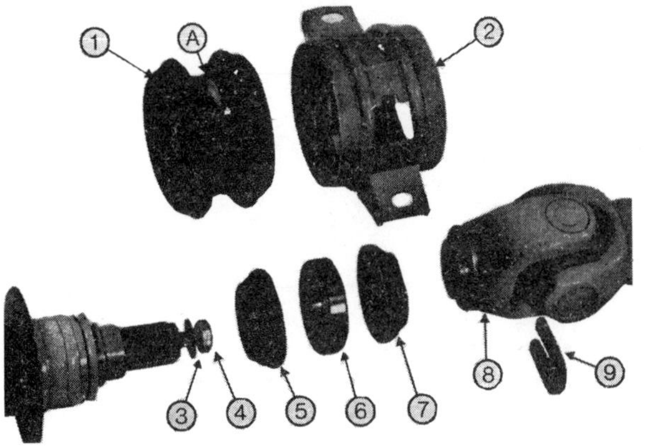

Fig. 7.4. Component parts of the centre bearing (Sec. 3)

A Mark for position of rubber insulator
1 Rubber insulator
2 Retainer
3 Lock plate
4 Bolt
5 Cap
6 Bearing
7 Cap
8 Yoke
9 U-retainer

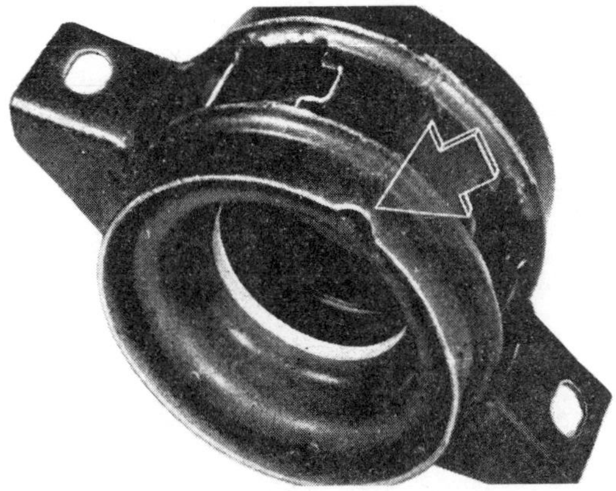

Fig. 7.5. Retainer recess mark (arrowed) (Sec. 3)

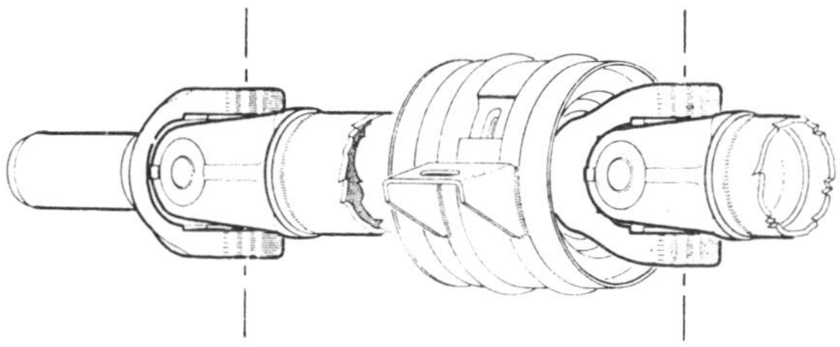

Fig. 7.6. The correct relationship between the joints (Sec. 3)

Fig. 7.7. The U-retainer (Sec. 3)

5 Fault diagnosis - Propeller shaft

Symptom	Reason/s
Vibration	Wear in sliding sleeve splines. Worn universal joint bearings. Propeller shaft out of balance. Distorted propeller shaft.
Knock or 'clunk' when taking up drive	Worn universal joint bearings. Worn rear axle drive pinion splines. Loose rear drive flange bolts. Excessive backlash in rear axle gears.

Chapter 8 Rear axle

Contents

Specifications

Axle designation	D (Salisbury)	
Vehicle application:		
Ford of Britain	1.6 GT, 2.0 engine	
Ford of Germany	1.6, 1.6 GT engine, Mercury Capri II	
Axle designation	J (Timken)	
Vehicle application:		
Ford of Britain	1.6 engine	
Ford of Germany	1.6, 1.6 GT engine	
Type D (Salisbury) axle		
Type	Hypoid semi-floating, integral differential	
Ratio:		
1.6 engine	3.75 : 1	
2.0 engine and Mercury Capri II	3.44 : 1	
Lubricant capacity	1.9 Imp. pints (1.1 litre, 2.3 US pints)	
Lubricant type	SAE 90EP gear oil	
Type J (Timken) axle		
Type	Hypoid semi-floating, detachable carrier differential	
Ratio	3.77 : 1	
Lubricant capacity	2.0 Imp. pints (1.14 litre, 2.4 US pints)	
Lubricant type	SAE 90EP gear oil	
Torque wrench settings	**lbf ft**	**kgf m**
Type D (Salisbury) axle		
Bearing cap to axle casing	44 to 50	6.1 to 6.9
Bearing cap to axle casing (Mercury Capri II)	15 to 18	2.08 to 2.48
Cover to axle casing	26 to 33	3.6 to 4.6
Crownwheel to differential case	59 to 64	8.2 to 8.8
Drive pinion flange bolts	44 to 48	6.1 to 6.6
Halfshaft retainer plate to axle flange	20 to 23	2.8 to 3.2
Drive pinion self-locking nut (early type axle)	74 to 88	10.2 to 12.2
Type J (Timken) axle		
Bearing cap to axle casing	46 to 51	6.4 to 7.0
Differential assembly to axle casing	26 to 30	3.6 to 4.1
Crownwheel to differential case	51 to 56	7.0 to 7.7
Drive pinion flange bolts	44 to 48	6.1 to 6.6
Halfshaft retainer plate to axle flange	15 to 18	2.1 to 2.5

1 General description

1 The rear axle is of hypoid semi-floating type and is located by the rear semi-elliptic leaf road springs in conjunction with a stabilizer bar.

2 Two types of rear axle may be encountered, according to model and manufacture source. One type has a completely detachable differential carrier (Timken or J type) and the other type is of integral design (Salisbury or D type) having only a removable cover plate on the rear face of the axle casing.

3 Unless the necessary tools and gauges are available, it is not recommended that the rear axle is overhauled, although the procedure is described later in this Chapter for those who have the necessary equipment.

4 With detachable differential type axle, it is recommended that the differential unit is either renewed on an exchange basis, or the original

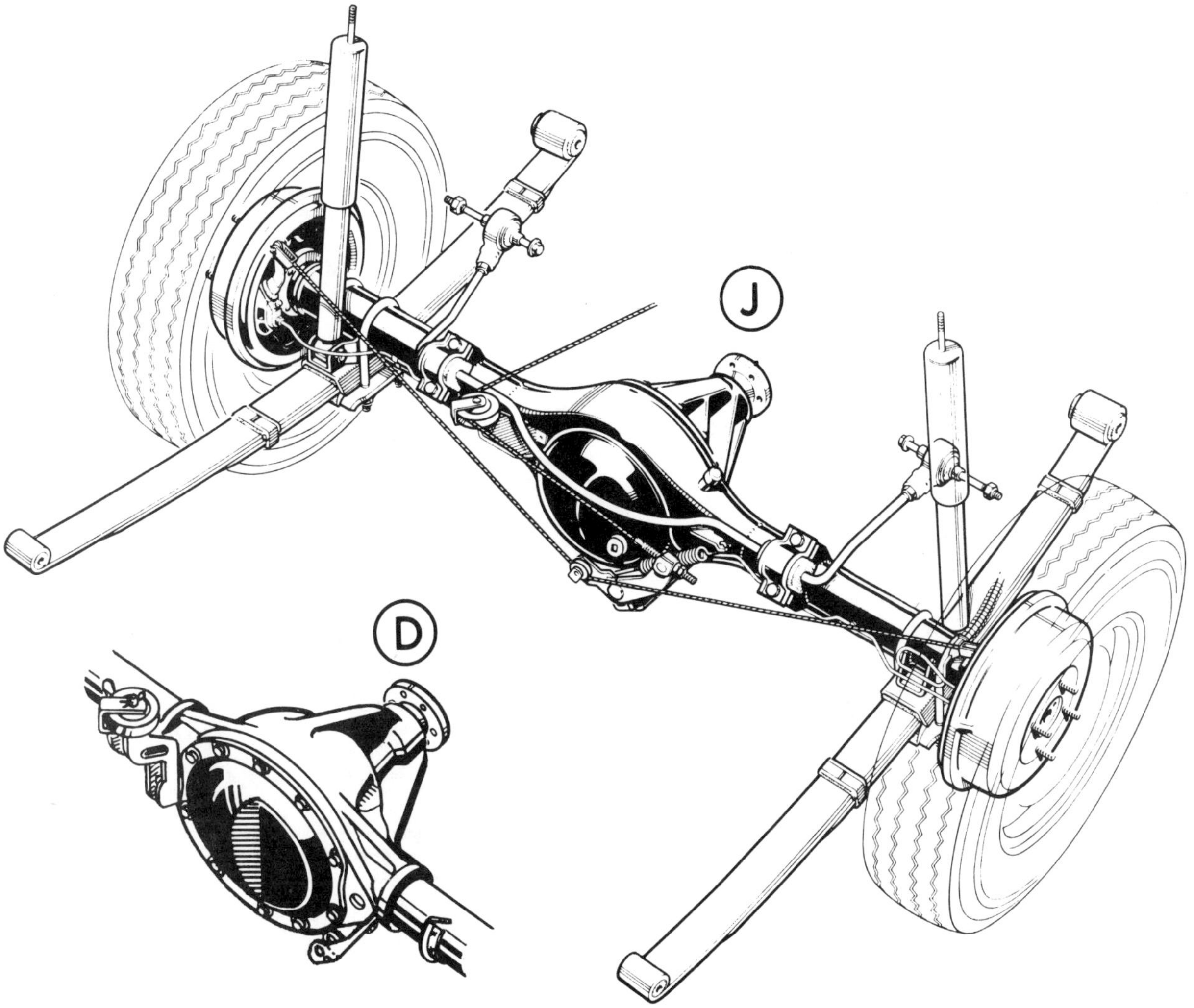

Fig. 8.1. Rear axle and suspension layout showing different axle types (Sec. 1)
D Salisbury *J Timken*

unit taken to your dealer for reconditioning.
5 Except on some early Salisbury rear axles, where there is a fixed length pinion bearing spacer, a collapsible spacer is used (see Sections 7, 13 and 14).

2 Rear axle (detachable differential) - removal and refitting

1 Remove the rear wheel hub caps (if fitted) then loosen the wheel nuts.
2 Raise and support the rear of the body and the differential casing with chocks or jacks so that the rear wheels are clear of the ground. This is most easily done by placing the jack under the centre of the differential, jacking-up the axle and then fitting chocks under the mounting points at the front of the rear springs to support the body.
3 Remove both rear wheels and place the wheel nuts in the hub caps for safe keeping.
4 Mark the propeller shaft and differential drive flanges to ensure replacement in the same relative positions. Undo and remove the nuts and bolts holding the two flanges together.
5 Release the handbrake and detach the cable from the axle (refer to Chapter 9, if necessary).
6 Unscrew the union on the brake pipe at the junction on the rear axle and have handy either a jar to catch the hydraulic fluid or a plug to block the end of the pipe.
7 Undo the nuts and bolts holding the shock absorber attachments to the spring seats and remove the bolts thus freeing the shock absorbers. It will probably be necessary to adjust the jack under the axle casing to free the bolts.
8 Disconnect the stabilizer bar brackets (see Chapter 11).
9 Unscrew the nuts from under the spring retaining plates. These nuts screw onto the ends of the inverted 'U' bolts which retain the axle to the spring.
10 The axle will now be resting free on the jack and can be removed by lifting it through one of the wheel arches.
11 Reassembly is a direct reversal of the removal procedure, but various points must be carefully noted.
12 The nuts on the 'U' bolts must be tightened to the specified torque.
13 Refit the stabilizer bar and shock absorber, referring to Chapter 11 for the method and tightening torques.
14 Bleed the brakes after reassembly, as described in Chapter 9.

3 Halfshaft (detachable differential) - removal and refitting

1 Raise the rear of the car and support the bodyframe and the axle casing securely.
2 Remove the roadwheel.
3 Remove the brake drum.
4 Remove the four self-locking nuts which retain the bearing retainer plate to the endface of the axle housing. These nuts are accessible through the hole in the halfshaft flange (Fig. 8.2).
5 A slide hammer must now be attached to the roadwheel studs and the halfshaft complete with bearing/seal assembly extracted from the axle casing.
6 It is sometimes possible to extract the halfshaft by bolting an old roadwheel onto the hub and then striking two opposite points on the

Fig. 8.2. Removing the bearing retainer plate nuts (Secs. 3 and 9)

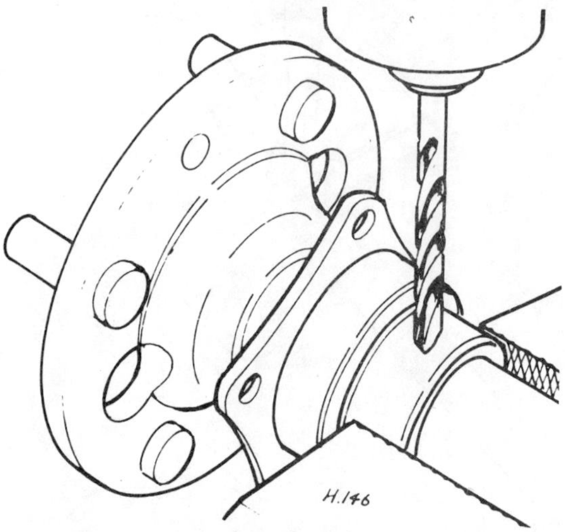

Fig. 8.3. Drilling a hole in the bearing inner ring prior to splitting with a cold chisel (Secs. 4 and 10)

Fig. 8.4. Identification marks on the bearing caps (Sec. 6)

inner rim simultaneously. A third method is to use two or three bolts placed between the axleshaft flange and the axle housing end flange. By unscrewing the nuts fitted to the bolts, the effective length of the bolts will be increased and the halfshaft forced outwards. Unless great care is taken, either of the last two methods can result in a bent halfshaft.
7 Refitting is simply a matter of inserting the shaft into the housing and holding it horizontally until the splines on the shaft can be felt to engage with those of the differential gears. A little grease should be smeared on the outer surface of the hub bearing to prevent future seizure by rust.

4 Halfshaft bearing/oil seal (detachable differential) - renewal

1 Withdraw the halfshaft, as described in the preceding Section.
2 Secure the assembly in a vice, the jaws of which have been fitted with soft metal protectors.
3 Drill a hole in the bearing securing collar and then remove the collar by splitting it with a cold chisel. Take care not to damage the shaft during these operations.
4 Using a suitable press, draw off the combined bearing/oil seal.
5 To the halfshaft install the bearing retainer plate, the new bearing (seal side towards differential) and a new bearing collar.
6 Apply pressure to the collar only, using a press or bearing puller, seat the components against the shoulder of the halfshaft flange.
7 Install the halfshaft, as described in the preceding Section.

5 Differential carrier - removal and refitting

1 To remove the differential carrier assembly, jack-up the rear of the vehicle, remove both roadwheels and brake drums and then partially withdraw both halfshafts as described in Section 3.
2 Disconnect the propeller shaft at the rear end, as described in Chapter 7.
3 Undo the eight self-locking nuts holding the differential carrier assembly to the axle casing. Pull the assembly slightly forward and allow the oil to drain in a suitable tray or bowl. The carrier complete with the crown wheel can now be lifted clear with the gasket.
4 Before refitting, carefully clean the mating surfaces of the carrier and the axle casing and always fit a new gasket. Replacement is then a direct reversal of the above instructions. The eight nuts retaining the differential carrier assembly to the axle casing should be tightened to the specified torque. Refill with oil.

6 Detachable type differential - overhaul

Most professional garages will prefer to renew the complete differential carrier assembly as a unit if it is worn, rather than to dismantle the unit to renew any damaged or worn parts. To do the job correctly 'according to the book' requires the use of special and expensive tools which the majority of garages do not have.

The primary object of these special tools is to enable the mesh of the crown wheel to the pinion to be very accurately set and thus ensure that noise is kept to a minimum. If any increase in noise cannot be tolerated (provided that the rear axle is not already noisy due to a defective part) then it is best to purchase an exchange built up differential unit.

The differential assembly should be stripped as follows:-
1 Remove the differential assembly from the rear axle, as described in Section 5.
2 With the differential assembly on the bench begin dismantling the unit.
3 Undo and remove the bolts, spring washers and lock plates securing the adjustment nuts to the bearing caps.
4 Release the tension on the bearing cap bolts and unscrew the differential bearing adjustment nuts. Note from which side each nut originated and mark with a punch or scriber.
5 Unscrew the bearing cap bolts and spring washers. Ensure that the caps are marked so that they may be fitted in their original positions upon reassembly.
6 Pull off the caps and then lever out the differential unit complete with crown wheel and differential gears.
7 Recover the differential bearing outer tracks and inspect the bearings for wear or damage. If evident the bearings will have to be renewed.
8 Using a universal puller and suitable thrust block draw off the old bearings.
9 Undo and remove the bolts and washers that secure the crown wheel to the differential cage. Mark the relative positions of the cage and crown wheel if new parts are not to be fitted and lift off the crown wheel.
10 Clamp the pinion flange in a vice and then undo the nut. Any damage caused to the edge of the flange by the vice should be carefully filed smooth.
11 With the nut removed pull off the splined pinion flange. Tap the end

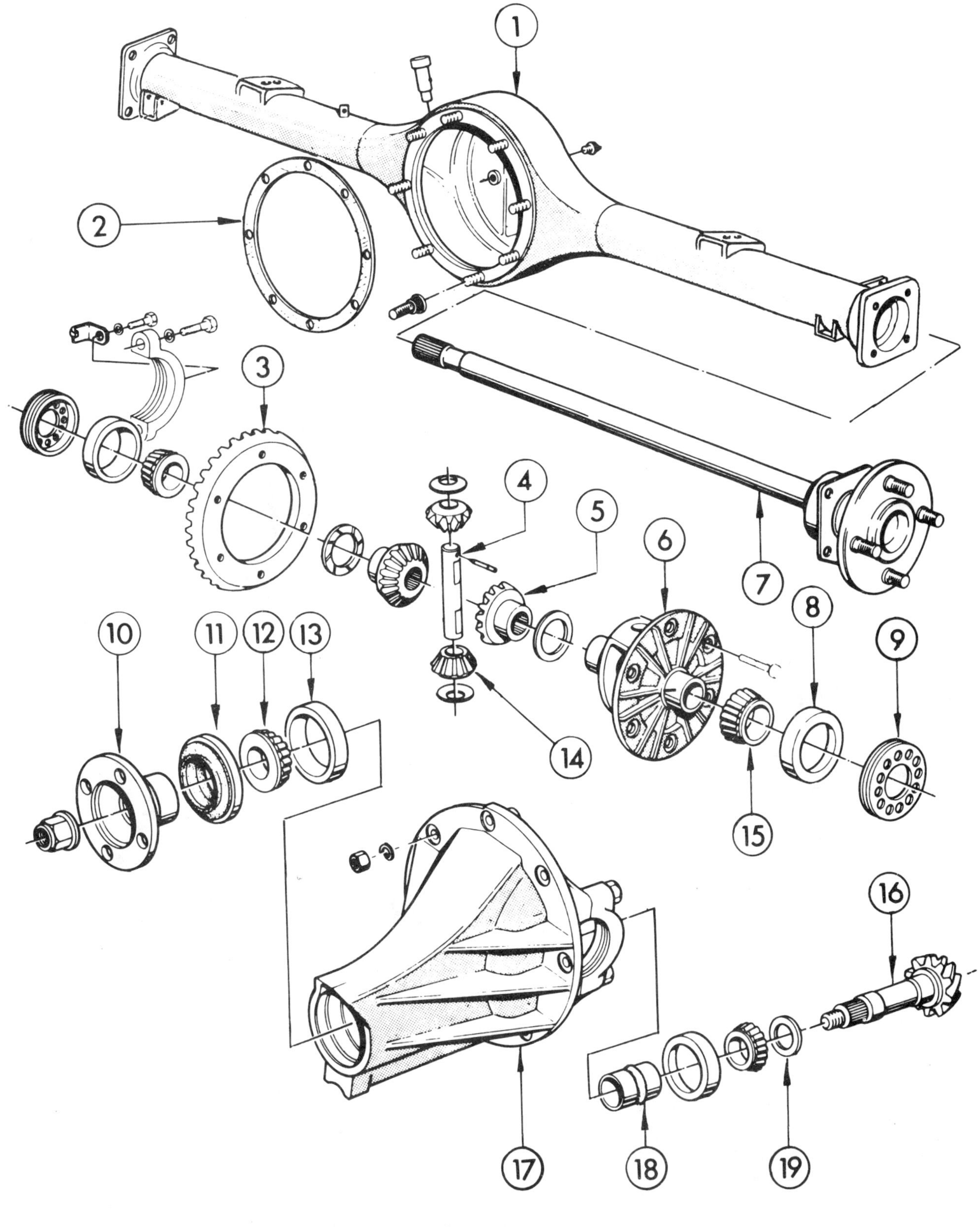

Fig. 8.5. Component parts of the detachable differential (Timken or type J) axle (Sec. 6)

1 Axle casing
2 Gasket
3 Crown wheel
4 Pinion gear shaft
5 Side gear
6 Casing
7 Half shaft
8 Outer cup of taper roller bearing
9 Adjusting nut
10 Drive pinion flange
11 Oil seal
12 Inner cup with taper rollers
13 Outer cup of taper roller bearing
14 Pinion gear
15 Inner cup with taper rollers
16 Drive pinion
17 Differential housing
18 Drive pinion collapsible spacer
19 Drive pinion shim

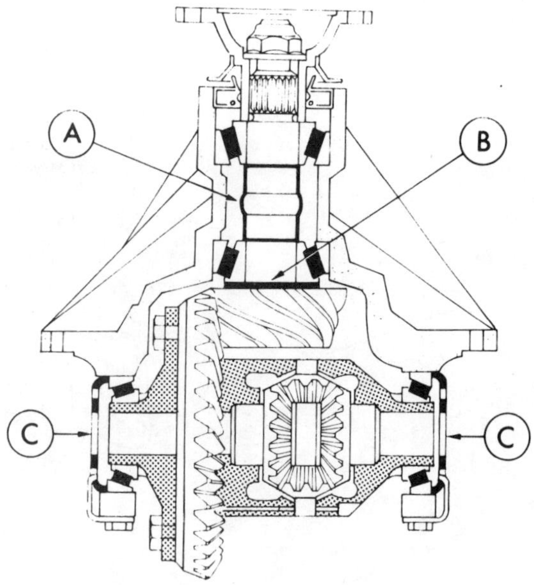

Fig. 8.6. Sectional view of the detachable differential type axle (Sec. 6)

A Collapsible spacer B Shim C Adjusting nuts

of the pinion shaft if the flange appears to be stuck.
12 The pinion complete with spacer and rear bearing cone may now be extracted from the rear of the housing.
13 Using a drift carefully tap out the pinion front bearing and oil seal.
14 Check the bearings for sign of wear and if evident the outer tracks must be removed using a suitable soft metal drift.
15 To dismantle the pinion assembly detach the bearing spacer and remove the rear bearing cone using a universal puller. Recover any shims found between the rear bearing and pinion head.
16 Tap out the differential pinion shaft locking pin which is tapered at one end and must be pushed out from the crown wheel side of the case.
17 Push the differential pinion shaft out of the case and rotate the pinions around the differential gears, so that they may be extracted through the apertures in the case. Cupped thrust washers are fitted between the pinions and the case and may be extracted after the pinions have been

Fig. 8.9. Installing the pinion gear shaft locking pin (Sec. 6)

Fig. 8.7. Component parts of the differential (Sec. 6)

Fig. 8.10. Fitting the collapsible spacer (Sec. 6)

Fig. 8.8. Measuring the play of the side gears (Sec. 6)

Fig. 8.11. Fitting an adjustment cup (Sec. 6)

removed.
18 Remove the differential gears and thrust washers from the differential case.
19 Wash all parts and wipe dry with a clean lint-free cloth.
20 Again check all bearings for signs of wear or pitting and if evident a new set of bearings should be obtained.
21 Examine the teeth of the crown wheel and pinion for pitting, score marks, chipping and general wear. If a crown wheel and pinion is required a mated crown wheel and pinion must be fitted and under no circumstances may only one part of the two be renewed.
22 Inspect the differential pinions and side gears for signs of pitting, score marks, chipping and general wear. Obtain new gears as necessary.
23 Inspect the thrust washers for signs of wear or deep scoring. Obtain new thrust washers as necessary.
24 Once the pinion oil seal has been disturbed it must be discarded and a new one obtained.
25 Commence reassembly by lubricating the differential gear thrust washers and then positioning a flat washer on each differential side gear. Position the two gears in the case.
26 Position the cupped thrust washers on the machined faces in the case and retain in position with a smear of grease.
27 Locate the pinion gears in the case diametrically opposite each other and rotate the gears to move the pinion gears in line with the holes in the shaft.
28 Check that the thrust washers are still in place and push the spider shaft through the case, thrust washers and pinions. If the pinions do not line up they are not diametrically opposite each other, and should be extracted and repositioned. Measure the play of the gears and, if necessary select new thrust washers to obtain 0.006 in. (0.15 mm) play.
29 Insert the locking pin (tapered end first) and lightly peen the case to prevent the pin working out.
30 Examine the bearing journals on the differential case for burrs, and refit the differential bearing cones onto the differential case using a suitable diameter tubular drift. Make sure they are fitted the correct way round.
31 Examine the crown wheel and differential case for burrs, score marks and dirt. Clean as necessary and then refit the crown wheel. Take care to line up the bolt holes and any previously made marks if the original parts are being refitted.
32 Refit the crown wheel to differential case securing bolts and tighten in a diagonal manner to the specified torque wrench setting.
33 Using a suitable diameter drift carefully drive the pinion bearing cups into position in the final drive housing. Make sure they are the correct way round.
34 Slide the shim onto the pinion shaft and locate behind the pinion head and then fit the inner cone and race of the rear bearing. It is quite satisfactory to drift the rear bearing on with a piece of tubing 12 to 14 inches long with sufficient internal diameter to just fit over the pinion shaft. With one end of the tube bearing against the race, tap the top end of the tube with a hammer, so driving the bearing squarely down the shaft and hard up against the underside of the thrust washer.
35 Slide a new collapsible type spacer over the pinion shaft and insert the assembly into the differential carrier.
36 Fit the pinion front bearing outer track and race, followed by a new pinion oil seal.
37 Fit the pinion drive flange and hold it still with a suitable tool and screw on the pinion self-locking nut until a pinion endfloat exists of between 0.002 and 0.005 in (0.05 and 0.13 mm). Tighten the nut only a fraction at a time and check the pinion turning torque after each tightening, using either a suitable torque gauge or a spring balance and length of cord wrapped round the pinion drive flange. The correct pinion turning torque should be:

Original bearings		
Torque wrench	*12 to 18 lbf in.*	*(0.14 to 0.216 kgfm)*
Pull on spring balance	*12 to 18 lb*	*(5 to 8 kg)*
New bearings		
Torque wrench	*20 to 26 lbf in.*	*(0.24 to 0.31 kgfm)*
Pull on spring balance	*20 to 26 lb*	*(9 to 11 kg)*

38 To the foregoing figures, add 3 lbf in (0.035 kgfm) if a new pinion oil seal has been fitted.
39 Throughout the nut tightening process, hold the pinion flange quite still with a suitable tool.
40 If the pinion nut is overtightened, the nut cannot be unscrewed to correct the adjustment as the pinion spacer will have been over-compressed and the assembly will have to be dismantled and a new collapsible type spacer fitted.
41 Fit the differential cage to the differential carrier and refit the two bearing caps, locating them in their original positions.
42 Tighten the bearing cap bolts finger-tight and then screw in the two adjustment cups.
43 It is now necessary to position the crown wheel relative to the pinion. If possible mount a dial indicator gauge, with the probe resting on one of the teeth of the crown wheel determine the backlash. Backlash may be varied by moving the whole differential assembly using the two adjustment cups until the required setting is obtained.
44 Tighten the bearing cap securing the bolts and recheck the backlash setting.
45 The best check the D-I-Y motorist can make to ascertain the correct meshing of the crownwheel and pinion is to smear a little engineer's blue onto the crown wheel and then rotate the pinion. The contact mark should appear right in the middle of the crown wheel teeth. If the mark appears on the toe or the heel of the crown wheel teeth then the crownwheel must be moved either nearer or further away from the pinion. The various tooth patterns that may be obtained are illustrated (Fig 8.12).
46 When the correct meshing between the crownwheel and pinion has been obtained refit the adjustment cup lock plates, bolts and spring washers.
47 The differential unit can now be refitted to the axle casing.

7 Pinion oil seal (detachable differential) - renewal

1 Jack-up the rear of the car and secure on stands both under the body-frame and axle casing.
2 Remove the roadwheels and brake drums.
3 Disconnect the propeller shaft from the pinion drive flange (refer to Chapter 7, if necessary).
4 Using either a spring balance and a length of cord wrapped round the drive pinion or a torque wrench (lbf in) check and record the turning torque of the pinion.
5 Hold the drive pinion flange quite still with a suitable tool and measure and remove the pinion self-locking nut.
6 Remove the washer, drive flange and dust deflector, and then prise out the oil seal. Do not damage or lever against the pinion shaft splines during this operation.
7 Tap in the new oil seal using a piece of tubing as a drift. Do not inadvertently knock the end of the pinion shaft.
8 Repeat the operations described in paragraphs 37 to 40 of Section 6, but ensuring that the final pinion turning torque figure agrees with that recorded before dismantling.
9 Refit the brake drums, propeller shaft and roadwheels and lower the car.

8 Rear axle (integral differential) - removal and refitting

1 The procedure is similar to that described in Section 2.

9 Halfshaft (integral differential) - removal and refitting

1 The procedure is similar to that described in Section 3.

10 Halfshaft bearing/oil seal (integral differential) - renewal

1 The procedure is similar to that described in Section 4.

11 Axle rear cover (integral differential) - removal and refitting

1 Wipe down the rear of the final drive housing to prevent the possibility of dirt entering the rear axle.
2 Release the handbrake cross cable from the rear of each brake back-plate by pulling out the small spring clips and withdrawing the clevis pins.
3 To give more room to work in, release the handbrake return spring from its bracket on the axle casing and then detach the operating lever from the casing.
4 Place a container of at least 2 imp. pints (1.14 litre; 2.4 US pints) capacity under the rear axle casing to catch the oil as the rear cover is released.

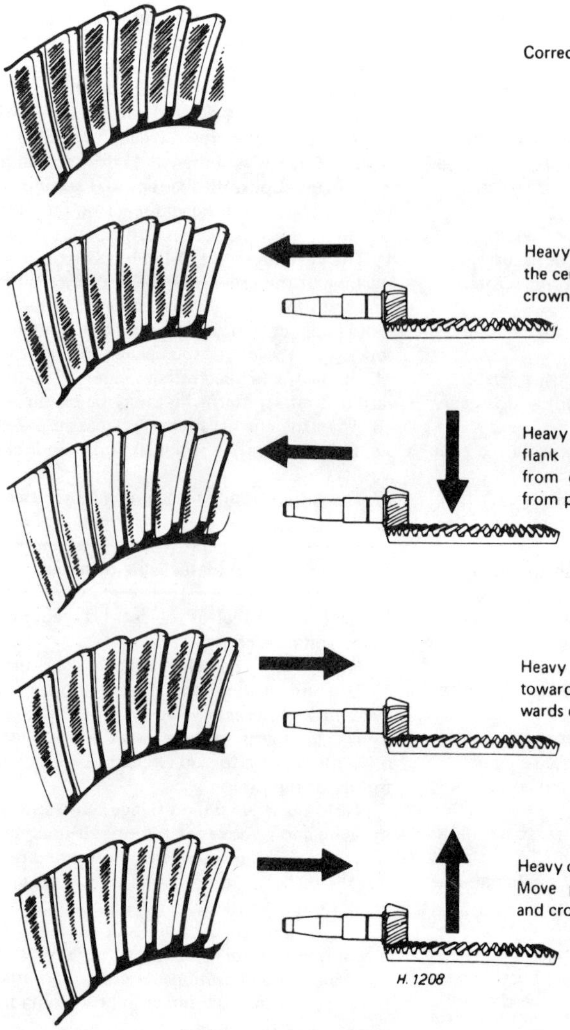

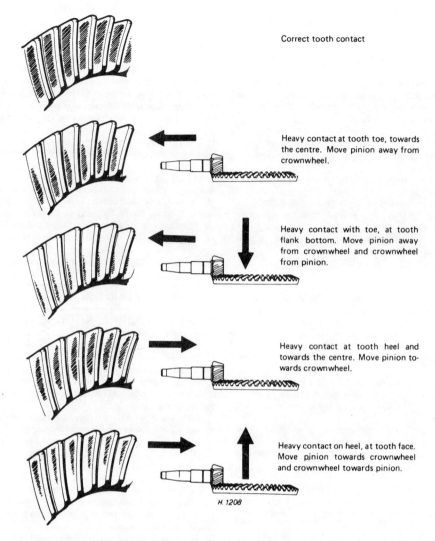

Correct tooth contact
Heavy contact at tooth toe, towards the centre. Move pinion away from crownwheel.
Heavy contact with toe, at tooth flank bottom. Move pinion away from crownwheel and crownwheel from pinion.
Heavy contact at tooth heel and towards the centre. Move pinion towards crownwheel.
Heavy contact on heel, at tooth face. Move pinion towards crownwheel and crownwheel towards pinion.
H. 1208

Fig. 8.12. Correct meshing of crownwheel and pinion and repositioning guide for incorrect tooth meshing (Sec. 6)

5 Undo and remove the ten bolts and spring washers that secure the rear cover to the final drive housing. Lift away the rear cover and its gasket.
6 Before refitting the rear cover make sure that the mating faces are free of the old gasket or jointing compound.
7 Fit a new gasket and then the rear cover and secure with the ten bolts and spring washers. The cover bolts protrude into the final drive housing so it is important that a suitable oil resistant sealing compound is smeared onto the threads of each bolt before it is fitted.
8 Tighten the cover securing bolts to the specified torque wrench setting.
9 Reconnect the handbrake operating lever, cross cable and return spring.
10 Do not forget to refill with the correct grade of oil.

12 Pinion oil seal (integral differential - early models) - renewal

1 This operation may be performed with the rear axle in position or on the bench.
2 Undo and remove the two bolts, spring and plain washers that secure the centre bearing support to the underside of the body.
3 With a scriber or file mark a line across the propeller shaft and pinion drive flanges so that they may be refitted together in their original positions.
4 Undo and remove the four bolts and spring washers securing the propeller shaft and pinion driving flanges and carefully lower the propeller shaft to the floor.
5 Carefully clean the front of the final drive housing as there will probably be a considerable amount of dirt and oil if the seal has been leaking for a while.
6 Using a suitable long handled tool or large wrench, grip the drive pinion flange and with a socket undo and remove the pinion flange retaining self locking nut. This nut must be discarded and a new one obtained ready for reassembly.
7 Place a container under the front of the final drive housing to catch any oil that may issue once the oil seal has been removed.
8 Using a universal puller and suitable thrust pad pull off the drive pinion flange from the drive pinion.
9 Using a screwdriver or small chisel carefully remove the old oil seal. It will probably be necessary to partially destroy it. Note the correct way round is with the lip facing inwards.
10 Before fitting a new seal apply some grease to the inner face between the two lips of the seal.
11 Apply a little jointing compound to the outer face of the seal.
12 Using a tubular drift of suitable diameter carefully drive the oil seal into the final drive housing.
13 Refit the drive pinion flange and once again hold squarely with the tool or wrench. Fit a new self locking nut and tighten to a torque wrench setting of 71 to 86 lbf ft (10 to 12 kgfm).
14 Reconnect the propeller shaft aligning the previously made marks on the flanges, and refit the bolts with new spring washers. Tighten to the specified torque wrench setting.
15 Refit the centre bearing support securing bolts, spring and plain washers and tighten to the specified torque wrench setting.
16 Finally check the oil level in the rear axle and top-up if necessary.

13 Pinion oil seal (integral differential - late models) - renewal

1 Late model rear axles are fitted with a collapsible type spacer on the pinion shaft. The procedure for renewing the oil seal is similar to that described in Section 7.

14 Integral type differential - overhaul

1 It is recommended that for complete overhaul the rear axle be removed from the car as described in Section 8. Before commencing work refer to the introduction to Section 6. In this case it would be better to look for a secondhand rear axle instead of just the differential unit.
2 Refer to Section 11 and remove the rear cover and then to Section 9 and withdraw the halfshafts by about 6 inches (152.4 mm).
3 Working inside the axle casing undo and remove the four bolts that hold the two 'U' shaped differential bearing caps in the casing.
4 With a scriber mark the relative positions of the two bearing caps so that they can be refitted in their original positions. Lift away the two end caps; there may already be mating numbers as shown in Fig. 8.13.
5 Obtain two pieces of 2 inch (50 mm) square wood at least 12 inches (300 mm) long and with a sharp knife, taper the ends along a length of 6 inches (150 mm).
6 Place the tapered ends of the wooden levers in the two cut-aways of the differential casing and using the rear cover face of the final drive housing as a fulcrum carefully lever the differential assembly from the final drive housing.
7 If it necessary to remove the two differential case bearings these may be removed next using a universal two legged puller and suitable thrust pad. Carefully ease each bearing from its location. Recover the shim packs from behind each bearing noting from which side they came.
8 Using a scriber mark the relative positions of the crownwheel and differential housing so that the crownwheel may be fitted in its original position, unless of course, it is to be renewed.
9 Undo and remove the eight bolts that secure the crownwheel to the differential housing. Using a soft faced hammer tap out the crownwheel from its location on the differential housing.
10 Using a suitable diameter paralled pin punch, tap out the pin that locks the differential pinion gear shaft to the differential housing. **Note:** The hole into which the peg fits is slightly tapered, and the opposite end may be lightly peened over and should be cleaned with a suitable diameter drill.
11 Using a soft metal drift tap out the differential pinion gear shaft. Lift away the differential pinion gears, side gears and thrust washers taking care to ensure that the thrust washers are left with their relative gears.
12 Professional fitters at the dealers use a special tool for holding the pinion drive flange stationary whilst the nut in the centre of the flange is unscrewed. Since it is tightened to a torque wrench setting of 71 to 86 lbf ft (10 to 12 kgf m), it will require some force to undo it. The average owner will not normally have the use of this special tool so, as an alternative method clamp the pinion flange in a vice and then undo the nut. Any damage caused to the edge of the flange by the vice should be carefully filed smooth. This nut must not be used again so a new one will be required during reassembly.
13 Using a universal two-legged puller and suitable thrust pad draw the pinion drive flange from the end of the pinion shaft.
14 The pinion shaft may now be removed from the final drive housing. Carefully inspect the large taper roller bearing behind the pinion gear and if it shows signs of wear or pitting on the rollers or cage the bearing must be renewed.
15 Using a universal two-legged puller and suitable thrust pad draw the bearing from the pinion shaft.
16 The smaller taper roller bearing and oil seal may next be removed from the final drive housing, pinion drive flange end. To do this use a soft metal drift with or tapered end or suitable diameter tube and working inside the housing tap the bearing circumference outwards so releasing first the oil seal and then the bearing.
17 Again using the soft metal drift and working inside the housing drift out the bearing cups. These must not be used with new bearings.
18 The final drive assembly is now dismantled and should be washed and dried with a clean lint-free rag ready for inspection.
19 Carefully inspect the parts, as described in Section 6.
20 When new parts have been obtained as required, reassembly can begin. First fit the thrust washers to the side gears and place them in position in the differential housing.
21 Place the thrust washers behind the differential pinion gears and mesh these two gears with the side gears through the two apertures in the differential housing. Make sure they are diametrically opposite to each other. Rotate the differential pinion gears through 10° so bringing them into line with the pinion gear shaft bore in the housing.
22 Insert the pinion gear shaft with the locking pin hole in line with the pin hole.
23 Using feeler gauges measure the endfloat of each side gear. The correct clearance is 0.006 inch (0.15 mm) and if this figure is exceeded new thrust washers must be obtained. Dismantle the assembly again and fit new thrust washers. (see Fig 8.8).
24 Lock the pinion gear shaft using the pin which should be tapped fully home using a suitable diameter parallel pin punch. Peen over the end of the pin hole to stop the pin working its way out.
25 The crownwheel may next be refitted. Wipe the mating faces of the crownwheel and differential housing and if original parts are being used place the crownwheel into position with the previously made marks aligned. Refit the eight bolts that secure the crownwheel and tighten these in a progressive and diagonal manner to a final torque wrench setting of 57 to 62 lbf ft (8 to 8.7 kgf m).
26 Place the shim packs back in their original fitted position on the differential housing bearing location. Using a peice of suitable diameter tube very carefully fit the differential housing bearings with the smaller diameter of the taper outwards. The bearing cage must not in any way be damaged.
27 Place the shims behind the head of the pinion gear and using a suitable diameter tube carefully fit the larger taper roller bearing onto the pinion shaft. The larger diameter of the bearing must be next to the pinion head.
28 Using suitable diameter tubes fit the two taper roller bearing cones

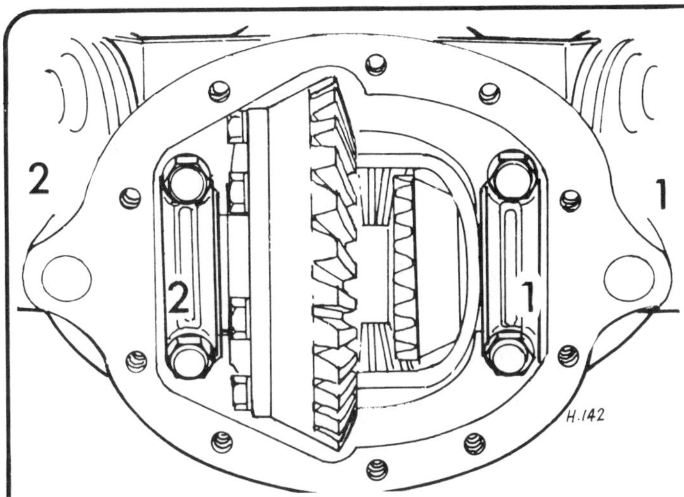

Fig. 8.13. Differential casing and end cap identification marks (Sec. 14)

Fig. 8.14. Removing the differential (Sec. 14)

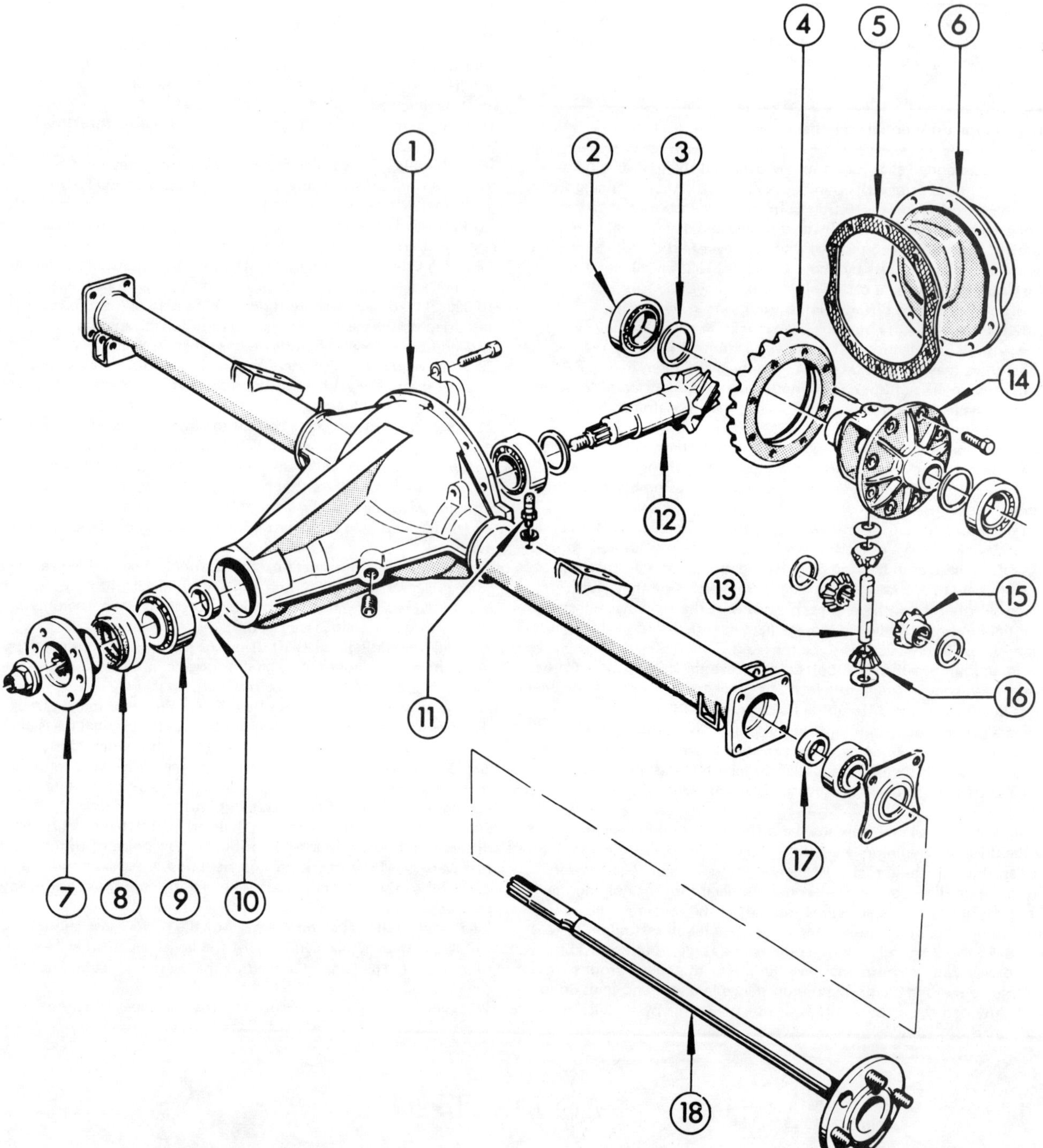

Fig. 8.15. Component parts of the integral differential (Salisbury or Type D) axle (Sec. 14)

1 Axle housing
2 Differential case taper roller bearing
3 Differential case shim
4 Crown wheel
5 Gasket
6 Cover
7 Drive pinion flange
8 Oil seal
9 Drive pinion taper roller bearing
10 Drive pinion spacer - fixed length or collapsible
11 Vent valve
12 Drive pinion
13 Pinion gear shaft
14 Differential case
15 Side gear
16 Differential pinion
17 Retaining ring
18 Half shaft

into the final drive housing making sure that they are fitted the correct way round.
29 Slide the shim and spacer onto the pinion shaft and insert into the final drive housing.
30 Refit the second and smaller diameter taper roller bearing onto the end of the pinion shaft and follow this with a new oil seal. Before the seal is actually fitted apply some grease to the inner face between the two lips of the seal.
31 Apply a little jointing compound to the outer face of the seal.
32 Using a tubular drift of suitable diameter carefully drive the oil seal into the final housing. Make quite sure that it is fitted squarely into the housing.
33 Refit the drive pinion flange and hold securely in a bench vice. On early models tighten the pinion nut to a torque wrench setting of between 74 and 88 lbf ft (10 and 12 kgf m). On later models with a collapsible spacer, tighten the nut and check the preload as described in Section 6, paragraphs 37 to 40.
34 Fit the bearing cones to the differential housing bearings and carefully ease the housing into position in the final drive housing.
35 Refit the bearing caps in their original positions. Smear a little jointing compound on the threads of each cap securing bolt and fit into position. When all four bolts have been refitted tighten these up in a diagonal and progressive manner to a final torque wrench setting of 43 to 50 lbf ft (6 to 6.8 kgf m).
36 If possible mount a dial indicator gauge so that the probe is resting on one of the teeth of the crownwheel and determine the backlash between the crownwheel and pinion. The backlash may be varied by decreasing the thickness of the shims behind one bearing and increasing the thickness of shims behind the other, thus moving the crownwheel into or out of mesh as required. The total thickness of the shims must not be changed.
37 The best check the do-it-yourself owner can make to ascertain the correct meshing of the crownwheel and pinion is to smear a little engineer's blue onto the crownwheel and pinion and then rotate the pinion. The contact mark should appear right in the middle of the crownwheel teeth. Refer to Fig 8.12 where the correct tooth pattern is shown. Also shown are incorrect tooth patterns and the method of obtaining the correct pattern. Obviously this will take time and further dismantling but will be worth it.
38 Before refitting the rear cover make sure that the mating faces are free from traces of the old gasket or jointing compound.
39 Fit a new gasket and then a rear cover and secure with the ten bolts and spring washers. The cover bolts protrude into the final drive housing so it is important that a suitable oil resistant sealing compound is smeared onto the threads of each bolt before it is fitted.
40 Tighten the cover securing bolts to the specified torque.
41 Refit the halfshafts and then the complete rear axle assembly.
42 Do not forget to refill with correct grade oil.

Fig. 8.16. Using a dial gauge to determine crownwheel/pinion backlash (Sec. 14)

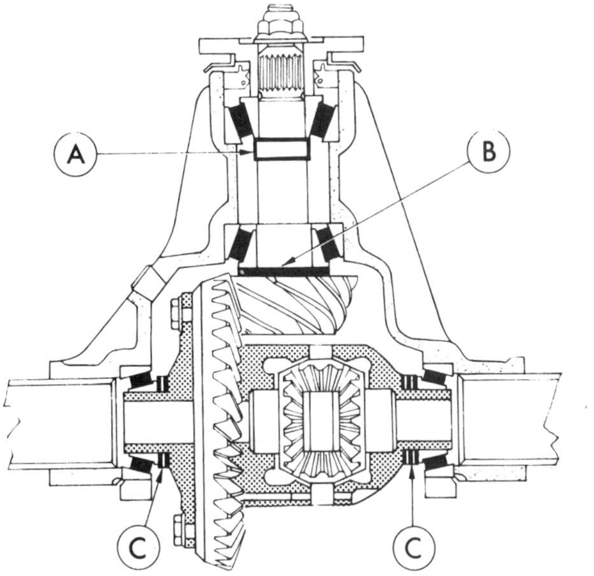

Fig. 8.17. Sectional view of the integral differential axle (early type with fixed length spacer) (Sec. 14)

A Spacer *B Shim* *C Shims*

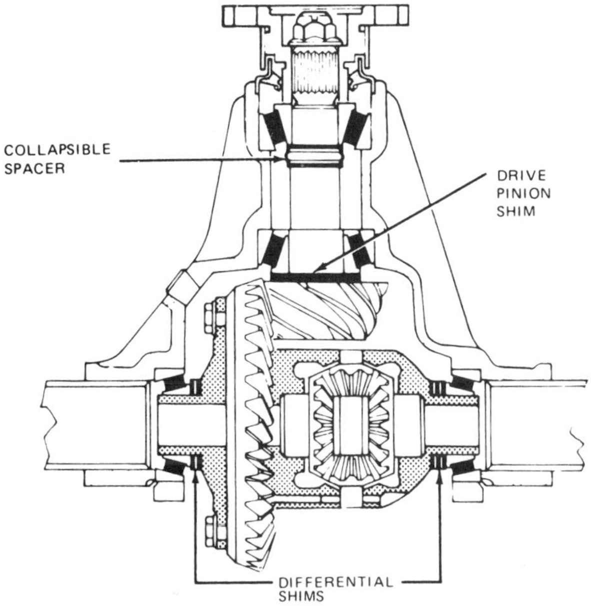

Fig. 8.18. Sectional view of the integral differential axle (Sec. 14) (later type with collapsible spacer)

15 Fault diagnosis - Rear axle

Symptom	Reason/s
Vibration	Worn axleshaft bearings Loose drive flange bolts. Out of balance propeller shaft. Wheels require balancing.
Noise	Insufficient lubricant. Worn gears and differential components generally.
'Clunk' on acceleration or deceleration	Incorrect crownwheel and pinion mesh. Excessive backlash due to wear in crownwheel and pinion teeth. Worn axleshaft or differential side gear splines. Loose drive flange bolts. Worn drive pinion flange splines.
Oil leakage	Faulty pinion or axleshaft oil seals. May be caused by blocked axle housing breather.

Chapter 9 Braking system

For modifications, and information applicable to later models, see Supplement at end of manual

Contents

Specifications

General

System type	Dual line, hydraulic with servo assistance
Front brakes	Disc, self-adjusting
Rear brakes	Drum, self-adjusting
Handbrake (parking brake)	Self-adjusting, cable operated to rear wheels

Front brakes

Disc diameter:	
Inner	5.1 in (129.5 mm)
Outer	9.6 in (244.5 mm)
Disc thickness:	
Nominal	0.5 in (12.7 mm)
Minimum	0.45 in (11.4 mm)
Disc run-out (max., including hub)	0.0035 in (0.09 mm)
Wheel cylinder diameter	2.12 in (54 mm)
Total swept brake area	190 sq in (1227 sq cm)

Rear brakes

Drum diameter	8.99 to 9.00 in (228.35 to 228.6 mm)
Shoe width	1.7 in (43.18 mm)
Wheel cylinder diameter	0.7 in (17.78 mm)
Total swept brake area	96.1 sq in (620 sq cm)

Master cylinder diameter ... 0.81 in (20.64 mm)

Servo boost ratio ... 4.3 : 1

Disc pads

Material:	
Ford of Britain (FOB)	Ferodo 2441F/1D341
Ford of Germany (FOG)	Textar/Mintex V1431
Minimum permissible thickness	1/8 inch (0.125 in/3.2 mm)
Rear brake linings, minimum permissible thickness (bonded linings)	1/32 in (0.03 in/0.8 mm)

Brake fluid specification ... To specification SAE J1703E, or ESEA-M6C-1001A or ESA-M6C25-A or C6AZ-19542-A

Torque wrench settings	lbf ft	kgf m
Caliper to front suspension unit	35 to 50	4.8 to 6.9
Brake disc to hub	30 to 34	4.1 to 4.7
Backplate to axle housing*:		
Type J (Timken) axle	15 to 18	2.1 to 2.5
Type D (Salisbury) axle	20 to 23	2.8 to 3.2
Hydraulic unions	5 to 7	0.7 to 1.0
Bleed valve	8 max	1.1 max
Master cylinder stopscrew (FOG)	4 to 7	0.6 to 1.0

** See Chapter 8 for axle applications.*

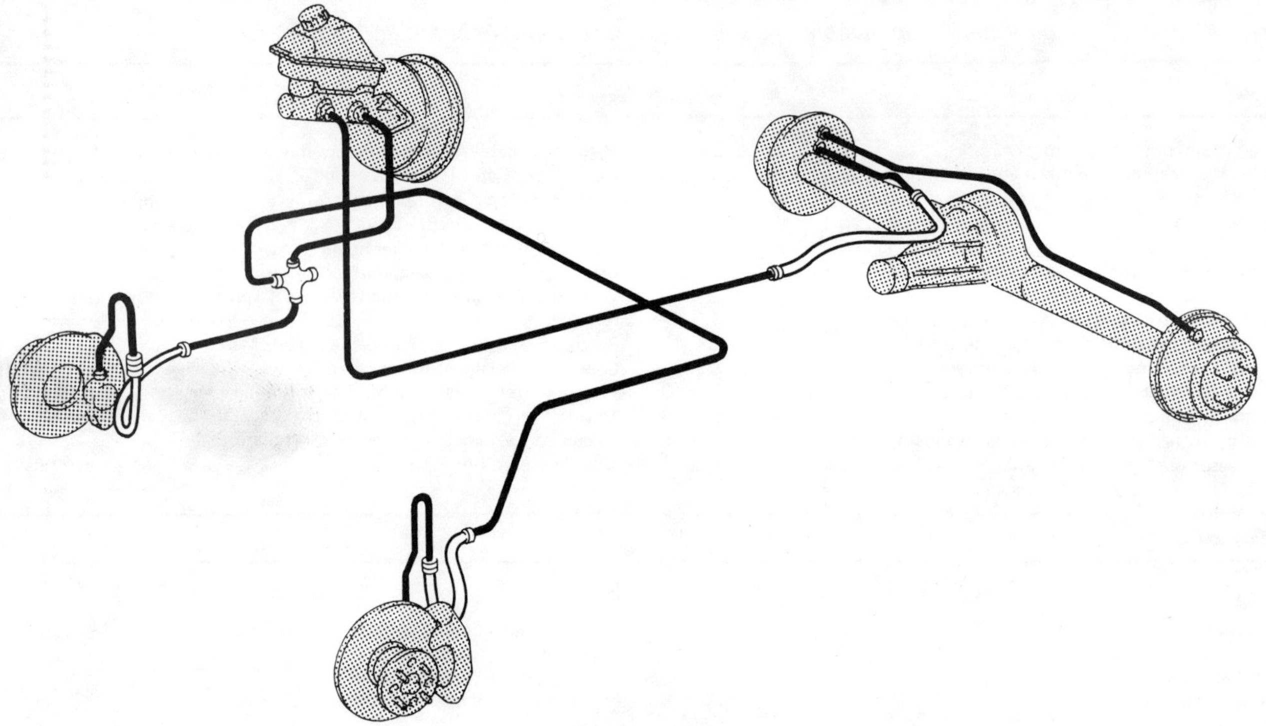

Fig. 9.1. Brake line layout (rhd)

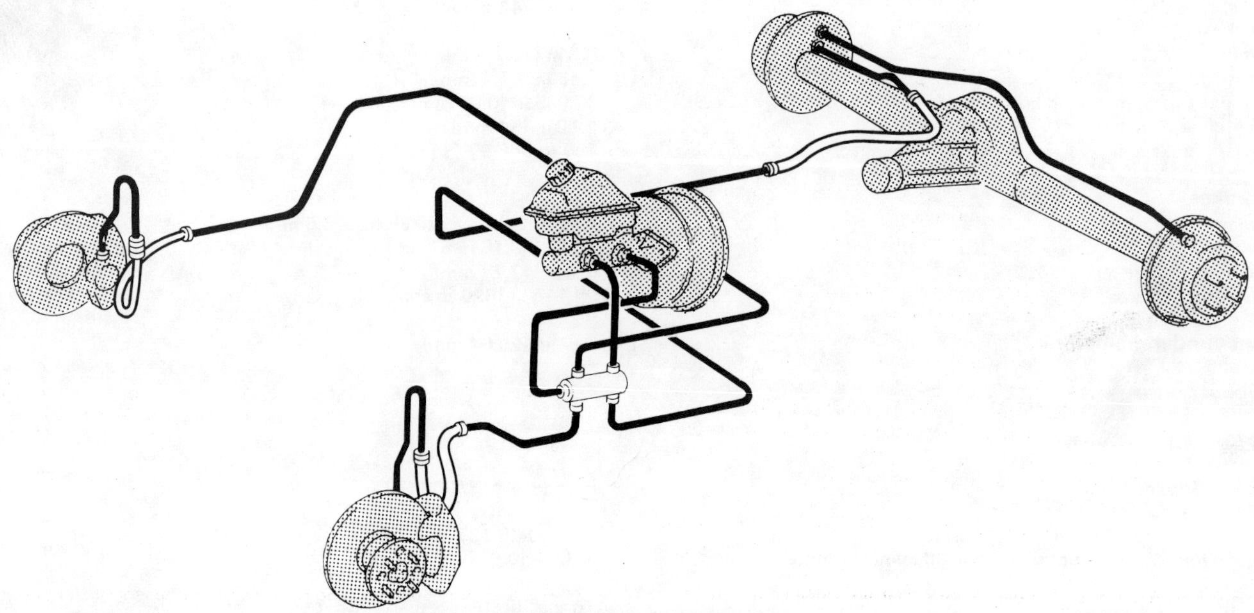

Fig. 9.2. Brake line layout (lhd)

1 General description

Disc brakes are fitted to the front wheels of all models together with single leading shoe drum brakes at the rear. The mechanically operated handbrake works on the rear wheels only.

The brakes fitted to the front wheels are of the rotating disc and static caliper type, with one caliper per disc, each caliper containing two piston operated friction pads, which on application of the footbrake pinch the disc rotating between them. The front brakes are of the trailing caliper type to minimise the entry of water.

Application of the footbrake creates hydraulic pressure in the master cylinder and fluid from the cylinder travels via steel and flexible pipes to the cylinders in each half of the calipers, thus pushing the pistons to which are attached the friction pads, into contact with either side of the disc.

Two seals are fitted to the operating cylinders, the outer seal prevents moisture and dirt entering the cylinder, while the inner seal which is retained in a groove inside the cylinder, prevents fluid leakage.

As the friction pads wear so the pistons move further out of the cylinders and the level of fluid in the hydraulic reservoir drops. Disc pad wear is therefore taken up automatically and eliminates the need for periodic adjustment by the owner.

All models use a floor mounted handbrake (parking brake) lever located between the front seats.

On Capri II models a single cable runs from the lever to a compensator mechanism on the back of the rear axle casing. From the compensator a single cable runs to the rear brake drums. As the rear brake shoes wear the handbrake cables operate a self adjusting mechanism in the rear brake drums thus doing away with the necessity for the owner to adjust the brakes on each rear wheel individually.

On Mercury Capri II models, a cable runs from the parking brake lever through an abutment bracket on the rear axle to the right-hand brake backplate. A transverse rod connects from the abutment to the left-hand brake backplate.

All models have the dual line braking system with a separate hydraulic system for the front and rear brakes, so that if failure of the hydraulic pipes to the front or rear brakes occurs half the braking system still operates. Servo assistance in this condition is still available. On some models a warning light is fitted on the facia which illuminates should either circuit fail. The bulb is connected to a pressure differential switch in the hydraulic line (see Section 15).

2 Front disc pads - inspection and renewal

1 Apply the handbrake, remove the front wheel trim (where applicable), slacken the wheel nuts, jack-up the front of the car and place on firmly based axle stands. Remove the front wheel.

2 Inspect the amount of friction material left on the pads. The pads must be renewed when the thickness of the friction material has been reduced to a minimum of 0.12 inches (3.00 mm).

3 If the fluid level in the master cylinder reservoir is high, when the pistons are moved into their respective bores to accommodate new pads the level could rise sufficiently for the fluid to overflow. Place absorbent cloth around the reservoir or syphon a little fluid out so preventing paintwork damage being caused by the hydraulic fluid.

4 Using a pair of long nosed pliers, extract the two small clips that hold the main retaining pins in place (photo).

5 Remove the main retaining pins which run through the caliper and the metal backing of the pads and the shims (Fig. 9.3).

6 The friction pads can now be removed from the caliper. If they prove difficult to remove by hand a pair of long nosed pliers can be used. Lift away the shims and tension springs (where fitted).

7 Carefully clean the recesses in the caliper in which the friction pads and shims lie, and the exposed faces of each piston from all traces of dirt or rust.

8 Using a piece of wood carefully retract the pistons.

9 Place the brake pad tension springs on the brake pads and shims and locate in the caliper. Insert the main pad retaining pins making sure that the tangs of the tension springs are under the retaining pins. Secure the pins with the small wire clips (Fig. 9.4).

10 Refit the road wheel and lower the car. Tighten the wheel nuts securely and replace the wheel trim.

11 To correctly seat the pistons pump the brake pedal several times and finally top up the hydraulic fluid level in the master cylinder

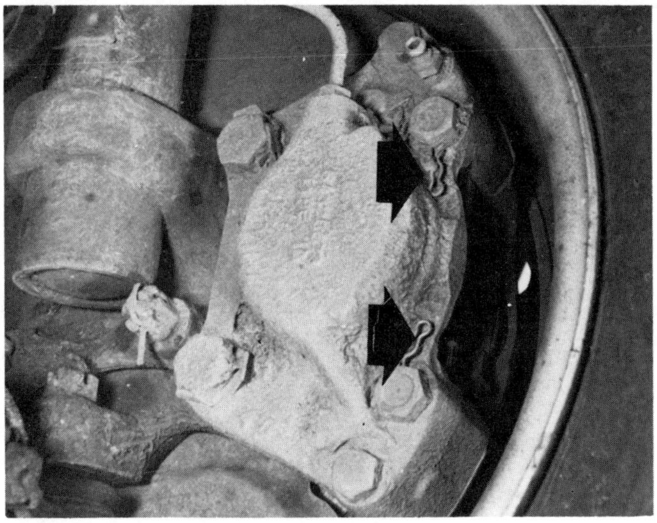

2.4 The main retaining pin clips (arrowed)

reservoir as necessary.

3 Front brake caliper - removal and refitting

1 Apply the handbrake, remove the front wheel trim, slacken the wheel nuts, jack-up the front of the car and place on firmly based axle stands. Remove the front wheel.

2 Wipe the top of the master cylinder reservoir and unscrew the cap. Place a piece of polythene sheet over the top of the reservoir and refit the cap. This will help to prevent loss of fluid by creating a vacuum.

3 Remove the friction pads, as described in Section 2.

4 If it is intended to fit new caliper pistons and/or seals, depress the brake pedal to bring the pistons into contact with the disc and assist subsequent removal of the pistons.

5 Wipe the area clean around the flexible hose bracket and detach the pipes as described in Section 13. Tape up the end of the pipe to stop the possibility of dirt ingress.

6 Using a screwdriver or chisel bend back the tabs on the locking plate and undo the two caliper body mounting bolts. Lift away the caliper from its mounting flange on the suspension leg (Fig. 9.5).

7 To refit the caliper, position it over the disc and move it until the mounting bolt holes are in line with the two front holes in the suspension leg mounting flange.

8 Fit the caliper retaining bolts through the two holes in a new locking plate and insert the bolts through the caliper body. Tighten the bolts to the specified torque wrench setting.

9 Using a screwdriver, pliers or chisel bend up the locking plate tabs so as to lock the bolts.

10 Remove the tape from the end of the flexible hydraulic pipe and reconnect it to the union on the hose bracket. Be careful not to cross the thread of the union nut during the initial turns. The union nut should be tightened securely using a spanner of short length.

11 Push the pistons into their respective bores so as to accommodate the pads. Watch the level of hydraulic fluid in the master cylinder reservoir as it can overflow if too high whilst the pistons are being retracted. Place absorbent cloth around the reservoir or syphon a little fluid out so preventing paintwork damage.

12 Fit the pads, shims and tension springs, as described in Section 2.

13 Remove the polythene from the reservoir cap. Bleed the hydraulic system, as described in Section 14. Replace the roadwheel and lower the car.

4 Front brake caliper - servicing

1 The pistons should be removed first. To do this half withdraw one piston from its bore in the caliper body.

2 Carefully remove the securing circlip and extract the sealing boot from its location in the lower part of the piston skirt. Completely remove the piston.

3 If difficulty is experienced in withdrawing the pistons use a jet of

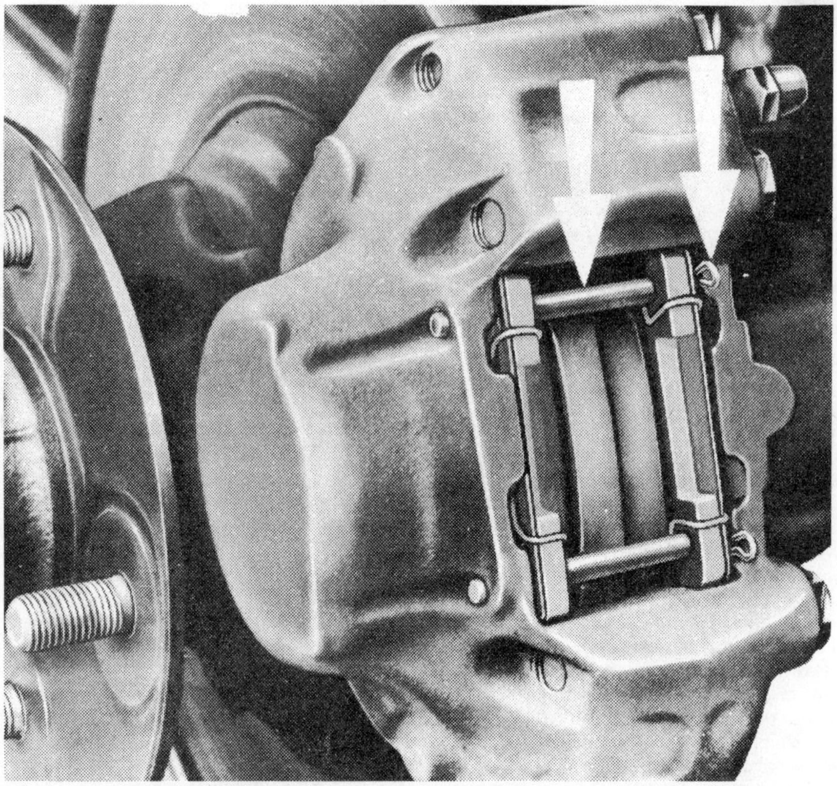

Fig. 9.3. Brake pad retaining pins and clips (arrowed) (Sec. 2)

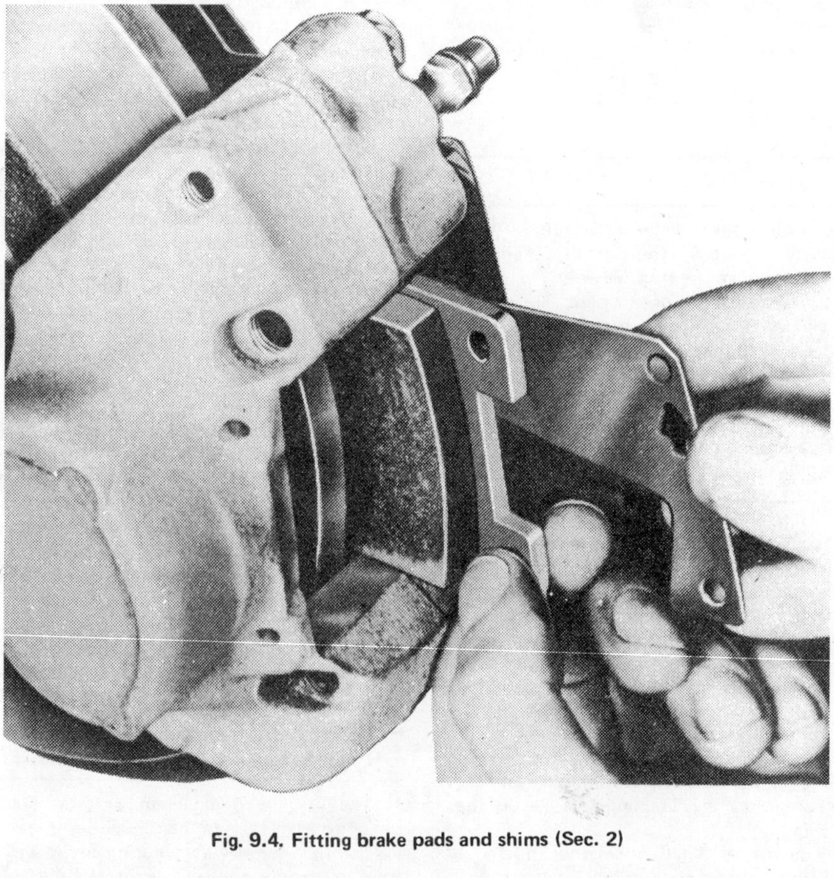

Fig. 9.4. Fitting brake pads and shims (Sec. 2)

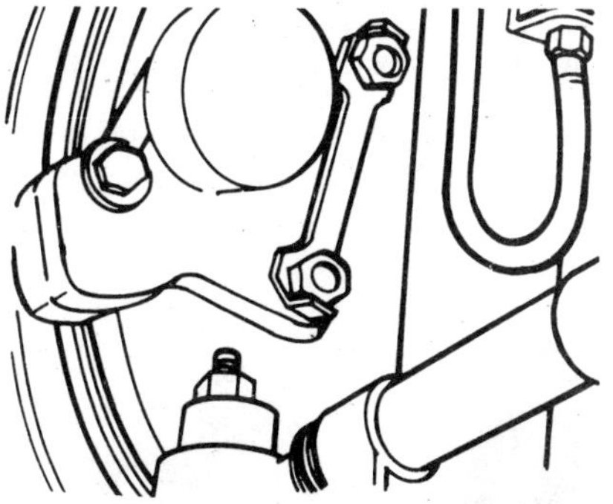

Fig. 9.5. Brake caliper mounting bolts (Sec. 3)

compressed air or foot pump to move it out of its bore.
4 Remove the sealing bellows from its location in the annular ring which is machined in the cylinder bore.
5 Remove the piston sealing ring from the cylinder bore using a small screwdriver but do take care not to scratch the fine finish of the bore.
6 To remove the second piston repeat paragraphs 1 to 5 inclusive.
7 It is important that the two halves of the caliper are not separated under any circumstances. If hydraulic fluid leaks are evident from the joint, the caliper must be renewed complete.
8 Thoroughly wash all parts in methylated spirit or clean hydraulic fluid. During reassembly new rubber seals must be fitted, these should be well lubricated with clean hydraulic fluid.
9 Inspect the pistons and bores for signs of wear, score marks or damage and, if evident, new parts should be obtained ready for fitting or a new caliper obtained.
10 To reassemble, fit one of the piston seals into the annular groove in the cylinder bore.
11 Fit the rubber boot to the cylinder bore groove so that the lip is turned outward.
12 Lubricate the seal and rubber boot with clean hydraulic fluid. Push the piston, crown first, through the rubber sealing bellows and then into the cylinder bore. Take care as it is easy for the piston to damage the rubber boot.
13 With the piston half inserted into the cylinder bore fit the inner edge of the boot into the annular groove in the piston skirt.
14 Push the piston down the bore as far as it will go. Secure the rubber boot to the caliper with the circlip.
15 Repeat paragraphs 10 to 14 inclusive for the second piston.
16 The caliper is now ready for refitting. It is recommended that the hydraulic pipe end is temporarily plugged to stop any dirt entering whilst it is being refitted, before the pipe connection is made.

5 Front disc (rotor) and hub - removal and installation

Note: Brake discs (rotors) are fitted as matched pairs and should therefore never be renewed or reground as single items.
1 After jacking-up the car and removing the front wheel, remove the caliper, as described in Section 4.
2 Tap off the dust cap from the centre of the hub.
3 Remove the split pin from the nut retainer and lift the retainer away.
4 Unscrew the adjusting nut and lift away the thrust washer and outer taper bearing.
5 Pull off the complete hub and disc assembly from the stub axle.
6 From the back of the hub assembly carefully prise out the grease seal and lift away the inner tapered bearing.
7 Carefully clean out the hub and wash the bearings with petrol making sure that no grease or oil is allowed to get onto the brake disc.
8 Should it be necessary to separate the disc from the hub for renewal or regrinding, first bend back the locking tabs and undo the four securing bolts. With a scriber mark the relative positions of the hub and disc to ensure refitting in their original positions and separate the disc from the hub.
9 Thoroughly clean the disc and inspect for signs of deep scoring, cracks or excessive corrosion. If these are evident, the discs may be reground but no more than a maximum total of 0.060 inch (1.524 mm) may be removed. It is however, desirable to fit new discs if at all possible.
10 To reassemble make quite sure that the mating faces of the disc and hub are very clean and place the disc on the hub, lining up any previously made marks.
11 Fit the four securing bolts and two new tab washers and tighten the bolts in a progressive and diagonal manner to the specified torque wrench setting. Bend up the locking tabs.
12 Work some grease well into the bearing, fully pack the bearing cages and rollers. **Note:** Leave the hub and grease seal empty to allow for subsequent expansion of the grease.
13 To reassemble the hub, first fit the inner bearing and then gently tap the grease seal into the hub. A new seal must always be fitted as, during removal, it was probably damaged or distorted. The lip must face inwards to the hub.
14 Replace the hub and disc assembly onto the stub axle and slide in

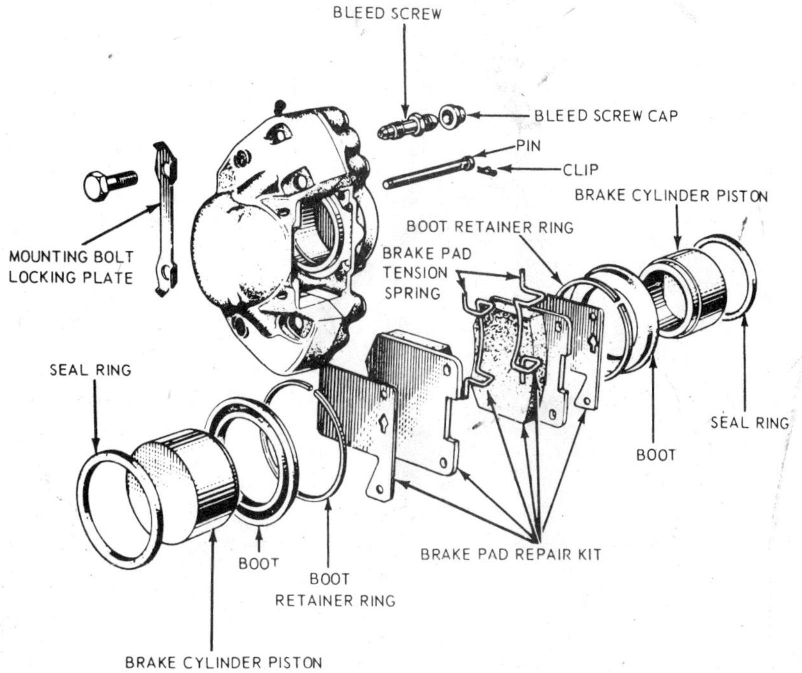

Fig. 9.6. Brake caliper - exploded view (Sec. 4)

the outer bearing and thrust washer.
15 Refit the adjusting nut and tighten it to a torque wrench setting of 27 lbf ft (3.7 kgf m) whilst rotating the hub and disc to ensure free movement and centralisation of the bearings. Slacken the nut back by 90° which will give the required endfloat of 0.001 - 0.005 in (0.03 - 0.13 mm). Fit the nut retainer and a new split pin, but at this stage do not lock the split pin.
16 If a dial indicator gauge is available, it is advisable to check the disc for run-out. The measurment should be taken as near to the edge of the worn yet smooth part of the disc as possible, and must not exceed 0.002 in (0.05 mm). If the figure obtained is found to be excessive, check the mating surfaces of the disc and hub for dirt or damage and check the bearing and cups for excessive wear or damage.
17 If a dial indicator gauge is not available the run-out can be checked by means of a feeler gauge placed between the casting of the caliper and the disc. Establish a reasonably tight fit with the feeler gauge between the top of the casting and the disc and rotate the disc and hub. Any high or low spots will immediately become obvious by extra tightness or looseness of the fit of the feeler gauge. The amount of run-out can be checked by adding or subtracting feeler gauges as necessary.
18 Once the disc run-out has been checked and found to be correct bend the ends of the split pin back and replace the dust cap.
19 Reconnect the brake hydraulic pipe and bleed the brakes as described in Section 14 of this Chapter.

6 Drum brake shoes - inspection and renewal

After high mileages, it will be necessary to fit replacement shoes with new linings. Refitting new brake linings to shoes is not considered economic, or possible, without the use of special equipment. However, if the services of a local garage or workshop having brake relining equipment are available then there is no reason why the original shoes should not be relined successfully. Ensure that the correct specification linings are fitted to the shoes.
1 Chock the front wheels, jack-up the rear of the car and place on firmly based axle stands. Remove the road wheel.

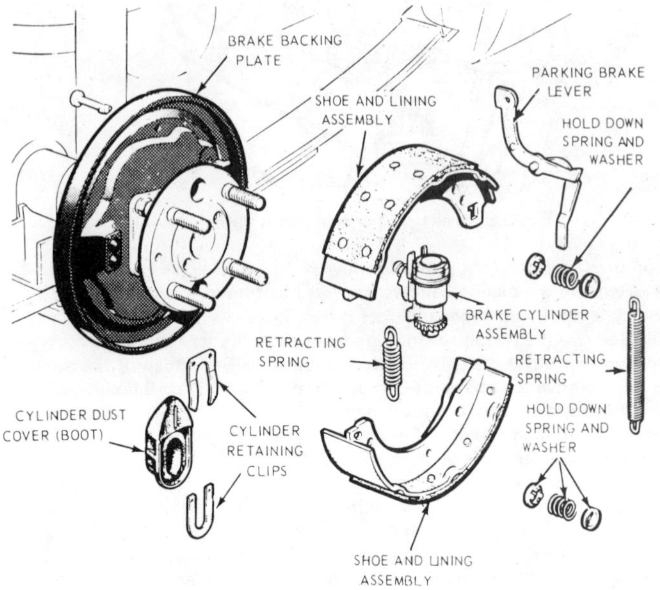

Fig. 9.7. Rear brake assembly (Capri II) - exploded view (Sec. 6)

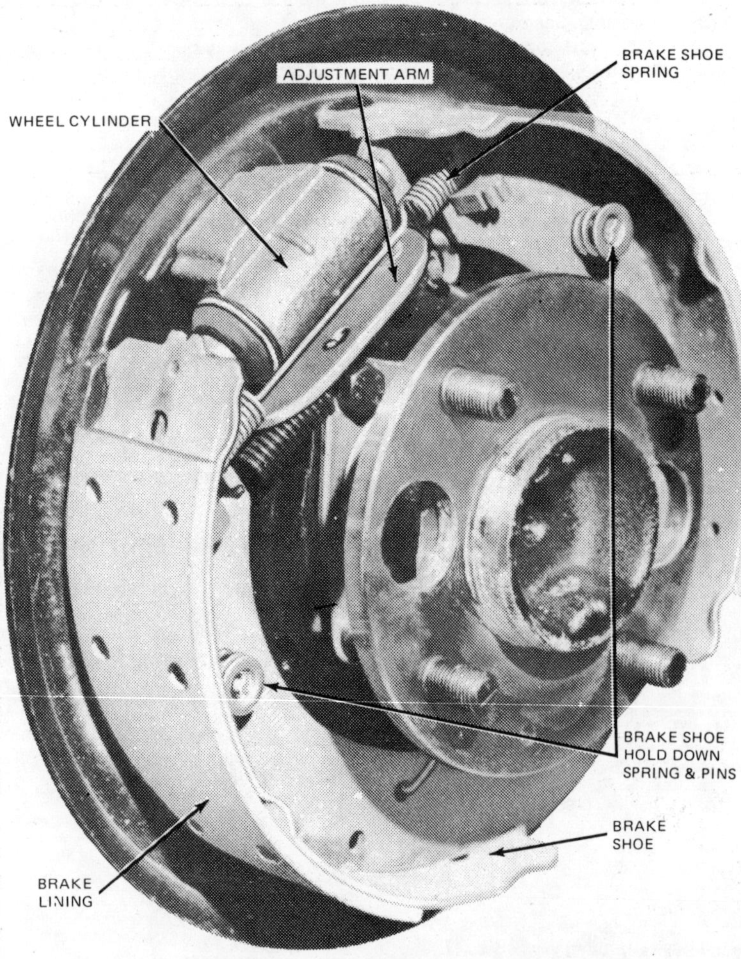

Fig. 9.8. Rear brake assembly (Mercury Capri II) (Sec. 6)

2 Release the brake drum retaining screw, and using a soft-faced hammer on the outer circumferance of the brake drum remove the brake drum. (photo).
3 The brake linings should be renewed if they are so worn that the rivet heads are flush with the surface of the lining. If bonded linings are fitted, they must be renewed when the lining material has worn down to the minimum specified thickness.
4 Depress each shoe holding down spring and rotate the spring retaining washer through 90° to disengage it from the pin secured to the backplate. Lift away the washer and spring.
5 Ease each shoe from its location slot in the fixed pivot and then detach the other end of each shoe from the wheel cylinder.
6 Note which way round and into which holes in the shoes the two retracting springs fit and detach the retracting springs.
7 Lift away the two brake shoes and retracting springs.
8 If the shoes are to be left off for a while, place a warning on the steering wheel. Also place an elastic band round the wheel cylinder to stop the piston falling out.
9 *Capri II:* Withdraw the ratchet wheel assembly from the wheel cylinder and rotate the wheel until it abuts the slot head bolt shoulder. If this is not done difficulty will arise in refitting the brake drum.
10 Thoroughly clean all traces of dust from the shoes, backplates and brake drums using a stiff brush. It is recommended that compressed air is not used as it blows up dust which should not be inhaled. Brake dust can cause judder, or squeal and, therefore, it is important to clean out as described.
11 Check that the piston is free in the cylinder, that the rubber dust covers are undamaged and in position, and that there are no hydraulic leaks.
12 Prior to reassembly smear a trace of brake grease on the shoe support pads, brake shoe pivots and on the ratchet wheel face and threads.
13 To reassemble first fit the retracting springs to the shoe webs in the same position as was noted during removal.
14 Fit the shoe assembly to the backplate by first positioning the rear shoe in its location on the fixed pivot and over the parking brake link. Follow this with the front shoe.
15 Secure each shoe to the backplate with the spring and dished washer dish facing inwards and turning through 90° to lock in position. Make sure that each shoe is firmly seated on the backplate.
16 *Mercury Capri II:* Reset the self-adjuster unit to its minimum setting by gently prying the adjuster arm from the adjuster wheel with a small screwdriver. Now push the adjuster arm towards the backplate until the arm reaches the top of its arc.
17 Refit the brake drum and push it up the studs as far as it will go. Secure with the retaining screw.
18 The shoes must next be centralised by the brake pedal being depressed firmly several times.
19 Pull on and then release the handbrake several times to reset the adjuster mechanism on Capri II models. It is important to note that with the ratchet wheel in the fully off adjustment position, it is possible for the indexing lever on the parking brake link to over-ride the ratchet and stay in this position. When operating the link lever it is necessary to ensure that it always returns to the fully off position each time.
20 Refit the roadwheel and lower the car. Road test to ensure correct operation of the brakes.

6.2 Rear brake with the drum removed (Capri II)

7 Drum brake wheel cylinder (Capri II) - removal, inspection and servicing

1 Refer to Section 6 and remove the brake drum and shoes. Clean down the rear of the backplate using a stiff brush. Place a quantity of rag under the backplate to catch any hydraulic fluid that may issue from the open pipe or wheel cylinder.
2 Wipe the top of the brake master cylinder reservoir and unscrew the cap. Place a piece of polythene sheet over the top of the reservoir and replace the cap.
3 Using an open ended spanner carefully unscrew the hydraulic pipe connection union at the rear of the wheel cylinder. To prevent dirt entering, tape over the end of the pipe.
4 Withdraw the split pin and clevis pin from the handbrake lever at the rear of the backplate.
5 Using a screwdriver carefully ease the rubber dust cover from the rear of the backplate and lift away.
6 Pull off the two 'U' shaped retainers holding the wheel cylinder to the backplate noting that the spring retainer is fitted from the handbrake link end of the wheel cylinder and the flat retainer from

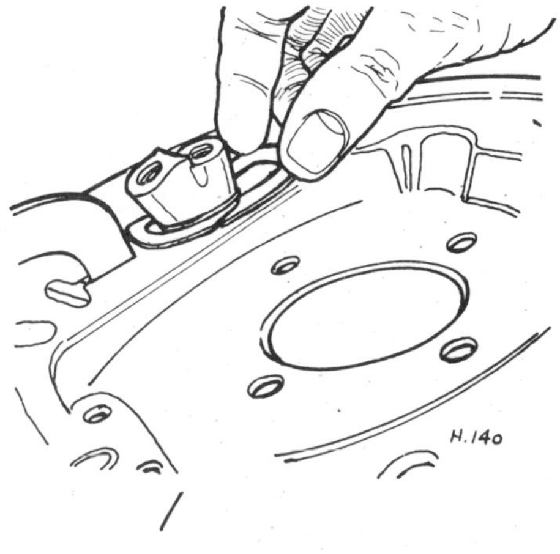

Fig. 9.9. Withdrawing rear wheel cylinder retaining plate (Capri II) (Sec. 7)

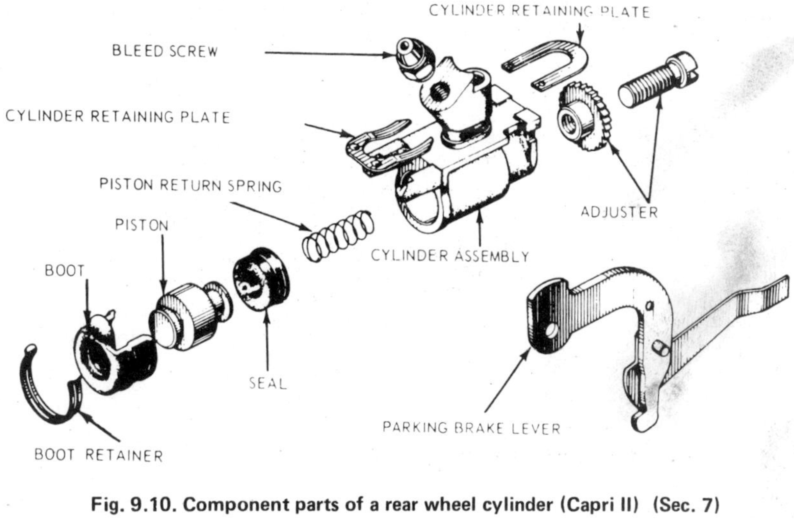

Fig. 9.10. Component parts of a rear wheel cylinder (Capri II) (Sec. 7)

the other end, the flat retainer being located between the spring retainer and the wheel cylinder.
7 The wheel cylinder and handbrake link can now be removed from the brake backplate.
8 To dismantle the wheel cylinder first remove the small metal clip holding the rubber dust cap in place then prise off the dust cap.
9 Take the piston complete with its seal out of the cylinder bore and then withdraw the spring. Should the piston and seal prove difficult to remove gentle pressure will push it out of the bore.
10 Inspect the cylinder bore for score marks caused by impurities in hydraulic fluid. If any are found the cylinder and piston will require renewal together, as a replacement unit.
11 If the cylinder bore is sound thoroughly clean it out with fresh hydraulic fluid.
12 The old rubber seal will probably be visibly worn or swollen. Detach it from the piston, smear a new rubber seal with hydraulic fluid and assemble it to the piston with the flat face of the seal next to the piston rear shoulder.
13 Reassembly is a direct reversal of the dismantling procedure. If the rubber dust cap appears to be worn or damaged it should also be renewed.
14 Before commencing refitting smear the area where the cylinder slides on the backplate and the brake shoe support pads, brake shoe pivots, ratchet wheel face and threads with brake grease.
15 Refitting is a straightforward reversal of the removal sequence but the following parts should be checked with extra care.
16 After fitting the rubber boot, check that the wheel cylinder can slide freely in the backplate and that the handbrake link operates the self adjusting mechanism correctly.
17 It is important to note that the self adjusting ratchet mechanism on the right-hand rear brake is right-hand threaded and the mechanism on the left-hand rear brake is left-hand threaded.
18 When refitting is complete, bleed the braking system as described in Section 14.

8 Drum brake wheel cylinder (Mercury Capri II) - removal, inspection and servicing

1 Initially proceed as described in paragraphs 1 to 3 of the previous Section, but do not pull the hydraulic pipe out of the rear of the wheel cylinder, as it may bend and be difficult to refit later.
2 Remove the wheel cylinder attaching bolts and washers. Remove the cylinder and tape over the end of the hydraulic pipe.
3 To dismantle the wheel cylinder, first remove the rubber dust covers.
4 Slide out the piston assemblies and remove the spring from the cylinder bore.
5 Where applicable, unscrew the bleed nipple.
6 Refer to the procedure given in paragraphs 10 to 12 in the previous Section, bearing in mind that there are two pistons and seals.
7 Reassembly of the wheel cylinder is the reverse of the dismantling procedure, ensuring that the parts are adequately lubricated with hydraulic fluid.
8 The wheel cylinder can now be refitted to the backplate following the reverse of the removal procedure. On completion, bleed the brakes, as described in Section 14.

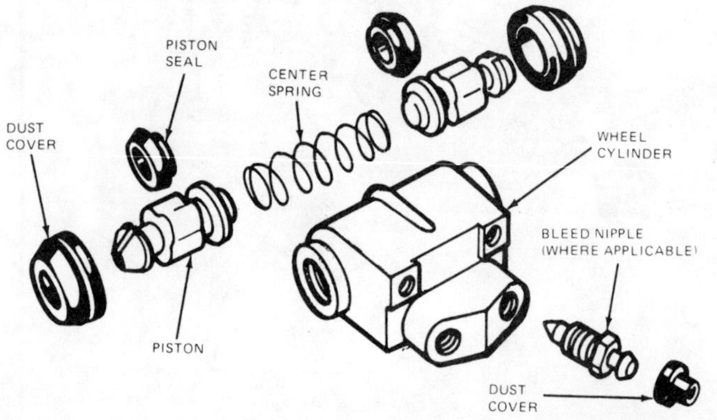

Fig. 9.11. Component parts of the rear wheel cylinder (Mercury Capri II) (Sec. 8)

9 Drum brake backplate - removal and refitting

1 To remove the backplate refer to Chapter 8 and remove the halfshaft.
2 Detach the handbrake cable from the handbrake relay lever on the backplate.
3 Wipe off the top of the master cylinder reservoir and unscrew the cap. Place a piece of polythene sheet over the top of the reservoir and replace the cap. This will prevent loss of fluid by creating a vacuum.
4 Using an open ended spanner, carefully unscrew the hydraulic pipe connection union to the rear of the wheel cylinder. To prevent dirt entering tape over the pipe ends.
5 The brake backplate may now be lifted away.
6 Refitting is the reverse sequence to removal. It will be necessary to remove the polythene from the reservoir cap and bleed the brake hydraulic system, as described in Section 14.

10 Master cylinder - removal and installation

1 Apply the handbrake and chock the front wheels. Drain the fluid from the master cylinder reservoir and master cylinder by attaching a plastic bleed tube to one of the front brake bleed screws. Undo the screw one turn and then pump the fluid out into a clean glass container by means of the brake pedal. Hold the brake pedal against the floor at the end of each stroke and tighten the bleed screw. When the pedal has returned to its normal position loosen the bleed screw and repeat the process. The above sequence should now be carried out on one of the rear brake bleed screws.
2 Wipe the area around the two union nuts on the side of the master cylinder body and using an open ended spanner undo the two union nuts. Tape over the ends of the pipes to stop dirt entering.
3 Undo and remove the two nuts and spring washers that secure the master cylinder to the rear of the servo unit. Lift away the master cylinder taking care not to damage the servo unit and ensure that no hydraulic fluid is allowed to drip onto the paintwork.
4 Refitting the master cylinder is the reverse sequence to removal. Always start the union nuts before finally tightening the master cylinder nuts. It will be necessary to bleed the complete hydraulic system: full details will be found in Section 14.

11 Master cylinder (FoG) - servicing

If a replacement master cylinder is to be fitted, it will be necessary to lubricate the seals before fitting to the car as they have a protective coating when originally assembled. Remove the blanking plugs from the hydraulic pipe union seatings. Inject clean hydraulic fluid into the master cylinder and operate the primary piston several times so that the fluid spreads over all the internal working surfaces.

If the master cylinder is to be dismantled after removal, proceed as follows:
1 The component parts are shown in Fig. 9.12.
2 Prior to dismantling, wipe the exterior of the master cylinder clean.
3 Using a clean metal rod of suitable diameter depress the primary piston until it reaches the stop so that the pressure of the intermediate piston is removed from the stop scew.
4 Unscrew the stop screw and remove the sealing washer. Release the pressure on the piston.
5 Lightly depress on the primary piston again to relieve the pressure on the circlip located in the bore at the flanged end of the cylinder. With a pair of pointed pliers remove the circlip taking care not to scratch the finely finished bore.
6 Lift away the stop washer, and withdraw the primary piston assembly.
7 Undo and remove the connecting screw and withdraw the deep spring retainer, spring, flat spring retainer, seal retainer, primary seal, seal protector and secondary seal from the piston.
8 The intermediate piston assembly may now be removed by lightly tapping on the master cylinder against a wooden base.
9 Withdraw the spring, spring retainer, seal retainer, primary cup seal, seal protector and the two secondary seals from the piston.
10 Thoroughly wash all parts in either methylated spirit or clean approved hydraulic fluid and place in order ready for inspection.
11 Examine the bores of the master cylinder carefully for any signs of scoring, ridges or corrosion and, if it is found to be smooth all over,

new seals can be fitted. If there is any doubt as to the condition of the bore, then a new assembly must be obtained.

12 If examination of the seals shows them to be apparently oversize or very loose on their seats, suspect oil contamination in the system. Oil will swell these rubber seals, and if one is found to be swollen it is reasonable to assume that all seals in the braking system will require attention.

13 Before reassembly again wash all parts in methylated spirit or clean approved hydraulic fluid. **Do not** use any other type of oil or cleaning fluid or the seals will be damaged.

14 Reassemble according to the piston assembly diagram noting the following points:

Dip all seals in clean hydraulic fluid before fitting.
Secondary seals are identified by a silver band.
Tighten the stop screw to the specified torque setting.

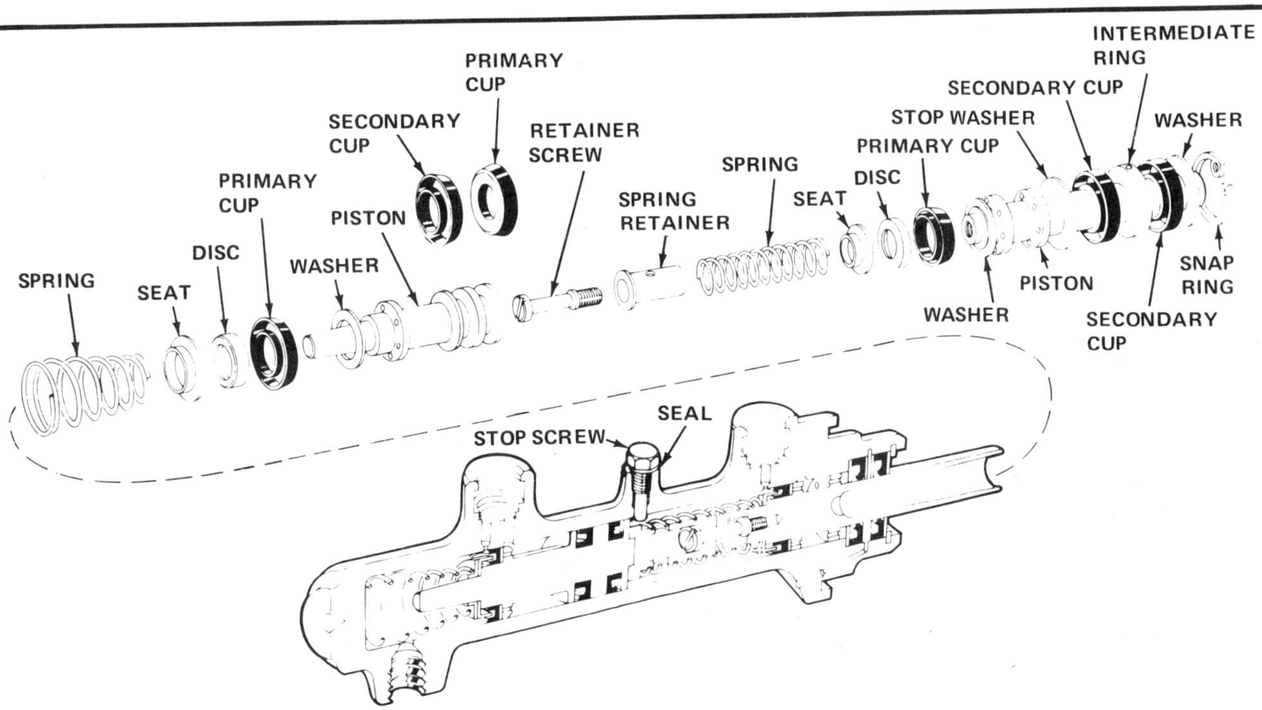

Fig. 9.12 Component parts of the master cylinder (FoG) (Sec. 11)

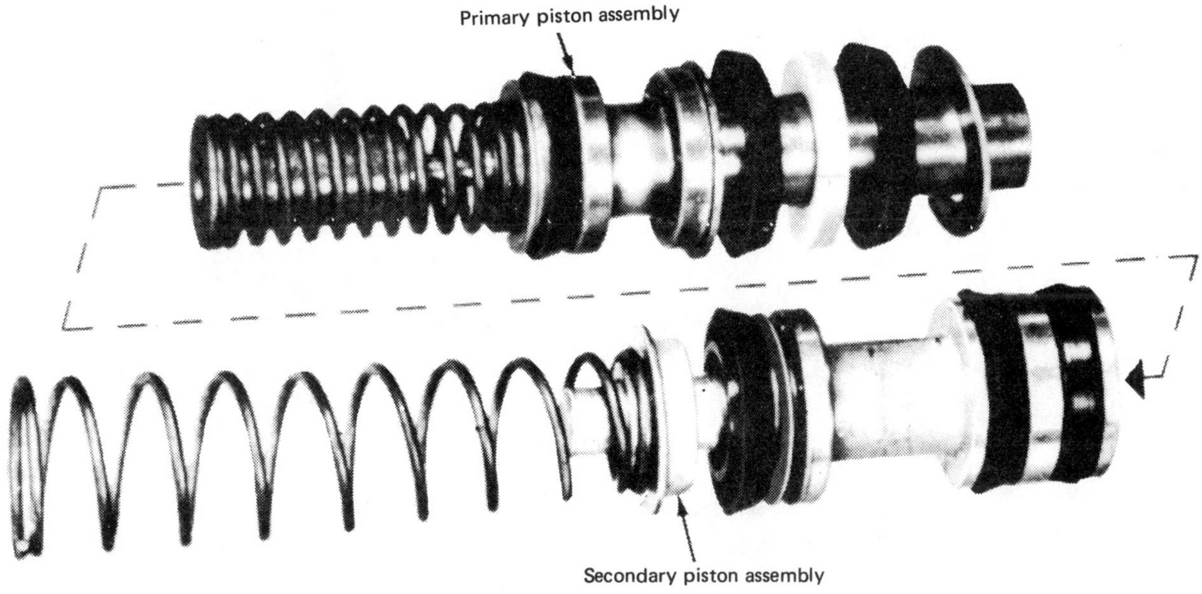

Fig. 9.13 Master cylinder piston assembly (FoG) (Sec. 11)

12 Master cylinder (FoB) - servicing

1 Refer to the introduction in Section 11.
2 The component parts are shown in Fig. 9.14.
3 Prior to dismantling wipe the exterior of the master cylinder clean.
4 Undo and remove the two screws and spring washers holding the reservoir to the master cylinder body. Lift away the reservoir. Using an Allen key, or wrench, unscrew the tipping valve nut and lift away the seal. Using a suitable diameter rod push the primary plunger down the bore, this operation enabling the tipping valve to be withdrawn.
5 Using a compressed air jet, very carefully applied to the rear outlet connection, blow out all the master cylinder internal components. Alternatively, shake out the parts. Take care that adequate precautions are taken to ensure all parts are caught as they emerge.
6 Separate the primary and secondary plungers from the intermediate spring. Use the fingers to remove the gland seal from the primary plunger.
7 The secondary plunger assembly should be separated by lifting the thimble leaf over the shouldered end of the plunger. Using the fingers, remove the seal from the secondary plunger.
8 Depress the secondary spring, allowing the valve stem to slide through the keyhole in the thimble, thus releasing the tension on the spring.
9 Detach the valve spacer, taking care of the spring washer which will be found located under the valve head.
10 For information on inspection refer to Section 11, paragraphs 10 to 13 inclusive.
11 All components should be assembled wet by dipping in clean brake fluid. Using fingers only, fit new seals to the primary and secondary plungers ensuring that they are the correct way round. Place the dished washer with the dome against the underside of the valve seat. Hold it in position with the valve spacer ensuring that the legs face towards the valve seal.
12 Replace the plunger return spring centrally on the spacer insert the thimble into the spring, and depress until the valve stem engages in the keyhole of the thimble.
13 Insert the reduced end of the plunger into the thimble until the thimble engages under the shoulder of the plunger, and press home the thimble leaf. Replace the intermediate spring between the primary and secondary plungers.
14 Check that the master cylinder bore is clean and smear with clean brake fluid. With the complete assembly suitably wetted with brake fluid carefully insert the assembly into the bore. Ease the lips of the piston seals into the bore taking care that they do not roll over. Push the assembly fully home.
15 Refit the tipping valve assembly and seal to the cylinder bore, and tighten the securing nut to a torque wrench setting of 27 to 35 lbf ft (3.7 to 4.7 kgf m).
16 Using a clean screwdriver push the primary piston in and out checking that the recuperating valve opens when the screwdriver is withdrawn and closes again when it is pushed in.
17 Check the condition of the front and rear reservoir gaskets and if there is any doubt as to their condition they must be renewed.
18 Replace the hydraulic fluid reservoir and tighten the two retaining screws.
19 The master cylinder is now ready for refitting to the servo unit. Bleed the complete hydraulic system and road test the car.

13 Flexible hose - inspection, removal and refitting

1 Inspect the condition of the flexible hydraulic hoses leading from under the front wings to the brackets on the front suspension units, and also the single hose on the rear axle casing. If they are swollen, damaged or chafed, they must be renewed.

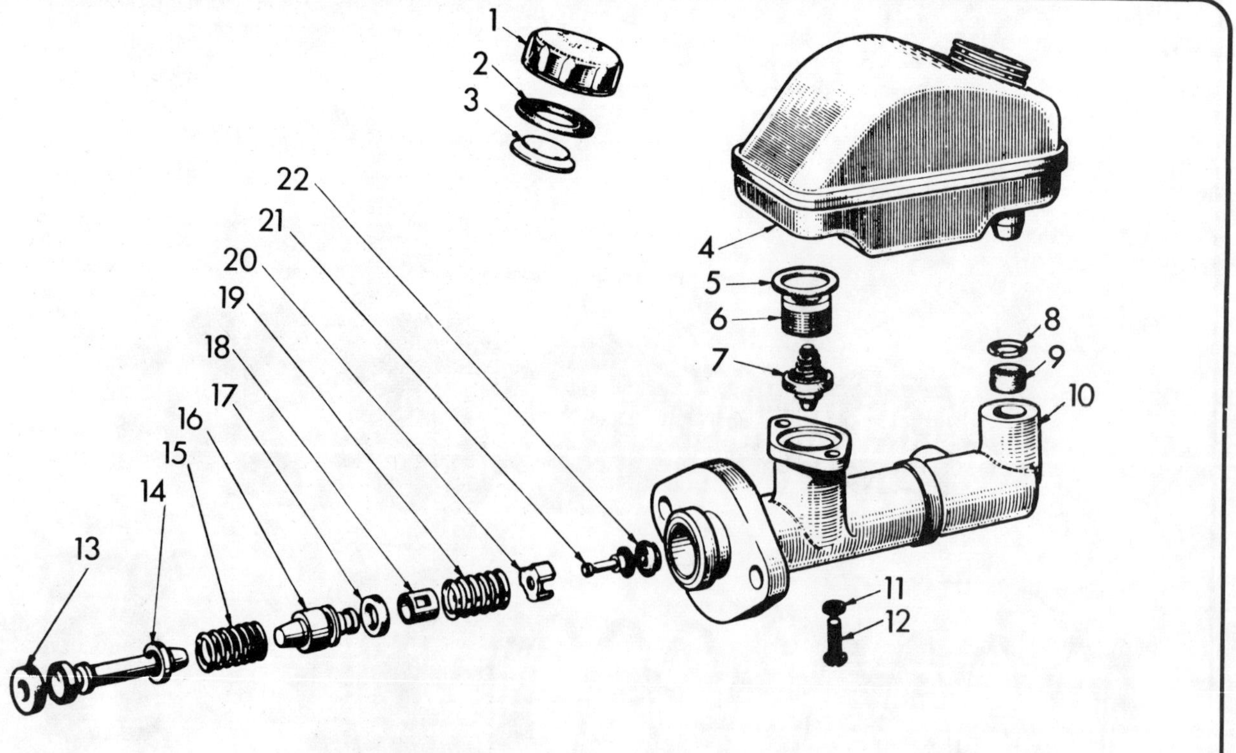

Fig. 9.14 Component parts of the master cylinder (FoB) (Sec. 12)

1 Reservoir cap
2 Cap seal
3 Seal retainer
4 Reservoir
5 Sealing ring
6 Tipping valve retainer
7 Tipping valve
8 Circlip
9 Gasket
10 Master cylinder body
11 Washer
12 Screw
13 Seal
14 Primary piston
15 Spring
16 Secondary piston
17 Seal
18 Spring retainer
19 Spring
20 Spring retainer
21 Valve
22 Seal

2 Undo the locknuts at both ends of the flexible hoses and then holding the hexagon nut on the flexible hose steady undo the other union nut and remove the flexible hose and washer.
3 Replacement is a reversal of the removal procedure, but carefully check that all the securing brackets are in a sound condition and that the locknuts are tight.

14 Bleeding the hydraulic system

1 Removal of all the air from the hydraulic system is essential to the correct working of the braking system, and before undertaking this, examine the fluid reservoir cap to ensure that both vent holes, one on top and the second underneath but not in line, are clear, check the level of fluid and top-up if required.
2 Check all brake line unions and connections for possible seepage, and at the same time check the condition of the rubber hoses, which may be perished.
3 If the condition of the wheel cylinders is in doubt, check for possible signs of fluid leakage.
4 If there is any possibility of incorrect fluid having been put into the system, drain all the fluid out and flush through with methylated spirit. Renew all piston seals and cups since these will be affected and could possibly fail under pressure.
5 Gather together a clean jar, a 9 inch (230 mm) length of tubing which fits tightly over the bleed nipples, and a tin of the correct brake fluid.
6 Centralise the piston in the pressure differential valve (see Section 15). To do this, modify the blade of a screwdriver as shown and after removing the rubber cover from the hose of the valve insert the screwdriver and wedge it to hold the piston centralised. (Fig 9.15).
7 Clean the dirt from around the front caliper bleed nipple which is furthest from the master cylinder (see Fig. 9.1 or 9.2). Fit one end of the tubing over the bleed nipple and put the other into the jar containing a little brake fluid. Ensure that this end remains immersed during the bleeding process.
8 Open the bleed valve with a spanner and then have an assistant quickly depress the brake pedal. After slowly releasing the pedal, for a moment to allow the fluid to recoup in the master cylinder and then depress again. This will force air from the system. Continue until no more air bubbles can be seen coming from the tube. At intervals make certain that the reservoir is kept topped up, otherwise air will enter at this point again.
9 Repeat this operation on the other front brake and the rear brakes (some models have one bleed nipple only on the rear brakes). When completed, check the level of the fluid in the reservoir and then check the feel of the brake pedal, which should be firm and free from any 'spongy' action, which is normally associated with air in the system.

15 Pressure differential switch - description and servicing

1 This device is incorporated in the hydraulic circuit on some models. It is a switch in which a piston is kept 'in balance' when the hydraulic pressure in the independent front and rear hydraulic brake circuits are equal. In the event of a drop in pressure in either circuit, the piston is displaced and makes an electrical contact to illuminate a warning light on the instrument panel.
2 To dismantle the switch, first disconnect the hydraulic pipes at their unions on the switch body. To prevent a loss of hydraulic fluid either place a piece of polythene under the cap of the master cylinder and screw it down tightly or plug the ends of the two pipes leading from the master cylinder.
3 Referring to Fig. 9.16 disconnect the wiring from the switch assembly.
4 Undo the single bolt holding the assembly to the rear of the engine compartment and remove it from the car.
5 To dismantle the assembly start by undoing the end plug and discarding the gasket.
6 Unscrew the switch assembly from the top of the unit then push the piston out of the bore taking extreme care not to damage the bore during this operation.
7 Take the small seals from the piston followed by the sleeves.
8 Carefully examine the piston and the bore of the actuator for score marks, scratches or damage; if any are found the complete unit must be exchanged for a new one. Also check that the piston retaining clips are secure and undamaged.
9 Reassembly of the unit is the reverse of the removal procedure, ensuring that all parts are adequately lubricated with hydraulic brake fluid.

16 Vacuum servo unit - description

1 A vacuum servo unit is fitted into the brake hydraulic circuit in series with the master cylinder, to provide assistance to the driver when the brake pedal is depressed. This reduces the effort required by the driver to operate the brakes under all braking conditions.
2 The unit operates by vacuum obtained from the induction manifold and comprises basically a booster diaphram and check valve. The servo unit and hydraulic master cylinder are connected together so that the servo unit piston rod acts as the master cylinder pushrod. The driver's braking effort is transmitted through another pushrod to the servo unit piston and its built-in control system. The servo unit piston does not fit tightly into the cylinder but has a strong diaphragm to keep its edges in constant contact with the cylinder wall, so assuring an air-tight seal between the two parts. The forward chamber is held under vacuum conditions created in the inlet manifold of the engine and, during periods when the brake pedal is not in use, the controls open a passage to the rear chamber so placing it under vacuum conditions as well. When the brake pedal is depressed, the vacuum passage to the rear chamber is cut off and the chamber exposed to atmospheric pressure. The consequent rush of air pushes the servo piston forward in the vacuum chamber and operates the main pushrod to the master cylinder.
3 The controls are designed so that assistance is given under all conditions and, when the brakes are not required, vacuum in the rear chamber is established when the brake pedal is released. All air from the atmosphere entering the rear chamber is passed through a small air filter.
4 Under normal operating conditions the vacuum servo unit is very reliable and does not require overhaul except at very high mileages. In this case it is far better to obtain a service exchange unit, rather than repair the original unit.

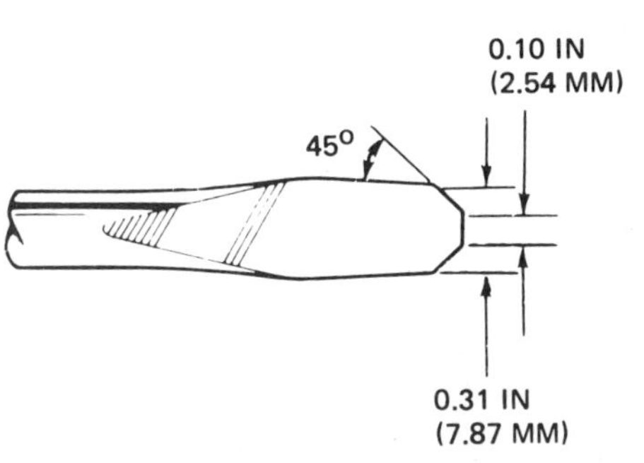

Fig. 9.15. Valve and switch assembly centralisation tool (Secs. 14 and 15)

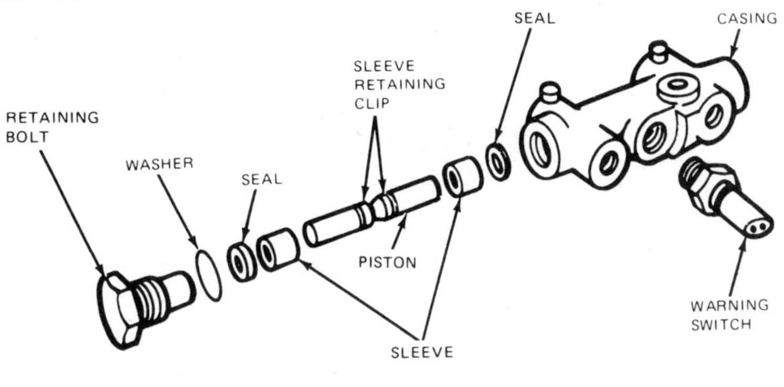

Fig. 9.16. Pressure differential valve - exploded view (Sec. 15)

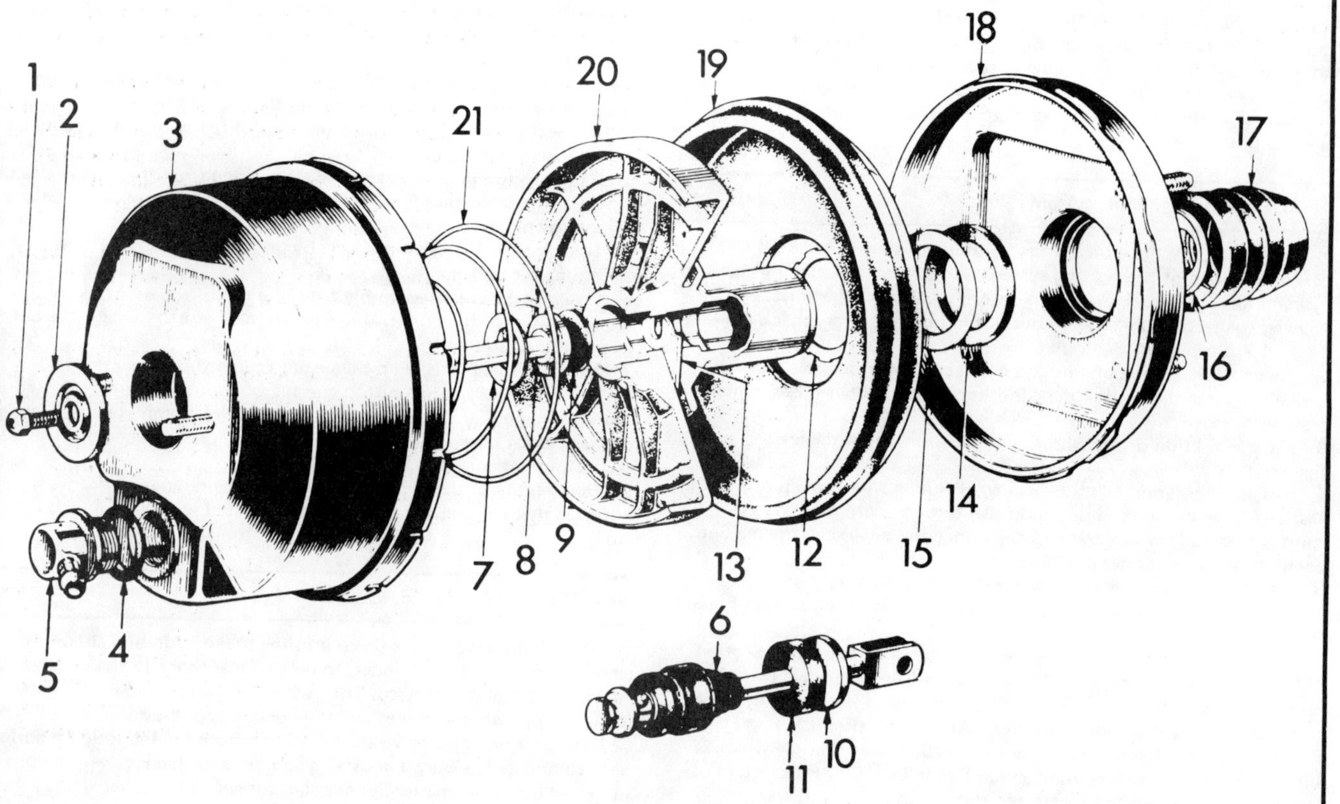

Fig. 9.17. The servo unit (brake booster) - component parts (Sec. 18)

1 Bolt
2 Seat assembly
3 Front shell
4 Seal
5 Valve assembly
6 Pushrod assembly
7 Dished washer
8 Brake servo pushrod
9 Reaction disc
10 Washer
11 Filter
12 Castellated washer
13 Stop key
14 Seal
15 Piston guide
16 Filter retainer
17 Dust cover
18 Rear shell
19 Diaphragm
20 Diaphragm plate
21 Spring

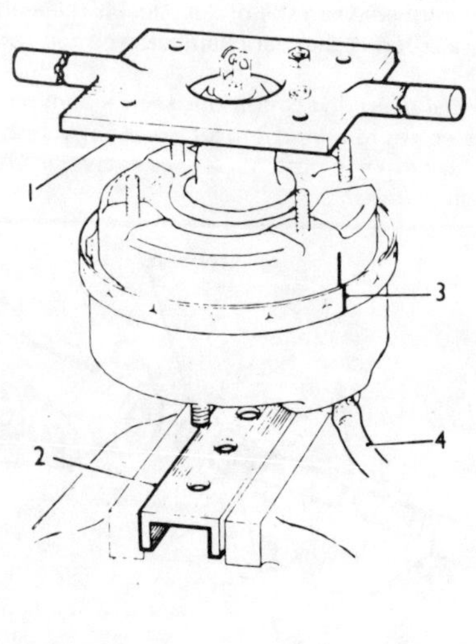

Fig. 9.18. Special tools required to dismantle the servo unit (Sec. 18)

1 Lever
2 Base plate
3 Scribed line
4 Vacuum connection

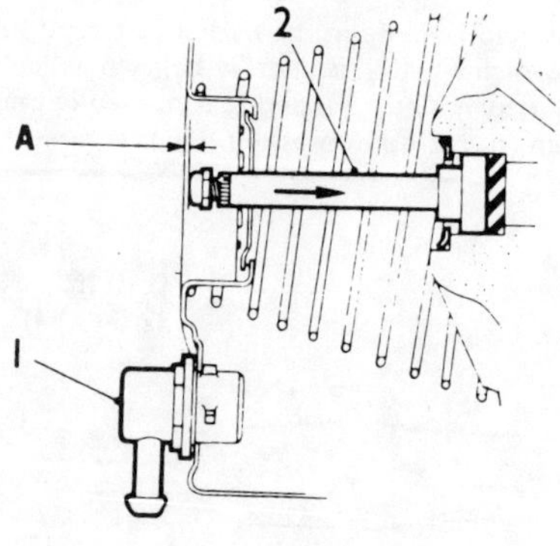

Fig. 9.19. Pushrod setting (Sec. 18)

A Setting gap 0.011 to 0.016 in (0.28 to 0.40 mm)
1 Vacuum applied to connection
2 Pushrod against reaction disc

17 Vacuum servo unit - removal and installation

1 Slacken the clip securing the vacuum hose to the servo unit carefully draw the hose from its union.
2 Refer to Section 10 and remove the master cylinder.
3 Using a pair of pliers remove the spring clip in the end of the brake pedal to pushrod clevis pin. Lift away the clevis pin and the bushes.
4 Undo and remove the nuts and spring washers securing the servo unit mounting bracket to the bulkhead. Lift away the servo unit and bracket.
5 Undo and remove the four nuts and spring washers that secure the bracket to the servo unit.
6 Refitting the servo unit is the reverse sequence to removal. It will be necessary to bleed the brake hydraulic system as described in Section 14.

18 Vacuum servo unit - servicing

Thoroughly clean the outside of the unit using a stiff brush and wipe with a non-fluffy rag. It cannot be too strongly emphasised that cleanliness is important when working on the servo. Before any attempt be made to dismantle, refer to Fig. 9.18, where it will be seen that two items of equipment are required. Firstly, a base plate must be made to enable the unit to be safely held in a vice. Secondly, a lever must be made similar to the form shown. Without these items it is impossible to dismantle satisfactorily.

To dismantle the unit proceed as follows:
1 Refer to Fig. 9.18 and, using a file or scriber, make a line across the two halves of the unit to act as a datum for alignment.
2 Fit the previously made base plate into a firm vice and attach the unit to the plate using the master cylinder studs.
3 Fit the lever to the four studs on the rear shell as shown.
4 Use a piece of long rubber hose and connect one end to the adaptor on the engine inlet manifold and the other end to the non-return valve. Start the engine and this will create a vacuum in the unit so drawing the two halves together.
5 Rotate the lever in an anticlockwise direction until the front shell indentations are in line with the recesses in the rim of the rear shell. Then press the lever assembly down firmly whilst an assistant stops the engine and quickly removes the vacuum pipe from the inlet manifold connector. Depress the operating rod so as to release the vacuum, whereupon the front and rear halves should part. If necessary, use a soft faced hammer and lightly tap the front half to break the bond.
6 Lift away the rear shell followed by the diaphragm return spring, the dust cap, end cap and the filter. Also withdraw the diaphragm. Press down the valve rod and shake out the valve retaining plate. Then separate the valve rod assembly from the diaphragm plate.
7 Gently ease the spring washer from the diaphragm plate and withdraw the pushrod and reaction disc.
8 The seal and plate assembly in the end of the front shell are a press fit. It is recommended that, unless the seal is to be renewed, they be left in-situ.
9 Thoroughly clean all parts, Inspect them for signs of damage, stripped threads etc., and obtain new ones as necessary. All seals should be renewed and for this a 'Major Repair Kit' should be purchased. This kit will also contain two separate greases which must be used as directed and not interchanged.
10 To reassemble first smear the seal and bearing with Ford grease numbered '64949008 EM - 1C - 14' and refit the rear shell positioning it such that the flat face of the seal is towards the bearing. Press into position and refit the retainer.
11 Lightly smear the disc and hydraulic pushrod with Ford grease number '64949008 EM - 1C - 14'. Refit the reaction disc and pushrod to the diaphragm plate and press in the large spring washer. The small spring washer supplied in the 'Major Repair Kit' is not required. It is important that the length of the pushrod is not altered in any way and any attempt to move the adjustment bolt will strip the threads. If a new hydraulic pushrod has been required the length will have to be reset. Details of this operation are given at the end of this Section.
12 Lightly smear the outer diameter of the diaphragm plate neck and the bearing surfaces of the valve plunger with Ford grease number '64949008 EM - 1C - 14'. Carefully fit the valve rod assembly into the neck of the diaphragm and fix with the retaining plate.
13 Fit the diaphragm into position and the non-return valve to the front shell. Next smear the seal and plate assembly with Ford grease numbered '64949008 EM - 1C - 15' and press into the front shell with the plate facing inwards.
14 Fit the front shell to the base plate and the lever to the rear shell. Reconnect the vacuum hose to the non-return valve and the adaptor on the engine inlet manifold. Position the diaphragm return spring in the front shell. Lightly smear the outer bead of the diaphragm with Ford grease numbered '64949008 EM - 1C - 14' and locate the diaphragm assembly in the rear shell. Position the rear shell assembly on the return spring and line up the previously made scribe marks.
15 The assistant should start the engine. Watching one's fingers very carefully, press the two halves of the unit together and, using the lever tool, turn clockwise to lock the two halves together. Stop the engine and disconnect the hose.
16 Press a new filter into the neck of the diaphragm plate, refit the end cap and position the dust cover onto the special lugs of the rear shell.
17 Hydraulic pushrod adjustment only applies if a new pushrod has been fitted. It will be seen from Fig. 9.19 that there is a bolt screwed into the end of the pushrod. The amount of protrusion has to be adjusted in the following manner: Remove the bolt and coat the threaded portion with Loctite Grade B. Reconnect the vacuum hose to the adaptor on the inlet valve and non-return valve. Start the engine and screw the prepared bolt into the end of the pushrod. Adjust the position of the bolt head so that it is 0.011 to 0.016 inch (0.28 to 0.40 mm) below the face of the front shell as shown by dimension A in Fig. 9.19. Leave the unit for a minimum of 24 hours to allow the Loctite to set hard.
18 Refit the servo unit to the car as described in the previous Section. To test the servo unit for correct operation after overhaul first start the engine and run for a period of two minutes and then switch off. Wait for ten minutes and apply the footbrake very carefully, listening to hear the rush of air into the servo unit. This will indicate that vacuum was retained and, therefore operating correctly.

19 Handbrake (Capri II - early models) - adjustment

1 Adjustment of the handbrake is normally automatically carried out by the action of the rear brake automatic adjusters. When new components have been fitted or where the handbrake cable has stretched, then the following operations should be carried out.
2 Chock the front wheels, jack-up the rear of the car and support on firmly based axle stands. Release the handbrake.
3 Slide under the car and check that the primary cable follows its correct run and is correctly in its guide. The cable guides must be kept well greased at all times.
4 First adjust the effective length of the primary cable by slackening the locknut on the end of the cable adjacent to the relay lever on the rear axle. (Fig 9.21).
5 Adjust the nut until the primary cable has no slack in it and the relay lever is just clear of the stop on the banjo casing bracket. Retighten the locknut.

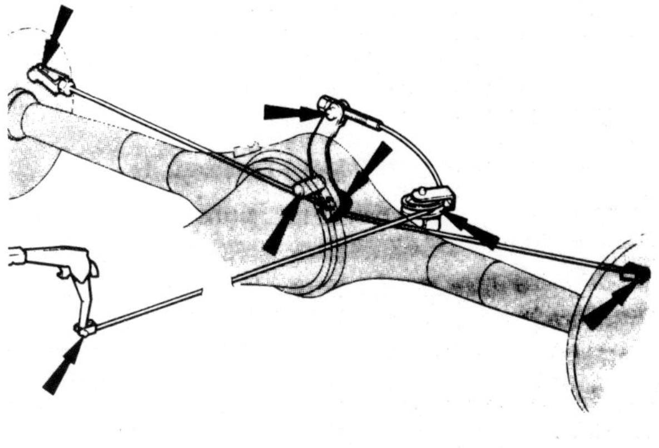

Fig. 9.20. Handbrake cable layout and lubrication points (arrowed) Capri II (Sec. 19)

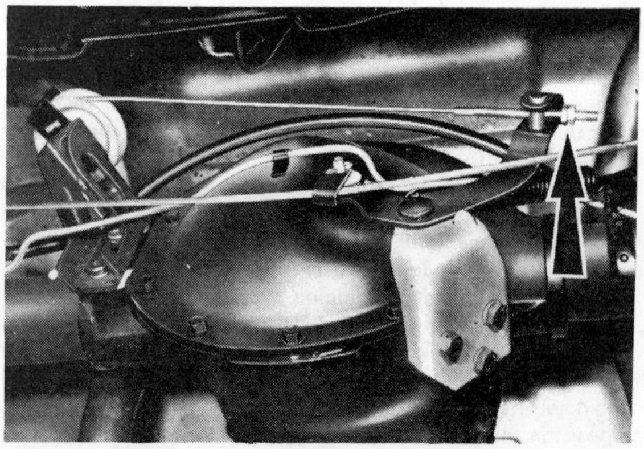

Fig. 9.21. Primary cable adjustment point (Capri II) (Sec. 19)

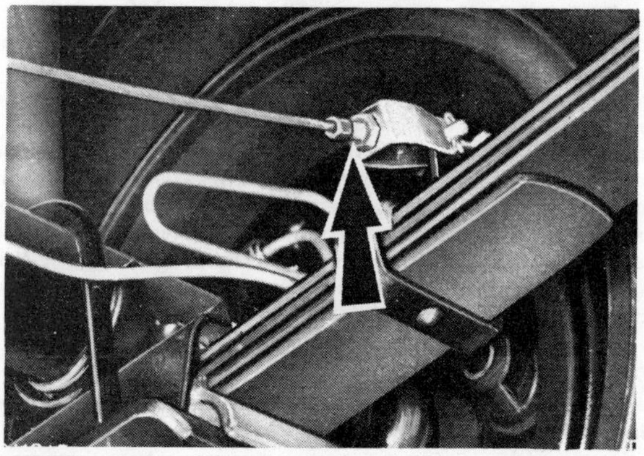

Fig. 9.22. Transverse cable adjustment point (Capri II) (Sec. 19)

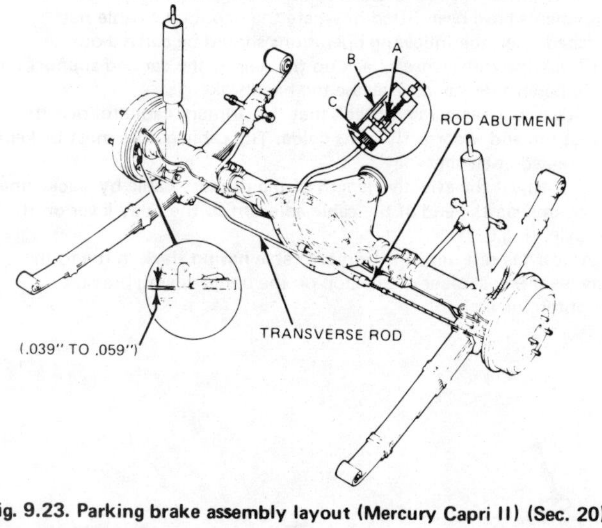

Fig. 9.23. Parking brake assembly layout (Mercury Capri II) (Sec. 20)

6 Slacken the locknut on the end of the transverse cable adjacent to the right-hand rear brake (Fig. 9.22). Check that the parking brake operating levers are in the fully 'off position, that is back on their stops, and adjust the cable so that there is no slack. Check that the operating levers are still on their stops and tighten the locknut.
7 Lower the car to the ground.

20 Parking brake (handbrake) (Mercury Capri II and late Capri II models) - adjustment

1 Adjustment of the parking brake is normally automatically carried out by the action of the rear brake automatic adjusters. When new components have been fitted or where the parking brake cable has stretched, then the following operations should be carried out.
2 Chock the front wheels, jack-up the rear of the car and support on firmly based axle stands. Release the parking brake.
3 First ensure that the primary cable is properly located, then engage the keyed sleeve 'A' into the abutment slot 'B' (Fig. 9.23).
4 Turn the adjuster nut 'C' until all cable slack is eliminated, and a clearance of 0.039 to 0.059 in. (1 to 1.5 mm) exists between the parking brake lever stop and the brake backplate.
5 Lower the car to the ground.

21.4 The hooked end of the brake primary cable

21 Handbrake (parking brake) control lever - removal and refitting

1 Chock the front wheels, jack-up the rear of the car and support on firmly based axle stands. Release the handbrake.
2 Working inside the car remove the carpeting from around the area of the handbrake lever.
3 Models fitted with a console: Refer to Chapter 12 and remove the console.
4 Remove the split pin and withdraw the clevis pin that connects the primary cable to the lower end of the handbrake lever; this protrudes under the floor panels. **Note:** On some models the cable hooks onto the end of the handbrake lever. (photo).
5 Undo and remove the six self-tapping screws which secure the handbrake lever rubber boot to the floor. Draw the rubber boot up the lever.
6 Undo and remove the two bolts that secure the handbrake lever assembly to the floor. Lift away the lever assembly.
7 Refitting the lever assembly is the reverse sequence to removal. The following additional points should be noted:

a) Apply some grease to the primary cable clevis pin.
b) Adjust the primary cable as described in Section 20.

22 Handbrake cable (Capri II - early models) - removal and refitting

Primary cable

1 Chock the front wheels, jack-up the rear of the car and support on firmly based axle stands. Release the handbrake.
2 Working under the car unscrew and remove the nuts that secure the end of the primary cable to the relay lever located at the rear of the axle casing.
3 Detach the primary cable from the end of the handbrake lever by removing the split pin and withdrawing the clevis pin. **Note:** On some models the cable hooks onto the end of the handbrake lever.
4 Detach the cable from its underbody guides and lift away.
5 Refitting the primary cable is the reverse sequence to removal but the following additional points should be noted:

a) Apply some grease to the cable guides and insert the cable. Also lubricate the front clevis pin.
b) Refer to Section 19 and adjust the primary cable.

Transverse cable

1 Chock the front wheels, jack-up the front of the car and support on firmly based axle stands. Release the handbrake.

2 Working under the car remove the split pin and withdraw the clevis pin that secures the transverse cable to the left-hand backplate.

3 Detach the cable from the right-hand rear backplate by removing the locknut and unscrewing the cable from the clevis.

4 Remove the pulley pins, split pin and withdraw the pulley pin. Lift away the little pulley wheel and transverse cable.

5 Refitting the transverse cable is the reverse sequence to removal but the following additional points should be noted:

a) Apply some grease to the pulley and pivot pin, the threaded end of the cable and the clevis pin.

b) Adjust the transverse cable as described in Section 19.

23 Parking brake (handbrake) cable and rod (Mercury Capri II & late Capri II models) - removal and refitting

Primary cable

1 Chock the front wheels, jack-up the rear of the car and support on firmly based axle stands. Release the parking brake.

2 Remove the spring clip and clevis pin connecting the parking brake cable to the lever of the parking brake handle.

3 Remove the spring clip and clevis pin from the right-hand rear brake lever, disconnect the cable.

4 Remove the parking brake cable-to-transverse rod retaining clip, then slide the cable clear of the rod bracket.

5 Slide the cable, adjusting nut and guide clear of the abutment bracket, and remove the assembly from the car.

6 Refitting is the reverse of the removal procedure. Apply a little general purpose grease to the rubbing and pivoting parts, then finally check the adjustment (Section 20).

Transverse rod

7 Initially proceed as described in paragraphs 1 and 2.

8 Remove the spring retaining clip which secures the parking brake cable to the transverse rod, and slide the cable assembly clear.

9 Remove the spring clip and clevis pin then disconnect the rod from the left-hand rear brake lever.

10 Slide the rod out of the bushing on the axle casing.

11 Refitting is the reverse of the removal procedure. Apply a little general purpose grease to the rubbing and pivoting parts, then finally check the adjustment (Section 20).

24 Fault diagnosis - Braking system

Before diagnosing faults from the following chart, check that any braking irregularities are not caused by:

1 Uneven and incorrect tyre pressures.
2 Incorrect 'mix' of radial and crossply tyres.
3 Wear in the steering mechanism.
4 Defects in the suspension and dampers.
5 Misalignment of the bodyframe.

Symptom	Reason/s
Pedal travels a long way before the brakes operate	Brake shoes set too far from the drums (auto. adjusters seized).
Stopping ability poor, even though pedal pressure is firm	Linings, discs or drums badly worn or scored. One or more wheel hydraulic cylinders seized, resulting in some brake shoes not pressing against the drums (or pads against discs). Brake linings contaminated with oil. Wrong type of linings fitted (too hard). Brake shoes wrongly assembled. Servo unit not functioning.
Car veers to one side when the brakes are applied	Brake pads or linings on one side are contaminated with oil. Hydraulic wheel cylinder(s) on one side partially or fully seized. A mixture of lining materials fitted between sides. Brake discs not matched. Unequal wear between sides caused by partially seized wheel cylinders.
Pedal feels spongy when the brakes are applied	Air is present in the hydraulic system.
Pedal feels springy when the brakes are applied	Brake linings not bedded into the drums (after fitting new ones). Master cylinder or brake backplate mounting bolts loose. Severe wear in brake drums causing distortion when brakes are applied. Discs out of true.
Pedal travels right down with little or no resistance and brakes are virtually non-operative	Leak in hydraulic system resulting in lack of pressure for operating wheel cylinders. If no signs of leakage are apparent the master cylinder internal seals are failing to sustain pressure.
Binding, juddering, overheating	One or a combination of reasons given in the foregoing Sections.

Chapter 10 Electrical system

For modifications, and information applicable to later models, see Supplement at end of manual

Contents

Specifications

System type ...	12 volt, negative earth (ground)

Battery

Battery type ...	Lead acid, 12 volt
Capacity (amp hr):	
1.6, Manual transmission (FOB) ...	38
1.6 GT and 2.0, Manual transmission (FOB) ...	44
1.6, Automatic transmission (FOB) ...	44
1.6 GT and 2.0, Automatic transmission (FOB) ...	55
1.6, 1.6 GT and 2.0 Manual transmission (FOG) ...	44
1.6 and 2.0 Automatic transmission (FOG) ...	55
Mercury Capri II, Manual transmission ...	55
Mercury Capri II, Automatic transmission ...	66

Note: A battery of higher capacity may be fitted for some markets, and in most cases is available as an optional fitment.

Starter motor (Bosch manufacture)

Type	EF 0.7	GF 1.0
Minimum brush length	0.4 in (10 mm)	0.4 in (10 mm)
Brush spring pressure	32 to 46 oz (900 to 1300 g)	32 to 46 oz (900 to 1300 g)
Commutator:		
Minimum diameter	1.291 in (32.8 mm)	1.291 in (32.8 mm)
Maximum out-of-round	0.012 in (0.3 mm)	0.012 in (0.3 mm)
Armature endfloat	0.004 to 0.012 in (0.1 to 0.3 mm)	0.004 to 0.012 in (0.1 to 0.3 mm)
Maximum power draw (on load)	2400 watts	2500 watts
Voltage	12V	12V
Output (on load)	515 watts	515 watts
Maximum power draw (off load)	540 watts	648 watts

Note: Starter motors used on Mercury Capri II may differ slightly from the above Specifications.

Starter motor (Lucas manufacture)

Type	M35J	5M90
Minimum brush length	0.374 in (9.5 mm)	0.354 in (9.0 mm)
Brush spring pressure	16.94 oz (480 g)	30 oz (850 g)
Commutator:		
Minimum diameter	1.339 in (34 mm)	–
Maximum out-of-round	0.003 in (0.075 mm)	–
Armature endfloat	0.004 to 0.012 in (0.1 to 0.3 mm)	0.004 to 0.012 in (0.1 to 0.3 mm)
Maximum power draw/on load, 44 A hr battery	2600 watts	2400 watts
Voltage	12	12
Maximum output	690 watts	820 watts
Maximum power draw (off load at 12 volts)	740 watts	900 watts

Alternator (Bosch manufacture)

Type	G1-28A	K1-35A	K1-55A
Output at 13.5V and 6000 rpm (nominal)	28 amp	35 amp	55 amp
Stator winding resistance per phase	0.2 to 0.21 ohms	0.13 to 0.137 ohm	0.01 to 0.017 ohms
Rotor winding resistance at 20°C (68°F)	4 to 4.4 ohms	4 to 4.4 ohms	4 to 4.4 ohms
Minimum protrusion of brushes in free position	0.197 in (5 mm)	0.197 in (5 mm)	0.197 in (5 mm)
Regulating voltage (model A01) 4000 rpm, 3 to 7 amp load	13.7 to 14.5 volt	13.7 to 14.5 volt	13.7 to 14.5 volt

Alternator (Femsa manufacture)

Type	ALD 12-32 or ALD 12-33
Output at 13.5V and 6000 rpm (nominal)	32 amp
Stator winding resistance per phase	0.173 ± 0.01 ohms
Rotor winding resistance at 20°C (68°F)	5.0 ± 0.15 ohms
Minimum protrusion of brushes in free position	0.28 in (7 mm)
Regulating voltage (model GRK 12-16), 4000 rpm, 3 to 7 amp load	13.7 to 14.5 volt
Field relay closing voltage	2.0 to 2.8 volt

Alternator (Lucas manufacture)

Type	15 ACR	17 ACR
Output at 13.5V and 6000 rpm (nominal)	28 amp	35 amp
Stator winding resistance per phase	0.198 ± 0.01 ohms	0.133 ± 0.007 ohms
Rotor winding resistance at 20°C (68°F)	3.27 ohms ± 5%	3.201 ohms ± 5%
Minimum protrusion of brushes in free position	0.2 in (5 mm)	0.2 in (5 mm)
Regulating voltage (model 14TR) 4000 rpm, 3 to 7 amp load	14.2 to 14.6 volt	14.2 to 14.6 volt

Windscreen wipers (front)

Type	Two speed electric, self parking

Windshield wiper (rear-optional and Ghia)

Type	Single speed electric, self parking

Horn

Type	4 in (102 mm) beep or projector
Current draw	4.5 to 5.0 amp

Bulb chart (Capri II)

Headlamp, except Ghia	45/40W
Headlamp, Ghia	60/55W halogen
Fog lamps	55W
Driving lamps	55W
Direction indicators	21W, bayonet
Stoplights	21W, bayonet

Front side and license plate lights	4W, bayonet
Reverse lamps	21W, bayonet
Interior lights:	
Front	6W, festoon
Rear (GT)	6W, festoon
Instrument panel warning lights	2W, wedge base
Instrument panel illumination	2W, wedge base
Electric clock	1.2W
Heated rear screen switch	1.2W

Bulb chart (Mercury Capri II)

Headlights (sealed beam)	5¾ inch S.B. Type 1 (high beam) 5¾ inch S.B. Type 2 (high and low beam)
Sidelights/front direction indicators	32 CP/4CP bayonet 15d/19
Rear direction indicator	32 CP bayonet 15d
Rear/stoplights	32 CP/4CP bayonet 15d/19
Rear number plate light	3 CP bayonet
Interior light	10W bayonet
Instrument panel lights	1 CP wedge-base
Side marker lights	2 CP wedge base
Back-up light	32 CP bayonet 15d

For lamps not listed consult your Ford dealer.

Fuses (Capri II)

	Fuse and rating	Circuits protected
Main fusebox on engine compartment bulkhead on driver's side	1 - 16 amp	Cigarette lighter, clock, interior light
	2 - 8 amp	License plate lights, instrument panel illumination
	3 - 8 amp	RH tail and side lights
	4 - 8 amp	LH tail and sidelights
	5 - 16 amp	Horn, blower motor
	6 - 16 amp	Wiper motor, reversing lights
	7 - 8 amp	Direction indicators, stoplights, instrument cluster
Fuses in dipper relay housing	8 - 16 amp	LH dipped headlamp
	9 - 16 amp	RH dipped headlamp
	10 - 16 amp	RH main beam
	11 - 16 amp	LH main beam
Fuses mounted under facia	12 - 8 amp	Within relay for heated rear screen
	13 - 2 amp	Radio circuit (medium-slow blow)
	14 - 8 amp	Within relay for driving lamps (RPO)
	15 - 8 amp	Within relay for fog lamps (RPO)

Fuses (Mercury Capri II)

	Fuse and rating	Circuits protected
Main fusebox on left-hand side of engine compartment on driver's side	1 - 8 amp	Clock, cigar lighter, interior light, hazard flasher
	2 - 8 amp	License plate lamp, map reading lamp, instrument illumination
	3 - 8 amp	RH tail, parking and side marker lights
	4 - 8 amp	LH tail, parking and side marker lights
	5 - 8 amp	Heater blower, horn
	6 - 16 amp	Wiper motors, back-up light, instrument cluster
	7 - 8 amp	Stoplights, turn signals

Torque wrench settings

	lbf ft	kgf m
Alternator pulley nut	25 to 29	3.5 to 4.0
Alternator mounting bolts	15 to 18	2.1 to 2.5
Alternator mounting bracket	20 to 25	2.8 to 3.5
Starter motor retaining bolts	20 to 25	2.8 to 3.5

1 General description

The major components of the 12 volt negative earth system comprise a 12 volt battery, an alternator (driven from the crankshaft pulley), and a starter motor.

The battery supplies a steady amount of current for the ignition, lighting and other electrical circuits and provides a reserve of power when the current consumed by the electrical equipment exceeds that being produced by the alternator.

The alternator has its own regulator which ensures a high output if the battery is in a low state of charge and the demand from the electrical equipment is high, and a low output if the battery is fully charged and there is little demand for the electrical equipment.

When fitting electrical accessories to cars with a negative earth system it is important, if they contain silicone diodes or transistors, that they are connected correctly; otherwise serious damage may result to the components concerned. Items such as radios, tape players, electric ignition systems, electric tachometer, automatic dipping etc, should all be checked for correct polarity.

It is important that the battery positive lead is always disconnected if the battery is to be boost charged, also if body repairs are to be carried out using electric welding equipment - the alternator must be disconnected otherwise serious damage can be caused. Whenever the battery has to be disconnected it must always be reconnected with the negative terminal earthed.

2 Battery - removal and refitting

1 The battery is on a carrier fitted to the left-hand wing valance of the engine compartment. It should be removed once every three months for cleaning and testing. Disconnect the negative and then the positive leads from the battery terminals by undoing and removing the plated nuts and bolts. Note that two cables are attached to the positive terminal.

2 Unscrew and remove the bolt, and plain washer that secures the battery clamp plate to the carrier. Lift away the clamp plate. Carefully lift the battery from its carrier holding it vertically to ensure that none of the electrolyte is spilled.

3 Refitting is a direct reversal of this procedure. **Note**: Refit the positive lead before the negative lead and smear the terminals with petroleum jelly to prevent corrosion. **Never** use an ordinary grease.

3 Battery - maintenance and inspection

1 Normal weekly battery maintenance consists of checking the electrolyte level of each cell to ensure that the separators are covered by ¼ inch (6.35 mm) of electrolyte. If the level has fallen top up the battery using distilled water only. Do not overfill. If a battery is overfilled or any electrolyte spilled, immediately wipe away and neutralize as electrolyte attacks and corrodes any metal it comes into contact with very rapidly.

2 If the battery has the Auto-fil device fitted, a special topping up sequence is required. The white balls in the Auto-fil battery are part of the automatic topping up device which ensures correct electrolye level. The vent chamber should remain in position at all times except when topping up or taking specific gravity readings. If the electrolyte level in any of the cells is below the bottom of the filling tube top up as follows :

a) *Lift off the vent chamber cover.*
b) *With the battery level, pour distilled water into the trough until all the filling tubes and trough are full.*
c) *Immediately replace the cover to allow the water in the trough and tubes to flow into the cells. Each cell will automatically receive the correct amount of water.*

3 As well as keeping the terminals clean and covered with petroleum jelly, the top of the battery, and especially the top of the cells, should be kept clean and dry. This helps prevent corrosion and ensures that the battery does not become partially discharged by leakage through dampness and dirt.

4 Once every three months remove the battery and inspect the battery securing bolts, the battery clamp plate, tray, and battery leads for corrosion (white fluffy deposits on the metal which are brittle to touch). If any corrosion is found, clean off the deposits with ammonia and paint over the clean metal with an anti-rust/anti acid paint.

5 At the same time inspect the battery case for cracks. If a crack is found, clean and plug it with one of the proprietary compounds marketed for this purpose. If leakage through the crack has been excessive then it will be necessary to refill the appropriate cell with fresh electrolyte as detailed later. Cracks are frequently caused to the top of the battery case by pouring in distilled water in the middle of winter *after* instead of *before* a run. This gives the water no chance to mix with the electrolyte and so the former freezes and splits the battery case.

6 If topping-up the battery becomes excessive and the case has been inspected for cracks that could cause leakage, but none are found, the battery is being overcharged and the voltage regulator will have to be checked and reset.

7 With the battery on the bench at the three monthly interval check, measure the specific gravity with a hydrometer to determine the state of charge and condition of the electrolyte. There should be very little variation between the different cells and if a variation in excess of 0.025 is present it will be due to either:

a) *Loss of electrolyte from the battery at sometime caused by spillage or a leak resulting in a drop in the specific gravity of the electrolyte, when the deficiency was replaced with distilled water instead of fresh electrolyte.*
b) *An internal short circuit caused by buckling of the plates or a similar malady pointing to the liklihood of total battery failure in the near future.*

8 The specific gravity of the electrolyte for fully charged conditions at the electrolyte temperature indicated, is listed in Table A. The specific gravity of a fully discharged battery at different temperatures of the electrolyte is given in Table B.

Table A

Specific Gravity - Battery Fully Charged

1.268 at 100°F or 38°C electrolyte temperature
1.272 at 90°F or 32°C electrolyte temperature
1.276 at 80°F or 27°C electrolyte temperature
1.280 at 70°F or 21°C electrolyte temperature
1.284 at 60°F or 16°C electrolyte temperature
1.288 at 50°F or 10°C electrolyte temperature
1.292 at 40°F or 4°C electrolyte temperature
1.296 at 30°F or-1.5°C electrolyte temperature

Table B

Specific Gravity - Battery Fully Discharged

1.098 at 100°F or 38°C electrolyte temperature
1.102 at 90°F or 32°C electrolyte temperature
1.106 at 80°F or 27°C electrolyte temperature
1.110 at 70°F or 21°C electrolyte temperature
1.114 at 60°F or 16°C electrolyte temperature
1.118 at 50°F or 10°C electrolyte temperature
1.122 at 40°F or 4°C electrolyte temperature
1.126 at 30°F or-1.5°C electrolyte temperature

4 Battery - electrolyte replenishment

1 If the battery is in a fully charged state and one of the cells maintains a specific gravity reading which is 0.025 or more lower than the others, and a check of each cell has been made with a voltmeter to check for short circuits (a four to seven second test should give a steady reading of between 12 to 18 volts) then it is likely that electrolyte has been lost from the cell with the low reading.

2 Top-up the cell with a solution of 1 part sulphuric acid to 2.5 parts of water. If the cell is already fully topped-up draw some electrolyte out of it with a pipette.

3 When mixing the sulphuric acid and water **never add water to sulphuric acid** - always pour the acid slowly onto the water in a glass container. **If water is added to sulphuric acid it will explode.**

4 Continue to top-up the cell with the freshly made electrolyte and then recharge the battery and check the hydrometer readings.

5 Battery - charging

1 In winter time when heavy demand is placed upon the battery, such as when starting from cold, and much electrical equipment is continually in use, it is a good idea to occasionally have the battery fully charged from an external source at the rate of 3.5 to 4 amps.

2 Continue to charge the battery at this rate until no further rise in specific gravity is noted over a four hour period.

3 Alternatively, a trickle charger charging at the rate of 1.5 amps can be safely used overnight.

4 Specially rapid 'boost' charges which are claimed to restore the power of the battery in 1 to 2 hours are most dangerous as they can cause serious damage to the battery plates through over-heating.

5 While charging the battery, note that the temperature of the electrolyte should never exceed 100°F (37.8°C).

6 Alternator - general

The alternator may be of Lucas, Femsa or Bosch manufacture according to the vehicle and production source (Fig. 10.1).

The main advantage of the alternator over its predecessor, the dynamo, lies in its ability to provide a high charge at low revolutions. Driving slowly in heavy traffic with a dynamo invariably means no charge is reaching the battery. In similar conditions even with the wiper, heater, lights and perhaps radio switched on the alternator will ensure a charge reaches the battery.

7 Alternator - routine maintenance

1 The equipment has been designed for the minimum amount of maintenance in service, the only items subject to wear being the brushes and bearings.

2 Brushes should be examined after about 75,000 miles (120,000 km)

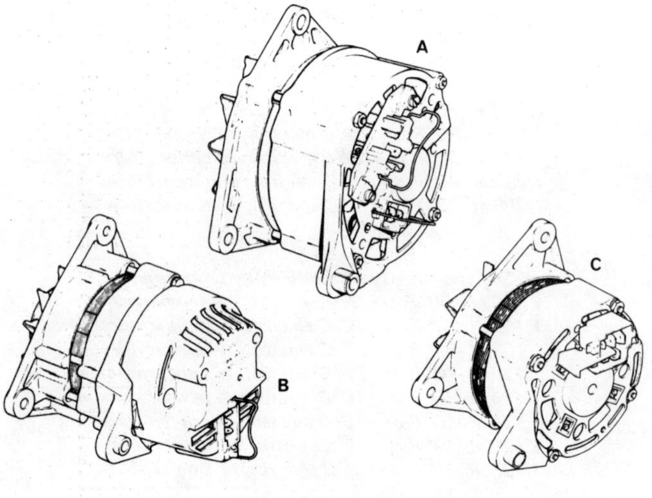

Fig. 10.1. Alternator recognition (Sec. 6)

A Bosch B Lucas C Femsa

and renewed if necessary. The bearings are prepacked with grease for life, and should not require further attention.

3 Check the fan belt every 3,000 miles (5,000 km) for correct adjustment which should be 0.5 inch (13 mm) total movement at the centre of the longest run between pulleys.

8 Alternator - special procedures

Whenever the electrical system of the car is being attended to, and external means of starting the engine is used, there are certain precautions that must be taken otherwise serious and expensive damage can result.

1 Always make sure that the negative terminal of the battery is earthed. If the terminal connections are accidentally reversed or if the battery has been reverse charged the alternator diodes will be damaged.

2 The output terminal on the alternator marked 'BAT' or 'B+' must never be earthed but should always be connected directly to the positive terminal of the battery.

3 Whenever the alternator is to be removed or when disconnecting the terminals of the alternator circuit, always disconnect the battery terminal earth first.

4 The alternator must never be operated without the battery to alternator cable connected.

5 If the battery is to be charged by external means always disconnect both battery cables before the external charger is connected.

6 Should it be necessary to use a booster charger or booster battery to start the engine always double check that the negative cable is connected to negative terminal and the positive cable to positive terminal.

9 Alternator - removal and refitting

1 Disconnect the battery leads.

2 Note the terminal connections at the rear of the alternator and disconnect the plug or multi pin connector. On Mercury Capri II models disconnect the heater hose bracket at the alternator.

3 Undo and remove the alternator adjustment arm bolt, slacken the alternator mounting bolts and push the alternator inward towards the engine. Lift away the fan belt from the pulley.

4 Remove the remaining two mounting bolts and carefully lift the alternator away from the car.

5 Take care not to knock or drop the alternator otherwise this can cause irreparable damage.

6 Refitting the alternator is the reverse sequence to removal.

7 Adjust the fan belt so that it has 0.5 inch (13 mm) total movement at the centre of the longest run between pulleys.

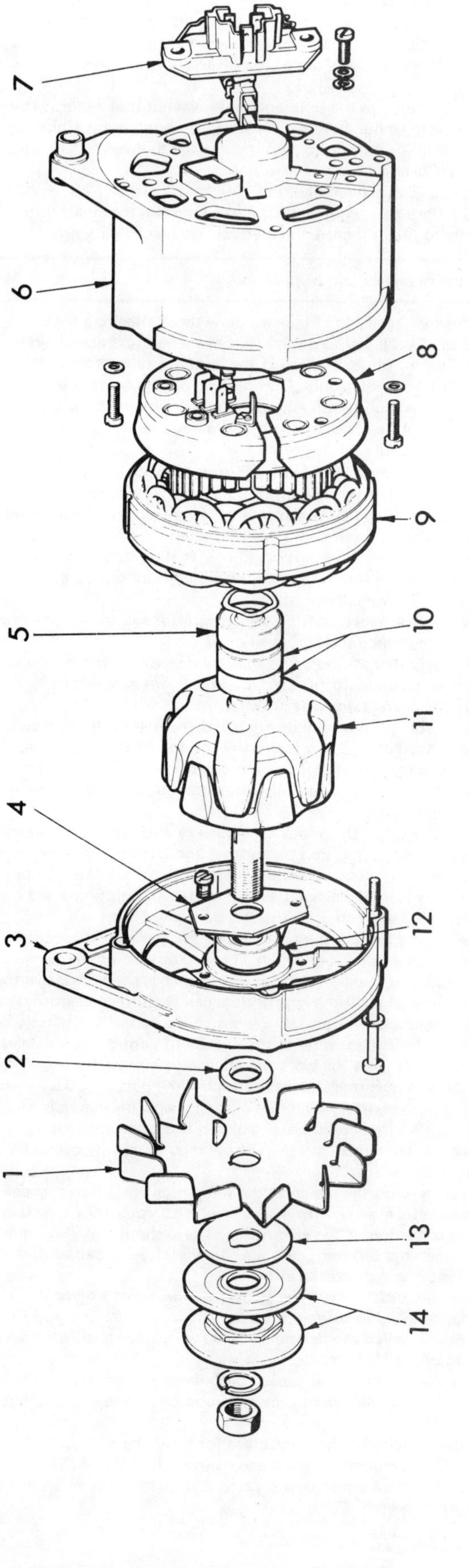

Fig. 10.2. Bosch alternator - exploded view

1 Fan
2 Spacer
3 Drive end housing
4 Thrust plate
5 Slip ring end bearing
6 Slip ring end housing
7 Brush box
8 Rectifier (diode) pack
9 Stator assembly
10 Slip rings
11 Rotor
12 Drive end housing
13 Spacer
14 Pulley

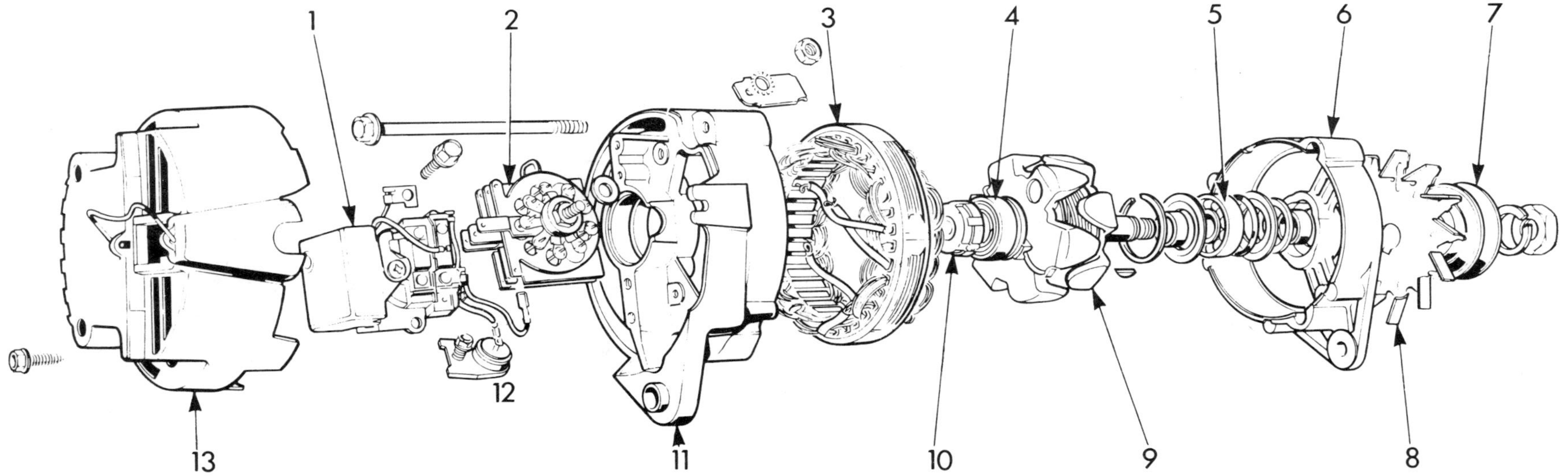

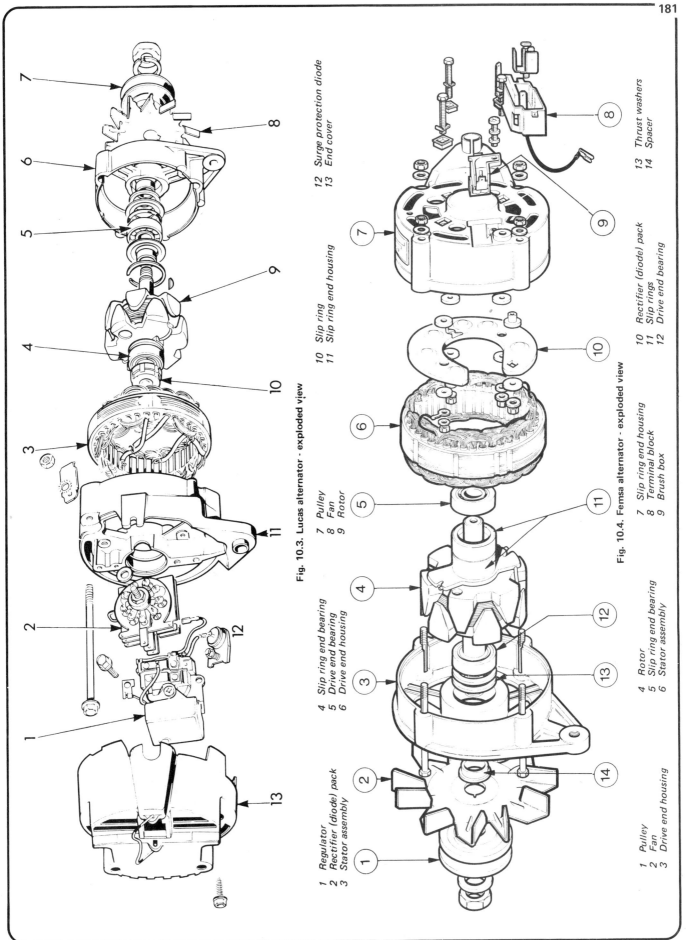

Fig. 10.3. Lucas alternator - exploded view

1 Regulator
2 Rectifier (diode) pack
3 Stator assembly
4 Slip ring end bearing
5 Drive end bearing
6 Drive end housing
7 Pulley
8 Fan
9 Rotor
10 Slip ring
11 Slip ring end housing
12 Surge protection diode
13 End cover

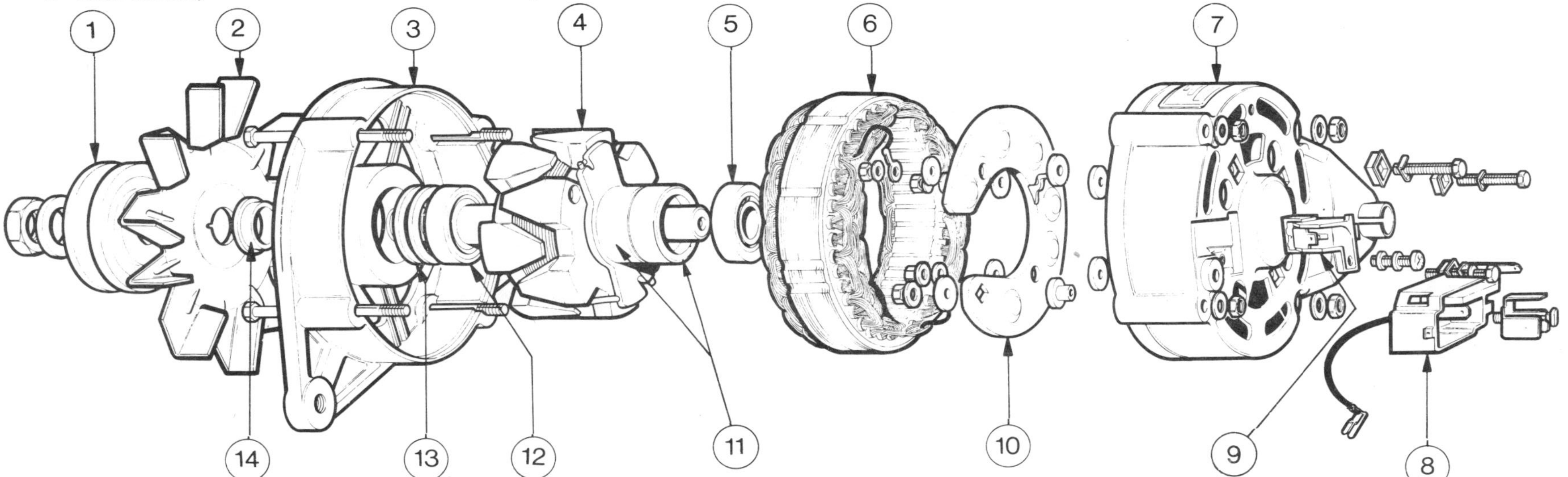

Fig. 10.4. Femsa alternator - exploded view

1 Pulley
2 Fan
3 Drive end housing
4 Rotor
5 Slip ring end bearing
6 Stator assembly
7 Slip ring end housing
8 Terminal block
9 Brush box
10 Rectifier (diode) pack
11 Slip rings
12 Drive end bearing
13 Thrust washers
14 Spacer

10 Alternator - fault diagnosis and repair

Due to the specialist knowledge and equipment required to test or service an alternator it is recommended that if the performance is suspect the car be taken to an automobile electrician who will have the facilities for such work. Because of this recommendation, information is limited to the inspection and renewal of the brushes. Should the alternator not charge or the system be suspect the following points may be checked before seeking further assistance:

1 *Check the fanbelt tension, as described in Section 7.*
2 *Check the battery, as described in Section 3.*
3 *Check all electrical cable connections for cleanliness and security.*

11 Alternator brushes (Lucas) - inspection, removal and refitting

1 Undo and remove the two screws and washers securing the end cover.
2 To inspect the brushes correctly the brush holder mountings should be removed complete by undoing the two bolts and disconnecting the 'Lucar' connection to the diode plates.
3 With the brush holder moulding removed and the brush assemblies still in position check that they protrude from the face of the moulding by at least 0.2 inches (5 mm). Also check that when depressed, the spring pressure is 7 to 10 ozs, when the end of the brush is flush with the face of the brush moulding. To be done with any accuracy this requires a push type spring gauge.
4 Should either of the foregoing requirements not be fulfilled the spring assemblies should be replaced.
5 This can be done by simply removing the holding screws of each assembly and replacing them.
6 With the brush holder moulding removed the slip rings on the face end of the rotor are exposed. These can be cleaned with a petrol soaked cloth and any signs of burning may be removed very carefully with fine glass paper. On no account should any other abrasive be used or any attempt at machining be made.
7 When the brushes are refitted they should slide smoothly in their holders. Any sticking tendency may first be rectified by wiping with a petrol soaked cloth or, if this fails, by carefully polishing with a very fine file where any binding marks may appear.
8 Reassemble in the reverse order of dismantling. Ensure that leads which may have been connected to any of the screws are reconnected correctly. Note:-

a) *If the charging system is suspect, first check the fan belt tension and condition - refer to Section 7 for details.*
b) *Check the battery - refer to Section 3 for details.*
c) *With an alternator the ignition warning light control feed comes from the centre point of a pair of diodes in the alternator via a control unit similar in appearance to an indicator flasher unit. Should the warning light indicate lack of charge, check this unit and if suspect replace it.*
d) *Should the above prove negative then proceed to check the alternator.*

12 Alternator brushes (Bosch) - inspection, removal and refitting

1 Undo and remove the two screws, spring and plain washers that secure the brush box to the rear of the brush end housing. Lift away the brush box.
2 Check that the carbon brushes are able to slide smoothly in their guides without any sign of binding.
3 Measure the length of brushes and if they have worn down to 0.35 inch (9 mm) or less, they must be renewed.
4 Hold the brush wire with a pair of engineer's pliers and unsolder it from the brush box. Lift away the two brushes.
5 Insert the new brushes and check to make sure that they are free to

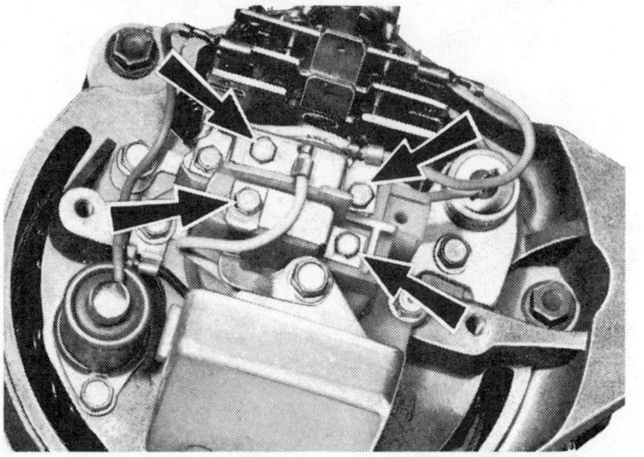

Fig. 10.5. Brush box retaining screws - Lucas alternator (Sec. 11)

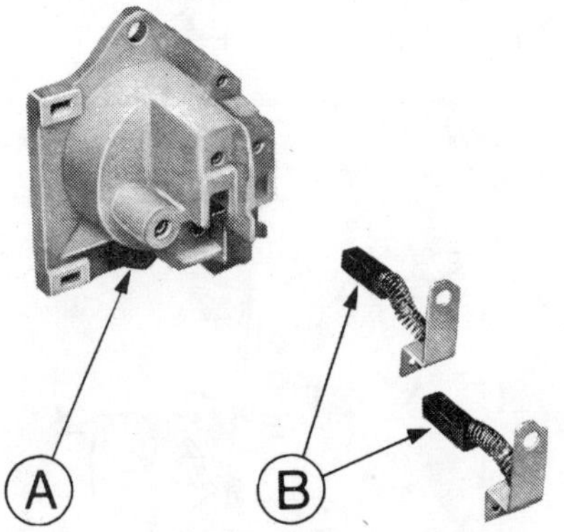

Fig. 10.6. Brush gear - Lucas alternator (Sec. 11)

A Brush box *B Brush assemblies*

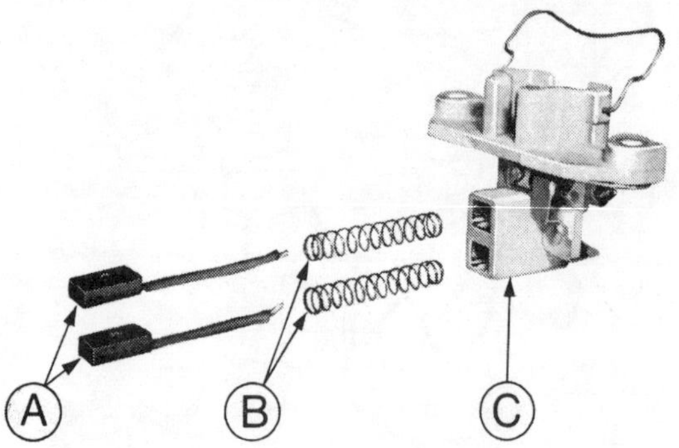

Fig. 10.7. Brush gear - Bosch alternator (Sec. 12)

A Brushes *B Springs* *C Brush box*

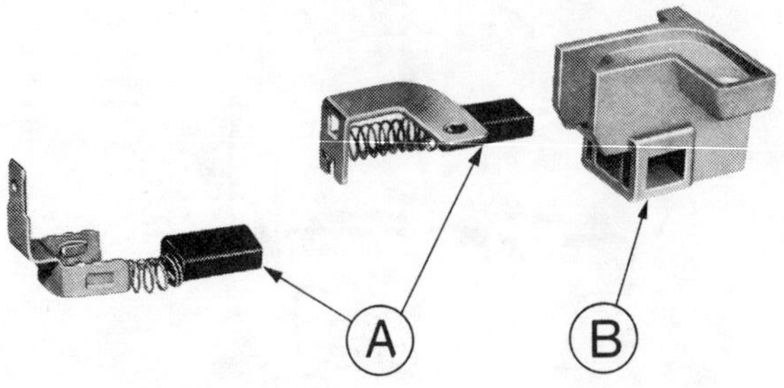

Fig. 10.8. Brush gear - Femsa alternator (Sec. 13)

move in their guides. If they bind, lightly polish with a very fine file.
6 Solder the brushwire ends to the brush box taking care that solder is allowed to pass to the stranded wire.
7 Whenever new brushes are fitted new springs should also be fitted.
8 Refitting the brush box is the reverse sequence to removal.

13 Alternator brushes (Femsa) - inspection, removal and refitting

1 Disconnect the single wire from the brush box.
2 Remove the crosshead retaining screw then withdraw the brush box.
3 Check that the carbon brushes are able to slide smoothly in their guides without any sign of binding.
4 Measure the amount by which the brushes protrude from the brush box. If this is less than 0.28 inch (7 mm), obtain and fit replacement brushes.
5 Refitting the brush box is a straightforward reversal of the removal procedure.

14 Starter motor - general description

The starter motor fitted to engines covered by this manual may be either of the inertia or pre-engaged type.

The pre-engaged type is recognisable by the solenoid assembly mounted on the motor body.

The principle of operation of the inertia type starter motor is as follows: When the ignition is switched on and the switch operated, current flows from the battery to the starter motor solenoid switch which causes it to become energised. Its internal plunger moves inwards and closes an internal switch so allowing full starting current to flow from the battery to the starter motor. This causes a powerful magnetic field to be induced into the field coils which causes the armature to rotate.

Mounted on helical spines is the drive pinion which, because of the sudden rotation of the armature, is thrown forward along the armature shaft and so into engagement with the flywheel ring gear. The engine crankshaft will then be rotated until the engine starts to operate on its own, and at this point, the drive pinion is thrown out of mesh with the flywheel ring gear.

The method of engagement on the pre-engaged starter differs considerably in that the drive pinion is brought into mesh with the starter ring gear before the main starter current is applied.

When the ignition is switched on, current flows from the battery to the solenoid which is mounted on the top of the starter motor. The plunger in the solenoid moves inwards so causing a centrally pivoted engagement lever to move in such a manner that the forked end pushes the drive pinion into mesh with the starter ring gear. When the solenoid reaches the end of its travel, it closes an internal contact and full starting current flows to the starter field coils. The armature is then able to rotate the crankshaft so starting the engine.

A special one way clutch is fitted to the starter drive pinion so that when the engine just fires and starts to operate in its own, it does not drive the starter motor.

15 Starter motor (inertia) - testing on engine

1 If the starter motor fails to operate, then check the condition of the battery by turning on the headlamps. If they glow brightly for several seconds and then gradually dim, the battery is in an uncharged condition.
2 If the headlamps continue to glow brightly and it is obvious that the battery is in good condition then check the tightness of the battery terminal to its connection on the body frame. Check the tightness of the connections at the relay switch and at the starter motor. Check the wiring with a voltmeter for breaks or shorts.
3 If the wiring is in order then check the starter motor switch is operating. To do this, press the rubber covered button in the centre of the relay switch under the bonnet. If it is working, the starter motor will be heard to 'click', as it tries to rotate. Alternatively, check it with a voltmeter.
4 If the battery is fully charged, the wiring in order, and the switch working but the starter motor fails to operate, then it will have to be removed from the car for examination. Before this is done, however, ensure that the starter pinion has not jammed in mesh with the flywheel. Check by turning the square end of the armature shaft with a spanner. This will free the pinion if it is stuck in engagement with the flywheel teeth.

16 Starter motor (inertia) - removal and refitting

1 Disconnect the positive and then the negative terminals from the battery. Also disconnect the starter motor cable from the terminal on the starter motor end cover.
2 Undo and remove the nuts, bolts and spring washers which secure the starter motor to the clutch and the flywheel housing. Lift the starter motor away by manipulating the drive gear out from the ring gear area and then from the engine compartment.
3 Refitting is the reverse procedure to removal. Make sure that the starter motor cable, when secured in position by its terminal, does not touch any part of the body or power unit which could damage the insulation.

17 Starter motor (inertia) - dismantling, overhaul and reassembly

1 The motor has four field coils, four pole pieces and four spring-loaded commutator brushes. Two of these brushes are earthed, and the other two are insulated and attached to the field coil ends.
2 The starter drive is a conventional pinion and spring engaging with a ring gear on either the flywheel or torque converter (automatic transmission).
3 The fully insulated brush gear is housed in a plastic brush box moulding riveted to the commutator end bracket. The wedge shaped brushes have keyways to ensure their correct fitting in the brush box and are kept in contact with the face type, moulded commutator, by small coil springs.
4 The field winding on this motor is continuously wound with no inter-connecting joints, one end terminating at the brush box moulding with the other end earthed to the yoke, or starter motor casing, via either a riveted eyelet, or soldered connection.
5 Unlike earlier versions of this starter motor the end brackets are held to the yoke independently of each other, each bracket being secured to its respective location with two screws. At the drive end these screws locate into the pole shoes while at the commutator end the screws locate in tapped holes in the yoke wall.
6 Secure the starter motor in the jaws of a vice. Then unscrew and remove the two screws which hold the drive endplate to the yoke.
7 Pull the end cap from the armature shaft, then extract the four commutator endplate screws and tap the plate free from the yoke. Pull it only sufficiently far to allow access to the brushes which should then be freed to enable the endplate to be completely withdrawn.
8 Remove the nut, washer and insulator from the terminal stud. Push the stud and the second insulator through the commutator endplate, then remove the stud and brushes.
9 The brush box can only be removed if the two securing rivets are first drilled out.
10 The drive pinion can be dismantled if the heavy spring is first compressed so that the circlip is exposed and can be removed. A suitable compressor will be required to compress the spring. Do not use makeshift methods as they can be dangerous.
11 To renew the non-detachable type field winding brushes, their flexible connecting leads must be cut to leave 0.25 in (6.0 mm) attached to the field coils.
12 Discard the old brushes and solder the new ones to the old studs. Check that the new brushes slide freely in their retainers.
13 The main terminal stud with its two earthed brushes are supplied as an assembly.
14 Clean the face type commutator with a fuel moistened cloth. If this fails to remove all the discoloured areas, gently polish with very fine glasspaper (not emery). Never undercut the insulating strips on the face type commutator.
15 With the starter motor stripped down, examine the drive end bush for wear. If the armature shaft can be moved frm side-to-side, within the bush, then the bush must be pressed or driven out and a new one fitted. As the bush is of the phosphor bronze type the new bush must be soaked in engine oil for 24 hours before fitting.
16 Reassembly is a reversal of dismantling, but make sure that the alignment notch and peg on the drive endplate and yoke are engaged correctly.

18 Starter motor (pre-engaged) - testing on engine

1 If the starter motor fails to operate then check the condition of the battery by turning on the headlamps. If they glow brightly for several seconds and then gradually dim the battery is in an uncharged condition.
2 If the headlights continue to glow brightly and it is obvious that the battery is in good condition, then check the tightness of the battery wiring connections (and in particular the earth lead from the battery terminal to its connection on the body frame). If the positive terminal on the battery becomes hot when an attempt is made to work the starter this is a sure sign of a poor connection on the battery terminal. To rectify remove the terminal, clean the mating faces thoroughly and reconnect. Check the connections on the rear of the starter solenoid. Check the wiring with a voltmeter or test lamp for breaks or shorts.
3 Test the continuity of the solenoid windings by connecting a test lamp circuit comprising a 12 volt battery and low wattage bulb between the 'STA' terminal and the solenoid body. If the two windings are in order the lamp will light. Next connect the test lamp (fitted with a high wattage bulb) between the solenoid main terminals. Energise the solenoid by applying a 12 volt supply between the unmarked Lucar terminal and the solenoid body. The solenoid should be heard to operate and the test bulb light. This indicates full closure of the solenoid contacts.
4 If the battery is fully charged, the wiring in order, the starter/ignition switch working and the starter motor still fails to operate then it will have to be removed from the car for examination. Before this is done ensure that the starter motor pinion has not jammed in mesh with the flywheel by engaging a gear (not automatic) and rocking the car to and fro. This should free the pinion if it is stuck in mesh with the flywheel teeth.

19 Starter motor (pre-engaged) - description, removal and refitting

1 The method of engagement of the pre-engaged starter is that the drive pinion is brought into mesh with the starter ring gear before the main starter current is applied.
2 When the ignition is switched on, the current flows from the battery to the solenoid which is mounted on the top of the starter motor body. The plunger in the solenoid moves inward so causing a centrally pivoted lever to move in such a manner that the forked end pushes the drive pinion into mesh with the starter ring gear. When the solenoid plunger reaches the end of its travel, it closes an internal contact and full starting current flows to the starter field coils. The armature is then able to rotate the crankshaft so starting the engine.
3 A special one way clutch is fitted to the starter drive pinion so that when the engine just fires and starts to operate on its own, it does not drive the starter motor.
4 Removal is basically identical to that for the inertia type starter motor with the exception of the cables at the rear of the solenoid. Note these connections and then detach the cable terminal from the solenoid.

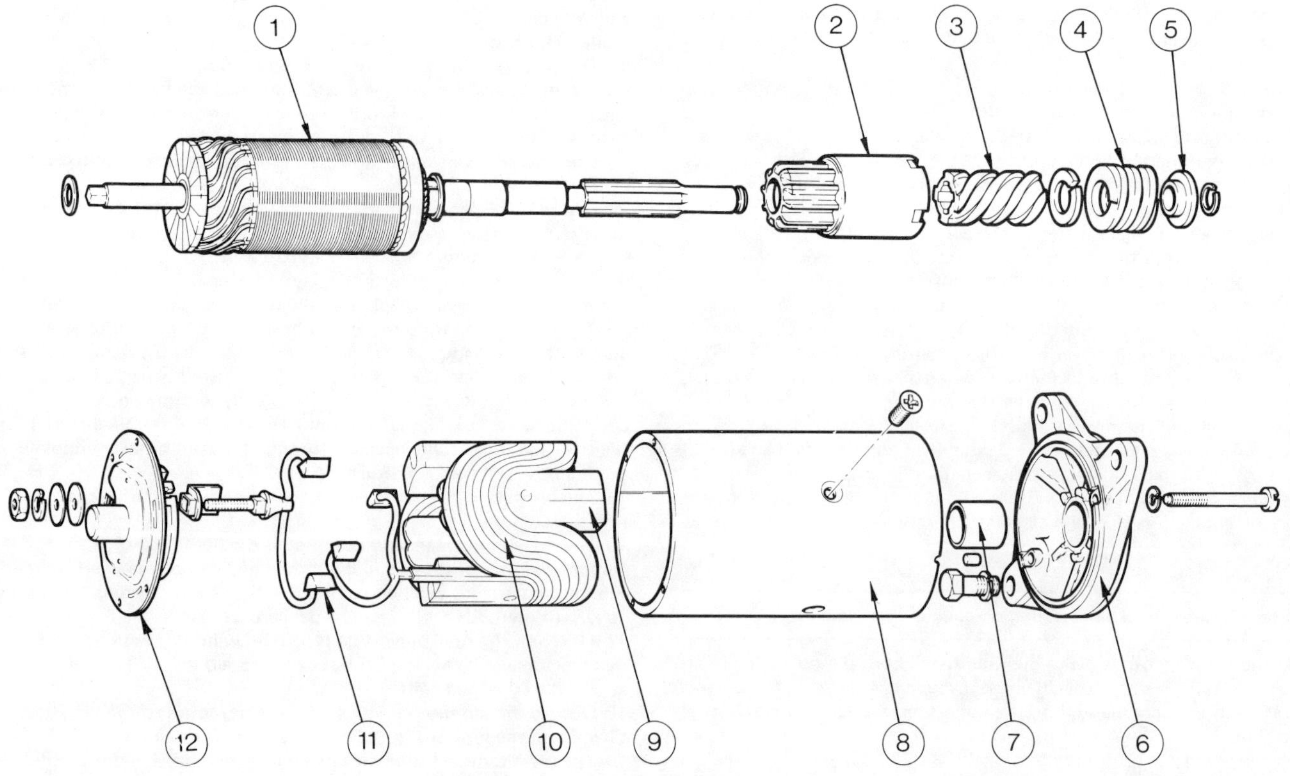

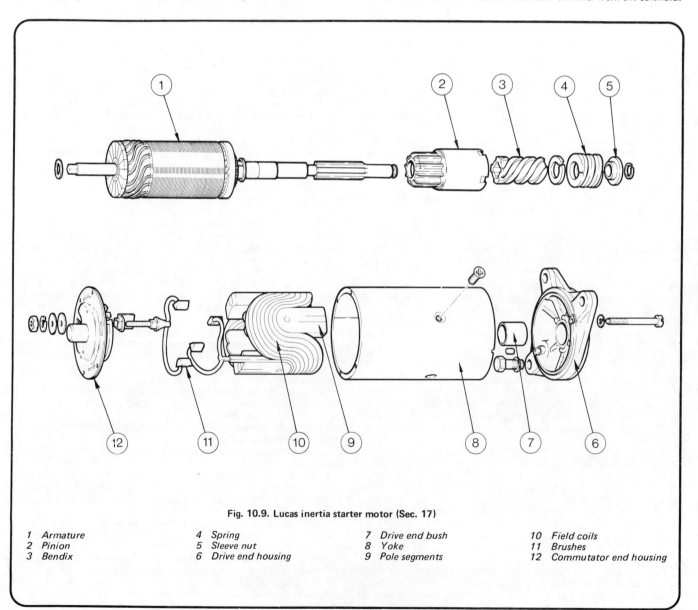

Fig. 10.9. Lucas inertia starter motor (Sec. 17)

1 Armature
2 Pinion
3 Bendix
4 Spring
5 Sleeve nut
6 Drive end housing
7 Drive end bush
8 Yoke
9 Pole segments
10 Field coils
11 Brushes
12 Commutator end housing

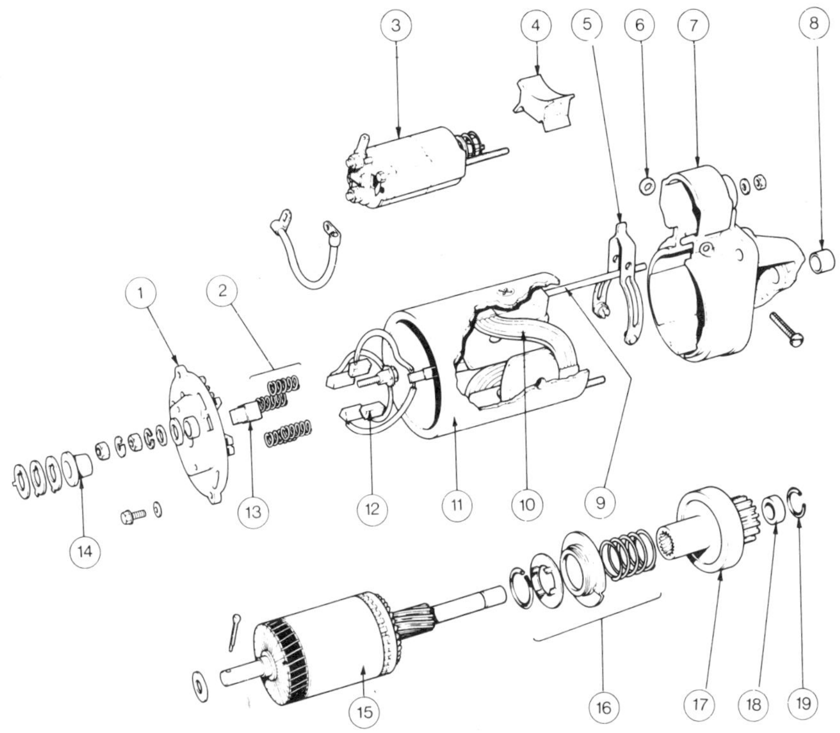

Fig. 10.10. Lucas pre-engaged starter motor (Sec. 20)

1 *Commutator end housing*
2 *Brush springs*
3 *Solenoid assembly*
4 *Grommet*
5 *Pivot lever*
6 *Pivot pin retaining clip*
7 *Drive end housing*
8 *Drive end bush*
9 *Through bolt*
10 *Field coil*
11 *Yoke*
12 *Brushes*
13 *Insulator*
14 *Commutator end bearing*
15 *Armature assembly*
16 *Drive plate and springs*
17 *Pinion*
18 *Thrust collar*
19 *Ring*

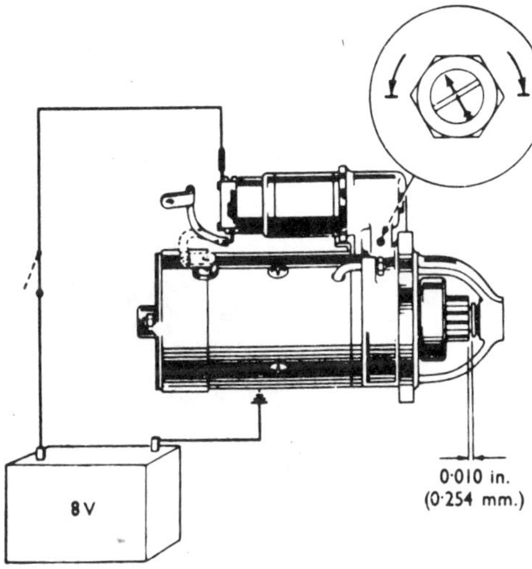

Fig. 10.10A Pre-engaged type starter endfloat (solenoid actuated) (Sec. 20)

20 Starter motor (Lucas pre-engaged) - dismantling, overhaul and reassembly

Due to the fact that this type of starter motor uses a face commutator, on which the brushes make contact end on, a certain amount of thrust is created along the armature shaft. A thrust bearing is therefore incorporated in the motor at the commutator end.

1 Remove the split pin from the end of the shaft and slide off the shim(s), washer and thrust plate.

2 Remove the two screws which retain the end plate and pull off the end plate complete with the brush holders and brushes.

3 If the brushes are badly worn, cut off the brush flexible connectors as near to their terminals as possible. Solder the new brush leads to the terminal posts.

4 Cut off the other two brush flexible connectors at a distance of 1/8 inch (3.2 mm) from their connection with the field windings. Solder the new brush leads into position, localise the heat applied.

5 To remove the armature, unscrew the nuts on the holding studs at the drive end bracket.

6 Withdraw the armature complete with the drive and the one-way clutch operating lever.

7 If necessary, clean the end face of the commutator with a petrol soaked cloth. It may be carefully polished with very fine glass paper - **never use emery cloth and never undercut the mica insulation.**

8 Reassembly is a direct reversal of the above procedure, but the armature end float should be measured as indicated in Fig. 10.10A. The correct endfloat should be 0.010 inch (0.254 mm) with an 8 volt current activating the solenoid. If the endfloat is found to be incorrect, it can be adjusted by fitting shims between the thrust plate and the split pin. After dismantling, always use a new split pin.

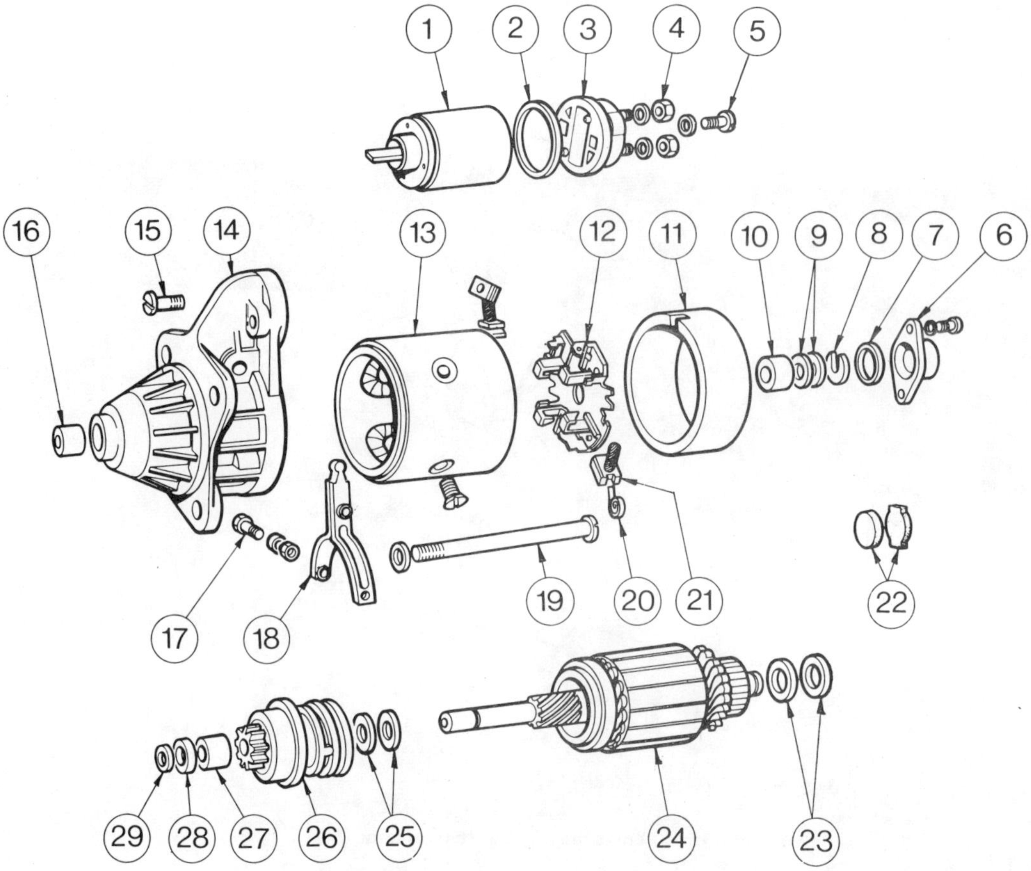

Fig. 10.11. Bosch pre-engaged starter motor (Sec. 21)

1 *Solenoid assembly*
2 *Packing ring*
3 *Switch contacts and cover*
4 *Nut*
5 *Screw*
6 *Cover*
7 *Washer*
8 *'U' shoe*
9 *Thrust washer*
10 *Commutator end bearing*
11 *Commutator end housing*
12 *Brush plate*
13 *Yoke*
14 *Drive end housing*
15 *Screw*
16 *Bush*
17 *Pivot pin*
18 *Pivot lever*
19 *Bolt*
20 *Brush spring*
21 *Brush*
22 *Lubricating pads*
23 *Thrust washers*
24 *Armature assembly*
25 *Packing rings*
26 *Drive assembly*
27 *Bush*
28 *Stop ring*
29 *Stop ring*

21 Starter motor (Bosch pre-engaged) - description, dismantling, overhaul and reassembly

1 The Bosch starter is a four pole, four brush motor utilising a series field and a solenoid controlled roller clutch drive.

2 The brush gear is again fully insulated and is made up of four brushes housed in a metal brush box riveted to the commutator end bracket. Small coil springs keep the brushes in contact with the axially moulded commutator.

3 The field windings are again continuously wound with no interconnecting joints, the end of the windings being connected to the brush gear, while the other is connected to the battery through the solenoid contacts.

4 The operating position of the pivot lever is preset in manufacture and cannot be adjusted. This approach eliminates the need to set the lever to obtain correct operation of the solenoid.

5 The overhaul procedure is similar to that described in the preceding Section but refer to the illustration for detail differences in component design (Fig. 10.11).

22 Headlamp assembly - removal and refitting

Capri II

1 Disconnect the battery earth lead and remove the headlamp cover

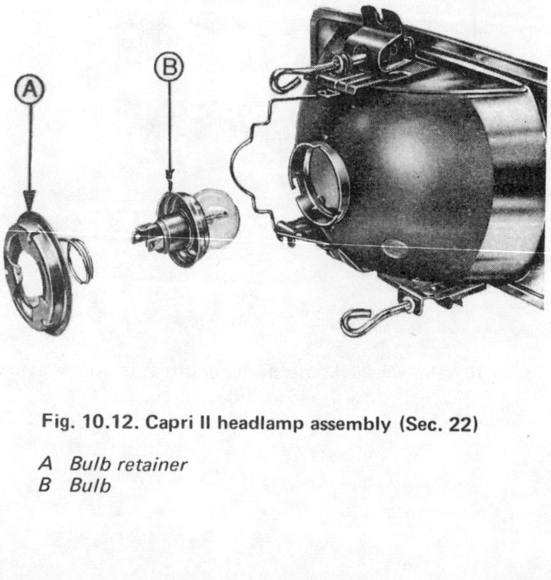

Fig. 10.12. Capri II headlamp assembly (Sec. 22)

A Bulb retainer
B Bulb

plate (photo).
2 Disengage the spring clip, then pull off the cap and multi-plug assembly (photo).
3 Remove the headlamp bulb retainer and bulb (photos).
4 Pull out the parking lamp bulb holder.
5 Remove the retaining screw and withdraw the headlamp assembly. If necessary, remove the adjusters and retaining clips from the lens and reflector assembly (photo).
6 Refitting is the reverse of the removal procedure, but it is recommended that beam alignment is checked, and adjusted if necessary as described in Section 23.

Mercury Capri II

7 Open the hood then remove the 4 bezel retaining screws (two at the top, two at the bottom).
8 Remove the bezel and the three foam insulators (Fig. 10.13).
9 Loosen the three screws from the headlamp retaining ring and remove the ring.
10 Withdraw the headlamp and disconnect the multi-way connector (Fig. 10.14).
11 Refitting is the reverse of the removal procedure, but it is recommended that beam alignment is checked, and adjusted if necessary.

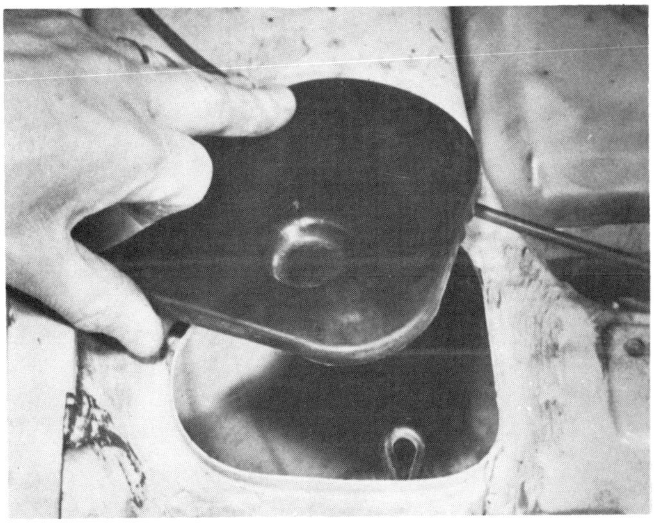

22.1 Removing the headlamp cover plate

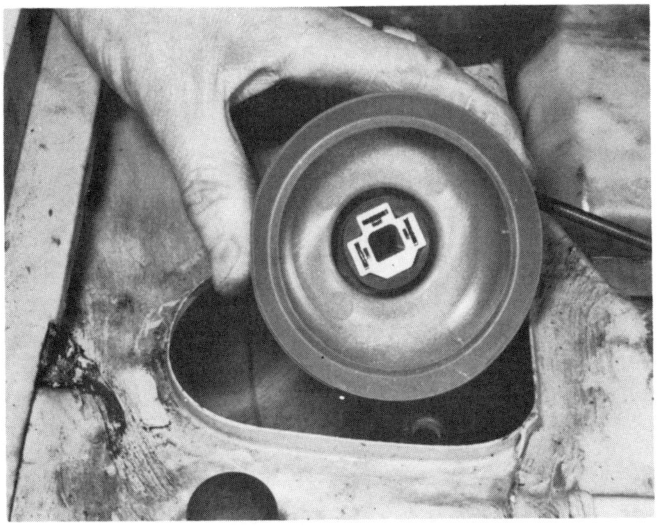

22.2 Headlamp cap and multi-plug

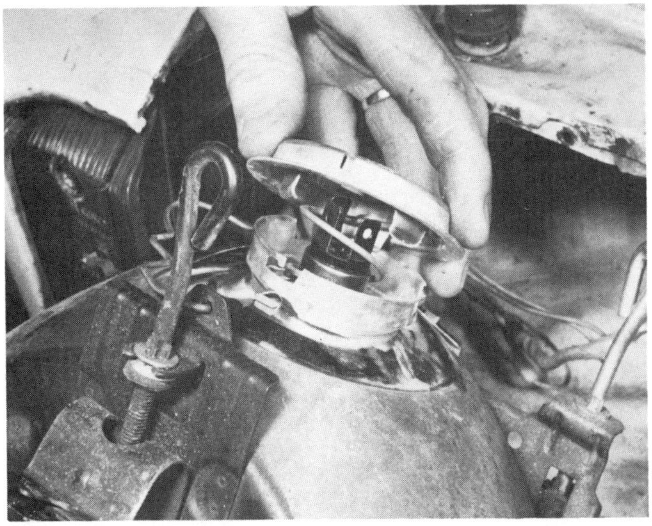

22.3a Remove the bulb retainer...

22.3b ... and bulb

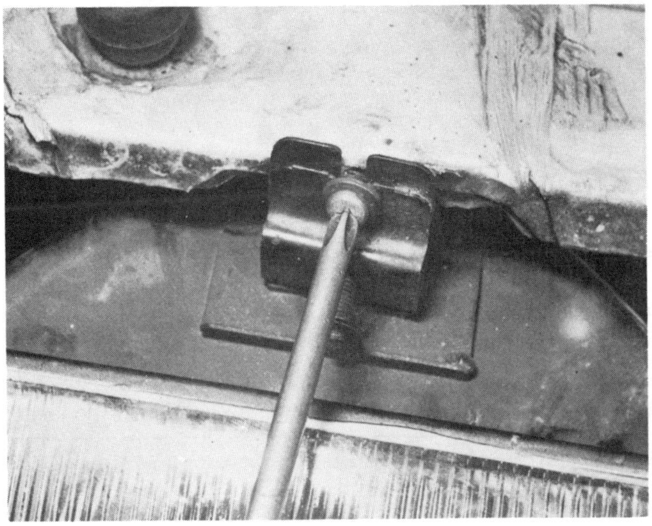

22.5 The headlamp retaining screw

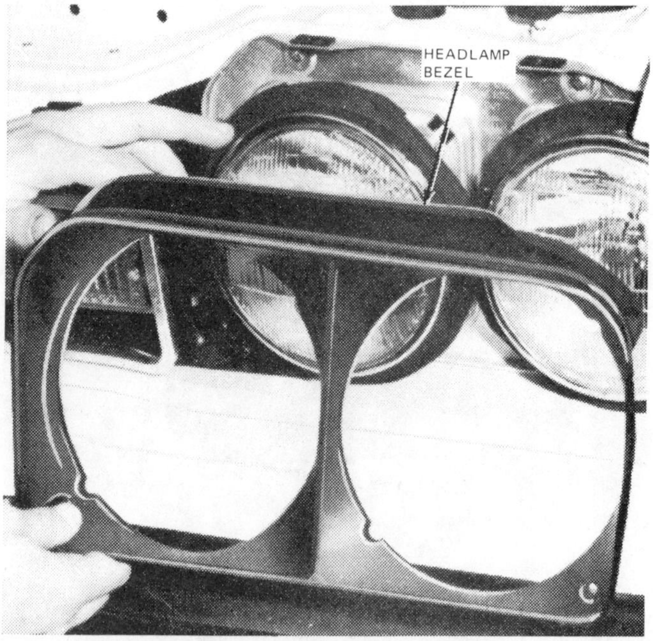

Fig. 10.13. Removing headlamp bezel - Mercury Capri II (Sec. 22)

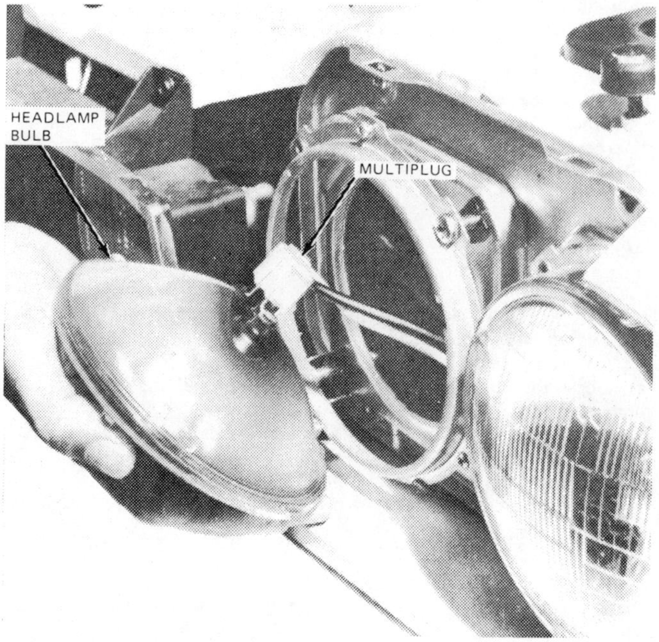

Fig. 10.14. Removing a headlamp unit - Mercury Capri II (Sec. 22)

23 Headlamp beam-alignment

1 The procedure given in this Section is satisfactory for most practical purposes, although it is not intended to replace the alignment procedure used by many dealers and garages who would use beam setting equipment.
2 Refer to Fig 10.15 which shows a beam setting chart for right-hand drive vehicles (for left-hand drive vehicles the chart is a mirror image)
3 Position the vehicle on flat, level ground 33 ft (10 m) from a wall on which the aiming chart is to be fixed. A suitable chart can be drawn using white chalk on any convenient flat wall such as a garage wall or door.
4 Bounce the front of the vehicle to ensure that the suspension has settled and measure the height from the headlamp centre to the ground (H).
5 Mark the centre of the front and rear screens (outside if a heated rear screen is fitted) using a soft wax crayon or masking tape and position the car at right-angles to the chart so that:

a) The vertical centre line and the window markings are exactly in line when viewed through the rear window and
b) the horizontal line is at height 'H-X' above the ground.

6 Remove the headlamp cover plate (Capri II), or the bezels (Mercury Capri II), cover the right headlamp and switch on the dipped beam.
7 Adjust the horizontal alignment of the left-hand headlamp so that the intersection of the horizontal and angled light pattern coincides with the vertical line on the aiming chart.
8 Adjust the vertical alignment so that the light/dark intersection of the beam pattern coincides with the dotted line on the aiming board.
9 Repeat the procedure for the left headlamp.
10 On completion, switch off the headlamps and refit the cover plates.

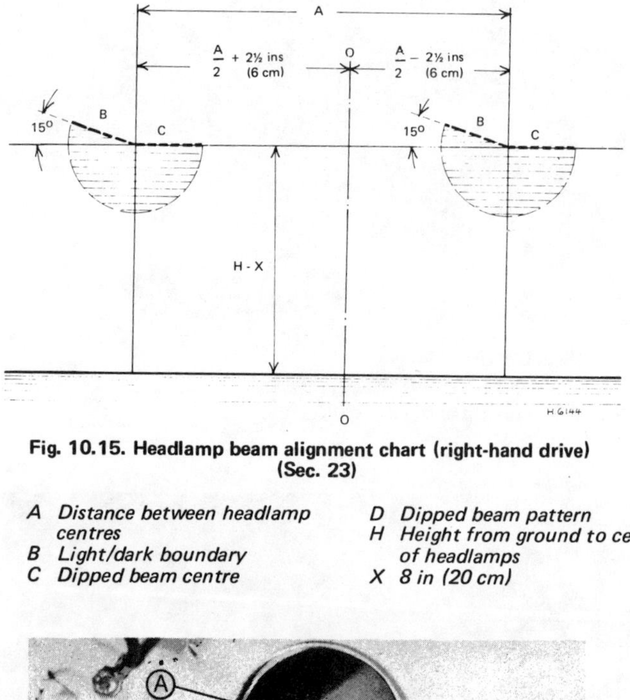

Fig. 10.15. Headlamp beam alignment chart (right-hand drive) (Sec. 23)

A Distance between headlamp centres
B Light/dark boundary
C Dipped beam centre
D Dipped beam pattern
H Height from ground to centre of headlamps
X 8 in (20 cm)

24 Parking lamp bulb (Capri II) - removal and refitting

1 Disconnect the battery earth lead and remove the headlamp cover plate.
2 Pull out the parking lamp bulb holder from the rear of the headlamp assembly.
3 Remove the parking lamp bulb.
4 Refitting is the reverse of the removal procedure.

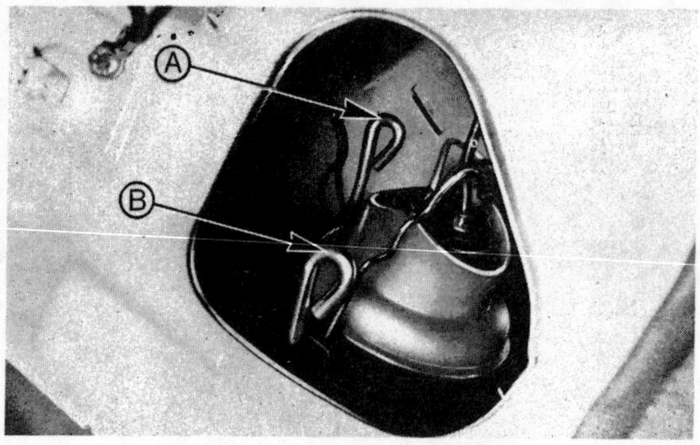

Fig. 10.16. Beam adjusting screws - Capri II (Sec. 23)

A Horizontal *B Vertical*

25 Front direction indicator assembly (Capri II) - removal and refitting

1 Disconnect the battery earth lead and remove the headlamp cover plate.
2 Remove the indicator lens (2 screws) and remove the bulb (photo).
3 Remove the reflector. The lower retaining screw is accessible by inserting a screwdriver between the headlamp and reflector body. Disconnect the wiring to permit the assembly to be withdrawn.
4 Refitting is the reverse of the removal procedure.

26 Front parking and turn signal lights (Mercury Capri II) - removal and refitting

1 To renew a bulb only, remove the two crosshead lens retaining screws and take off the lens. The bayonet fitting bulb can now be removed.
2 If the complete light assembly is to be removed, remove the radiator grille, as described in Chapter 12.
3 Remove the bulb socket from the rear of the light body, then the two body retaining nuts.
4 Refitting is the reverse of the removal procedure.

27 Side marker lights (Mercury Capri II) - removal and refitting

Bulbs renewal - front

1 From behind the fender (wing), pull back the bulb holder protective boot.
2 Turn the bulb holder counter-clockwise and pull the lamp from the body. Pull the bulb out of its holder.
3 Refitting is the reverse of the removal procedure.

Bulb renewal - rear

4 Open the tailgate door and remove the floor panel.
5 Reach under the side panel to the marker light bulb, turn the bulb counter-clockwise to remove it, then remove the dust cover and connector (If a rear window washer is fitted, the reservoir will need to be removed on the left-hand side).
6 Refitting is the reverse of the removal procedure.

Light body - front

7 From behind the fender (wing), remove the securing nuts, clamps and washers, withdraw the light unit from the fender.
8 Slide back the rubber boot and disengage the bulb from the holder.
9 Installation is the reverse of the removal procedure.

Light body - rear

10 Remove the rear panel trim, 'B' post trim, and upper quarter window trim. Remove the side panel retaining screws for access to the rear of the marker lamp (for further information on these operations, see Chapter 12).
11 Remove the two light retaining bolts then remove the light body from outside the car.
12 Installation is the reverse of the removal procedure.

28 Rear lamp assembly - removal and refitting

1 Disconnect the battery earth lead.
2 Open the tailgate, where applicable remove the tailgate trim panel, and remove the rear lamp retaining screws (Fig. 10.19).
3 Carefully lever out the rear lamp assembly and disconnect the wiring. Take care that the paintwork is not damaged during this operation (Fig. 10.20).
4 Clean off any caulking compound from the lamp body.
5 Installation is the reverse of the removal procedure, but to ensure a weather proof joint a caulking compound should be applied around the lamp body prior to its installation.

29 Rear lamp assembly - bulb renewal

1 Remove the four lens retaining screws and take off the lens (photo).
2 Remove and discard the bulbs as appropriate.
3 Refitting is the reverse of the removal procedure.

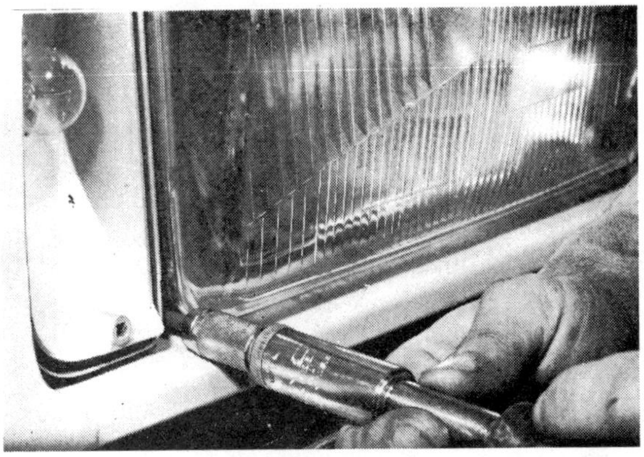

Fig. 10.17. Access to the direction indicator lamp lower screw (Sec. 25)

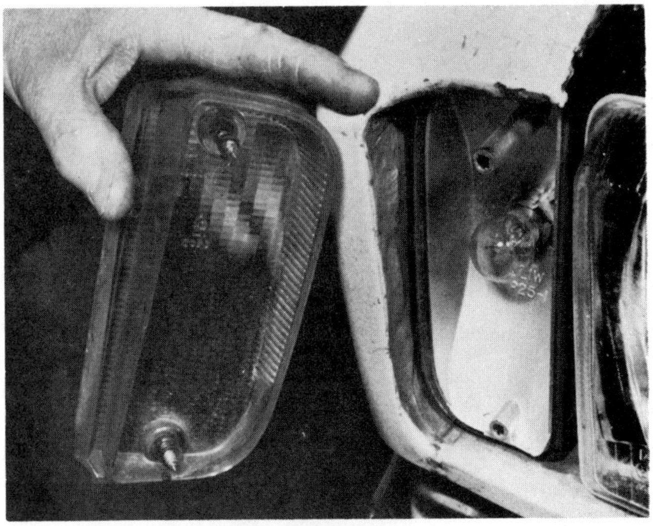

25.2 The indicator lens removed (Capri II)

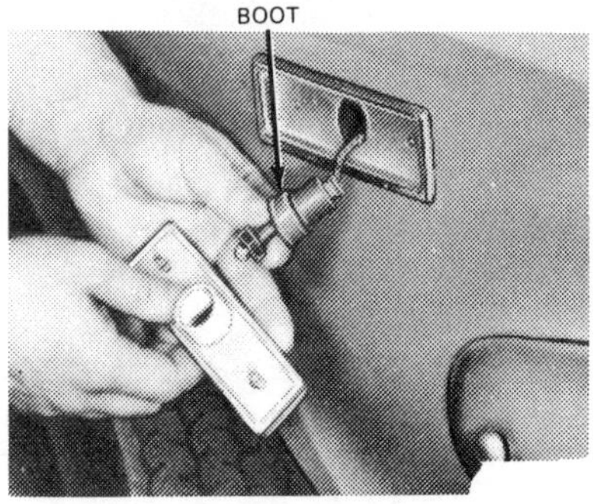

Fig. 10.18. Front side marker light (Mercury Capri II) (Sec. 27)

30 Licence plates (number plates) lamp assembly - removal and refitting

1 Disconnect the battery earth lead.
2 Open the tailgate, lift up the carpet and remove the spare wheel cover.
3 Remove the lamp lens (2 screws).
4 Disconnect the wiring and attach a length of cord to the lamp assembly lead to assist when installing so that the lead can be pulled

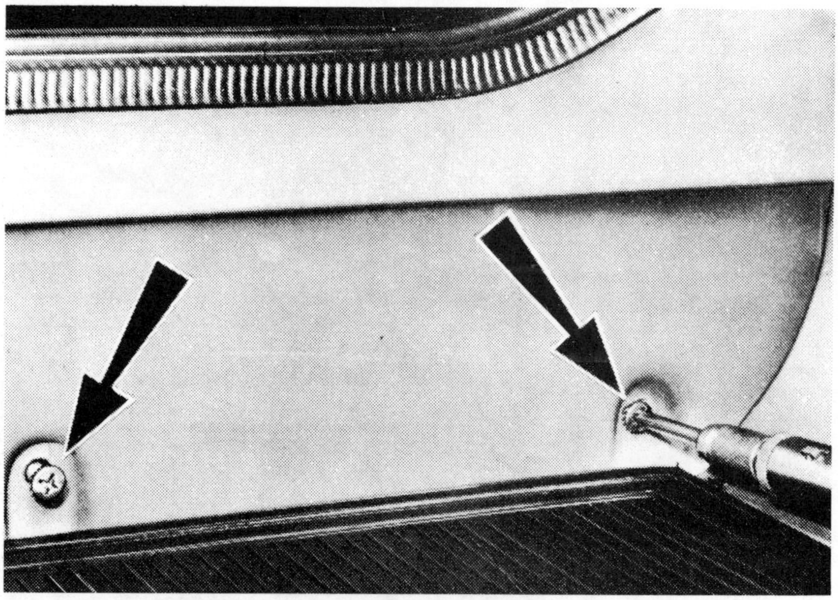

Fig. 10.19. Rear lamp assembly retaining screws (Sec. 28)

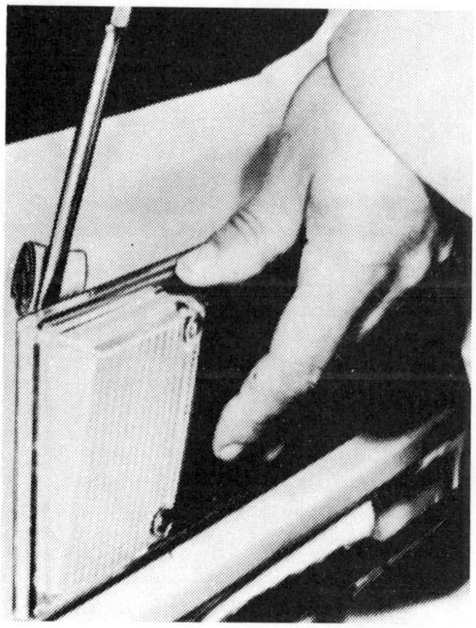

Fig. 10.20. Rear lamp assembly removal (Sec. 28)

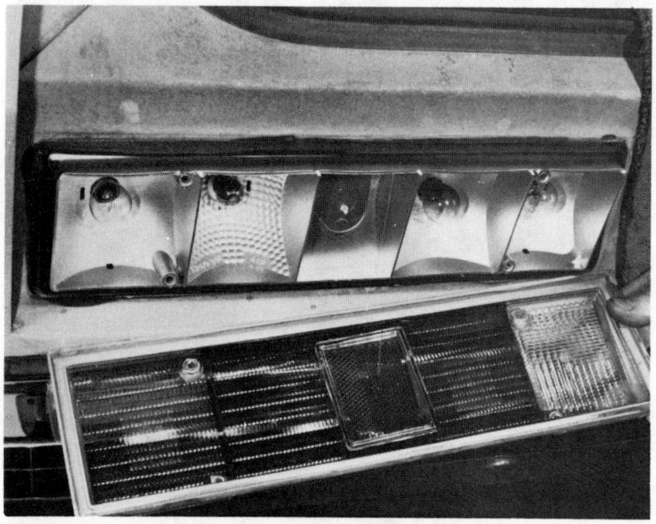

29.1 The rear lamp assembly lens removed

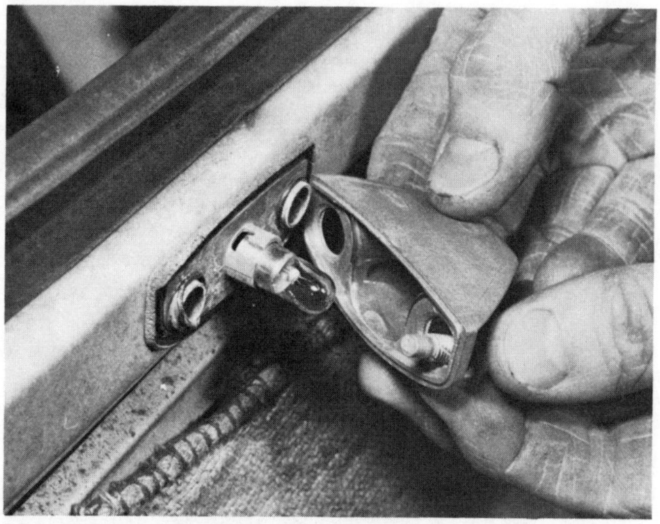

30.6 Access to the number plate lamp bulb

through the body section. Remove the lamp body.
5 Refitting is the reverse of the removal procedure.
6 For access to the bulb only, remove the two crosshead screws and take off the lens (photo).

31 Windscreen wiper motor and linkage (rear) - removal and refitting

1 Disconnect the battery earth lead.
2 Remove the wiper arm and blade.
3 Open the tailgate, and remove the tailgate trim panel.
4 Disconnect the wiring at the wiper motor, noting the respective position of the leads.
5 Remove the wiper spindle retaining nut and the three motor bracket retaining screws. Remove the motor and linkage assembly from the tailgate.
6 Remove the drive spindle nut and the three retaining bolts to detach the motor from the bracket.
7 Remove the circlip at the wiper spindle end and detach the linkage from the bracket.
8 Refitting is the reverse of the removal procedure, adjustment of motor bracket being made before the bolts are finally tightened.

32 Windscreen washer pump (rear) - removal and refitting

1 Disconnect the battery earth lead.
2 Open the tailgate and remove the spare wheel cover.
3 Remove the washer pipes and leads, noting their installed positions to prevent mix-up when refitting.
4 Remove the pump mounting screws and lift off the pump.
5 Refitting is the reverse of the removal procedure.

33 Windscreen washer nozzle (rear) - removal and refitting

1 Open the tailgate, remove the weather strip and pull down the headlining for access to the washer nozzle. Remove the nozzle.
2 Refitting is the reverse of the removal procedure.

34 Windscreen wiper motor and linkage (front) - removal and refitting

1 Disconnect the battery earth lead.
2 Remove the windscreen wiper arm and blades. (Refer to Section 40,

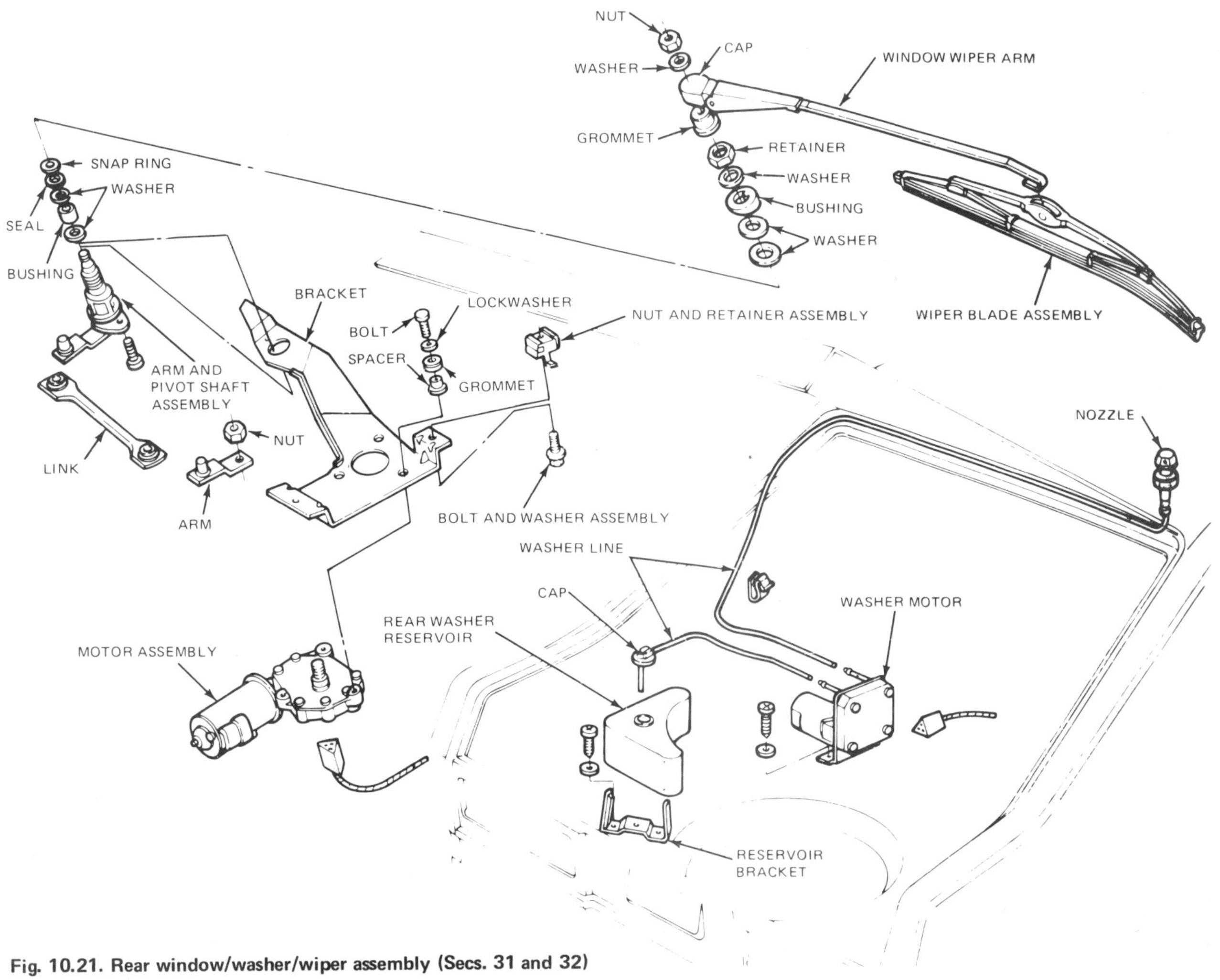

Fig. 10.21. Rear window/washer/wiper assembly (Secs. 31 and 32)

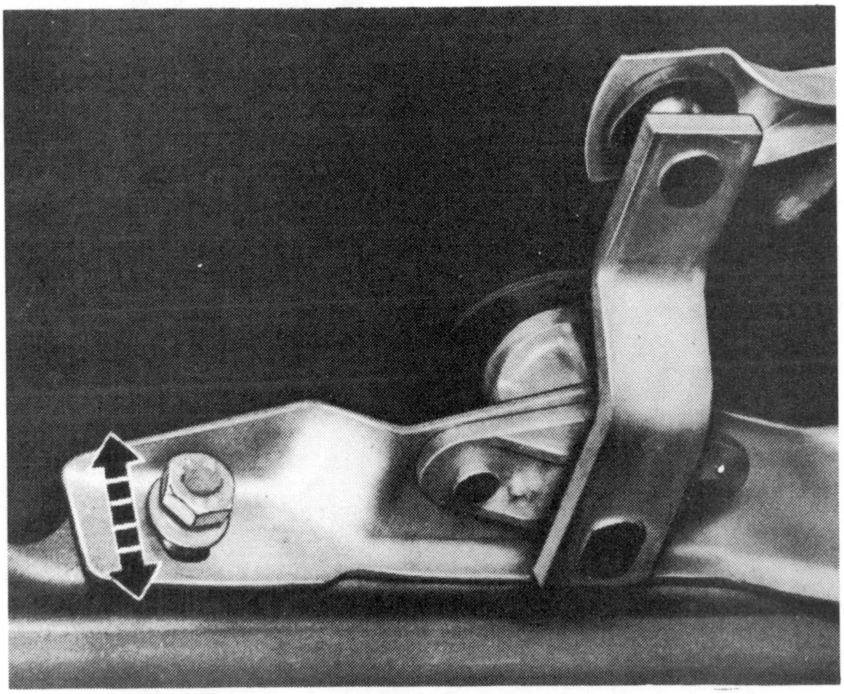

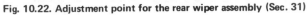

Fig. 10.22. Adjustment point for the rear wiper assembly (Sec. 31)

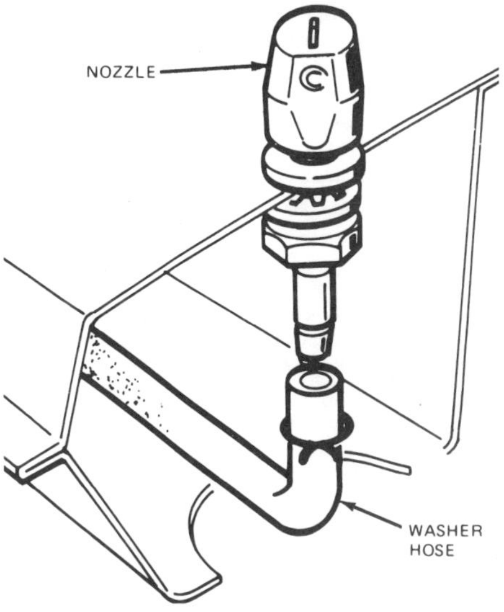

Fig. 10.23. Rear window washer nozzle (Sec. 33)

Fig. 10.24. Removing the windscreen wiper motor (Sec. 34)

if necessary).

3 Remove the air cleaner and disconnect the choke cable at the carburettor (Capri II only).

4 Remove the steering column shroud.

5 Remove the retaining screws, and pull the lower dash insulating panel and cover panel assembly clear of the dash panel.

6 Disconnect the cigar lighter wiring and withdraw the panel assembly, complete with choke cable, away from the vehicle.

7 Remove the instrument cluster bezel and the instrument cluster. Refer to Section 43, if necessary.

8 Remove the glovebox catch striker and glovebox assembly. Disconnect the light wiring.

9 Disconnect the cable from the heater controls.

10 Disconnect the driver's side demister tube connector from the heater box, and remove the connector and tube.

11 Disconnect and remove the driver's side face level vent tube.

12 Disconnect the wiring at the wiper motor and heater.

13 Remove the driver's side demister vent (1 screw).

14 Remove the wiper spindle retaining nuts, and the motor bracket retaining screw. Remove the motor and linkage from the vehicle.

15 If necessary, separate the motor from the linkage.

16 Refitting is the reverse of the removal procedure, but ensure that the heater control cable and the choke operating cable are correctly adjusted.

35.2 Removing the front washer pump leads (Capri II)

35 Windscreen washer pump (front) - removal and refitting

Capri II

1 The front windscreen washers on Capri II models are operated from a facia mounted wash/wipe switch (see Section 60), and an integral pump and reservoir mounted at the front right-hand side of the engine compartment.

2 To remove the pump and reservoir, pull off the electrical connections lift up the reservoir and disconnect the flexible pipe from the reservoir. The pump can be removed from the reservoir if necessary (photo).

Mercury Capri II

3 The front windscreen washers on Mercury Capri II models are operated from a floor mounted wash/wipe foot pump. The reservoir is mounted in the engine compartment.

4 To remove the washer pump, disconnect the battery ground cable then pull back the floor covering from around the washer pump.

5 Remove the two crosslead screws then disconnect the flexible hose and lead, and remove the pump.

6 Refitting is the reverse of the removal procedure.

36 Windscreen washer nozzles (front) - removal and refitting

1 Disconnect the battery earth lead.

2 Remove the retaining screws, withdraw the nozzles and disconnect the pipes.

3 Refitting is the reverse of the removal procedure.

37 Windscreen wiper mechanism - fault diagnosis and rectification

1 Should the windscreen wipers fail, or work very slowly, then check the terminals on the motor for loose connections, and make sure the insulation of all the wiring is not cracked or broken thus causing a short circuit. If this is in order then check the current the motor is taking by connecting an ammeter in the circuit and turning on the wiper switch. Consumption should be between 2.3 to 3.1 amps.

2 If no current is passing through the motor, check that the switch is operating correctly.

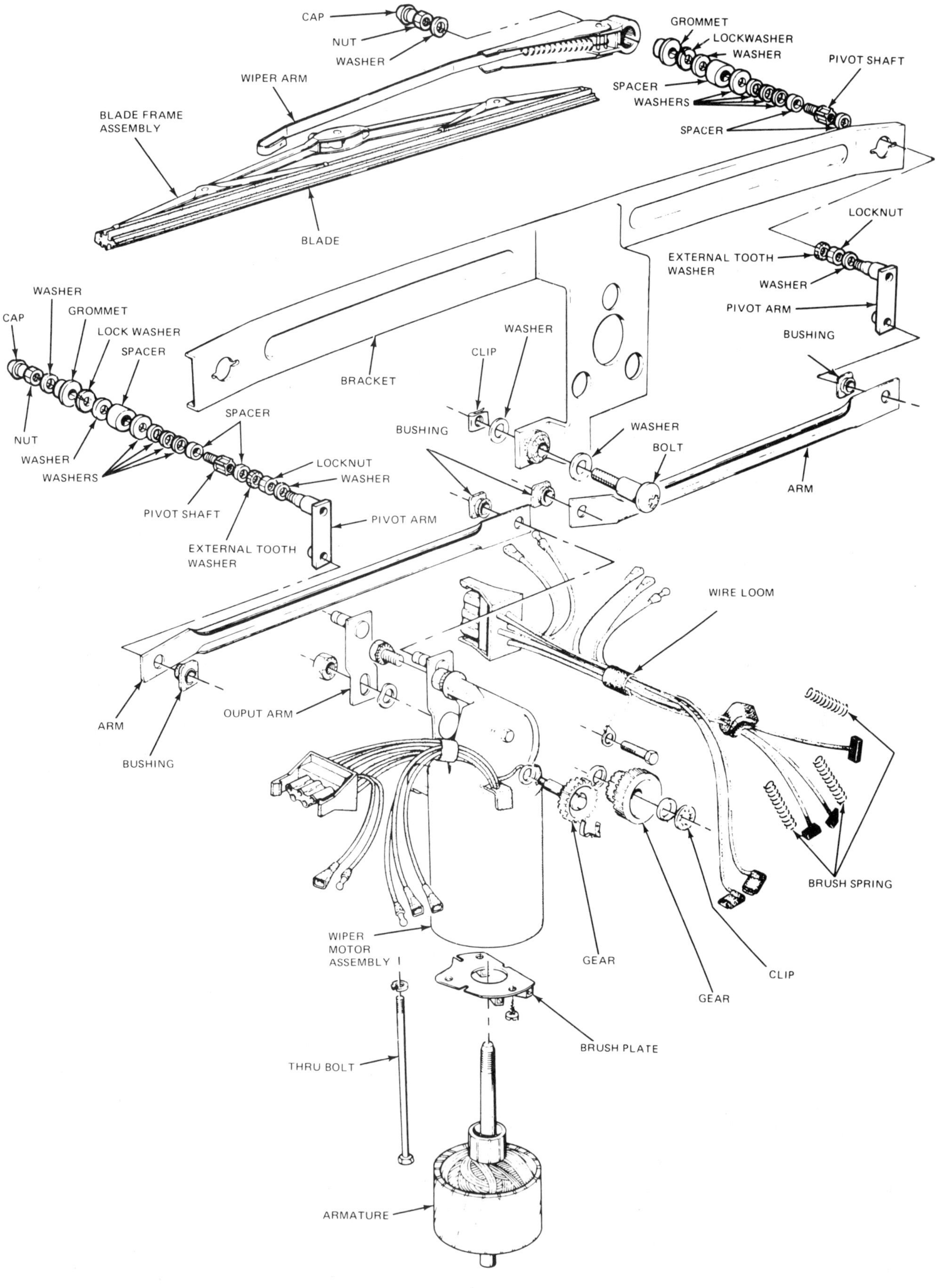

Fig. 10.25. Major parts of the windscreen wiper and linkage (Secs. 38 and 39)

3 If the wiper motor takes a very high current check the wiper blades for freedom of movement. If this is satisfactory check the gearbox cover and gear assembly for damage.
4 If the motor takes a very low current ensure that the battery is fully charged. Check the brush gear and ensure the brushes are bearing on the commutator. If not, check the brushes for freedom of movement and, if necessary, renew the tension springs. If the brushes are very worn they should be replaced with new ones. Check the armature by substitution if this unit is suspect.

38 Windscreen wiper motor - brush renewal

1 Remove the two motor case/gear housing screws and withdraw the case and armature together.
2 Withdraw the brushes from the holders and remove the springs.
3 Remove the three brush mounting plate to wiper gear housing screws. Pull the wiring plug out of the side of the housing and remove the brush mounting plate.
4 Remove the screw and earth wire in the gear housing cover plate. Loosen the second screw and slide the cover plate away.
5 Disconnect the white/green and black/green leads from the terminals on the switch cover assembly then remove the wiring assembly from the motor.
6 Disconnect the motor multi-pin connector from the harness and remove the motor feed wires and brushes.
7 Connect the replacement motor feed wire and brush assembly into the harness via the multi-pin connector.
8 Connect the black/green wire to the terminal marked 'black' and the white/green wire to the terminal marked 'green' on the switch cover assembly.
9 Slide the gear housing cover plate into position, ensuring that the wires are correctly positioned in the cut-out on the cover plate.

39 Windscreen wiper motor - dismantling and reassembly

1 Separate the motor from the linkage.
2 Remove the brushes, wiring harness and brush mounting plate, referring to the previous Section as necessary.
3 Remove the remaining screw securing the gear housing cover plate and switch assembly. Remove the assembly.
4 Remove the spring steel armature stop from the gear housing.
5 Remove the spring clip and washer which secure the pinion gear; withdraw the gear and washers.
6 Remove the nut securing the motor output arm. Remove the arm, spring and flat washers.
7 Remove the output gear, and the parking switch assembly and washer from the gear housing.
8 Reassembly is the reverse of the removal procedure, referring to the previous Section as necessary for the brush gear connections.

40 Windscreen wiper arms and blades - removal and refitting

1 To remove a wiper blade, raise the wiper arm away from the windscreen then, either slide the blade out of the hooked end of the arm or remove it from the spring clip in the centre of the blade. Refitting of the blade is straightforward (photo).
2 To remove a wiper arm, lift up the cap at the spindle and, remove the nut and carefully prise off the arm. When refitting, position the arm as necessary to obtain a satisfactory sweep on the windscreen (photo).

41 Horn - fault finding and rectification

1 If the horn works badly or fails completely, check the wiring leading to the horn plug located on the body panel next to the horn itself. Also check that the plug is properly pushed home and is in a clean condition free from corrosion etc.
2 Check that the horn is secure on its mounting and that there is nothing lying on the horn body.
3 If the fault is not an external one, remove the horn cover and check the leads inside the horn. If they are sound, check the contact breaker contacts. If these are burnt or dirty clean them with a fine file and wipe all traces of dirt and dust away with a petrol moistened rag.

42 Fuses

1 If a fuse blows, always trace and rectify the cause before renewing it with one of the same rating.
2 The fuse block is located within the engine compartment on the side apron.
3 The fuse ratings and circuits protected vary according to model and reference should be made to 'Specifications' Section at the beginning of this Chapter.

43 Instrument cluster - removal and refitting

Capri II

1 Disconnect the battery earth lead.
2 Remove the steering column shroud. The bottom half is retained by two screws and the top half can then be pushed out.
3 Remove eight screws from the lower dash trim panel, ease the panel over the ignition switch and allow it to hang freely.

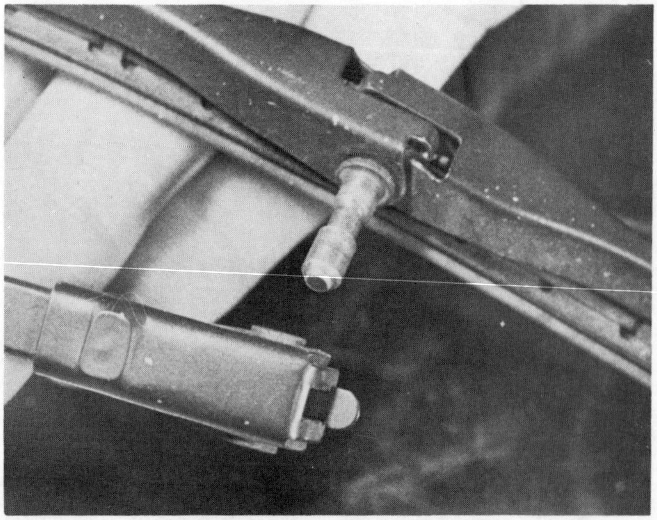

40.1 Spring clip type wiper blade attachment

40.2 Wiper arm securing nut

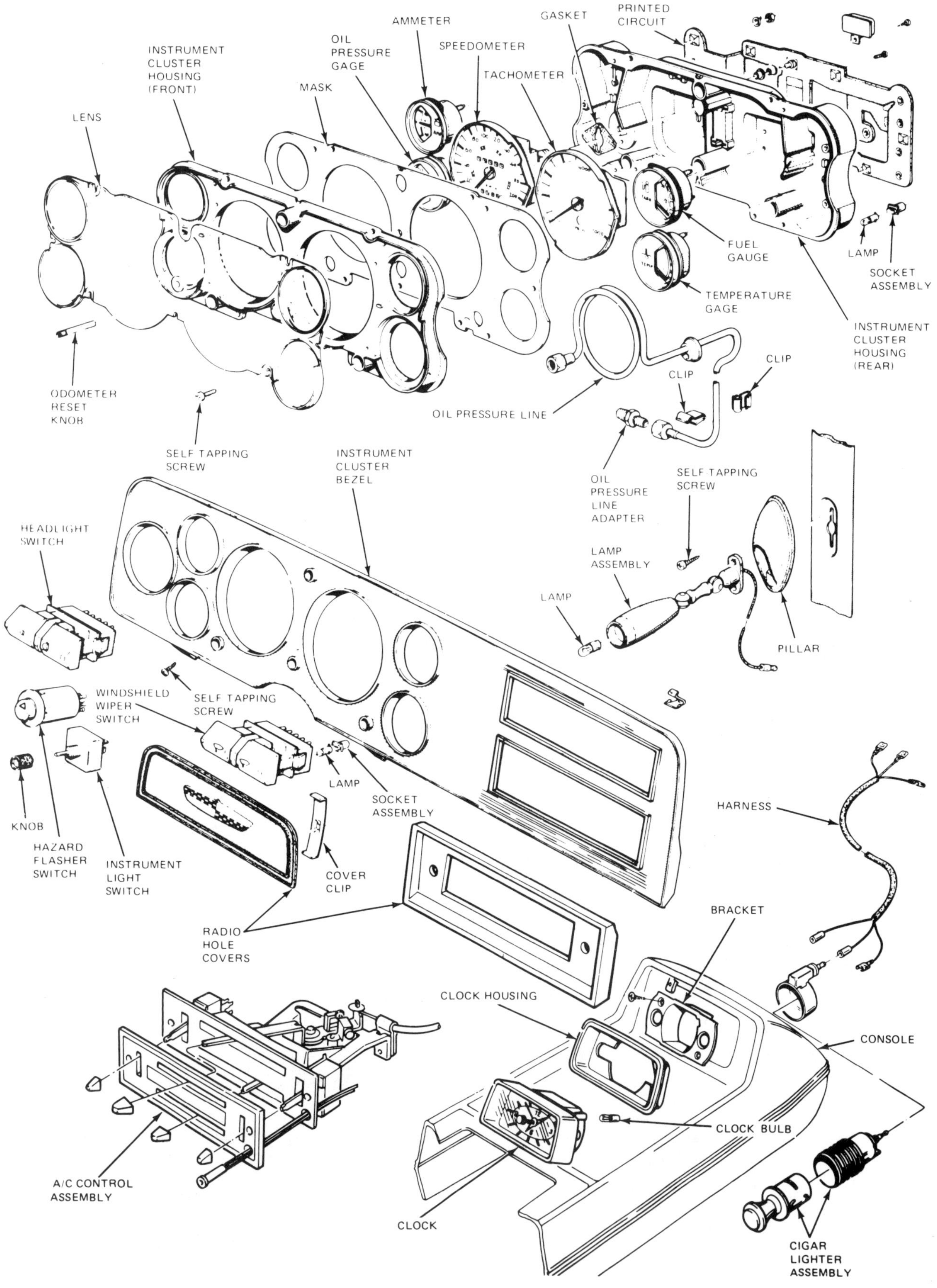

Fig. 10.26. Instrument cluster - Mercury Capri II with air conditioning (Sec. 43)
The rhd model is opposite hand in most respects

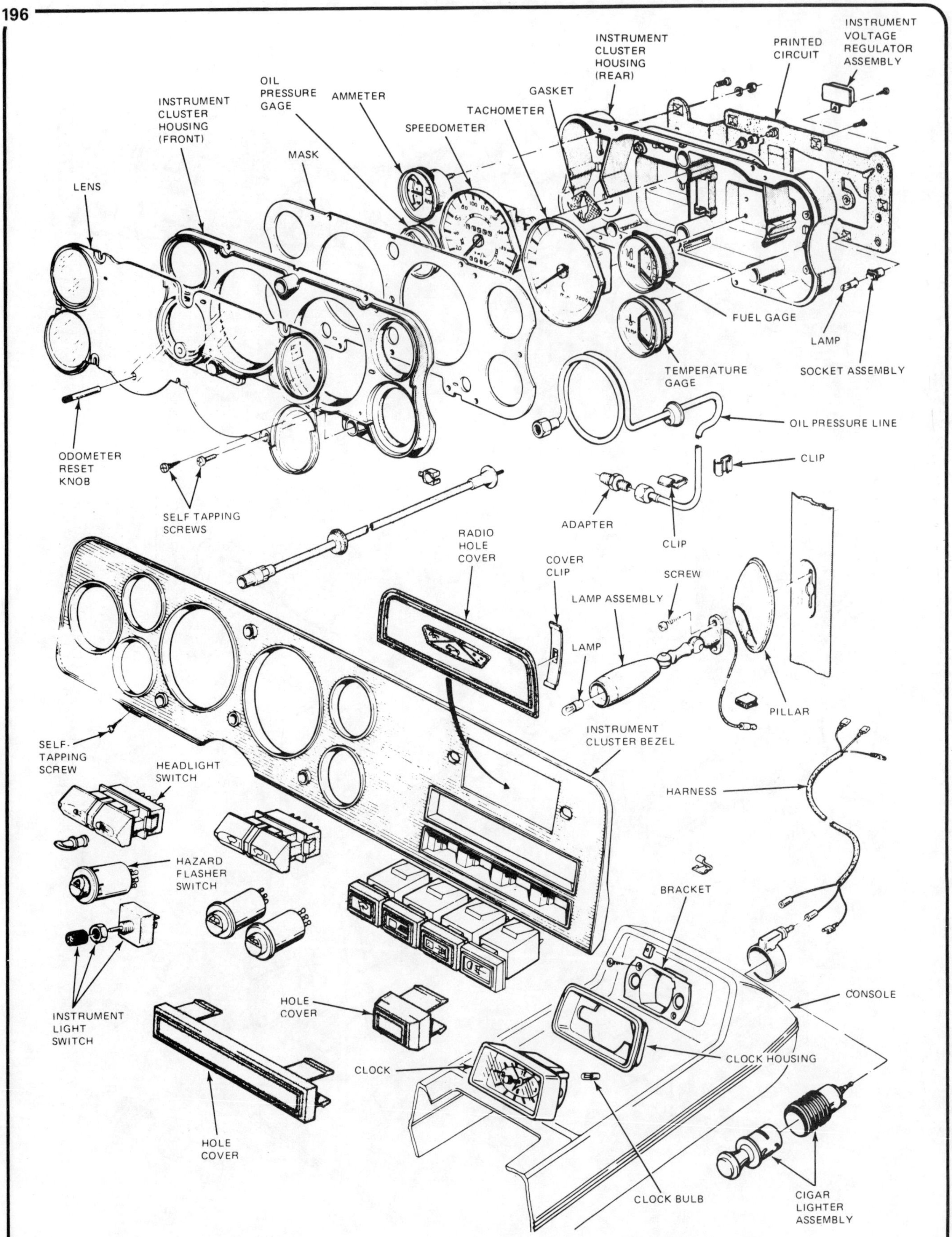

Fig. 10.27 Instrument cluster - Mercury Capri II without air conditioning (Sec. 43)

4 Where applicable, pull out the two radio control knobs, remove three screws and disconnect the switch multi-plugs. Remove the facia panel.
5 Remove the four instrument cluster retaining screws and ease the cluster forwards. Disconnect the speedometer cable, oil pressure gauge feed pipe (where applicable) and the wiring loom multi-plug.
6 Refitting is the reverse of the removal procedure.

Mercury Capri II (without air conditioning)

7 Follow the procedure given for the Capri II models with the following additions:

a) Take out the ashtray.
b) Withdraw the hazard flasher switch and disconnect the wiring.
c) Remove the direction indicator switch and allow it to hang by its leads.
d) Disconnect the cigar lighter and clock cable connectors, and completely remove the lower trim panel.
e) Pull off the instrument panel illumination control knob.
f) Remove the lower screws securing the instrument cluster bezel and release the bezel from its upper location by pulling down.

Also disconnect the seat belt warning light at the connector.

8 Refitting is the reverse of the removal procedure.

Mercury Capri II (with air conditioning)

9 Initially refer to paragraph 1 and 2 of this Section.
10 Remove the lower left side dash trim panel screws. Withdraw the hazard switch and disconnect the cable connector.
11 Remove the turn signal switch screws, leaving the switch hanging by the wiring harness.
12 Remove the two bottom screws on the right lower dash trim panel. Remove the air-conditioning panel assembly and remove the two screws securing the assembly to the dash.
13 Where applicable, pull the trim panel forwards and down, and remove the cigar lighter and rear window wash/wiper switch connectors. Remove the trim panel.
14 Pull out the panel illumination control knob and radio control knobs.
15 Now follow the procedure given in paragraph 7f) followed by paragraph 5.
16 Refitting is the reverse of the removal procedure.

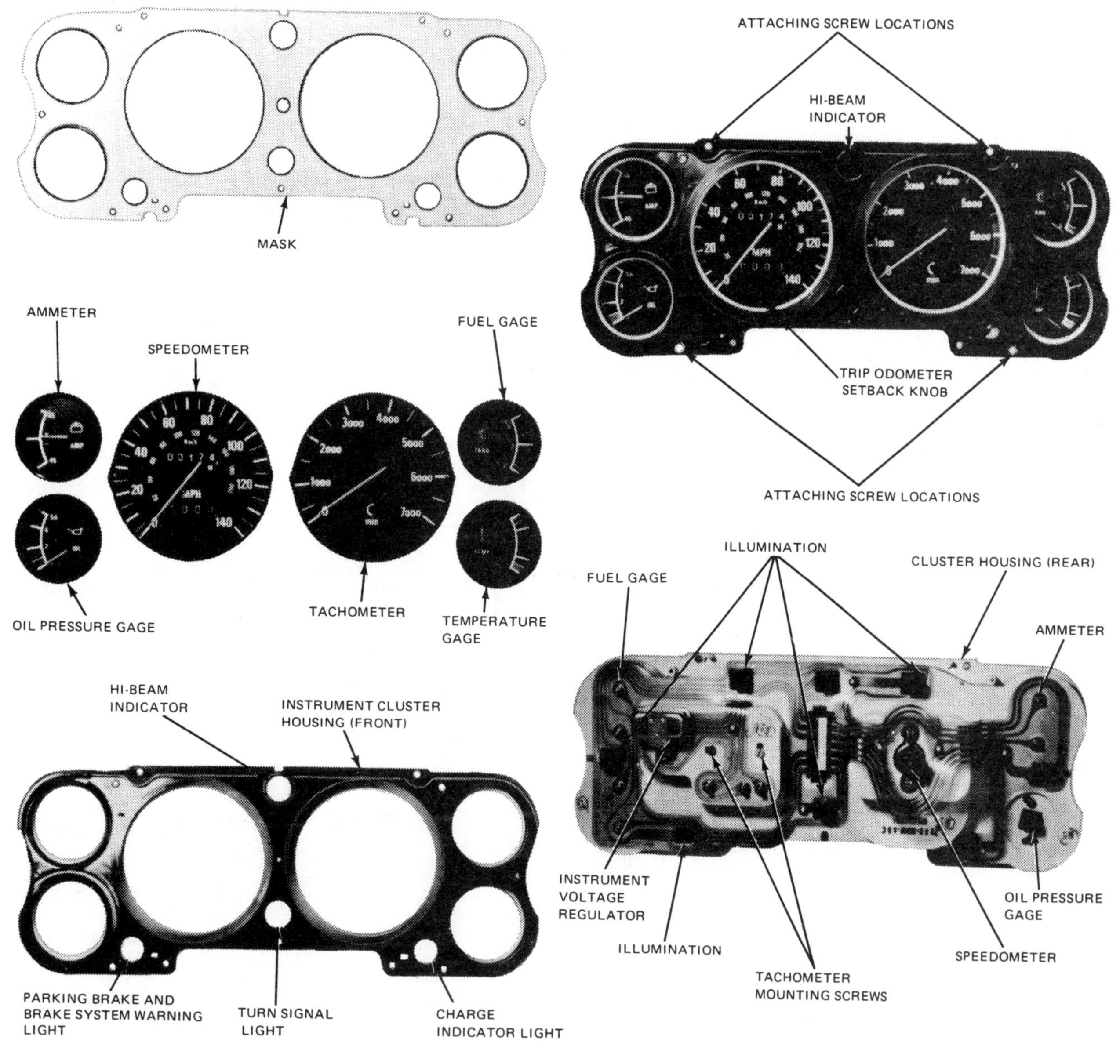

Fig. 10.28. The parts of the cluster assembly (Sec. 43)
(On right-hand drive models the speedometer and tachometer are reversed)

44 Clock (console mounted) - removal and refitting

Refer to the procedure given for removing the centre console in Chapter 12 where this item is listed.

45 Hazard warning switch - removal and refitting

1 Pull the switch from the lower dash trim panel and disconnect the wiring harness.
2 When refitting, connect the wiring harness and press the switch into the trim panel to retain it.

46 Steering column multi-function switch - removal and refitting

1 Disconnect the battery earth lead.
2 Remove the steering column shroud. The bottom half is retained by two screws and the top half can then be pulled out.
3 Remove the switch retaining screws, disconnect the multi-plug then detach the switch from the steering column.
4 Refitting is the reverse of the removal procedure.

47 Flasher unit

1 The flasher unit is mounted behind the lower dash trim panel and access can be gained by removing the panel.
2 In the event of failure of a particular piece of equipment always check the connecting wiring, bulbs and fuses before assuming that it is the relay or flasher unit that is at fault. Take the relay or flasher unit to your dealer for testing or check the circuit by substituting a new component.

48 Speedometer cable - renewal

1 Chock the front wheels, jack-up the rear of the car and support on firmly based stands.
2 Working under the car carefully remove the snap-ring that secures the speedometer cable to the transmission. Detach the cable.
3 Now working in the engine compartment remove the speedometer cable clip located on the engine bulkhead.
4 Ease the speedometer cable rubber grommet from the engine bulkhead.
5 Refer to Section 43 and move the instrument cluster by a sufficient amount to gain access to the rear of the speedometer.
6 Detach the cable from the rear of the speedometer.
7 Refitting is the reverse sequence to removal. For reliable operation it is very important that there are no sharp bends in the cable run.

49 Instrument voltage regulator - removal and refitting

1 Remove the instrument panel cluster as described in Section 43.
2 Unscrew and remove the single screw that retains the instrument voltage regulator to the rear of the instrument panel and withdraw the regulator.
3 Refitting is a reversal of the removal procedure.

50 Cigar lighter - removal and refitting

1 Initially proceed as described in paragraph 1 to 4 of Section 56.
2 Unclip the cigar lighter illumination bulb from the unit body.
3 Working from behind the instrument panel, unscrew and remove the lighter body. Remove the front Section through the instrument panel.
4 Refitting is the reverse of the removal procedure.

51 Ignition switch - removal and refitting

1 Disconnect the battery earth lead.
2 Remove the steering column shroud. The bottom half is retained by two screws and the top half can then be pulled out.
3 Set the ignition key to the 'O' position.
4 Note the location of the cables at the ignition switch and then detach the cables.
5 Undo and remove the two screws that secure the ignition switch to the lock. Lift away the switch.
6 Refitting the ignition switch is the reverse of the removal procedure.

52 Steering column lock (up to mid 1976) - removal and refitting

1 Disconnect the battery earth lead.
2 Remove the steering column shroud. The bottom half is retained by two screws and the top half can then be pushed out.
3 Undo and remove the two screws that secure the upper steering column support bracket.
4 Turn the column until it is possible to gain access to the headless bolts.
5 Note the location of the cables to the ignition switch terminals and lock body, and then detach the cables.
6 Using a suitable diameter drill remove the headless bolts that clamp the lock to the steering column. Alternatively use a centre punch to rotate the bolts.
7 Lift away the lock assembly and clamp bracket.
8 Refitting the lock assembly is the reverse sequence to removal. Make sure that the pawl enters the steering shaft. It will be necessary to use new shear bolts which must be tightened equally before the heads are separated from the shank.
9 For procedure for later models, see Chapter 13.

53 Key-in-lock warning buzzer (Mercury Capri II) - removal and refitting

1 Disconnect the battery ground lead.
2 Remove the lower left-hand dash trim panel.
3 Disconnect the buzzer connector (located on the steering column bracket) and remove the buzzer retaining scew.
4 Refitting is the reverse of the removal procedure.

54 Door pillar switches - removal and refitting

1 Disconnect the battery earth lead.
2 Prise the appropriate switch out of the door pillar, disconnect the lead and remove the switch.
3 Refitting is the reverse of the removal procedure.

55 Interior light - removal and refitting

1 To remove the interior light lens, switch, and/or body, carefully prise the lens away from the light body.

56 Map light (Mercury Capri II) - removal and refitting

1 Disconnect the battery earth lead.
2 Remove the steering column shroud. The bottom half is retained by two screws and the top half can then be pushed out.
3 Remove the screws retaining the direction indicator switch and allow the switch to hang by the wiring harness.
4 Remove the lower dash panel screws, pull the panel forwards and downwards to gain access to the clock and cigar lighter cable connectors. Disconnect the cables and remove the trim panel.
5 Remove the glovebox (refer to Chapter 12, if necessary).
6 Disconnect the map light harness at the harness connector under the instrument panel crash pad on the right-hand side.
7 Remove the retaining screws, and remove the map light complete with harness. A length of cord can be tied to the end of the harness lead and drawn through the pillar to act as an aid to installation.
8 Refitting is the reverse of the removal procedure.

57 Instrument illumination and warning lamp bulbs (general) - renewal

1 Refer to Section 43 and move the instrument cluster by a sufficient amount to gain access to the bulb holder(s),
2 Extract the appropriate bulb from its holder.

Fig. 10.29. Door pillar switches (Sec. 54)

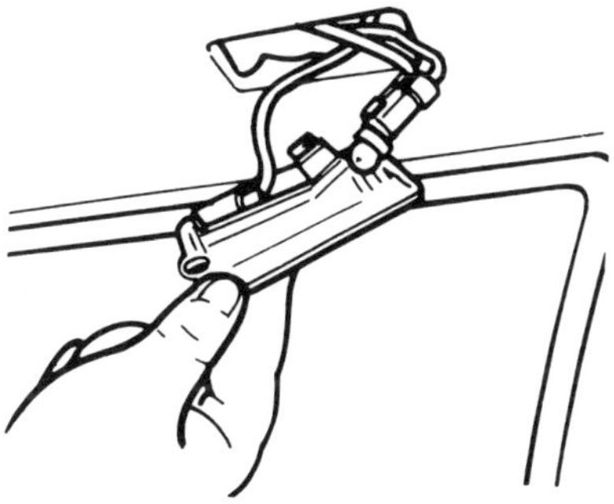
Fig. 10.30. Interior light (Sec. 55)

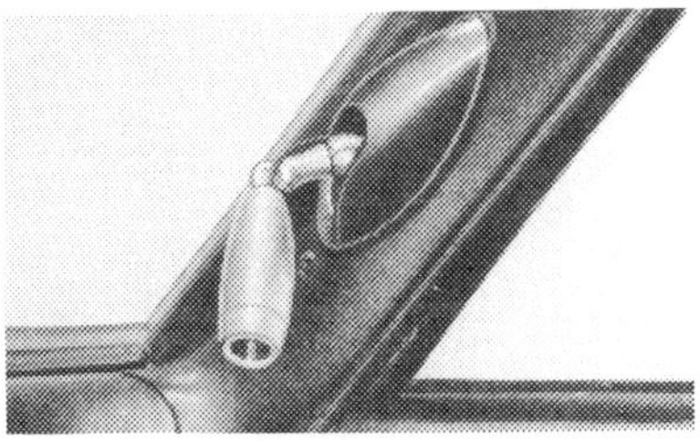
Fig. 10.31. Map light (Sec. 56)

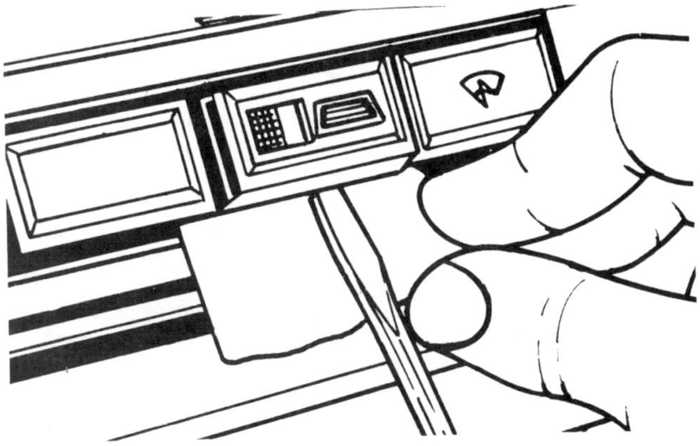
Fig. 10.32. Removing a facia mounted heated rear window warning light bulb or a facia mounted windscreen washer switch (Secs. 58 and 59)

Fig. 10.33. Removing the luggage compartment lamp (Sec. 63)

3 Refitting is the reverse of the removal procedure.

58 Handbrake warning light bulb - renewal

1 Disconnect the battery earth lead.
2 Remove the steering column shroud. The bottom half is retained by two screws and the top half can then be pushed out.
3 Remove the ashtray.
4 Remove all the screws along the upper edge and glove compartment edge of the lower panel, and also those on the lower edge (outboard of the steering column) so that the lower panel can be pulled down and clear of the steering lock.
5 Reach up under the facia panel and apply sideways pressure to the bulb holder to release it from the instrument cluster.
6 Installation is the reverse of the removal procedure, but ensure that the bulb holder electrical contacts are horizontal to mate with the printed circuit contacts.

59 Facia mounted heated rear window warning light bulb - renewal

1 Using a piece of thick paper or a piece of card to prise against, use a screwdriver to prise out the switch assembly from the multi-plug.
2 Withdraw the bulb holder and remove the bulb.
3 Installation is the reverse of the removal procedure.

60 Facia mounted heated rear window switch and windscreen washer switch (front) - removal and refitting

1 Follow the procedure given in the previous Section for warning light bulb renewal.

61 Rear window washer and wiper switches - removal and refitting

1 Remove the lower dash trim panel, as described in Section 43.
2 Disconnect the switch leads then press the switch(es) out of the trim panel.
3 Installation is the reverse of the removal procedure.

62 Heated rear window switch (Mercury Capri II with air-conditioning) - removal and refitting

1 Remove the two screws securing the air-conditioning assembly to the lower dash panel.
2 Partially pull out the assembly, disconnect the bulb housing connectors and withdraw the plastic bulb housing.
3 Remove the switch knob, remove the switch retaining capscrew and remove the switch.
4 Refitting is the reverse of the removal procedure.

63 Luggage compartment lamp - removal and refitting

1 Disconnect the battery earth lead.
2 Open the tailgate and pull out the lamp from the trim panel.
3 Note the relative positions of the electrical connections then remove them from the lamp.
4 Refitting is the reverse of the removal procedure.

64 Light and windscreen wiper (front) switches - removal and refitting

1 Disconnect the battery earth lead.
2 Slacken the three screws on the lower panel.
3 Fully depress one of the switches of the pair to be removed, then insert a suitably cranked tool such as a piece of bent rod into the exposed hole in the switch centre web (Fig. 10.34).
4 Hold down the lower panel and gently pull out the switches.
5 When refitting, first connect the plug, then install the switch and tighten the parcel screws.
6 Finally reconnect the battery earth lead.

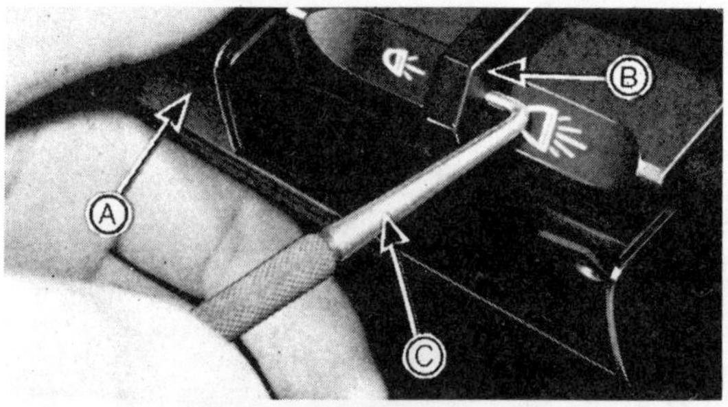

A Lower panel

B Centre web

C Cranked tool

Fig. 10.34. Light and windscreen wiper (front) switch removal (Sec. 64)

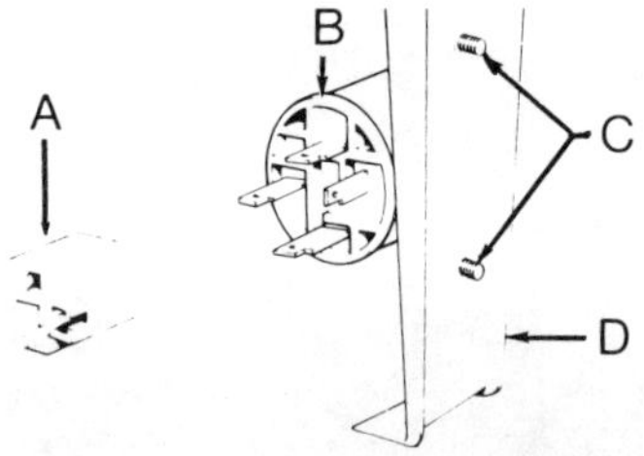

Fig. 10.35. Heated rear window relay (Sec. 65)

A Multi-plug
B Relay
C Retaining screws
D Bracket

65 Heated rear window relay - removal and refitting

1 Disconnect the battery earth lead.
2 Remove the steering column shroud. The bottom half is retained by two screws and the top half can then be pushed out.
3 Remove the lower panel retaining screws, disconnect the cigar lighter and remove the panel.
4 Disconnect the multi-plug and remove the relay.
5 Installation is the reverse of the removal procedure.

66 Seat belt/starter interlock system

1 This system is installed on North American cars (not Canada) and is designed to prevent operation of the car unless the front seat belts have been fastened.
2 If either of the front seats is occupied and the seat belts have not been fastened, then, as the ignition key is turned to the 'II' (ignition on) position, a warning lamp will flash and a buzzer will sound.
3 If the warning is ignored, further turning of the key to the start position will not actuate the starter motor.
4 In an emergency, and in the event of a failure in the system, an override switch is located under the bonnet. One depression of the switch will permit one starting sequence of the engine without the front seat belts being fastened.
5 If a fault develops in the system, first check the fuse and then the security of all leads and connections.

67 Seat belt warning buzzer (Mercury Capri II) - removal and refitting

1 Initially proceed as described in paragraph 1 through 4 of Section 56.
2 Remove the buzzer-to-steering column mounting screw(s), disconnect the wiring and remove the buzzer.
3 Refitting is the reverse of the removal procedure.

68 Radios and tape players - fitting (general)

A radio or tape player is an expensive item to buy and will only give its best performance if fitted properly. It is useless to expect concert hall performance from a unit that is suspended from the dash panel on string with its speaker resting on the back seat or parcel shelf! If you do not wish to do the installation yourself there are many in-car entertainment specialists' who can do the fitting for you.

Make sure the unit purchased is of the same polarity as the car, and ensure that units with adjustable polarity are correctly set before commencing installation.

It is difficult to give specific information with regard to fitting, as final positioning of the radio/tape player, speakers and aerial is entirely a matter of personal preference. However, the following paragraphs give guidelines to follow, which are relevent to all installations.

Radios

Most radios are a standardised size of 7 inches wide, by 2 inches deep - this ensures that they will fit into the radio aperture provided in most cars. If your car does not have such an aperture, then the radio must be fitted in a suitable position either in, or beneath, the dashpanel. Alternatively, a special console can be purchased which will fit between the dashpanel and the floor, or on the transmission tunnel. These consoles can also be used for additional switches and instrumentation if required. Where no radio aperture is provided, the following points should be borne in mind before deciding exactly where to fit the unit:

a) The unit must be within easy reach of the driver wearing a seat belt.
b) The unit must not be mounted in close proximity to an electric tachometer, the ignition switch and its wiring, or the flasher unit and associated wiring.
c) The unit must be mounted within reach of the aerial lead, and in such a place that the aerial lead will not have to be routed near the components detailed in the preceding paragraph 'b'.
d) The unit should not be positioned in a place where it might cause injury to the car occupants in an accident; for instance, under the dashpanel above the driver's or passengers' legs.
e) The unit must be fitted really securely.

Some radios will have mounting brackets provided together with instructions: others will need to be fitted using drilled and slotted metal strips, bent to form mounting brackets - these strips are available from most accessory shops. The unit must be properly earthed, by fitting a separate earthing lead between the casing of the radio and the vehicle frame.

Use the radio manufacturers' instructions when wiring the radio into the vehicle's electrical system. If no instructions are available refer to the relevant wiring diagram to find the location of the radio 'feed' connection in the vehicle's wiring circuit. A 1-2 amp 'in-line' fuse must be fitted in the radio's 'feed' wire - a choke may also be necessary (see next Section).

The type of aerial used, and its fitted position is a matter of personal preference. In general the taller the aerial, the better the reception. It is best to fit a fully retractable aerial - especially, if a mechanical car-wash is used or if you live in an area where cars tend to be vandalised. In this respect electric aerials which are raised and lowered automatically when switching the radio on or off are convenient, but are more likely to give trouble than the manual type.

When choosing a site for the aerial the following points should be considered:

a) The aerial lead should be as short as possible - this means that the aerial should be mounted at the front of the car.
b) The aerial must be mounted as far away from the distributor and HT leads as possible.
c) The part of the aerial which protrudes beneath the mounting point must not foul the roadwheels, or anything else.
d) If possible the aerial should be positioned so that the coaxial lead does not have to be routed through the engine compartment.
e) The plane of the panel on which the aerial is mounted should not be so steeply angled that the aerial cannot be mounted vertically (in relation to the 'end-on' aspect of the car). Most aerials have a small amount of adjustment available.

Having decided on a mounting position, a relatively large hole will have to be made in the panel. The exact size of the hole will depend upon the specific aerial being fitted, although, generally, the hole required is of ¾ inch (19 mm) diameter. On metal bodied cars, a 'tank-cutter' of the relevant diameter is the best tool to use for making the hole. This tool needs a small diameter pilot hole drilled through the panel, through which, the tool clamping bolt is inserted. When the hole has been made the raw edges should be de-burred with a file and then painted, to prevent corrosion.

Fit the aerial according to the manufacturer's instructions. If the aerial is very tall, or if it protrudes beneath the mounting panel for a considerable distance it is a good idea to fit a stay between the aerial and the vehicle frame. This stay can be manufactured from the slotted and drilled metal strips previously mentioned. The stay should be securely screwed or bolted in place. For best reception it is advisable to fit an earth lead between the aerial and the vehicle frame.

It will probably be necessary to drill one or two holes through bodywork panels in order to feed the aerial lead into the interior of the car. Where this is the case ensure that the holes are fitted with rubber grommets to protect the cable, and to stop possible entry of water.

Positioning and fitting of the speaker depends mainly on its type. Generally, the speaker is designed to fit directly into the aperture already provided in the car (usually in the shelf behind the rear seats, or in the top of the dashpanel). Where this is the case, fitting the speaker is just a matter of removing the protective grille from the aperture and screwing or bolting the speaker in place. Take great care not to damage the speaker diaphragm whilst doing this. It is a good idea to fit a 'gasket' between the speaker frame and the mounting panel, in order to prevent vibration - some speakers will already have such a gasket fitted.

If a 'pod' type speaker was supplied with the radio, the best acoustic results will normally be obtained by mounting it on the shelf behind the rear seat. The pod can be secured to the mounting panel with self-tapping screws.

When connecting a rear mounted speaker to the radio, the wires should be routed through the vehicle beneath the carpets or floor mats - preferably the middle, or along the side of the floorpan, where they will not be trodden on by passengers. Make the relevant connections as directed by the radio manufacturer.

By now you will have several yards of additional wiring in the car, use PVC tape to secure this wiring out of harm's way. Do not leave electrical leads dangling. Ensure that all new electrical connections are properly made (wires twisted together will not do) and completely secure.

The radio should now be working, but before you pack away your tools it will be necessary to 'trim' the radio to the aerial. If specific instructions are not provided by the radio manufacturer, proceed as follows. Find a station with a low signal strength on the medium-wave band, slowly, turn the trim screw of the radio in, or out, until the loudest reception of the selected station is obtained - the set is then trimmed to the aerial.

Tape players

Fitting instructions for both cartridge and cassette stereo tape players are the same and in general the same rules apply as when fitting a radio. Tape players are not usually prone to electrical interference like radio - although it can occur - so positioning is not so critical. If possible the player should be mounted on an 'even-keel'. Also, it must be possible for a driver wearing a seat belt to reach the unit in order to change or turn over tapes.

For the best results from speakers designed to be recessed into a panel, mount them so that the back of the speaker protrudes into an enclosed chamber within the car (eg; door interiors or the boot cavity).

To fit recessed type speakers in the front doors first check that there is sufficient room to mount the speakers in each door without it fouling the latch or window winding mechanism. Hold the speaker against the skin of the door, and draw a line around the periphery of the speaker. With the speaker removed draw a second 'cutting' line, within the first, to allow enough room for the entry of the speaker back, but at the same time providing a broad seat for the speaker flange. When you are sure that the 'cutting-line' is correct, drill a series of holes around its periphery. Pass a hacksaw blade through one of the holes and then cut through the metal between the holes until the centre section of the panel falls out.

De-burr the edges of the hole and then paint the raw metal to prevent corrosion. Cut a corresponding hole in the door trim panel - ensuring that it will be completely covered by the speaker grille. Now drill a hole in the door edge and a corresponding hole in the door surround. These holes are to feed the speaker leads through - so fit grommets. Pass the speaker leads through the door trim, door skin and out through the holes in the side of the door and door surround. Refit the door trim panel and then secure the speaker to the door using self-tapping screws. Note: If the speaker is fitted with a shield to prevent water dripping on it, ensure that this shield is at the top.

Pod type speakers can be fastened to the shelf behind the rear seat, or anywhere else offering a corresponding mounting point on each side of the car. If the pod speakers are mounted on each side of the shelf behind the rear seat, it is a good idea to drill several large diameter holes through to the boot cavity beneath each speaker - this will improve the sound reproduction. Pod speakers sometimes offer a better reproduction quality if they face the rear window - which then acts as a reflector - so it is worthwhile to do a little experimenting before finally fixing the speaker.

69 Radios and tape players - suppression of interference (general)

To eliminate buzzes and other unwanted noises, costs very little and is not as difficult as sometimes thought. With a modicum of common sense and patience and following the instructions in the following paragraphs, interference can be virtually eliminated.

The first cause for concern is the generator. The noise this makes over the radio is like an electric mixer and the noise speeds up when you rev up (if you wish to prove the point, you can remove the drive-belt and try it). The remedy for this is simple; connect a 1.0 uf-3.0 uf capacitor between earth, probably the bolt that holds down the generator base, and the *large* terminal on the dynamo or alternator. This is most important for if you connect it to the small terminal, you will probably damage the generator permanently (see Fig. 10.36).

A second common cause of electrical interference is the ignition system. Here a 1.0 ohm capacitor must be connected between earth and the 'SW' or '+' terminal on the coil (see Fig 10.37). This may stop the tick-tick-tick sound that comes over the speaker. Next comes the spark itself.

There are several ways of curing interference from the ignition HT system. One is to use carbon film HT lead but these have a tendency to 'snap' inside and you don't know then, why you are firing on only half your cylinders. So the second, and more successful method is to use resistive spark plug caps (see Fig. 10.38) of about 10,000 ohm to 15,000 ohm resistance. If, due to lack of room, these cannot be used, an alternative is to use 'in-line' suppressors (Fig 10.38) - if the interference is not too bad, you may get away with only one suppressor in the coil to distributor line. If the interference does continue (a 'clacking' noise) then doctor all HT leads.

At this stage it is advisable to check that the radio is well earthed, also the aerial, and to see that the aerial plug is pushed well into the set and that the radio is properly trimmed (see preceding Section). In addition, check that the wire which supplies the power to the set is as short as possible and does not wander all over the car. At this stage it is a good idea to check that the fuse is of the correct rating. For most sets this will be about 1 to 2 amps.

At this point the more usual causes of interference have been suppressed. If the problem still exists, a look at the causes of interference may help to pinpoint the component generating the stray electrical discharges.

The radio picks up electromagnetic waves in the air; now some are made by radio stations and other broadcasters and some, not wanted, are made by the car. The home made signals are produced by stray electrical discharges floating around the car. Common producers of these signals are electric motors; ie, the windshield wipers, electric screen washers, electric window winders, heater fan or an electric aerial if fitted. Other sources of interference are electric fuel pumps, flashing turn signals, and instruments. The remedy for these cases is shown in Fig 10.39 for an electric motor whose interference is not too bad and Fig 10.40 for instrument suppression. Turn signals are not normally suppressed. In recent years, radio manufacturer's have included in the line (live) of the radio, in addition to the fuse, an 'in-line' choke. If your installation lacks one of these, put one in as shown in Fig 10.41.

All the foregoing components are available from radio shops or accessory shops. For a transistor radio, a 2A choke should be adequate If you have an electric clock fitted this should be suppressed by connecting a 0.5 uf capacitor directly across it as shown for a motor in Fig 10.39.

If after all this, you are still experiencing radio interference, first assess how bad it is, for the human ear can filter out unobtrusive unwanted noises quite easily. But if you are still adamant about eradicating the noise, then continue.

As a first step, a few 'experts' seem to favour a screen between the radio and the engine. This is O.K. as far as it goes, literally! - for the whole set is screened and if interference can get past that then a small piece of aluminium is not going to stop it.

A more sensible way of screening is to discover if interference is

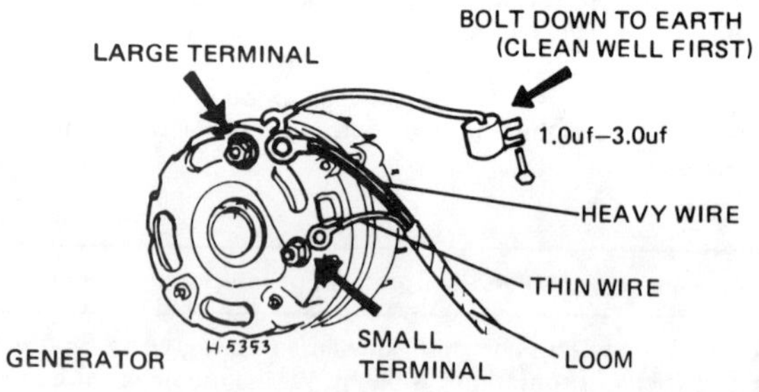

Fig. 10.36. The correct way to connect a capacitor to the generator

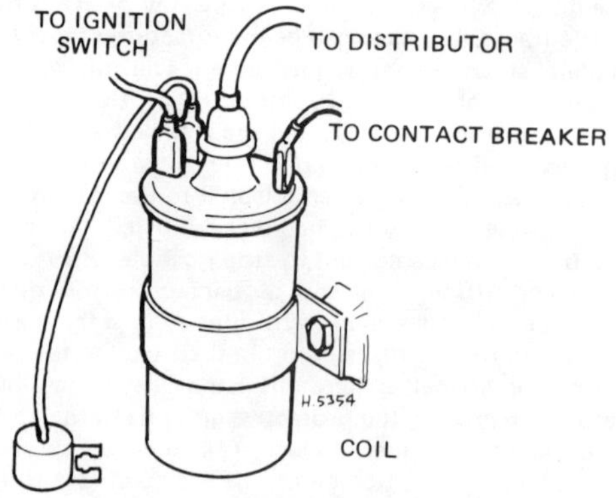

Fig. 10.37. The capacitor must be connected to the ignition switch side of the coil

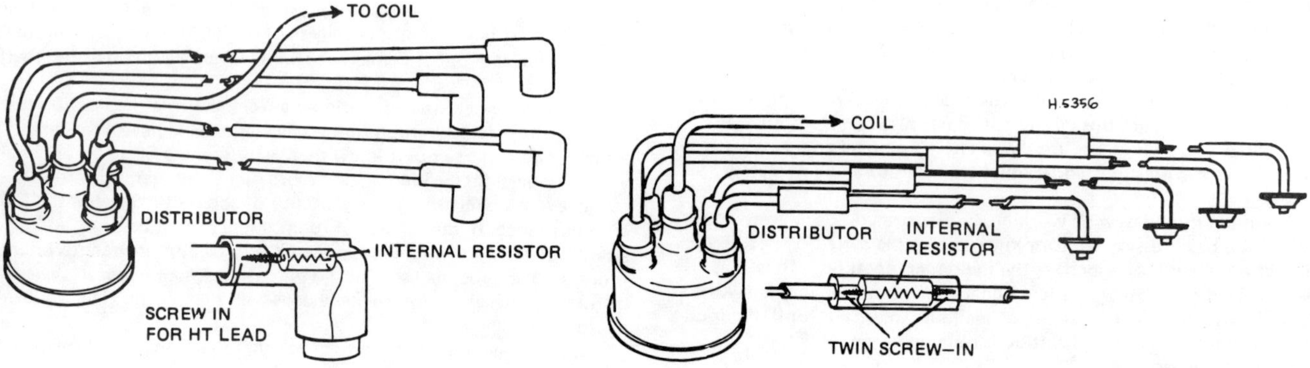

Resistive spark plug caps

Fig. 10.38. Ignition HT lead suppressors

'In-line' suppressors

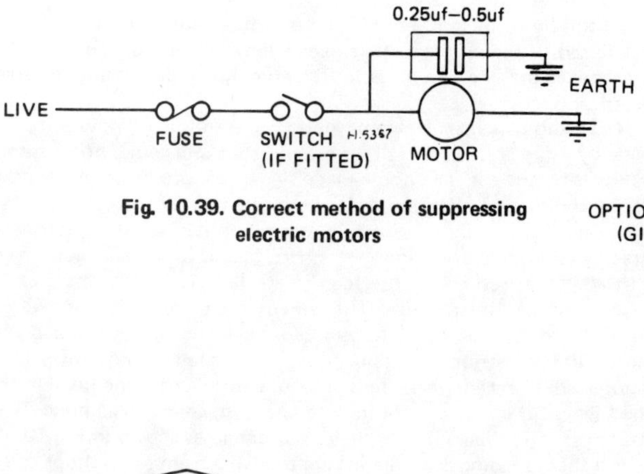

Fig. 10.39. Correct method of suppressing electric motors

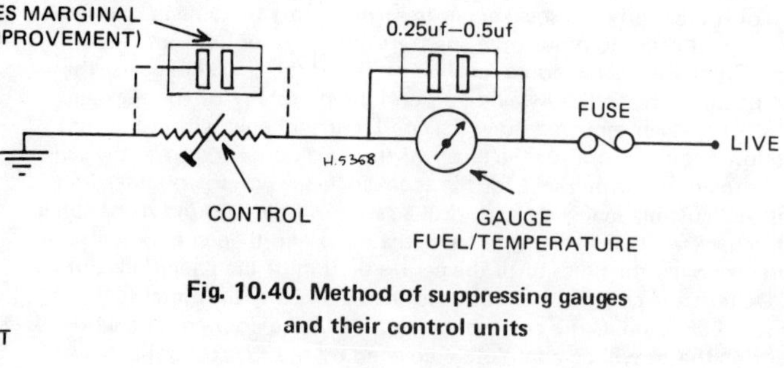

Fig. 10.40. Method of suppressing gauges and their control units

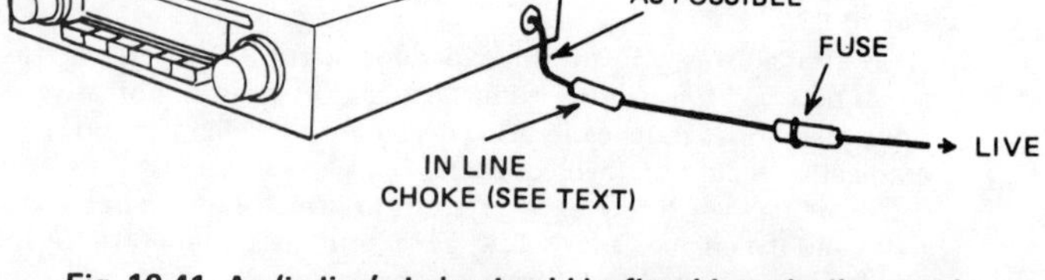

Fig. 10.41. An 'in-line' choke should be fitted into the live supply lead as close to the unit as possible

coming down the wires. First, take the live lead; interference can get between the set and the choke (hence the reason for keeping the wires short). One remedy here is to screen the wire and this is done by buying screened wire and fitting that. The loudspeaker lead could be screened also to prevent 'pick-up' getting back to the radio - although this is unlikely.

Without doubt, the worst source of radio interference comes from the ignition HT leads, even if they have been suppressed. The ideal way of suppressing these is to slide screening tubes over the leads themselves. As this is impractical, we can place an aluminium shield over the majority of the lead areas. In a vee - or twin-cam engine, this is relatively easy but for a straight engine the results are not particularly good.

Now for the really impossible cases, here are a few tips to try out. Where metal comes into contact with metal, an electrical disturbance is caused which is why good clean connections are essential. To remove interference due to overlapping or butting panels you must bridge the join with a wide braided earth strap (like that from the frame to the engine/transmission). The most common moving parts that could create noise and should be strapped are, in order of importance:

a) Silencer to frame.
b) Exhaust pipe to engine block and frame.
c) Air cleaner to frame.
d) Front and rear bumpers to frame.
e) Steering column to frame.
f) Hood and trunk lids to frame.
g) Hood frame to frame on soft tops.

These faults are most pronounced when (1) the engine is idling, (2) labouring under load. Although the moving parts are already connected with nuts, bolts, etc, these do tend to rust and corrode, thus creating a high resistance interference source.

If you have a 'ragged' sounding pulse when mobile, this could be wheel or tyre static. This can be cured by buying some anti-static powder and sprinkling it liberally inside the tyres.

If the interference takes the shape of a high pitched screaching noise that changes its note when the car is in motion and only comes now and then, this could be related to the aerial, especially if it is of the telescopic or whip type. This source can be cured quite simply by pushing a small rubber ball on top of the aerial (yes, really!) as this breaks the electric field before it can form; but it would be much better to buy yourself a new aerial of a reputable brand. If, on the other hand, you are getting a loud rushing sound every time you brake, then this is brake static. This effect is most prominent on hot dry days and is cured only by fitting a special kit, which is quite expensive.

In conclusion, it is pointed out that it is relatively easy, and therefore cheap to eliminate 95 per cent of all noises, but to eliminate the final 5 per cent is time and money consuming. It is up to the individual to decide if it is worth it. Please remember also, that you will not get concert hall performance from a cheap radio.

Finally at the beginning of this Section are mentioned tape players; these are not usually affected by interference but in a very bad case, the best remedies are the first three suggestions plus using a 3 - 5 amp choke in the 'live' line and in incurable cases screen the live and speaker wires.

Note: If your car is fitted with electronic ignition, then it is not recommended that either the spark plug resistors nor the ignition coil capacitor be fitted as these may damage the system. Most electronic ignition units have buit-in suppression and should, therefore, not cause interference.

70 Fault diagnosis - Electrical system

Symptom	Reason/s
No voltage at starter motor	Battery discharged. Battery defective internally. Battery terminal leads loose or earth lead not securely attached to body. Loose or broken connections in starter motor circuit. Starter motor switch or solenoid faulty.
Voltage at starter motor: faulty motor	Starter motor pinion jammed in mesh with flywheel gear ring. Starter brushes badly worn, sticking, or brush wires loose. Commutator dirty, worn or burnt. Starter motor armature faulty. Field coils earthed.
Electrical defects	Battery in discharged condition. Starter brushes badly worn, sticking, or brush wires loose. Loose wires in starter motor circuit.
Dirt or oil on drive gear	Starter motor pinion sticking on the screwed sleeve.
Mechanical damage	Pinion or flywheel gear teeth broken or worn.
Lack of attention or mechanical damage	Pinion or flywheel gear teeth broken or worn. Starter drive main spring broken. Starter motor retaining bolts loose.
Wear or damage	Battery defective internally. Electrolyte level too low or electrolyte too weak due to leakage. Plate separators no longer fully effective. Battery plates severely sulphated.
Insufficient current flow to keep battery charged	Fan belt slipping. Battery terminal connections loose or corroded. Alternator not charging properly. Short in lighting circuit causing continual battery drain. Regulator unit not working correctly.
Alternator not charging*	Fan belt loose and slipping, or broken. Brushes worn, sticking, broken or dirty. Brush springs weak or broken.

**If all appears to be well but the alternator is still not charging, take the car to an automobile electrician for checking of the alternator and regulator.*

Symptom	Reason/s
Battery will not hold charge for more than a few days	Battery defective internally. Electrolyte level too low or electrolyte too weak due to leakage. Plate separators no longer fully effective. Battery plates severely sulphated. Fan/alternator belt slipping. Battery terminal connections loose or corroded. Alternator not charging properly. Short in lighting circuit causing continual battery drain. Regulator unit nor working correctly.
Ignition light fails to go out, battery runs flat in a few days	Fan belt loose and slipping or broken. Alternator faulty.

Failure of individual electrical equipment to function correctly is dealt with alphabetically, below.

Symptom	Reason/s
Fuel gauge gives no reading	Fuel tank empty! Electric cable between tank sender unit and gauge earthed or loose. Fuel gauge case not earthed. Fuel gauge supply cable interrupted. Fuel gauge unit broken.
Fuel gauge registers full all the time	Electric cable between tank unit and gauge broken or disconnected.
Horn operates all the time	Horn push either earthed or stuck down. Horn cable to horn push earthed.
Horn fails to operate	Blown fuse. Cable or cable connection loose, broken or disconnected. Horn has an internal fault.
Horn emits intermittent or unsatisfactory noise	Cable connections loose. Horn incorrectly adjusted.
Lights do not come on	If engine not running, battery discharged. Light bulb filament burnt out or bulbs broken. Wire connections loose, disconnected or broken. Light switch shorting or otherwise faulty.
Lights come on but fade out	If engine not running battery discharged.
Lights give very poor illumination	Lamp glasses dirty. Reflector tarnished or dirty. Lamps badly out of adjustment. Incorrect bulb with too low wattage fitted. Existing bulbs old and badly discoloured. Electrical wiring too thin not allowing full current to pass.
Lights work erratically - flashing on and off, especially over bumps	Battery terminals or earth connections loose. Lights not earthing properly. Contacts in light switch faulty.
Wiper motor fails to work	Blown fuse. Wire connections loose, disconnected or broken. Brushes badly worn. Armature worn or faulty. Field coils faulty.
Wiper motor works very slowly and takes excessive current	Commutator dirty, greasy or burnt. Drive to spindles bent or unlubricated. Drive spindle binding or damaged. Armature bearings dry or unaligned. Armature badly worn or faulty.
Wiper motor works slowly and takes little current	Brushes badly worn. Commutator dirty, greasy or burnt. Armature badly worn or faulty.
Wiper motor works but wiper blades remain static	Linkage disengaged or faulty. Drive spindle damaged or worn. Wiper motor gearbox parts badly worn.

The following codes are applicable to all the circuit diagrams on pages 205 - 218

Wire codes

54 - 16 sw/gr-rt 2.5

- 2.5 — Wire cross-section in mm^2. Unmarked wires have 0.75 mm^2 cross-section
- gr-rt — Wire colour code - secondary colours
- sw — Wire colour code - main colour
- 54 - 16 — Wire number

Wiring colour	Code	Wiring colour	Code
Blue	bl	Pink	rs
Brown	br	Red	rt
Yellow	ge	Black	sw
Grey	gr	Violet	vi
Green	gn	White	ws

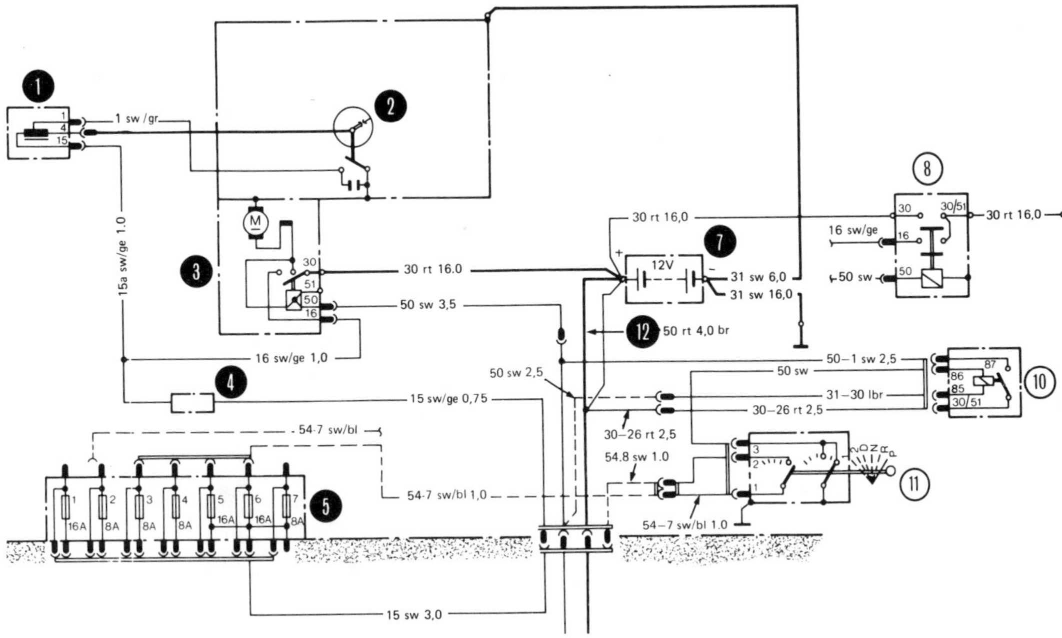

Item Number	Item
1	Coil
2	Distributor
3	Starter Motor
4	Ballast Resistance – Ignition Coil.
5	Fuse Box
6	Steering Lock Ignition Switch
7	Battery
8	Solenoid Starting Switch
9	Starter Motor
10	Relay – Automatic Transmission
11	Inhibitor Switch – Automatic Transmission
12	Fuse Link Wire – British sourced vehicles only

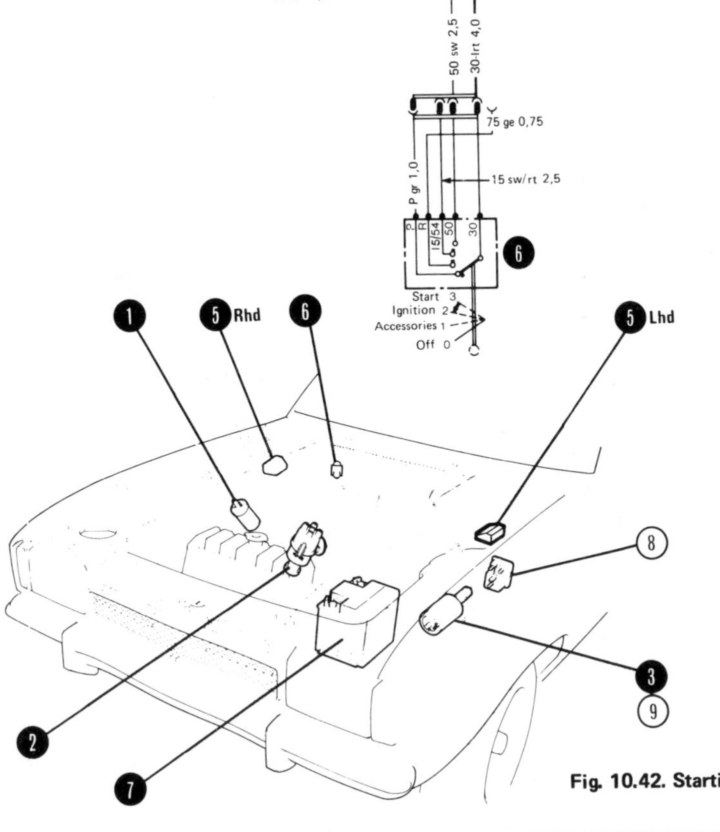

● Standard Equipment

○ Optional Extra Equipment

Fig. 10.42. Starting and ignition circuits, L and XL models

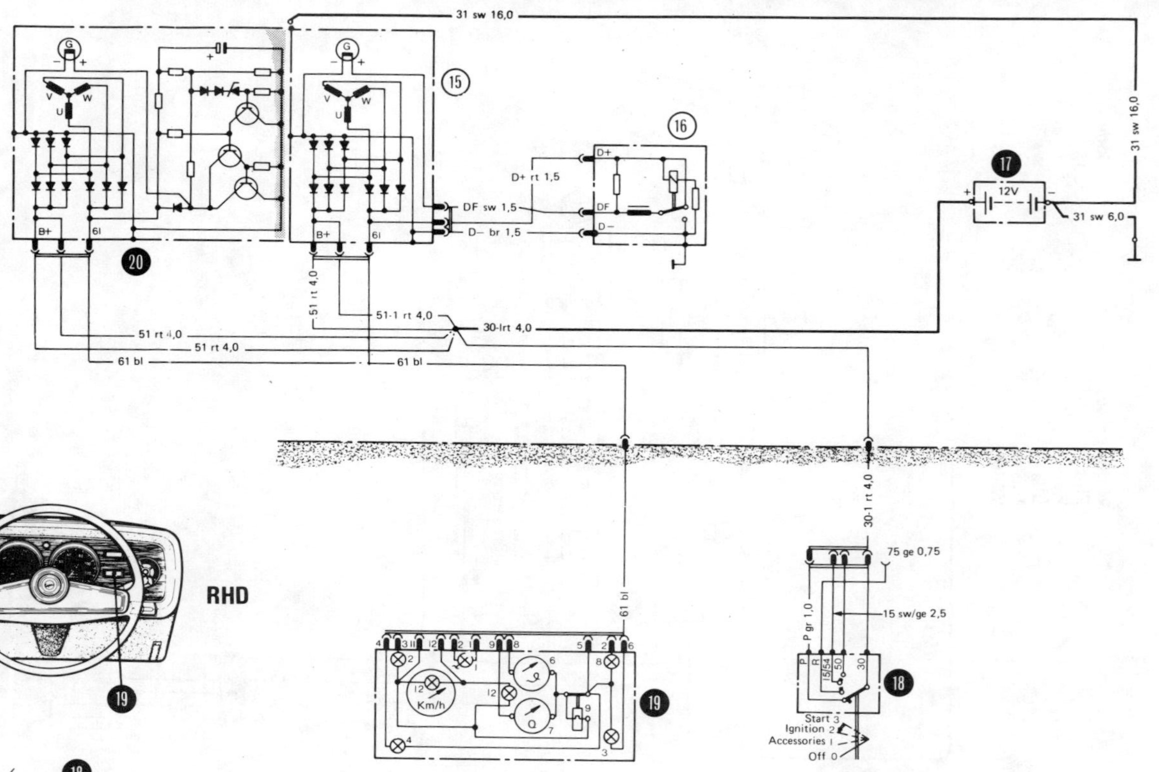

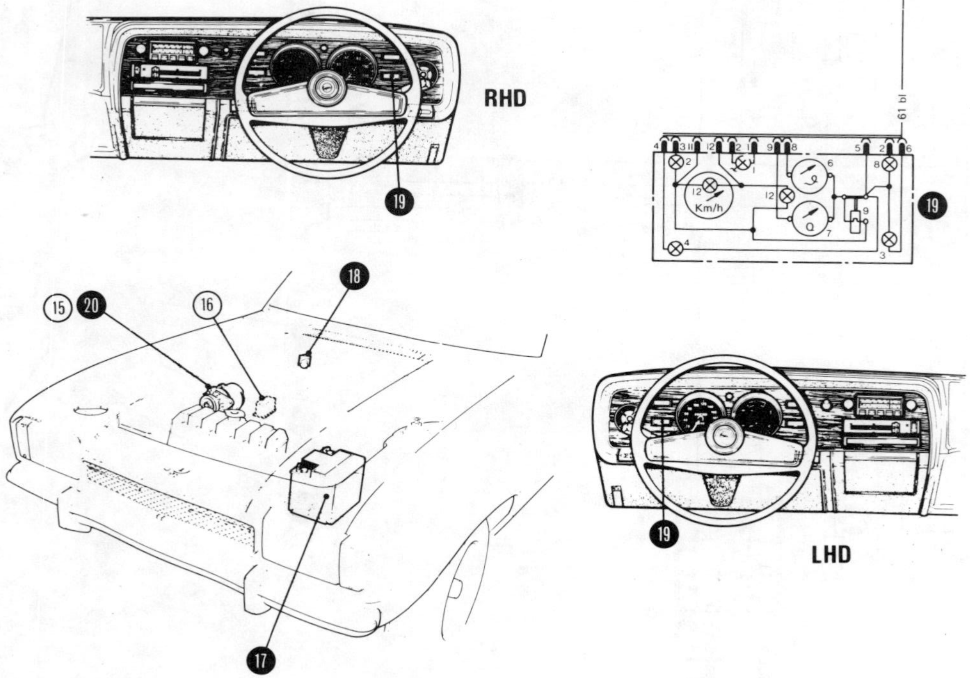

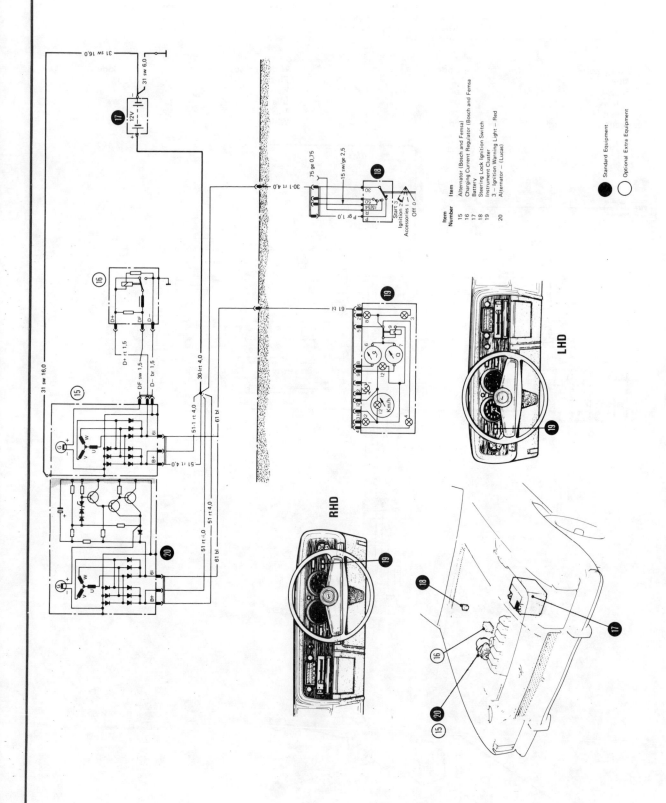

Item Number	Item
15	Alternator (Bosch and Femsa)
16	Charging Current Regulator (Bosch and Femsa
17	Battery
18	Steering Lock Ignition Switch
19	Instrument Cluster 3 – Ignition Warning Light – Red
20	Alternator – (Lucas)

● Standard Equipment

○ Optional Extra Equipment

Fig. 10.43. Charging circuits. L and XL models (see page 205 for wiring codes)

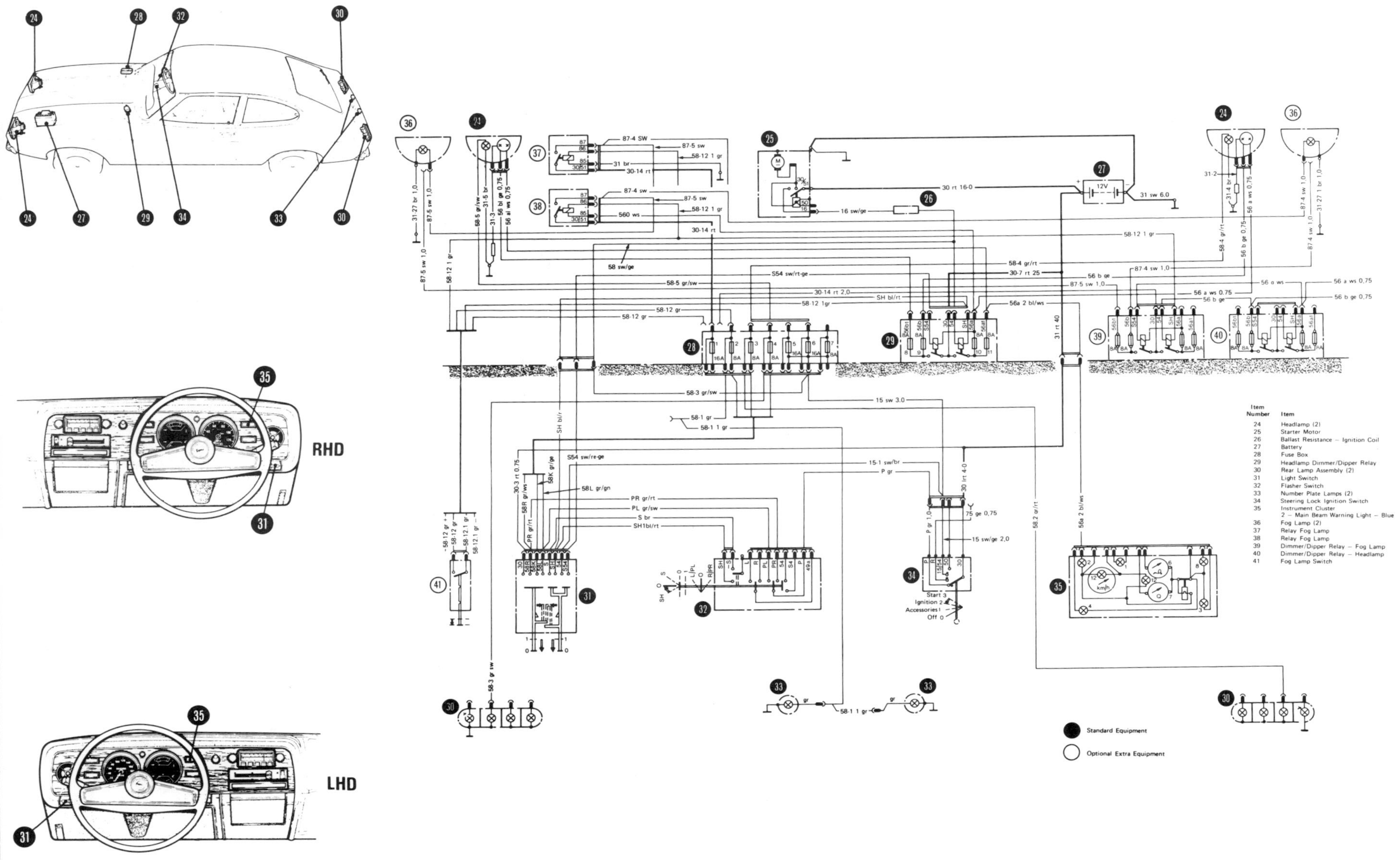

Item Number	Item
24	Headlamp (2)
25	Starter Motor
26	Ballast Resistance – Ignition Coil
27	Battery
28	Fuse Box
29	Headlamp Dimmer/Dipper Relay
30	Rear Lamp Assembly (2)
31	Light Switch
32	Flasher Switch
33	Number Plate Lamps (2)
34	Steering Lock Ignition Switch
35	Instrument Cluster 2 – Main Beam Warning Light – Blue
36	Fog Lamp (2)
37	Relay Fog Lamp
38	Relay Fog Lamp
39	Dimmer/Dipper Relay – Fog Lamp
40	Dimmer/Dipper Relay – Headlamp
41	Fog Lamp Switch

Fig. 10.44. Exterior light circuits. L and XL models (see page 205 for wiring codes)

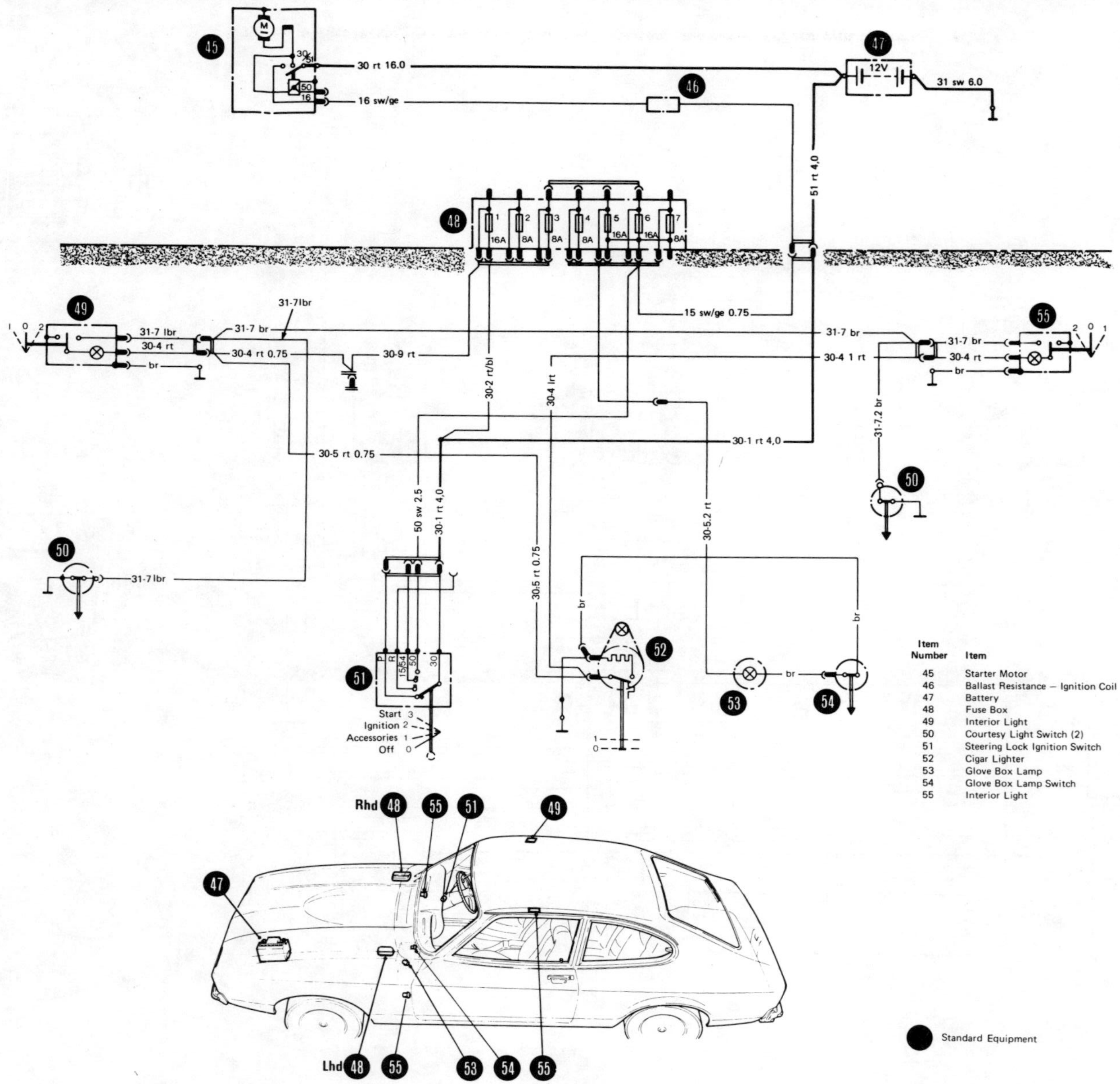

Item Number	Item
45	Starter Motor
46	Ballast Resistance – Ignition Coil
47	Battery
48	Fuse Box
49	Interior Light
50	Courtesy Light Switch (2)
51	Steering Lock Ignition Switch
52	Cigar Lighter
53	Glove Box Lamp
54	Glove Box Lamp Switch
55	Interior Light

Fig. 10.45. Interior light circuits. L and XL models (see page 205 for wiring codes)

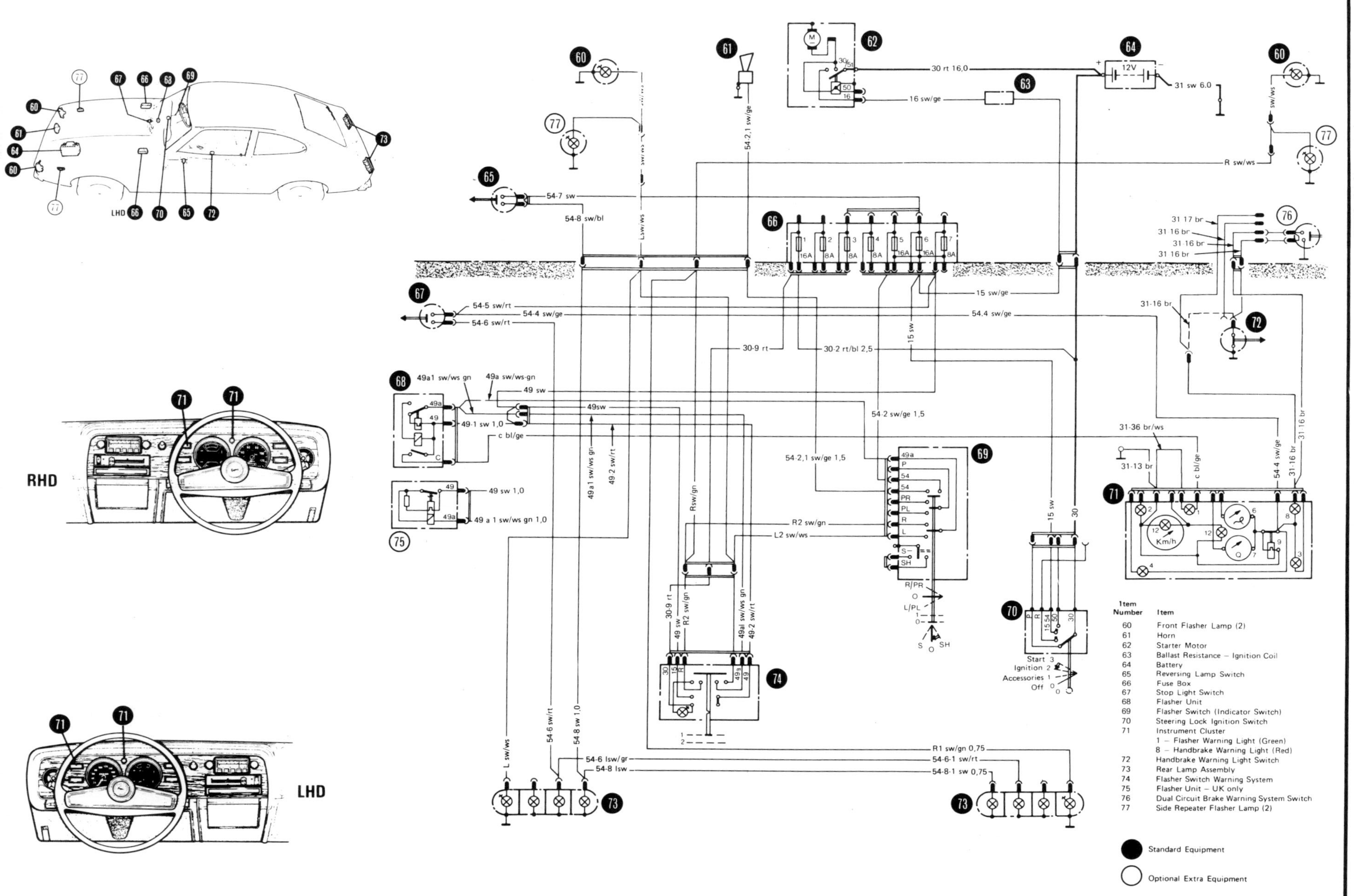

Item Number	Item
60	Front Flasher Lamp (2)
61	Horn
62	Starter Motor
63	Ballast Resistance – Ignition Coil
64	Battery
65	Reversing Lamp Switch
66	Fuse Box
67	Stop Light Switch
68	Flasher Unit
69	Flasher Switch (Indicator Switch)
70	Steering Lock Ignition Switch
71	Instrument Cluster
	1 – Flasher Warning Light (Green)
	8 – Handbrake Warning Light (Red)
72	Handbrake Warning Light Switch
73	Rear Lamp Assembly
74	Flasher Switch Warning System
75	Flasher Unit – UK only
76	Dual Circuit Brake Warning System Switch
77	Side Repeater Flasher Lamp (2)

● Standard Equipment

○ Optional Extra Equipment

Fig. 10.46. Horn, indicator and hazard light circuits. L and XL models (see page 205 for wiring codes)

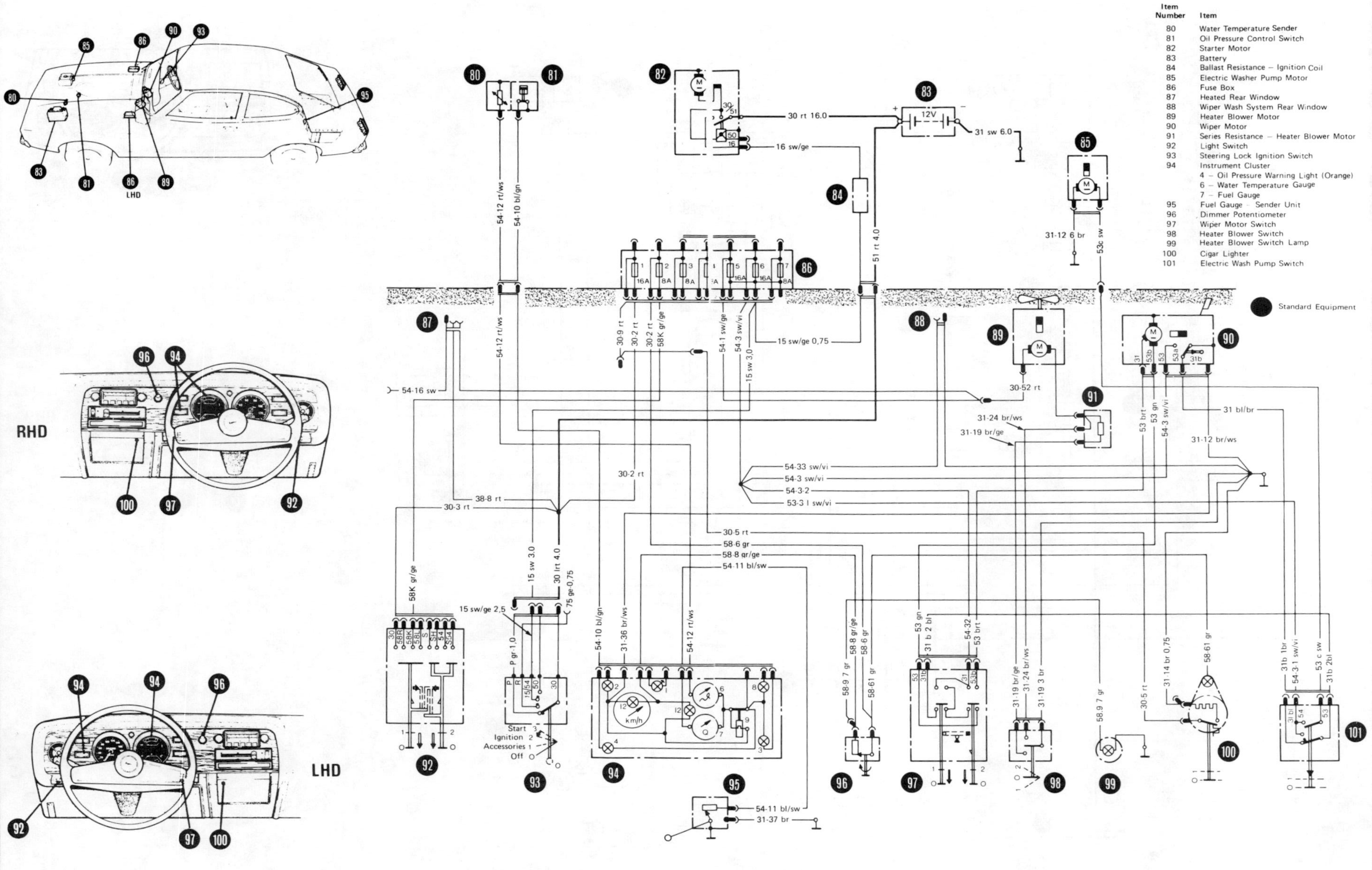

Item Number	Item
80	Water Temperature Sender
81	Oil Pressure Control Switch
82	Starter Motor
83	Battery
84	Ballast Resistance – Ignition Coil
85	Electric Washer Pump Motor
86	Fuse Box
87	Heated Rear Window
88	Wiper Wash System Rear Window
89	Heater Blower Motor
90	Wiper Motor
91	Series Resistance – Heater Blower Motor
92	Light Switch
93	Steering Lock Ignition Switch
94	Instrument Cluster 4 – Oil Pressure Warning Light (Orange) 6 – Water Temperature Gauge 7 – Fuel Gauge
95	Fuel Gauge – Sender Unit
96	Dimmer Potentiometer
97	Wiper Motor Switch
98	Heater Blower Switch
99	Heater Blower Switch Lamp
100	Cigar Lighter
101	Electric Wash Pump Switch

Fig. 10.47. Heater, wipers and ancillary circuits. L and XL models (see page 205 for wiring codes)

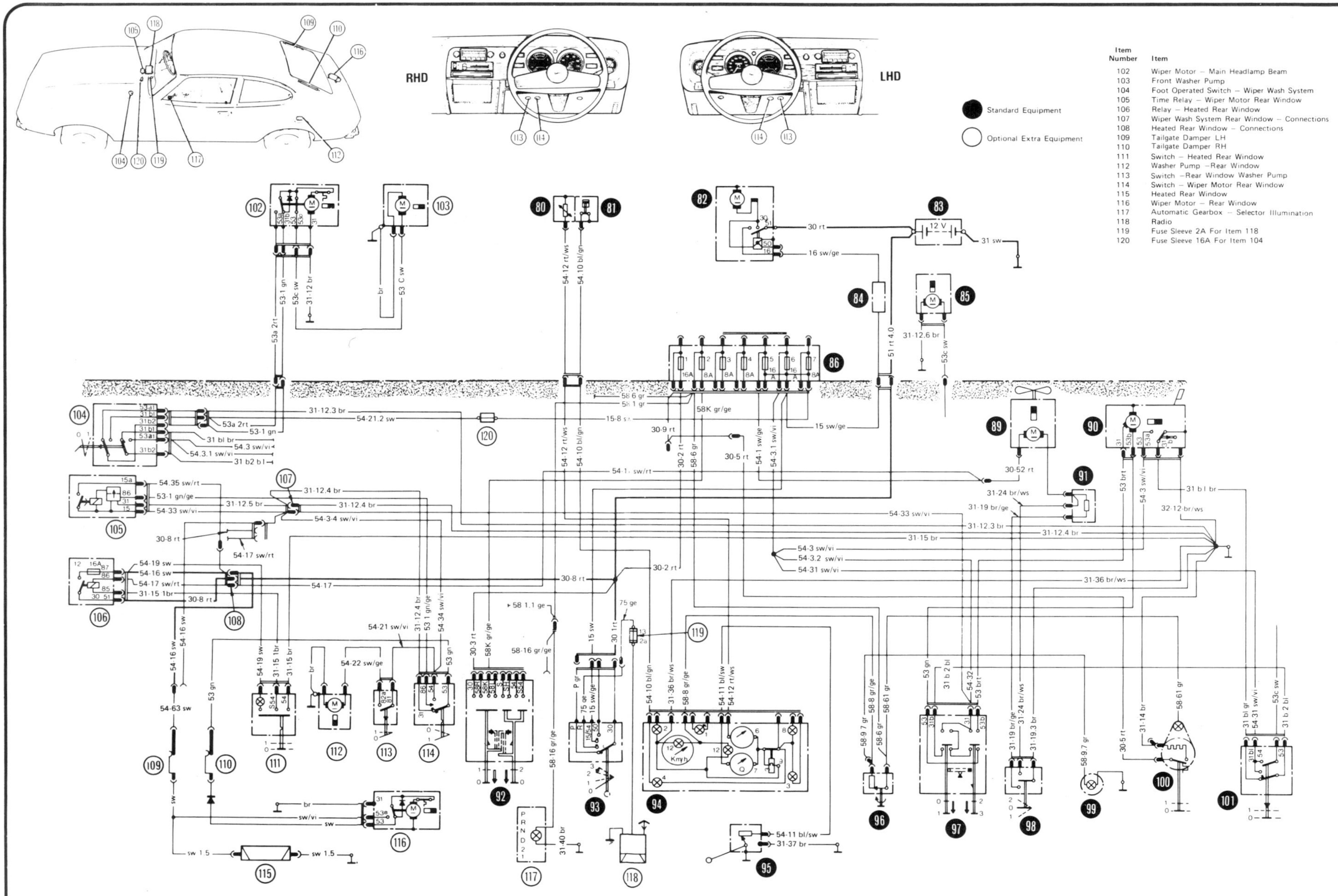

Item Number	Item
102	Wiper Motor – Main Headlamp Beam
103	Front Washer Pump
104	Foot Operated Switch – Wiper Wash System
105	Time Relay – Wiper Motor Rear Window
106	Relay – Heated Rear Window
107	Wiper Wash System Rear Window – Connections
108	Heated Rear Window – Connections
109	Tailgate Damper LH
110	Tailgate Damper RH
111	Switch – Heated Rear Window
112	Washer Pump –Rear Window
113	Switch –Rear Window Washer Pump
114	Switch – Wiper Motor Rear Window
115	Heated Rear Window
116	Wiper Motor – Rear Window
117	Automatic Gearbox – Selector Illumination
118	Radio
119	Fuse Sleeve 2A For Item 118
120	Fuse Sleeve 16A For Item 104

Fig. 10.48. Regular production option circuits, additional to Fig. 10.47. L and XL models (see page 205 for wiring codes)

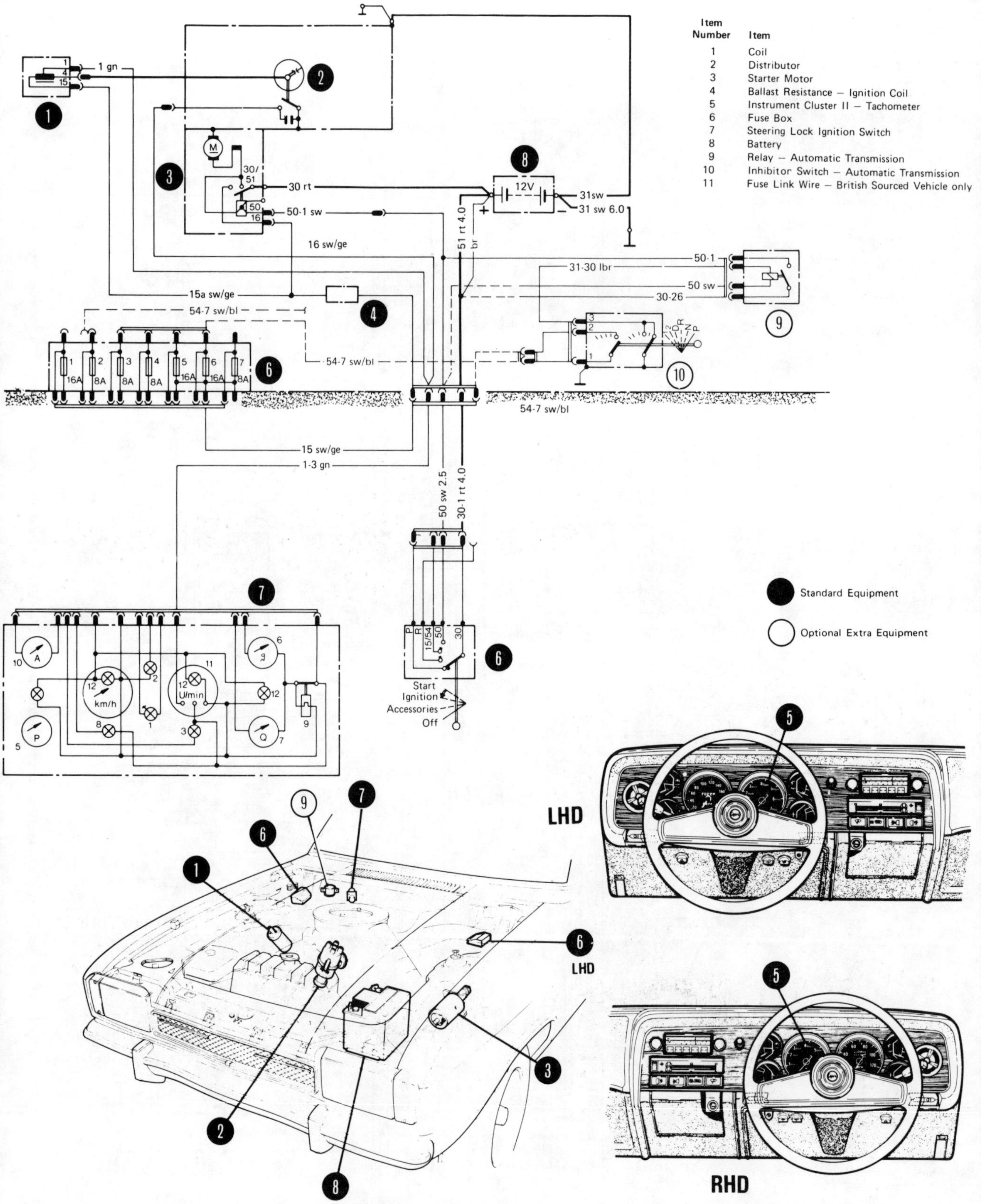

Item Number	Item
1	Coil
2	Distributor
3	Starter Motor
4	Ballast Resistance – Ignition Coil
5	Instrument Cluster II – Tachometer
6	Fuse Box
7	Steering Lock Ignition Switch
8	Battery
9	Relay – Automatic Transmission
10	Inhibitor Switch – Automatic Transmission
11	Fuse Link Wire – British Sourced Vehicle only

Fig. 10.49. Starting and ignition circuits, GT and Ghia models (see page 205 for wiring codes)

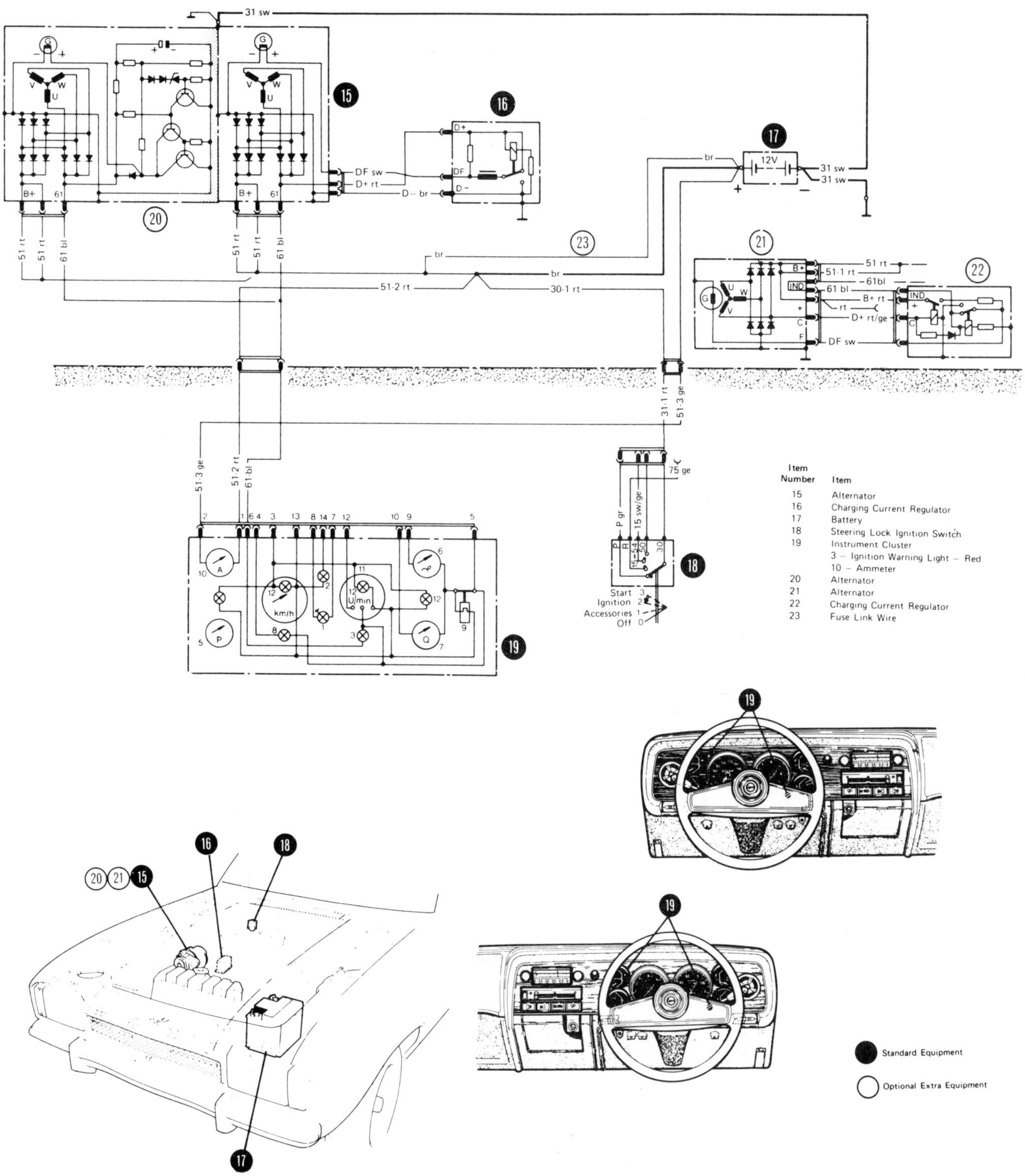

Fig. 10.50. Charging circuits, GT and Ghia models (see page 205 for wiring codes)

Item Number	Item
24	Headlamp (2)
25	Starter Motor
26	Ballast Resistance – Ignition Coil
27	Battery
28	Fuse Box
29	Headlamp Dimmer/Dipper Relay
30	Rear Lamp Assembly (2)
31	Light Switch
32	Flasher Switch
33	Number Plate Lamps (2)
34	Steering Lock Ignition Switch
35	Instrument Cluster
	2 – Main Beam Warning Light – Blue
36	Fog Lamp (2)
37	Relay Fog Lamp
38	Relay Fog Lamp
39	Dimmer/Dipper Relay – Fog Lamp
40	Dipper/Dipper Relay – Headlamp
41	Fog Lamp Switch

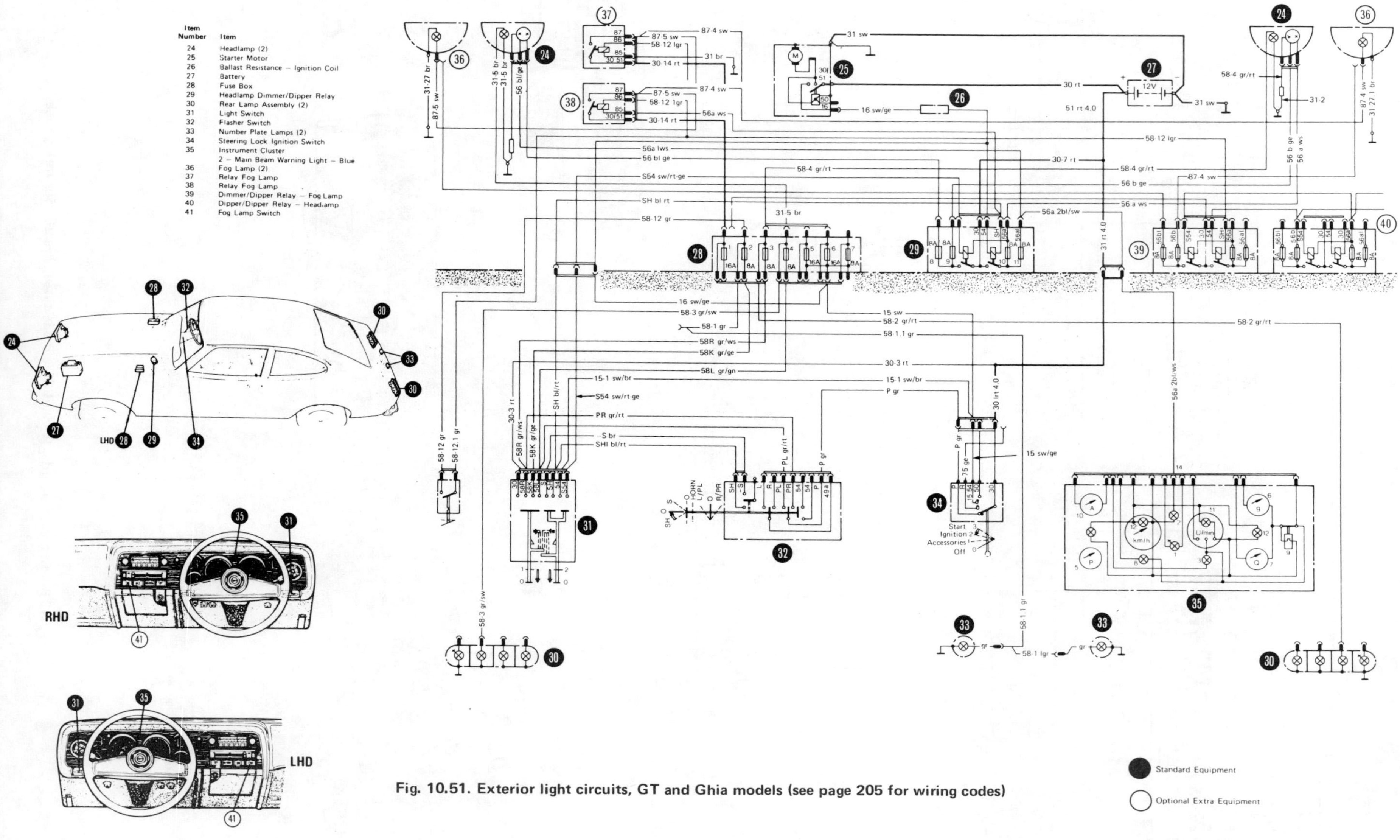

Fig. 10.51. Exterior light circuits, GT and Ghia models (see page 205 for wiring codes)

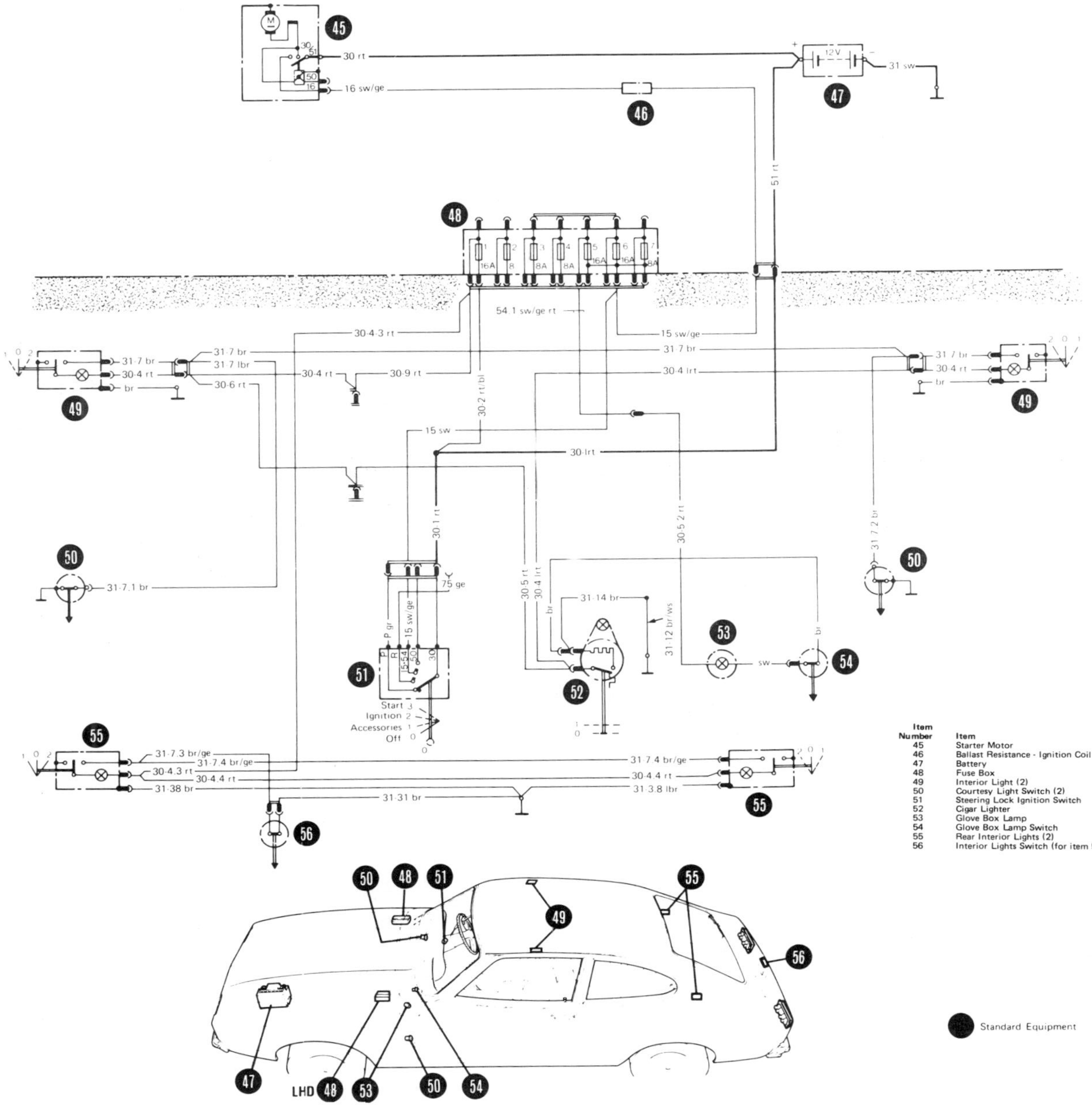

Item Number	Item
45	Starter Motor
46	Ballast Resistance - Ignition Coil
47	Battery
48	Fuse Box
49	Interior Light (2)
50	Courtesy Light Switch (2)
51	Steering Lock Ignition Switch
52	Cigar Lighter
53	Glove Box Lamp
54	Glove Box Lamp Switch
55	Rear Interior Lights (2)
56	Interior Lights Switch (for item 55)

Fig. 10.52. Interior light circuits. GT and Ghia models (see page 205 for wiring codes)

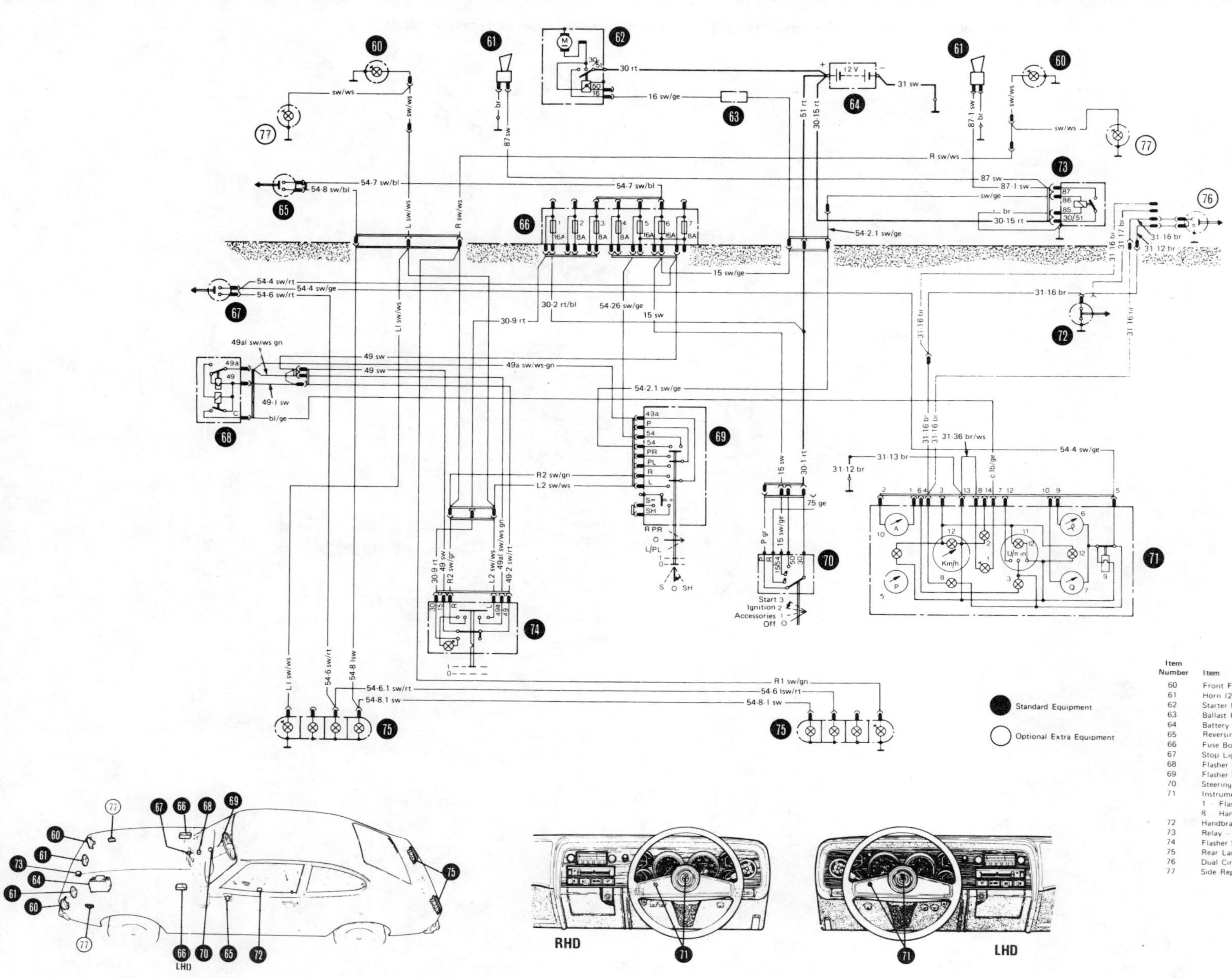

Fig. 10.53. Horn, indicator and hazard light circuits, GT and Ghia models (see page 205 for wiring codes)

Item Number	Item
60	Front Flasher Lamp (2)
61	Horn (2)
62	Starter Motor
63	Ballast Resistance – Ignition Coil
64	Battery
65	Reversing Lamp Switch
66	Fuse Box
67	Stop Light Switch
68	Flasher Unit
69	Flasher Switch (Indicator Switch)
70	Steering Lock Ignition Switch
71	Instrument Cluster 1 – Flasher Warning Light (Green) 8 – Handbrake Warning Light (Red)
72	Handbrake Warning Light Switch
73	Relay – Two Tone Horn
74	Flasher Switch Warning System
75	Rear Lamp Assembly
76	Dual Circuit Brake Warning System Switch
77	Side Repeater Flasher Lamp (2)

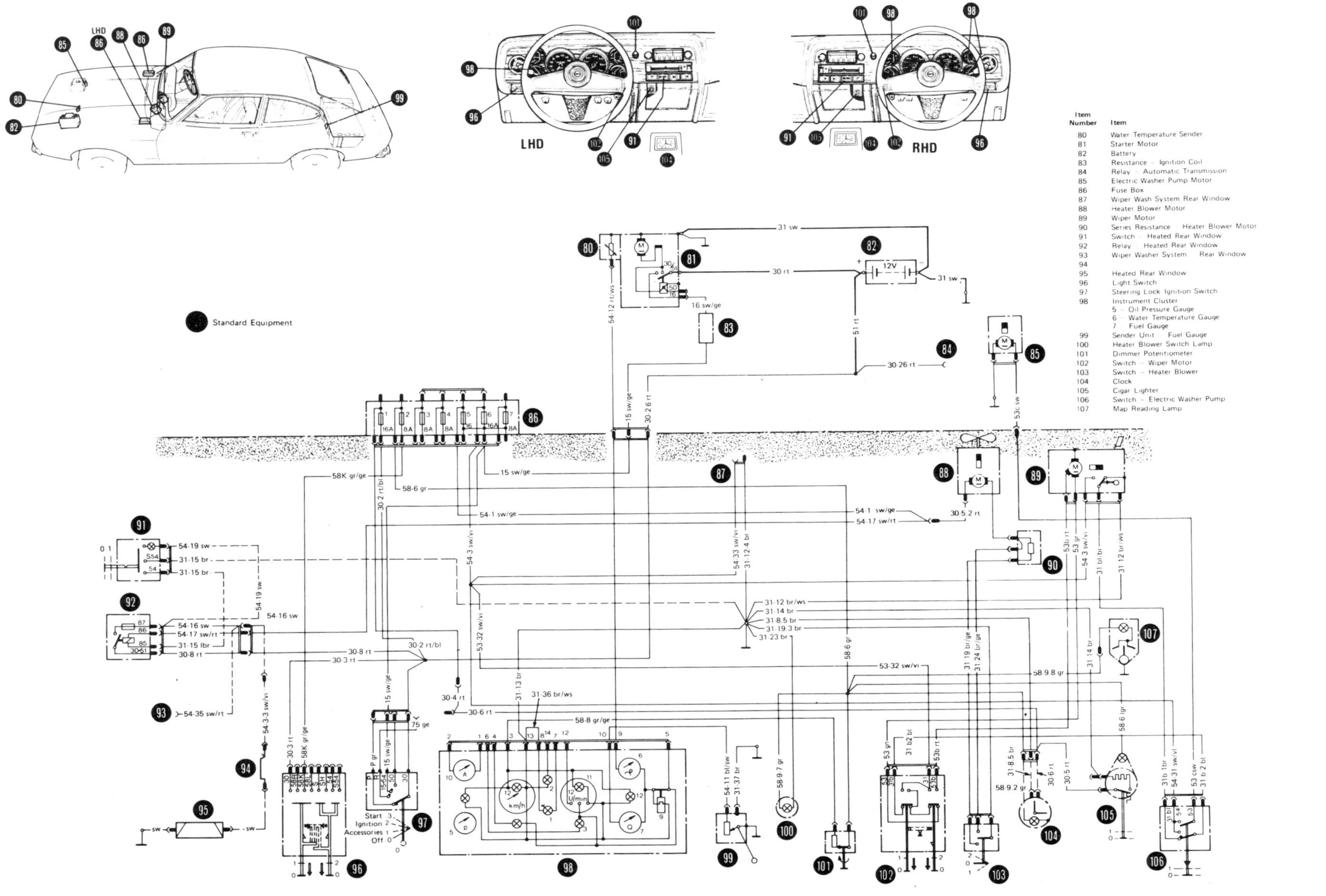

Item Number	Item
80	Water Temperature Sender
81	Starter Motor
82	Battery
83	Resistance – Ignition Coil
84	Relay – Automatic Transmission
85	Electric Washer Pump Motor
86	Fuse Box
87	Wiper Wash System Rear Window
88	Heater Blower Motor
89	Wiper Motor
90	Series Resistance – Heater Blower Motor
91	Switch – Heated Rear Window
92	Relay – Heated Rear Window
93	Wiper Washer System – Rear Window
94	
95	Heated Rear Window
96	Light Switch
97	Steering Lock Ignition Switch
98	Instrument Cluster 5 – Oil Pressure Gauge 6 – Water Temperature Gauge 7 – Fuel Gauge
99	Sender Unit – Fuel Gauge
100	Heater Blower Switch Lamp
101	Dimmer Potentiometer
102	Switch – Wiper Motor
103	Switch – Heater Blower
104	Clock
105	Cigar Lighter
106	Switch – Electric Washer Pump
107	Map Reading Lamp

Fig. 10.54. Heater, wipers and ancillary circuits, GT and Ghia models (see page 205 for wiring codes)

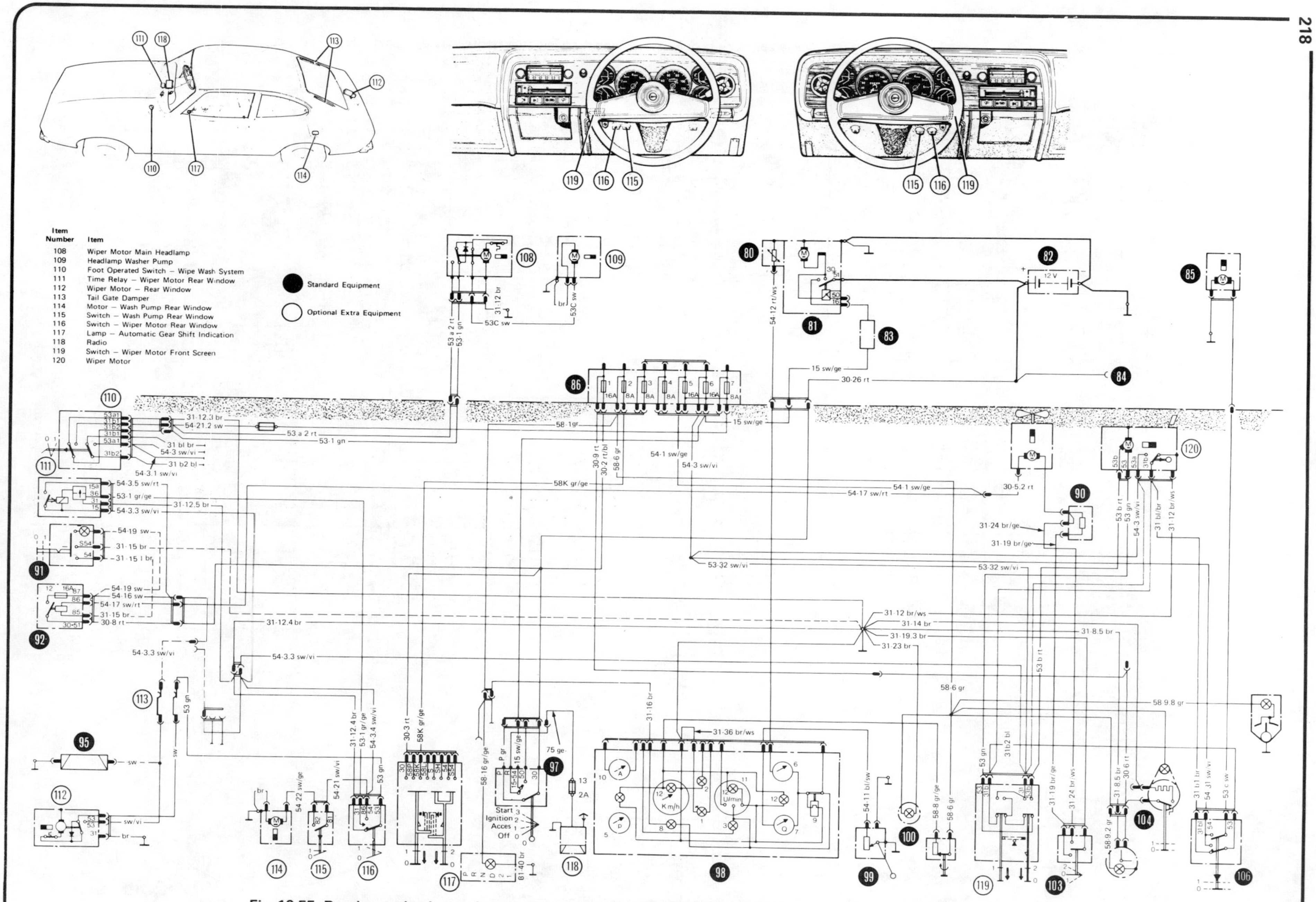

Item Number	Item
108	Wiper Motor Main Headlamp
109	Headlamp Washer Pump
110	Foot Operated Switch – Wipe Wash System
111	Time Relay – Wiper Motor Rear Window
112	Wiper Motor – Rear Window
113	Tail Gate Damper
114	Motor – Wash Pump Rear Window
115	Switch – Wash Pump Rear Window
116	Switch – Wiper Motor Rear Window
117	Lamp – Automatic Gear Shift Indication
118	Radio
119	Switch – Wiper Motor Front Screen
120	Wiper Motor

Fig. 10.55. Regular production option circuits, additional to Fig. 10.54 GT and Ghia models (see page 205 for wiring codes)

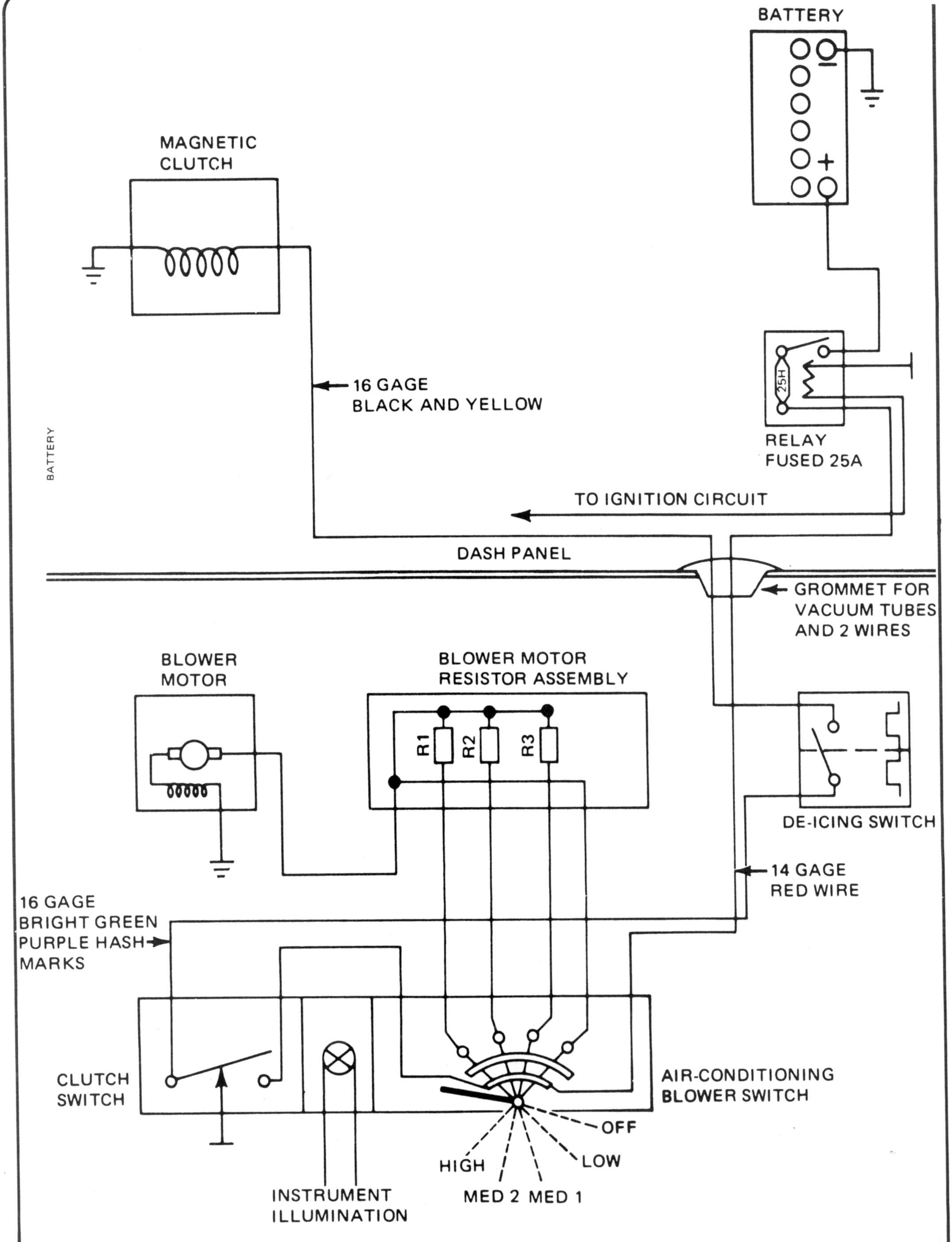

Fig. 10.56. Air conditioning circuit wiring diagram

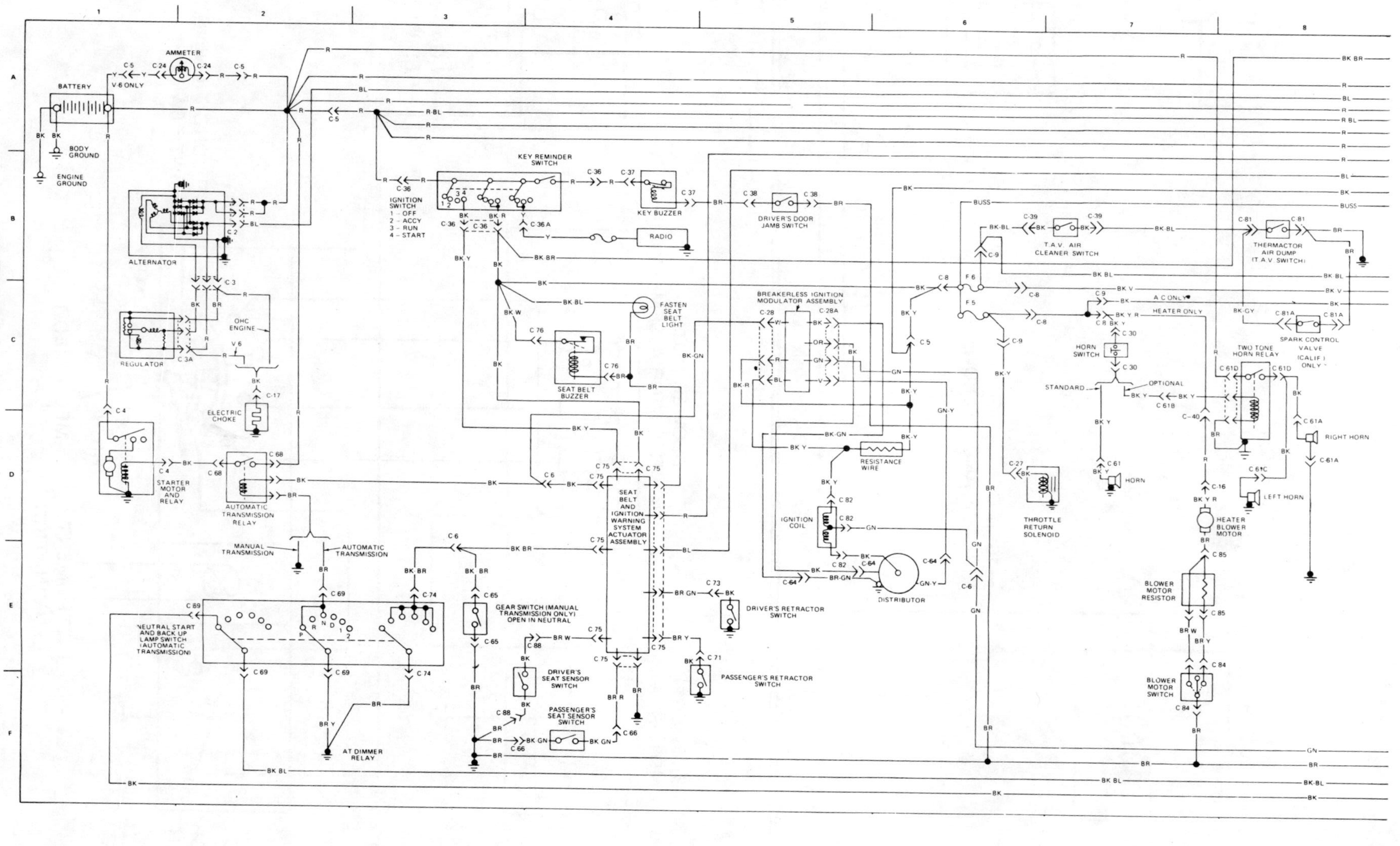

Fig. 10.57. Circuit diagram - Mercury Capri II to 1976
(see page 224 for wiring codes)

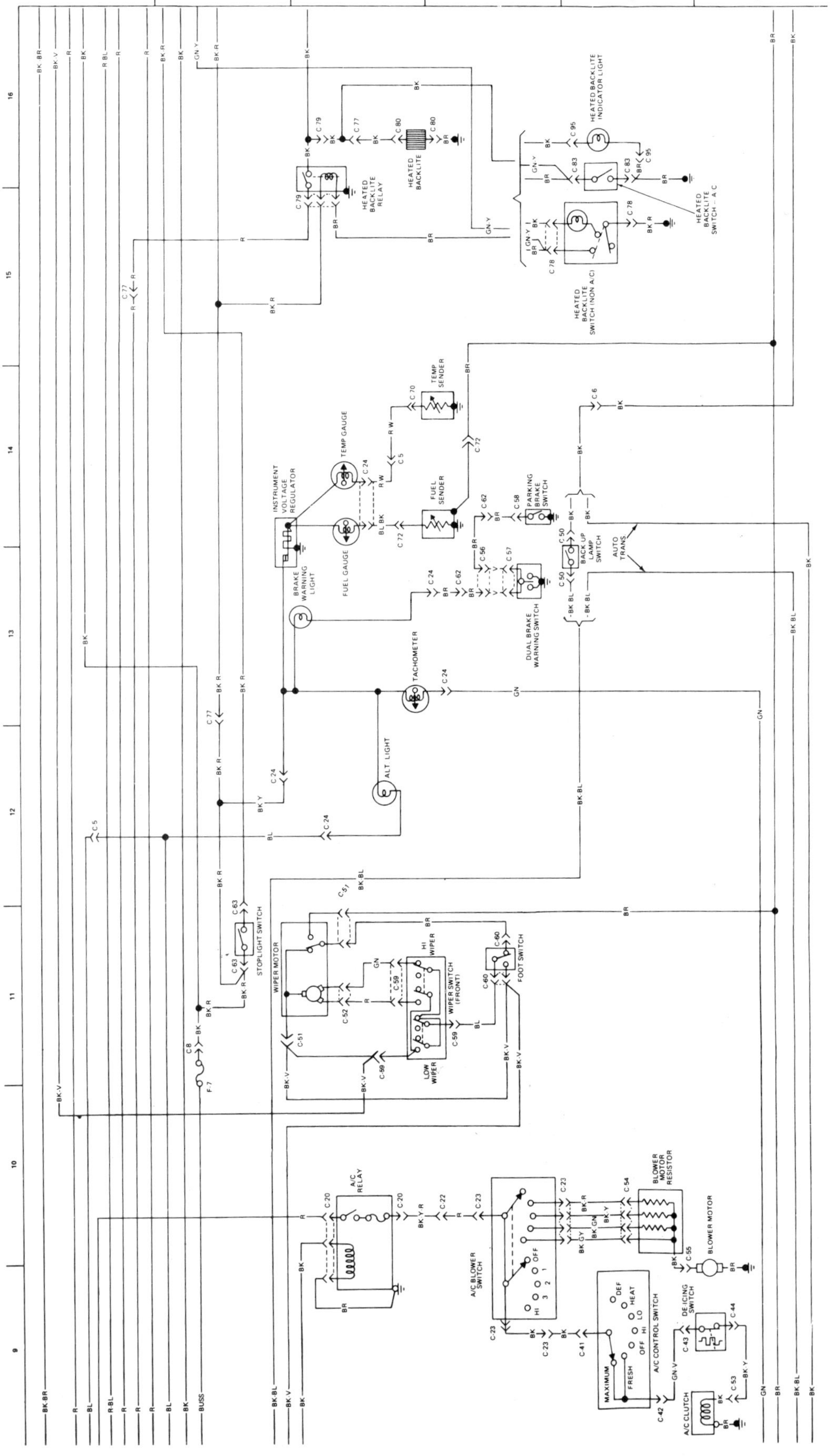

Fig. 10.58. Circuit diagram (continued) - Mercury Capri II to 1976
(see page 224 for wiring codes)

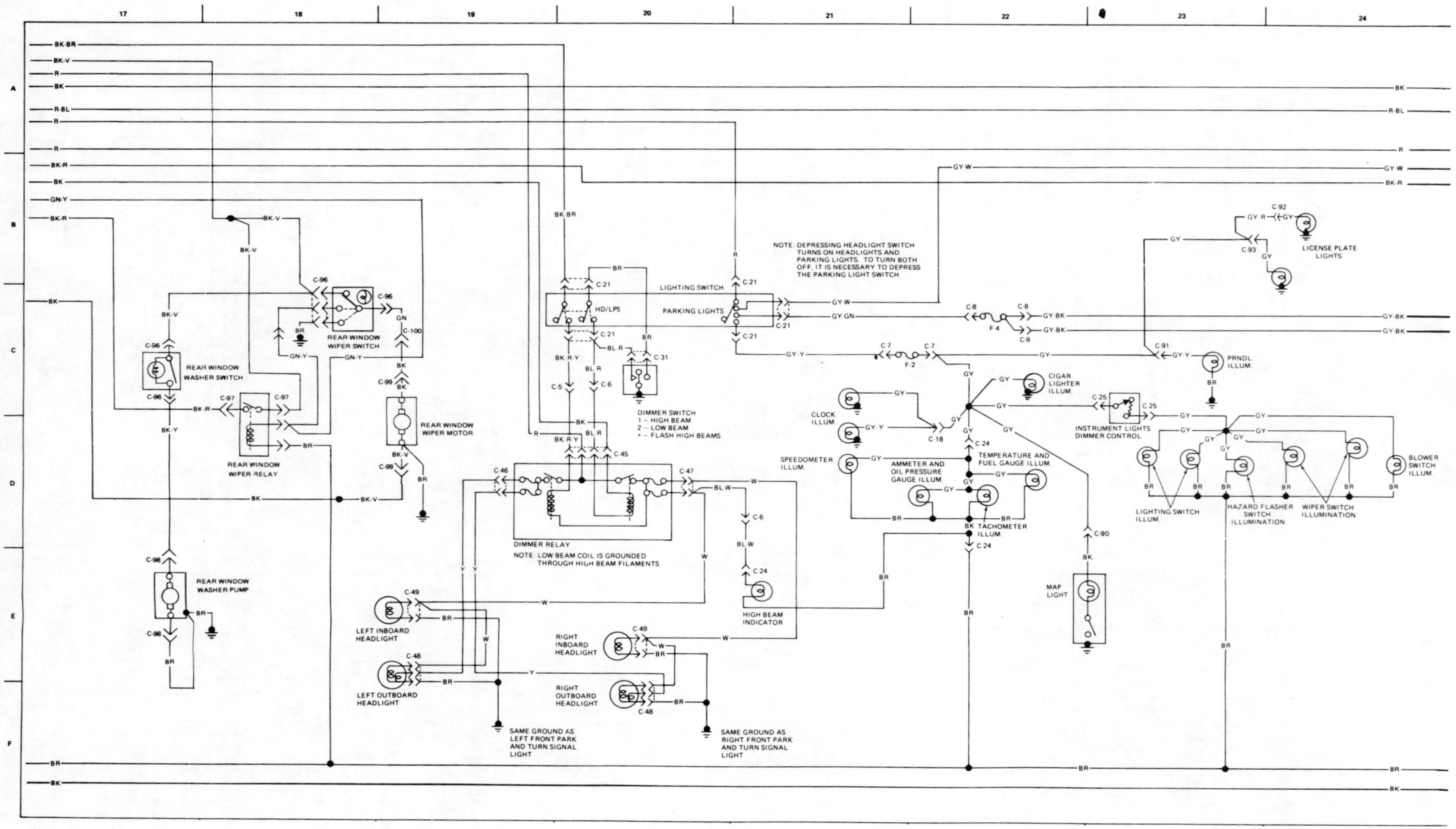

Fig. 10.59. Circuit diagram (continued) - Mercury Capri II to 1976
(see page 224 for wiring codes)

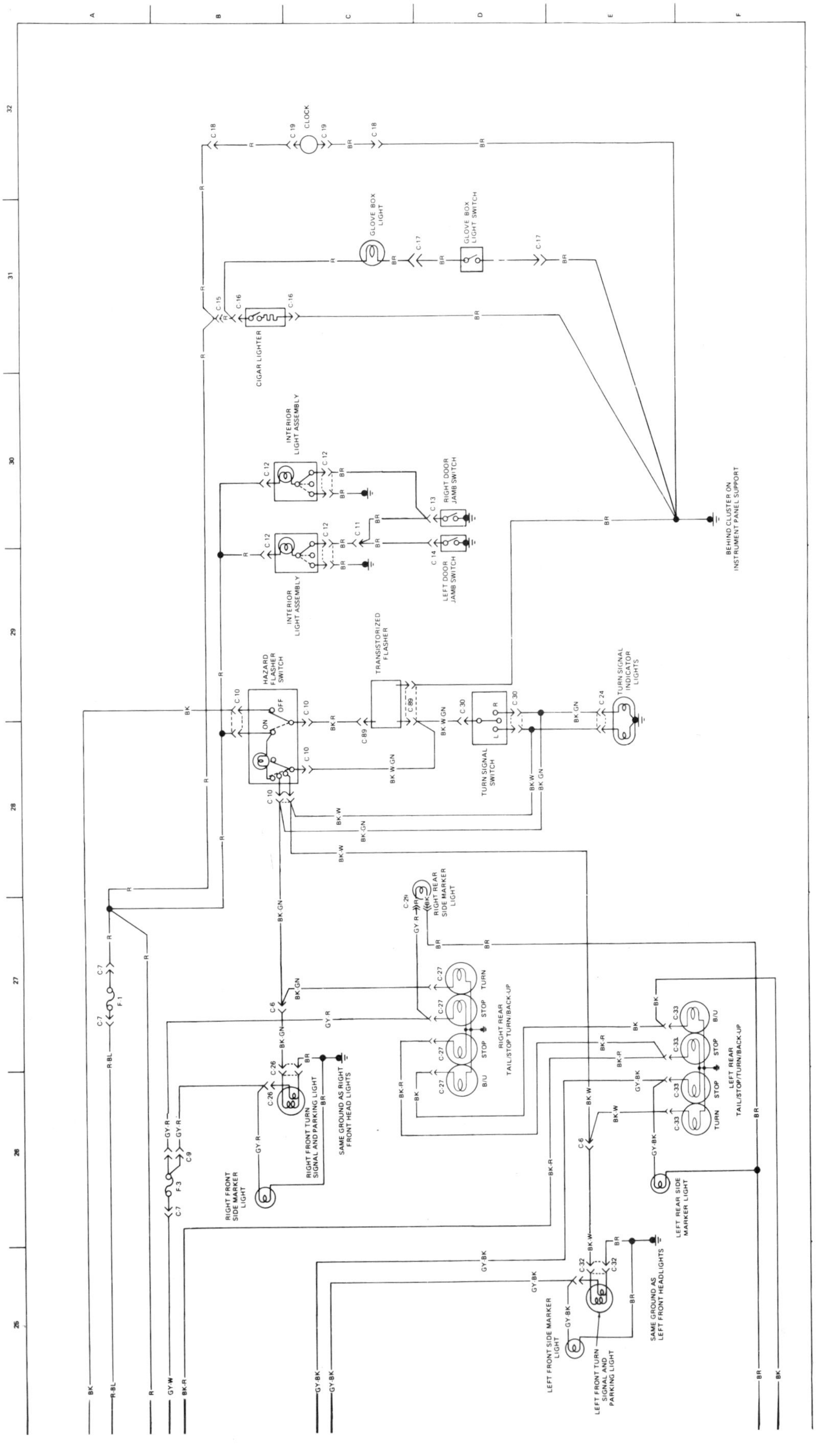

Fig. 10.60. Circuit diagram (continued) - Mercury Capri II to 1976

Code relating to circuit diagrams on pages 220 - 223

Component	Location
Air conditioner clutch	F-9
Alternator	B-1
Alternator regulator	C-1
Battery	A-1
Buzzers	
Key reminder	B-4
Seat belt	C-4
Cigar lighter	B-31
Clock	C-32
Distributor	E-6
Exterior lights	
Back-up	D-26, F-27
Headlights	
Left	E-19
Right	E-20
License plate	B-24
Park and turn signal	
Left	E-25
Right	C-26
Side marker	
Left front	E-25
Left rear	E-26
Right front	B-26
Right rear	C-28
Stop lights	
Left	E-26
Right	D-27
Taillights	
Left	F-26
Right	D-27
Rear turn signal	
Left	F-26
Right	D-27
Flashers	
Hazard flasher	B-28
Turn signal	D-28
Gauges	
Ammeter	A-2
Fuel	C-14
Tachometer	C-13
Temperature	C-14
Heated backlight	C-16
Heater blower motor	D-7
Heater blower motor resistor	E-7
Horns	D-7, D-8
Ignition coil	D-5
Ignition resistor wire	D-5
Illumination lights	
Ammeter and oil pressure gauge	D-21
Blower switch	D-24
Cigar lighter	C-22
Clock	D-21
Dome	B-29
Fuel gauge	D-22
Glove box	C-31
Hazard flasher	B-28
Lighting switch	D-23
Map	E-22
PRND21	C-23
Tachometer	D-22
Temperature gauge	D-22
Windshield wiper switch	D-24

Component	Location
Indicator lights	
Alternator	C-12
Brake warning	C-13
Heated backlight	E-16
High beam	E-21
Seat belt	C-4
Turn signal	E-28
Instrument voltage regulator	B-14
Motors	
A/C blower	F-8
Heater blower	D-7
Starter	D-1
Windshield wiper (front)	B-11
Windshield wiper (rear)	D-18
Radio	B-4
Relays	
Air conditioning	C-10
Automatic transmission	D-19
Dimmer	D-20
Heated backlight	C-16
Starter motor	D-1
Two-tone horn and ignition warning actuator	C-8
Seat belt logic box	D-4
Senders	
Fuel gauge	D-14
Water temperature gauge	D-14
Switches	
A/C blower	D-9
A/C control	E-9
Dimmer	
Instrument panel illumination	C-23
High beam	C-20
Door jamb	
Driver's	D-30
Passenger's	D-30
Door jamb - key buzzer	B-5
Dual brake warning	D-13
Gear	E-3
Glove box lamp	D-31
Hazard flasher	B-28
Heated backlight	E-15
Heater blower	F-7
Horn	C-7
Ignition	B-3
Lighting	C-20
Neutral start	E-2
Parking brake	D-13
Seat belt retractor	
Driver's	E-5
Passenger's	F-5
T.A.V. air cleaner	B-7
Thermactor air dump	B-8
Throttle return	D-6
Turn signal	D-28
Seat sensor	
Driver's	E-3
Passenger's	F-4
Spark control valve	
Stoplight	B-11
Windshield wiper (front)	D-11
Foot switch	D-11
Windshield wiper (rear)	C-18
Rear washer switch	C-17

Wiring colour code

BK	Black
R	Red
Y	Yellow
BL	Blue
W	White
GN	Green
GY	Grey
BR	Brown
V	Violet
O	Orange

Chapter 11 Suspension and steering

For modifications, and information applicable to later models, see Supplement at end of manual

Contents

Specifications

Front suspension

Type	Independent, MacPherson strut
Lateral control	Track control arms
Longitudinal control	Stabilizer bar
Shock absorbers	Hydraulic, telescopic, double-acting
Fluid type:	
FOB	SM6C-1003-A
FOG	GES-M6C-4503-A
Fluid capacity:	
FOB	325 ± 15 cc (0.18 Imp. pint, approx/0.22 US pint approx.)
FOG	340 ± 15 cc (0.19 Imp. pint, approx/0.23 US pint approx.)
Spring rating	The spring rating varies according to the vehicle and intended market. When replacements are required, consult a Ford dealer for further information.

Rear suspension

Type	Semi-elliptic, leaf spring with rigid axle and stabilizer bar.
Shock absorbers	Hydraulic, telescopic, double-acting
Spring rating	The spring rating varies according to the vehicle and intended market. When replacements are required, consult a Ford dealer for further information

Manual steering gear

Type	Rack and pinion.
Rack travel (lock-to-lock)	5.08 in (129 mm)
Steering wheel turns (lock-to-lock)	3.36
Turning circle (between kerbs)	32.8 ft (10.0 m)
Teeth on pinion (helical)	5 Capri II; 6 Mercury Capri II
Lubricant type	SAE 90 EP gear oil
Lubricant capacity	0.15 litre (0.25 Imp. pint/0.3 US pint)
Steering gear adjustment	By shims
Pinion bearing shim thicknesses	0.005, 0.007, 0.010, 0.090 in (0.127, 0.178, 0.254, 2.286 mm)
Rack slipper bearing shim thicknesses	0.002, 0.005, 0.010, 0.015, 0.020 in (0.051, 0.127, 0.254, 0.381, 0.508 mm)

Power steering gear

Pump type	Hobourn-Eaton roller pump
Ratio	16.8 : 1
Steering wheel turns (lock-to-lock)	3.23
Turning circle (between kerbs)	32.0 ft (9.7 m)
Lubricant type	SAE 40 or 20W/50 oil
Lubricant capacity	0.19 litre (0.33 Imp. pint/0.4 US pint)
Fluid type	Automatic transmission fluid, ESWM-2C-33E or SQM-2C9007 AA or D2AZ-19582-A
Fluid capacity	0.5 litre (0.9 Imp. pint/1.1 US pint)

Front wheel alignment (unladen)

Castor angle	0° 30' to 1° 45' positive
Maximum difference (side to side)	0° 45'
Camber angle	0° 18' to 1° 48' positive
Maximum difference (side to side)	1° 0'
Toe-in	0 to 0.28 in (0 to 7.0 mm)

Wheels

L versions	Pressed steel } 5 J x 13
Other versions (except Ghia types)	Pressed steel, sports style } 5 J x 13
Ghia types	Cast aluminium 5½ J x 13

Tyres

Size	165SR13 or 185/70 HR13	
Pressures:	Front	Rear
Load up to 3 persons	24 lbf/in² (1.7 kgf/cm²)	27 lbf/in² (1.9 kgf/cm²)
Load in excess of 3 persons	27 lbf/in² (1.9 kgf/cm²)	31 lbf/in² (2.2 kgf/cm²)

Note 1: *For sustained high speeds in excess of 100 mph, consult the tyre manufacturer or a Ford dealer.*
Note 2: *Where there is a tyre chart on the inside of the glove compartment door, refer to this for recommended tyre pressures and loads.*

Torque wrench settings

	lbf ft	kgf m
Suspension unit upper mounting bolts	15 to 18	2.1 to 2.5
Spindle to top mount assembly *	29 to 33	4.0 to 4.6
Track control arm ball stud nut	30 to 35	4.1 to 4.8
Stabilizer bar attachment clamps **	21 to 24	2.9 to 3.3
Stabilizer bar to track control arm nut **	14 to 45	1.9 to 6.2
Track control arm inner bushing **	18 to 22	2.5 to 3.0
Front suspension crossmember to body sidemember	29 to 37	4.0 to 5.1
Shock absorber to rear axle	39 to 46	5.4 to 6.4
Shock absorber to floor assembly **	20 to 24	2.8 to 3.3
Stabilizer bar to axle tube **	29 to 37	4 to 5.1
Stabilizer bar to side member **	26 to 30	3.6 to 4.1
Locknut on stabilizer bar end-piece **	29 to 37	4 to 5.1
Spring U-bolts **	18 to 27	2.5 to 3.7
Front of rear spring **	26 to 30	3.6 to 4.1
Rear of rear spring **	8 to 10	1.1 to 1.4
Steering arm to suspension unit	30 to 34	4.1 to 4.7
Steering gear to crossmember	15 to 18	2.1 to 2.5
Trackrod-end to steering arm	18 to 22	2.5 to 3.0
Coupling to pinion spline	12 to 15	1.6 to 2.1
Universal joint to steering shaft spline	17 to 22	2.3 to 3.0
Steering wheel to shaft	20 to 25	2.8 to 3.5
Steering column tube to pedal box	15 to 18	2.1 to 2.5
Power steering fluid pressure lines	19 to 23	2.6 to 3.2
Power steering fluid return lines	12 to 15	1.6 to 2.1
Pinion bearing cover plate bolts (14 ball lower bearing)	7 to 9	1 to 1.2
Pinion bearing cover plate bolts (11 ball lower bearing)	13 to 18	1.7 to 2.4
Rack slipper cover plate bolts (14 ball lower bearing)	7 to 9	1 to 1.2
Rack slipper cover plate bolts (11 ball lower bearing)	13 to 18	1.7 to 2.4
Wheelnuts (conical face)	63 to 85	8.7 to 11.8
Wheelnuts (flat face)	85 to 103	11.8 to 14.2

* *These are to be tightened with the wheels in the 'straight-ahead' position and the weight of the car resting on its wheels. They are to be locked by punching the nut intc the slot using a 0.10 in (3 mm) diameter ball ended punch.*
** *These are to be tightened with the weight of the car resting on its wheels.*

1 General description

Each of the independent front suspension MacPherson strut units consists of a vertical strut enclosing a double acting damper surrounded by a coil spring.

The upper end of each strut is secured to the top of the wing valance under the bonnet by rubber mountings.

The wheel spindle carrying the brake assembly and wheel hub is forged integrally with the suspension unit foot.

The steering arms are connected to each unit which is in turn connected to trackrods and thence to the rack and pinion steering gear.

The lower end of each suspension unit is located by a track control arm. A stabilising torsion bar is fitted between the outer ends of each track control arm and secured at the front to mountings on the body front member.

A rubber rebound stop is fitted inside each suspension unit thus preventing the spring becoming over-extended and jumping out of its mounting plates. Upward movement of the wheel is limited by the spring becoming fully compressed but this is damped by the addition of a rubber bump stop fitted around the suspension unit piston rod which comes into operation before the spring is fully compressed.

Whenever repairs have been carried out on a suspension unit it is essential to check the wheel alignment as the linkage could be altered which will affect the correct front wheel settings.

Every time the car goes over a bump vertical movement of a front wheel pushes the damper body upwards against the combined resistance of the coil spring and the damper piston.

Hydraulic fluid in the damper is displaced and forced through the compression valve into the space between the inner and outer cylinder. On the downward movement of the suspension, the road spring forces the damper body downwards against the pressure of the hydraulic fluid which is forced back again through the rebound valve. In this way the natural oscillations of the spring are damped out and a comfortable ride is obtained.

On the front uprights it is worth noting that there is a shroud inside the coil spring which protects the machined surface of the piston rod from road dirt.

The steering gear is of the rack and pinion type and is located on the front crossmember by two 'U' shaped clamps. The pinion is connected to the steering column by a flexible coupling. On Mercury Capri II models an optional power steering unit is available.

The steering wheel is mounted on a convoluted collapsible can which is designed to collapse progressively in the event of impact damage, thus protecting the driver to some degree.

Turning the steering wheel causes the rack to move in a lateral direction and the trackrods attached to each end of the rack pass this movement to the steering arms on the suspension/axle nuts thereby moving the roadwheels.

Two adjustments are possible on the steering gear, namely rack damper adjustment and pinion bearing pre-load adjustment, but the steering gear must be removed from the car to carry out these adjustments. Both adjustments are made by varying the thickness of shim-packs.

At the rear, the axle is located by two inverted 'U' bolts at each end of the casing to underslung semi-elliptic leaf springs which provide both lateral and longitudinal location. Lateral movement of the rear axle is further controlled by fitting a stabilizer bar.

Double acting telescopic shock absorbers are fitted between the spring plates on the rear axle and reinforced mountings in the boot of the car. These shock absorbers work on the same principle as the front shock absorbers.

In the interests of lessening noise and vibration, the spring and dampers are mounted on rubber bushes. A rubber spacer is also incorporated between the axle and the springs.

2 Front hub bearings – adjustment

1 To check the condition of the hub bearings, jack-up the front of the car and support on firmly based stands. Grasp the roadwheel at two opposite points to check for any rocking movement in the wheel hub. Watch carefully for any movement in the steering gear which can easily be mistaken for hub movement.

2 If a front wheel hub has excessive movement, this is adjusted by removing the hub cap and then tapping and levering the dust cap from the centre of the hub.

3 Remove the split pin from the nut retainer and lift away the adjusting nut retainer.

4 If a torque wrench is available tighten the centre adjusting nut to a torque wrench setting of 27 lbf ft (3.73 kgf m), and then slacken the nut back 90° which will give the required endfloat. Replace the nut retainer and lock with a new split pin.

5 Assuming a torque wrench is not available however, tighten the centre adjusting nut until a slight drag is felt on rotating the wheel. Then loosen the nut very slowly until the wheel turns freely again and there is just a perceptible endfloat. Refit the nut retainer and lock with a new split pin.

6 Refit the dust cap to the centre of the hub.

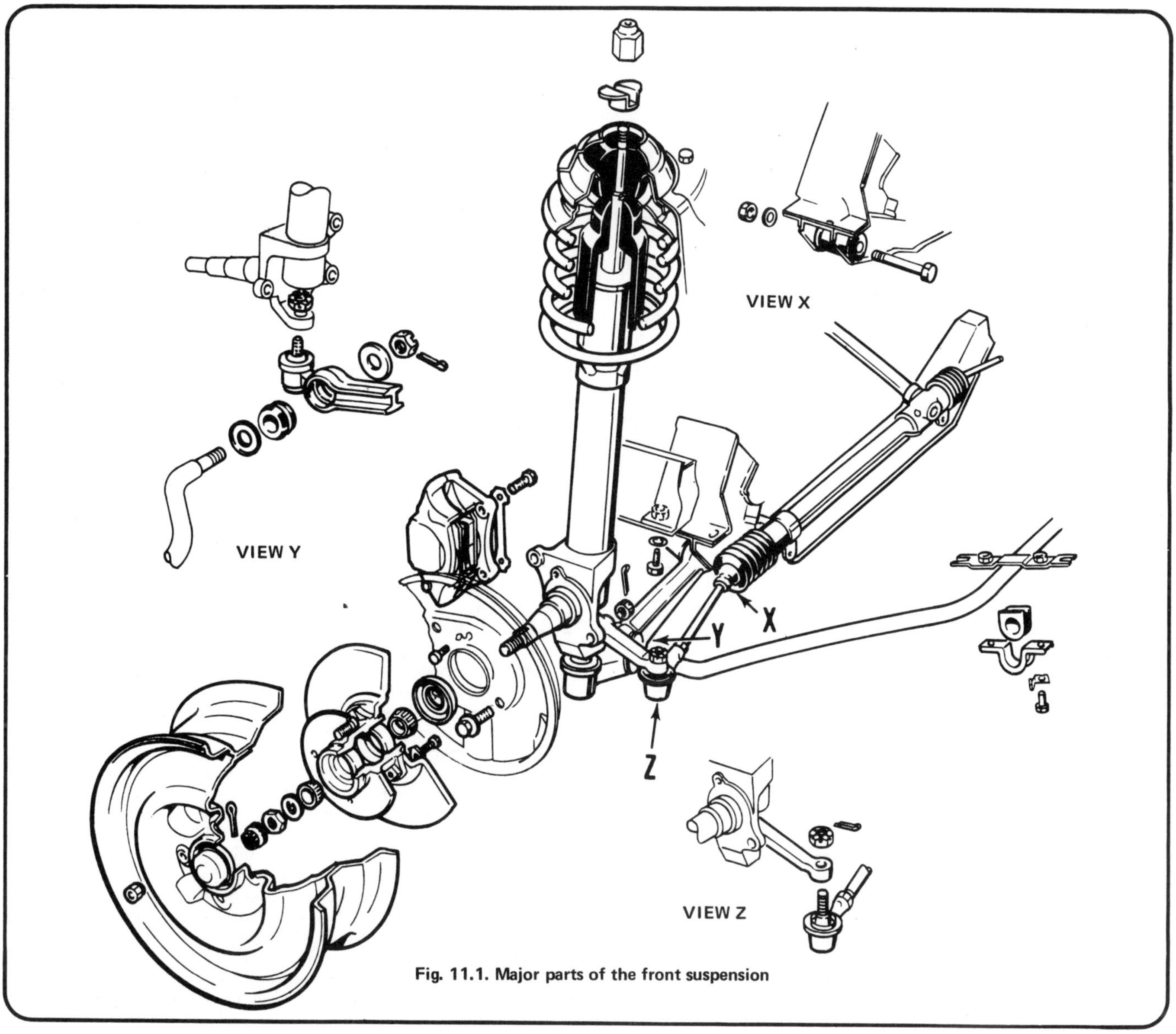

Fig. 11.1. Major parts of the front suspension

3 Front hub bearings and oil seal - renewal

1 Raise the front of the car and remove the roadwheels.
2 Disconnect the hydraulic brake pipe at the union on the suspension strut and plug the pipe ends.
3 Unbolt and remove the brake caliper (see Chapter 9).
4 Tap the dust cap from the end of the hub, extract the split-pin, remove the nut retainer, the nut and the thrust washer.
5 Pull the hub/disc towards you to displace the outer bearing. Be ready to catch it.
6 Prise out the oil seal and remove the inner bearing.
7 Drive out the bearing tracks from the hub using a brass drift. Clean out the grease from the hub interior.
8 If the disc is to be renewed because of deep scoring, bend down the tabs of the lockplates and unbolt it from the hub.
9 Reassembly is a reversal of removal. Do not mix up the bearing components as new kits are supplied as matched sets. Half fill the hub interior with grease and work some into the bearing races. Fit a new oil seal. Use new disc locking plates. Fit and adjust the hub as described in the preceding Section. On completion, bleed the brakes.

4 Front suspension strut - removal and refitting

1 It is difficult to work on the front suspension without one or two special tools, the most important of which is a set of adjustable spring clips which is Ford tool No. P.5045 (USA tool number T70P-5045). This tool or similar clips or compressors are vital and any attempt to dismantle the units without them may result in personal injury.
2 Get someone to sit on the wing of the car and with the spring partially compressed in this way, securely fit the spring clips.
3 Jack-up the car and remove the roadwheel, then disconnect the brake pipe at the bracket on the suspension leg and plug the pipes or have a jar handy to catch the escaping hydraulic fluid.
4 Disconnect the trackrod from the steering arm (see Section 11, paragraph 4), thus leaving the steering arm attached to the suspension unit.
5 Remove the outer end of the track control arm from the base of the suspension strut unit (for further information see Section 7).
6 Working under the bonnet, undo the three bolts holding the top end of the suspension strut to the side panel and lower the unit complete with the brake caliper away from the car.
7 Refitting is a direct reversal of the removal sequence but remember to use a new split pin on the steering arm to track rod nut and also on the track control arm to suspension unit nut.
8 The top suspension unit mounting bolts, the track control arm to suspension strut nut, and the steering arm to trackrod end nut must all be tightened to the specified torque.

5 Front coil spring - removal and refitting

1 Get someone to sit on the front wing of the car and with the spring partially compressed in this way securely fit spring clips or a roadspring compressor. (See Fig. 11.2).
2 Jack-up the front of the car, fit stands, and remove the road wheel
3 Working under the bonnet remove the piston nut and the cranked retainer.
4 Undo and remove the three bolts securing the top of the suspension unit to the side panel.
5 Push the piston rod downwards as far as it will go. It should now be possible to remove the top mounting assembly, the dished washer and the upper spring seat from the top of the spring.
6 The spring can now be lifted off its bottom seat and removed over the piston assembly.
7 If a new spring is being fitted check extremely carefully that it is of the same rating as the spring on the other side of the car. The colour coding of the springs can be found in the Specifications at the beginning of this Chapter.
8 Before fitting a new spring it must be compressed with the adjustable restrainers and make sure that the clips are placed on the same number of coils, and in the same position as on the spring that has been removed.
9 Place the new spring over the piston and locate it on its bottom seat, then pull the piston and fit the upper spring seat so that it locates correctly on the flats cut on the piston rod.
10 Fit the dished washer to the piston rod ensuring that the convex side faces upwards.
11 Now fit the top mounting assembly. With the steering in the straight-ahead position, fit the cranked retainer so that the ear on the retainer faces inwards and is at 90° to the centre-line of the car. Later models have retainers which incorporate two ears. Screw the piston rod nut on having previously applied Loctite or a similar compound to the threads. Do not fully tighten the piston nut at this stage.
12 If necessary pull the top end of the unit upward until it is possible to locate correctly the top mount bracket and fit the three retaining bolts from under the bonnet. These nuts must be tightened down to the specified torque.
13 Remove the spring clips, fit the roadwheel and lower the car to the ground.
14 Finally slacken off the piston rod nut, get an assistant to hold the upper spring seat to prevent it turning and retighten the nut to the specified torque. Ensure that the cranked retainer faces inwards (ie; towards the engine). (photo).

6 Front stabilizer bar - removal and refitting

1 Jack-up the front of the car, support the car on suitable stands and remove both front roadwheels.
2 Working under the car at the front, knock back the locking tabs on the four bolts securing the two front clamps that hold the stabilizer bar to the frame and then undo the four bolts and remove the clamps and rubber insulators.
3 Remove the split pins from the castellated nuts retaining the stabilizer bar to the track control arms then undo the nuts and pull off the large washers, carefully noting the way in which they are fitted.
4 Pull the stabilizer bar forward out of the two track control arms and remove from the car.
5 With the stabilizer bar out of the car remove the sleeve and large washer from each end of the bar again noting the correct fitting positions.
6 Reassembly is a reversal of the above procedure, but new locking tabs must be used on the front clamp bolts and new split pins on the castellated nuts. The nuts on the clamps and the castellated nuts on each end of the stabilizer bar must be fully tightened down until the car is resting on its wheels.
7 Once the car is on its wheels the castellated nuts on the ends of the stabilizer bar should be tightened down to the specified torque and the new split pins fitted. The four clamp bolts on the front mounting points must be tightened down to the specified torque and the locking tabs knocked up.

7 Track control arm (suspension arm) - removal and refitting

1 Jack-up the front of the car, support it on suitable stands and remove the front wheel.
2 Working under the car remove the split pin and unscrew the castellated nut that secures the track control arm to the stabilizer bar.
3 Lift away the large dished washer noting which way round it is fitted.
4 Remove the self-lock nut and flat washer from the back of the track control arm pivot bolt. Release the inner end of the track control arm.
5 Withdraw the split pin and unscrew the nut securing the track control arm balljoint to the base of the suspension unit. Separate the joint using a balljoint separator or wedges.
6 To refit the track control arm first assemble the track control arm ball stud to the base of the suspension unit.
7 Refit the nut and tighten to the specified torque. Secure with a new split pin.
8 Place the track control arm so that it correctly locates over the stabilizer bar and then secure the inner end.
9 Slide the pivot bolt into position from the front and secure with the flat washer and a new self-locking nut. The nut must be to the rear. Tighten the nut to the specified torque when the car is on the ground.
10 Fit the dished washer to the end of the stabilizer bar making sure it is the correct way round and secure with the castellated nut. This must be tightened when the car is on the ground, to the specified torque. Lock the castellated nut with a new split pin.

8 Rear shock absorber - removal and refitting

1 Remove the back seat after having removed the two screws from the floor assembly crossmember.
2 Remove the screws securing the seat belt to the top of the 'B' pillar.
3 Detach the 'B' pillar cover (2 screws).
4 Remove the top trim from the side window (4 screws).

5.14 Suspension unit cranked retainer - installed position

5 Remove the two screws from the rocker panel at the rear end and pull off the door weatherstrip in the region of the side trim.
6 Take out the boot side trim (2 screws) and the carpet.
7 Remove the lining of the rear panel (5 screws) and of the side panel (10 screws) folding the rear seat forward for access.
8 Note the position of the steel and rubber washer at the wheel arch and axle mounting, then remove the shock absorber.
9 Refitting is a direct reversal of the removal procedure, but ensure that the rubber and steel washers are correctly positioned (where these are showing signs of deterioration, replacement items should be used). Commence the refitting by first connecting the shock absorber at the axle end then extending it for fitting at the wheel arch end.

9 Rear stabilizer bar - removal, renewal of bushes and refitting

1 Chock the front wheels to prevent the car moving, the jack-up the rear of the car for access to the rear axle and stabilizer bar mountings.
2 Using a multi-grip wrench or similar tool to hold the stabilizer bar towards the axle tube, remove the two bolts at each stabilizer bar-to-axle tube bracket.
3 Disconnect the nut and bolt at each end of the stabilizer bar where it is attached to the floor assembly.
4 To renew a stabilizer bar mounting bush, remove the locknut at one end and unscrew the end piece. Remove the nut and withdraw both rubber bushes from the stabilizer bar.
5 Dip the new rubber bushes in glycerine or brake fluid, ensure that the stabilizer bar surface is clean and not scored, then slide on the bushes and refit the end piece. When fitted, the endpiece should be positioned as shown in Fig. 11.6, and the difference between the two sides must not be greater than 0.1 inch (2.5 mm).
6 If the bushes in the end pieces require renewal, it may be found more convenient to remove the end pieces from the stabilizer bar although this is not essential. The bushes can be pressed out using a

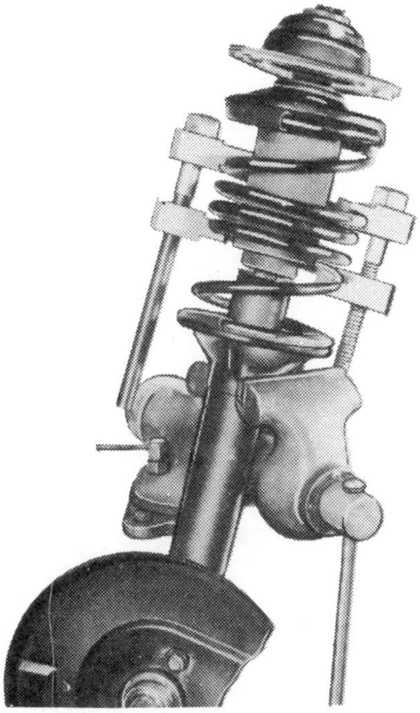

Fig. 11.2. Front strut supported in vice with special tool compressing coil spring (Sec. 4 and 5)

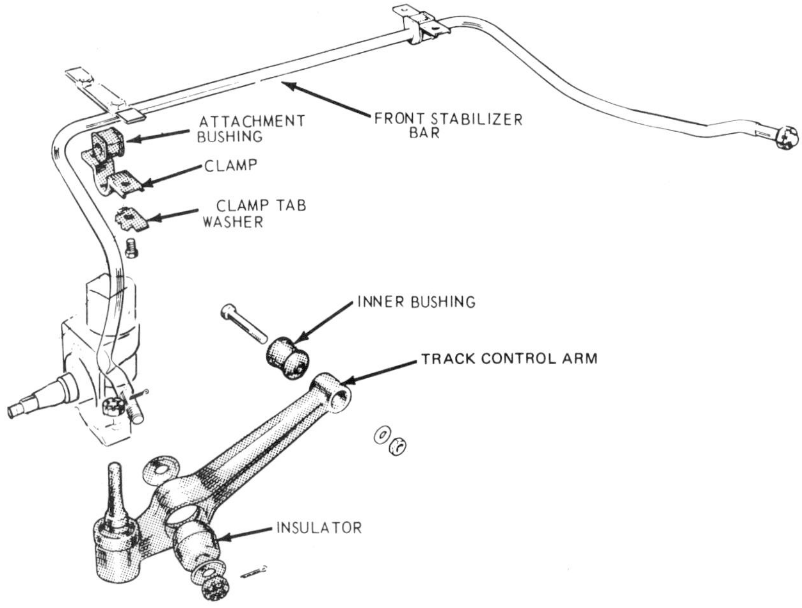

Fig. 11.3. The track control arm and stabilizer bar (Secs. 6 and 7)

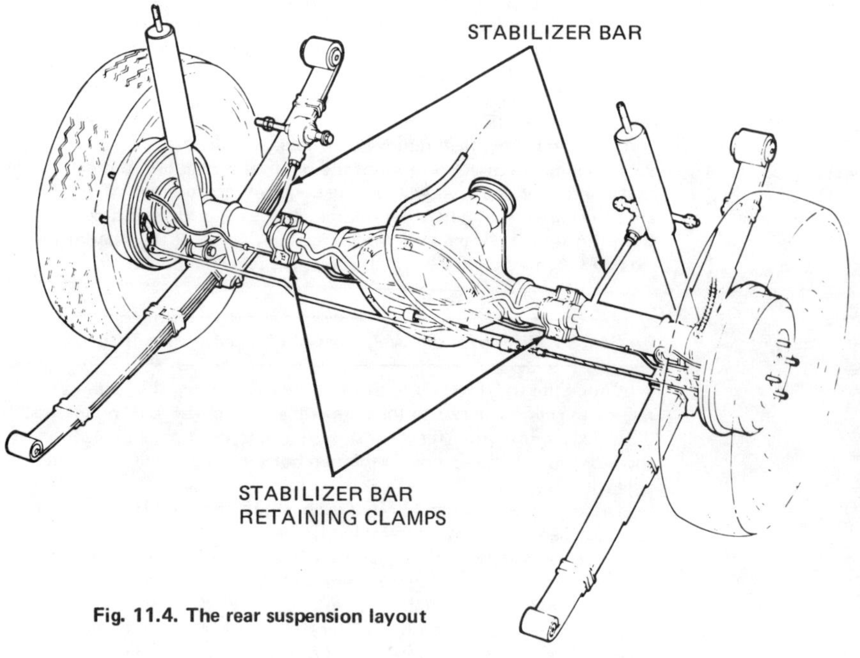

Fig. 11.4. The rear suspension layout

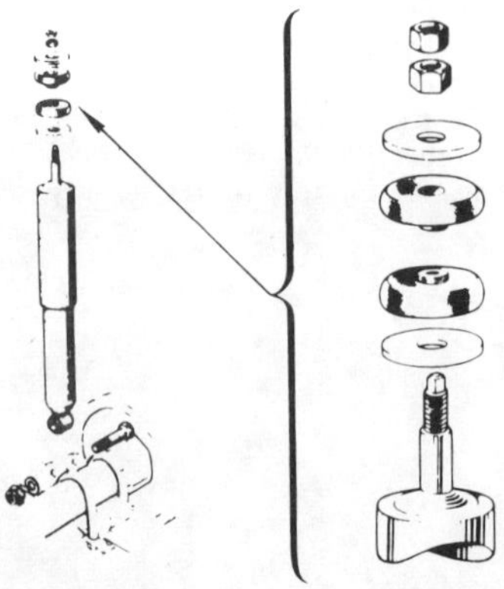

Fig. 11.5. The rear shock absorber mountings (Sec. 8))

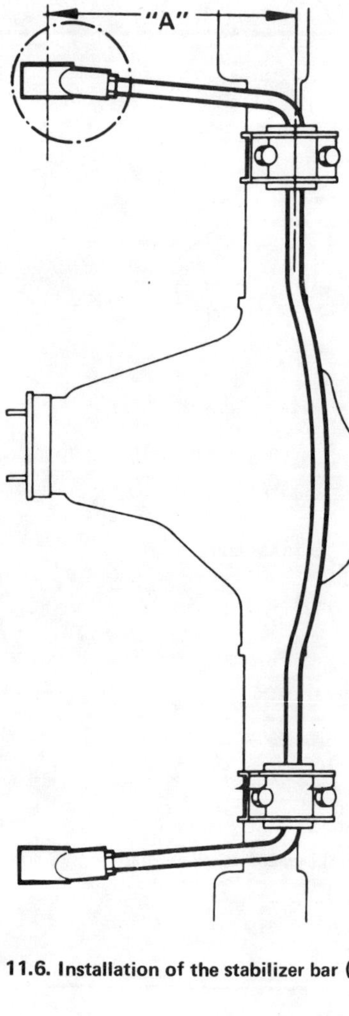

Fig. 11.6. Installation of the stabilizer bar (Sec. 9)

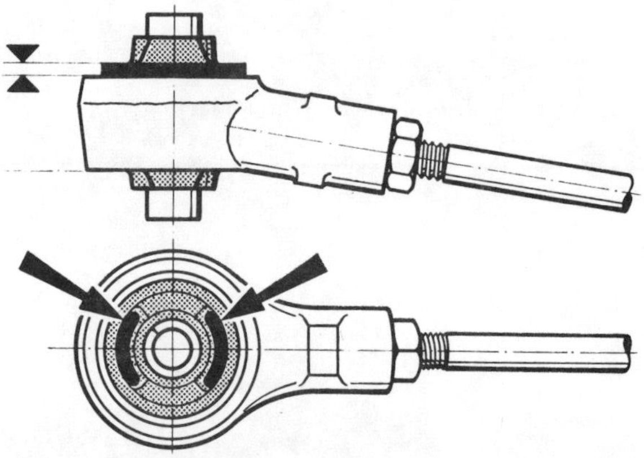

Fig. 11.7. The stabilizer bar rubber bush correctly positioned (Sec. 9)

suitable drift whilst the endpiece is supported on a suitable diameter tube. Installation is straightforward, the new bushes being pressed in until the steel case on the outside of the bush is flush with the inside of the end piece. Note the position of the semi-circular recess in the bush as shown in Fig. 11.7.

7 When refitting the stabilizer bar it should be fitted at the floor end first with the washers and self-locking nuts loosely installed.

8 The bar is then fitted to the axle tube using a suitable tool to pull it towards the axle. The brackets, clamps and rubber insulators should now be fitted and the bolts tightened to the specified torque.

9 Lower the vehicle to the ground then load the vehicle so that the centre of the axle tube and the spring rear eye are on the same horizontal level (the weight required is approximately that of two adults). The nuts and bolts securing the stabilizer bar to the floor can now be torque tightened to the specified value.

10 Rear leaf spring - removal, renewal of bushes and refitting

1 Chock the front wheels to prevent the car moving, then jack-up the rear of the car and support it on suitable stands. To make the springs more accessible remove the roadwheels.

2 Then place a trolley jack underneath the differential housing to support the rear axle assembly when the springs are removed. Do not

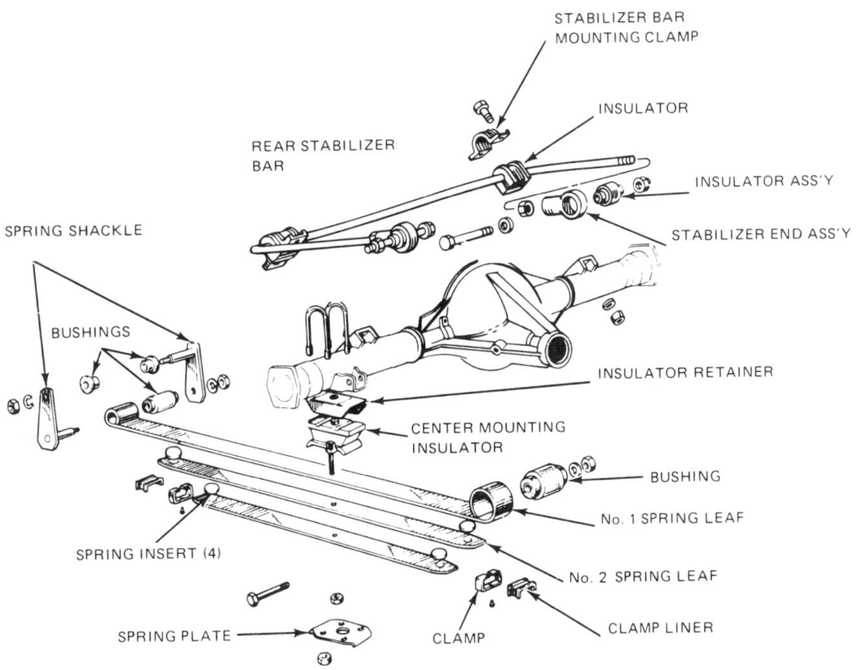

Fig. 11.8. Rear suspension - exploded view

raise the jack under the differential housing so that the springs are flattened, but raise it just enough to take the full weight of the axle with the springs fully extended.

3 Undo the rear shackle nuts and remove the combined shackle bolt and plate assemblies. Then remove the rubber bushes.

4 Undo the nut from the front mounting and take out the bolt running through the mounting.

5 Undo the nuts on the ends of the four 'U' bolts and remove the 'U' bolts together with the attachment plate and rubber spring insulators.

6 The rubber bushes can be pressed or driven out, and replacements fitted as described for the bushes in the stabilizer bar and end pieces in the previous Section. A little glycerine or brake fluid will allow the bushes to be pressed in more easily. Note that the front bushes are 7/16 inch (11 mm) diameter and the rear bushes are 5/16 inch (8 mm) diameter.

7 Refitting the spring is the reverse of the removal procedure. The nuts on the 'U' bolts, spring front mounting and rear shackles must be torqued down to the figures given in the Specifications at the beginning of this Chapter only **after** the car has been lowered onto its wheels.

11.2 Steering column clamp nut and bolt (arrowed)

11 Steering gear - removal and refitting

1 Before starting this job, set the front wheels in the straight-ahead position. Then jack-up the front of the car and place blocks under the wheels; lower the car slightly on the jack so that the trackrods are in a near horizontal position.

2 Remove the nut and bolt from the clamp at the front of the flexible coupling on the steering column. This clamp holds the coupling to the pinion splines. (photo).

3 Working on the front crossmember, knock back the locking tabs on the two nuts on each rack housing 'U' clamp, undo the nut and remove the locking tabs and clamps.

4 Remove the split pins and castellated nuts from the ends of each trackrod where they join the steering arms. Separate the trackrods from the steering arms using a ball joint separator or wedges and lower the steering gear downwards out of the car.

5 Before refitting the steering gear make sure that the wheels have remained in the straight-ahead position. Also check the condition of the mounting rubbers round the housing and if they appear worn or damaged renew them.

6 Check that the steering gear is also in the straight-ahead position. This can be done by ensuring that the distances between the ends of both trackrods and the steering gear housing on both sides are the same.

7 Place the steering gear in its location on the crossmember and at the same time mate up the splines on the pinion with the splines in the clamp on the steering column flexible coupling.

8 Refit the two 'U' clamps using new locking tabs under the bolts, tighten down the bolts to the specified torque.

9 Refit the trackrod ends into the steering arms, refit the castellated nuts and tighten them to the specified torque. Use new split pins to retain the nuts.

10 Tighten the clamp bolt on the steering column flexible coupling to the specified torque, having first made sure that the pinion is correctly located in the splines.

11 Jack-up the car, remove the blocks from under the wheels and lower the car to the ground. It is advisable at this stage to take the car to your local dealer and have the toe-in checked (see Section 19).

12 Steering gear - adjustments

1 For the steering gear to function correctly, two adjustments are

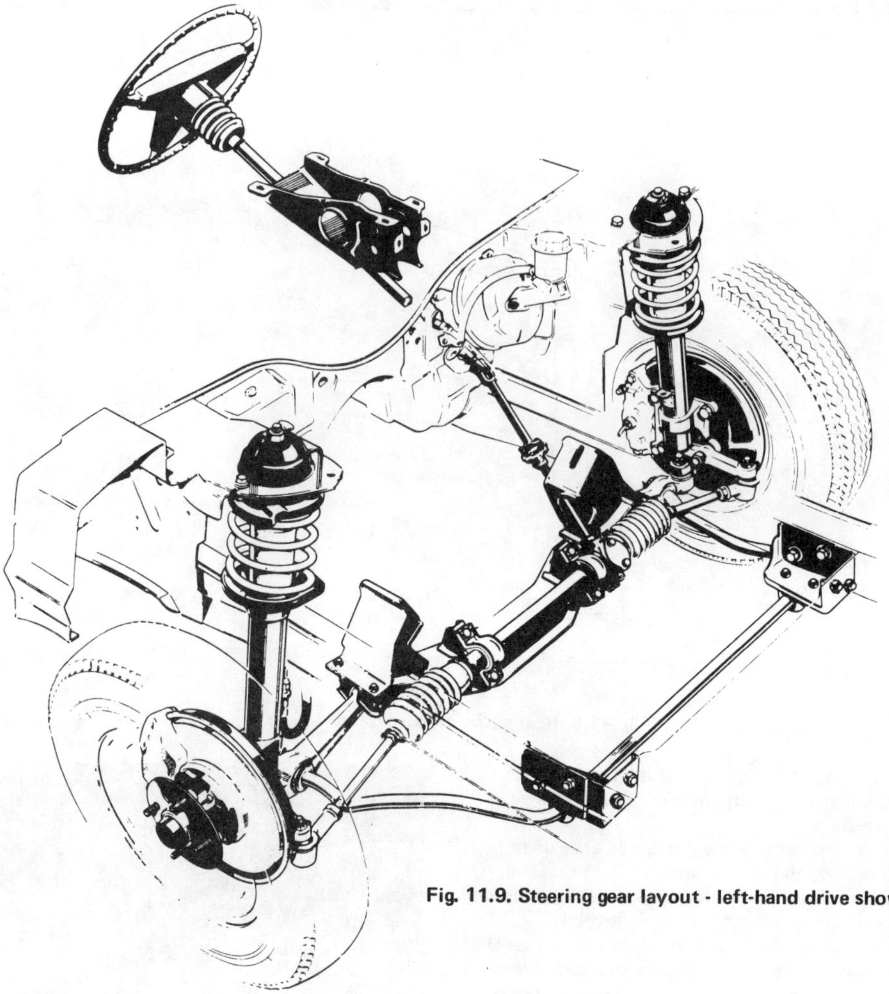

Fig. 11.9. Steering gear layout - left-hand drive shown (Sec. 11)

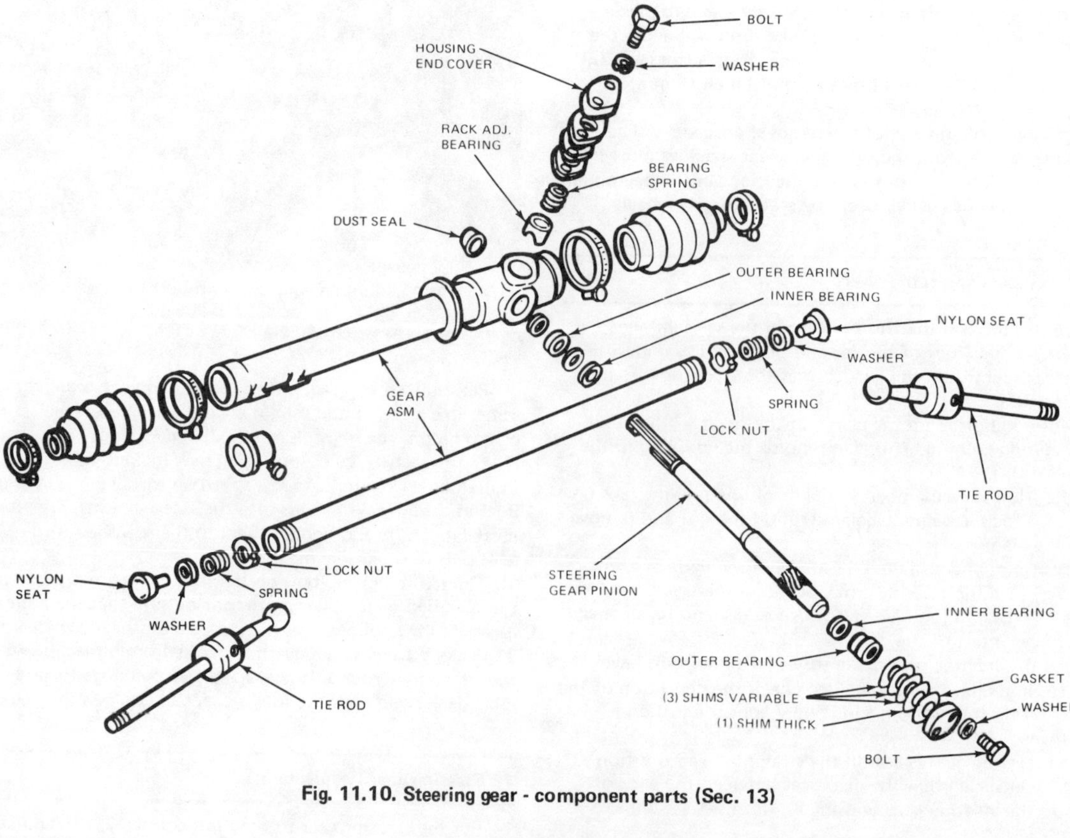

Fig. 11.10. Steering gear - component parts (Sec. 13)

necessary. These are pinion bearing preload and rack slipper adjustment. Ideally this will require the use of a dial gauge and mounting block, a surface table, a torque gauge and a splined adaptor. It is felt that most people will be able to suitably improvise using other equipment, but if this cannot be done and the equipment listed is not available, the job should be entrusted to your local vehicle main dealer.

2 To carry out these adjustments, remove the steering gear from the car as described in the previous Section. Mount the assembly in a soft jawed vice then remove the rack slipper cover plate, shim pack gasket and spring.

3 Remove the pinion bearing cover plate, shim pack and gasket. Check the number of balls in the lower bearing as the torque on reassembly will depend on this.

Pinion bearing preload

4 Place the shim pack and cover plate on the bearing, tighten the bolts then slacken them so that the cover plate touches the shim. The shim pack must comprise at least three shims one of which must be 0.093 inch (2.35 mm), this being immediately against the cover plate.

5 Measure the cover plate-to-housing gap, and if outside the range 0.011 to 0.013 inch (0.28 to 0.33 mm) reduce the shim pack thickness (if the gap is too large) or increase it (if the gap is too small) until this gap is obtained. Remember that the 0.093 inch (2.35 mm) shim must remain immediately against the cover plate.

6 When the correct gap is obtained, remove the cover plate, install the gasket and refit the cover plate. Apply a sealer such as Loctite to the cover bolt threads, fit them and torque tighten to the specified setting.

Rack slipper adjustment

7 Having set the pinion bearing preload measure the height of the slipper above the main body of the rack as the rack is transversed from lock-to-lock by turning the pinion. Note the height reading obtained.

8 Prepare a shim pack which, including the thickness of the rack slipper bearing gasket, is 0.002 to 0.006 inch (0.05 to 0.15 mm) thicker than the dimension noted in paragraph 7.

9 Fit the spring, gasket, shim pack and cover plate to the rack housing (gasket nearest housing). Apply a sealer such as Loctite to the cover bolt threads, fit them and torque tighten to specification.

10 Measure the torque required to turn the pinion throughout its range of travel. This should be 10 to 18 lbf inch (11.5 to 20.7 kg cm); if outside this range, faulty components, lack of lubricant, etc., should be suspected.

13 Steering gear - dismantling, overhaul and reassembly

Note: The procedure given may be beyond the capabilities of many d-i-y motorists. Read through the Section before commencing any work and if not considered to be feasible, entrust the job to your local vehicle main dealer.

1 Remove and discard the wire retaining clips, remove the bellows and drain the lubricant.

2 Mount the steering gear in a soft-jawed vice and drill out the pins securing the trackrod housings to the locknuts. Centre-punch the pins before drilling then use a 4 mm (5/32 inch or No. 22) drill but do not drill too deeply.

3 It is now necessary to unscrew the housings from the ball joints so that the trackrods, housings, locknuts, ball seats, washers and springs can be removed. Ideally this requires the use of special tools which should be available from a vehicle main dealer but if improvised grips or wrenches are used take care that no parts are damaged (if parts are damaged, replacement items must be obtained).

4 Remove the rack slipper cover plate, shim pack, gasket and slipper.

5 Remove the pinion bearing preload cover plate, shim pack, gasket and lower bearing.

6 Using a screwdriver or similar tool, prise out the pinion oil seal.

7 Clean all dirt and paint from the pinion shaft then push the pinion out of the housing.

8 Take out the pinion upper bearing and washer.

9 Clean and inspect all the parts for damage and wear. Examine the bush in the end of the rack tube furthest from the pinion; if worn it can be pressed out and a replacement fitted.

10 Commence reassembly by fitting the pinion upper bearing and washer into the housing.

11 Position the rack into the housing, and leave it in the central position.

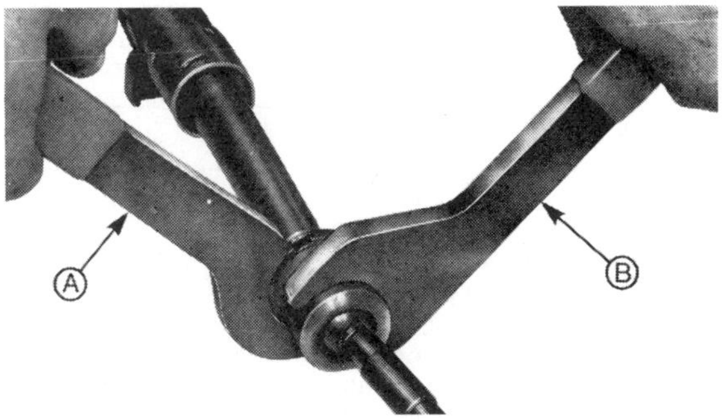

Fig. 11.11. Removing a track rod (Sec. 13)
A and B are special tools available for the purpose

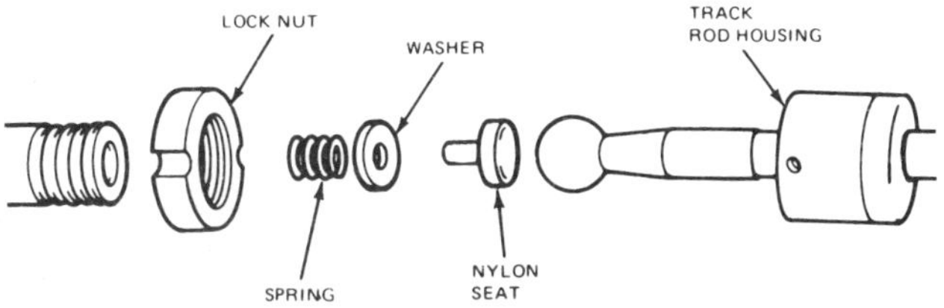

Fig. 11.12. Tie rod (track rod or connecting rod) ball joint - exploded view (Sec. 13)

12 Install the pinion, ensuring that after installation the flat is towards the right-hand side of the vehicle (irrespective of right or left-hand drive vehicles).

13 Fit the pinion lower bearing cover plate and adjust the preload as described in the previous Section.

14 Assemble the rack slipper, spring, gasket, shim pack and cover plate, adjusting as described in the previous Section.

15 Lubricate the ball seats, balls and housings with SAE 90 EP gear oil. Screw the locknuts onto the ends of the steering rack.

16 Assemble the springs, washers, ball seats, trackrod ends and housing. Tighten the housings to obtain a rotational torque of 5 lbf ft (0.7 kgf m) then lock them with the locknuts. Recheck the torque after tightening the locknut.

17 Drill new holes (even if the old holes are in alignment), 4 mm (5/32 inch or No. 22 drill) diameter x9 mm (0.38 inch) deep along the break lines between the housing and the locknut, approximately opposite the spanner locating hole in the housing.

18 Fit new retaining pins and peen over the surrounding metal to retain them.

19 Lightly grease the inside of the bellows where they will contact the trackrods, install one bellows ensuring that it locates in the trackrod groove; then fit a new retaining clip.

20 Add the specified quantity of steering gear oil, operating the rack over its range of travel to assist the lubricant in flowing. Do not overfill.

21 Fit the other bellows.

22 Check the pinion turning torque, as described in paragraph 10 of the previous Section.

14 Power steering - general description

1 The power steering system available on Mercury Capri II cars has a pulley-driven Hobourn-Eaton series 110 roller pump. This pump delivers fluid to a servo assisted rack and pinion gear assembly.

2 Servo assistance is obtained through a piston mounted on the rack and running in the rack tube. The degree of assistance is controlled by a spool valve mounted concentrically with the input and pinion shaft.

3 The power steering pump incorporates an integral fluid reservoir.

4 Owing to the complexity of the power steering system it is recommended that servicing etc., is limited to that given in the following

Sections. In the event of a fault occurring it is recommended that repair or overhaul is entrusted to a specialist in this type of work.

15 Power steering - bleeding

1 The power steering system will only need bleeding in the event of air being introduced into the system ie; where pipes have been disconnected or where a leakage has occurred. To bleed the system proceed as described in the following paragraphs.
2 Open the bonnet (hood) and check the fluid level in the integral reservoir. Top-up if necessary using the specified type of fluid.
3 If fluid is added, allow two minutes then run the engine at approximately 1500 rpm. Slowly turn the steering wheel from lock-to-lock, whilst checking and topping-up the fluid level until the level remains steady and no more bubbles appear in the reservoir.
4 Clean and refit the reservoir cap, and close the bonnet.

16 Power steering pump - removal and refitting

1 Disconnect the battery earth lead.
2 Raise the car on a hoist or place it over an inspection pit if possible. Alternatively, the car must be jacked-up to provide the working room beneath.
3 Where applicable, remove the engine splash shield.
4 Loosen the alternator mounting bolts and remove the drivebelt (refer to Chapter 10 if necessary).
5 Disconnect the power system fluid lines and drain the fluid into a suitable container.
6 Remove the fuel pump from the engine, but do not disconnect the fuel lines. Move the pump away from the power steering bolts. (Refer to Chapter 3 for further information, if necessary).
7 Remove the power steering pump. As applicable, remove the pump pulley and adaptor bracket.
8 Refitting is a direct reversal of the removal procedure. Ensure that the fluid lines are tightened to the specified torque, top-up the system with an approved fluid, adjust the alternator drivebelt tension (see Chapter 10), then bleed the system, as described in the previous Section 15.

17 Power steering gear - removal and refitting

1 The procedure for removing the power steering gear is similar to that described in Section 11 for the manual steering gear with the additional task of disconnecting the pump lines. When refitting, ensure that the fluid lines are tightened to the specified torque, top-up the system with an approved fluid, adjust the alternator drivebelt tension, see Chapter 10, then bleed the system, as described in Section 15.

18 Steering column - removal, dismantling, reassembly and refitting

1 Disconnect the battery earth lead.
2 Remove the upper and lower steering coupling clamp bolts, and tap the coupling shaft down the pinion shaft to disconnect the coupling shaft from the column.
3 Carefully prise out the motif from the centre of the steering wheel and then unscrew the wheel retaining nut (photo).
4 Ensure that the roadwheels are in the straight-ahead position then pull off the steering wheel.
5 Remove the direction indicator actuator cam.
6 Remove the steering column shroud (2 screws at the bottom, then pull out at the top) and lower the dash panel trim.
7 Disconnect the direction indicator switch from the column (two bolts - see Fig. 11.15).
8 Disconnect the loom wiring from the ignition switch.
9 Remove the two steering column retaining bolts (see Fig. 11.16) and pull the column assembly from the vehicle. Push the grommet out of the floor pan.
10 Drill off the steering column lockbolt heads, or tap them round with a pin punch, then use suitable grips to pull out the bolt shanks. Remove the steering lock (refer to Chapter 10, if necessary).
11 Remove the circlip snap ring, washer and spring from the lower end of the column.
12 Tap the lower end of the shaft with a soft-faced hammer to remove the shaft and bearing from the top of the column.
13 Using the shaft as a drift, tap the lower bearing out of the column.
14 Inspect all the parts for wear and damage, renewing if necessary.
15 Commence reassembly by positioning the shaft in the column, then assemble the lower bearing (smaller diameter towards the column), spring, washer and circlip to the shaft. Push the assembly into the column to locate the bearing against the stops.
16 Press the upper bearing onto the column.
17 Secure the steering lock to the column and shear the bolts.
18 Use the steering lock to locate the shaft in the column, then fit the direction indicator actuating cam and steering wheel (check that the roadwheels are still in the 'straight-ahead' position).
19 Install the steering column grommet at the lower end.
20 Locate the column assembly and secure it with the two mounting bolts.
21 The remainder of the refitting procedure is the reverse of the removal procedure.

19 Steering angles and front wheel alignment

1 Accurate front wheel alignment is essential for good steering and tyre wear. Before considering the steering angle, check that the tyres are correctly inflated, that the front wheels are not buckled, the hub bearings are not worn or incorrectly adjusted and that the steering linkage is in good order, without slackness or wear at the joints.
2 Wheel alignment consists of four factors:

Camber which is the angle at which the front wheels are set from the vertical when viewed from the front of the car. Positive camber is the amount (in degrees) that the wheels are tilted outwards at the top from the vertical.

Castor is the angle between the steering axis and a vertical line when viewed from each side of the car. Positive castor is when the steering axis is inclined rearwards.

Steering axis inclination is the angle when viewed from the front of the car, between the vertical and an imaginary line drawn between the upper and lower suspension strut pivots.

Toe-in is the amount by which the distance between the **front** inside edges of the roadwheels (measured at hub height) is less than the distance measured between the **rear** inside edges.

3 The angles of camber, castor and steering axis are set in production and are not adjustable.
4 Front wheel alignment (toe-in) checks are best carried out with modern setting equipment but a reasonably accurate alternative is by means of the following procedure.
5 Place the car on level ground with the wheels in the 'straight-ahead' position. It should be unladen apart from the spare wheel, jack and wheelspanner. Tyre pressures should be normal. Bounce the car, front and rear, up and down about 2 ins (50 mm) to settle the suspension. Don't disturb the ride height by jacking or sitting in the car before the toe-in checks are done.
6 Obtain or make a toe-in gauge. One may easily be made from a length of rod or tubing, cranked to clear the sump or bellhousing and having a setscrew and locknut at one end.
7 With the gauge, measure the distance between the two inner wheel rims at hub height at the front of the wheel.
8 Rotate the roadwheel through 180^{o}(half a turn) by pushing or pulling the car and then measure the distance again at hub height between the inner wheel rims at the rear of the roadwheel. This measurement should either be the same as the one just taken or greater by not more than 0.28 inch (7 mm).
9 Where the toe-in is found to be incorrect slacken the locknuts on each trackrod, also the flexible bellows clips and rotate each trackrod by an equal amount until the correct toe-in is obtained. Tighten the trackrod-end locknuts while the ball joints are held in the centre of their arcs of travel. It is imperative that the lengths of the trackrods are always equal otherwise the wheel angles on turns will be incorrect. If new components have been fitted, set the roadwheels in the 'straight-ahead' position and also centralise the steering wheel. Now adjust the lengths of the trackrods by turning them so that the trackrod-end ball joint studs will drop easily into the eyes of the steering arms. Measure the distances between the centres of the ball joints and the grooves on the inner ends of the trackrods and adjust, if necessary so that they are equal. This is an initial setting only and precise adjustment must be carried out as described in earlier paragraphs of this Section.

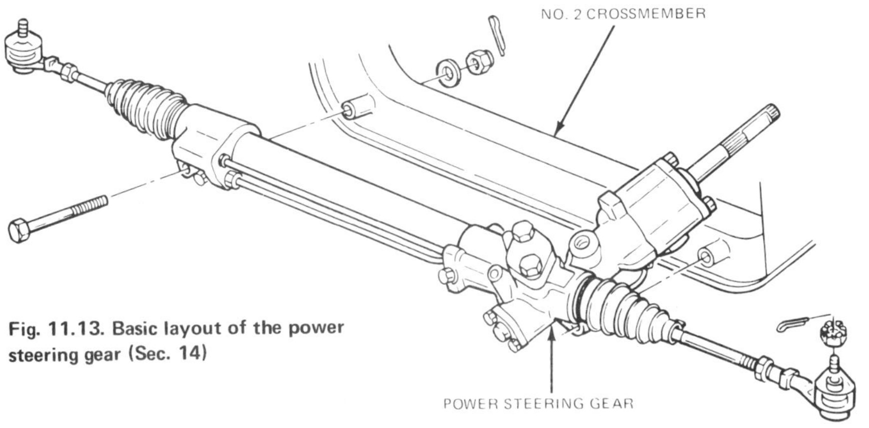

Fig. 11.13. Basic layout of the power steering gear (Sec. 14)

Fig. 11.14. Power steering reservoir and dipstick (Sec. 15)

18.3 Removal of the steering wheel motif

Fig. 11.15. Retaining bolts for direction indicator switch (arrowed) (Sec. 18)

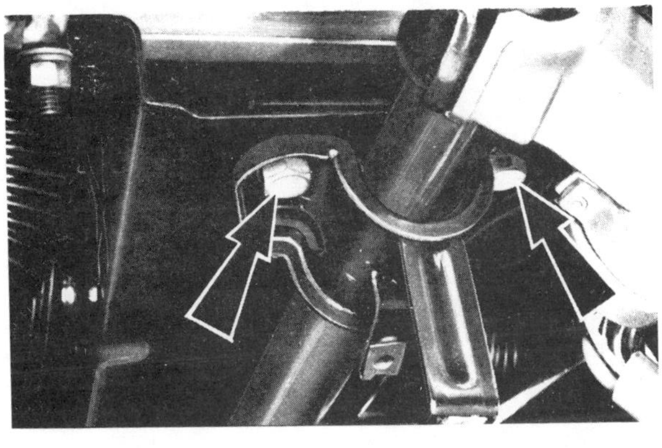

Fig. 11.16. Retaining bolts for the steering column (arrowed) (Sec. 18)

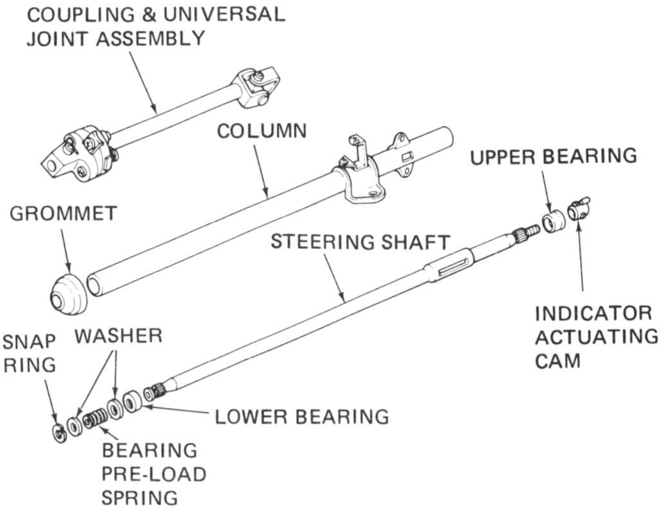

Fig. 11.17. The steering column assembly (Sec. 18)

20 Wheels and tyres

1 Check the tyre pressures weekly (when they are cold).
2 Frequently inspect the tyre walls and treads for damage and pick out any large stones which have become trapped in the tread pattern.
3 If the wheels and tyres have been balanced on the car then they should not be moved to a different axle position. If they have been balanced off the car then, in the interests of extending tread life, they can be moved between front and rear on the same side of the car and the spare incorporated in the rotational pattern.
4 Never mix tyres of different construction or very dissimilar tread patterns.
5 Always keep the roadwheels tightened to the specified torque and if the bolt holes become elongated or flattened, renew the wheel.
6 Occasionally, clean the inner faces of the roadwheels and if there is any sign of rust or corrosion, paint them with metal preservative paint. **Note:** Corrosion on aluminium alloy wheels may be evidence of a more serious problem which could lead to wheel failure. If corrosion is evident, consult your Ford dealer for advice.
7 Before removing a roadwheel which has been balanced on the car, always mark one wheel stud and bolt hole so that the roadwheel may be refitted in the same relative position to maintain the balance.

21 Fault diagnosis - Suspension and steering

Before diagnosing faults from the following chart, check that any irregularities are not caused by:

1. *Binding brakes.*
2. *Incorrect 'mix' of radial and crossply tyres.*
3. *Incorrect tyre pressures.*
4. *Misalignment of the bodyframe.*

Symptom	Reason(s)
Steering wheel can be moved considerably before any sign of movement of the roadwheels is apparent	Wear in the steering linkage, gear and column coupling.
Vehicle difficult to steer in a consistent straight line - wandering	As above. Wheel alignment incorrect (indicated by excessive or uneven tyre wear). Front wheel hub bearings loose or worn. Worn ball joints.
Steering stiff and heavy	Incorrect wheel alignment (indicated by excessive or uneven tyre wear). Excessive wear or seizure in one or more of the joints in the steering linkage or suspension. Excessive wear in the steering gear. Failure of power steering gear pump.
Wheel wobble and vibration	Roadwheels out of balance. Roadwheels buckled. Wheel alignment incorrect. Wear in the steering linkage, suspension ball joints or track control arm pivot. Broken front spring
Excessive pitching and rolling on corners and during braking	Defective shock absorbers and/or broken spring.

Chapter 12 Bodywork and fittings

For modifications, and information applicable to later models, see Supplement at end of manual

Contents

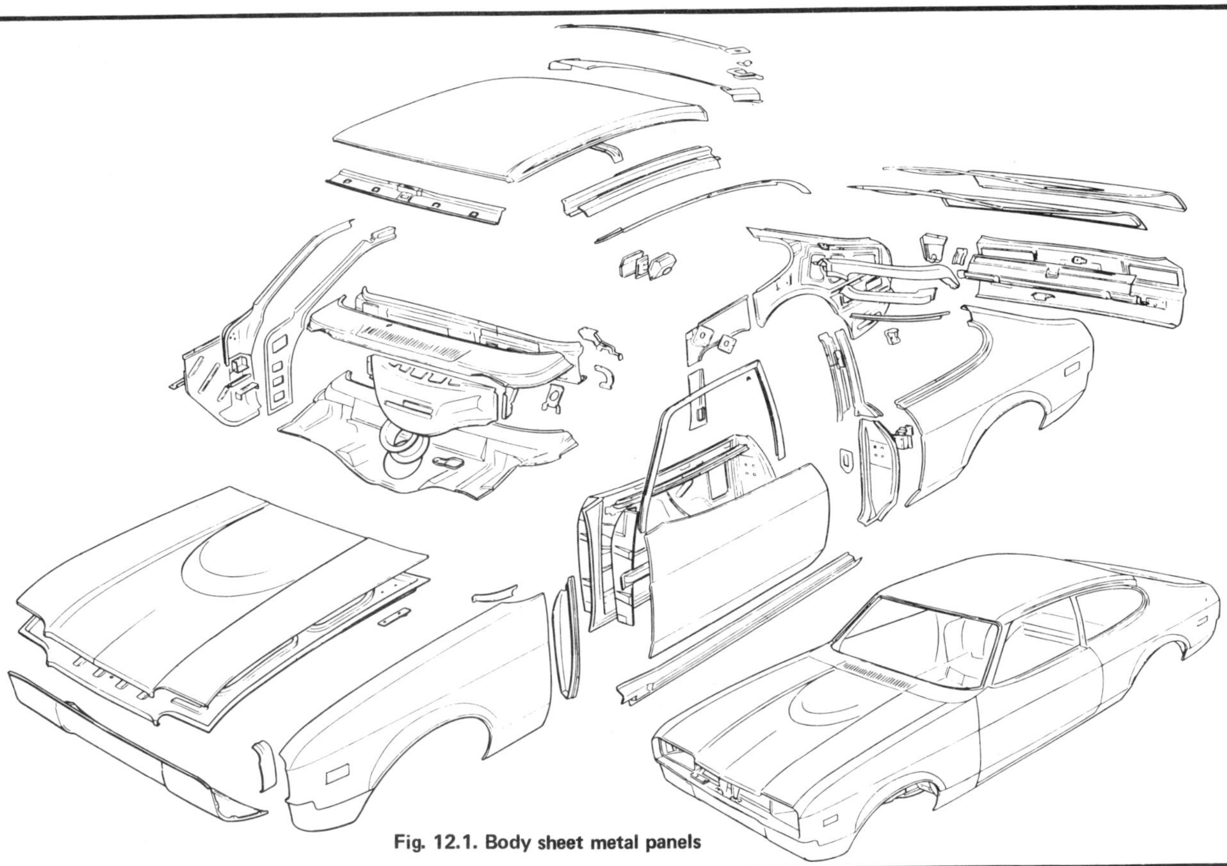

Fig. 12.1. Body sheet metal panels

1 General description

The body is of a monocoque all-steel, welded construction with impact absorbing front and rear sections.

The car has 2 side doors and a full-length lifting tailgate for easy access to the rear compartment. The side doors are fitted with anti-burst locks and incorporate a key operated lock in each handle; window frames are adjustable for position. The tailgate hinges are bolted to the underside of the roof panel and to the tailgate itself. Gas-filled dampers support the tailgate in the open position; when closed it is fastened by a key-operated lock incorporating a release pushbutton.

An automatic bonnet (hood) locking mechanism operates when the bonnet is closed, a release lever being fitted at the edge of the instrument panel on the driver's side. The bonnet (hood) is hinged at the rear and is held in the open position by a support stay.

A cable-operated sliding roof is available as an option, this being controlled by a handle fitted flush to the head lining.

Toughened safety glass is fitted to all windows, the windscreen having an additional 'zone' toughened band in front of the driver. In the event of the windscreen shattering this zone crazes into large sections to give a greater degree of visibilty as a safety feature. An optional glass/plastic/glass laminated windscreen is available at extra cost on early UK models. All North American and later UK models have a laminated screen as standard to comply with modern safety standards; this has the advantage of cracking only, to give an even greater degree of visibility in the event of accidental damage. The front door windows have a convenient winding mechanism. On certain variants, frameless opening rear quarter windows are fitted. These are hinged at the forward edge and are operated from an 'over-centre' type latch. A heated rear window is available as an optional extra throughout the range.

All vehicles have individual reclining front bucket seats. GT versions have individual rear folding seats whereas a folding rear bench seat is used on other models. The standard seat and panel upholstery is a vinyl material but a cloth fabric trim is available for all models.

A padded facia crash panel is standard equipment together with deep pile wall-to-wall carpeting. Inertia reel seatbelts are fitted to all models.

To prevent damage under minor impacts, rubber faced bumpers are used, with rubber overriders on GT models.

All models are fitted with a heating and ventilating system which operates by ram air when the car is moving, or by a blower when stationary or for increased airflow. The heater is operated from a central control panel and airflow is directed to the windscreen or car interior according to the control lever settings. A heavy duty heater is available for some markets, and USA models can be supplied with an optional air conditioning system.

2 Maintenance - bodywork and underframe

1 The condition of your car's bodywork is of considerable importance as it is on this that the secondhand value of the car will mainly depend. It is very much more difficult to repair neglected bodywork than to renew mechanical assemblies. The hidden portions of the body, such as the wheel arches and the underframe and the engine compartment are equally important though obviously not requiring such frequent attention as the immediately visible paintwork.

2 Once a year or every 12,000 miles (19000 km), it is a sound scheme to visit your local main agent and have the underside of the body steam cleaned. This will take about 1½ hours. All traces of dirt and oil will be removed and the underside can then be inspected carefully for rust, damaged hydraulic pipes, frayed electrical wiring and similar maladies.

3 At the same time the engine compartment should be cleaned in the same manner. If steam cleaning facilities are not available then brush a water soluble cleanser over the whole engine and engine compartment with a stiff paintbrush, working it well in where there is an accumulation of oil and dirt. Do not paint the ignition system but protect it with oily rags when the cleanser is washed off. As the cleanser is washed away it will take with it all traces of oil and dirt, leaving the engine looking clean and bright.

4 The wheel arches should be given particular attention as undersealing can easily come away here and stones and dirt thrown up from the road wheels can soon cause the paint to chip and flake, and so allow rust to set in. If rust is found, clean down to the bare metal with wet and dry paper, paint on an anti-corrosive coating and renew the paintwork and undercoating.

5 The bodywork should be washed once a week or when dirty. Thoroughly wet the car to soften the dirt and then wash the car down with a soft sponge and plenty of clean water. If the surplus dirt is not washed off very gently, in time it will wear the paint down as surely as wet and dry paper. It is best to use a hose if this is available. Give the car a final wash down and then dry with a soft chamois leather to prevent the formation of spots.

6 Spots of tar and grease thrown up from the road can be removed with a rag dampened with petrol.

7 Once every six months, or every three months, if wished, give the bodywork and chromium trim a thoroughly good wax polish. If a chromium cleaner is used to remove rust or any of the car's plated parts remember that the cleaner also removes part of the chromium so use sparingly.

3 Maintenance - upholstery and carpets

1 Remove the carpets and thoroughly vacuum clean the interior of the car every three months or more frequently if necessary.

2 Beat out the carpets and vacuum clean them if they are very dirty. If the headlining or upholstery is soiled apply an upholstery cleaner with a damp sponge and wipe off with a clean dry cloth.

4 Maintenance - vinyl roof covering

Under no circumstances try to clean any external vinyl roof covering with detergents, caustic soaps or spirit cleaners. Plain soap and water is all that is required with a soft brush to clean dirt that may be ingrained. Wash the covering as frequently as the rest of the car.

5 Minor body damage - repair

Repair of minor scratches in the car's bodywork

If the scratch is very superficial and does not penetrate to the metal of the bodywork, repair is very simple. Lightly rub the area of the scratch with a paintwork renovator, or a very fine cutting paste, to remove loose paint from the scratch and to clear the surrounding bodywork of wax polish. Rinse the area with clean water.

Apply touch-up paint to the scratch using a thin paintbrush, continue to apply thin layers of paint until the surface of the paint in the scratch is level with the surrounding paintwork. Allow the new paint at least two weeks to harden; then blend it into the surrounding paintwork by rubbing the paintwork, in the scratch area with a paintwork renovator, or a very fine cutting paste. Finally apply wax polish.

Where the scratch has penetrated right through to the metal of the bodywork, causing the metal to rust, a different repair technique is required. Remove any loose rust from the bottom of the scratch with a penknife, then apply rust inhibiting paint to prevent the formation of rust in the future. Using a rubber nylon applicator, fill the scratch with bodystopper paste. If required, this paste can be mixed with cellulose thinners to provide a very thin paste which is ideal for filling narrow scratches. Before the stopper-paste in the scratch hardens, wrap a piece of smooth cotton rag around the top of a finger. Dip the finger in cellulose thinners and then quickly sweep it across the surface of the stopper-paste in the scratch; this will ensure that the surface of the stopper-paste is slightly hollowed. The scratch can now be painted over as described earlier in this Section.

Repair of dents in the car's bodywork

When deep denting of the car's bodywork has taken place, the first task is to pull the dent out, until the affected bodywork almost attains its original shape. There is little point in trying to restore the original shape completely, as the metal in the damaged area will have stretched on impact and cannot be reshaped fully to its original contour. It is better to bring the level of the dent up to the point which is about

1/8 inch (3 mm) below the level of the surrounding bodywork. In cases where the dent is very shallow anyway, it is not worth trying to pull it out at all.

If the underside of the dent is accessible, it can be hammered out gently from behind, using a mallet with a wooden or plastic head. Whilst doing this, hold a suitable block of wood firmly against the impact from the hammer blows and thus prevent a large area of bodywork from being 'belled-out'.

Should the dent be in a section of the bodywork which has a double skin or some other factor making it inaccessible from behind, a different technique is called for. Drill several small holes through the metal inside the dent area - particularly in the deeper sections. Then screw long self-tapping screws into the holes just sufficiently for them to gain a good purchase in the metal. Now the dent can be pulled out by pulling on the protruding heads of the screws with a pair of pliers.

The next stage of the repair is the removal of the paint from the damaged area, and from an inch or so of the surrounding 'sound' bodywork. This is accomplished most easily by using a wire brush or abrasive pad on a power drill, although it can be done just as effectively by hand using sheets of abrasive paper. To complete the preparations for filling, score the surface of the bare metal with a screwdriver or the tang of a file, or alternatively, drill small holes in the affected area. This will provide a really good 'key' for filler paste.

To complete the repair see the Section on filling and respraying.

Repair of rust holes or gashes in the car's bodywork

Remove all paint from the affected area and from an inch or so of the surrounding 'sound' bodywork, using an abrasive pad or a wire brush on a power drill. If these are not available a few sheets of abrasive paper will do the job just as effectively. With the paint removed you will be able to gauge the severity of the corrosion and therefore decide whether to replace the whole panel (if this is possible) or to repair the affected area. Replacement body panels are not as expensive as most people think and it is often quicker and more satisfactory to fit a new panel than to attempt to repair large areas of corrosion.

Remove all fittings from the affected area except those which will act as a guide to the original shape of the damaged bodywork (eg; headlamp shells etc.). Then, using tin snips or a hacksaw blade, remove all loose metal and any other metal badly affected by corrosion. Hammer the edges of the hole inwards in order to create a slight depression for the filler paste.

Wire brush the affected area to remove the powdery rust from the surface of the remaining metal. Paint the affected area with rust inhibiting paint; if the back of the rusted area is accessible treat this also.

Before filling can take place it will be necessary to block the hole in some way. This can be achieved by the use of one of the following materials: Zinc gauze, Aluminium tape or Polyurethane foam.

Zinc gauze is probably the best material to use for a large hole. Cut a piece to the approximate size and shape of the hole to be filled, then position it in the hole so that its edges are below the level of the surrounding bodywork. It can be retained in position by several blobs of filler paste around its periphery.

Aluminium tape should be used for small or very narrow holes. Pull a piece off the roll and trim it to the approximate size and shape required, then pull off the backing paper (if used) and stick the tape over the hole; it can be overlapped if the thickness of one piece is insufficient. Burnish down the edges of the tape with the handle of a screwdriver or similar, to ensure that the tape is securely attached to the metal underneath.

Polyurethane foam is best used where the hole is situated in a section of bodywork of complex shape, backed by a small box section (eg; where the sill panel meets the rear wheel arch - most cars). The usual mixing procedure for this foam is as follows: Put equal amounts of fluid from each of the two cans provided in the kit, into one container. Stir until the mixture begins to thicken, then quickly pour this mixture into the hole, and hold a piece of cardboard over the larger apertures. Almost immediately the polyurethane will begin to expand, gushing frantically out of any small holes left unblocked. When the foam hardens it can be cut back to just below the level of the surrounding bodywork with a hacksaw blade.

Bodywork repairs - filling and re-spraying

Before using this Section, see the Sections on dent, deep scratch, rust hole, and gash repairs.

Many types of bodyfiller are available, but generally speaking those proprietary kits which contain a tin of filler paste and a tube of resin hardener are best for this type of repair. A wide, flexible plastic or nylon applicator will be found invaluable for imparting a smooth and well contoured finish to the surface of the filler.

Mix up a little filler on a clean piece of card or board - use the hardener sparingly (follow the maker's instructions on the packet) otherwise the filler will set very rapidly.

Using the applicator, apply the filler paste to the prepared area; draw the applicator across the surface of the filler to achieve the correct contour and to level the filler surface. As soon as a contour that approximates to the correct one is achieved, stop working the paste - if you carry on too long the paste will become sticky and begin to 'pick-up' on the applicator. Continue to add thin layers of filler paste at twenty-minute intervals until the level of the filler is just 'proud' of the surrounding bodywork.

Once the filler has hardened, excess can be removed using a metal plane or file. From then on, progressively finer grades of abrasive paper should be used, starting with a 40 grade production paper and finishing with 400 grade 'wet-and-dry' paper. Always wrap the abrasive paper around a flat rubber, cork or wooden block - otherwise the surface of the filler will not be completely flat. During the smoothing of the filler surface the 'wet-and-dry' paper should be periodically rinsed in water. This will ensure that a very smooth finish is imparted to the filler at the final stage.

At this stage the 'dent' should be surrounded by a ring of bare metal, which in turn should be encircled by the finely 'feathered' edge of the good paintwork. Rinse the repair area with clean water, until all of the dust produced by the rubbing-down operation is gone.

Spray the whole repair area with a light coat of grey primer - this will show up any imperfections in the surface of the filler. Repair these imperfections with fresh filler paste or bodystopper, and once more smooth the surface with abrasive paper. If bodystopper is used, it can be mixed with cellulose thinners to form a really thin paste which is ideal for filling small holes. Repeat this spray and repair procedure until you are satisfied that the surface of the filler, and the feathered edge of the paintwork are perfect. Clean the repair area with clean water and allow to dry fully.

The repair area is now ready for spraying. Paint spraying must be carried out in a warm, dry, windless and dust free atmosphere. This condition can be created artificially if you have access to a large indoor working area, but if you are forced to work in the open, you will have to pick your day very carefully. If you are working indoors, dousing the floor in the work area with water will 'lay' the dust which would otherwise be in the atmosphere. If the repair area is confined to one body panel, mask off the surrounding panels; this will help to minimise the effects of a slight mis-match in paint colours. Bodywork fittings (eg; chrome strips, door handles etc.), will also need to be masked off. Use genuine masking tape and several thicknesses of newspaper for the masking operation.

Before commencing to spray, agitate the aerosol can thoroughly, then spray a test area (an old tin, or similar) until the technique is mastered. Cover the repair area with a thick coat of primer; the thickness should be built up using several thin layers of paint rather than one thick one. Using 400 grade 'wet-and-dry' paper, rub down the surface of the primer until it is really smooth. While doing this, the work area should be thoroughly doused with water, and the 'wet-and-dry' paper periodically rinsed in water. Allow to dry before spraying on more paint.

Spray on the top coat, again building up the thickness by using several thin layers of paint. Start spraying in the centre of the repair area and then, using a circular motion, work outwards until the whole repair area and about 2 inches of the surrounding original paintwork is covered. Remove all masking material 10 to 15 minutes after spraying on the final coat of paint.

Allow the new paint at least 2 weeks to harden fully; then, using a paintwork renovator or a very fine cutting paste, blend the edges of the new paint into the existing paintwork. Finally, apply wax polish.

6 Major body damage - repair

1 Because the body is built on the monocoque principle and is integral with the underframe, major damage must be repaired by competent mechanics with the necessary welding and hydraulic straightening

equipment.
2 If the damage has been serious it is vital that the body is checked for correct alignment as otherwise the handling of the car will suffer and many other faults such as excessive tyre wear and wear in the transmission and steering may occur.
3 There is a special body jig which most large body repair shops have and to ensure that all is correct it is important that this jig be used for all major repair work.

7 Maintenance - locks and hinges

Once every 6 months or 6000 miles (10000 km) the door, bonnet and tailgate hinges should be lubricated with a few drops of engine oil. Door striker plates can be given a thin smear of grease to reduce wear and ensure free movement.

8 Bumpers - removal and refitting

Front bumper (Capri II)
1 Initially disconnect the battery earth lead.
2 Remove the radiator cover which is retained by five screws.
3 Remove the four bumper retaining screws and lift away the bumper.
4 Refitting is the reverse of the removal procedure, but do not fully tighten the bolts until the bumper is correctly aligned.

Front bumper (Mercury Capri II)
9 Remove the nuts from the bolts securing the bumper to the bumper brackets and lift the bumper away.
10 Remove the front license plate brackets.
11 Remove the bolts securing the bumper reinforcement then lift the reinforcement away.
12 Refitting is a direct reversal of the removal procedure but do not fully tighten the bolts until the bumper is correctly aligned.

Rear bumper (Capri II)
5 Open the tailgate, then remove the mat and the sub-floor.
6 Remove the jack and washer water reservoir (where applicable).
7 Remove two nuts, spring washer and flat washers at each end and lift away the bumper.
8 Refitting is the reverse of the removal procedure, but do not fully tighten the nuts until the bumper is correctly aligned.

Rear bumper (Mercury Capri II)
13 Remove the eight bolts and washers securing the bumper assembly to the brackets then remove the assembly.
14 Remove the special bolts securing the bumper reinforcement to the bumper.
15 Refitting is a direct reversal of the removal procedure but do not fully tighten the bolts until the bumper is correctly aligned.

Bumper trim strips
16 The bumper trim strips can be removed, and replacements fitted, by prising them in and out of the retaining grooves. The job is made a little easier if a soap and water solution is applied to the T-shaped retaining groove.

9 Radiator grille - removal and refitting

1 Initially disconnect the battery earth lead.
2 Remove the eight screws and washers and lift away the grill. On Mercury Capri II models it is necessary to disconnect the turn signal leads before the grille can be removed fully.
3 When refitting, ensure that the eight special nuts are correctly positioned on the front and lower crossmembers, then align and secure the bumper with the screws and washers. On Mercury Capri II models the turn signal leads must be connected before the grille is fitted.
4 Reconnect the battery earth lead.

10 Windscreen - removal and refitting

1 If you are unfortunate enough to have a windscreen shatter, or should you wish to renew your present windscreen, fitting a replacement is one of the few jobs which the average owner is advised to leave to a professional but for the owner who wishes to attempt the job himself the following instructions are given.
2 Cover the bonnet with a blanket or cloth to prevent accidental damage and remove the windscreen wiper blades and arms as detailed in Chapter 10.

Windscreen intact
3 Put on a pair of lightweight shoes and get into one of the front seats. With a piece of soft cloth between the soles of your shoes and the windscreen glass, place both feet in one top corner of the windscreen and push firmly. (See Fig. 12.6).
4 When the weatherstrip has freed itself from the body flange in that area, repeat the process at frequent intervals along the top edge of the windscreen until, from outside the car, the glass and weatherstrip can be removed together.

Windscreen shattered
5 If you are having to replace your toughened windscreen due to shattering, remove all traces of sealing compound and broken glass from the weatherstrip and body flange.
6 Gently prise out the clip which covers the joint of the chromium finisher strip and pull the finisher strip out of the weatherstrip. Then remove the weatherstrip from the glass or, if it is still on the car (as in the case of a shattered screen) remove it from the body flange.
7 To fit a new windscreen start by fitting the weatherstrip around the new windscreen glass.
8 Apply a suitable sealer to the weatherstrip to body groove. In this groove then fit a fine but strong piece of cord right the way round the groove allowing an overlap of about 6 in (15 cm) at the joint.
9 From outside the car place the windscreen in its correct position making sure that the loose end of the cord is inside the car.
10 With an assistant pressing firmly on the outside of the windscreen get into the car and slowly pull out the cord thus drawing the weatherstrip over the body flange. (See Fig. 12.7).
11 Apply a further layer of sealer to the underside of rubber to glass groove from outside the car.
12 Replace the chromium finisher strip into its groove in the weatherstrip and replace the clip which covers its joint.
13 Carefully clean off any surplus sealer from the windscreen glass before it has a chance to harden and then replace the windscreen wiper arms and blades. Retrieve the tax disc from the old screen.

11 Tailgate window glass - removal and refitting

1 Where applicable, remove the window glass wiper arm and blade, and carefully disconnect the heater element connections.
2 Carefully prise out the bright trim from the rubber moulding.
3 If possible, obtain help from an assistant and carefully use a blunt bladed screwdriver to push the weatherstrip lip along the upper transverse section under the tailgate aperture flange. When approximately two thirds of the weatherstrip lip has been treated in this manner, pressure should be applied to the glass from inside the car. The glass and weatherstrip can then be removed from the outside.
4 Clean the lip of the window aperture, and the glass and weatherstrip if they are to be used again. Do not use solvents such as petrol or white spirit on the weatherstrip as this may cause deterioration of the rubber.
5 When refitting, initially fit the weatherstrip to the glass then insert a drawcord in the rubber-to-body groove so that the cord ends emerge at the bottom centre with approximately 6 in (15 cm) of overlap. During this operation it may help to retain the weatherstrip to the glass by using short lengths of masking tape.
6 On British built vehicles only, apply a suitable sealer to the body flange. Position the glass and weatherstrip assembly to the body aperture and push up until the weatherstrip groove engages the top transverse flange of the body aperture. Ensure that the ends of the draw cord are inside the car, then get the assistant to push the window firmly at the base whilst one end of the draw cord is pulled from the weatherstrip groove. Ensure that the cord is pulled at right-angles to the flange (ie; towards the centre of the glass) and that pressure is always being applied on the outside of the glass in the vicinity of the point where the draw cord is being pulled.
7 When the glass is in position, remove any masking tape which may have been used then seal the weatherstrip to the glass.
8 Lubricate the bright trim with a rubber lubricant and refit it.
9 Refit the wiper arm and blade (where applicable), and reconnect the heater element connections.

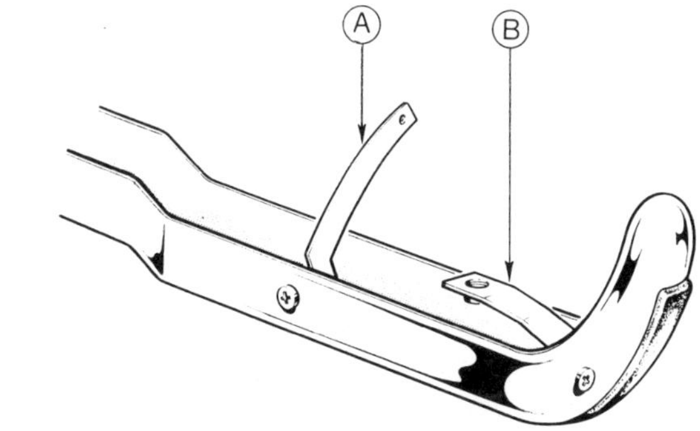

Fig. 12.2. Front bumper mounting - Capri II (Sec. 8)

A Mounting bracket - inner *B Mounting bracket - outer*

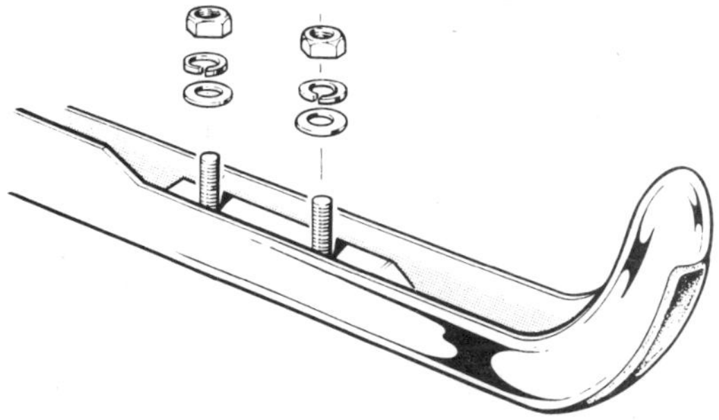

Fig. 12.3. Rear bumper mounting - Capri II (Sec. 8)

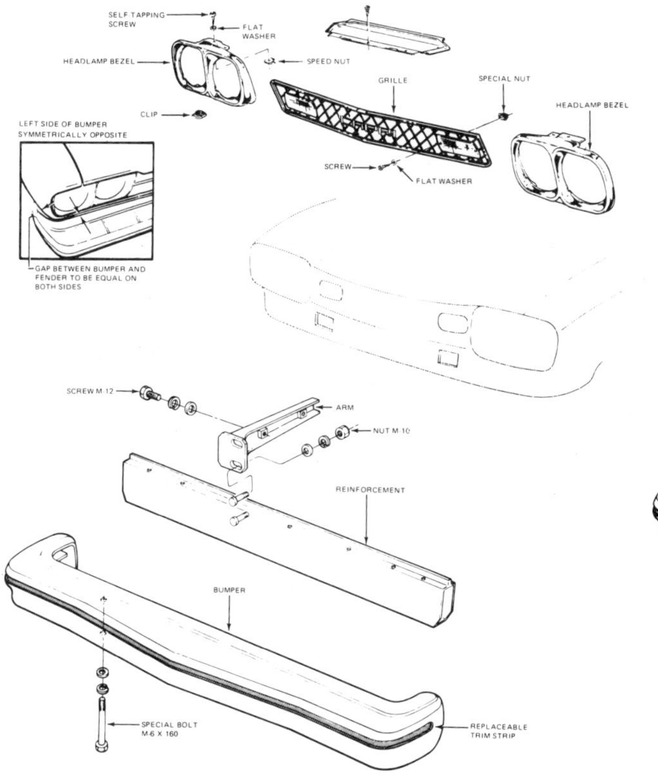

Fig. 12.4. Front bumper and grille - Mercury Capri II (Sec. 8)

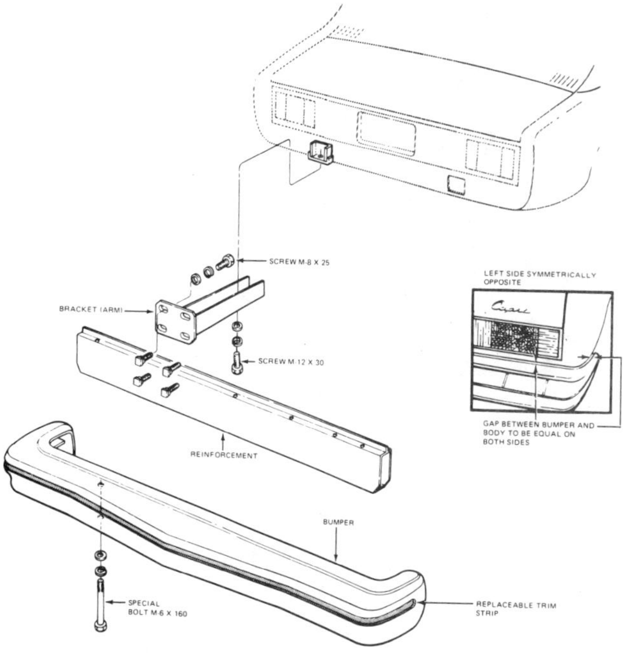

Fig. 12.5. Rear bumper - Mercury Capri II (Sec. 8)

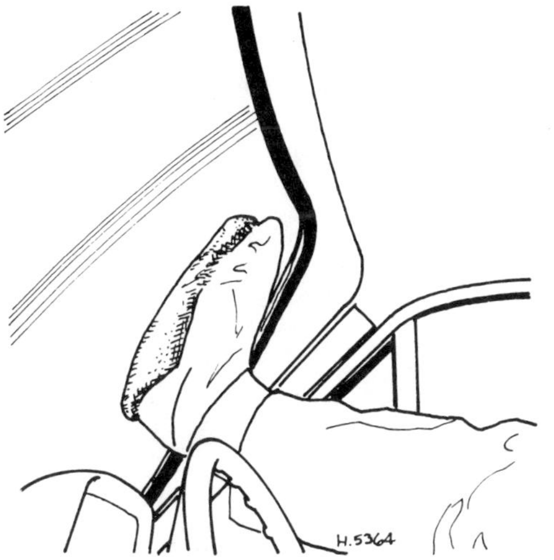

Fig. 12.6. Windscreen removal (Sec. 10)

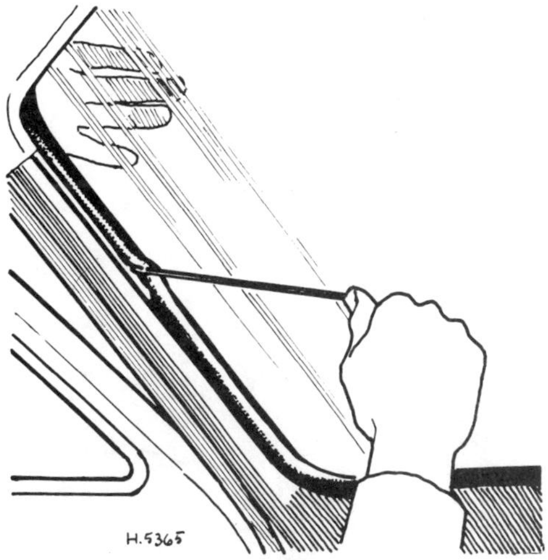

Fig. 12.7. Windscreen fitting using a length of cord (Sec. 10)

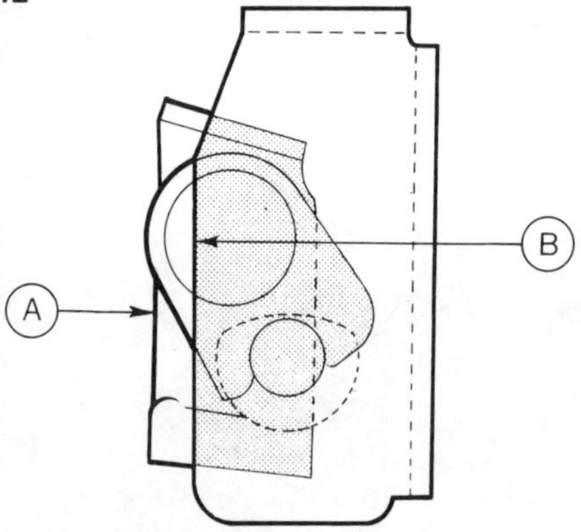

Fig. 12.8. Aligning the striker to lock support plate (Sec. 12)

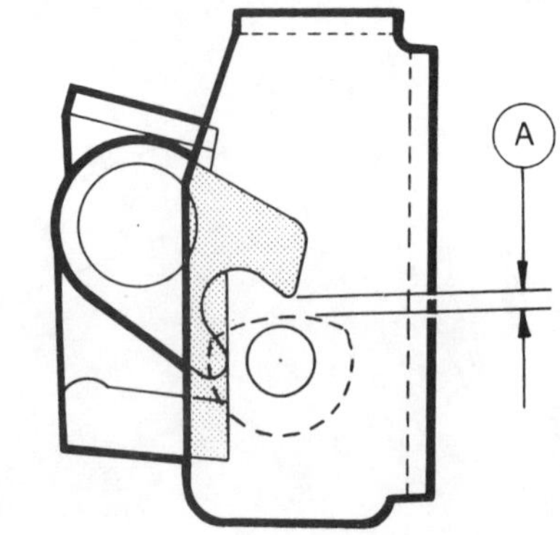

Fig. 12.9. Lock claw to striker clearance (Sec. 12)

13.3a Lift the protective cap off the rear of the remote control handle...

13.3b ... and twist the assembly to disengage it from the operating rod

13.4 The remote control handle protective cap

14.4 Removing the remote control bezel

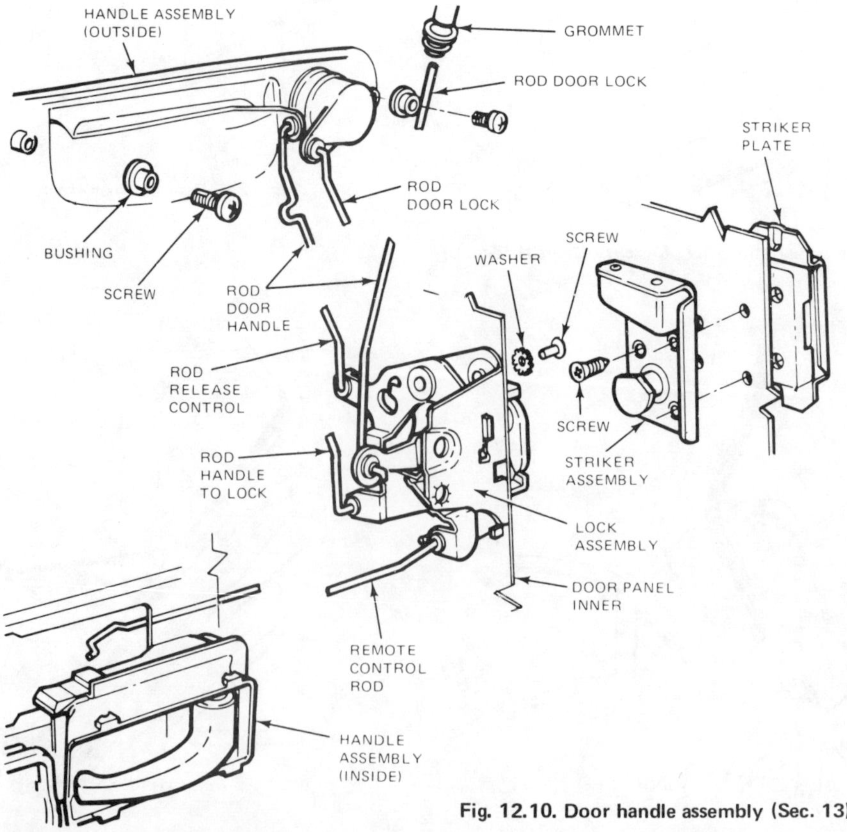

Fig. 12.10. Door handle assembly (Sec. 13)

12 Door rattles - tracing and rectification

1 The most common cause of door rattles is a misaligned, loose or worn striker plate. However, other causes may be:

a) *Loose door or window winder handles.*
b) *Loose or misaligned door lock components.*
c) *Loose or worn remote control mechanism.*

2 It is quite possible for rattles to be the result of a combination of the above faults so a careful examination should be made to determine the exact cause.
3 If it is found necessary to adjust the striker plate, close the door to the first of the two locking positions. Visually check the relative attitude of the striker outside edge to the lock support plate edge. The edges 'A' and 'B' (Fig. 12.8) should be parallel and can be checked by shining a torch through the door gap from above and below the striker.
4 Also check the amount by which the door stands proud of the adjacent panel. Adjust the striker plate as necessary to obtain a dimension of 0.24 in (6 mm).
5 With the lock in the open position check the lock claw striker clearance (dimension 'A' in Fig. 12.9). This should be 0.28 in (7 mm) and can be checked by placing a small ball of plasticine or similar on the striker post and checking its height after gently closing the door. The striker plate can be repositioned vertically to obtain this dimension but take care not to disturb any previous initial settings of the plate.

13 Door remote control handle - removal and refitting

1 Remove the door trim panel, as described in Section 14.
2 Push the remote control handle assembly towards the front of the car and pull it out of the opening in the door inner panel.
3 Lift the protective cap off the rear and twist the assembly to disengage it from the operating rod (photos).
4 Remove the protective cap from the operating rod (photo).
5 Refitting is the reverse of the removal procedure.

14 Door trim panel - removal and refitting

1 Carefully lift up and remove the window winder handle insert strip.
2 Remove the winder handle retaining screw and pull off the handle and escutcheon.
3 Remove the two armrest retaining screws, turn the armrest through 90° and pull out the top fixing.
4 Carefully prise out the remote control bezel and unscrew the private lock button (photo).
5 Taking care that no damage to the panel or paintwork occurs, carefully prise the trim panel from the door panel.
6 When refitting, press in the panel so that it is secured by its clips.
7 Refit the lock button, then position the bezel on the door remote control housing, push the trim pad clear of the housing and push the bezel rearwards to secure.
8 Position the spacer over the armrest stud. Position the armrest to the door and push the stud to secure it. Secure the armrest with the two screws.
9 Assemble the escutcheon over the winder shaft and install the winder so that when the window is closed the winder is in the lower vertical position. Secure the winder with the screw and refit the insert strip.

15 Door window regulator assembly - removal and refitting

1 Remove the door trim panel, as described in the previous Section.
2 Peel off the plastic sheet.
3 Temporarily refit the winder handle and lower the window. Remove the four gear plate fixing screws and the three pivot plate screws.
4 Draw the regulator assembly towards the rear of the door to disengage it from the runner at the base of the window.
5 Push the window glass up and use adhesive tape on each side of the glass and over the window frame to retain it. If it is to be left for any length of time, additionally use a wooden support.
6 Withdraw the regulator from the door.
7 Installation is the reverse of the removal procedure, alignment being obtained by adjusting the pivot plate as necessary.

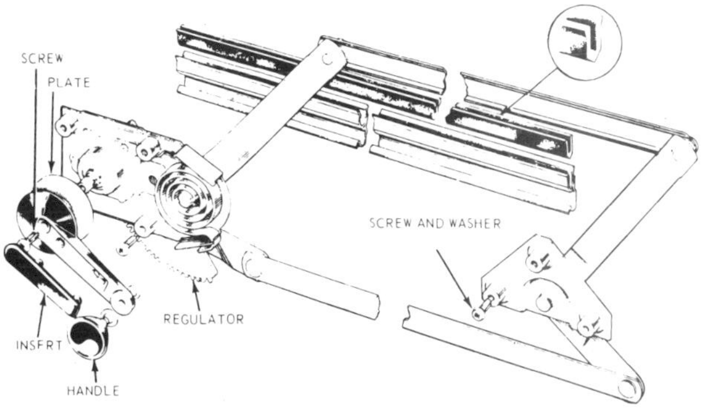

Fig. 12.11. Door window regulator assembly (Sec. 15)

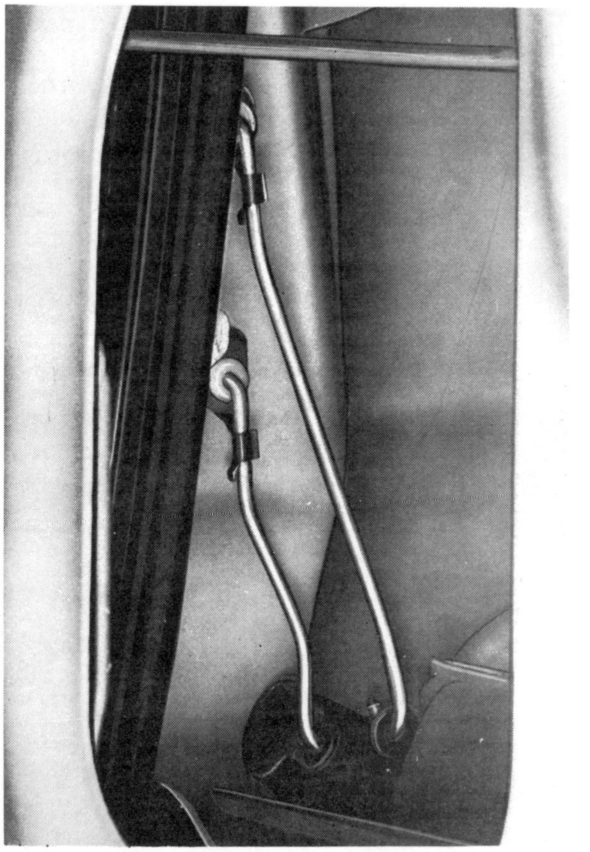
Fig. 12.12. Door lock to handle connecting links (Sec. 16)

16 Exterior door handle - removal and refitting

1 Remove the door trim panel, as previously described.
2 Pull back the plastic sheet behind the exterior handle then disconnect the two connecting links from the door lock to the exterior handle.
3 Remove the two handle retaining bolts and withdraw the handle.
4 Installation is the reverse of the removal procedure but do not forget to install the bushes for the link rods. A little petroleum jelly on the rod ends will assist with their installation.

17 Door lock assembly - removal and refitting

1 Remove the door trim panel as previously described, and remove the plastic sheeting.
2 Remove the remote control handle and two window frame bolts.
3 Using a screwdriver, prise the clips from the exterior handle rod and detach the rods from the lock.
4 Remove the crosshead screws securing the lock to the shell and the plastic clips securing the remote control rod to the inner panel.
5 Remove the lock from the door through the lower rear access

aperture.

6 When refitting, insert the remote control rod through the door aperture ensuring that the rod lies against the door inner panel. Locate the lock on the door shell, pushing the frame towards the outer panel to enable the lock to be correctly positioned on the rear shell.

7 Secure the lock with the three screws, and the remote control rod to the inner panel with the two plastic clips.

8 Replace the exterior handle rods in their respective lock locations. Position the black bush 'A' and white bushes 'B' as shown in Fig. 12.13.

9 The remainder of the refitting procedure is the reverse of the removal procedure.

18 Door window glass - removal and refitting

1 Remove the door trim panel, as previously described, then peel the plastic sheeting away from the door panel apertures.

2 Remove the door belt moulding/weatherstrip assembly (see Fig. 12.14).

3 Wind up the window glass then remove the pivot plate screws. Remove the four regulator gear plate securing screws, then disengage the studs and rollers of the regulator arms from the door glass channel and carefully lift out the glass. Allow the regulator to fall away, pivoting on the regulator handle shaft.

4 When refitting, initially insert a small block of wood in the bottom of the door assembly. Locate the glass in the door panel so that it is resting on the wooden block.

5 Locate the studs and rollers of the regulator arm into the door glass channel then temporarily install the winder handle and turn it to align the gear plate with the panel fixings. Secure the plate to the inner panel.

6 Loosely assemble the pivot plate then wind up the glass and align it in the frame. Tighten the pivot plate screws.

7 The remainder of the refitting procedure is the reverse of the removal procedure.

19 Door window frame - removal and refitting

1 Remove the door trim panel as previously described then peel the plastic sheeting away from the lower door panel apertures.

2 Remove the door belt moulding/weatherstrip assembly (see Fig. 12.14).

3 Lower the window glass, then peel back the lower front corner of the plastic sheeting and remove the reflector (where applicable) to gain access to the front and rear lower fixing bolts.

4 Remove the five bolts and frame seals to free the frame from the shell. Push the glass out of the frame at the rear of the door so that the frame lies between the glass and the outer panel. Repeat for the front of the door.

5 Pull the rear of the frame from the shell whilst guiding the front of the frame rearwards past the first door bolt moulding retaining clip to enable the frame to be lifted clear.

6 When refitting, insert the front of the frame so that the vertical leg lies to the rear of the first moulding clip.

7 Spring the rear of the frame into the shell so that the frame lies between the glass and the outer panel whilst springing the frame front vertical leg past the moulding clip so that this also lies between the glass and the inner panel.

8 Spring the frame around the glass and secure it with the five bolts.

9 Pull the weatherstrip from the door aperture flange, then shut the door and adjust the frame to obtain a gap between the frame and flange (in and out) of 0.4 to 0.56 in (10 to 14 mm) and between the frame and the 'A' pillar (fore and aft) of 0.32 to 0.48 in (8 to 12 mm). Tighten the bolts.

10 The remainder of the refitting procedure is the reverse of the removal procedure.

20 Window frame mouldings and door weatherstrips - removal and refitting

1 Where applicable wind the window down to its fullest extent. Carefully prise the weatherstrip out of the groove in the door outer bright metal finish moulding.

2 When refitting, correctly position the weatherstrip over its groove.

Fig. 12.13. The black (A) and white (B) door lock bushes (Sec. 17)

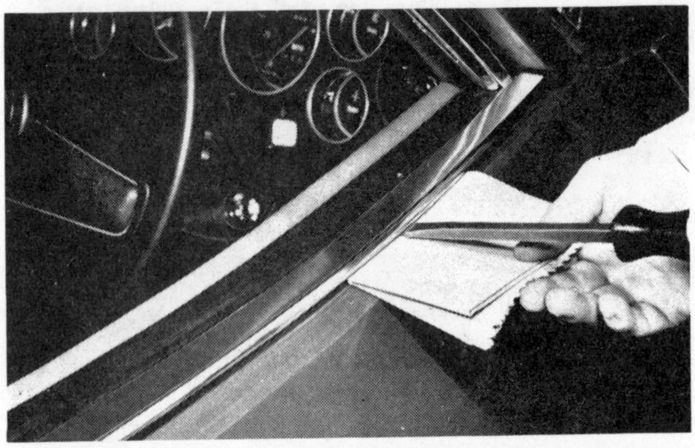

Fig. 12.14. Removing the door moulding (Sec. 18)

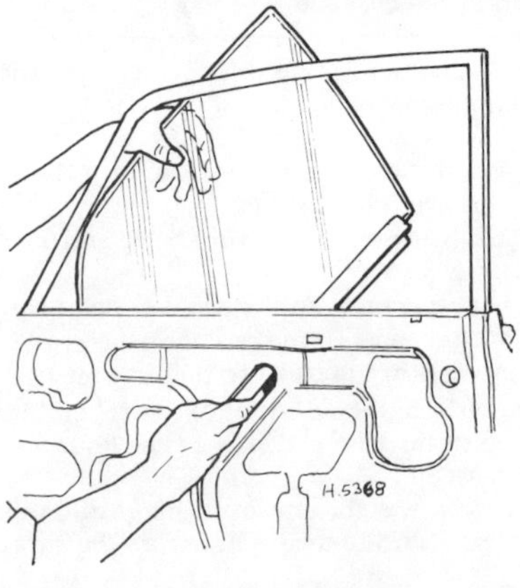

Fig. 12.15. Door window glass removal (Sec. 18)

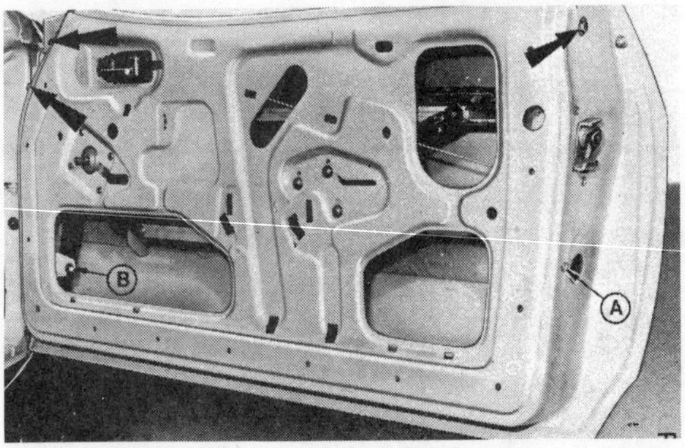

Fig. 12.16. Window frame retaining bolts at A, B and as indicated by arrows (Sec. 19)

With the thumbs, carefully press the strip fully into the groove.
3 Wind the window up (where applicable) and check that the weatherstrip is correctly fitted.

21 Rear quarter trim panel - removal and refitting

1 Remove the screws retaining the window quarter trim and lift away the trim.
2 Remove the 'B' pillar vertical trim and the seatbelt screw (where applicable) (photo).
3 Remove the two screws (A in Fig. 12.17) and remove the rear seat cushion. Where applicable, feed the seatbelt and buckle assemblies through the opening in the cushion.
4 Remove the three trim panel screws and the step plate. Also, where applicable, remove the luggage compartment hook. Carefully prise away the trim panel.
5 Installation is the reverse of the removal procedure, but on completion tighten the seatbelt bolt to a torque of 15 to 20 lb f ft (2.1 to 2.9 kg fm).

22 Opening rear quarter glass assembly - removal and refitting

1 Remove the trim covers from the 'B' panel and the quarter window surround (trim).
2 Remove the two toggle retaining screws and remove the toggle from the rear 'C' pillar.
3 Remove the window frame weatherstrip then drive out the toggle-to-catch retaining pin, remove the toggle.
4 Refitting is the reverse of the removal procedure, but lubricate the 'B' pillar hinge pivots with a soap solution prior to fitting the glass assembly. Adjust the toggle or weatherstrip flange to achieve 0.32 to 0.39 in (8 to 10 mm) gap between the glass and the weatherstrip flange.

23 Load space trim panel - removal and refitting

1 Remove the rear quarter trim panel, as previously described.
2 Pull the seat forward and remove the ten securing screws. It may also be necessary to detach the back trim panel (five screws).
3 Remove the panel after removing the interior light connection and the seatback lock knob.
4 Refitting is the reverse of the removal procedure. Ensure that the sound deadening material is correctly positioned and that the trim panel does not foul the seat release hinge mechanism.

24 Bonnet (hood) release cable - removal and refitting

1 In the event of the release cable breaking it is possible to remove the radiator grille to operate the lock spring by hand. Grille removal is dealt with in Section 9, but since it is not possible to open the bonnet it will be found a little difficult (though not impossible) to gain access to the upper retaining screws.
2 To remove the release cable in normal circumstances, remove the radiator upper cowl panel.
3 From inside the car remove both the clevis pins and the spring, and disconnect the release cable from the control lever.
4 Slacken the cable adjuster clamp and release the cable from the hood lock spring.
5 Remove the cable retaining clips then pull the cable through the dashpanel to remove it.
6 Refitting of the cable is essentially the reverse of the removal procedure, adjusting, as necessary, to remove any cable slack. For further information on this refer to paragraph 6, of the following Section.

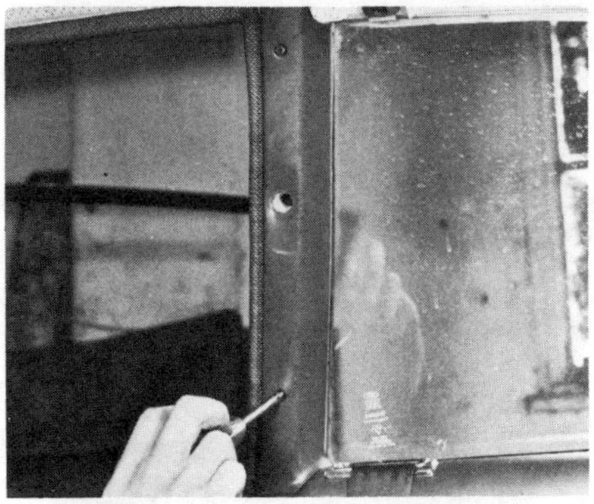

21.2 Removing the 'B' pillar vertical trim

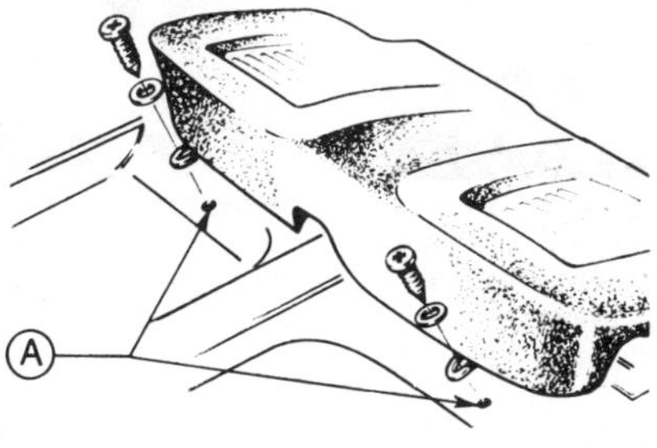

Fig. 12.17. Seat cushion securing screws (Sec. 21)

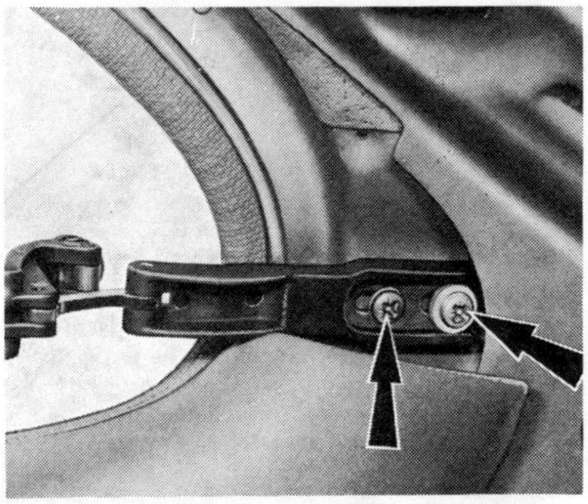

Fig. 12.18. Quarter window toggle fixing screws (Sec. 22)

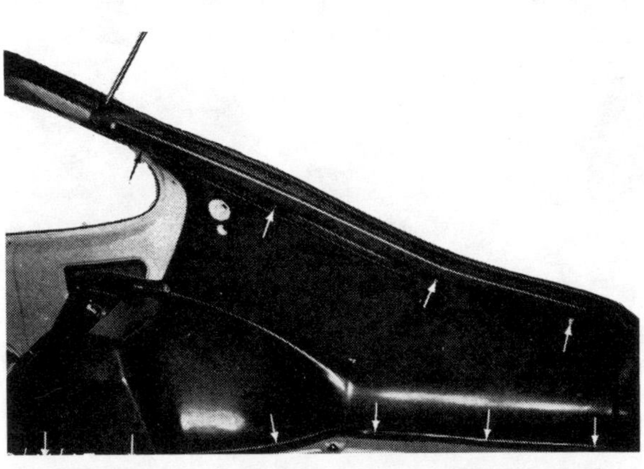

Fig. 12.19. Load space trim panel fixing points (Sec. 23)

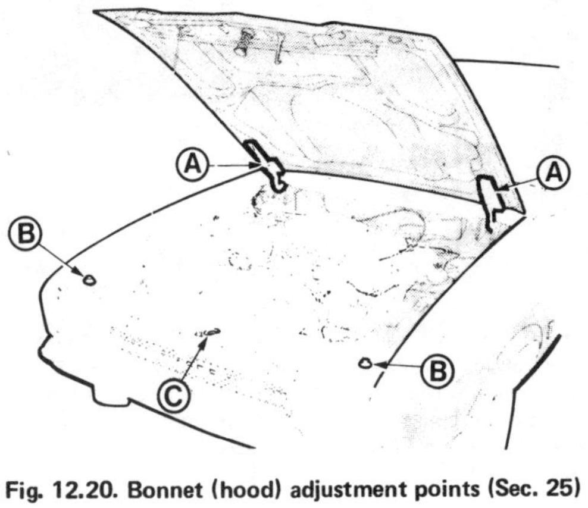

Fig. 12.20. Bonnet (hood) adjustment points (Sec. 25)

A Hinge *B Bump rubber* *C Striker*

This sequence of photographs deals with the repair of the dent and paintwork damage shown in this photo. The procedure will be similar for the repair of a hole. It should be noted that the procedures given here are simplified – more explicit instructions will be found in the text

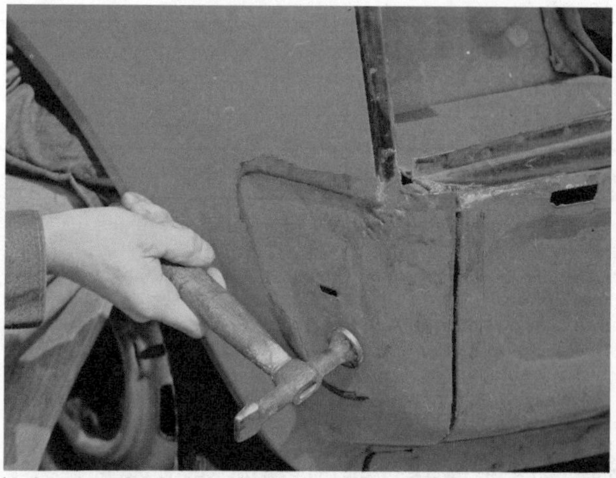

In the case of a dent the first job – after removing surrounding trim – is to hammer out the dent where access is possible. This will minimise filling. Here, the large dent having been hammered out, the damaged area is being made slightly concave

Now all paint must be removed from the damaged area, by rubbing with coarse abrasive paper. Alternatively, a wire brush or abrasive pad can be used in a power drill. Where the repair area meets good paintwork, the edge of the paintwork should be 'feathered', using a finer grade of abrasive paper

In the case of a hole caused by rusting, all damaged sheet-metal should be cut away before proceeding to this stage. Here, the damaged area is being treated with rust remover and inhibitor before being filled

Mix the body filler according to its manufacturer's instructions. In the case of corrosion damage, it will be necessary to block off any large holes before filling – this can be done with zinc gauze or aluminium tape. Make sure the area is absolutely clean before...

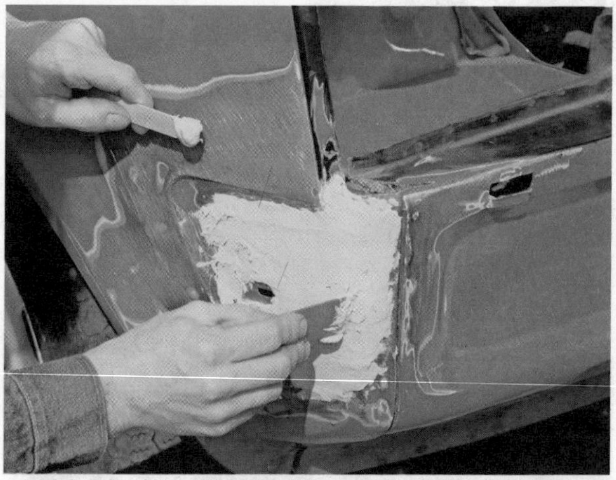

...applying the filler. Filler should be applied with a flexible applicator, as shown, for best results; the wooden spatula being used for confined areas. Apply thin layers of filler at 20-minute intervals, until the surface of the filler is slightly proud of the surrounding bodywork

Initial shaping can be done with a Surform plane or Dreadnought file. Then, using progressively finer grades of wet-and-dry paper, wrapped around a sanding block, and copious amounts of clean water, rub down the filler until really smooth and flat. Again, feather the edges of adjoining paintwork

The whole repair area can now be sprayed or brush-painted with primer. If spraying, ensure adjoining areas are protected from over-spray. Note that at least one inch of the surrounding sound paintwork should be coated with primer. Primer has a 'thick' consistency, so will fill small imperfections

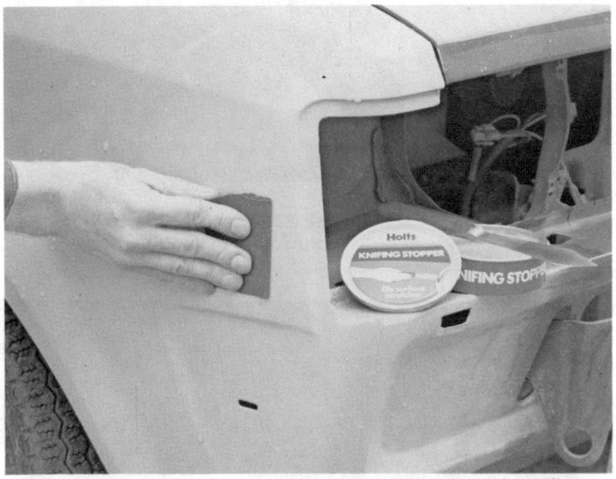

Again, using plenty of water, rub down the primer with a fine grade of wet-and-dry paper (400 grade is probably best) until it is really smooth and well blended into the surrounding paintwork. Any remaining imperfections can now be filled by carefully applied knifing stopper paste

When the stopper has hardened, rub down the repair area again before applying the final coat of primer. Before rubbing down this last coat of primer, ensure the repair area is blemish-free – use more stopper if necessary. To ensure that the surface of the primer is really smooth use some finishing compound

The top coat can now be applied. When working out of doors, pick a dry, warm and wind-free day. Ensure surrounding areas are protected from over-spray. Agitate the aerosol thoroughly, then spray the centre of the repair area, working outwards with a circular motion. Apply the paint as several thin coats

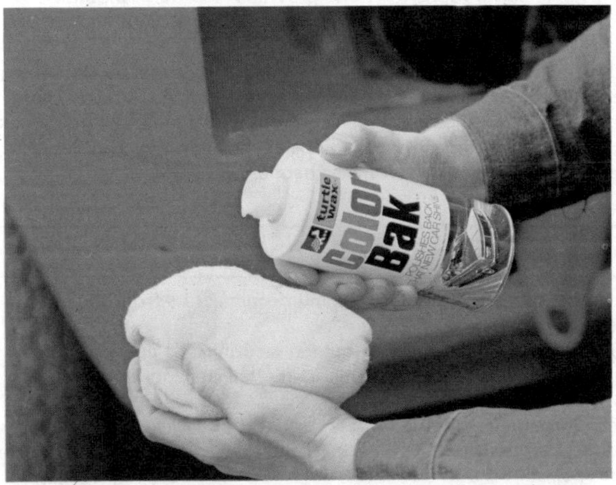

After a period of about two weeks, which the paint needs to harden fully, the surface of the repaired area can be 'cut' with a mild cutting compound prior to wax polishing. When carrying out bodywork repairs, remember that the quality of the finished job is proportional to the time and effort expended

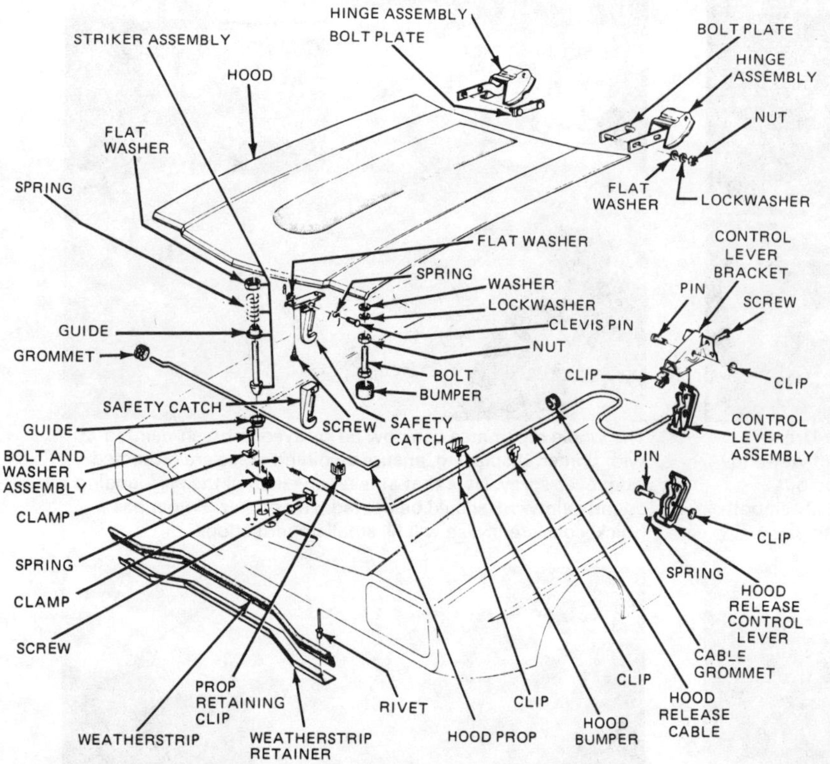

Fig. 12.21. Bonnet assembly - component parts (Sec. 24)

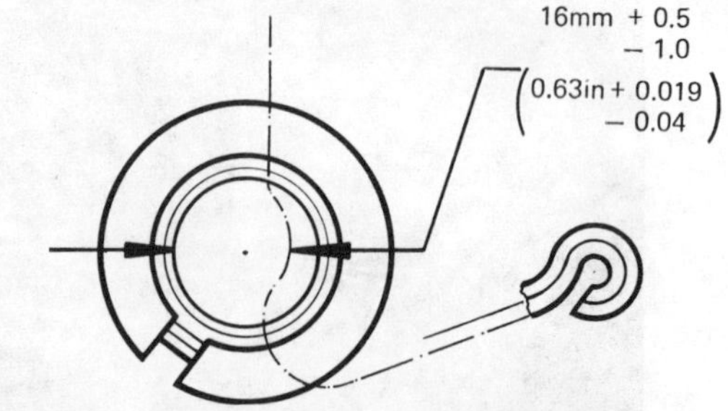

Fig. 12.22. Hood lock spring setting dimension (Sec. 25)

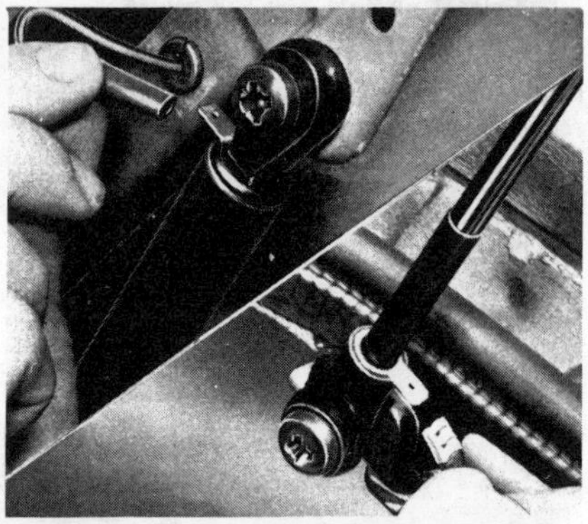

Fig. 12.23. The damper (strut) in-line connectors (Sec. 26)

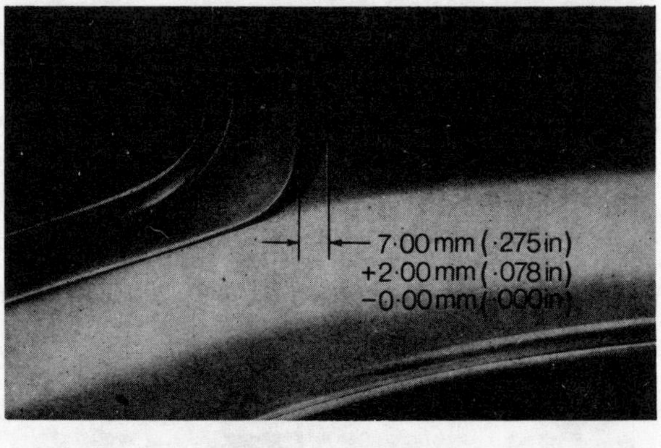

Fig. 12.24. Tailgate to roof edge alignment (Sec. 26)

25 Bonnet (hood) - removal, refitting and adjustment

1 Open the bonnet to its fullest extent. Using a suitable implement scribe a line around the hinges.

2 Remove the two bolts and washers on each side securing the bonnet to its hinges. With assistance it can now be lifted off.

3 Replacement is a reversal of the removal procedure. However, before fully tightening the securing bolts, ensure that the hinges are aligned with the scribed marks. This will ensure correct alignment.

4 If it is found that the bonnet requires adjustment, this can be effected in the vertical plane by slackening the catch post locknut and screwing the catch post in or out. Fore-and-aft adjustment can be effected by slackening the hinge bolts.

5 Adjustable bump rubbers are also provided, and these should be positioned as necessary to stop vibration but at the same time must allow the bonnet to be closed easily.

6 Adjustment of the bonnet locking spring can be made by slackening the cable clamp on the upper crossmember and sliding the outer cable through the clip as necessary. When correctly positioned, the hood lock spring/cable setting dimension should be as shown in Fig. 12.22. Tighten the clamp screw when the adjustment is satisfactory.

26 Tailgate assembly - removal and refitting

1 Open the tailgate and detach the inline connectors from the damper(s)/strut(s).

2 Detach each damper by removing the securing bolt at each end.

3 With help from an assistant, support the tailgate and remove it by removing the hinge bolts.

4 When installing, align the tailgate so that the edges are flush with the rear of the roof and the 'C' pillar sides, and the gap between the tailgate and the roof edge is 0.275 to 0.353 in (7 to 9 mm) - see Fig. 12.24.

5 Align the lower edges of the tailgate so that it is flush with the rear corners of the body with the striker plate in the upper central position.

6 Pads can be used beneath the 'C' pillar bumpers for alignment of the tailgate sides with the 'C' pillar slope. Note that the thick end of the bumper faces towards the front of the vehicle.

7 On completion, refit the dampers. Assemble the spacer to the screw, then locate the screw and spacer through the pushrod end of the damper. Secure the damper to the 'C' pillar bracket, with the terminals facing

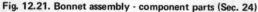

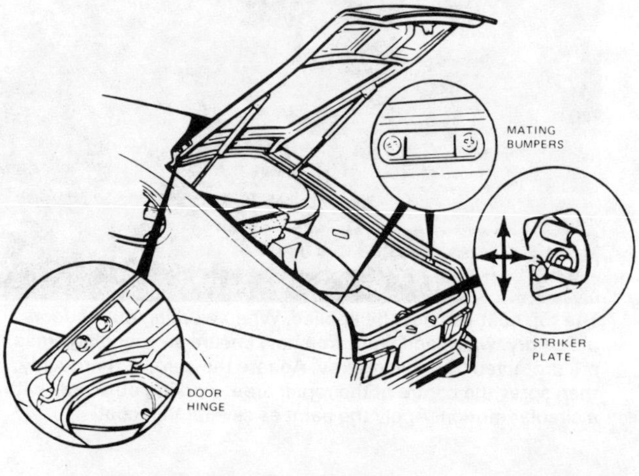

Fig. 12.25. Tailgate adjustment points (Secs. 26 and 28)

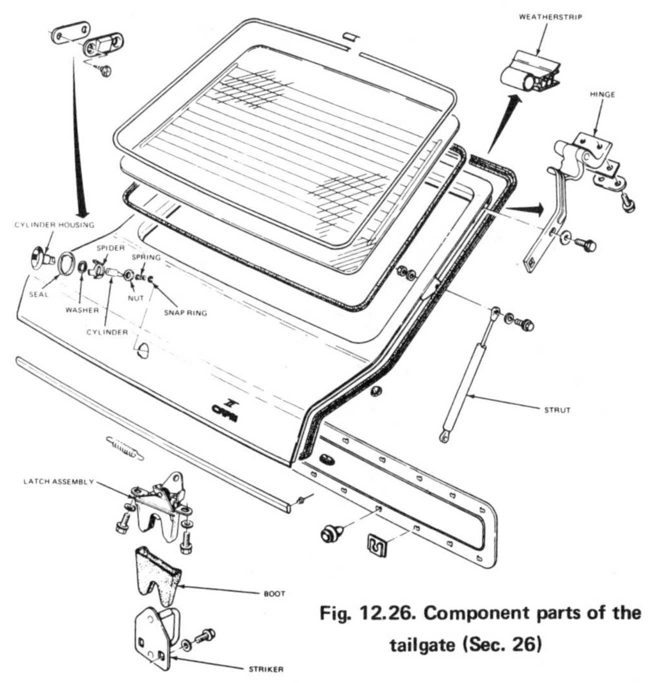

Fig. 12.26. Component parts of the tailgate (Sec. 26)

rearwards.

8 Align the damper to the tailgate bracket and secure it with the remaining screw and spacer.

9 Reconnect the electrical connections to the dampers.

27 Tailgate lock assembly - removal and refitting (including removal of the lock barrel)

1 Open the tailgate and remove the latch (three bolts and washers).
2 Remove the lock cylinder retaining nut, then turn the lock spider to detach it from the lock cylinder and outer panel.
3 Installation is the reverse of the removal procedure.
4 If it is found necessary to remove the lock barrel, this can be done after it has been removed by removing the circlip (snap-ring) from the barrel housing. The spring, barrel and spider can then be detached and a replacement barrel fitted by reversing this procedure.

28 Tailgate striker plate - removal and refitting

1 Open the tailgate then carefully scribe a mark around the striker to facilitate refitting.
2 Remove the single bolt and washer and take off the striker plate.
3 Refitting is the reverse of the removal procedure, following which adjustment can be made if found necessary to obtain satisfactory opening and closing of the tailgate.

29 Fuel filler flap - removal and refitting

1 Remove the loadspace trim panel, as previously described.
2 Remove the two screws indicated in Fig. 12.27 and lift away the filler flap.
3 Installation is the reverse of the removal procedure.

30 Instrument panel crash pad - removal and refitting

1 Disconnect the battery earth lead.
2 Remove the steering column shroud retaining screws. Remove the lower half and release the upper half retaining lug from its spring clip by pulling sharply upwards.
3 Remove the instrument cluster, as described in Chapter 10.
4 Detach the flexible pipes from the dashpanel vents and defrosters.
5 Remove the left and right-hand 'A' pillar trims (2 screws each) -

Fig. 12.27. Fuel filler flap retaining screws (Sec. 29)

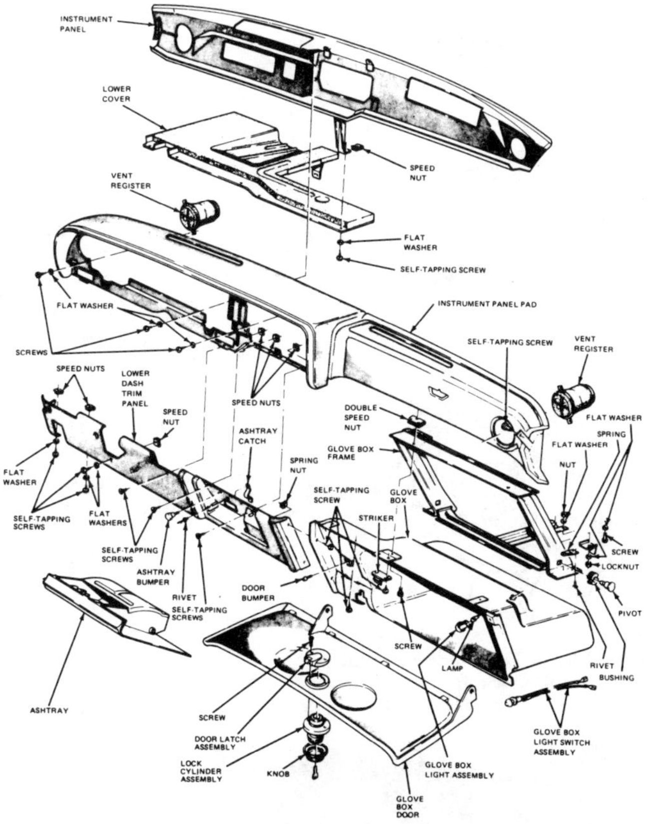

Fig. 12.28. Instrument panel crash pad and glove box (cars without air conditioning (Sec. 30)

also the grab handle if fitted.

6 Remove the instrument panel pad retaining screws and lift the pad away. If appropriate, remove the dash panel vents and transfer them to the new instrument panel.

7 Installation is essentially the reverse of the removal procedure, but connect the flexible pipes to the vents and defrosters before the crash pad is fitted.

31 Centre console - removal and refitting

Basic type

1 Lift the carpet from around the front of the console then push the clock and bezel out of the housing. Disconnect the clock leads.
2 Remove two screws at the rear end and two more from the clock end to release the console.
3 Remove the gear lever knob or T-handle.
4 Lift off the console. As applicable, remove the clock mounting plate screws and/or gearshift lever boot.
5 Installation is the reverse of the removal procedure.

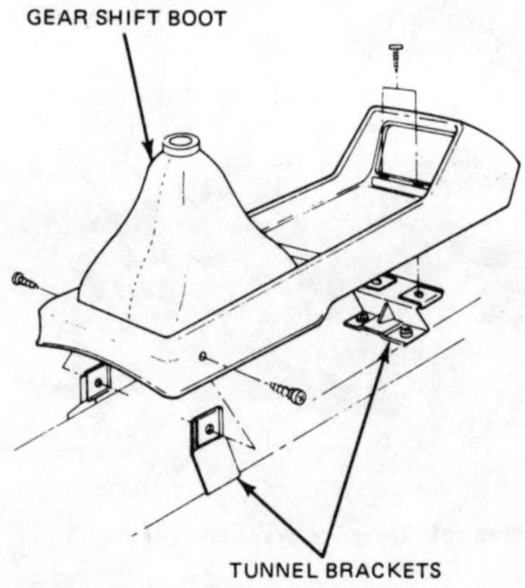

Fig. 12.29. Centre console - basic type (Sec. 31)

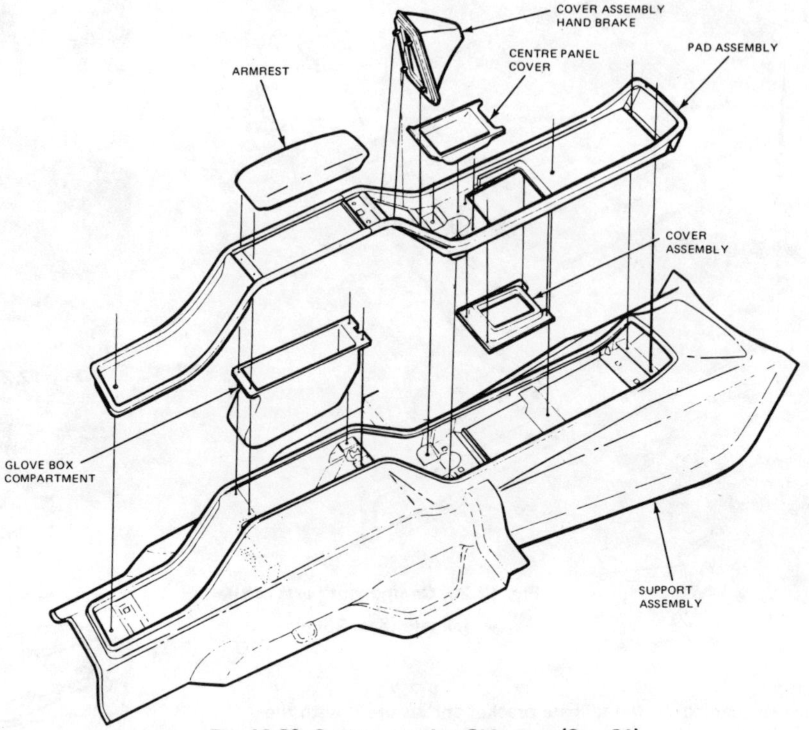

Fig. 12.30. Centre console - Ghia type (Sec. 31)

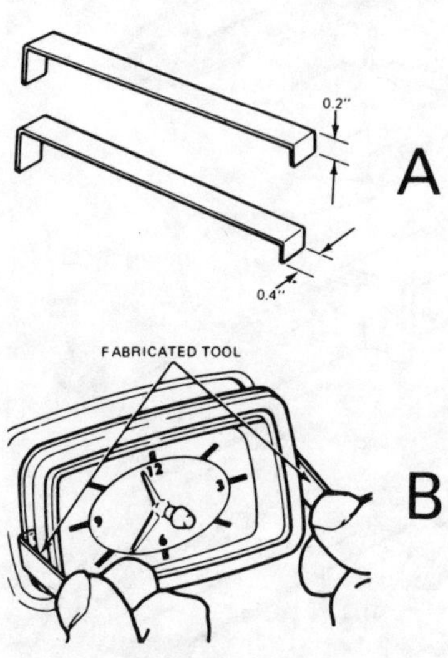

Fig. 12.31. A Tools for removal of the Ghia console clock, B The tools in use (Sec. 31)

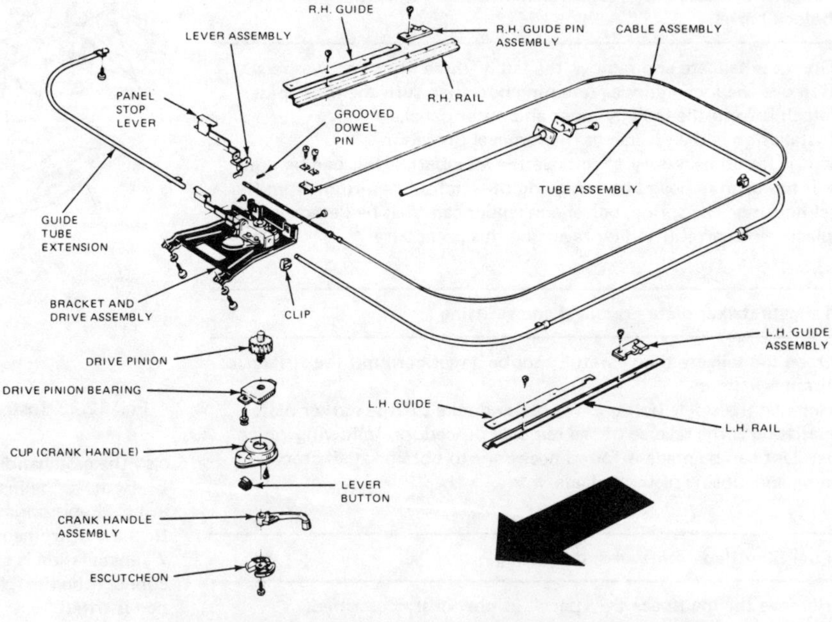

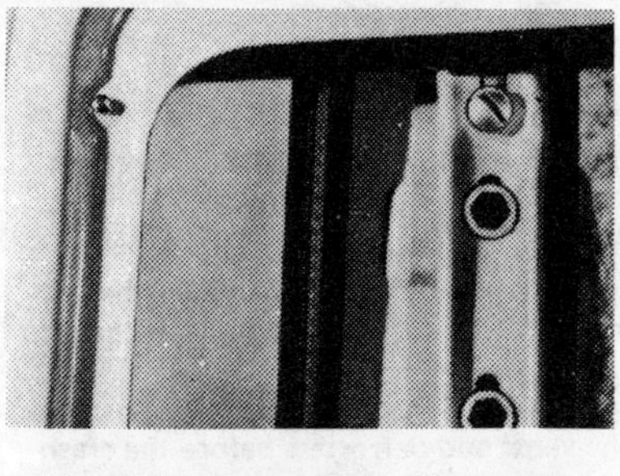

Fig. 12.33. Sunroof gap adjustment - front (Sec. 32)

Fig. 12.32. The sunroof control mechanism (Secs. 32 and 33)

Ghia type

6 Lift the carpet from around the front of the console.

7 Fabricate two small brackets from 1/16 in (1.5 mm) sheet steel (see Fig. 12.31A) and insert these behind the black bezel tc remove the clock (Fig. 12.31B).

8 Remove the two console retaining screws then prise out the cap in front of the gearshift lever and remove the screw beneath.

9 Carefully prise the handbrake lever boot and bezel assembly from the console and remove it.

10 Carefully prise out the centre panel cover from behind the gear lever.

11 Lift up the centre armrest and remove the screw from the bottom of the compartment.

12 Remove the armrest hinge screws and place the armrest in the compartment.

13 Remove the two screws at the front end of the armrest.

14 Prise out the cap at the rear of the console and remove the screw.

15 Carefully lift out the rear section, front section and console compartment.

16 Remove the heat insulating pad from beneath the console compartment area.

17 As applicable, remove the electrical connector from the base of each

seatbelt stalk and remove the stalk fixing bolt through the top of the console. Remove the stalk assembly through the inside console support.
18 Pull the carpet away from the sides of the support assembly then detach the support by removing the eight securing screws.
19 Installation is basically the reverse of the removal procedure but first ensure that all the spire nuts are correctly located on the brackets. Tighten the seatbelt stalks to a torque of 26 to 31 lb f ft (3.6 to 4.3 kg fm).

32 Sunroof panel - adjustments

Gap adjustment

1 When closed, a gap of 0.23 to 0.27 in (5.8 to 6.9 mm) should exist between the sunroof and the car roof. If a vinyl roof cover is fitted this gap should be reduced by 0.07 in (1.78 mm). If adjustment is required, proceed as described below.
2 With the sunroof half open, remove the sunroof headlining frame.
3 Close the sunroof then pull the headlining from the rear and remove it.
4 To adjust the front of the sunroof, loosen the front guide retaining screws then whilst pressing the guides inwards tighten the screws.
5 To adjust the rear, loosen the two fixing screws at each side of the adjusting base, then press the rear slides inwards and tighten.
6 Fit the headlining and headlining frame.
7 If the adjustment is still incorrect, remove the weatherstrip from the roof panel and bend its mounting flange as necessary.

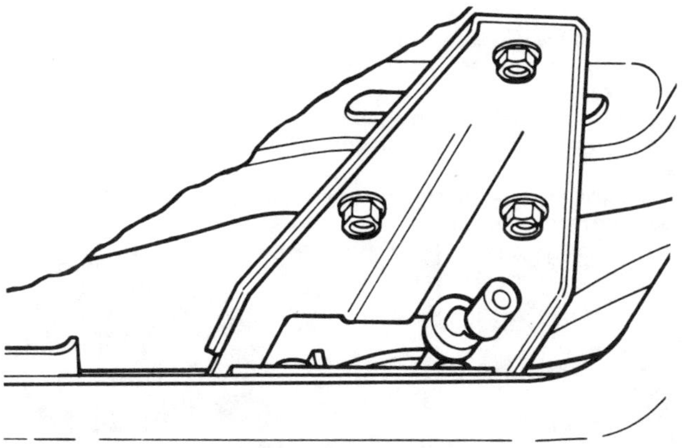

Fig. 12.34. Sunroof gap adjustment - rear (Sec. 32)

Height adjustment

8 The front edge of the sunroof should be flush with or 0.04 in (1 mm) below the edge of the car roof. The rear edge should be flush with or 0.04 in (1 mm) above the car roof. If adjustment is required, proceed as described below.
9 Proceed as described in paragraphs 1 to 4 inclusive, but before tightening the screws adjust the sunroof height by turning the adjusting screw (Fig. 12.35) as necessary; tighten the guide retaining screws.
10 To adjust the rear end, loosen the adjusting screws on the link assemblies (on the inner side of the panel). Adjust the height and tighten the screws.
11 Check for leaks and noises, adjusting again, if necessary.
12 Fit the headlining and headlining frame.

33 Sunroof - removal and refitting

1 Open the sunroof then mark the position of both guide pin assemblies. Remove the guide pins and guides.
2 Close the sunroof then push the button upwards to the tilt position.
3 Lift the front of the sunroof out of its opening whilst turning the handle until the screws fastening the cable to the base assembly are accessible.
4 Unscrew the cable and lift out the complete sunroof including the base assembly.
5 Unscrew the handle assembly, pull out the handle and escutcheon then remove the button control. Remove the cup.
6 Unscrew the gear bearing then remove it together with the pinion.
7 Move the cable so that the grooved dowel pin appears in the opening of the pinion. Pull out the pin and discard it. The operating cable can now be pulled out of the tube assembly.
8 To refit the sunroof, install the operating cable into the tube assembly. Turn the cable at its T-formed end and fit a new grooved dowel pin. Smear a little general purpose grease on the cable where it will contact the pinion, then assemble the pinion and bearing.
9 Fit the handle cup and fit the button to the lever.
10 Fit the handle and escutcheon, then check the handle position as follows:

- *a) Pull the button down and turn the handle fully clockwise which should now be approximately 30 degrees ahead of its original position opposite the cup of the handle (Fig. 12.36).*
- *b) Push the button up and turn the handle fully anticlockwise which should now be approximately 30 degrees ahead of its original position. The handle can be reset on the pinion splines as necessary.*

11 Insert the sunroof into the opening and attach the cable to the base assembly.
12 Carefully move the sunroof to the rear by turning the handle then screw on the guide pin assemblies with the pin outwards, to coincide

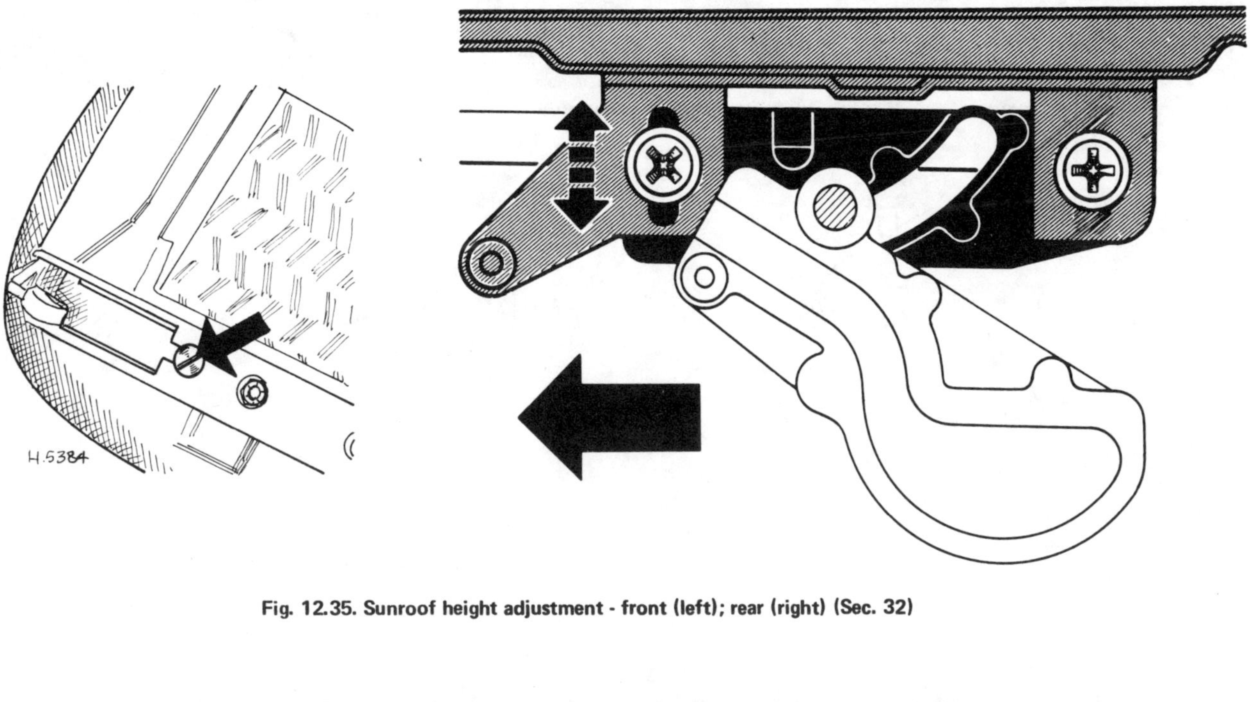

Fig. 12.35. Sunroof height adjustment - front (left); rear (right) (Sec. 32)

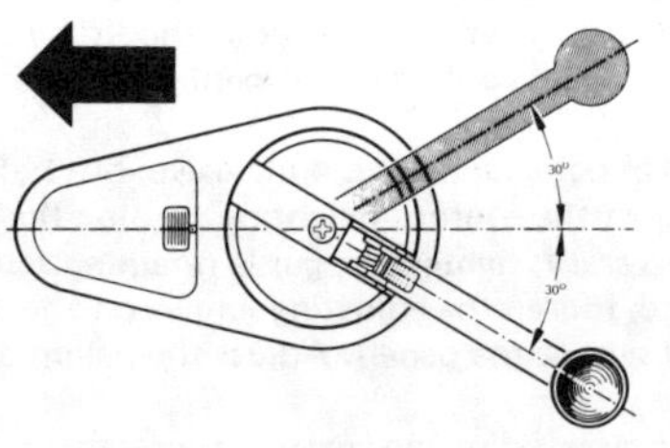

Fig. 12.36. Checking the handle alignment (Sec. 33)

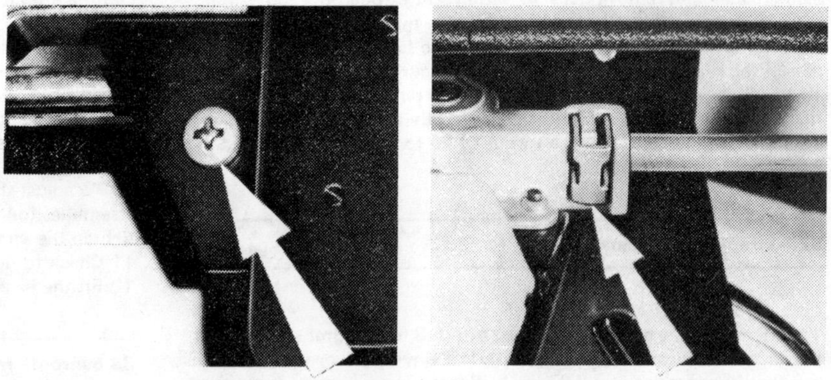

Fig. 12.37. Tube guide screw and clip (Sec. 34)

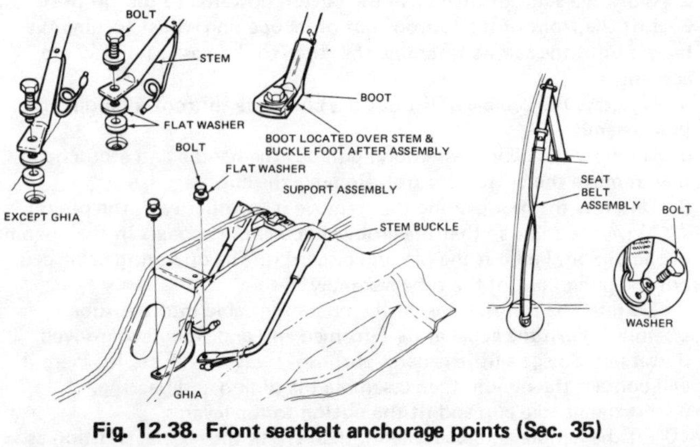

Fig. 12.38. Front seatbelt anchorage points (Sec. 35)

with the marks made when removed. Note that the left and right-hand guides are not interchangeable.

13 Adjust the roof, as described in the previous Section.

34 Sunroof bracket and drive assembly - removal and refitting

1 Remove the crank handle, the pinion drive and the bearing.

2 Remove the covering strip then remove the mirror, courtesy light and sun visors.

3 Remove the windscreen, as described in Section 10.

4 Carefully remove the headlining from above the middle of the windscreen.

5 Pull the grooved dowel pin out of the actuating cable and discard it.

6 Pull back on the cable slightly to clear the drive assembly of the cable.

7 Remove the tube guide screw (right-hand side) and clip (left-hand side), and remove the tubes.

35.4a Anchor plate stud nuts

35.4b Feeding the belt through the slot in the inner panel

35.4c Lowering the inertia reel through the slot in the inner panel

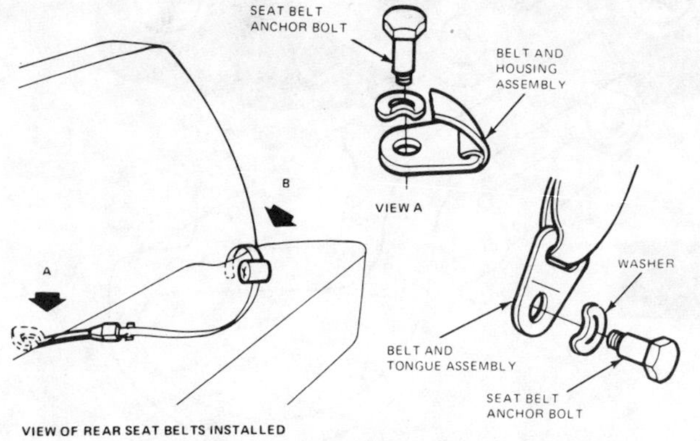

Fig. 12.39. Rear seatbelt anchorage points (Sec. 35)

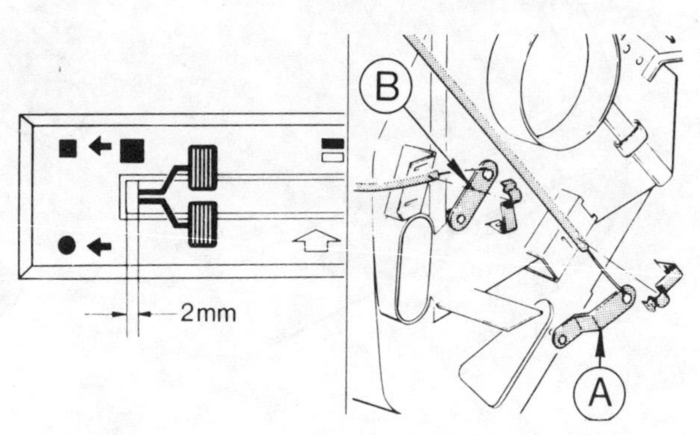

Fig. 12.40. Standard heater, control cable adjustment (Sec. 36)

A Distributor flap control lever *B Regulator flap control lever*

8 Remove the screws to release the bracket and drive assembly.
9 Refitting the bracket and drive assembly is the reverse of the removal procedure, using a new grooved dowel pin. Check the handle position, as described in paragraph 10 of the previous Section, and adjust the roof, if necessary, as described in Section 32.

35 Seatbelts - general

1 Mercury Capri II models will normally be fitted with a seatbelt interlock and warning buzzer system. Further information on these will be found in Chapter 10.
2 All models are fitted with inertia reel seatbelts for the front seats. Rear seatbelts of a similar type are also available.
3 Fig. 12.38 shows the floor mounted front seatbelt stalk. Removal of the basic type fixing is straightforward, but for Ghia models the centre console must be partly removed, as described in Section 31.
4 To remove the front seatbelt inertia reel, remove the rear quarter trim panel, as described in Section 21, then remove the three nuts from the anchor plate and lower the assembly through the aperture, whilst feeding the belt through the slot in the inner panel (photos).
5 If the seatbelt fixings are removed, they should be torque tightened to the following values on installation. (**Note:** This does not include the inertia reel anchor plate):

Front stalks	*26 to 31 lb f ft (3.6 to 4.3 kg fm)*
Other fixings	*15 to 20 lb f ft (2.1 to 2.9 kg fm)*

36 Heater controls - adjustment

1 Initially disconnect the battery earth lead, then remove the glove compartment by unscrewing 7 screws at the top and 2 nuts at the bottom. Also disconnect the glove compartment lighting leads.
2 Move the heater controls to a point 0.08 in (2 mm) from the end position, then remove both outer cable clips (see Figs. 12.40, 12.41 or 12.42 as appropriate).
3 *Standard heater:* Check that the distributor and regulator flap levers are at the end of their travel and clamp the outer cables in this position (Fig. 12.40).
4 *Heavy duty heater:* Check that the distributor flap lever (Fig. 12.41) and water control lever (Fig. 12.42) are at the end of their travel and clamp the outer cables in this position.
5 On completion, reconnect the glove compartment lighting leads, then refit the glove compartment and reconnect the battery earth lead.

37 Heater controls - removal and refitting

1 Initially disconnect the battery earth lead.
2 Remove the steering column shroud (2 screws at the bottom, then pull out at the top). Lower the steering column (leaving the two bolts in position), sufficiently to allow the instrument cluster trim to be removed.
3 Disconnect the switch leads and remove the instrument cluster trim complete with cowl trim (11 screws). Remove the instrument cluster bezel (3 screws).
4 Using a large pair of pliers, break the heater control knobs and remove the controls (4 screws). Do not disconnect the control cables at the heater.
5 Remove the heater control panel (2 screws). Remove the blower switch and lighting leads.
6 Disconnect the cables from the heater controls.
7 Refitting is the reverse of the removal procedure, during which it will be necessary to adjust the cables, as described in the previous Section. Also it will be necessary to obtain replacement heater control knobs.

38 Heater water valve (heavy duty heater) - removal and refitting

1 Drain the engine coolant and disconnect the lower hose from the radiator (refer to Chapter 2, if necessary).

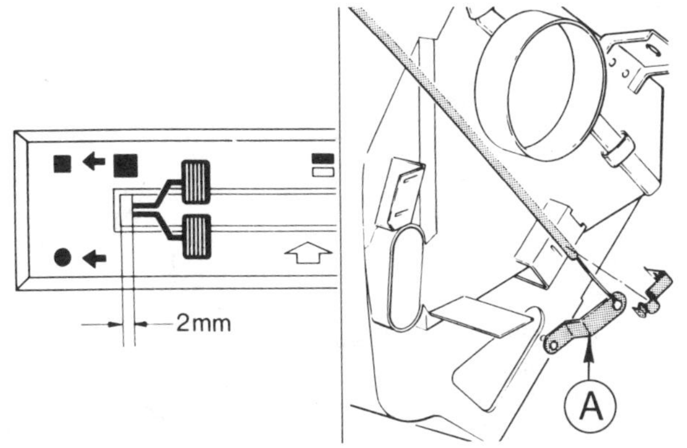

Fig. 12.41. Heavy duty heater, control cable adjustment (Sec. 36)

A Distributor flap control lever

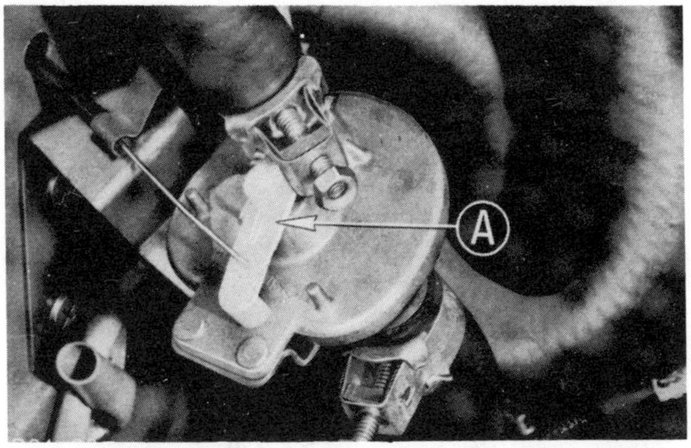

Fig. 12.42. Heavy duty heater, water valve (Sec. 36)

A Valve control lever

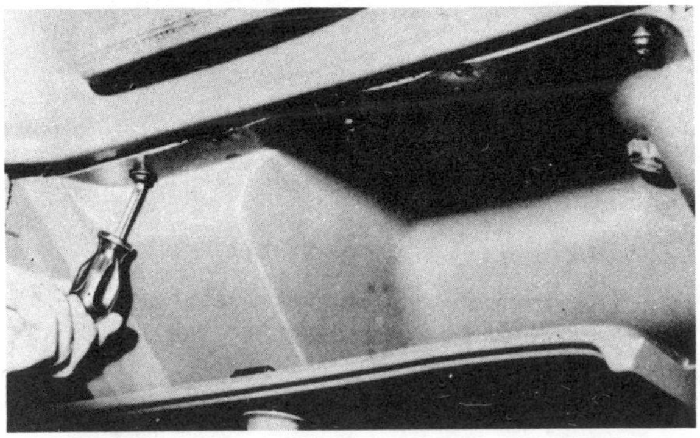

Fig. 12.43. Removing the glove compartment (Sec. 36)

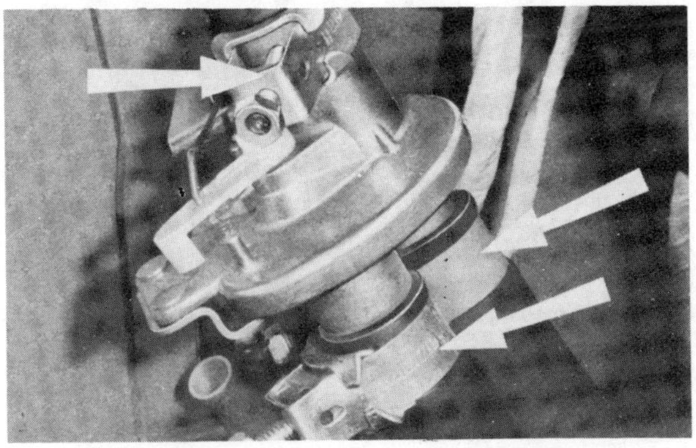

Fig. 12.44. The water valve hoses (arrowed) (Sec. 38)

2 Disconnect the three water hoses from the water valve.
3 Remove the outer cable from the clip on the water valve bracket then remove the assembly from the bulkhead (2 screws).
4 Twist the water valve to disconnect the cable from the operating lever.
5 Installation is the reverse of the removal procedure, during which adjustment should be made, as described in Section 36 for the heavy duty heater. On completion, refit the radiator hose and fill the cooling system, as described in Chapter 2.

39 Heater assembly - removal and refitting

1 Initially disconnect the battery earth lead.
2 Drain the coolant, referring to Chapter 2, if necessary.
3 Disconnect the water hoses from the heater heat exchanger. If practicable, blow through the heat exchanger with compressed air to remove any coolant remaining; alternatively place cloths and/or newspapers beneath to absorb any spillage.
4 Remove the cover panel together with the heat exchanger-to-water connection gasket from the bulkhead (2 screws).
5 Slacken the gearlever locknut then remove the gearlever. The locknut requires a special peg spanner available from Ford, but it is not difficult to fabricate a tool which will do the job.
6 Remove the parcel tray (4 screws); where there is a centre console this must be removed also (refer to Section 31).
7 Remove the steering column shroud (2 screws at the bottom, then pull out at the top). Lower the steering column (leaving the two bolts

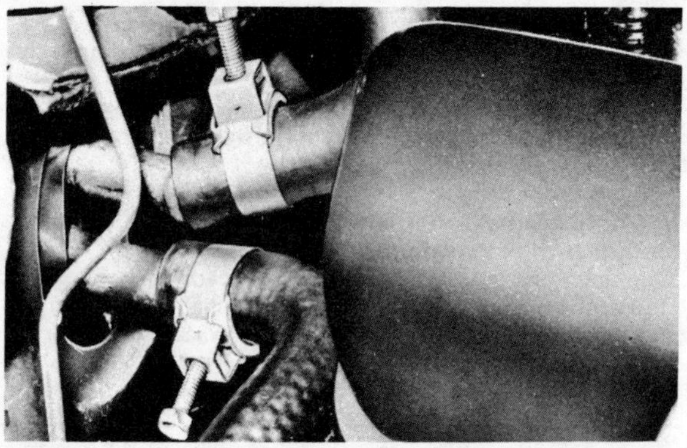

Fig. 12.45. Heat exchanger hoses (Sec. 39)

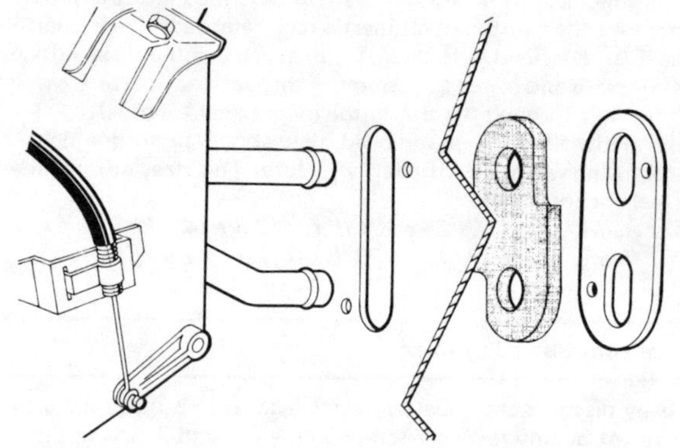

Fig. 12.46. Heat exchanger gasket and cover panel (Sec. 39)

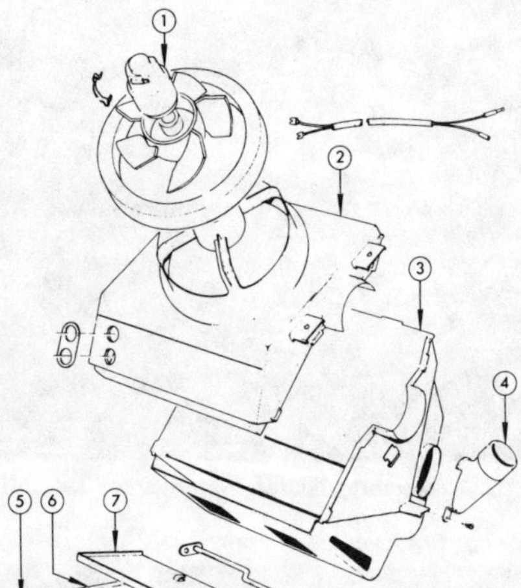

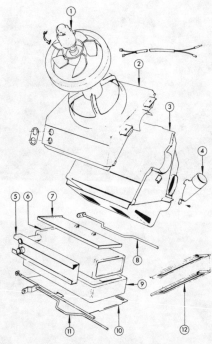

Fig. 12.47. Standard heater (Behr) (Sec. 40)

1 Motor and fan
2 Upper housing
3 Lower housing
4 Demister hose connection
5 Heat exchanger cover plate
6 Heat exchanger
7 Control flap
8 Control flap shaft
9 Heat exchanger seal
10 Distributor flap
11 Distributor flap shaft
12 Heat exchanger case

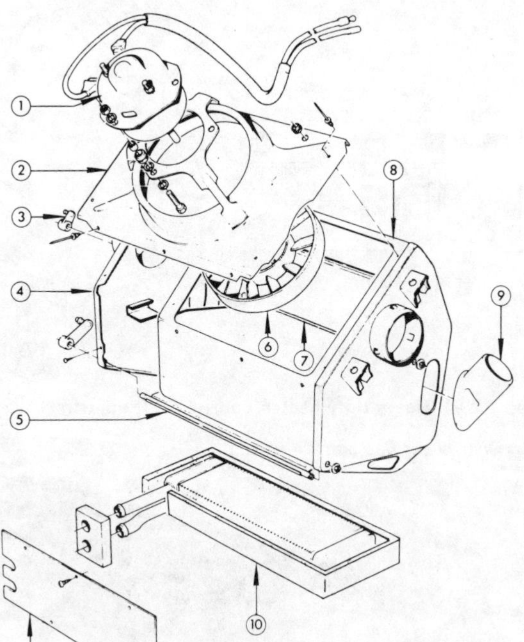

Fig. 12.48. Standard heater (Smiths) (Sec. 41)

1 Motor assembly
2 Cover and bracket assembly
3 Control valve operating lever
4 Right-hand housing cover
5 Distributor flap
6 Fan
7 Control valve
8 Housing
9 Demister hose connection
10 Heat exchanger seal
11 Plenum chamber cover

in position), sufficiently to allow the instrument cluster to be removed.
8 Remove the lower dash panel complete with cover panel (9 screws). Remove the ashtray and cigarette lighter, and disconnect the switches.
9 Remove the glove compartment by unscrewing the 7 screws at the top and 2 nuts at the bottom. Also disconnect the glove compartment lighting leads.
10 Disconnect the demister nozzle hoses together with their connections (1 screw each).
11 Disconnect the facia vent hoses from the heater. There are 2 on the standard heater and 4 on the heavy duty heater.
12 Remove the lower dash panel support stay (1 screw).
13 Disconnect the control cables from the heater, and the heater blower leads.
14 Remove the demister nozzles (refer to Section 42, if necessary).
15 Remove the windscreen wiper motor bracket from its mounting.
16 Remove the 4 heater securing screws then pull the heater far enough rearward for the water connection pipes to clear the bulkhead. Tilt the top of the heater upward and forward, and withdraw it sideways; remove the foam gasket also.
17 Refitting is the reverse of the removal procedure, during which it will be necessary to adjust the heater controls as described in Section 36. Do not forget to tighten the gearlever locknut. On completion fill the cooling system, as described in Chapter 2.

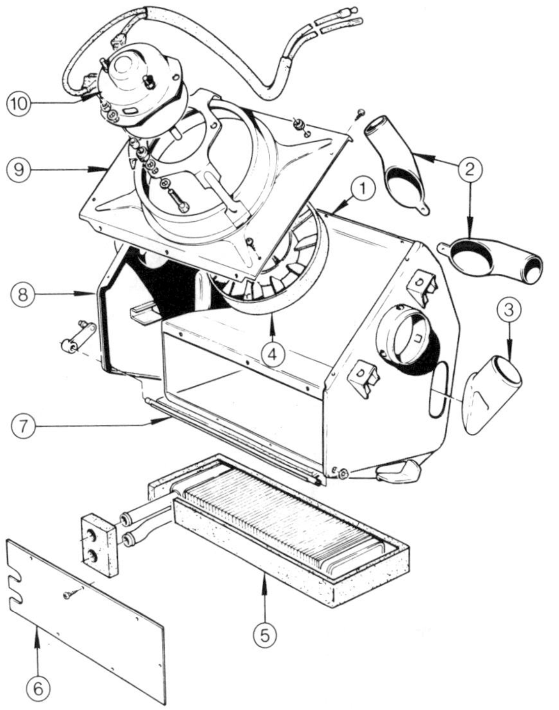

Fig. 12.49. Heavy duty heater (Smiths) (Sec. 41)

1 *Housing*
2 *Hot air supply to facia connection*
3 *Demister hose connection*
4 *Fan*
5 *Heat exchanger seal*
6 *Plenum chamber cover*
7 *Distributor flap*
8 *Right-hand housing cover*
9 *Cover and bracket assembly*
10 *Motor assembly*

40 Heater assembly (Behr) - dismantling and reassembly

1 Remove the distributor flap shaft (1 clip). Note that the flap remains in the lower section of the housing.
2 Remove the clamps securing the two halves of the housing, using circlip pliers. Remove the upper section, complete with the motor, from the lower section.
3 Remove the heat exchanger and frame from the lower section of the housing, then remove the heat exchanger from the frame and take off the foam packing.
4 To remove the distributor flap from the housing, remove the clip and withdraw the control lever sideways.
5 Remove the regulator flap from the lower section of the housing. Bend back the 2 clamping straps sufficiently to enable the control lever to be withdrawn after it has been turned towards the side, then remove the regulating flap.
6 Remove the retaining straps for the blower motor cap by pressing outwards from the inside using a screwdriver (see Fig. 12.50).
7 Detach the motor from the upper section. Disconnect the motor leads, remove the 4 retaining clamps and remove the motor and fan inwards.
8 When reassembling, position the blower motor so that the electrical connections face towards the cable fastening at the upper section. Secure the motor and connect the leads, then fit the motor cap.
9 Position the regulating flap in the lower section and insert the control lever by turning it from the side as necessary and swing it round into the straps. Close the straps using pliers.
10 Position the distributor flap in the lower section and insert the control lever from the side.
11 The remainder of the reassembly procedure is the reverse of the removal procedure.

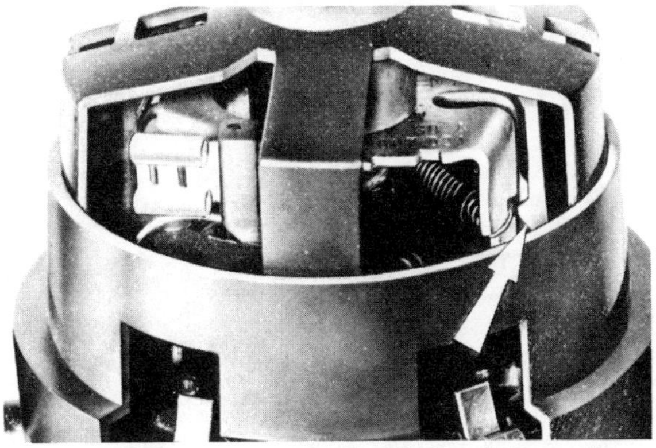

Fig. 12.50. Blower motor cap retaining strap (Sec. 40)

41 Heater assembly (Smiths standard and heavy duty) - dismantling and reassembly

1 *Standard heater:* Remove clips 'A' and 'B' (Fig. 12.52) and remove the heater housing side cover complete with flaps (15 screws).
2 *Heavy duty heater:* Remove clip 'A' (Fig. 12.52) and remove the heater housing side cover complete with flaps (15 screws).
3 Remove the heat-exchanger and foam seal.
4 Prise off the circlip and remove the fan from the blower motor shaft.
5 Detach the blower motor from the support (3 nuts and bolts).
6 Reassembly is the reverse of the dismantling procedure.

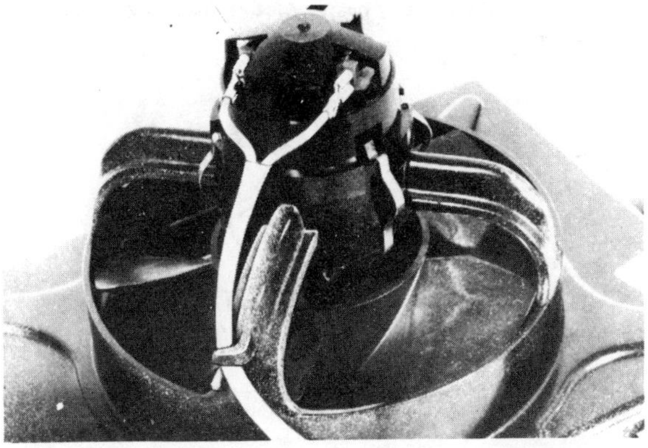

Fig. 12.51. The installed position of the blower motor (Secs. 40 and 41)

42 Demister nozzles - removal and refitting

Passenger's side

1 Remove the glove compartment by unscrewing the 7 screws at the

top and 2 nuts at the bottom. Also disconnect the glove compartment lighting leads.
2 Withdraw the hose from the demister nozzle and remove the nozzle (1 screw).
3 Installation is the reverse of the removal procedure.

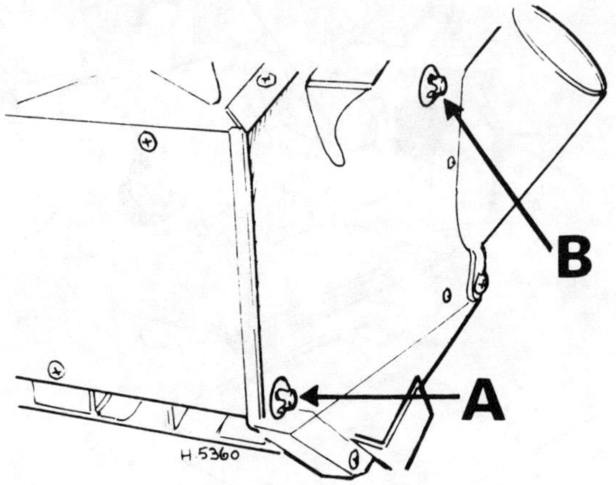

Fig. 12.52. Distributor flap (A) and regulator flap (B) clips (Sec. 41) (Smiths heaters)

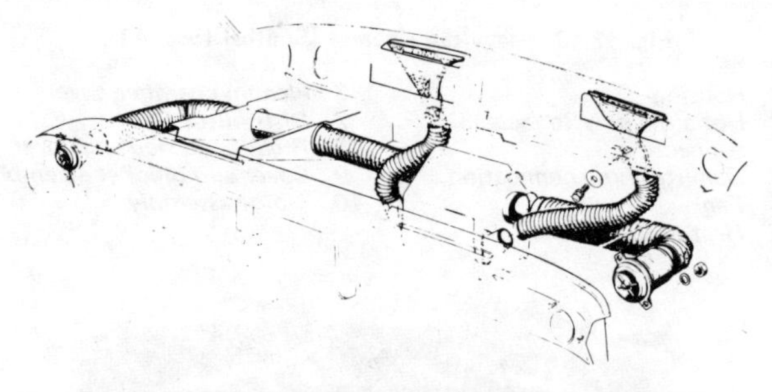
Fig. 12.53. Standard heater ducting (Secs. 42 and 43)

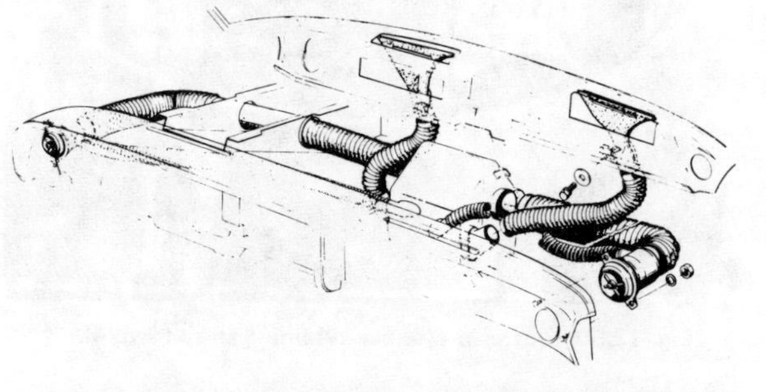
Fig. 12.54. Heavy duty heater ducting (Secs. 42 and 43)

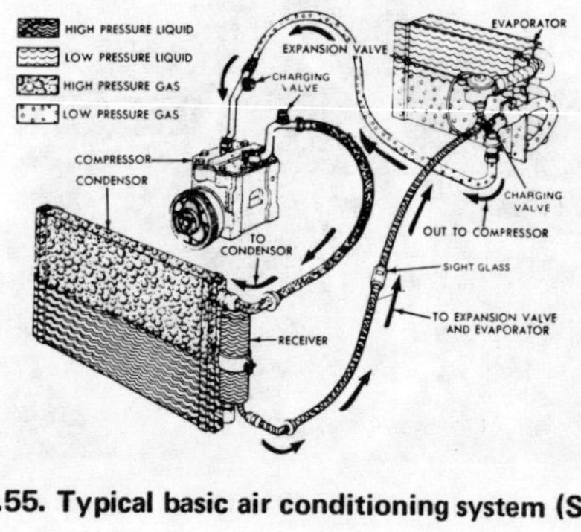

Fig. 12.55. Typical basic air conditioning system (Sec. 45)

Driver's side

4 Initially proceed as described in paragraphs 1, 2 and 3 of Section 37. Additionally remove the ashtray and cigar lighter.
5 Remove the instrument cluster (4 screws), disconnecting the speedometer drive cable and electrical connections. If there is any doubt about the position of any of the electrical connections, make a note of them first of all.
6 Withdraw the demister nozzle hose and remove the demister nozzle (1 screw), turning it upward and outward so that the inlet side of the nozzle can come out first from the instrument cluster opening.
7 Refitting is the reverse of the removal procedure.

43 Face level vents (vent registers) - removal and refitting

Passenger's side

1 Remove the glove compartment by unscrewing 7 screws at the top and 2 nuts at the bottom. Also disconnect the glove compartment lighting leads.
2 Withdraw the hose(s) from the vent.
3 Remove the vent by unscrewing the 2 nuts which are accessible from the rear of the panel.
4 Installation is the reverse of the removal procedure.

Driver's side

5 Initially proceed as described in paragraphs 1, 2 and 3 of Section 37. Additionally remove the 9 screws at the top of the instrument panel trim.
6 Withdraw the hose(s) from the vent.
7 Remove the vent by unscrewing the 2 nuts which are accessible from the rear of the panel.
8 Installation is the reverse of the removal procedure.

44 Fault diagnosis - heating system

Symptom	Reason
Insufficient heat	Faulty engine coolant reservoir cap. Faulty cooling system thermostat Kink in heater hose. Faulty control lever or cable. Heat exchanger blocked. Blower fuse blown. Low engine coolant level.
Inadequate defrosting or general heat circulation	Incorrect setting of deflector doors. Disconnected ducts. Carpet obstructing airflow outlet.

45 Air-conditioning system - general

1 Where the car is equipped with an air-conditioning system, the checks and maintenance operations must be limited to the following items. No part of the system must be disconnected due to the danger from the refrigerant which will be released. Your Ford dealer or a refrigeration engineer must be employed if the system has to be evacuated or recharged.
2 Regularly check the condition of the system hoses and connections.
3 Inspect the fins of the condenser (located ahead of the radiator) and brush away accumulations of flies and dirt.
4 Check the compressor drivebelt adjustment. There should be a total deflection of ½ in (12.7 mm) at the centre of the longest run of the belt. Where adjustment is required, move the position of the idler pulley.
5 Keep the air-conditioner drain tube clear. This expels condensation produced within the unit to a point under the car.
6 When the system is not in use, move the control to the 'OFF' position. During the winter period operate the unit for a few minutes every three or four weeks to keep the compressor in good order.
7 Every six months, have your Ford dealer check the refrigerant level in the system and the compressor oil level.

Chapter 13 Supplement: Revisions and information on later models

Contents

1 Introduction

Since their introduction in 1974 the Capri II models have had a number of modifications and improvements in order to keep pace with current technical and servicing innovations. The most significant changes on UK models result from the European Economic Community regulations designed to reduce toxic emissions from motor vehicles. In May 1975, in this respect, the manufacturer started to introduce modified carburettors known as Sonic Idle or Increased Severity Emission carburettors together with other related changes, and a year later further alterations to the carburettors were made giving them the name of Tamperproof carburettors. From May 1979 modified engines were introduced to give improvements in performance and economy, and to permit the use of regular grade petrol. Later the same year the Ford Variable Venturi (VV) carburettor was introduced to enable the manufacturers to meet the more stringent exhaust emission regulations expected in the future. Details of these carburettors are given in the Supplement together with their servicing procedures, as well as details of other changes.

In order to use the Supplement to the best advantage, it is suggested that it is referred to before the main Chapters of the manual; this will ensure that any relevant information can be collected and accommodated into the procedures given in Chapters 1 to 12. Time and cost will therefore be saved and the particular job will be completed correctly.

2 Specifications

The specifications listed here are revised or supplementary to the main specifications given at the beginning of each Chapter.

Engine

Alterations to engine specification from 1979 model year on

Engine identification:

1.6 litre, low compression (LC)	LAN
1.6 litre, high compression (HC)	LCN
1.6 litre, GT	LEN
2.0 litre, high compression (HC)	NEN
Compression ratio:	
1.6 litre LC	8.2 : 1
1.6 litre HC & GT and 2.0 litre HC	9.2 : 1
Compression pressure at cranking speed:	
1.6 litre LC	128 to 156 lbf/in^2 (9 to 11 kgf/cm^2)
1.6 litre HC & GT and 2.0 litre HC	157 to 184 lbf/in^2 (11 to 13 kgf/cm^2)
Engine idle speed	800 $\pm$ 25 rpm
Max. continuous engine speed:	
1.6 litre HC and LC	5800 rpm
1.6 litre GT	6300 rpm
2.0 litre HC	5800 rpm
Engine horsepower (DIN):	
1.6 litre LC	68 BHP at 5300 rpm
1.6 litre HC	72 BHP at 5300 rpm
1.6 litre GT	91 BHP at 5700 rpm
2.0 litre HC	101 BHP at 5200 rpm
Torque (DIN):	
1.6 litre LC	83.4 lbf ft (11.5 kgf m) at 2800 rpm
1.6 litre HC	86.3 lbf ft (11.9 kgf m) at 2700 rpm
1.6 litre GT	92.3 lbf ft (12.7 kgf m) at 4000 rpm
2.0 litre HC	113 lbf ft (15.6 kgf m) at 4000 rpm

Camshaft

Cam heel-to-toe dimension:	
1.6 litre LC, HC and GT	1.399 to 1.413 in (35.894 to 36.234 mm)
2.0 litre HC	1.414 to 1.427 in (36.260 to 36.600 mm)
Camshaft endfloat	0.004 to 0.007 in (0.104 to 0.204 mm)

Pistons

Ring gap position	Equally spaced around piston with oil control ring ends abutting, not overlapping

Cylinder head

Cast identification number:	
1.6 litre LC, HC and GT	6
2.0 litre HC	20
Valve seat angle	46°
Parent bore for camshaft bearing liners:	
Front	1.757 to 1.758 in (45.072 to 45.102 mm)
Centre	1.859 to 1.861 in (47.692 to 47.722 mm)
Rear	1.874 to 1.875 in (48.072 to 48.102 mm)

Inlet valve

Length:	
1.6 litre LC, HC and GT	4.39 to 4.43 in (112.65 to 113.65 mm)
2.0 litre HC	4.31 to 4.35 in (110.65 to 111.65 mm)
Head diameter	1.630 to 1.645 in (41.80 to 42.20 mm)
Stem diameter:	
Standard	0.313 to 0.314 in (8.025 to 8.043 mm)
Oversize 0.2	0.320 to 0.321 in (8.225 to 8.243 mm)
Oversize 0.4	0.328 to 0.329 in (8.425 to 8.443 mm)
Oversize 0.6	0.336 to 0.337 in (8.625 to 8.643 mm)
Oversize 0.8	0.344 to 8.345 in (8.825 to 8.843 mm)
Valve lift (excluding clearance):	
1.6 litre LC, HC and GT	0.370 in (9.503 mm)
2.0 litre HC	0.394 in (10.121 mm)
Spring load, valve open	132.75 to 146.25 lbf (59 to 65 kgf)
Spring load, valve closed	61.65 to 70.65 lbf (29.4 to 31.4 kgf)
Free spring length	1.716 in (44.0 mm)
Spring length, compressed	0.936 in (24.0 mm)

Exhaust valve

Length	4.295 to 4.330 in (110.15 to 111.05 mm)

Head diameter	1.396 to 1.412 in (35.80 to 36.20 mm)
Stem diameter:	
Standard	0.312 to 0.314 in (7.999 to 8.017 mm)
Oversize 0.2	0.319 to 0.320 in (8.199 to 8.217 mm)
Oversize 0.4	0.327 to 0.328 in (8.399 to 8.417 mm)
Oversize 0.6	0.335 to 0.336 in (8.599 to 8.617 mm)
Oversize 0.8	0.343 to 0.344 in (8.799 to 8.817 mm)
Valve lift (excluding clearance)	0.395 in (10.121 mm)
Spring load, valve open	132.75 to 146.25 lbf (59 to 65 kgf)
Spring load, valve closed	61.65 to 70.65 lbf (29.4 to 31.4 kgf)
Free spring length	1.833 in (47 mm)
Spring length, compressed	0.936 in (24 mm)

Engine lubrication data

Minimum oil pressure (SAE10W/30) at:	
750 rpm, 80°C	29.4 lbf/in^2 (2.1 kgf/cm^2)
2000 rpm, 80°C	35 lbf/in^2 (2.5 kgf/cm^2)

Fuel system

Motorcraft 1V, 1976 model year (Sonic Idle carburettor)

Engine	1600 cc	1600 cc	1600 cc
Transmission	Manual	Manual	Manual
Type	75HF-9510-KEA	75HF-9510-KKA	75HF-9510-KDA
Throttle barrel diameter (mm)	36.0	36.0	36.0
Venturi diameter (mm)	27.0	27.0	27.0
Main jet	135	135	135
Idle speed (rpm)	800 ± 25	800 ± 25	800 ± 25
Mixture % CO	0.5% ± 0.1	0.5% ± 0.1	0.5% ± 0.1
Fast idle (rpm)	1000 ± 100	2000 ± 100	2200 ± 100
Float level setting	29.0 ± 0.75 mm (1.14 ± 0.03 in)	29.0 ± 0.75 mm (1.14 ± 0.03 in)	29.0 ± 0.75 mm (1.14 ± 0.03 mm)
Choke plate pull down setting	3.3 ± 0.25 mm (0.13 ± 0.01 in)	3.8 ± 0.25 mm (0.15 ± 0.01 in)	3.0 ± 0.25 mm (0.12 ± 0.01 in)
De-choke	–	5.3 ± 0.5 mm (0.21 ± 0.02 in)	5.3 ± 0.5 mm (0.21 ± 0.02 in)
Accelerator pump stroke	2.9 ± 0.13 mm (0.11 ± 0.005 in)	2.9 ± 0.13 mm (0.11 ± 0.005 in)	2.9 ± 0.13 mm) 0.11 ± 0.005 in)
Vacuum piston link hole	–	Outer	Outer
Thermostatic spring slot	–	Centre	Centre
V-mark setting	–	5.0 mm (0.20 in)	4.5 mm (0.18 in)

Weber 2V, 1976 model year (Sonic Idle carburettor)

Engine	1600 cc	1600 cc
Transmission	Manual	Auto
Type	76HF-9510-JA/JB	76HF-9510-KA/KB
Throttle barrel diameter	32/36 mm	32/36 mm
Venturi diameter	26/27 mm	26/27 mm
Main jet	130/125	130/125
Idle speed (rpm)	800 ± 20	800 ± 20
Mixture % CO	1.5 ± 0.25	1.5 ± 0.25
Fast idle speed (rpm)	2000 ± 100	2000 ± 100
Float level setting		
Brass float	41.0 ± 0.3 mm (1.61 ± 0.01 in)	41.0 ± 0.3 mm (1.61 ± 0.01 in)
Plastic float	35.3 ± 0.5 mm (1.39 ± 0.02 in)	35.3 ± 0.5 mm (1.39 ± 0.02 in)
Choke plate pull down setting	6 mm (max) (0.24 in)	6 mm (max) (0.24 in)
Choke phasing	2.25 ± 0.25 mm (0.09 ± 0.001 in)	2.25 ± 0.25 mm (0.09 ± 0.001 in)

Motorcraft 1V, 1977 model year (Tamperproof carburettor)

Engine	1600 cc	1600 cc	1600 cc
Transmission	Manual	Manual	Auto
Type	77HF-9510-KBA	77HF-9510-KCA	77HF-9510-KDA
Choke	Manual	Auto	Auto
Main jet	137	137	135
Choke plate pull down setting (manual choke)	3.5 mm (0.14 in)	–	–

Note: *All other specifications identical to Sonic Idle 1V carburettor*

Weber 2V, 1977 model year (Tamperproof carburettor)

Engine	1600 cc	1600 cc	2000 cc	2000 cc
Transmission	Manual	Auto	Manual	Auto
Type	77HF-9510-JA	77HF-9510-KA	77HF-9510-CA	77HF-9510-DA
Choke	Auto	Auto	Auto	Auto
Main jet	130/125	130/125	137/127	135/127
Max vacuum pull down	6.0 mm (0.24 in)	6.0 mm (0.24 in)	7.0 mm (0.28 in)	7.0 mm (0.28 in)
Choke phasing	2.3 mm (0.09 in)	2.3 mm (0.09 in)	2.8 mm (0.11 in)	2.8 mm (0.11 in)
Bi-metal adjustment	On index	On index	On index	On index

Note: *All other specifications identical to Sonic Idle 2V carburettor*

Idle adjustments, 1979 on except VV carburettor

	Idle speed	CO level
1600 cc	800 rev/min	1.0%
2000 cc	800 to 825 rev/min	1.5%

Ford variable venturi (VV) carburettor 1980 model year on

Idle speed	800 $\pm$ 25 rpm
Idle CO%	1.5 $\pm$ 0.5
Operating fuel level	1.4 to 1.6 in (35 to 41 mm) from fuel to top of casting
Diaphragm lever setting dimension	0.47 in (12 mm)
Choke gauging twist drill diameter	0.135 in (3.4 mm)
Choke fast idle/pulldown twist drill diameter:	
Early housing	0.144 in (3.7 mm)
Later housing	0.167 in (4.3 mm)
Air valve maximum opening	0.9 in (23 mm)

Ignition system

Dwell angle (all models)	48 to 52°
Ignition timing:	
1600 cc:	
Up to 1979	6° to 8°
1979 on (VV carburettor)	12°
2000 cc:	
Up to 1979 (distributor No 73BB-AA)	4°
1979 on (distributor No 76HF-DA)	8°

Automatic transmission

Fluid type (see text):	
Up to 1981	Ford type G (SQM-2C9007-AA)
1981 on	Ford type CJ (SQM-209010-A)

Suspension and steering

Front wheel alignment (1978 on):	
Toe setting	2.0 mm (0.078 in) toe-in to 5.0 mm (0.195 in) toe-out
Castor angle:	
Standard	0° to 1°45' positive
Heavy duty	0°35' to 2°20' positive
Maximum difference (side to side)	0°45'
Camber angle:	
Standard	-0°15' to +1°15'
Heavy duty	+0°15' to + 1°45'
Maximum difference (side to side)	1°0'

3 Engine (Capri II)

Revised cylinder head valve seat angles

1 Should it be necessary to carry out repair or overhaul work to the cylinder head combustion chambers or valve seats, the dimensions and angles shown in Fig. 13.1 should be used. Note also that the valve seat angle has been revised and is now 46° for both inlet and exhaust valve seats.

4 Fuel system (Capri II)

PART A MOTORCRAFT SINGLE VENTURI AUTOMATIC CHOKE CARBURETTOR

Adjustment

1 A revised procedure has been introduced for adjusting the vacuum choke plate pull down on '1V' automatic choke carburettors. A pre-load tool weighing between 50 and 65 grams is required to make the adjustment and it is suggested that enquiries are made at the local Ford garage or have a tool made up to suit. The adjustment is carried out with the engine running, and is therefore more accurate than the method described in Chapter 3, Section 14.

2 First remove the air cleaner (Chapter 3), and run the engine until it has reached the normal operating temperature.

3 Switch off the engine and position the fast idle cam so that the arrow is pointing towards the top of the fast idler lever.

4 Connect a tachometer to the engine and check that the fast idle speed is correct (see Specifications); adjust if necessary by bending the adjusting tag.

5 With the engine switched off, unscrew and remove the three retaining screws and withdraw the choke housing and bi-metal spring assembly, carefully placing it to one side.

6 The choke lever is now exposed and the pre-load tool can now be positioned on the lever as shown in Fig. 13.2.

7 Start the engine and make sure it is still at the normal operating

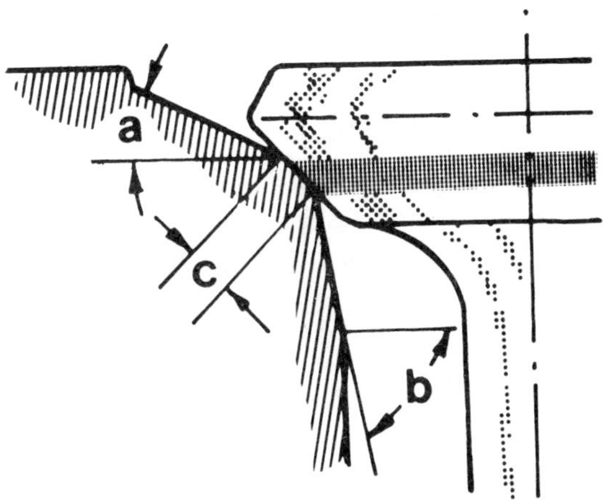

Fig. 13.1 Revised valve seat angles and dimensions

Inlet	Exhaust
a 35°	*a 35°*
b 65° (FoG), 78 to 82° (FoB)	*b 65°*
c 1.5 to 2.0 mm	*c 1.5 to 2.0 mm*

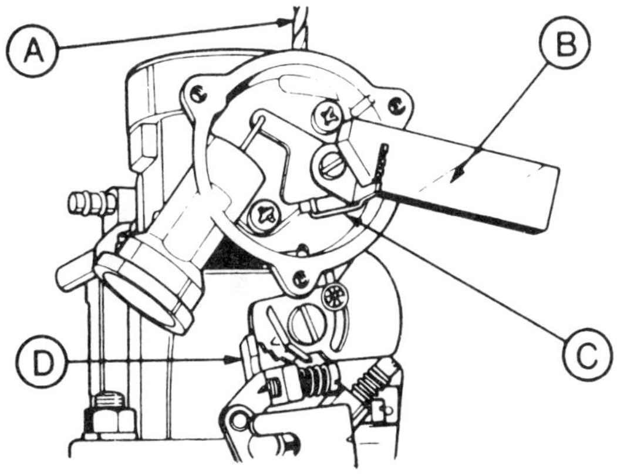

Fig. 13.2 Vacuum choke plate pulldown adjustment – (1V) carburettor

A Gauge (twist drill)
B Automatic choke preload tool
C Pulldown lever
D Throttle high cam setting

temperature, and then move the throttle to the high cam position.

8 The preload tool should now be floating, and the specified clearance between the choke plate and carburettor wall can be checked using the shank of a suitable twist drill. If adjustment is required, switch off the engine, and bend the pull down lever accordingly.

9 After checking the adjustment, refit the choke housing and bi-metal spring assembly, making sure that the alignment marks coincide and that the bi-metal spring is located in the centre slot on the choke operating link. Tighten the retaining screws evenly and refit the air cleaner.

PART B SONIC IDLE CARBURETTORS (1V)

Description and adjustment

1 From May 1975, the Ford 'Bypass' (Sonic) Idle carburettor was progressively introduced on Capri II models. The carburettor idle system differs from the conventional type in that the majority of the idle air flow and all of the idle fuel flow passes through the bypass system. The remaining airflow flows past the carburettor butterfly which is held in a slightly open position.

2 During the idle, with the butterfly almost closed, air is drawn into the bypass system (see Fig. 13.3). This air travels along the distribution channel and mixes with the fuel entering via the mixture screw; the resulting mixture is drawn into the engine via the Sonic discharge tube.

3 The Sonic Idle carburettor may be instantly recognised by the following:-

(a) Seven screws retaining the upper body, compared with six on previous units
(b) The distributor advance/retard vacuum pick-up tube is increased in length from 14 mm (0.52 in) to 35 mm (1.37 in)
(c) The idle mixture screw is repositioned to a point just above where the vacuum pick-up tube was previously situated
(d) The vacuum pick-up tube is repositioned to a point just above where the idle mixture screw was previously situated

4 Adjustment procedures for the Sonic Idle carburettor are as given in Chapter 3, Section 14 (except where a tamperproof carburettor is fitted), and all specification details are given in the Specifications section of this Supplement. It should be remembered that where a Sonic Idle carburettor is fitted, the following amendments will apply:-

(a) A revised inlet manifold (which may also be used with earlier single venturi carburettors). The carburettor flange gasket must be fitted with the tab towards the front of the engine
(b) A revised initial advance ignition timing of 6° to 8° BTDC at 800 rpm

PART C SONIC IDLE CARBURETTOR (2V)

Description and adjustment

1 The Weber dual venturi carburettor described in Chapter 3 was modified in May 1975 and progressively introduced on the appropriate Capri II models. In addition to the Bypass Idle characteristic, the modified Weber 2V carburettor includes a fuel return system and on some models (mainly automatic transmission) an anti-stall device.

2 The fuel return system ensures that the temperature of fuel entering the float chamber is maintained at a constant level at all times, and this in turn keeps the quantity of fuel vapour from the float chamber to the engine constant. Previously, if the engine was left idling for long periods, the idle mixture became over-rich.

3 Refer to Fig. 13.4 and observe that, on the Weber Bypass Idle system, fuel is initially supplied via the float chamber to the secondary main jet (A). Fuel then travels up to the secondary idle jet (B) where air is introduced into the system through the drilling (C). The air/fuel mixture then passes through a restrictor and is atomised as it enters the main bypass air flow (D). The mixture then passes through the fixed discharge channel (F) and the bypass discharge channel (G), the latter being adjustable by the bypass idle screw (E), and thence to the engine.

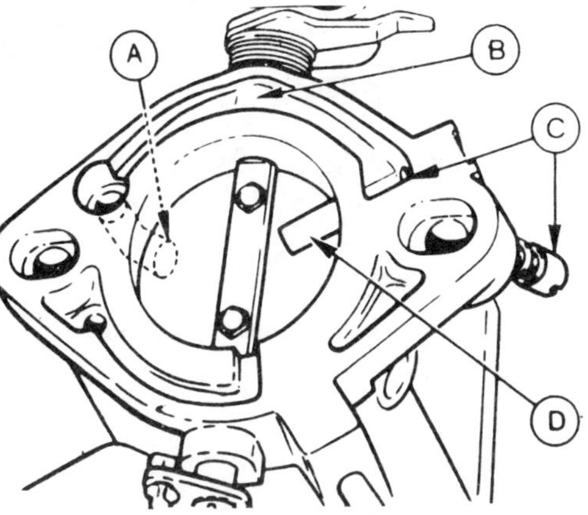

Fig. 13.3 Sonic idle type carburettor

A Air entry into bypass system
B Air distribution channel
C Fuel mixture screw
D Sonic discharge tube

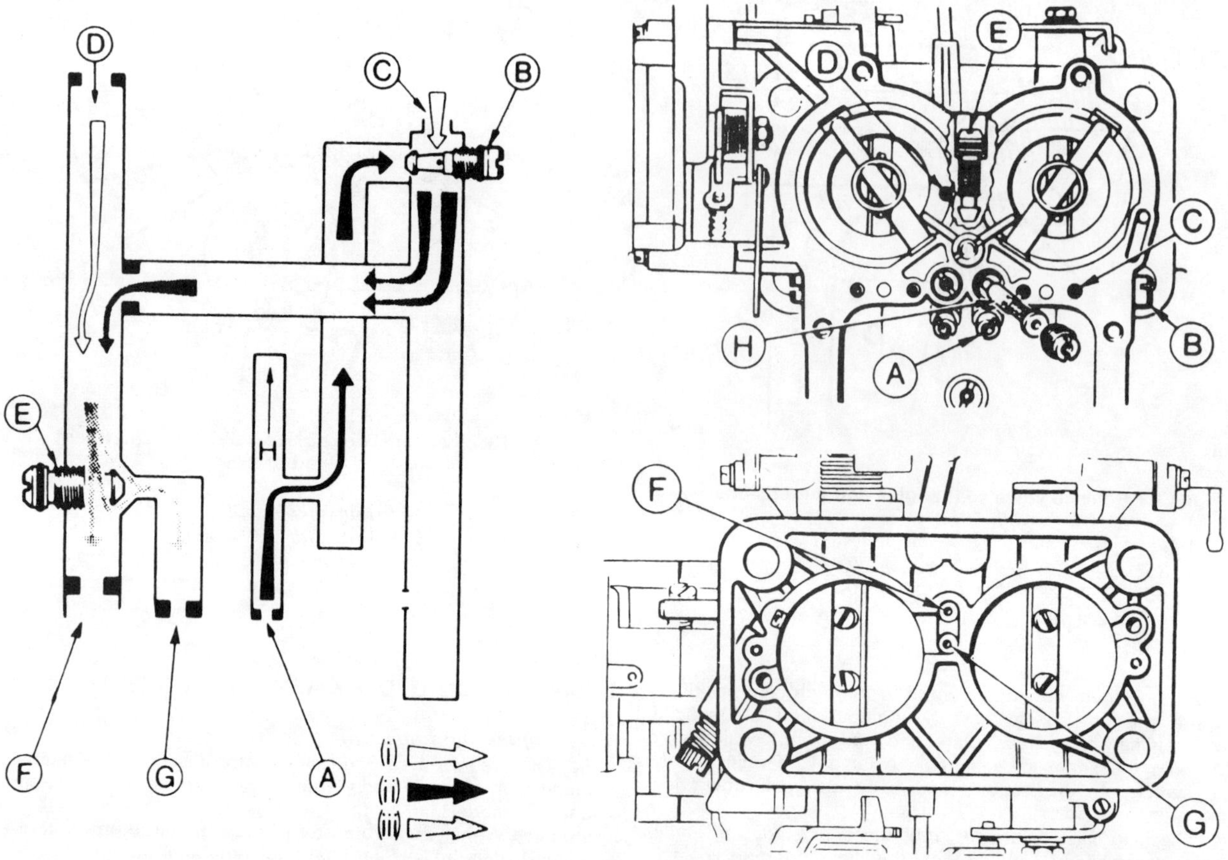

Fig. 13.4 Weber Bypass Idle system

(i) *Air supply*
(ii) *Fuel supply*
(iii) *Air/fuel mixture*
A *Main jet*
B *Idle jet*
C *Air bleed*
D *Main air supply*
E *Bypass idle screw*
F *Fixed discharge channel*
G *Bypass discharge channel*
H *Secondary emulsion tube*

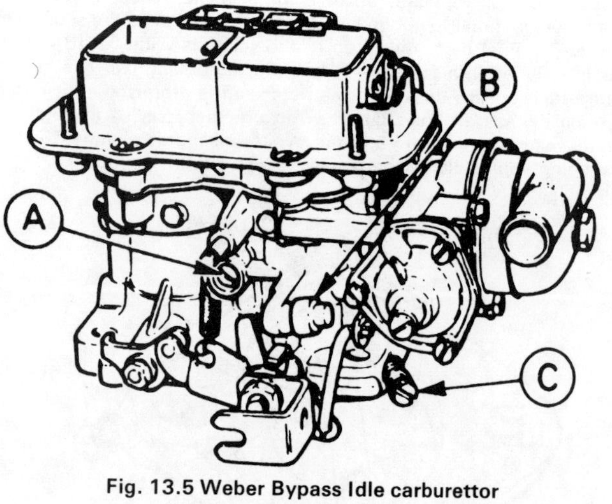

Fig. 13.5 Weber Bypass Idle carburettor

A *Bypass idle speed screw*
B *Basic idle speed screw*
C *Mixture screw*

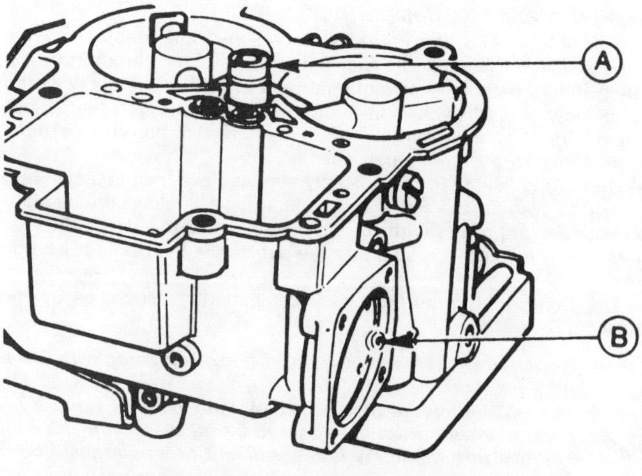

Fig. 13.6 Location of Weber anti-stall device

A *Discharge tube*
B *Fuel inlet*

4 Adjustment of the modified Weber 2V carburettor is similar to that described in Chapter 3, but it should be remembered that the basic idle speed screw (Fig. 13.5) should not be adjusted during normal routine servicing; it should only require adjustment after a carburettor overhaul or if the correct idle speed is impossible to achieve using the bypass idle screw. It is also imperative that an exhaust gas analyser is used to make the adjustment to the mixture screw.

5 The anti-stall device fitted to some models consists of a housing, diaphragm and spring. Engine vacuum is applied by an external tube to one side of the diaphragm which is then pulled back against spring tension. This action draws fuel from the accelerator pump reservoir to the opposite side of the diaphragm. If the engine attempts to stall, there will be an initial drop in engine vacuum and immediately this occurs, the diaphragm will be released and spring pressure will pump a quantity of fuel through the accelerator pump discharge tube, thus temporarily enriching the mixture and overcoming the stall.

6 Where an anti-stall device is fitted (mainly automatic transmission models) it is important to set the engine speed correctly; if it is too low, the anti-stall device will give an intermittent fuel delivery causing 'hunting'.

PART D TAMPERPROOF CARBURETTORS

Description and adjustment

1 From May 1976, all carburettors will not only be of the Sonic Idle type, but will also be tamperproof in respect of the idle mixture adjustment. This is effected by a plastic plug being installed over the idle mixture adjustment screw, and has been introduced to comply with EEC regulations.

2 The carburettor body is slightly modified to accommodate the recessed idle mixture screw which is beneath a white plastic plug. The carburettor is so designed that after the initial running-in period of a new engine, the percentage of carbon monoxide (CO) in the exhaust gas will be in accordance with a predetermined requirement (this may mean that during running-in, the requirement may not be met). Therefore, in order to comply with the regulations, adjustment should only be made with an exhaust gas analyser coupled to the car exhaust system.

3 Should adjustment be necessary, the white plastic plug may be punctured in its centre using a small screwdriver, and then prised out. Where this adjustment has been found necessary, a blue replacement plug should be pressed in on completion.

4 It is not essential for satisfactory operation of the carburettor to have the plastic plug fitted after any adjustment, but future legislation may (officially) restrict the adjustment procedure and supply of replacement plastic plugs to authorised dealers. Where adjustment is carried out, the exhaust gas CO content at idle speed is given in the Specifications Section.

5 When using an exhaust gas analyser on tamperproof carburettors it is imperative to obtain the correct reading, due to the fine CO percentage limits imposed on them. The engine must be at its normal operating temperature and the CO meter and exhaust gas analyser must be connected to the engine in accordance with the manufacturers' instructions.

6 Run the engine at 3000 rpm for approximately 30 seconds then allow it to idle. Then, as soon as the meters have stabilised, and within 10 to 30 seconds, record the CO percentage. If it takes longer than 30 seconds to make any adjustment, the engine should be run at 3000 rpm for 30 seconds again.

7 If it is found impossible to adjust the carburettor within the specification limits, the ignition timing, valve clearances, and general engine conditions should be checked.

PART E VARIABLE VENTURI (VV) CARBURETTOR

Air cleaner element renewal

1 Unscrew the retaining screws and unclip the cover. If the main body comes free, disconnect the vacuum hoses and ducting.

2 Remove the element and discard it.

3 Wipe clean the air cleaner body, then insert the new element.

4 Refit the body and/or cover in reverse order, making sure that the gasket is correctly positioned on the top of the carburettor.

5 This gasket is fitted with the orange-coloured resin side uppermost on early models but due to the fact that when the air cleaner is removed pieces of gasket can fall into the carburettor intake, it is recommended that the gasket is inverted to place the resin-coated side downwards.

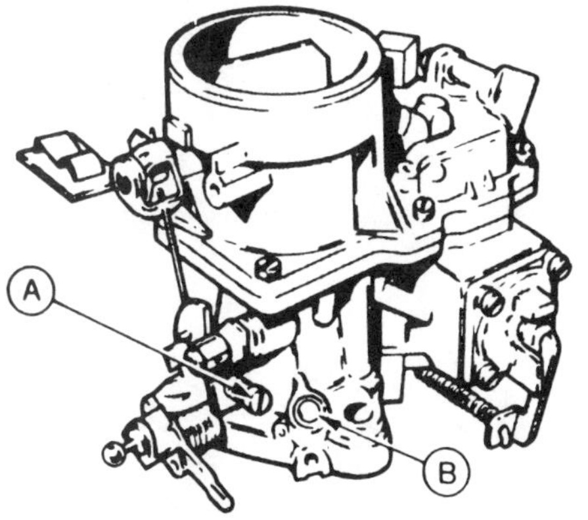

Fig. 13.7 Tamperproof carburettor (1V)

A *Idle speed screw* B *Sealing plug*

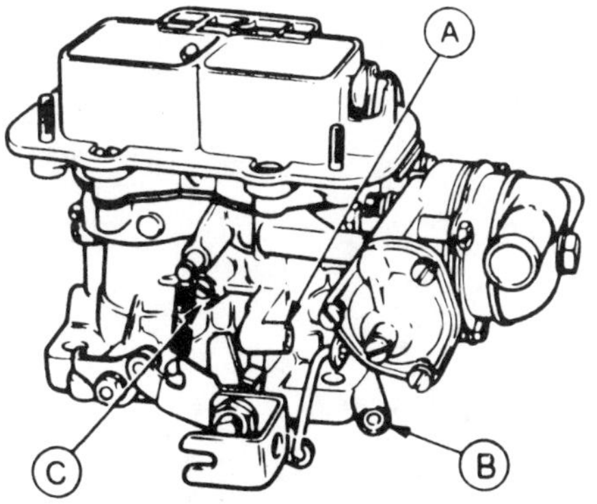

Fig. 13.8 Tamperproof carburettor (2V)

A *Idle speed screw* C *Bypass idle speed screw*
B *Fuel mixture screw*

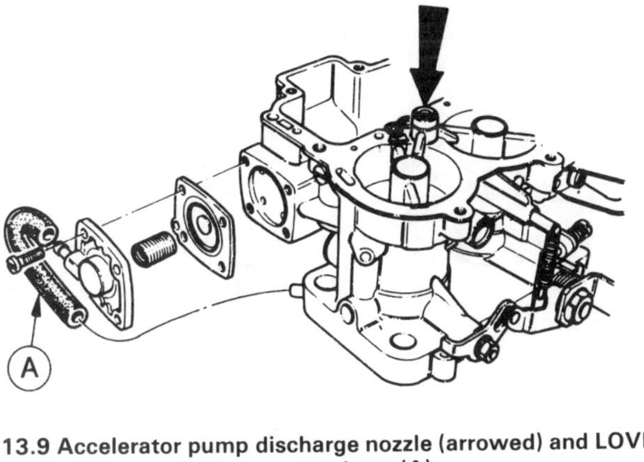

Fig. 13.9 Accelerator pump discharge nozzle (arrowed) and LOVE device vacuum hose (A)

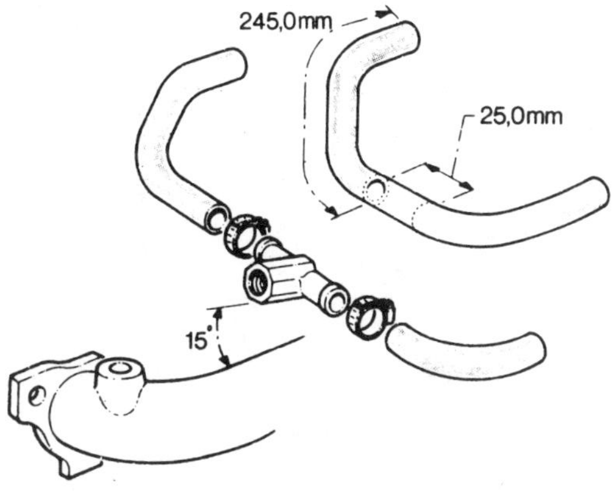

Fig. 13.10 PVS vacuum hoses and switch adaptor

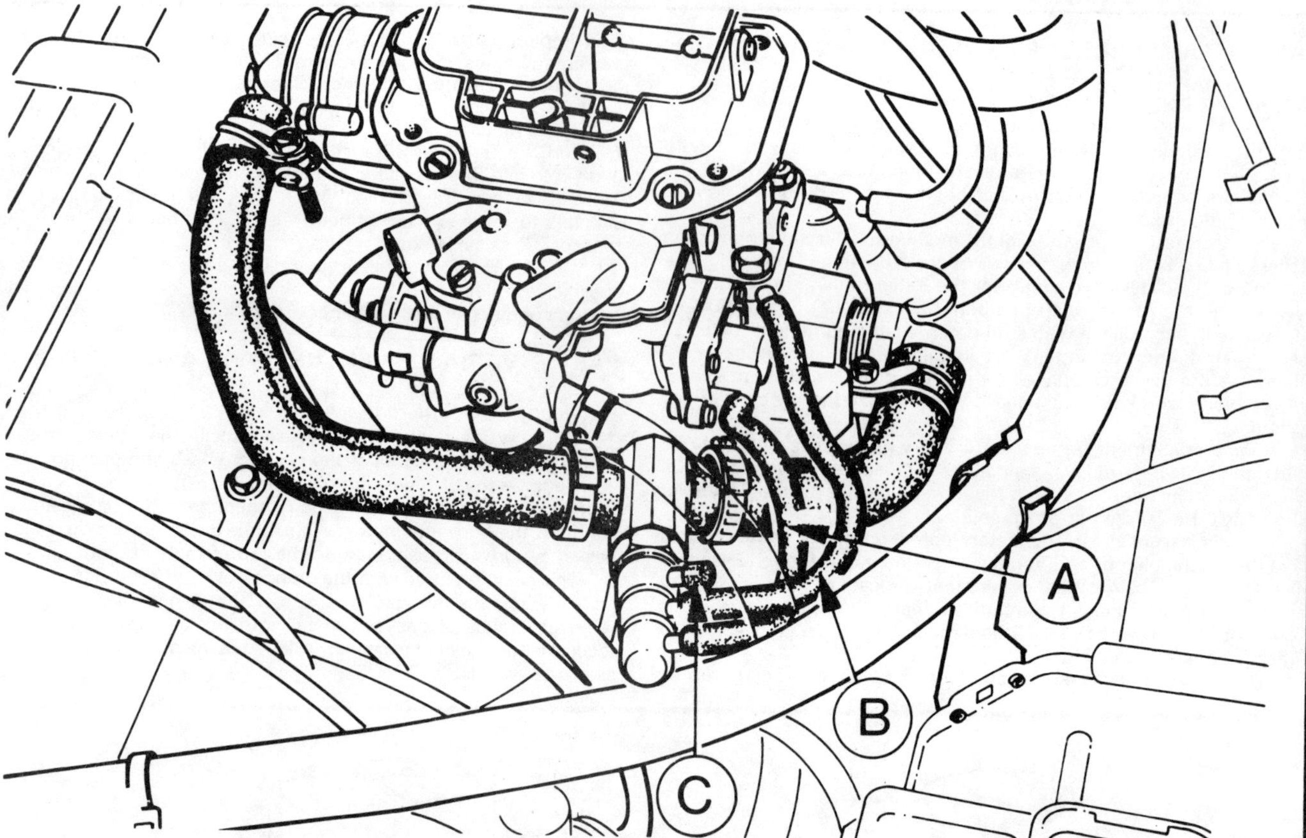

Fig. 13.11 PVS switch installation

A Vacuum hose (160 mm long) *B* Vacuum hose (200 mm long) *C* Blanking cap

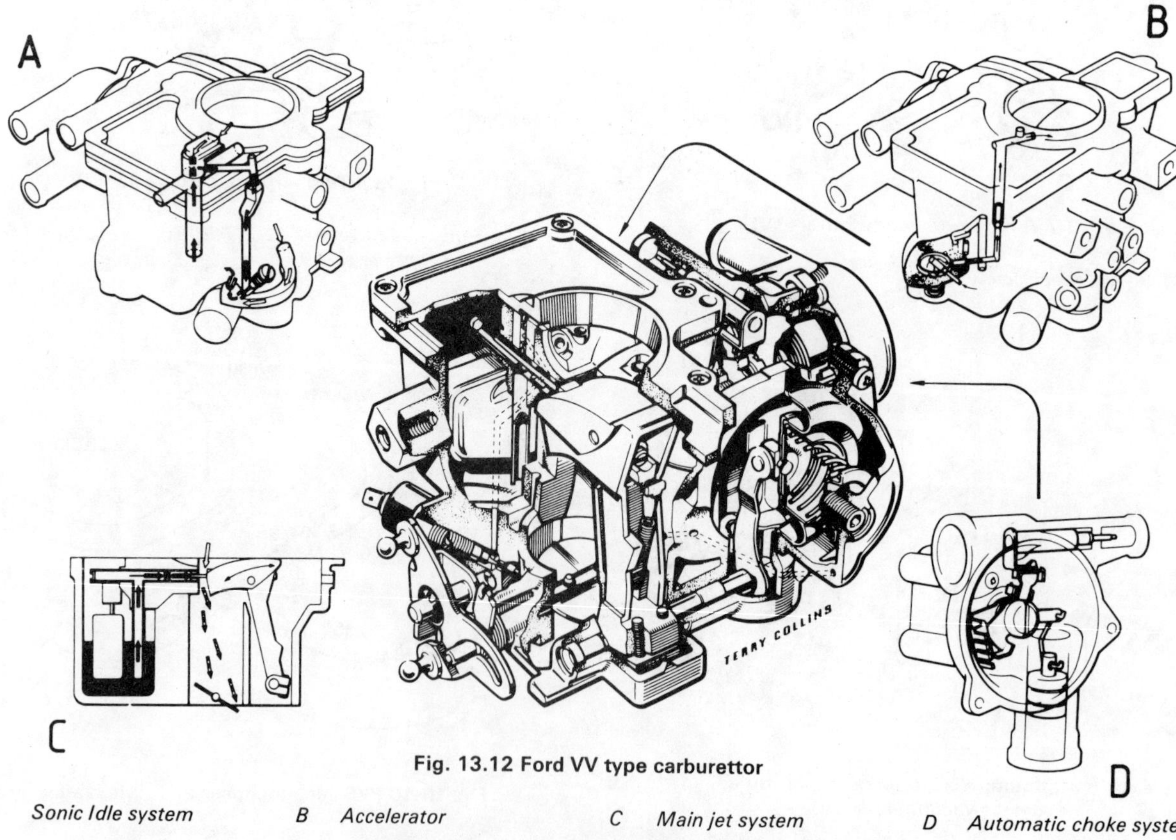

Fig. 13.12 Ford VV type carburettor

A Sonic Idle system *B* Accelerator *C* Main jet system *D* Automatic choke system

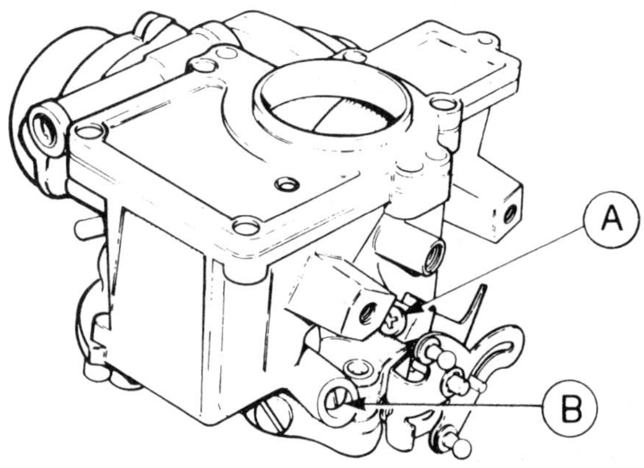

Fig. 13.13 Location of adjusting screws (VV carburettor)

A Idle speed screw *B Mixture screw (plugged)*

PART F WEBER 2V CARBURETTOR (2.0 L ENGINE)

System modifications

1 In order to eliminate hesitation during warm-up, vehicles built after May 1981 with 2.0 l engines have a modified accelerator pump discharge nozzle, low vacuum enrichment device and the inclusion of a manifold-mounted temperature sensitive ported vacuum switch (PVS).

2 Earlier vehicles may be modified by carrying out the following operations.

3 Disconnect the battery.

4 Remove the air cleaner.

5 Remove the carburettor upper body after first unscrewing the six screws and extracting the choke operating rod circlip.

6 Remove the accelerator discharge nozzle and fit a new nozzle (Part No. 78HF-9A574-BA). Fit new sealing rings if originally installed.

7 Refit the carburettor upper body and reconnect any hoses which may have been disconnected.

8 Now disconnect and discard the hose (A) for the low vacuum enrichment device (LOVE).

9 Unscrew and remove the diaphragm cover from the LOVE device housing taking care to catch the coil spring and diaphragm.

10 A new diaphragm cover (Part No. 75IF-9P788-BA) should now be

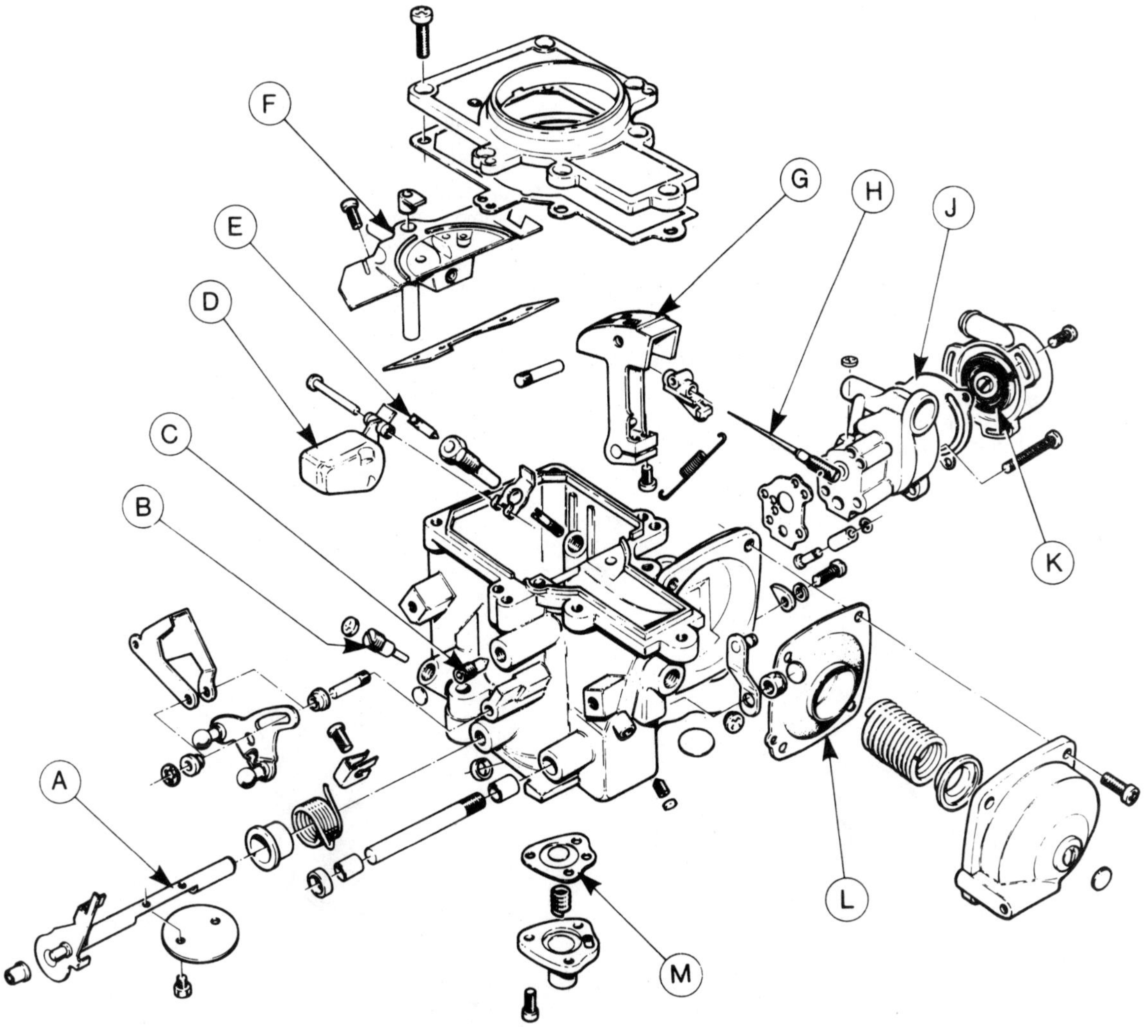

Fig. 13.14 Exploded view of VV carburettor

A Throttle spindle
B Fuel mixture screw
C Bypass leak adjuster
D Float
E Fuel inlet needle valve
F Main jet body
G Air valve
H Metering needle
J Choke assembly
K Bi-metal coil
L Vacuum diaphragm
M Accelerator pump diaphragm

fitted after first locating the spring and the diaphragm.
11 Having purchased a PVS (Part No. D7LE-8A564-AIA) and an adaptor (Part No. 74HF-9C704-AA), screw the switch into the adaptor and tighten to a torque of 27 Nm (19 lbf ft). Slight further tightening may be done if necessary to bring the hose stubs on the switch into the correct position for connection to the vacuum hoses (see Fig. 13.11).
12 Remove the radiator cap to depressurise the cooling system.
13 Now mark the hose which runs from the carburettor to the inlet manifold at a point 245 mm (9.65 in) from the carburettor.
14 Now measure 25 mm (0.98 in) from this first mark and make a second mark.
15 Raise the marked section of the hose as high as possible to minimise coolant loss and cut out the section of hose between the two marked points.
16 Fit the adaptor/switch into the cut hose so that the switch hose stubs point towards the engine compartment rear bulkhead.
17 Obtain a blanking cap (Part No. 757F-9A476-AA) and fit it to the hose stub on the switch nearest to the joint with the adaptor.
18 Obtain sufficient vacuum hose (Part No. 0710112 or 81 HF-12226-AA) to be able to cut two lengths of hose 160.0 mm (6.3 in) and 200.0 mm (7.9 in).
19 Now connect the starter hose to the uppermost of the two remaining unblanked stubs on the switch and the longer hose to the next lower one.
20 Connect the other end of the shorter hose from the switch to the cover of the LOVE diaphragm housing.
21 Connect the longer hose to the vacuum pipe stub on the carburettor.
22 Top up the cooling system, refit the radiator cap and reconnect the battery.
23 Fit the air cleaner.

Part G VARIABLE VENTURI (VV) CARBURETTOR

Description

24 As from November 1979 on, the variable venturi (VV) carburettor is fitted in place of the Motorcraft fixed venturi carburettor on 1.6 litre models. The new carburettor gives increased performance and improved fuel consumption largely due to better fuel atomisation and air/fuel control.
25 Unlike other types of variable venturi carburettors in current use, the Ford concept employs an air valve which is pivoted. The valve incorporates a tapered needle which is positioned in the main and secondary fuel jets to provide the correct amount of fuel in relation to the volume of air entering the engine.
26 The valve is actuated through a pivot and lever, by a diaphragm and spring which is in turn activated by the vacuum within the carburettor. This arrangement ensures that the correct air/fuel mixture is supplied to the engine during all operational conditions.
27 The carburettor incorporates a sonic idle system which operates in an identical manner to the system fitted to the fixed jet carburettor described earlier in this Supplement.
28 An indirect throttle control is fitted which is of the progressive cam and roller type. During initial throttle pedal movement the throttle valve movement is small but, as the pedal approaches maximum travel, the throttle valve movement increases. The arrangement aids economy, and enables the same carburettor to be fitted to other models in the range.
29 Damping of the air valve to prevent a flat spot, is provided by a restrictor in the vacuum passage to the control diaphragm. When the throttle valve is opened quickly, the restrictor prevents the air valve responding simultaneously which would otherwise provide a weak mixture temporarily.
30 A diaphragm type accelerator pump is fitted, similar to that fitted to the fixed venturi carburettor.
31 The automatic choke is of the coolant sensitive, bi-metallic spring type, and incorporates its own variable needle jet. A vacuum choke pull-down system is employed whereby the choke is released under cruising conditions.
32 An anti-dieseling (anti-run-on) solenoid valve is fitted to cut off the idle mixture supply when the ignition is switched off. The solenoid plunger blocks off the sonic idle discharge tube.

Starting procedure

33 A normal characteristic of this type of carburettor is that engine starting is not so instantaneous as should be the case with other designs.
34 To minimise this disadvantage, it is important that the correct starting technique is observed.

Engine cold

35 Simply turn the ignition key without having depressed the accelerator pedal. The engine should fire within ten seconds. If it does not, return the key to position 1 and try again.
36 If the engine does not start after two attempts, the cylinders must be assumed to be flooded. Depress the accelerator pedal slowly to the floor and hold it there while the engine is again cranked on the starter. As soon as the engine fires, gradually release the accelerator pedal.

Engine hot or warm

37 Slowly depress the accelerator pedal to the halfway position and hold it there. Operate the starter and if the engine does not fire within ten seconds, return the key to position 1 then try again. If the engine fails to start after three attempts, the cylinders must be assumed to be flooded and the procedure described in paragraph 36 should be followed.

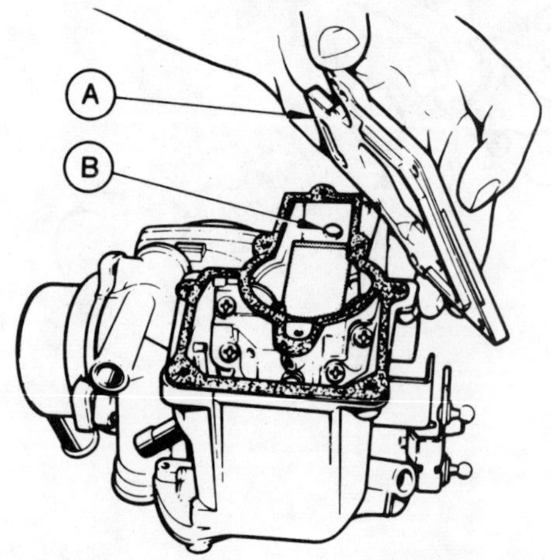

Fig. 13.15 Removing top cover (VV carburettor)

A Cover *B Metering needle tamperproof plug*

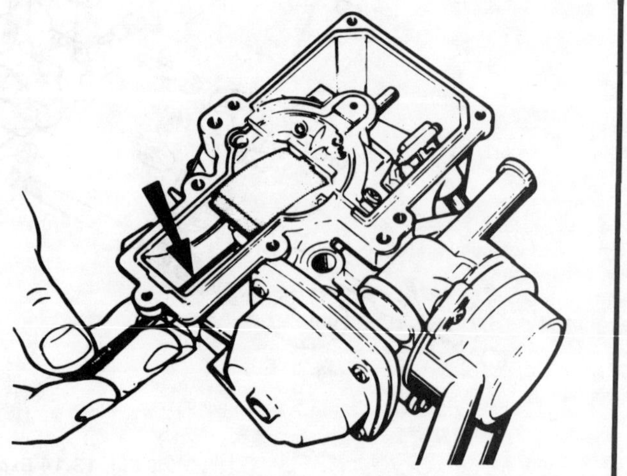

Fig. 13.16 Removing metering needle (arrowed) from VV carburettor

Adjustment

38 Run the engine until it reaches normal operating temperature.

39 Two adjustments are necessary for normal maintenance; these are idle speed adjustment and mixture setting. The idle speed adjustment procedure is identical to that described in Chapter 3, but requires a tachometer to set it accurately to between 775 and 825 rpm.

40 The mixture adjustment screw is 'tamperproof' and it is not normally necessary to remove the plug as the adjustment is preset during manufacture. However, the plug can be prised free to adjust the CO level. It is preferable to use an exhaust gas analyser, but if not available adjust the screw to achieve the smoothest idle. Turn the screw clockwise to weaken the mixture and anti-clockwise to enrich it. It may be necessary to readjust the idle speed.

41 The correct CO level with the engine idling is between 1.0 and 2.0%.

Removal and refitting

42 Remove the air cleaner but do not unclip the cover.

43 Disconnect the wire to the anti-run-on solenoid.

44 Disconnect and plug the main fuel supply pipe.

45 Prise the clip from the carburettor end of the throttle cable, then compress the plastic clip to release the cable from the support.

46 Pull off the distributor vacuum pipe at the carburettor.

47 With the cooling system cool, temporarily release the radiator filler cap. Disconnect and plug the two hoses from the automatic choke housing after identifying them for position.

48 Remove the two nuts and washers, and withdraw the carburettor over the studs. Remove the gasket from the inlet manifold.

49 Refitting is a reversal of removal, but note the following additional points:

- *(a) Clean the carburettor and manifold mating faces and always use a new gasket*
- *(b) Do not overtighten the retaining nuts*
- *(c) Discard the crimped type fuel hose clamp if fitted, and fit a worm drive clip*
- *(d) Adjust the idle speed and mixture setting as described in paragraphs 40 and 41*

Dismantling and reassembly

50 Clean the exterior of the carburettor with paraffin and wipe dry with a lint-free cloth.

51 Unscrew the seven screws and lift off the cover. Remove the gasket.

52 Drain the fuel from the float chamber. Prise the plug from the body and unscrew the metering needle from the air valve.

53 Remove the four screws and withdraw the main jet body from the top of the carburettor together with the gasket.

54 Invert the carburettor and remove the accelerator pump outlet one-way valve ball and weight.

55 Extract the float pivot pin, and remove the float and inlet valve needle.

56 Remove the four screws and withdraw the control diaphragm housing, spring and seat.

57 Pull back the diaphragm, prise out the C-clip, and lift out the diaphragm assembly.

58 Remove the three screws and withdraw the accelerator pump housing, spring and diaphragm.

59 Note the cover-to-body alignment marks, then remove the screws and withdraw the automatic choke cover, housing, and gasket.

60 Unscrew the anti-run-on solenoid. The carburettor is now dismantled and the individual components can be cleaned and examined. Check each item for wear and damage, particularly linkages and moving parts. If the main and secondary jets are worn oval, renew the main jet body. Thoroughly check the diaphragm for splits or perishing. Make sure that the metering needle spring is correctly fitted. Obtain a kit of gaskets and diaphragms for fitting during reassembly.

61 Commence reassembly by locating the gasket face of the accelerator pump diaphragm on the housing, followed by the spring and cover. Insert and tighten the retaining screws.

62 Reconnect the control diaphragm assembly, ensuring that the double holes on one corner will align with those on the carburettor.

63 Locate the spring, seat, and cover over the diaphragm, then insert and tighten the retaining screws evenly in a diagonal sequence.

64 If the mixture adjustment screw tamperproof plug is removed, lightly tighten the screw then back it off three full turns.

65 Insert the needle valve needle with the spring loaded ball toward

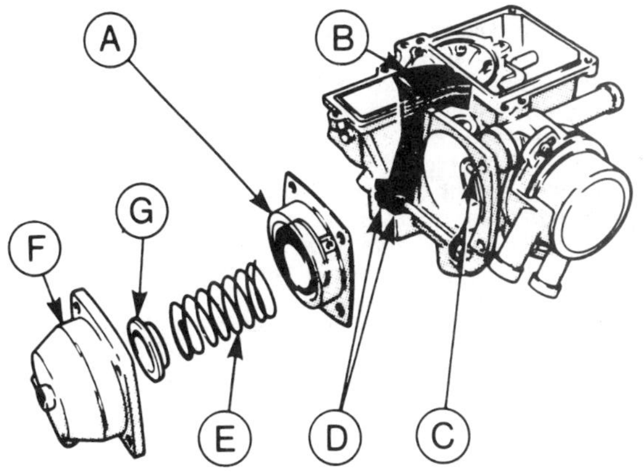

Fig. 13.17 VV carburettor control diaphragm components

A Control diaphragm
B Air valve
C Pin
D Clamp screw
E Spring
F Cover
G Seat

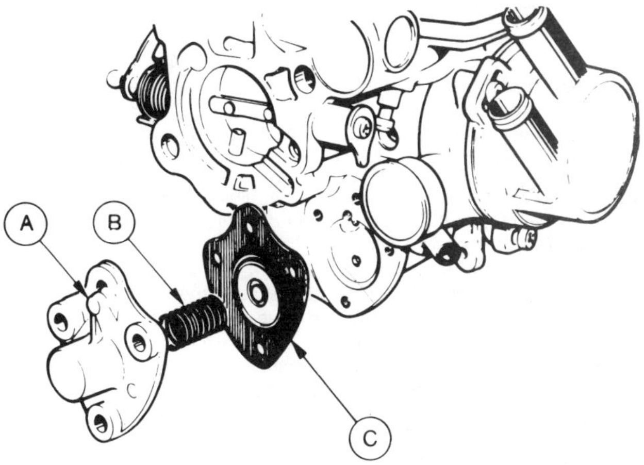

Fig. 13.18 VV carburettor accelerator pump components

A Cover
B Return spring
C Diaphragm

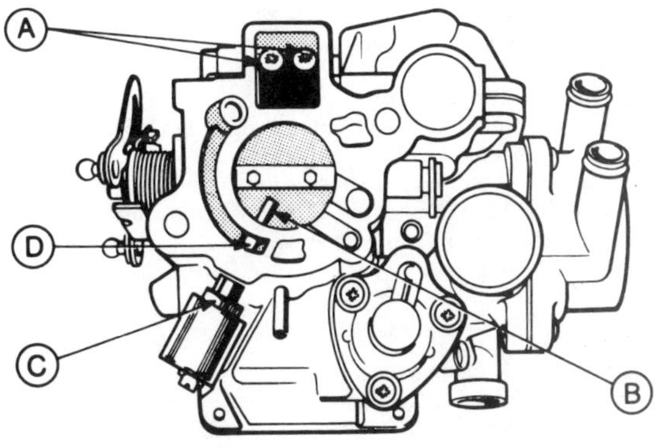

Fig. 13.19 Underside of VV carburettor

A Air valve adjusting screws
B Sonic Idle tube
C Solenoid
D Solenoid plunger

the float. Refit the float and pivot pin.
66 Insert the accelerator pump outlet one-way valve ball and weight into the discharge gallery.
67 Refit the main jet body with a new gasket, and tighten the retaining screws lightly in a diagonal sequence. Do not fully tighten the screws at this stage.
68 Slide the metering needle into the air valve and tighten it until the shoulder is aligned with the main jet body vertical face. Install the plug, using a liquid locking agent to secure it.
69 Open and close the air valve several times to centralise the main jet then, with the valve fully closed, tighten the main jet body screws in diagonal sequence.
70 Refit the top cover with a new gasket, and tighten the retaining screws evenly.
71 Refit the automatic choke housing using a new gasket, and tighten the retaining screws.
72 Engage the bi-metal coil in the cover with the middle slot in the choke lever, as the cover is fitted to the housing with a new gasket.
73 Align the cover-to-housing marks, and tighten the screws.
74 The carburettor is now ready to be fitted to the engine.

Automatic choke

Adjustment

75 One of two types of automatic choke may be met with. Earlier assemblies are marked with the letter A stamped on the choke housing. Later assemblies are either marked with the letter M or with blue and white colour spots on top of the choke housing. Refer to the following table for diameters of gauge tool for the particular choke housing.

	Early housing	Later housing
Choke mixture gauge (dia)	3.4 mm	3.4 mm
Choke pull-down gauge (dia)	3.7 mm	4.3 mm
Choke lever to be held	Anti-clockwise	Clockwise
Choke housing alignment	Index	Index

Note: *The following procedure assumes that the carburettor is fitted to the engine although the adjustment can be made during reassembly of the carburettor on the bench*
76 Remove the air cleaner.
77 Note the position of the alignment marks, then remove the screws and withdraw the automatic choke cover.
78 Prise the plug from the top of the carburettor behind the automatic choke housing. Look through the aperture and turn the automatic choke lever until the drilling in the shaft is in alignment. Insert a specified diameter twist drill fully into the drilling.
79 Loosen the nut on the end of the choke shaft. Turn the choke lever clockwise to its stop, then retighten the nut. This is the choke mixture adjustment.
80 Remove the twist drill, then bend the pull-down lever slightly downwards to ensure that it does not restrict the vacuum piston movement.
81 Look through the top aperture again and turn the lever to align the drilling. Insert a specified diameter twist drill fully into the drilling, then push the vacuum piston down to the bottom of its travel whilst holding the choke lever in the fully anti-clockwise position on early housings and fully clockwise on later units. Note that there must be a clearance between the choke lever and pull-down lever, then bend back the pull down lever so that it just touches the choke lever. This is the choke fast idle/pull down adjustment.
82 Remove the twist drill and fit a new plug to the top of the carburettor.
83 Refit the automatic choke cover with the previously noted marks aligned (see Fig. 13.22) and the bi-metal spring engaged with the central slot. Tighten the screws evenly.
84 Refit the air cleaner.

Removal and refitting

85 Remove the air cleaner assembly.
86 With the engine cold, release the pressure in the cooling system by temporarily removing the radiator cap. Disconnect and plug the hoses from the automatic choke cover after identifying them for position.
87 Note the cover-to-body alignment marks, then remove the screws and withdraw the cover.
88 Remove the three screws and withdraw the housing and gasket.
89 Refitting is a reversal of removal, but adjust the choke as

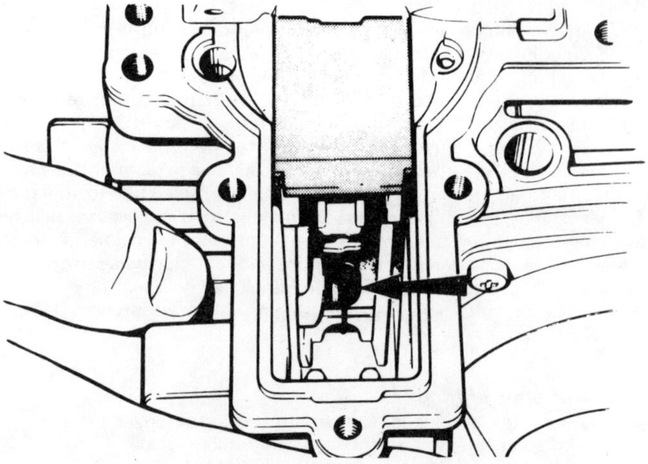

Fig. 13.20 VV carburettor air valve spring (arrowed)

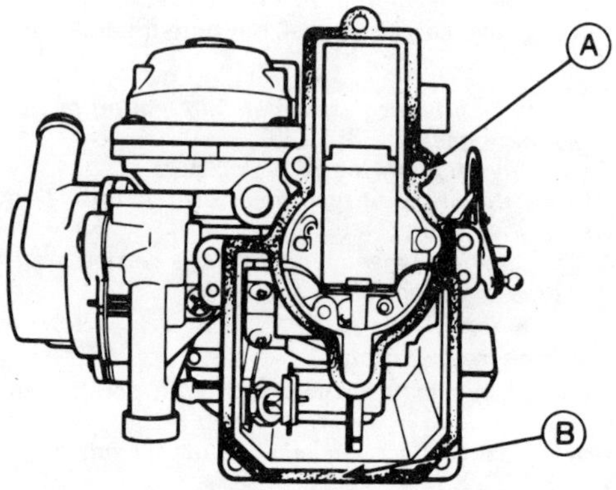

Fig. 13.21 VV carburettor top cover gasket. Check alignment at points A and B

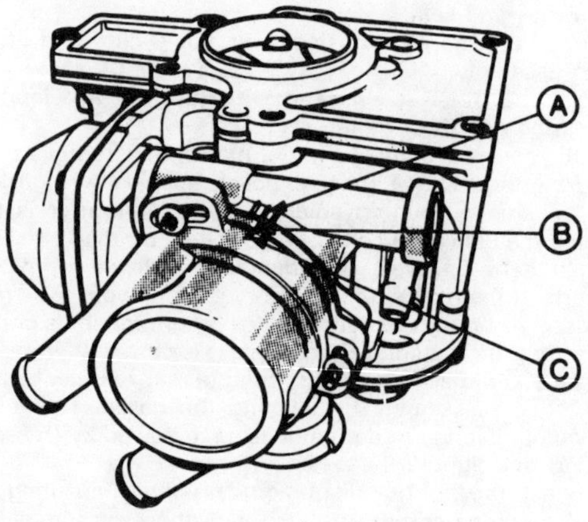

Fig. 13.22 Automatic choke alignment marks (VV carburettor)

A Centre index
B Alignment mark (groove)
C Cast rib (not for alignment)

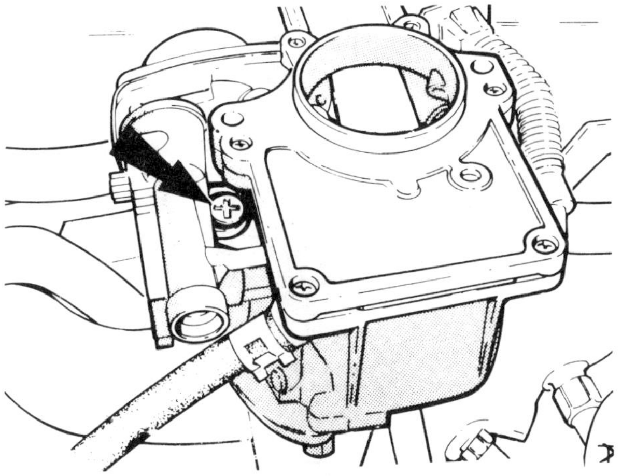

Fig. 13.23 Location of choke adjustment aperture plug (arrowed) on VV carburettor

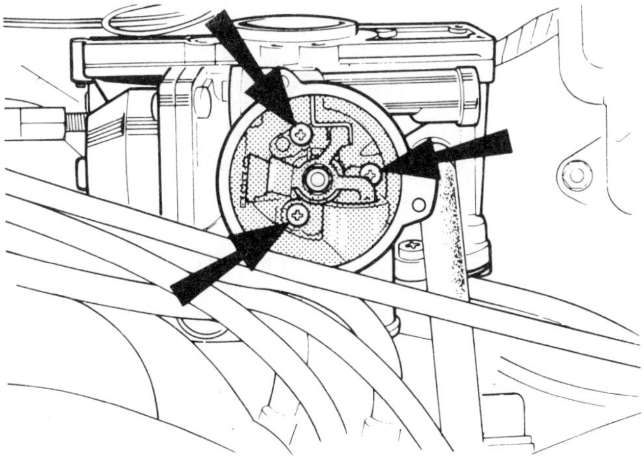

Fig. 13.25 Choke housing retaining screws (VV carburettor)

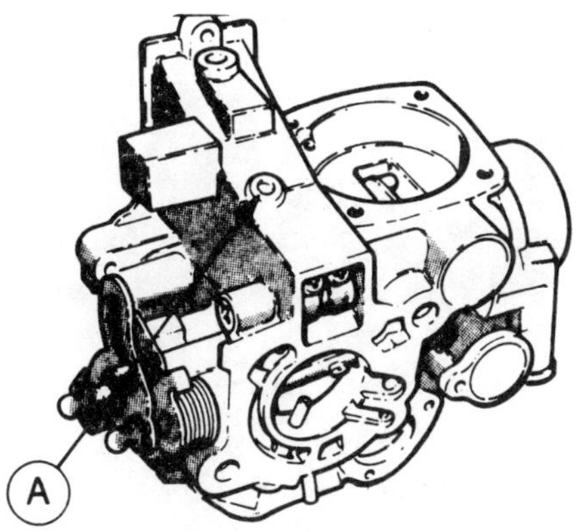

Fig. 13.27 Location of air valve maximum setting adjusting screw (A) on VV carburettor

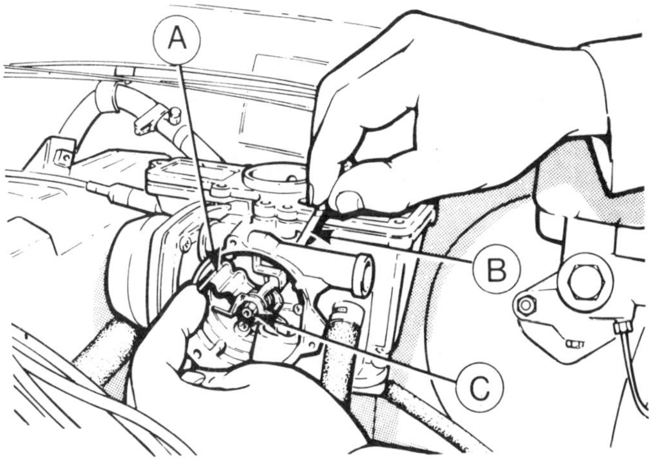

Fig. 13.24 Adjusting automatic choke mixture (VV carburettor)

A Choke lever
B Twist drill
C Shaft nut

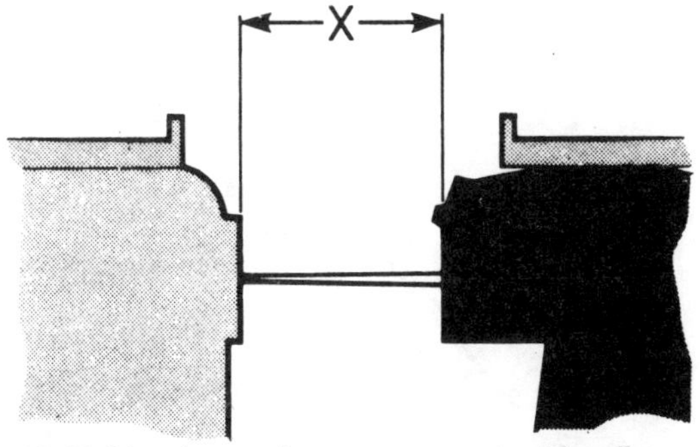

Fig. 13.26 Air valve maximum movement setting dimension

X 23.0 mm (0.9 in)

described earlier. Make sure that the bi-metal spring engages with the central slot in the choke lever. Top up the cooling system if necessary.

Float level check

90 If poor fuel consumption and difficult starting are experienced, the operating fuel level should be checked as follows.
91 Start the engine and run it at 3000 rpm for one minute, then switch off.
92 Remove the carburettor cover as previously described, and measure the distance from the fuel to the top of the casting. If the distance is not as given in the Specifications, remove the float and check it for leakage. Renew it if necessary.
93 Refit the carburettor cover.

Air valve adjustment

94 Two adjustments are possible; these are the maximum air valve movement, and the air valve-to-diaphragm lever setting.
95 To check the air valve movement, first remove the carburettor and withdraw the top cover as previously described.
96 With the air valve held fully open, measure the distance from the air valve to the main jet body. If this is not as given in the Specifications, remove the tamperproof plug and air valve stop screw, then coat the screw with a liquid locking agent and reinsert it to its correct position.
97 Fit a new plug and refit the carburettor.
98 To adjust the air valve-to-diaphragm lever setting, first remove the carburettor then dismantle the control diaphragm housing, spring, and diaphragm as previously described.
99 From under the carburettor loosen the two air valve screws.
100 Set the control diaphragm lever so that the distance from the housing mating face to the nearer edge of the diaphragm lever pin is as given in the Specifications.
101 Tighten the air valve screws and reassemble the control diaphragm housing components in reverse order.

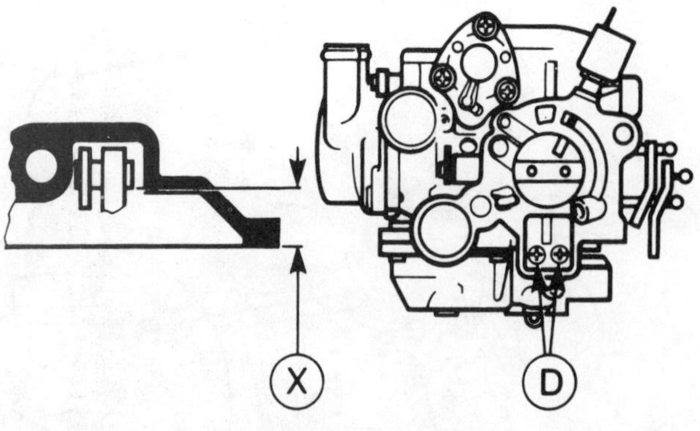

Fig. 13.28 Air valve to diaphragm lever setting (VV carburettor)

D Air valve screws X 0.9 in (23 mm)

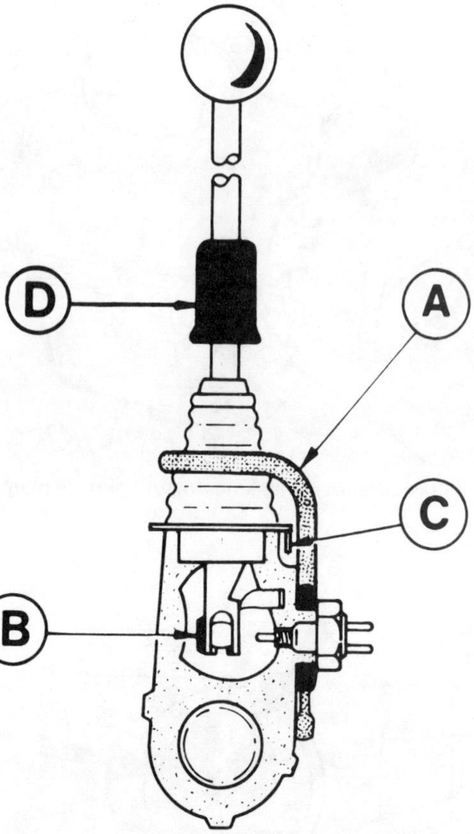

Fig. 13.29 Sectional view of modified gear lever

A Rubber strap C Tab washer
B Damping bush D Metal cup

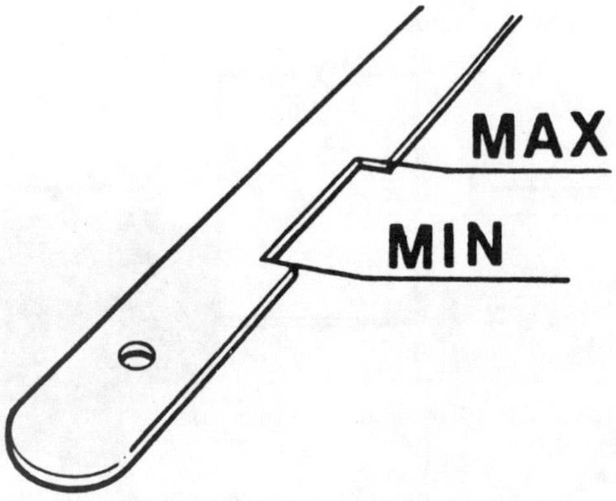

Fig. 13.30 New type automatic transmission fluid dipstick

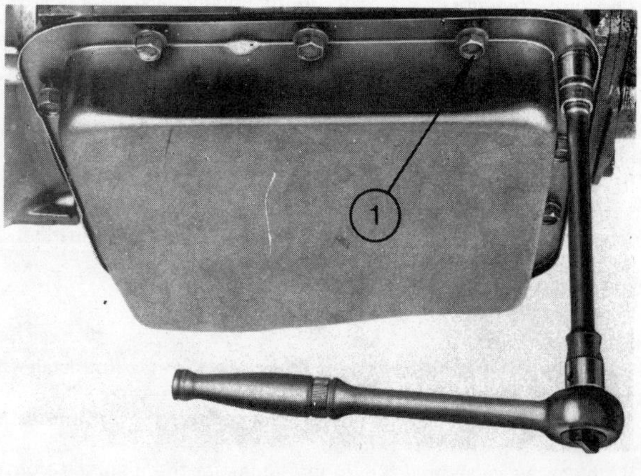

Fig. 13.31 Unbolting automatic transmission sump pan

Fig. 13.32 Automatic transmission fluid filter (1)

5 Manual transmission (Capri II)

Gear lever – modification

1 As from August 1980, an improved gear lever assembly is fitted as shown in Fig. 13.29. The modified lever can be identified by checking the metal cup which fits over the rubber gaiter on the gear lever; if it does not incorporate inward protruding tabs, it is of the modified type.
2 If gear lever rattles are experienced, remove it as described in the following paragraphs and fit the modified components.
3 Remove the gear lever as described in Chapter 6.
4 Substitute a rubber damper bush (Part No. 793T-7K382-AA) for the original bush (B).
5 Apply grease to the gear lever fork, refit the lever and secure with the tab washer (C).
6 It may be found easier to install both the bush and the gear lever if 3rd gear is selected before the work begins.
7 If not already fitted, pass a rubber strap (Part No. 743T-7227-AA) over the gear lever and secure on the reverse lamp switch.
8 If the foregoing operations do not eliminate gear lever rattles, then fitting a new gear lever (Part No. 803T-7K387-AA) will be the only solution.

6 Automatic transmission (Capri II)

Transmission fluid capacity

1 As from August 1979, the fluid capacity has been increased and in consequence a new dipstick is used.

2 To check the fluid level, have the fluid at normal operating temperature and, with the engine idling, move the selector three times through all positions. Select P and wait two minutes.

3 Withdraw the dipstick, wipe it clean, re-insert it and withdraw it again. The level should be within the cut-out section of the dipstick. Top up, if necessary, through the dipstick guide tube.

Automatic transmission fluid types

4 Consequent upon the introduction of a new grade of Ford automatic transmission fluid (Type CJ) it is important that the new fluid and existing Type G fluid are only used in accordance with the following recommendations.

5 Never mix the two fluids in the same transmission.

6 If a new torque converter or transmission is being fitted, always drain the torque converter and the fluid cooler and pipes, and flush through with paraffin if the new assemblies require the addition of the newer type CJ fluid.

C3 transmission up to 1981, tag mark up to 80 DT, having black knob to dipstick and black or bright metal dipstick guide tube – use only Ford G (SQM-2C9007-AA) fluid

C3 transmission 1981 on, tag mark 81 DT on having red cap to dipstick and red dipstick guide tube – use only Ford CJ (SQM-209010-A) fluid

Fig. 13.33 Valve control block bolts

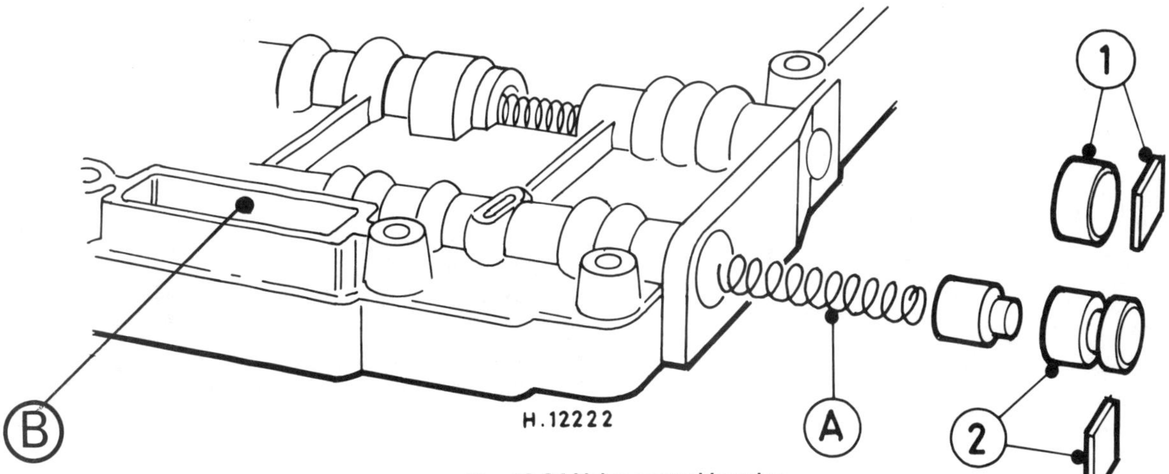

Fig. 13.34 Valve control housing

A Spring B Rectangular aperture 1 Early type valve and retainer 2 Later type

Rectification of harsh change (1st/2nd speed)

7 Some automatic transmissions are inclined to give a harsh change from 1st to 2nd speed. Where this is evident, an improvement may be made by changing the valve body spring in the following way.

8 With the transmission cool, unbolt the fluid sump pan, lower it and pour the fluid into a clean container.

9 Unbolt the fluid filter and remove it together with its gasket.

10 Now take a sheet of paper and press it against the valve control housing and by rubbing with the finger, make an impression on the paper of the location of the bolt heads.

11 Unscrew the valve control housing securing bolts and as each one is removed, push it through the paper template in its appropriate location.

12 When lifting the control housing away, disconnect the selector lever connecting rod.

13 Peel away the gasket.

14 Remove the existing coil spring and renew it with a yellow coded one (Part No. 74DT-7A289-AA).

15 Refit the valve control housing using a new gasket. Tighten the bolts to between 9 and 12 Nm (7 and 9 lbf ft).

16 Refit the oil pan again using a new gasket. Tighten the fixing screws to between 16 and 23.5 Nm (12 and 17 lbf ft).

17 Adjust the front brake band. If the special torque wrench (17-005) is not available, release the adjuster screw locknut which is located just below the inhibitor switch and tighten the adjuster screw to a torque of 14 Nm (10 lbf ft). Now unscrew the adjuster screw through 1¾ turns, and retighten the locknut.

18 Refill with transmission fluid as necessary to the MAX mark on the dipstick.

7 Braking system

Handbrake – revised adjustment procedure (Capri II)

1 Follow the instructions given in Chapter 9, Section 19, paragraphs 1 to 4 inclusive, and then turn the adjusting nut to remove all slack from the mechanism; this is indicated by a total clearance of 4.0 to 5.0 mm (0.16 to 0.20 in) existing at the handbrake actuating lever abutment points ('C' Fig. 13.36). It is in order for a 'nil' clearance to exist on one side and the maximum total clearance on the other side, as both will equalise when the handbrake is operated.

2 Fully apply the handbrake, then release it fully to settle the mechanism. Then check that the sum of the abutment clearances at each side totals between 3.0 and 4.5 mm (0.12 and 0.18 in); again it is in order for a clearance of 'nil' to exist on one side.

3 The handbrake cable should not be tightened outside the above limits otherwise the self-adjusting mechanism will not operate correctly; with this system it is in order for the handbrake lever to travel up to 10 notches before the rear brakes are fully applied.

Fig. 13.35 Front brake band adjuster screw and locknut

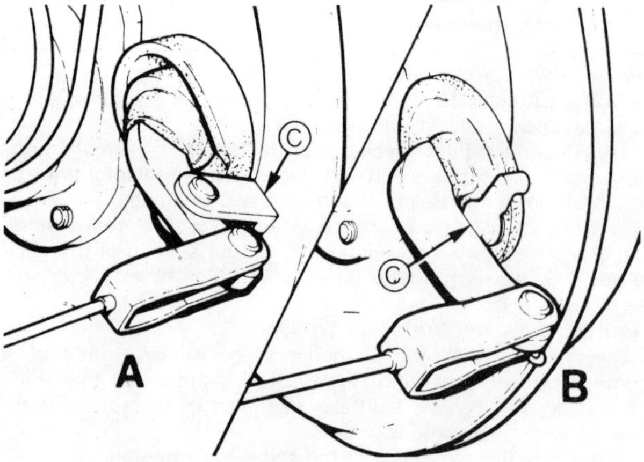

Fig. 13.36 Zero movement at handbrake lever arm

A 8 in (203 mm) B 9 in (227 mm)

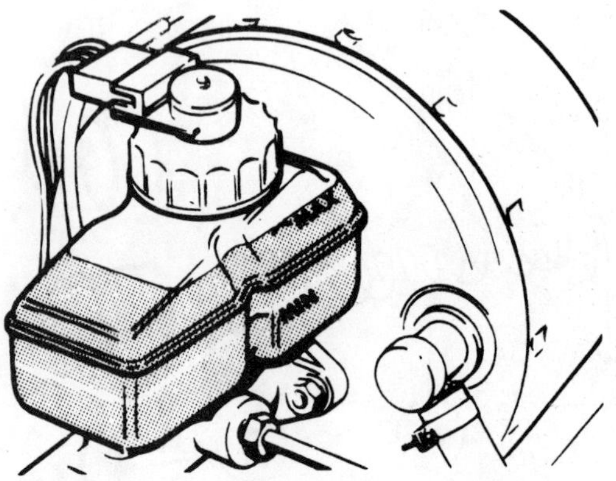

Fig. 13.37 Brake master cylinder reservoir with warning switch

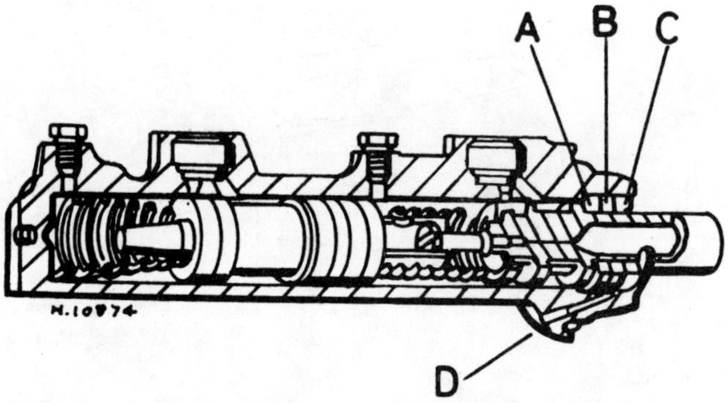

Fig. 13.38 ATE (Teves) type master cylinder

A Secondary seal C Vacuum seal
B Spacer D Drain hole

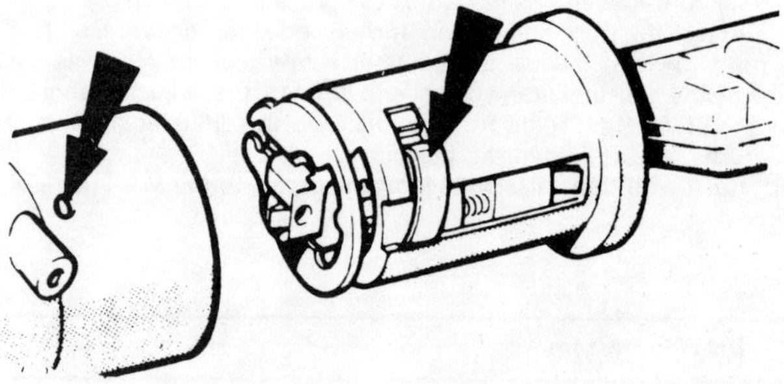

Fig. 13.39 Ignition switch cylinder retaining spring

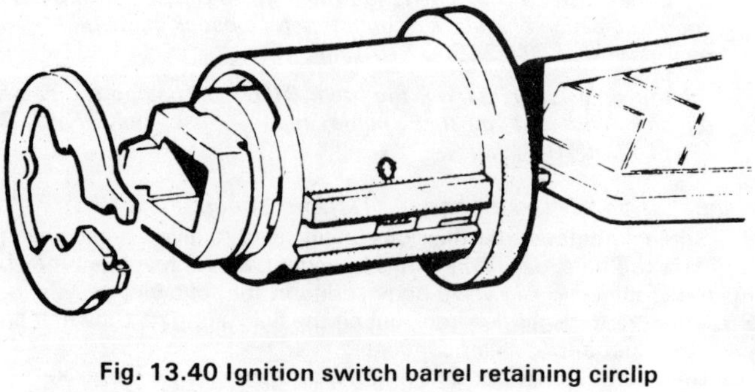

Fig. 13.40 Ignition switch barrel retaining circlip

Brake hydraulic system – revised bleeding procedure

4 If the master cylinder has been disconnected and reconnected then the complete system (both circuits) must be bled.

5 If only a component of one circuit has been disturbed, only that particular circuit need be bled.

6 If the entire system is being bled, the sequence of bleeding should be carried out by starting at the bleed screw furthest from the master cylinder and finishing at the one nearest to it. Unless the pressure bleeding method is being used, do not forget to keep the fluid level in the master reservoir topped up to prevent air from being drawn into the system which would make any work done worthless.

7 Before commencing operations, check that all system hoses and pipes are in good condition with all unions tight and free from leaks.

8 Take great care not to allow hydraulic fluid to come into contact with the vehicle paintwork as it is an effective paint stripper. Wash off any spilled fluid immediately with cold water.

9 If the system incorporates a vacuum servo, destroy the vacuum by giving several applications of the brake pedal in quick succession.

Bleeding – two man method

10 Gather together a clean glass jar and a length of rubber or plastic tubing which will be a tight fit on the brake bleed screws.
11 Engage the help of an assistant.
12 Push one end of the bleed tube onto the first bleed screw and immerse the other end in the glass jar which should contain enough hydraulic fluid to cover the end of the tube.
13 Open the bleed screw $\frac{1}{2}$ turn and have your assistant depress the brake pedal fully then slowly release it. Tighten the bleed screw at the end of each pedal downstroke to obviate any chance of air or fluid being drawn back into the system.
14 Repeat this operation until clean hydraulic fluid, free from air bubbles, can be seen coming through into the jar.
15 Tighten the bleed screw at the end of a pedal downstroke and remove the bleed tube. Bleed the remaining screws in a similar way.

Bleeding – using one-way valve kit

16 There are a number of one-man, one-way brake bleeding kits available from motor accessory shops. It is recommended that one of these kits is used wherever possible as it will greatly simplify the bleeding operation and also reduce the risk of air or fluid being drawn back into the system quite apart from being able to do the work without the help of an assistant.
17 To use the kit, connect the tube to the bleed screw and open the screw $\frac{1}{2}$ turn.
18 Depress the brake pedal fully and slowly release it. The one-way valve in the kit will prevent expelled air from returning at the end of each pedal downstroke. Repeat this operation several times to be sure of ejecting all air from the system. Some kits include a translucent container which can be positioned so that the air bubbles can actually be seen being ejected from the system.
19 Tighten the bleed screw, remove the tube and repeat the operations on the remaining brakes.
20 On completion, depress the brake pedal. If it still feels spongy repeat the bleeding operation as air must still be trapped in the system.

Bleeding – using a pressure bleeding kit

21 These kits too are available from motor accessory shops and are usually operated by air pressure from the spare tyre.
22 By connecting a pressurised container to the master cylinder fluid reservoir, bleeding is then carried out by simply opening each bleed screw in turn and allowing the fluid to run out, rather like turning on a tap, until no air is visible in the expelled fluid.
23 By using this method, the large reserve of hydraulic fluid provides a safeguard against air being drawn into the master cylinder during bleeding which often occurs if the fluid level in the reservoir is not maintained.
24 Pressure bleeding is particularly effective when bleeding 'difficult' systems or when bleeding the complete system at time of routine fluid renewal.

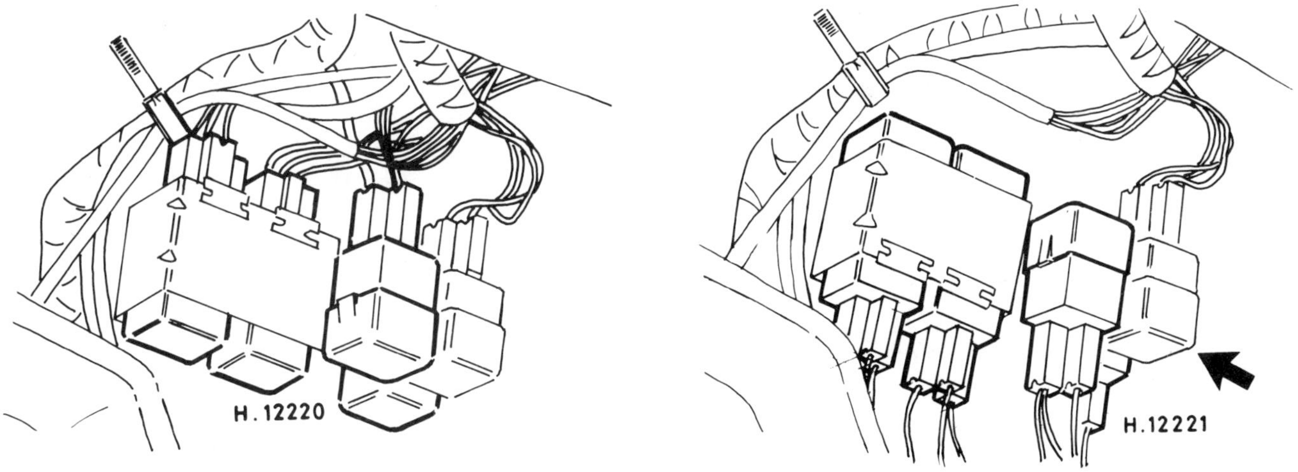

Fig. 13.41 Mounting of relays A (before 1978), B (after 1978). Heated rear window relay arrowed

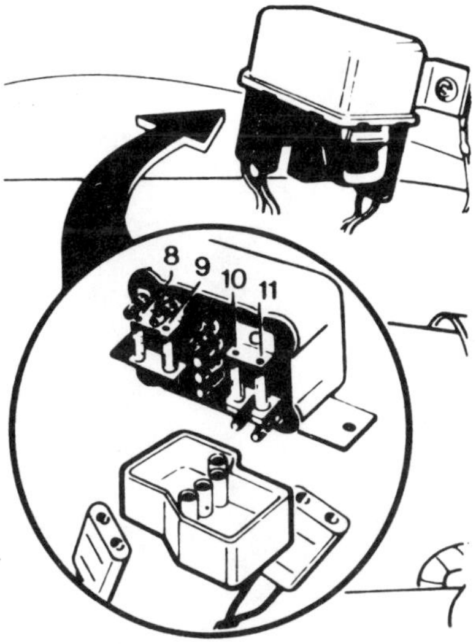

Fig. 13.42 Location of headlamp fuses
For key see text

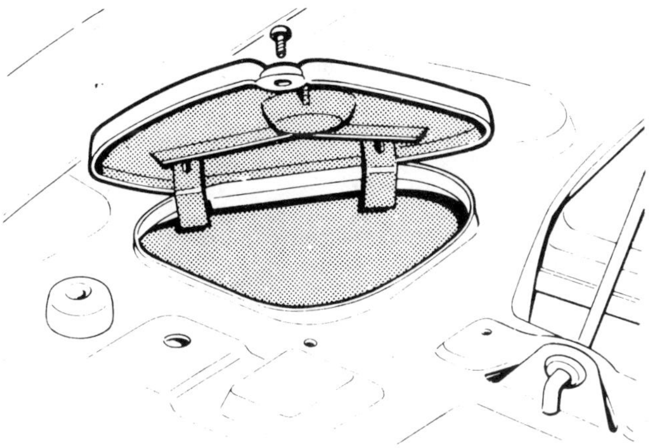

Fig. 13.43 Headlamp access cover plate

Bleeding – all methods

25 When bleeding is completed, check and top up the fluid level in the master cylinder reservoir.
26 Check the 'feel' of the brake pedal. If it feels at all spongy, air must still be present in the system and further bleeding is indicated. Failure to bleed satisfactorily after a reasonable repetition of the bleeding operations may be due to worn master cylinder seals.
27 Discard brake fluid which has been expelled. It is almost certain to be contaminated with moisture, air and dirt making it unsuitable for further use. Clean fluid should always be stored in an airtight container as it absorbs moisture readily (ie is hygroscopic) which lowers its boiling point and could affect braking performance under severe conditions.

Fluid level warning indicator – description (Capri II)

28 As from October 1978, a fluid level warning indicator system is fitted, which consists of a float and switch assembly incorporated in the master cylinder reservoir cap; it is connected electrically to a warning light on the instrument panel.
29 The warning light is illuminated when the fluid level reaches the predetermined minimum level, as would occur if a leak was present in one of the hydraulic circuits.
30 The same warning light is also illuminated by the handbrake when on; therefore a check should be made that the handbrake is fully off before assuming that there is a hydraulic fluid leak.

Teves (ATE) master cylinder – description (Capri II)

31 Teves (ATE) master cylinders fitted to some models manufactured from November 1978 on incorporate an additional seal in the mouth of the cylinder. The inner seal now retains the hydraulic fluid and the outer seal maintains vacuum in the vacuum servo.
32 The two seals are separated by a spacer which is vented to atmosphere by a small hole which also acts as a drain hole.
33 After a moderate period of use it is normal for a small accumulation of fluid to pass down the drain hole and stain the vacuum servo unit, but this does not indicate a faulty seal. Action should only be taken if droplets appear, in which case the master cylinder should be dismantled and overhauled, or renewed.

8 Electrical system

Ignition switch cylinder assembly – removal and refitting (Capri II)

1 Models manufactured since mid-1976 are fitted with a revised steering column lock assembly, and the switch cylinder and barrel can be withdrawn without the need to detach the complete switch.
2 First disconnect the battery negative lead.
3 Remove the steering column shroud as described in Chapter 10. Section 51, then insert the ignition key and turn it to the accessory position '1'.
4 Locate the small hole in the switch perimeter and insert a suitable small diameter tool to depress the lock spring, at the same time pull the key and cylinder away from the housing. It may be necessary to turn the key slightly in both directions while removing the cylinder.
5 The cylinder can be removed from the barrel by first ensuring that the key is fully entered. Then carefully remove the retaining circlip and withdraw the key 5 mm (0.2 in); the barrel can now be separated from the cylinder.
6 Reassembling and refitting the switch is a reversal of the removal procedure, but make sure that the barrel is refitted to the cylinder in its original position. Turn the key to the accessory position '1' in order to fit the retaining circlip. When the assembly is refitted, check its operation in all the positions before finally reconnecting the battery negative lead.

Relays and fuses (Capri II)

7 Various relays are located either under the facia panel or within the engine compartment, to protect the accessories fitted according to model.
8 Fuses are located under the headlamp relay within the engine compartment as follows:

8	*Headlamp (LH dipped)*	*16 amp*
9	*Headlamp (RH dipped)*	*16 amp*
10	*Headlamp (RH main)*	*16 amp*
11	*Headlamp (LH main)*	*16 amp*

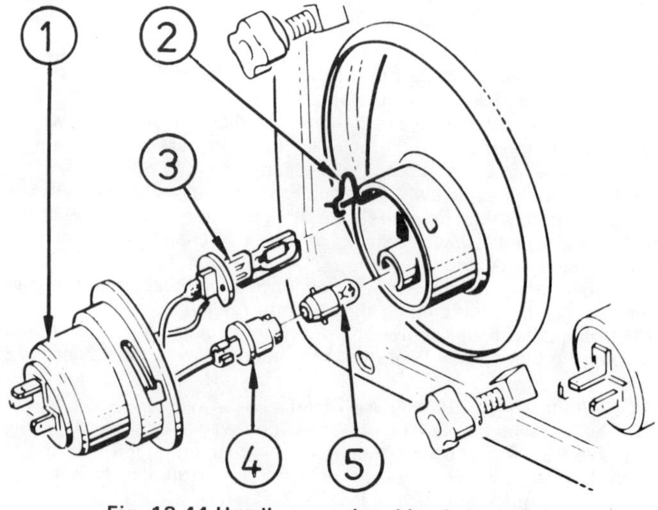

Fig. 13.44 Headlamp and parking lamp bulbs

1 Cap
2 Clip
3 Headlamp bulb
4 Parking lamp bulb socket
5 Parking lamp bulb

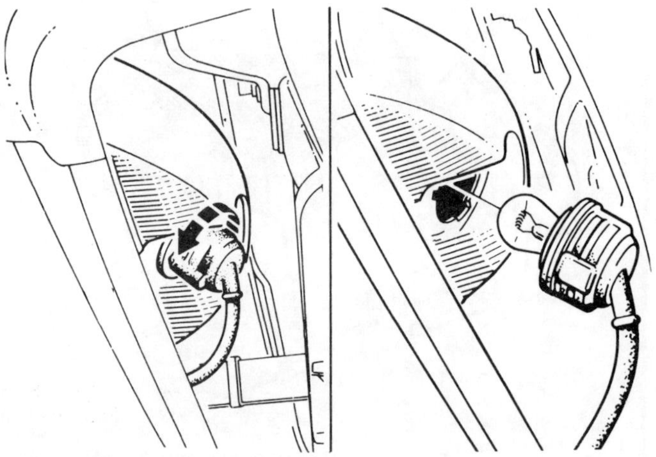

Fig. 13.45 Front direction indicator bulb

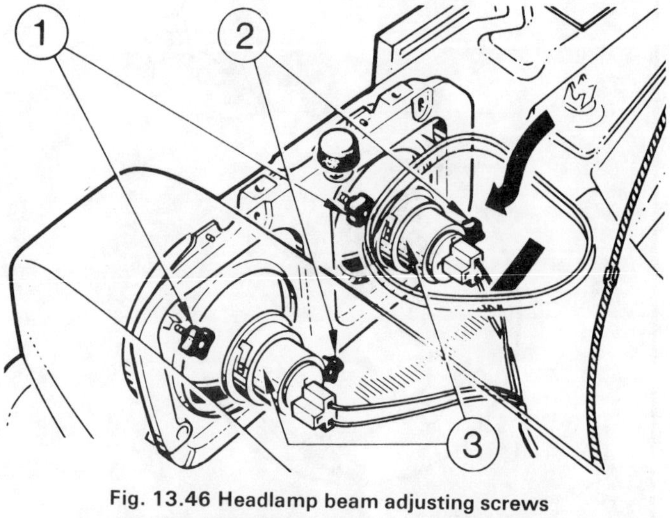

Fig. 13.46 Headlamp beam adjusting screws

1 Vertical adjustment
2 Horizontal adjustment
3 Clip

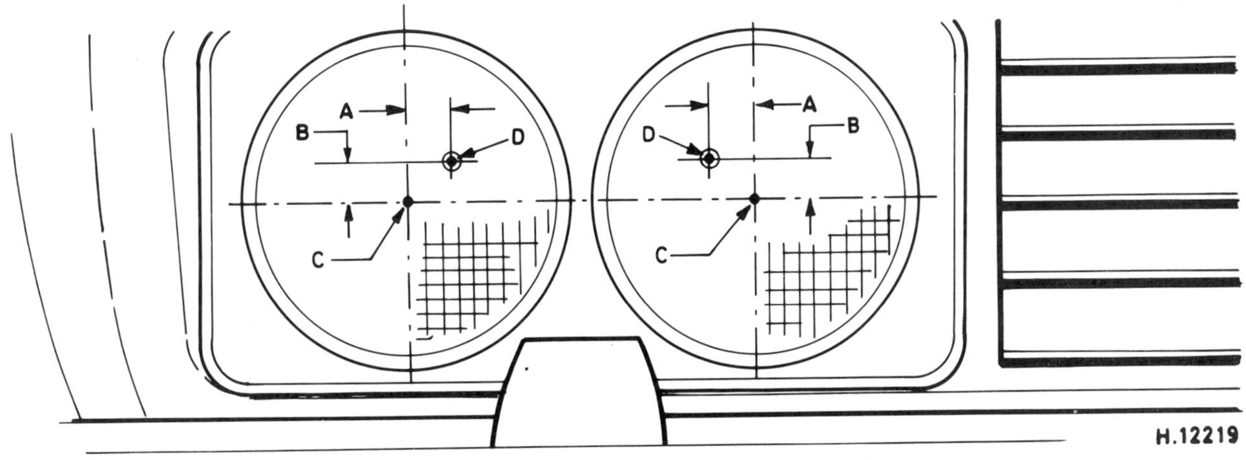

Fig. 13.47 Headlamp washer nozzle/jet adjustment setting diagram

A 10.0 mm (0.4 in)
B 10.0 mm (0.4 in)
C Centre of lens
D Jet impact point

Headlamp bulb – renewal (Capri II)

9 Extract the fixing screw and remove the triangular cover panel from the inner wing.
10 Remove the cap from the rear of the lamp by turning it in an anti-clockwise direction.
11 Release the retaining clip and swivel it upwards.
12 Withdraw the bulb from the headlamp reflector but do not finger the glass of the bulb.
13 Pull off the wiring connector plug.
14 Refit by reversing the removal operations but make sure that the guide pegs and the flat on the bulb flange are correctly aligned in the reflector socket.

Front parking bulb – removal (Capri II)

15 The initial operations are as for renewal of the headlamp bulb. Then simply pull the bulb holder from the headlamp reflector; the bulb is of bayonet fitting type.

Front direction indicator – bulb renewal (Capri II)

16 Access to the bulb is obtained by reaching under the bumper and turning the bulb holder in an anti-clockwise direction and pulling it from the lamp body. The bulb is of bayonet fitting type.

Headlamp beam – adjustment (Capri II)

17 This is best carried out by a service station having the necessary optical beam setting equipment.
18 In an emergency, the beams can be adjusted both in the vertical and horizontal planes by turning the screws with the plastic knobs at the rear of the lamps.

Headlamp washers (Capri II)

19 A headlamp wash system is fitted as standard to Ghia versions, and is an option on all other models.
20 The washer nozzles should be adjusted so that the jets of washer fluid strike the headlamp lenses at the points marked D (Fig. 13.47). This position can be marked on the glass with a grease pencil.

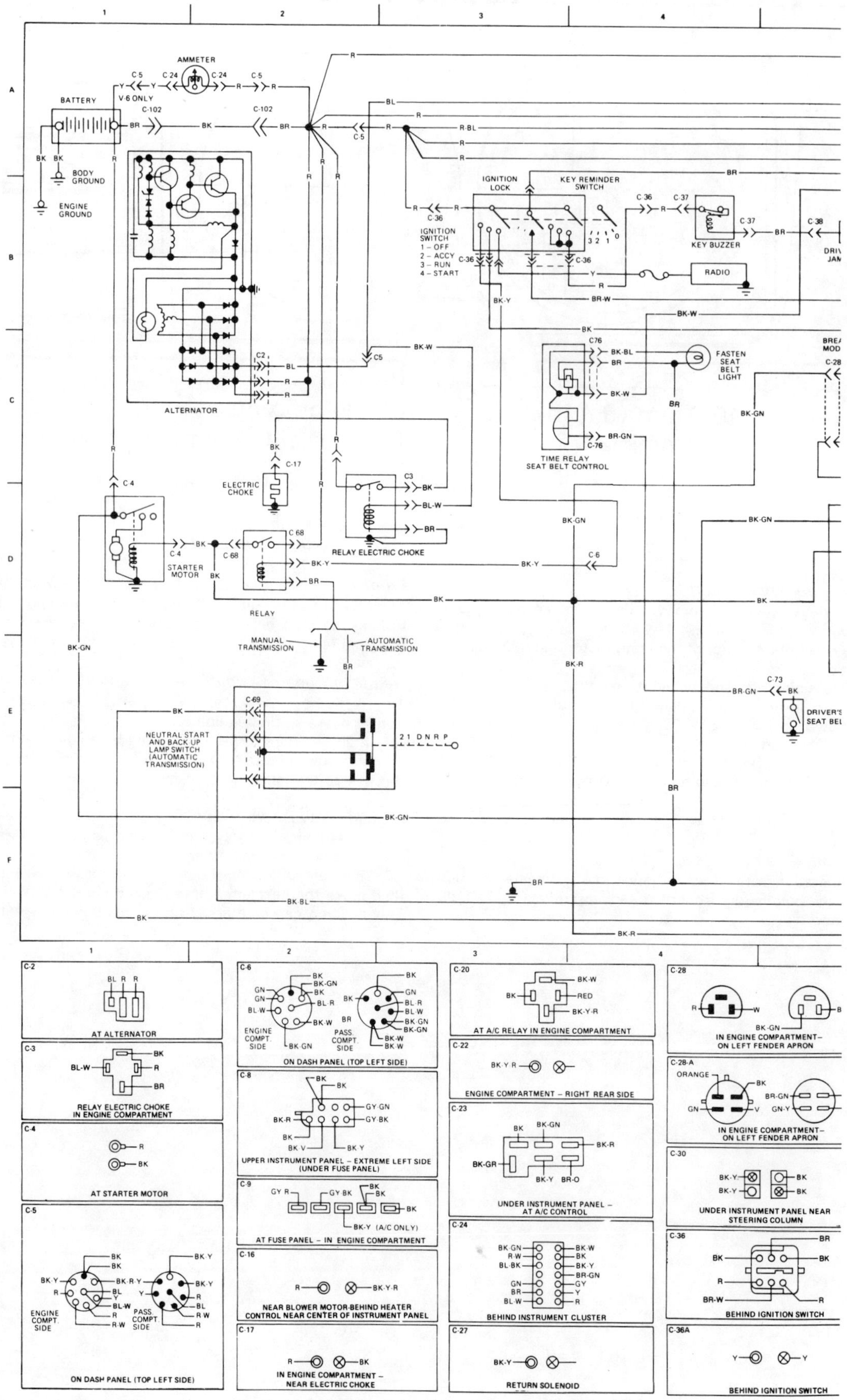

Fig. 13.48A Circuit diagram – Mercury Capri II, 1977/1978

See page 284 for wiring codes

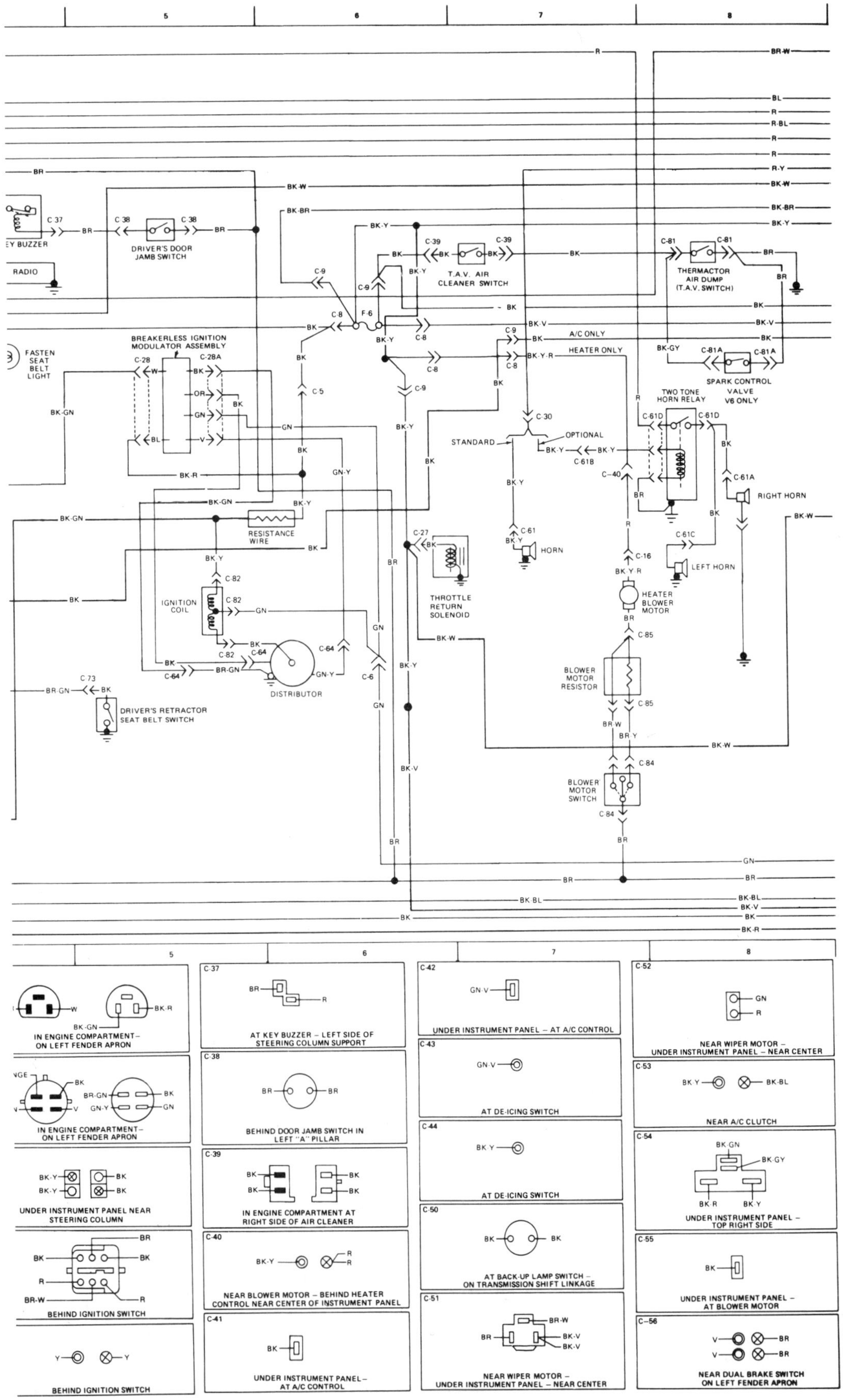

Fig. 13.48B Circuit diagram – Mercury Capri II, 1977/1978 (continued)
See page 284 for wiring codes

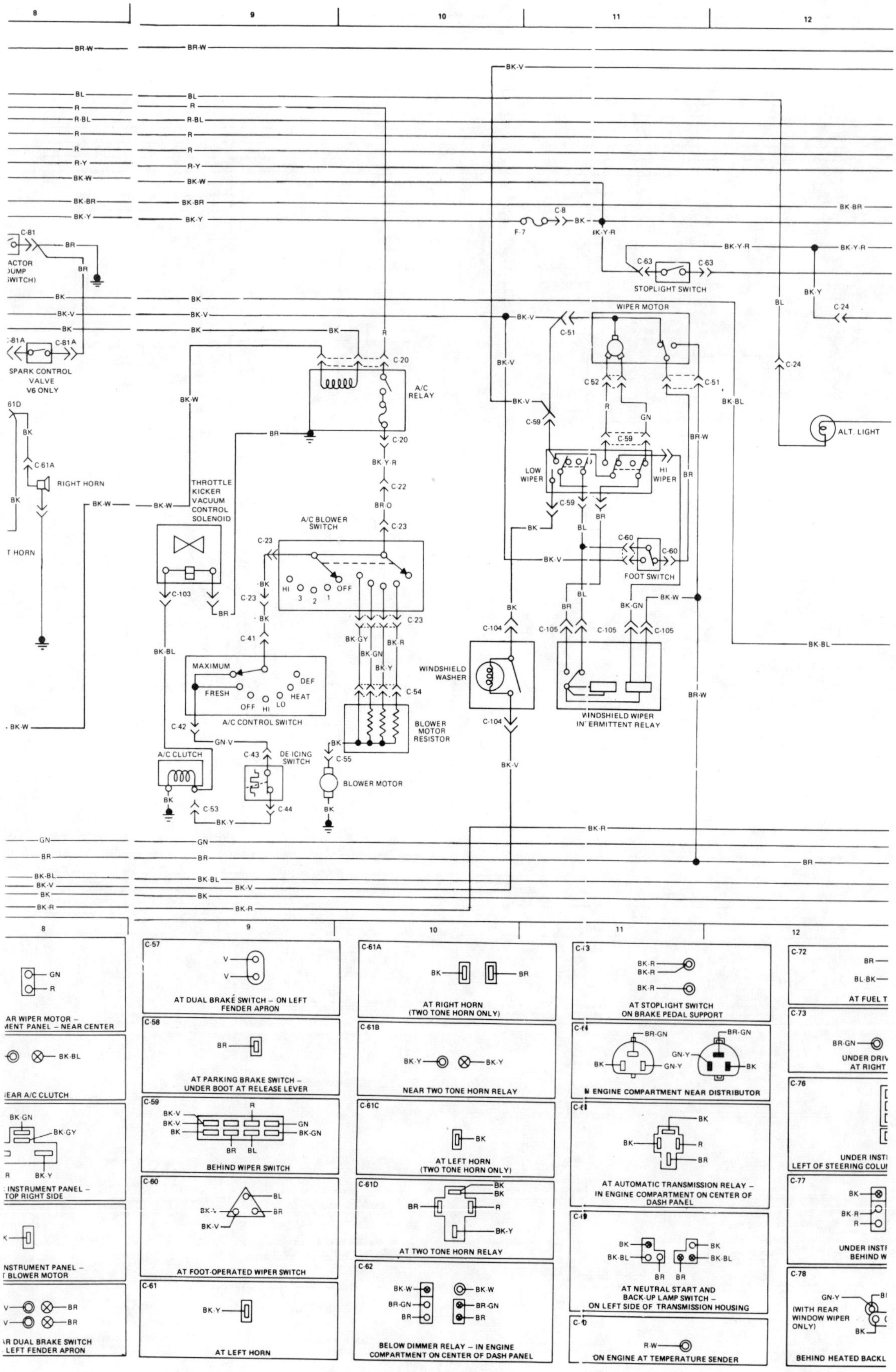

Fig. 13.48C Circuit diagram – Mercury Capri II, 1977/1978 (continued)

See page 284 for wiring codes

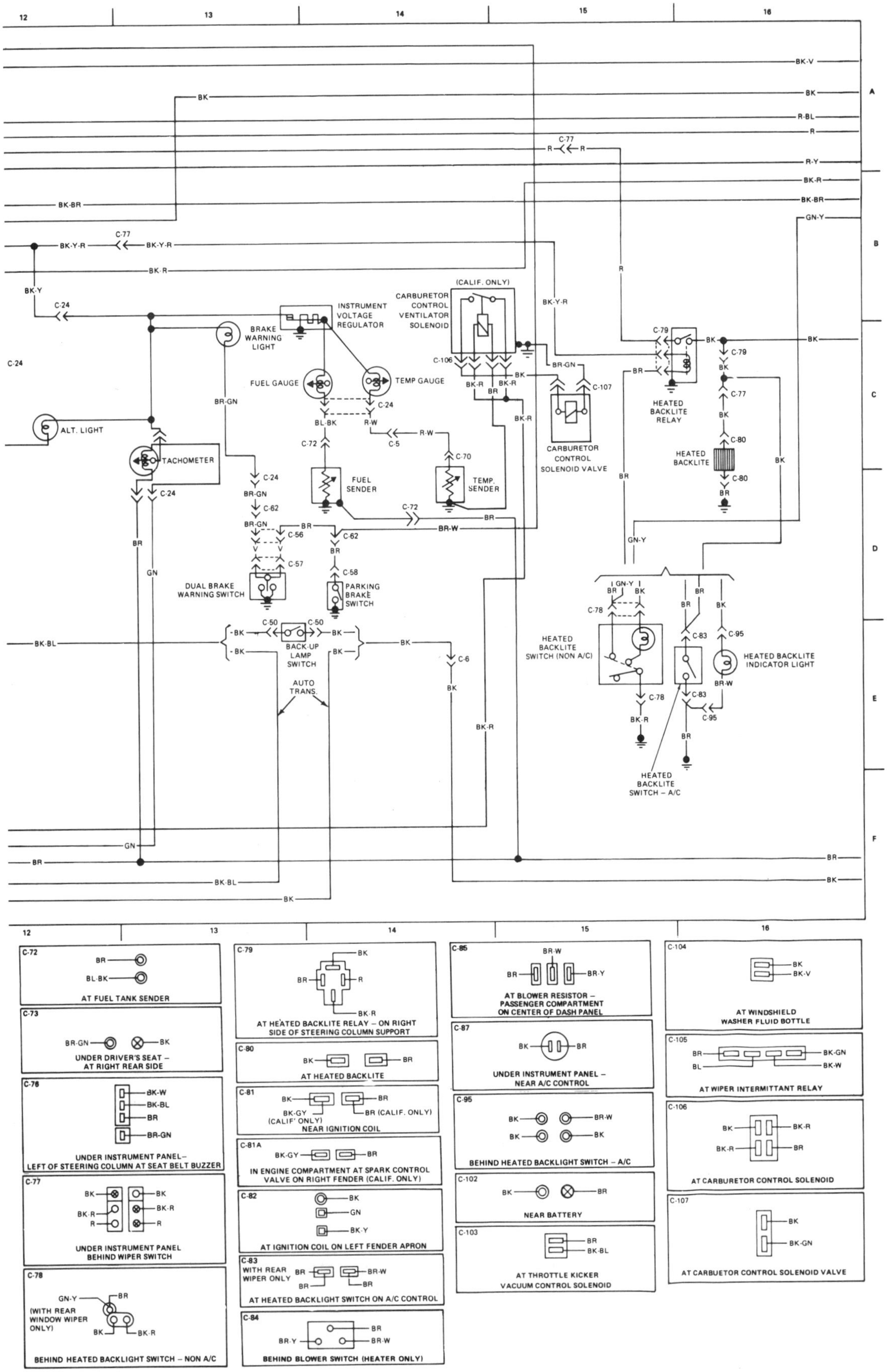

Fig. 13.48D Circuit diagram – Mercury Capri II, 1977/1978 (continued)

See page 284 for wiring codes

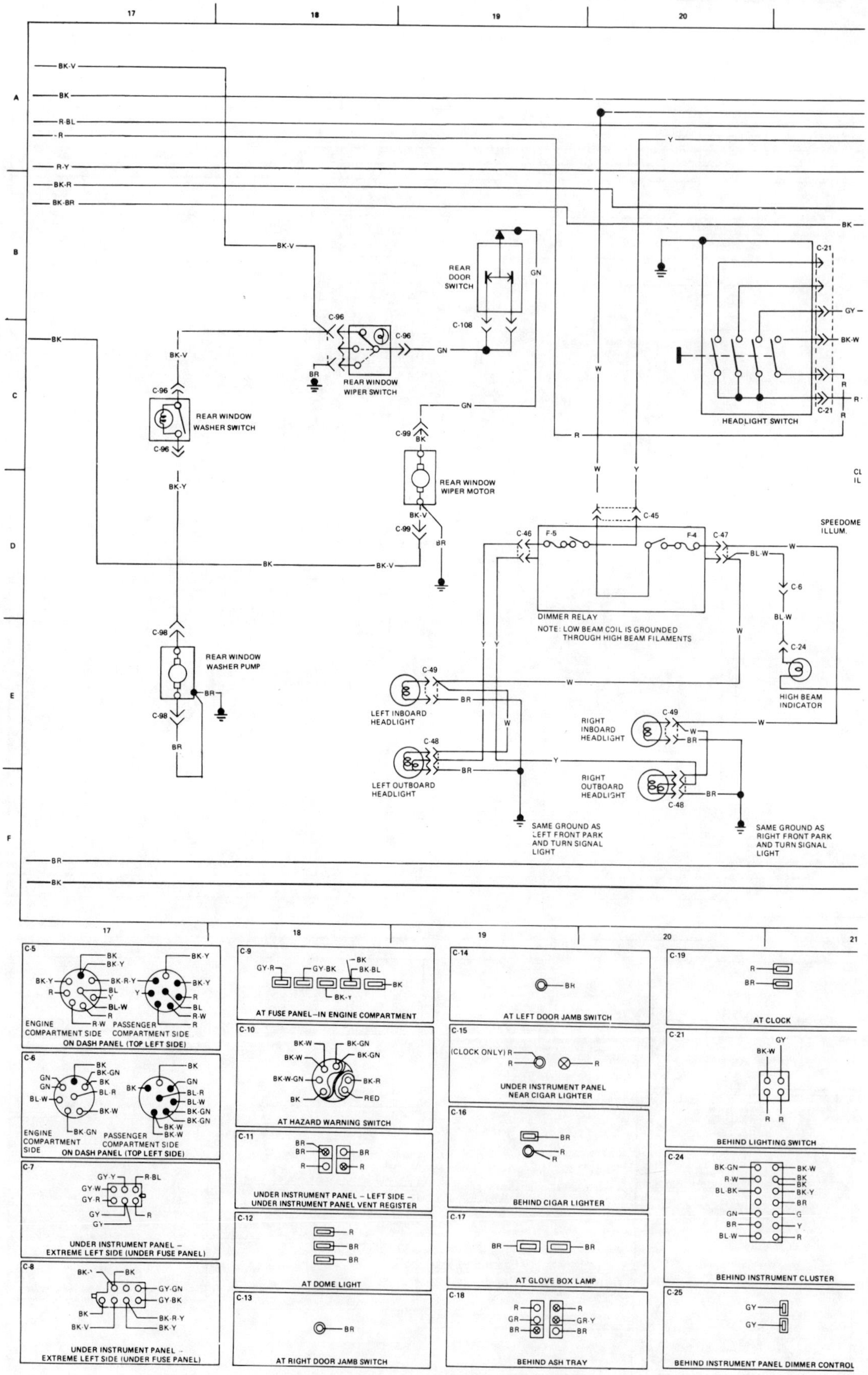

Fig. 13.48E Circuit diagram – Mercury Capri II, 1977/1978 (continued)

See page 284 for wiring codes

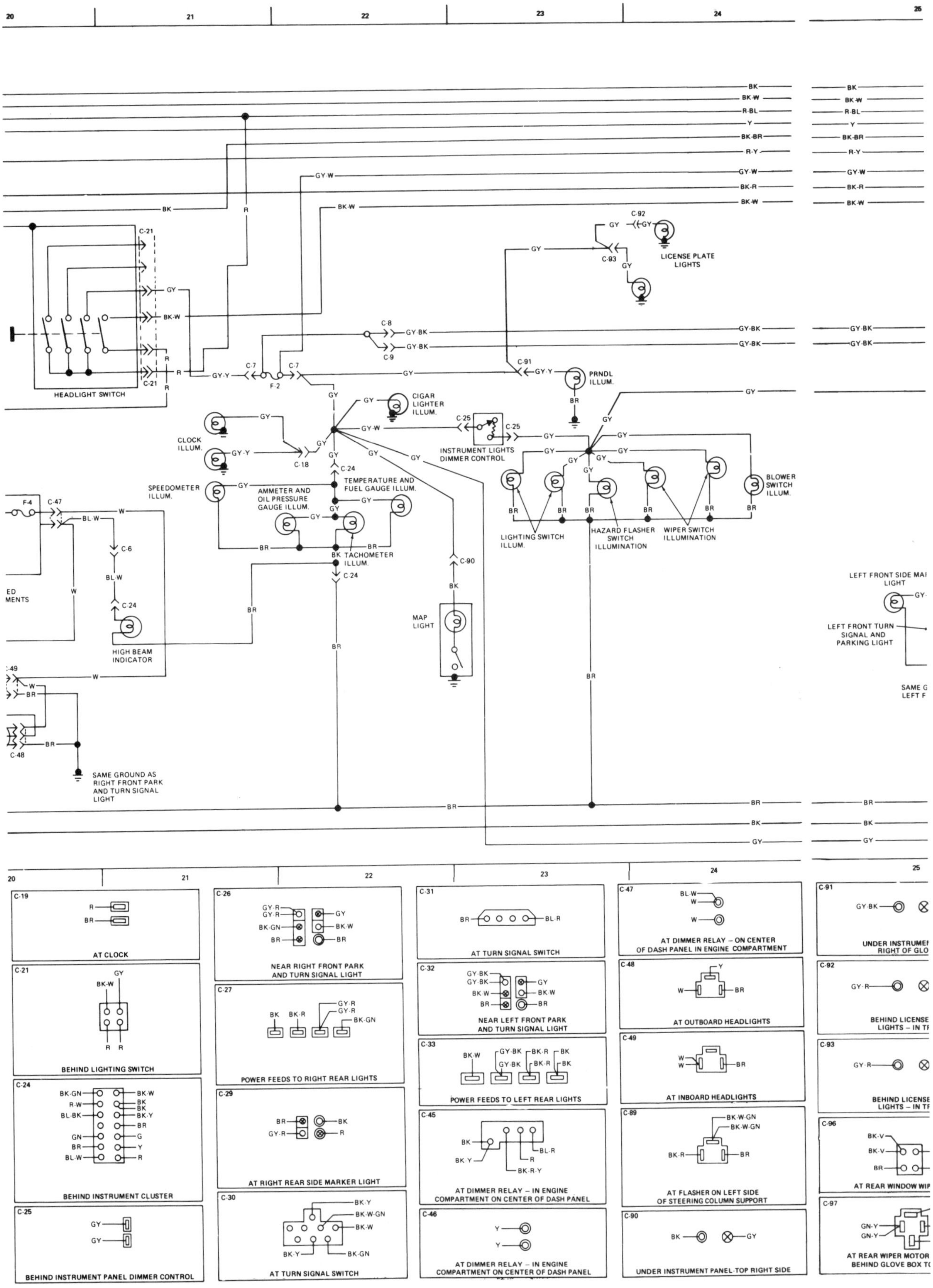

Fig. 13.48F Circuit diagram – Mercury Capri II, 1977/1978 (continued)

See page 284 for wiring codes

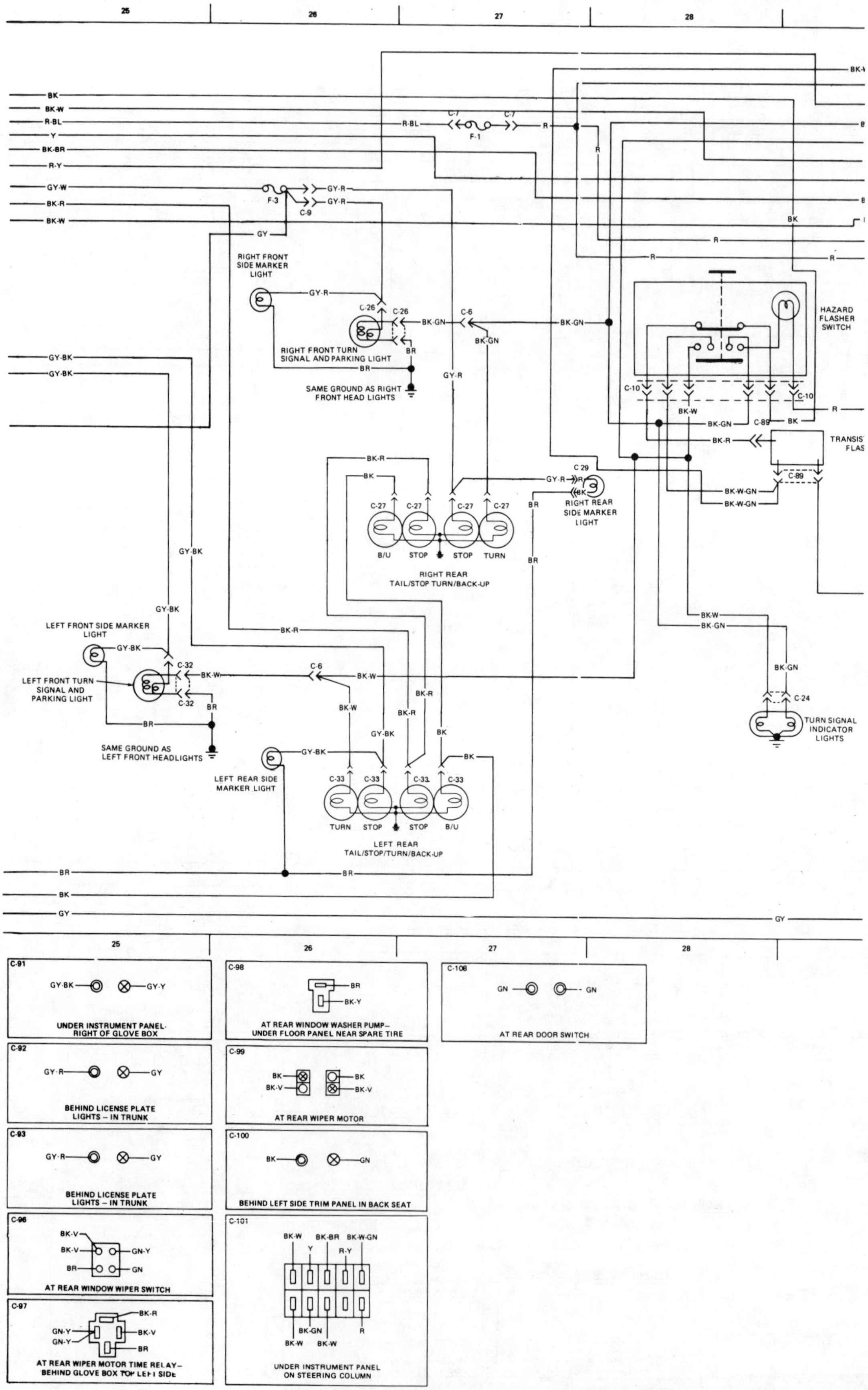

Fig. 13.48G Circuit diagram – Mercury Capri II, 1977/1978 (continued)

See page 284 for wiring codes

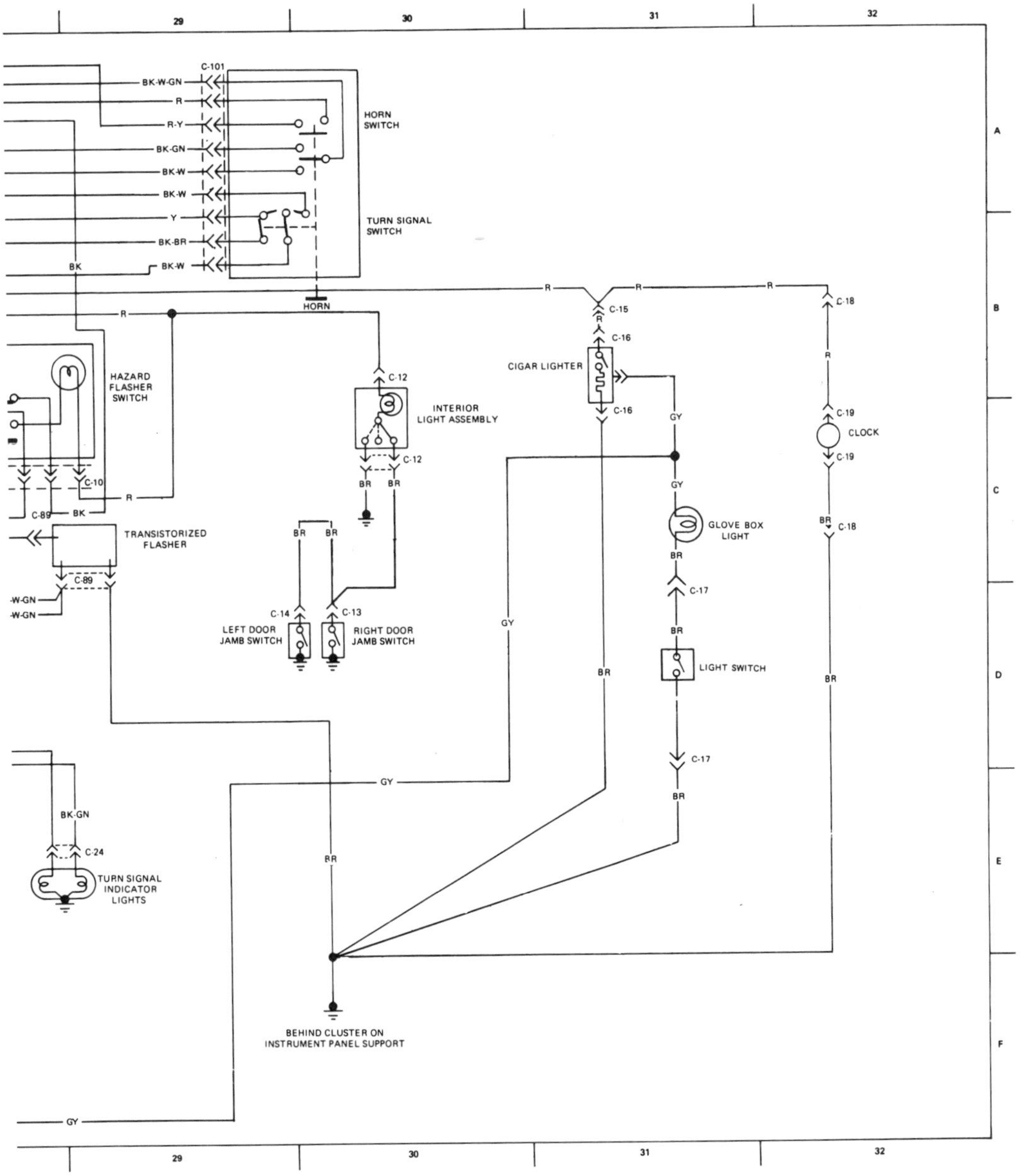

Fig. 13.48H Circuit diagram – Mercury Capri II, 1977/1978 (continued)

See page 284 for wiring codes

Code relating to circuit diagrams on pages 276 to 283

Component	Location
Air conditioner clutch	F–9
Alternator	B–1
Alternator regulator	C–1
Battery	A–1
Buzzers	
Key reminder	B–4
Seat belt	C–4
Cigar lighter	B–31
Clock	C–32
Distributor	C–32
Exterior lights	
Back-up	D–26, F–27
Headlights	
Left	E–19
Right	E–20
License plate	B–24
Park and turn signal	
Left	E–25
Right	C–26
Side marker	
Left front	E–25
Left rear	E–26
Right front	B–26
Right rear	C–28
Stoplights	
Left	E–26
Right	D–27
Tail-lights	
Left	F–26
Right	D–27
Rear turn signal	
Left	F–26
Right	D–27
Flashers	
Hazard flasher	B–28
Turn signal	E–28
Gauges	
Ammeter	A–2
Fuel	C–14
Tachometer	C–13
Temperature	C–14
Heated backlight	C–16
Heated blower motor	D–7
Heated blower motor resistor	E–7
Horns	D–7, D–8
Ignition coil	D–5
Ignition resistor wire	D–5
Illumination lights	
Ammeter and oil pressure gauge	D–21
Blower switch	D–24
Cigar lighter	C–22
Clock	D–21
Dome	B–29
Fuel gauge	D–22
Glove box	C–31
Hazard flasher	D–23
Lighter switch	D–23
Map	E–22
PRND21	C–23
Tachometer	D–22
Temperature gauge	D–22
Windshield wiper switch	D–24
Indicator lights	
Alternator	C–12

Component	Location
Brake warning	C–13
Seatbelt	C–4
Starter motor	D–1
Two-tone horn	C–8
Seatbelt logic box	D–4
Senders	
Fuel gauge	D–14
Water temperature gauge	D–14
Switches	
A/C blower	D–9
A/C control	E–9
Dimmer	
Instrument panel illumination	C–23
High beam	C–20
Door jamb	
Drivers	D–30
Passengers	D–30
Door jamb - key buzzer	B–5
Dual brake warning	D–13
Gear	E–13
Glove box lamp	D–31
Hazard flasher	B–28
Heated backlight	E–15
Heated blower	F–7
Horn	A–30
Ignition	B–3
Lighting	B–20
Neutral start	E–2
Parking brake	D–13
Seatbelt retractor	
Drivers	E–5
T.A.V. air cleaner	B–7
Thermactor air dump	B–8
Throttle return	D–6
Turn signal	A–30
Rear door	B–19
Seat sensor	
Drivers	E–5
Spark control valve	
Stoplight	B–11
Windshield wiper (front)	D–11
Footswitch	D–11
Windshield wiper (rear)	C–18
Rear washer switch	C–17
Windshield washer switch	E–10
Heated backlight	E–16
High beam	E–21
Seat belt	C–4
Turn signal	E–28
Instrument voltage regulator	B–14
Motors	
A/C blower	F–8
Heater blower	D–7
Starter	D–1
Windshield wiper (front)	B–11
Windshield wiper (rear)	D–18
Radio	B–4
Relays	
Air conditioning	C–10
Automatic transmission	D–19
Dimmer	D–20
Heated backlight	C–16
Intermittent wiper	E–11

9 Suspension and steering

Power steering pump drivebelt – tensioning (Mercury Capri II)

1 When moving the pump body away from the engine to adjust belt tension it is important to use the correct method of levering, thus preventing damage. This is shown in Fig. 13.49 and only sufficient force should be used to get the right tension. Don't use any incorrect methods such as gripping the neck of the reservoir or the flexible pipes, and don't use a wooden block or metal lever against the sheet metal canister of the pump body.

Power steering system – bleeding (Mercury Capri II)

2 A revised method of bleeding the power steering system is now recommended for all models.
3 Check that the level in the fluid reservoir is correct, neither under nor overfilled. This should be carried out immediately after stopping the engine.
4 Remove the sump undershield and examine all hoses and unions for leakage. Tighten unions where necessary.
5 Drive the car for a short distance carrying out at least one U-turn and several sharp turns to left and to right. If the fluid level has decreased but no external leaks are visible, this may indicate an internal leak in the steering system.
6 If the results of the tests described in the preceding paragraphs are satisfactory, then carry out the bleeding procedure proper.
7 With the engine switched off, turn the steering wheel from lock-to-lock three or four times. Keep the roadwheels on the ground during this work.
8 Check the reservoir fluid level. If topping-up is required, allow the car to stand motionless for at least two minutes before proceeding.
9 Disconnecting the negative LT lead from the coil, operate the ignition key to crank the engine for short two-second periods whilst at the same time turning the steering wheel slowly from lock-to-lock.
10 Keep the fluid reservoir topped-up all the time. Discontinue the bleeding once the fluid level ceases to fall and air bubbles no longer appear in the fluid.
11 Refit the coil lead and the reservoir cap.

Power steering gear – modified pinion valve cover (Mercury Capri II)

12 To overcome fluid seepage from early type valve pinion cover oil seals, a modified cover is fitted to later cars. This new assembly can be fitted to earlier models.
13 Clean away all external dirt.
14 Disconnect and remove the steering column universal joint and coupling assembly.
15 Unscrew the three bolts and withdraw the pinion valve cover taking great care that dirt does not enter the interior of the power steering assembly.
16 Clean the mating faces of the new type cover and the power steering gear.
17 Check that the O-ring seal is located on the underside of the cover. Then pack the spaces between the bearing and seal, and the seal and the cover with silicone grease.
18 Before fitting the cover, tape the pinion shaft splines to prevent them cutting into the cover seal.
19 Make sure that the spool valve bias spring has its smaller diameter uppermost and is not trapped between the valve body and the cover during the fitting of the cover.
20 Tighten the cover bolts to between 15 and 18 lbf ft (2.1 and 2.5 kgf m).
21 Refit the steering shaft coupling/universal joint assembly but only tighten the bolts to the specified torque when the weight of the car is on the roadwheels. The torque wrench setting for the coupling to the pinion shaft and coupling to the steering shaft is 18 to 22 lbf ft (2.5 to 3.0 kgf m).
22 Bleed the steering system as described earlier.

Condition of front suspension top mounts

23 Small surface cracks or slight damage to the rubber insert in the front suspension top mounts do not indicate the need for replacement. If the condition of the top mounts is suspect, measure between the top of the winged washer and the body of the top mount after making sure that the car is at kerb weight and the front of the car has been bounced several times.

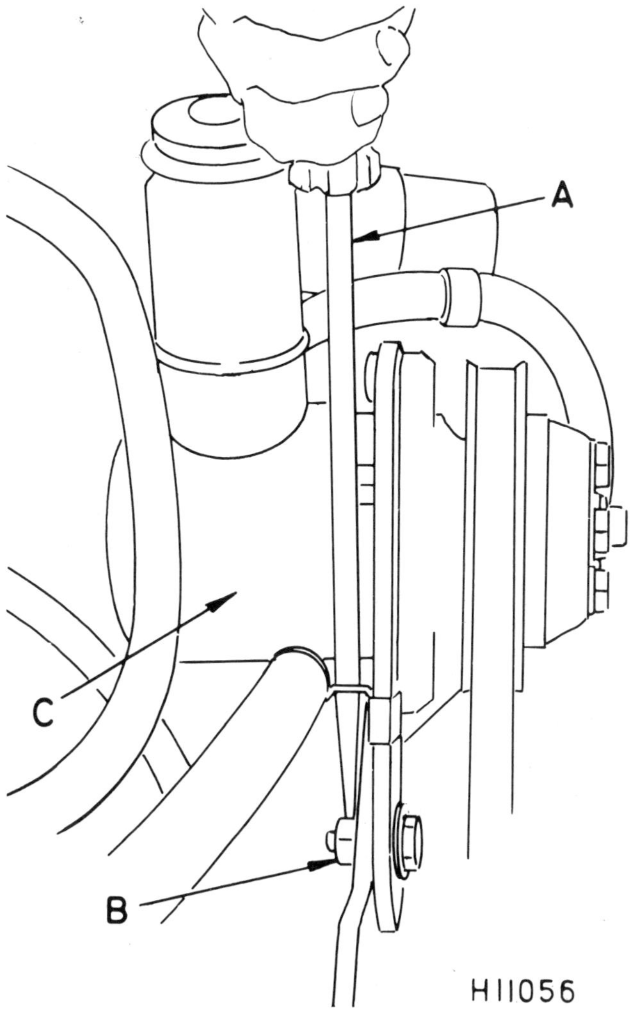

Fig. 13.49 Power steering pump drivebelt tensioning

A Screwdriver (as lever)
B Pinch bolt
C Fragile metal canister

24 If this dimension exceeds 1.06 in (27 mm) the mount should be changed, otherwise the surface condition of the rubber can be ignored.

Rear shock absorber top mounts

25 After April 1975 a redesign of the rear load space trim panels permits removal of the rear shock absorbers without having to remove the trim panel. A removable blanking plug is located near the top mount nut of each rear shock absorber and the following procedure for removal and installation of the unit can be used.
26 Fold the rear seat forward and remove the blanking plug from near the top end of the shock absorber. Remove the shock absorber top mount nut and locknut.
27 Jack-up the rear of the car and support it on axle stands.
28 Remove the shock absorber lower mounting on the rear axle and remove the shock absorber.
29 To install a shock absorber, fit and secure the lower mounting. Tighten to the specified torque.
30 Lower the car to the ground.
31 Fit the top mount nut and locknut, tightening to the specified torque.
32 Refit the trim panel blanking plug and refit the back of the rear seat.

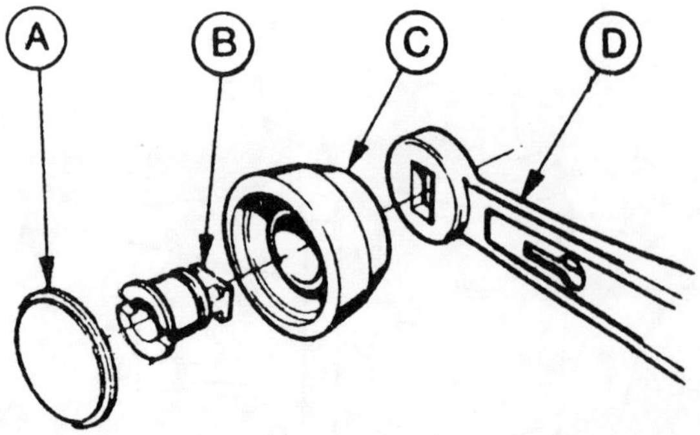

Fig. 13.50 Later type door window regulator handle

A Blanking cap *C Knob*
B Retainer *D Arm*

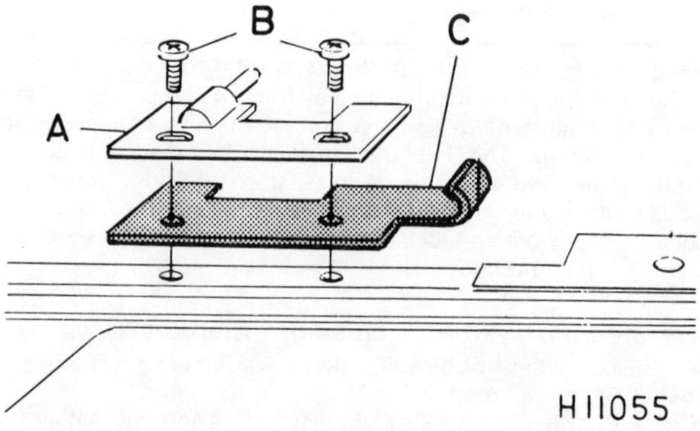

Fig. 13.51 Sunroof additional guide plates

A Original guide plate *C Additional guide plate*
B Fixing screws

Revised design wheelnuts

33 New style wheelnuts were introduced in 1975 which are longer than the earlier nuts. They also have a black plastic cap.

34 With the new nut fitted, if the black cap is removed, it would appear that the wheelstuds are too short as one or two threads can be seen in the nut. Providing they have been tightened to the correct torque this is acceptable.

10 Bodywork and fittings

Door window regulator knob

1 From September 1977 a break-off knob was fitted to the door window regulator to conform with EEC regulations. If the knob is accidentally knocked off a new retainer can be fitted.

2 Remove the door window regulator handle (Chapter 12, Section 14). and from the underside of the handle remove the remaining part of the knob retainer by turning it anti-clockwise with a screwdriver (Fig. 13.50).

3 Place the knob face down over the end of a suitable tube (about $1\frac{1}{8}$ in, 28 mm internal diameter) and push out the broken retainer and the cap of the knob. Don't try to prise the cap off as this would damage the knob and the cap.

4 Put a new retainer in the knob and feed the end into the rectangular hole in the regulator arm. Rotate the retainer one eighth of a turn clockwise and refit the cap to the knob. Refit the regulator arm.

Sunroof panel guide plates

5 In 1976 additional guideplates were introduced for the sun-roof panel to reduce noise and water leaks. These plates can be fitted to earlier models if these problems exist (Fig. 13.51). The left and right plates are similar except for being handed.

Use of English

As this book has been written in England, it uses the appropriate English component names, phrases, and spelling. Some of these differ from those used in America. Normally, these cause no difficulty, but to make sure, a glossary is printed below. In ordering spare parts remember the parts list will probably use these words:

English	American	English	American
Aerial	Antenna	Layshaft (of gearbox)	Countershaft
Accelerator	Gas pedal	Leading shoe (of brake)	Primary shoe
Alternator	Generator (AC)	Locks	Latches
Anti-roll bar	Stabiliser or sway bar	Motorway	Freeway, turnpike etc
Battery	Energizer	Number plate	License plate
Bodywork	Sheet metal	Paraffin	Kerosene
Bonnet (engine cover)	Hood	Petrol	Gasoline
Boot lid	Trunk lid	Petrol tank	Gas tank
Boot (luggage compartment)	Trunk	'Pinking'	'Pinging'
Bottom gear	1st gear	Propeller shaft	Driveshaft
Bulkhead	Firewall	Quarter light	Quarter window
Cam follower or tappet	Valve lifter or tappet	Retread	Recap
Carburettor	Carburetor	Reverse	Back-up
Catch	Latch	Rocker cover	Valve cover
Choke/venturi	Barrel	Roof rack	Car-top carrier
Circlip	Snap-ring	Saloon	Sedan
Clearance	Lash	Seized	Frozen
Crownwheel	Ring gear (of differential)	Side indicator lights	Side marker lights
Disc (brake)	Rotor/disk	Side light	Parking light
Drop arm	Pitman arm	Silencer	Muffler
Drop head coupe	Convertible	Spanner	Wrench
Dynamo	Generator (DC)	Sill panel (beneath doors)	Rocker panel
Earth (electrical)	Ground	Split cotter (for valve spring cap)	Lock (for valve spring retainer)
Engineer's blue	Prussian blue	Split pin	Cotter pin
Estate car	Station wagon	Steering arm	Spindle arm
Exhaust manifold	Header	Sump	Oil pan
Fast back (Coupe)	Hard top	Tab washer	Tang; lock
Fault finding/diagnosis	Trouble shooting	Tailgate	Liftgate
Float chamber	Float bowl	Tappet	Valve lifter
Free-play	Lash	Thrust bearing	Throw-out bearing
Freewheel	Coast	Top gear	High
Gudgeon pin	Piston pin or wrist pin	Trackrod (of steering)	Tie-rod (or connecting rod)
Gearchange	Shift	Trailing shoe (of brake)	Secondary shoe
Gearbox	Transmission	Transmission	Whole drive line
Halfshaft	Axleshaft	Tyre	Tire
Handbrake	Parking brake	Van	Panel wagon/van
Hood	Soft top	Vice	Vise
Hot spot	Heat riser	Wheel nut	Lug nut
Indicator	Turn signal	Windscreen	Windshield
Interior light	Dome lamp	Wing/mudguard	Fender

Miscellaneous points

An 'oil seal' is fitted to components lubricated by grease!

A 'damper' is a 'shock absorber', it damps out bouncing, and absorbs shocks of bump impact. Both names are correct, and both are used haphazardly.

Note that British drum brakes are different from the Bendix type that is common in America, so different descriptive names result. The shoe end furthest from the hydraulic wheel cylinder is on a pivot; interconnection between the shoes as on Bendix brakes is most uncommon. Therefore the phrase 'Primary' or 'Secondary' shoe does not apply. A shoe is said to be 'Leading' or 'Trailing'. A 'Leading' shoe is one on which a point on the drum, as it rotates forward, reaches the shoe at the end worked by the hydraulic cylinder before the anchor end. The opposite is a 'Trailing' shoe, and this one has no self servo from the wrapping effect of the rotating drum.

Safety first!

Professional motor mechanics are trained in safe working procedures. However enthusiastic you may be about getting on with the job in hand, do take the time to ensure that your safety is not put at risk. A moment's lack of attention can result in an accident, as can failure to observe certain elementary precautions.

There will always be new ways of having accidents, and the following points do not pretend to be a comprehensive list of all dangers; they are intended rather to make you aware of the risks and to encourage a safety-conscious approach to all work you carry out on your vehicle.

Essential DOs and DON'Ts

DON'T rely on a single jack when working underneath the vehicle. Always use reliable additional means of support, such as axle stands, securely placed under a part of the vehicle that you know will not give way.

DON'T attempt to loosen or tighten high-torque nuts (e.g. wheel hub nuts) while the vehicle is on a jack; it may be pulled off.

DON'T start the engine without first ascertaining that the transmission is in neutral (or 'Park' where applicable) and the parking brake applied.

DON'T suddenly remove the filler cap from a hot cooling system – cover it with a cloth and release the pressure gradually first, or you may get scalded by escaping coolant.

DON'T attempt to drain oil until you are sure it has cooled sufficiently to avoid scalding you.

DON'T grasp any part of the engine, exhaust or catalytic converter without first ascertaining that it is sufficiently cool to avoid burning you.

DON'T syphon toxic liquids such as fuel, brake fluid or antifreeze by mouth, or allow them to remain on your skin.

DON'T inhale brake lining dust – it is injurious to health.

DON'T allow any spilt oil or grease to remain on the floor – wipe it up straight away, before someone slips on it.

DON'T use ill-fitting spanners or other tools which may slip and cause injury.

DON'T attempt to lift a heavy component which may be beyond your capability – get assistance.

DON'T rush to finish a job, or take unverified short cuts.

DON'T allow children or animals in or around an unattended vehicle.

DO wear eye protection when using power tools such as drill, sander, bench grinder etc, and when working under the vehicle.

DO use a barrier cream on your hands prior to undertaking dirty jobs – it will protect your skin from infection as well as making the dirt easier to remove afterwards; but make sure your hands aren't left slippery.

DO keep loose clothing (cuffs, tie etc) and long hair well out of the way of moving mechanical parts.

DO remove rings, wristwatch etc, before working on the vehicle – especially the electrical system.

DO ensure that any lifting tackle used has a safe working load rating adequate for the job.

DO keep your work area tidy – it is only too easy to fall over articles left lying around.

DO get someone to check periodically that all is well, when working alone on the vehicle.

DO carry out work in a logical sequence and check that everything is correctly assembled and tightened afterwards.

DO remember that your vehicle's safety affects that of yourself and others. If in doubt on any point, get specialist advice.

IF, in spite of following these precautions, you are unfortunate enough to injure yourself, seek medical attention as soon as possible.

Fire

Remember at all times that petrol (gasoline) is highly flammable. Never smoke, or have any kind of naked flame around, when working on the vehicle. But the risk does not end there – a spark caused by an electrical short-circuit, by two metal surfaces contacting each other, or even by static electricity built up in your body under certain conditions, can ignite petrol vapour, which in a confined space is highly explosive.

Always disconnect the battery earth (ground) terminal before working on any part of the fuel system, and never risk spilling fuel on to a hot engine or exhaust.

It is recommended that a fire extinguisher of a type suitable for fuel and electrical fires is kept handy in the garage or workplace at all times. Never try to extinguish a fuel or electrical fire with water.

Fumes

Certain fumes are highly toxic and can quickly cause unconsciousness and even death if inhaled to any extent. Petrol (gasoline) vapour comes into this category, as do the vapours from certain solvents such as trichloroethylene. Any draining or pouring of such volatile fluids should be done in a well ventilated area.

When using cleaning fluids and solvents, read the instructions carefully. Never use materials from unmarked containers – they may give off poisonous vapours.

Never run the engine of a motor vehicle in an enclosed space such as a garage. Exhaust fumes contain carbon monoxide which is extremely poisonous; if you need to run the engine, always do so in the open air or at least have the rear of the vehicle outside the workplace.

If you are fortunate enough to have the use of an inspection pit, never drain or pour petrol, and never run the engine, while the vehicle is standing over it; the fumes, being heavier than air, will concentrate in the pit with possibly lethal results.

The battery

Never cause a spark, or allow a naked light, near the vehicle's battery. It will normally be giving off a certain amount of hydrogen gas, which is highly explosive.

Always disconnect the battery earth (ground) terminal before working on the fuel or electrical systems.

If possible, loosen the filler plugs or cover when charging the battery from an external source. Do not charge at an excessive rate or the battery may burst.

Take care when topping up and when carrying the battery. The acid electrolyte, even when diluted, is very corrosive and should not be allowed to contact the eyes or skin.

If you ever need to prepare electrolyte yourself, always add the acid slowly to the water, and never the other way round. Protect against splashes by wearing rubber gloves and goggles.

Mains electricity

When using an electric power tool, inspection light etc, which works from the mains, always ensure that the appliance is correctly connected to its plug and that, where necessary, it is properly earthed (grounded). Do not use such appliances in damp conditions and, again, beware of creating a spark or applying excessive heat in the vicinity of fuel or fuel vapour.

Ignition HT voltage

A severe electric shock can result from touching certain parts of the ignition system, such as the HT leads, when the engine is running or being cranked, particularly if components are damp or the insulation is defective. Where an electronic ignition system is fitted, the HT voltage is much higher and could prove fatal.

Fault diagnosis

Introduction

The vehicle owner who does his or her own maintenance according to the recommended schedules should not have to use this section of the manual very often. Modern component reliability is such that, provided those items subject to wear or deterioration are inspected or renewed at the specified intervals, sudden failure is comparatively rare. Faults do not usually just happen as a result of sudden failure, but develop over a period of time. Major mechanical failures in particular are usually preceded by characteristic symptoms over hundreds or even thousands of miles. Those components which do occasionally fail without warning are often small and easily carried in the vehicle.

With any fault finding, the first step is to decide where to begin investigations. Sometimes this is obvious, but on other occasions a little detective work will be necessary. The owner who makes half a dozen haphazard adjustments or replacements may be successful in curing a fault (or its symptoms), but he will be none the wiser if the fault recurs and he may well have spent more time and money than was necessary. A calm and logical approach will be found to be more satisfactory in the long run. Always take into account any warning signs or abhormalities that may have been noticed in the period preceding the fault – power loss, high or low gauge readings, unusual noises or smells, etc – and remember that failure of components such as fuses or spark plugs may only be pointers to some underlying fault.

The pages which follow here are intended to help in cases of failure to start or breakdown on the road. There is also a Fault Diagnosis Section at the end of each Chapter which should be consulted if the preliminary checks prove unfruitful. Whatever the fault, certain basic principles apply. These are as follows:

Verify the fault. This is simply a matter of being sure that you know what the symptoms are before starting work. This is particularly important if you are investigating a fault for someone else who may not have described it very accurately.

Don't overlook the obvious. For example, if the vehicle won't start, is there petrol in the tank? (Don't take anyone else's word on this particular point, and don't trust the fuel gauge either!) If an electrical fault is indicated, look for loose or broken wires before digging out the test gear.

Cure the disease, not the symptom. Substituting a flat battery with a fully charged one will get you off the hard shoulder, but if the underlying cause is not attended to, the new battery will go the same way. Similarly, changing oil-fouled spark plugs for a new set will get you moving again, but remember that the reason for the fouling (if it wasn't simply an incorrect grade of plug) will have to be established and corrected.

Don't take anything for granted. Particularly, don't forget that a 'new' component may itself be defective (especially if it's been rattling round in the boot for months), and don't leave components out of a fault diagnosis sequence just because they are new or recently fitted. When you do finally diagnose a difficult fault, you'll probably realise that all the evidence was there from the start.

Electrical faults

Electrical faults can be more puzzling than straightforward mechanical failures, but they are no less susceptible to logical analysis if the basic principles of operation are understood. Vehicle electrical wiring exists in extremely unfavourable conditions – heat, vibration and chemical attack – and the first things to look for are loose or corroded connections and broken or chafed wires, especially where the wires pass through holes in the bodywork or are subject to vibration.

All metal-bodied vehicles in current production have one pole of the battery 'earthed', ie connected to the vehicle bodywork, and in nearly all modern vehicles it is the negative (–) terminal. The various electrical components – motors, bulb holders etc – are also connected to earth, either by means of a lead or directly by their mountings. Electric current flows through the component and then back to the battery via the bodywork. If the component mounting is loose or corroded, or if a good path back to the battery is not available, the circuit will be incomplete and malfunction will result. The engine and/or gearbox are also earthed by means of flexible metal straps to the body or subframe; if these straps are loose or missing, starter motor, generator and ignition trouble may result.

Assuming the earth return to be satisfactory, electrical faults will be due either to component malfunction or to defects in the current supply. Individual components are dealt with in Chapters 10 and 13. If supply wires are broken or cracked internally this results in an open-circuit, and the easiest way to check for this is to bypass the suspect wire temporarily with a length of wire having a crocodile clip or suitable connector at each end. Alternatively, a 12V test lamp can be used to verify the presence of supply voltage at various points along the wire and the break can be thus isolated.

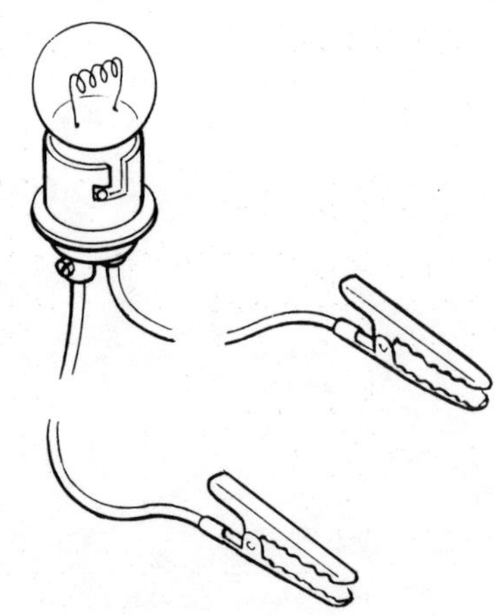

A simple test lamp is useful for investigating electrical faults

If a bare portion of a live wire touches the bodywork or other earthed metal part, the electricity will take the low-resistance path thus formed back to the battery: this is known as a short-circuit. Hopefully a short-circuit will blow a fuse, but otherwise it may cause burning of the insulation (and possibly further short-circuits) or even a fire. This is why it is inadvisable to bypass persistently blowing fuses with silver foil or wire.

Spares and tool kit

Most vehicles are supplied only with sufficient tools for wheel changing; the *Maintenance and minor repair* tool kit detailed in *Tools and working facilities,* with the addition of a hammer, is probably sufficient for those repairs that most motorists would consider attempting at the roadside. In addition a few items which can be fitted without too much trouble in the event of a breakdown should be carried. Experience and available space will modify the list below, but the following may save having to call on professional assistance:

Spark plugs, clean and correctly gapped
HT lead and plug cap – long enough to reach the plug furthest from the distributor
Distributor rotor, condenser and contact breaker points

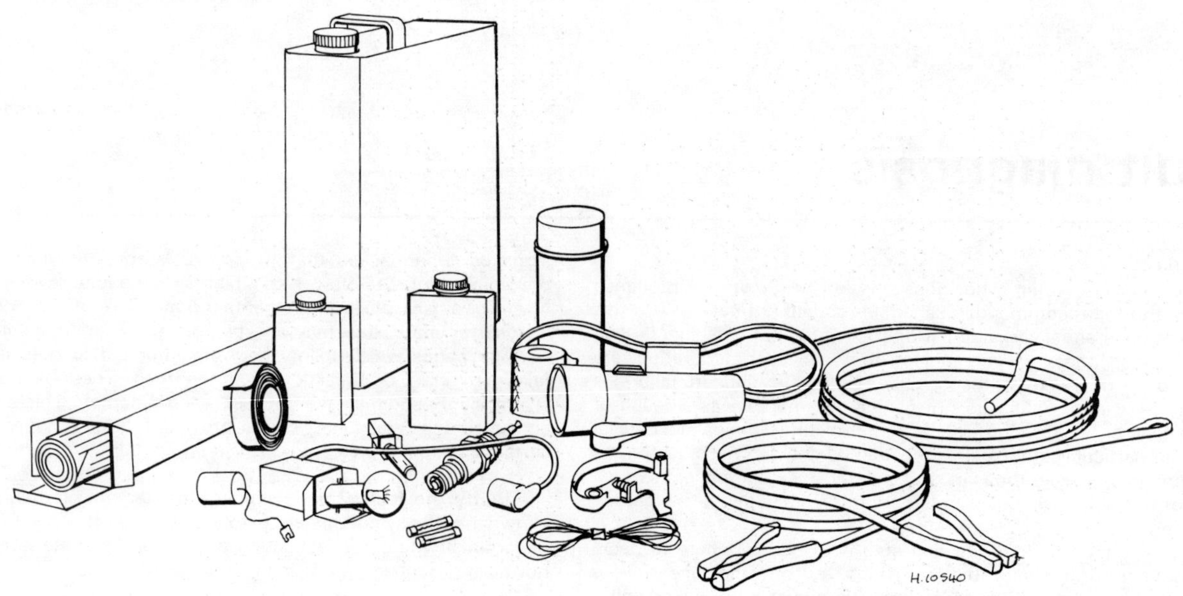

Carrying a few spares may save you a long walk!

Drivebelt(s) – emergency type may suffice
Spare fuses
Set of principal light bulbs
Tin of radiator sealer and hose bandage
Exhaust bandage
Roll of insulating tape
Length of soft iron wire
Length of electrical flex
Torch or inspection lamp (can double as test lamp)
Battery jump leads
Tow-rope
Ignition waterproofing aerosol
Litre of engine oil
Sealed can of hydraulic fluid
Emergency windscreen
'Jubilee' clips
Tube of filler paste

If spare fuel is carried, a can designed for the purpose should be used to minimise risks of leakage and collision damage. A first aid kit and a warning triangle, whilst not at present compulsory in the UK, are obviously sensible items to carry in addition to the above.

When touring abroad it may be advisable to carry additional spares which, even if you cannot fit them yourself, could save having to wait while parts are obtained. The items below may be worth considering:

Clutch and throttle cables
Cylinder head gasket
Dynamo or alternator brushes
Fuel pump repair kit
Tyre valve core

One of the motoring organisations will be able to advise on availability of fuel etc in foreign countries.

Engine will not start

Engine fails to turn when starter operated
Flat battery (recharge, use jump leads, or push start)
Battery terminals loose or corroded
Battery earth to body defective
Engine earth strap loose or broken
Starter motor (or solenoid) wiring loose or broken
Automatic transmission selector in wrong position, or inhibitor switch faulty
Ignition/starter switch faulty
Major mechanical failure (seizure)
Starter or solenoid internal fault (see Chapter 10)

Starter motor turns engine slowly
Partially discharged battery (recharge, use jump leads, or push start)
Battery terminals loose or corroded
Battery earth to body defective
Engine earth strap loose
Starter motor (or solenoid) wiring loose
Starter motor internal fault (see Chapter 10)

Starter motor spins without turning engine
Flat battery
Starter motor pinion sticking on sleeve
Flywheel gear teeth damaged or worn
Starter motor mounting bolts loose

Engine turns normally but fails to start
Damp or dirty HT leads and distributor cap (crank engine and check for spark)
Dirty or incorrectly gapped distributor points (if applicable)
No fuel in tank (check for delivery at carburettor)
Excessive choke (hot engine) or insufficient choke (cold engine)
Fouled or incorrectly gapped spark plugs (remove, clean and regap)
Other ignition system fault (see Chapter 4)
Other fuel system fault (see Chapter 3)

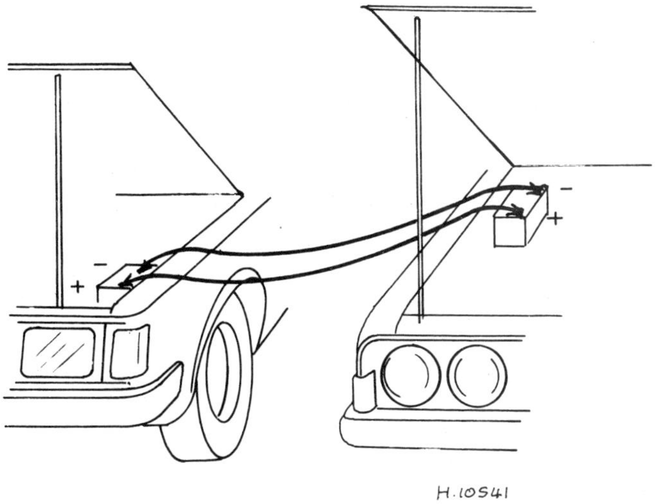

Correct way to connect jump leads. Do not allow car bodies to touch!

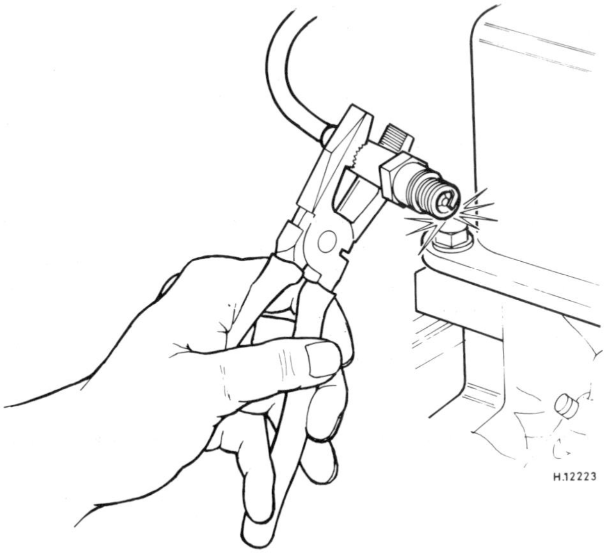

Crank engine and check for a spark. Note use of insulated pliers – dry cloth or a rubber glove will suffice

Poor compression (see Chapter 1)
Major mechanical failure (eg camshaft drive)

Engine fires but will not run
Insufficient choke (cold engine)
Air leaks at carburettor or inlet manifold
Fuel starvation (see Chapter 3)
Ballast resistor defective, or other ignition fault (see Chapter 4)

Engine cuts out and will not restart

Engine cuts out suddenly – ignition fault
Loose or disconnected LT wires
Wet HT leads or distributor cap (after traversing water splash)
Coil or condenser failure (check for spark)
Other ignition fault (see Chapter 4)

Engine misfires before cutting out – fuel fault
Fuel tank empty
Fuel pump defective or filter blocked (check for delivery)

Fuel tank filler vent blocked (suction will be evident on releasing cap)
Carburettor needle valve sticking
Carburettor jets blocked (fuel contaminated)
Other fuel system fault (see Chapter 3)

Engine cuts out – other causes

Serious overheating
Major mechanical failure (eg camshaft drive)

Engine overheats

Ignition (no-charge) warning light illuminated

Slack or broken drivebelt – retension or renew (Chapter 2)

Ignition warning light not illuminated

Coolant loss due to internal or external leakage (see Chapter 2)
Thermostat defective
Low oil level
Brakes binding
Radiator clogged externally or internally
Engine waterways clogged
Ignition timing incorrect or automatic advance malfunctioning
Mixture too weak

Note: *Do not add cold water to an overheated engine or damage may result*

Low engine oil pressure

Gauge reads low or warning light illuminated with engine running

Oil level low or incorrect grade
Defective gauge or sender unit
Wire to sender unit earthed
Engine overheating
Oil filter clogged or bypass valve defective
Oil pressure relief valve defective
Oil pick-up strainer clogged
Oil pump worn or mountings loose
Worn main or big-end bearings

Note: *Low oil pressure in a high-mileage engine at tickover is not necessarily a cause for concern. Sudden pressure loss at speed is far more significant. In any event, check the gauge or warning light sender before condemning the engine.*

Engine noises

Pre-ignition (pinking) on acceleration

Incorrect grade of fuel
Ignition timing incorrect
Distributor faulty or worn
Worn or maladjusted carburettor
Excessive carbon build-up in engine

Whistling or wheezing noises

Leaking vacuum hose
Leaking carburettor or manifold gasket
Blowing head gasket

Tapping or rattling

Incorrect valve clearances
Worn valve gear
Worn timing chain or belt
Broken piston ring (ticking noise)

Knocking or thumping

Unintentional mechanical contact (eg fan blades)
Worn fanbelt
Peripheral component fault (generator, water pump etc)
Worn big-end bearings (regular heavy knocking, perhaps less under load)
Worn main bearings (rumbling and knocking, perhaps worsening under load)
Piston slap (most noticeable when cold)

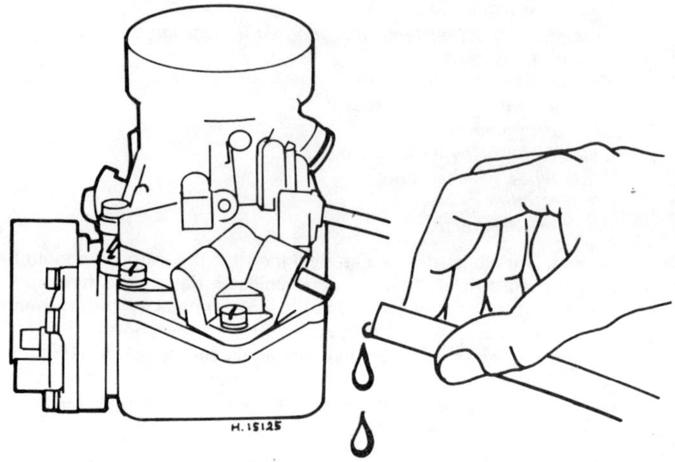

Remove pipes from carburettor and check that fuel is being delivered

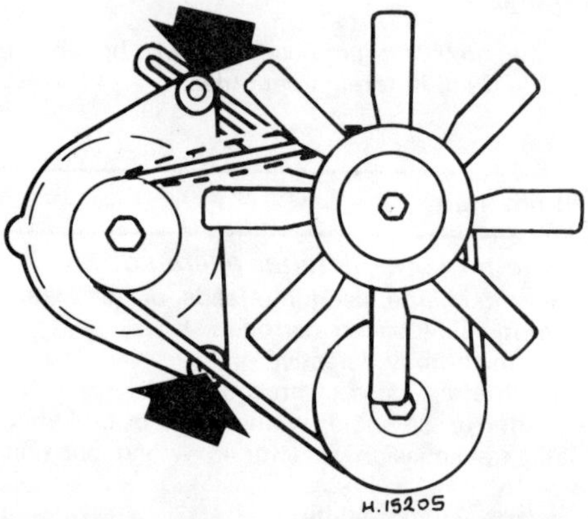

A slack drivebelt may cause overheating and battery charging problems. Slacken bolts (arrowed) to adjust

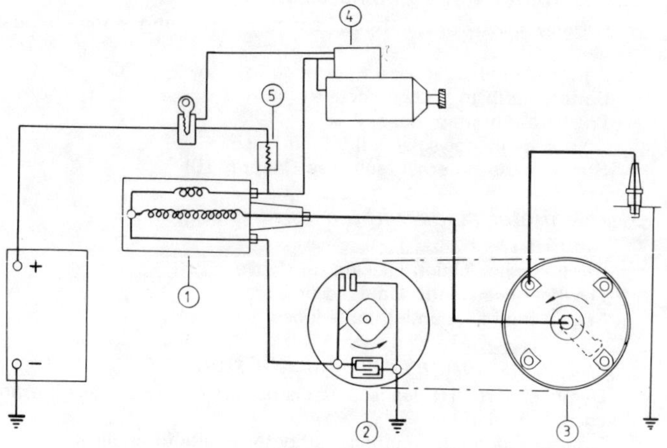

Ignition system schematic diagram. Ballast resistor is bypassed when starter motor operates

1 *Coil*
2 *Distributor (LT section)*
3 *Distributor (HT section)*
4 *Starter motor*
5 *Ballast resistor*

Conversion factors

Length (distance)					
Inches (in)	X 25.4	= Millimetres (mm)	X 0.0394	= Inches (in)
Feet (ft)	X 0.305	= Metres (m)	X 3.281	= Feet (ft)
Miles	X 1.609	= Kilometres (km)	X 0.621	= Miles
Volume (capacity)				
Cubic inches (cu in; in^3)	X 16.387	= Cubic centimetres (cc; cm^3)	X 0.061	= Cubic inches (cu in; in^3)
Imperial pints (Imp pt)	X 0.568	= Litres (l)	X 1.76	= Imperial pints (Imp pt)
Imperial quarts (Imp qt)	X 1.137	= Litres (l)	X 0.88	= Imperial quarts (Imp qt)
Imperial quarts (Imp qt)	X 1.201	= US quarts (US qt)	X 0.833	= Imperial quarts (Imp qt)
US quarts (US qt)	X 0.946	= Litres (l)	X 1.057	= US quarts (US qt)
Imperial gallons (Imp gal)	X 4.546	= Litres (l)	X 0.22	= Imperial gallons (Imp gal)
Imperial gallons (Imp gal)	X 1.201	= US gallons (US gal)	X 0.833	= Imperial gallons (Imp gal)
US gallons (US gal)	X 3.785	= Litres (l)	X 0.264	= US gallons (US gal)
Mass (weight)				
Ounces (oz)	X 28.35	= Grams (g)	X 0.035	= Ounces (oz)
Pounds (lb)	X 0.454	= Kilograms (kg)	X 2.205	= Pounds (lb)
Force				
Ounces-force (ozf; oz)	X 0.278	= Newtons (N)	X 3.6	= Ounces-force (ozf; oz)
Pounds-force (lbf; lb)	X 4.448	= Newtons (N)	X 0.225	= Pounds-force (lbf; lb)
Newtons (N)	X 0.1	= Kilograms-force (kgf; kg)	X 9.81	= Newtons (N)
Pressure				
Pounds-force per square inch (psi; lbf/in^2; lb/in^2)	X 0.070	= Kilograms-force per square centimetre (kgf/cm^2; kg/cm^2)	X 14.223	= Pounds-force per square inch (psi; lbf/in^2; lb/in^2)
Pounds-force per square inch (psi; lbf/in^2; lb/in^2)	X 0.068	= Atmospheres (atm)	X 14.696	= Pounds-force per square inch (psi; lbf/in^2; lb/in^2)
Pounds-force per square inch (psi; lbf/in^2; lb/in^2)	X 0.069	= Bars	X 14.5	= Pounds-force per square inch (psi; lbf/in^2; lb/in^2)
Pounds-force per square inch (psi; lbf/in^2; lb/in^2)	X 6.895	= Kilopascals (kPa)	X 0.145	= Pounds-force per square inch (psi; lbf/in^2; lb/in^2)
Kilopascals (kPa)	X 0.01	= Kilograms-force per square centimetre (kgf/cm^2; kg/cm^2)	X 98.1	= Kilopascals (kPa)
Torque (moment of force)				
Pounds-force inches (lbf in; lb in)	X 1.152	= Kilograms-force centimetre (kgf cm; kg cm)	X 0.868	= Pounds-force inches (lbf in; lb in)
Pounds-force inches (lbf in; lb in)	X 0.113	= Newton metres (Nm)	X 8.85	= Pounds-force inches (lbf in; lb in)
Pounds-force inches (lbf in; lb in)	X 0.083	= Pounds-force feet (lbf ft; lb ft)	X 12	= Pounds-force inches (lbf in; lb in)
Pounds-force feet (lbf ft; lb ft)	X 0.138	= Kilograms-force metres (kgf m; kg m)	X 7.233	= Pounds-force feet (lbf ft; lb ft)
Pounds-force feet (lbf ft; lb ft)	X 1.356	= Newton metres (Nm)	X 0.738	= Pounds-force feet (lbf ft; lb ft)
Newton metres (Nm)	X 0.102	= Kilograms-force metres (kgf m; kg m)	X 9.804	= Newton metres (Nm)
Power				
Horsepower (hp)	X 745.7	= Watts (W)	X 0.0013	= Horsepower (hp)
Velocity (speed)				
Miles per hour (miles/hr; mph)	X 1.609	= Kilometres per hour (km/hr; kph)	X 0.621	= Miles per hour (miles/hr; mph)
Fuel consumption*				
Miles per gallon, Imperial (mpg)	X 0.354	= Kilometres per litre (km/l)	X 2.825	= Miles per gallon, Imperial (mpg)
Miles per gallon, US (mpg)	X 0.425	= Kilometres per litre (km/l)	X 2.352	= Miles per gallon, US (mpg)

Temperature

Degrees Fahrenheit = (°C x 1.8) + 32

Degrees Celsius (Degrees Centigrade; °C) = (°F - 32) x 0.56

**It is common practice to convert from miles per gallon (mpg) to litres/100 kilometres (l/100km), where mpg (Imperial) x l/100 km = 282 and mpg (US) x l/100 km = 235*

Index

C

D

W

Printed by
Haynes Publishing Group
Sparkford Yeovil Somerset
England